BANNED BOOKS

LITERATURE SUPPRESSED ON

Sexual Grounds

Third Edition

DAWN B. SOVA

Preface by
KEN WACHSBERGER

Facts On File
An Infobase Learning Company

Facts On File, Inc.
An imprint of Infobase Learning
132 West 31st Street
New York NY 10001

Library of Congress Cataloging-in-Publication Data
Sova, Dawn B.
Literature suppressed on sexual grounds / Dawn B. Sova; preface by Ken Wachsberger.—3rd ed.
p. cm.—(Banned books)
Includes bibliographical references and index.
ISBN 978-0-8160-8229-2 (acid-free paper)
1. Erotic literature—Censorship—United States—History. 2. Prohibited books—United States—History. 3. Erotic literature—Censorship—History.
4. Prohibited books—History. I. Title.
PN56.E7S68 2011
809'.933538—dc22   2010040118

Facts On File books are available at special discounts when purchased in bulk quantities for businesses, associations, institutions, or sales promotions. Please call our Special Sales Department in New York at (212) 967-8800 or (800) 322-8755.

You can find Facts On File on the World Wide Web at
http://www.infobaselearning.com

Text design by Cathy Rincon
Compostion by Publication Services, Inc.
Cover printed by Yurchak Printing, Landisville, Pa.
Book printed and bound by Yurchak Printing, Landisville, Pa.
Date printed: June 2011

Printed in the United States of America

10 9 8 7 6 5 4 3 2 1

This book is printed on acid-free paper.

To my son, Robert Gregor, and to all young people who will try to make the world they have inherited a better place

There is no freedom either in civil or ecclesiastical [affairs], but where the liberty of the press is maintained.
—Matthew Tindal

If all mankind minus one were of one opinion, and only one person were of the contrary opinion, mankind would be no more justified in silencing that one person, than he, if he had the power, would be justified in silencing mankind.
—John Stuart Mill

Dare to think for yourself.
—Voltaire

CONTENTS

ACKNOWLEDGMENTS

The long history of censorship has created many heroes, both famous and obscure, authors and publishers who have dared to defy the restrictions of their respective ages in order to reveal truth in their writings. The works of some appear in this volume, but many more have been silenced and their works destroyed. To all, however, this book owes both life and purpose. Had they acquiesced to those who challenge, censor, and ban books containing ideas or language that displease vocal minorities, our intellectual universe would be significantly smaller.

I treasure my association with Bert Holtje, whose support and advice as both literary agent and friend helped me to maintain perspective throughout this lengthy project. His insight and literate commentary helped to resolve seemingly insurmountable problems. Gene Brissie of James Peter Associates, Inc., brought his patience and his considerable knowledge of the publishing world to ensuing editions of the work. I am grateful to know him. My sincere appreciation also belongs to Facts On File editor Jeff Soloway.

Actual works were used to create entries in this volume, giving this book an authenticity that the use of mere summaries could not. This literature, often difficult to locate, would not have been available to me without the efforts of I. Macarthur Nickles, director of the Garfield (New Jersey) Library, a man whose professional expertise and insight were invaluable. He made certain that my sometimes obscure research requests were satisfied and introduced innovations in my hometown library. I am also grateful to reference experts Kathleen Zalenski and Karen Calandriello, who tracked down unusual books and odd quotations, dates, and notes, always persevering long after I had given up the chase.

In my personal life, no one has meant more to me than my son, Rob Gregor, who helped me to organize my thoughts, contributed insights on various works, and kept me human. I appreciate greatly the support of my parents, my mother, Violet Sova, and my late father, Emil Sova, whose pride in my accomplishments and unwavering confidence in my abilities have always sustained me.

Finally, although I can never meet them, I appreciate the efforts of the many authors over the centuries who risked their livelihoods and lives to stand strong against the oppressive efforts of those who would silence all who refuse to conform.

PREFACE

We Americans are proud of our Constitution, especially its Bill of Rights. The First Amendment right to freedom of speech and religion has inspired dissenters and nonconformists everywhere. Censored writers such as Salman Rushdie, Pramoedya Ananta Toer, and Aleksandr Solzhenitsyn have looked to our country's example for strength as they battled for their rights to express their own thoughts, and that of others to read them, even at the risk of their lives.

Yet censorship has been a major part of American history from the time of Roger Williams and other early colonial freethinkers. Many of our richest literary works—*Adventures of Huckleberry Finn*, *The Color Purple*, *The Grapes of Wrath*, *The Jungle*, *Uncle Tom's Cabin*, *Tropic of Cancer*—have been censored at one time or another. Even today, school boards, local governments, religious organizations, and moral crusaders attempt to restrict our freedom to read or to learn alternative viewpoints. Witness the Texas State Board of Education's attempts to revise American history and tear down the wall separating church and state through its revisionist textbooks. Advancing technology has provided more diverse targets—the record, film, and television industries and the Internet—for the censors and would-be censors to aim at, as they work their strategies to restrict free expression and the freedom to read, watch, and listen, dumbing down material in order to shield their children, and you, from original or disturbing thoughts.

The history of books depicting sexual acts—whether the chosen word was *pornography*, *erotica* or *obscenity*—is a fascinating ride through our country's court system, as Dawn Sova shows in this volume of books censored for erotic reasons. It includes such major works as *Fanny Hill: Memoirs of a Woman of Pleasure*, *Lady Chatterley's Lover*, *Lolita*, *Tropic of Cancer*, *Candide*, *Ulysses*, and others that survived court challenges and went on to become recognized as literary classics, not to mention best sellers. In this third edition of the Facts On File Banned Books series, Sova adds both books that have been around long enough to be known as literary classics and others that were published only recently. These new entries include *The Awakening*; *Native Son*; *Song of Solomon*; *Their Eyes Were Watching God*; *Bless Me, Ultima*; *How the García Girls Lost Their Accents*; *The Epic of Gilgamesh*; Gossip Girls series; *The Perks of Being a Wallflower*; *This Boy's Life*; and the Twilight series.

A message from those books that survived the challenges is that there is no better publicity, no more solid guarantee of best-seller status, than a good court fight. But these victories would be impossible without the First Amendment, the United States's greatest gift to civilization, as well as heroic groups and individuals who are willing to take up the struggle to defend the First Amendment.

Fortunately, our country has a strong tradition of fighting censorship as well. Groups such as the National Coalition Against Censorship, the American Library Association's Office for Intellectual Freedom, People for the American Way, the American Civil Liberties Union, the PEN American Center, and the National Writers Union exist to defend the First Amendment and support independent writers, through legal action and by raising public awareness.

The first edition of the Facts On File Banned Books Series came out as a four-volume hardcover set in 1998. The second edition, which was published in 2006, added 50 additional titles to the list. The four volumes in this dynamic revised and expanded third edition add to our rich First Amendment tradition by spotlighting approximately 500 works that have been censored for their political, social, religious, or erotic content, in the United States and around the world, from biblical times to the present day. While many of these have been legally "banned"—or prohibited "as by official order"—all indeed have been banned or censored in a broader sense: targeted for removal from school curricula or library shelves, condemned in churches and forbidden to the faithful, rejected or expurgated by publishers, challenged in court, even voluntarily rewritten by their authors. Censored authors have been verbally abused, physically attacked, shunned by their families and communities, excommunicated from their religious congregations, and shot, hanged, or burned at the stake by their enemies, who thus made them heroes and often enough secured their memory for posterity. Their works include novels, histories, biographies, children's books, religious and philosophical treatises, dictionaries, poems, polemics, and every other form of written expression.

It is illuminating to discover in these histories that such cultural landmarks as the Bible, the Qur'an, the Talmud, and the greatest classics of world literature have often been suppressed or censored from the same motives, and by similar forces, as those we see today seeking to censor such books as *Daddy's Roommate* and *Heather Has Two Mommies*. Every American reading these volumes will find in their pages books they love and will be thankful that their authors' freedom of expression and their own freedom to read are constitutionally protected. But at the same time, how many will be gratified by the cruel fate of books we detest? Reader-citizens capable of acknowledging their own contradictions will be grateful for the existence of the First Amendment and will thank its guardians, including the authors of this series, for protecting us against our own worst impulses.

It is to Facts On File's credit that they have published this new version of the original Banned Books series. May the day come when an expanded series is no longer necessary.

* * *

To prevent redundancy, works banned for multiple reasons appear in only one volume apiece, based on the judgment of the editor and the volume authors. The alphabetical arrangement provides easy access to titles. Works whose titles appear in SMALL CAPITAL LETTERS within an entry have entries of their own elsewhere in the same volume. Those whose titles appear in *ITALICIZED SMALL CAPITAL LETTERS* have entries in one of the other volumes. In addition, each volume carries complete lists of the works discussed in the other volumes.

—Ken Wachsberger

Ken Wachsberger is a longtime author, editor, educator, and member of the National Writers Union. He is the editor of the four-volume Voices from the Underground series, a landmark collection of insider histories about the Vietnam era underground press (www.voicesfromtheundergroundpress.com).

INTRODUCTION

Changing social mores have moved many books formerly forbidden because of explicit sexual content out of locked cabinets and onto the open shelves of libraries and bookstores. Many such books have also entered high school and college classrooms to be read by students who little realize their notorious pasts.

A changed society has taken literary criticism out of the courts. In 1961, the United States Supreme Court was asked to rule if D. H. Lawrence's *Lady Chatterley's Lover* was lewd or literary. By 1969, the novel was required reading in college literature courses. The same is true of other works, such as James Joyce's *Ulysses*, Vladimir Nabokov's *Lolita*, Henry Miller's *Tropic of Cancer*, and Voltaire's *Candide*, all once banned and considered indecent. When did the "obscene" and the "pornographic" become the "erotic" and the "classic?"

Dirty words alone are not enough to make a work erotic, although many books in the 19th and early 20th centuries were banned simply for that reason. Similarly, many books have been banned because they discussed or alluded to such familiar social phenomena as prostitution, unwed pregnancy, and adultery, among them Thomas Hardy's *Jude the Obscure* and Nathaniel Hawthorne's *Scarlet Letter*. Neither can reasonably be termed an erotic or pornographic work, yet both books were banned for their presumed sexual content.

In 1957, the U.S. Supreme Court changed its definition of obscenity to refer to works that had sexual content but no "redeeming social importance." This redefinition sent Americans in search of works both erotically interesting and socially redeeming, and thus legally sexually titillating. Anonymous Victorian novels, the underground pornography of their day, joined art books with lavish reproductions of Japanese and Indian erotic painting and sculpture and explicit psychological case studies of sexually "abnormal" behavior as the standard middle-class erotica of the early to mid-20th century. During that time, American courts tried obscenity cases and pondered the literary merits of *Fanny Hill: Memoirs of a Woman of Pleasure*, *Lady Chatterley's Lover*, *Ulysses*, and *Tropic of Capricorn*.

By 1970, the barriers were down and the Report of the United States President's Commission on Obscenity noted that "Virtually every English language book thought to be obscene when published, and many similar books translated into English, have been reissued by secondary publishers. The entire stockpile of 'classic erotic literature' (e.g., *The Kama Sutra*, Frank Harris, de Sade, etc.) published over centuries has thus come onto the market."

As formerly banned works gained acceptance, many novels published in the last several decades have benefited and freely include sexual detail and sometimes gratuitous sex scenes. Society's view of sex has changed and many books that would once have been condemned as pornographic or obscene now become best sellers. Even cheaply produced "adult" books that do not pretend to any purpose other than sexual arousal are now easily available to willing buyers through direct mail and retail stores. The legal line between pornography and erotica has disappeared, and the differences are now defined more according to aesthetic appeal than to content.

But how is "erotic" different from "pornographic?" Nineteenth-century booksellers coined the term *erotica* to describe risqué writing found in such classics as the poems of Catullus, the satires of Juvenal, and love manuals such as the *Kama Sutra*, as well as that perennial favorite, *Fanny Hill, or Memoirs of a Woman of Pleasure* (1748–49), the subject of the first U.S. obscenity trial in 1821. These early works bore no resemblance to the cheaply produced, and cheap-looking, books of the mid-20th century. The market catered to men of means who could well afford the lavishly illustrated deluxe editions that satisfied what was termed their "curious" tastes. Early patrons paid handsomely for their pleasure.

The growth of mass demand for erotica required mass production, and cheaply produced pulp novels with lurid covers and plotless texts appeared in great number. These contrasted strongly in appearance with the lavishly illustrated and expensively produced gentlemen's erotica of the 19th century, but they were identical in purpose. Price was the primary distinguishing factor. The differences became so blurred that the 1970 Report of the United States President's Commission on Obscenity struggled and failed to define what was obscene and pornographic, and thus illegal.

The definitions were no clearer in 1986, when the Attorney General's Commission on Pornography (often called the Meese Commission) revealed that its findings were inconclusive regarding the dangers of pornography. Although the Commission recommended intensified enforcement against child pornography and material showing sexual violence, the Commission members hedged in their recommendations regarding all-text materials. The panel recommended "extraordinary caution" in regard to prosecuting those who distributed materials that contained no photographs, pictures, or drawings. "The written word has had and continues to have a special place in this and any other civilization." The Commission designated as among the "least harmful" types of pornography "books consisting of the printed text only" and observed that such text might not always meet its criteria for pornography, that it be "sexually explicit and intended primarily for the purpose of sexual arousal."

Thus, with the conclusion of investigations by the Meese Commission, the century and a half of obscenity trials regarding literature came to a halt, and the old argument was invalidated. Those who could read could indulge themselves in the provocative power of words that arouse, stimulate, and titillate—they were consumers of "erotica." The less literate, more likely to view X-rated videos or picture magazines that arouse, stimulate and titillate, were indulging in "pornography." The appeal of the categories is the same, but their audiences differed, as did the assumed consequences.

The goal of this volume on works censored for having sexual content is neither to deride nor defend either the mainstream erotica or the pulp pornography that has been published over the centuries. Instead, it is to illuminate changing cultural attitudes toward the erotic, through a survey of the legal fate of classic representative works in centuries past as well as the present day.

NOTES ON THE THIRD EDITION

This third edition contains 11 new entries and updates the censorship histories of many existing entries to include new cases and challenges and additional information on already presented material. New entries examine the challenging of longtime classics such as Kate Chopin's *The Awakening*, Richard Wright's *Native Son*, Zora Neale Hurston's *Their Eyes Were Watching God*, and *The Epic of Gilgamesh*; modern classics such as Toni Morrison's *Song of Solomon* and Rudolfo Anaya's *Bless Me, Ultima;* and more contemporary books such as *How the García Girls Lost Their Accents* by Julia Alvarez, *The Perks of Being a Wallflower* by Stephen Chbosky, the Gossip Girl series by Cecily von Ziegesar, *This Boy's Life* by Tobias Wolff, and Stephenie Meyer's Twilight series. Existing entries updated with new information on challenges or censorship include the Alice series, Toni Morrison's *The Bluest Eye*, Judy Blume's *Forever*, Margaret Atwood's *The Handmaid's Tale*, Robie Harris's *It's Perfectly Normal*, David Guterson's *Snow Falling On Cedars*, and James Joyce's *Ulysses*. Many of the newer challenges contain the increasingly vague charge of "explicit sexuality," which often proves to be indefensible.

Some attempts to censor and to limit the freedom of others to read what they choose seem amusing to everyone except to those who are the objects of the challenges and, of course, to those who have launched the challenges. In 2010, Apple Computers revived the controversy over James Joyce's *Ulysses*, which many thought had been put to rest in 1933. The company refused to add the graphic version of the novel to its iPads and iPhones unless the creators of the application revised the material and deleted the cartoon sketch of a naked Buck Mulligan diving into the sea. They reversed the decision after readers around the world filled Internet Web sites with criticism regarding the furor over what many opponents of the ban termed "the cartoon penis" incident.

Other challenges are inspiring to many observers. The highly popular Twilight series contains a brooding and moody but attractive vampire who expresses what many conservative readers view as the moral high ground when he refuses to have a sexual relationship until marriage. Despite this stance, parents have raised an outcry regarding the erotic undercurrent that exists in the novels, and their challenges have resulted in the temporary removal of some or all volumes in the series from school libraries.

The number of challenges reported annually appears to have decreased in recent years, but the reason for this decrease may simply lie in the practice of preventive banning, in which officials in school and public library systems neglect to purchase a book that has aroused controversy. Nonetheless, perceptions have changed to some extent. With increasing frequency, review committees appointed by school districts or county school boards report having taken the time to read material being challenged and, after sometimes prolonged debate, have returned the books to classrooms or to school library shelves, albeit sometimes with certain restrictions, such as setting minimum age requirements for checkout or demanding written permission from parents. Such capitulation does not constitute total victory over the efforts of those who seek to deny others the freedom to read what they choose nor does it suggest that efforts to fight censorship should be relaxed. Instead, the lower number of reported challenges should make us increasingly vigilant to the subtle ways in which others can suppress our right to read.

WORKS DISCUSSED IN THIS VOLUME

THE BLUEST EYE
Toni Morrison

BOY
James Hanley

THE BUFFALO TREE
Adam Rapp

CANDIDE
Voltaire (François Marie Arouet Voltaire)

CANDY
Maxwell Kenton

THE CARPETBAGGERS
Harold Robbins

CASANOVA'S HOMECOMING (CASANOVA'S HEIMFAHRT)
Arthur Schnitzler

THE CHINESE ROOM
Vivian Connell

CHRISTINE
Stephen King

THE CLAN OF THE CAVE BEAR
Jean Auel

CONFESSIONS
Jean-Jacques Rousseau

THE DECAMERON
Giovanni Boccaccio

THE DEER PARK
Norman Mailer

THE DEVIL RIDES OUTSIDE
John Howard Griffin

THE DIARY OF SAMUEL PEPYS
Samuel Pepys

DROLL STORIES
Honoré de Balzac

DUBLINERS
James Joyce

EAT ME
Linda Jaivin

THE EPIC OF GILGAMESH
Unknown

FANNY HILL, OR MEMOIRS OF A WOMAN OF PLEASURE
John Cleland

THE FIFTEEN PLAGUES OF A MAIDENHEAD
Anonymous

FLOWERS FOR ALGERNON
Daniel Keyes

THE FLOWERS OF EVIL (LES FLEURS DU MAL)
Charles Baudelaire

FOREVER
Judy Blume

FOREVER AMBER
Kathleen Winsor

FROM HERE TO ETERNITY
James Jones

THE GENIUS
Theodore Dreiser

THE GILDED HEARSE
Charles O. Gorham

THE GINGER MAN
J. P. Donleavy

THE GOATS
Brock Cole

LITERATURE
SUPPRESSED ON
SEXUAL GROUNDS

ALICE SERIES

Author: Phyllis Reynolds Naylor
Original date and place of publication: 1985–2005, New York
Original publisher: Atheneum
Literary form: Young adult novel series

SUMMARY

The 24 books in the Alice series by Phyllis Reynolds Naylor are very popular among teenage girls, many of whom write letters to the author, participate in "Alice" chat boards, and post blog entries stating how closely the experiences and concerns of the central character Alice McKinley mirror their own. Naylor portrays Alice and her friends as normal adolescents, talking about boys, cosmetics, and clothes; more important, she allows her characters to discuss the weightier issues as well. Their discussions include sex, body image, pregnancy, homosexuality, puberty, menstruation, and how a girl goes about buying a bra.

Alice McKinley is growing up without her mother, who died when Alice was four years old. As Alice continues through adolescence, she becomes increasingly aware that, however much her father and her older brother love her, there are some questions she is just not comfortable asking them. Her Aunt Sally did care for her for a few years after her mother's death, but Alice became the only female in the household when she was 10 years old and her family moved to Silver Springs because of her father's work. Alice has only vague memories of her mother, and her tendency to mix up the memories of what she and Aunt Sally shared with what she and her mother shared distresses her father.

Alice wants a mother, and she seems to be always on the lookout for a mother substitute. She would like to have someone who can take her shopping for jeans, teach her how to become a young woman, and explain to her how and why her body is changing. Throughout the series, Alice struggles with the normal issues and questions of every adolescent girl. She has numerous friends, but her closest are Elizabeth Price and Pamela Jones, with whom she can share her fears and concerns and from whom she receives support and advice. In many ways, their mothers serve as surrogates to Alice, who may not always speak with them directly but who receives information conveyed through Elizabeth and Pamela.

The books in the series are the following: *The Agony of Alice* (1985), *Alice in Rapture, Sort of* (1989), *Reluctantly Alice* (1989), *All but Alice* (1992), *Alice in April* (1993), *Alice In-Between* (1994), *Alice the Brave* (1995), *Alice in Lace* (1996), *Outrageously Alice* (1997), *Achingly Alice* (1998), *Alice on the Outside* (1999), *The Grooming of Alice* (2000), *Alice Alone* (2001), *Simply Alice* (2002), *Starting with Alice* (2002), *Alice in Blunderland* (2003), *Patiently Alice* (2003), *Including Alice*

(2004), *Lovingly Alice* (2004), *Alice on Her Way* (2005), *Alice in the Know* (2006), *Dangerously Alice* (2007), *Almost Alice* (2008), and *Intensely Alice* (2009).

CENSORSHIP HISTORY

The Alice series was number seven on the American Library Association's list of the top 10 banned books in 2002 and moved up to the number one position in 2003. Although the series did not appear among the top 10 challenged works in 2004 and 2005, it did occupy the third position in 2006. Since then, Alice has continued to generate controversy. Most challenges reported by libraries concern only one or two of the books, but in many instances libraries have withdrawn all books in the series while the specific book challenged is under review.

In 2002, Sonja Sullivan, the mother of a 12-year-old girl attending Blackman Middle School in Murfreesboro, Tennessee, complained about *Alice on the Outside* and requested its removal from all of the libraries in the Rutherford County school district. Her daughter had checked the book out from the Blackman Middle School library. In her complaint, Sullivan claimed that the book was "too sexually explicit" and thus inappropriate for her middle school–age daughter. The district review committee considered the complaint and recommended that the book remain on the shelves.

Also in 2002, parents in Webb City, Missouri, formally complained to the school board that all books in the Alice series should be removed from the school libraries because they are "immoral." The complaint, signed by several parents in the school district and supported by members of the state chapter of Concerned Women for America, asserted that one instance in which Alice befriends a girl being bullied in the restroom promotes homosexuality and that other books discuss topics "such as menstruation, puberty and sex that are best left to parents." In June 2002, the school board, whose members had not read the books, voted to remove all of them from school libraries despite a six-teacher review committee's recommendation to retain the books. At the next school board meeting, the board rescinded its vote and decided to read the books before taking further action. On August 13, 2002, the school reconsidered the fate of the Alice books in front of more than 50 citizens. Charles Moore, one resident who spoke against the books, said that he objected to the books "on moral grounds" and stated, "God tells us some of the things in these books is [*sic*] an abomination, like homosexuality and certain acts between men and women." School superintendent Ron Lankford told a reporter for the *Columbia Daily Tribune*, "A lot of name-calling has gone on . . . and remarks about people's 'commitment to religion.' " The school board voted to retain most of the books in the Alice series in the elementary school libraries and allow them to be taken out by students with parental permission but to remove the books *Achingly Alice*, *Alice in Lace*, and *Grooming Alice* completely. The local library in Webb City told reporters that after the ban the books were constantly checked out, and there were long waiting lists for each. As public librarian Sue Oliveira told an Associate Press reporter, "The surest way to get everyone to read a book is to ban it."

The American Civil Liberties Union stated in its report "Banned and Challenged Books in Texas Public Schools 2002–2003" that several Texas school districts banned or restricted books in the series during 2002–2003. The series was banned from the North East Independent School District in San Antonio, Humble Independent School District, and Linden-Kildare Independent School District in Linden. In Pleasant Grove Independent School District, *Achingly Alice* was restricted to students who had obtained signed parental permission. Challenges were also raised on one or more Alice books in Columbia-Brazoria Independent School District (West Columbia) and McKinney Independent School District.

In 2004, school officials in Mesquite, Texas, received a complaint about *Alice the Brave* from the mother of a fifth-grade student who submitted a written complaint that the book contained "inappropriate sexual references" and who requested the removal of the book from district's school libraries. School administrators at the Pirrung Elementary School referred the book to the district review committee, which was expected either to remove the book from the elementary school libraries and place copies only in the middle school or to pull it completely from the district libraries. Katherine Oates Cernosek told a writer for the *School Library Journal*, "Most likely, the committee will make a recommendation about removing it from the elementary level."

In 2005, parents Joe and Candy Riley in Shelbyville, Kentucky, submitted a formal complaint to the East Middle School Book Challenge Committee charging that *Alice on the Outside* "is too sexually explicit for middle school students." They objected specifically to instances in the book in which Alice questions an adult family member about sex, including how it feels to have intercourse and to masturbate. The Rileys also objected to the author's use of graphic terms and charged that "the author advocates lesbianism and multiple sex partners."

The book challenge committee was composed of the school principal Patty Meyer, librarian Louise Watts, seventh-grade teachers Debbie Meredith and Suzanne Guelda, and parents Sandy Phillips and Angela Best. The parents were vehement in wanting to remove the book from the school library; as Best noted, "the sex is way too much for this age group. I wouldn't want my daughter to read it." Phillips expressed concern "with the words the author used." The committee voted 3-3 to keep the book available, but superintendent Elaine Farris determined that the book would be available only in the librarian's office and students could request it only with parental permission.

In 2006, parents of students attending public schools in Wake County, North Carolina, submitted formal complaints to school districts officials to request the district remove five popular and classics books that they asserted contain "vulgar and sexually explicit language": THE CHOCOLATE WAR by Robert Cormier, IN THE NIGHT KITCHEN by Maurice Sendak, *Cassell's*

Dictionary of Slang by Jonathan Green, *Junie B. Jones and Some Sneaky, Peaky Spying* by Barbara Park, and *Reluctantly Alice* (1989) by Phyllis Naylor. Supported by the local Christian activist group name Called2Action, the parents complained that the books contain "graphic sexual descriptions" and, because of the content, they should have been informed of the reading assignments in advance. The ABC television local affiliate WTVD reported in a story televised on Thursday, June 22, 2006, that "School board members met with school administrators and recommended a revision of the existing book-use policy. Administrators then created a new policy to appease the angry parents." The new policy required teachers to provide parents with reading lists at the beginning of each school year. In order to use books not previously approved by the school district, teachers were required to complete forms and to provide reviews from professional sources to justify their use of specific materials in the classroom. They were also required to identify in advance "possible challenges that may come up during lessons such as sexuality, violence, adult language, and ethnic issues." As reporter Ed Crump stated, "Obtaining book lists would provide parents with time to request an alternate assignment, request the book be removed from the classroom, or simply discuss the book with their children. Parents who opposed the change in policy expressed concern that the new policy "could be the first step to censorship" and said that they "doubt the principal will approve most of the books, possibly for fear of more controversy."

In 2008, in Leavenworth, Washington, protests by parents against free access to *Alice on Her Way* (2005) led to borrowing restrictions at the Icicle River Middle School library that limited access to the book to students who had written parental consent. Parents told a reporter for the *Wenatchee World Online* that they objected to its "depiction of sexuality." The school board asked a review committee to study the book and to return with a determination regarding whether to retain the book in the middle school library or to remove it. After the committee returned its recommendation, the school board voted unanimously on March 24, 2008, to retain the book but provided a compromise solution for parents who challenged the book. District librarian John Mausser expressed some concern over the restriction and told a reporter that the board had "struggled with that for a while."

FURTHER READING

"*Alice on Her Way* Gets Waylaid in Washington." Available online. URL: www.ala. org/ala/alonline/currentnews/newsarchive/2008/march2008/alicewaylaid.cfm. Accessed September 20, 2010.

American Civil Liberties Union. *Banned and Challenged Books in Texas Public Schools 2002–2003: A Report of the American Civil Liberties Union of Texas.* Austin, Tex: ACLU, 2003.

"Censorship Dateline: Libraries." *Newsletter on Intellectual Freedom* 54 (May 2005): 107.

Crump, Ed. "Wake County Schools Revise Book Policy." WTVD-TV Raleigh-Durham, N.C. (June 22, 2006). Formerly available online. URL: http://abclocal.go.com/wtvd/story?section=news/local&id=4292888. Accessed September 20, 2010.

"Mesquite, TX: School Officials at Pirrung Elementary School Are Reviewing *Alice the Brave*." *School Library Journal* 50 (November 2004): 23.

"Missouri Librarians Latest to Discover: Banning Makes Books Popular." Associated Press. Available online. URL: www.freedomforum.org/templates/document.asp?documentID=17008&printerfriend. Accessed December 10, 2009.

"Murfreesboro, TN: A Book Review Committee Is Considering Whether to Remove *Alice on the Outside*." *School Library Journal* 49 (April 2003): 30.

"Webb City District Bans Trio of Books." *Columbia Daily Tribune* (August 15, 2002). Available online. URL: http://archive.showmenews.com/2002/Aug/20020815news017.asp. Accessed August 12, 2010.

ALWAYS RUNNING—LA VIDA LOCA: GANG DAYS IN L.A.

Author: Luis T. Rodriguez
Original date and place of publication: 1993, Willimantic, Connecticut
Original publisher: Curbstone Press
Literary form: Autobiography

SUMMARY

Always Running is the memoir of a former Los Angeles gang member that takes readers deep into the poverty, crime, and despair of the barrios of Los Angeles and reveals the often frightening and brutal world in which surviving is a daily struggle. With honesty and eloquence, Luis Rodriguez writes of surviving the gang lifestyle, "the crazy life." He reveals in the prologue how he managed to finally break free from gang life and explains what enabled him to begin focusing on being creative and to work for the advancement of the Chicano people. He explains clearly that, however important, these are not his main reasons for writing the book. Instead, he was motivated to tell his story when he realized that his young son, Ramiro, to whom the book is dedicated, was being swept up in the gang culture. His main concern was to save his son from the suffering he experienced and the threats of violence and death associated with the gang lifestyle.

The memoir begins with Rodriguez's parents' move from Mexico when the author was very young and outlines his early years living in the Watts section of Los Angeles; however, it covers primarily the years he was active in gang life in the Las Lomas barrio, from ages 12 through 18. The author states in the preface that this is a nonfiction work, but he admits that he has changed names and stories to protect people from being hurt by revelations about their lives. "I've changed names and synthesized events and circumstances in keeping with the integrity of a literary dramatic work, as an artist does in striving for that rare instance when, as a critic once said, 'something of beauty collides with something of truth.' "

Luis and his sisters and brothers were born in El Paso, Texas, but the family moved back and forth between there and Mexico while he was a baby. His father, a teacher, was sent to jail in Mexico for reasons that were never clearly revealed to the family. After he was released, the family left Mexico and ended up in Watts, one of the poorest sections of Los Angeles. Young Luis soon found himself surrounded by *la vida loca*, or "the crazy life," a world filled with violence, sex, suicide, drugs, prison, and death.

Luis's attempts to stay in school became increasingly difficult, as Latino students attended school where facilities and learning materials were outdated and the schools were surrounded by drug dealing and violence. The predominantly black and Latino schools of the author's experience did not receive the same funding as schools in other areas of the city, and in the late sixties and early seventies racial and gang-related confrontations were daily occurrences. Luis began a cycle of being suspended from school, then being expelled, and then ending up in jail or on drugs. When he was approximately 14, he began "sniffing" anything he could get his hands on: "I stole cans of anything that could give a buzz: carbono, clear plastic, paint or gasoline. Sometimes I'd mix it up in a concoction and pour it on a rag or in a paper bag we sniffed from." He refers to these mixtures as "spray" and describes their effects on his and his friends' brains in graphic language: "The world became like jello, like clay, something which could be molded and shaped. . . . With spray I became water."

Rodriguez's parents became disgusted with the lack of respect he showed toward the family and their house, so they made him move out of the house and live in their small garage. Soon after, he was initiated into the Lomas gang, and with several friends he began wreaking havoc on the lives of rival gang members, participating in beatings and riots, and having sex with multiple partners. With the increasing accessibility of heroin and PCP on the poverty-stricken streets of Los Angeles, the author's drug use became increasingly self-destructive. He describes his lingering depression throughout his high school years and his two attempts at suicide.

I tried to commit suicide. I had come home in a stupor from pills, liquor and from sniffing aerosol can spray. I had slithered into the house around 3 a.m. and made it to the bathroom. Everyone else slept. Leaning on a washbasin, I looked into the mirror and stared into a face of weariness, of who-cares, of blood-shot eyes, prickly whiskers poking out of the chin, an unruly mustache below a pimpled nose, a face that as much as I tried could not be washed away.

I staggered out of the house and crossed into a backyard with lemon trees and decayed avocados on the ground, and a tiled ramada with hanging vines. I entered my room in the garage, grabbed the pail I used to pee in, and filled it with water from a faucet on a rusted outdoor pipe. I planned to thrust my arm into the water after I cut an artery (I didn't want any blood on the floor—even at this moment I feared Mama cursing about the mess).

I pressed my street-scarred and tattooed body against the wall and held a razor to my wrist. Closed my eyes. Hummed a song—I don't know what song. But I couldn't do it.

He acknowledges that several times he wanted to leave the gang life but it always managed to pull him back in. He also describes the terrifying brutality of the police, who justified their actions by claiming that their treatment of gang members helped protect the law-abiding citizens of Los Angeles. According to Rodriguez, what they did not admit was that anyone whose skin was brown was likely to get stopped, harassed, and probably arrested.

Rodriguez reveals that from the age of 15, he was writing in his mind and in personal notes what became the beginning of *Always Running*. As he grew older, he tried to remove himself from the gang life, but making the change was very difficult for him. He bounced from school to school and eventually became involved in Chicano organizations. This new interest put some stability into his life, but the deaths of several friends and family members left him feeling empty. At the same time, his family was in the process of breaking down. His sister became involved in the gang life and his brother was murdered shortly after. His father continued to experience frustration in attempting to become an American teacher, and his mother struggled for years to learn English.

Rodriguez never glamorizes the gang lifestyle, but he explains why he could not avoid becoming involved in it. The reader begins to understand that his volatile behavior is a reaction against his young life and that of his fellow gang members. Violent passages such as the following one have been highlighted by opponents of the book: "The dude looked at me through glazed eyes, horrified at my presence, at what I held in my hands, at this twisted, swollen face that came at him through the dark. *Do it!* were the last words I recalled before I plunged the screwdriver into flesh and bone, and the sky screamed."

The author eventually found comfort in writing poetry, and through involvement in volunteer organizations he became involved in helping Chicano people advance. He learned that his organizational skills are far more helpful to his people than a gun or a knife in his hand. He successfully struggled to leave the gang, but his life came full circle when his young son joined a gang. After reading a poem written by his son, Ramiro, Luis helped his son leave his gang and realize that his life was more valuable to his family than to his gang.

CENSORSHIP HISTORY

Luis Rodriguez admits that *Always Running* is "a hard-core book" and presents "a lot of graphic material." He denies that any of the graphic material is gratuitous, claiming that "There's no way you can write this kind of book without getting as close to what these young people are going through." The book won the Carl Sandburg Literary Arts Award, and a *Chicago Sun-Times*

Book Award, and it was lavishly praised in reviews by the *New York Times*, the *Washington Post*, and the *National Catholic Reporter*. Parents and educators in several school districts have disagreed with that viewpoint and have banned the book.

In 1996, *Always Running* was the first book ever banned in the Rockford, Illinois, school district. Parents complained to school district officials that passages in the book contained "extreme violence, sexually graphic descriptions, and anti-family rhetoric." The story was picked up by Judy Howard, a local columnist who was affiliated with the conservative organization Citizens for Excellence in Education, and the controversy accelerated. On June 11, 1996, the Rockford School District school board voted 4-3 to remove the book from school libraries throughout the district. In the discussion preceding the vote, school board member David Strommer, who voted against keeping the book, spoke of *Always Running* as "irreligious, anti-family, left-wing, anti-American and radical. . . . What's in the book is harmful, ungodly and wrong." Ed Sharp, another board member who voted against the book, stated, "I challenge anyone who knows how the mind works, after reading this book, not to be more likely to assume the lifestyle of a gang person and not to be more likely to have sex in the back of a car."

In October 1998, controversy over the book arose in San Jose, California, when parent Sarah Gama told school officials that her daughter, a student at Lincoln High School, had complained that the book she had chosen from the supplemental reading list "was not clean" and claimed that a male classmate had made "a sexually explicit comment" to her on the school bus. *Always Running* had appeared on the supplemental reading lists for Lincoln High School and Broadway High School in the San Jose Unified School District for several years without controversy. Lincoln High School has a zero-tolerance policy on sexual harassment, but officials could do nothing because Gama and her daughter refused to identify the boy who had made the comment, "saying only that he was inspired to make the comment by *Always Running*." The school district gave Gama's daughter the opportunity to select another book, which she did, but Gama insisted that the district remove the book from the classrooms and libraries. When school officials refused to comply, she appeared on a local radio talk show and accused the district of "supplying pornography to children." The appearance triggered numerous angry telephone calls to school district officials. The *San Francisco Chronicle* reported on May 16, 1998, that a group called the Justice Institute threatened the school district with legal action, claiming that the district was promoting child pornography by keeping the book on the reading list. School officials yielded to the protestors and removed the book from school classroom and library shelves until a 10-member panel of parents, teachers, and community members could hear public testimony and readings of controversial passages. San Jose resident Adele Hernandez read aloud a long passage "detailing a variety of sexual acts in the back seat of a car" and then told members of the panel, "I'm sure none of you are exactly shocked by this. But I was. I'm sure there's a lot more out there other than this to teach our children." At the hearing, the chair of the English department at Lincoln High School, Kris Morrella, stated, "This book is an easy target. It's easy to take those few passages out of context." The panel recommended that the school district retain *Always Running*, but the book remained on junior and senior reading lists, and students who wished to read alternative books would have that option.

A May 1998 meeting was attended by nearly 100 people and lasted two-and-a-half hours, during which parents, teachers, and community members expressed heated opinions. In the end, the school board agreed with the panel's decision and voted to keep the book on the reading list. After two students spoke and defended the book, parent Rene Moncada stated to those present that teenagers are at "the stupidest time of their life. To me, their opinion doesn't count." He then read aloud an obscenity-filled passage from the book. Another parent, Deborah García, claimed that she was "embarrassed to read the book out loud" and said that she disliked the negative manner in which Hispanics are portrayed in the book: "I'm a proud American, but my history is Mexico, and the people and culture I know is very different from this." On July 23, 1998, a group of San Jose parents called the Parental Rights Organization, formed right after the school board voted to keep the book on the supplemental reading list, officially informed three board members that they would be subjected to a recall campaign.

In Modesto, California, in spring 2003, Patricia LaChapell, the parent of a home-schooled student in the school district, discovered that the supplemental reading lists for three advanced English classes at Beyer High School taught by teacher Melissa Cervantes contained *Always Running*. LaChappell contacted the board of education and requested that the board remove the book from the advanced English classes and from the approved list on which it appeared. The seven-member board declined to do so and, instead, recommended that administrators provide parents with more information about books, including a summary of the text. They also asserted that parents can choose to excuse their child from any assignment they find objectionable. In October 2003, LaChappell approached school administrators to complain a second time about the book. As the American Library Association Office on Intellectual Freedom reported, "After taking a second look at the board-approved book, district administrators told Cervantes that she could no longer use the book in her class." In defending the move, David Cooper, director of secondary education in the district, said the book was "not well-written and does not have the same literary value as other novels."

The swift and unilateral action by school district administrators outraged Barney Hale, executive director of the 1,800-member Modesto Teacher's Association. He said that the administrators had violated their own policy by pulling the book without going through the appropriate channel of taking the matter back to the board that had already approved it. To quell the uproar, the district sent the book for review to a committee of high school English department chairs. Members of the committee disagreed with the complaint and recommended reinstatement of the book, which is on a state-approved book list. In a vote of 4-3, the school board reaffirmed the decision to retain the book.

FURTHER READING

"Censorship Dateline: Schools: Modesto, California." *Newsletter on Intellectual Freedom* 53 (March 2004): 51–52.

Frey, Christine. "Parents Notify 3 SJUSD Trustees of Their Intention to Recall Them." *Willow Glen Resident*, July 29, 1998.

Gaura, Maria Alicia. "Parents in San Jose Criticize School Book—District Reviewing Use of Explicit Novel." *San Francisco Chronicle*, May 16, 1998.

"Modesto School Board Votes to Allow Controversial Book to Stay on List." KXTV News 10 Broadcast, December 16, 2003.

"Success Stories—Libraries: Modesto, California." *Newsletter on Intellectual Freedom* 53 (January 2004).

Sullivan, Patrick. "Luis Rodriguez Casts a Skeptical Eye on Attempts to Ban His Autobiography." *Sonoma County Independent*, February 4–10, 1999.

AMERICA (THE BOOK): A CITIZEN'S GUIDE TO DEMOCRACY INACTION

Authors: Jon Stewart, Ben Karlin, and David Javerbaum
Original date and place of publication: 2004, New York
Original publisher: Warner Books
Literary form: Nonfiction humor

SUMMARY

America (The Book) is an irreverent look at American history written in the form of a high school civics textbook. Jon Stewart, with the help of several of the writers of the popular television program *The Daily Show*, which gives a satiric edge to contemporary news, lambastes the intentions of the Founding Fathers and repeatedly takes aim at all three branches of the contemporary United States government and its policies.

The book is faithful in mimicking the textbook format, beginning with a "Study Guide" that provides bulleted highlights of each of the nine chapters, followed by a foreword by a noted individual (Thomas Jefferson). Chapter 1, "Democracy before America," provides a historical perspective complete with pie graphs and a mock "Timeline of Democracy," and the book continues through the founding of America to the present. Famous quotations and observations are given a new and comedic interpretation and illustrations and cartoons are juxtaposed with facts and statistics to provide a fractured and thought-provoking view of history. Photographs of presidents and other government officials appear throughout the book, as well as the photograph that created the greatest furor among challengers—a photograph of the Supreme Court justices without their clothes. Each chapter ends with a section of "Discussion Questions" and a page of "Classroom Activities." The final page of the book is an official-looking "Certificate of Completion" which states that "_____ has hereby completed *America (The Book)* and is thus fully qualified to practice, participate in, or found a democracy. Awarded this 221st page of *America (The Book)*."

As do most civics textbooks, *America* includes a number of maps of other nations, as well as the requisite foldout pages. Maps of Latin America, Russia, the Middle East, and Europe identify such important places and events as the "most seizable city," the level of "funness" to be found in various places, types of liquor found, the birthplace of the wet t-shirt contest, and other dubiously notable places or incidents. The large foldout poster is solely concerned with the United States. One side of the large poster contains a carefully illustrated and labeled diagram of "The Shadow Government," starting from the top with the White House and moving to the lowest level containing "CIA Drug Distribution," "The Voices in Your Head," "Virgin Mary Image Placement Division," "Illuminating Jews from the Center of the Earth," and "Halliburton." The other side of the poster advertises a boxing match, entitled "Skull vs. Bones: The Thrilla in Vanilla," and features manipulated images containing the heads of Senator John Kerry and President George W. Bush superimposed on the bodies of boxers wearing gloves and boxing shorts. The top of the poster announces "*The Daily Show* with Jon Stewart and The Founding Father Present" and the line above the proposed date, November 2, states "This Time It's Presidential." For added effect, the poster notes "Every Citizen Guaranteed a Vote" but in small print at the bottom adds "Vote not guaranteed to count."

The mock foreword sets the tone for the book. Signed "As Always, Thomas 'T. J.' Jefferson," the foreword labels John Adams "an unbearable prick [who] squealed girlishly whenever he saw a bug," and notes about Ben Franklin that "If crack existed in our day, that boozed-up snuff machine would weigh 80 pounds and live outside the Port Authority." About himself, "T. J." writes, "And I had slaves. Damn, I can't believe I had slaves!" He also questions in a postscript if it is true that actress Halle Berry is again single and claims that he would "be forever in your debt if you would put in a good word for T. J. Oh how I loves [*sic*] the mochachina."

Each of the nine chapters follows the methodical format of a textbook. The chapters open with an introductory page that provides an overview of the material covered; subheadings divide the material, and quotations from officials and presidents in the given era are provided in sidebars. Chapters also contain sketches and mock floor plans of government buildings that are labeled with innovative humorous uses for commonplace devices, such as the

"Video Uplink—For receiving ransom demands from super villains" found in the layout of "The Cabinet: Yes-Men of Freedom." Photograph captions identify the subject, but with a twist, as in the caption for a portrait of President John F. Kennedy: "John F. Kennedy (1917–1963), whose idealism and/or sexual escapades inspired a generation." Sidebars in each chapter provide "Were You Aware?" questions and "Quoting the President" statements, as well as the occasional "Congressional Glossary" to enrich the text.

Among "Were You Aware?" items are the following: "In pre-Colonial times, 'Colonial Williamsburg' was seen as a glorious vision of future utopia"; "Despite working long hours in grueling conditions, most slaves received absolutely no college credit for their unpaid labor"; "During the average president's first four-year term, he spends 1,241 days figuring out how to get a second four-year term"; "Campaign-finance laws do not specifically bar the donation of lottery tickets"; "Though they may grimace and roll their eyes, each of the Supreme Court justices secretly likes it when you shout 'Here comes da judge!' " In Chapters 8 and 9, the questions change to "Will You Be Aware?": "There was once a time when it was not only legal to talk about urning-bay the ag-flay but even doing so"; "The Social Security Administration once granted retirees a monthly check, instead of just a coupon good for a free side salad at Denny's"; and more.

America (The Book) spares no level of government, past or present, in its satiric look at "democracy inaction." Prominent figures are described with slang terminology, the character and the intentions of America's founders are questioned, and contemporary figures are ridiculed.

Chapter 1, for example, asks readers to "[i]magine a system in which anyone could wind up serving on the Supreme Court. *Anyone.* Think about your own family. Friends. The guys you knew in college who would eat dog feces for ten dollars." The chapter also offers a quiz to allow readers to determine "What type of government best suits you?" in which such grave concerns as the following appear: "Your typical day," "Your favorite kind of war," "Your standard breakfast," "Your pet peeves," "Your take on genital mutilation," and others.

Chapter 2, "The Founding of America," presents a chart of "Your Unelectable Founders—The Founding Fathers: Young, Gifted, and White." The chart identifies each founder's achievements and the reason each would be unelectable today. Benjamin Franklin "[l]oved the ladies. Loved 'em old, young, fat, thin, whatever. Couldn't get enough. Just loved 'em. Also, once wrote, 'As to Jesus . . . I have some doubts as to his divinity.' Kiss red states goodbye." George Washington had "[b]ad teeth and syphilis." John Adams "[a]ctually made principled, unpopular decisions." Alexander Hamilton was "[b]orn in West Indies, so constitutionally impossible. Had unfortunate tendency to duel . . . and lose." James Madison was "5'4", and would weigh 108 pounds even *after* the camera added ten pounds." Founding mothers fare little better: The book claims that Abigail Adams "was a dyke," and if Betsy Ross were alive and sewing flags today "she'd be a 13-year-old Laotian boy." The chapter also tells the "facts" behind the "fiction" of the founding fathers' notable accomplishments.

Chapter 3, "The President: King of Democracy," debunks the myth that everyone can become president, explains "why people should really stop spreading that rumor," and calls upon readers to "[d]iscover that most of what you've seen on *The West Wing* is total fucking bullshit." Readers are also offered the opportunity to "read who our gayest president was," to "take a ride in Stagecoach One," and to "lose your virginity (maybe, if you play your cards right)."

Chapter 4, "Congress: Quagmire of Freedom," invites readers to "compare and contrast the soulless gray-faced bureaucrats of the Senate with the soulless gray-faced bureaucrats of the House" and criticizes the manner in which Congress often hides unpopular or frivolous appropriations in bills containing important legislation. The McCarthy hearings of the 1950s also come under close scrutiny, as *America (The Book)* asks readers to embark on "an exotic journey of the senses as you are exposed as a leftist and homosexual."

Chapter 5, "The Judicial Branch: It Rules," tackles the Supreme Court of the United States and contains the photograph that fueled challenges to the book and the refusal of one large department store chain to carry the book. Readers are told that in this chapter they will learn how to desegregate a school and "learn how to operate a gavel responsibly and safely—even a stretch gavel." The book also invites readers to "See all nine Supreme Court justices naked (see pp. 98–99)" and "Discover how to know pornography when you see it (see pp. 98–99)." The pages listed function as paper doll books might, with nine black robes with tabs on the left-hand page to be matched to the nine naked justices on the right-hand page.

Chapter 6, "Campaigns and Elections: America Changes the Sheets," suggests that readers will "[g]o negative" and helps them "[l]earn why their vote counts, but not nearly as much as [their] money." Readers will also "[c]ontinue to be bored by the issue of campaign finance reform" and "[l]earn the hottest new debate techniques from *Dirty Dancing* choreographer Kenny Ortega." Included are several illustrations of mock campaign buttons and bumper stickers: "I Schtupped President Kennedy and I VOTE," "Catch the Dukakis Magic! Then, let us know where you found it," "Yo, Fuck McKinley," and "Life-Long Retired Palm Beach Jews for Buchanan."

Chapter 7, "The Media: Democracy's Valiant Vulgarians," attacks the news media in general and singles out specific self-promoting contemporary media figures. In a satiric swipe at conservative media critics, the book suggests that readers will "[l]earn how to identify political bias in today's liberal, bleeding-heart, Jew and gay-run media," "[b]ecome an unnamed source," and "[c]reate your own 'no-spin zone.'" The chapter contains numerous historical political cartoons from 19th-century newspapers, with references to the way in which presidents have used the news media to advance their plans, and discusses contemporary political interviewers such as Ted Koppel ("a shapeshifter"), Tim Russert ("Holding your own against Russert is a political rite akin to the Masai teenage-warrior circumcision ritual and only slightly easier on your penis"), Larry King ("it's easy to cry on the show because Larry King smells like onions"), and Geraldo Riviera ("an incredible asshole").

Chapter 8, "The Future of Democracy: Four Score and Seven Years from Now," asks that readers "[a]ngrily say loud, '*Future* of democracy? How 'bout some democracy right friggin' now?' " and allows readers to "[t]ake a look at the Washington of the future, and the crumbums of the future who occupy it." Further, readers will take a different view of ethnic diversity, one that appreciates how it will "enhance [their] take-out options." Warnings abound about such "emerging issues" as global warming ("Non-issue. Red herring. Not happening"), new global trouble spots ("Southern Ireland: Tired of being ignored, they start killing each other"), "Paraguay and Uruguay: War breaks out in 2030 over who is 'guayer,' " "India: Chaos reigns c. 2015 after running out of Gandhis," "Ibiza: Girls go wild; thousands killed"), distribution of wealth ("By 2050, it is believed the meek shall inherit, at best, a shit-sandwich"), and demographics ("In the 1990s, the Hispanic population of the U.S. rose 38%, comprising 12% of the populace by 2000. If these growth rates remain constant, 124% of all Americans will be Hispanic by 2060").

The final chapter, "The Rest of the World: International House of Horrors," purports to introduce readers to "the rest of the world in 22 pages" and allows readers to "see most common stereotypes reinforced." In this chapter, the book presents misidentified maps of Africa, Australia, New Zealand, South Pacific Islands, China, "Old Europe," Japan, Latin America, Central America, the Middle East, Russia, Eastern Europe, Scandinavia, and Southern Asia. Each map is accompanied by satiric comments about the social problems, government structures, and industrial concerns of the region.

CENSORSHIP HISTORY

America (The Book) contains so many instances of irreverence toward long-honored U.S. institutions, historical giants, and contemporary political and media figures that dozens of objections might have been raised to its publication and circulation. In an article published on November 2, 2004, *USA Today* derided the best-selling satire as "chock-full of four-letter words and bodily functions," further reasons that some might give to ban the book. Instead, the reason that Wal-Mart, a major retail chain, and the Jackson-George Regional Library System in Mississippi refused to offer the book was nudity—the book pretends to depict the nine Supreme Court justices naked and invites the reader to dress them in their appropriate robes as one might do with paper dolls. The obviously doctored picture contains the heads of the justices superimposed on nude bodies from photographs located at ClothesFree.com, a nudist Web site, but nudity, not the justices' dignity, is at the root of the opposition.

The *New York Times* reported on October 22, 2004, that Wal-Mart ordered thousands of copies of *America (The Book)* and then decided not to put the book on its store shelves because of "a photograph that it said customers might deem offensive." The retailer canceled its order because the book "didn't meet their criteria on potentially offensive material." A spokesperson for the retailer, Karen Burk, told a reporter for *USA Today*, "We felt a majority of our customers would not be comfortable with the image of the naked justices." In another interview published in the *Daily Cardinal* on October 22, 2004, an unnamed Wal-Mart spokesperson cited the photograph in the book as "too inappropriate for release in stores." The retailer issued a press release regarding the decision on October 21, 2004, which claimed that the majority of their customers would be uncomfortable with the work and stated that "it makes good business sense" to sell only products that appeal to the consumer.

Critics of the action, such as Allen Ruff of Rainbow Books, called the ban "censorship" and claimed that "it sends out immense messages about what's permissible and what's not permissible for people to look at, to read, to open. It's absurd." Other critics viewed it as "conspicuously insincere" that Wal-Mart banned the book from in-store sales yet made it available through its Internet outlet. As Greg Porter of the *Daily Cardinal* wrote, "Wal-Mart stores still sell the movie *About Schmidt*, which features Kathy Bates in the nude, and sexually explicit romance novels, such as those written by Danielle Steele." According to Porter, critics "suggest the retailers have an ulterior motive" and one bookseller cited Stewart's criticism of "the conservative regime in this country" as an attendant reason for the ban. Wal-Mart's cancellation of the order for in-store sales made little impact on the success of the book, although as *USA Today* reports, "Wal-Mart can account for as much as 20% of sales of popular books."

Because of the media attention generated by Wal-Mart's ban, Jon Stewart publicly invited other outlets to ban his book. Within months, the Jackson-George Regional Library System, which includes eight libraries near the Gulf Coast of Mississippi, appeared to accept the offer. Robert Willits, director of the Jackson-George Regional Library System, decided not to circulate the seven copies of the book, which the library had ordered without knowing about the nude photographs of the Supreme Court justices. Once Willits saw the photograph, he decided not to allow the books to circulate. He later told a reporter, "I've been a librarian for 40 years and this is the only book I've objected to so strongly that I wouldn't allow it to circulate." During a December 14, 2004, meeting of the library board, trustees affirmed the director's decision to withhold the book from circulation and agreed with his decision that the doctored photograph of the justices was the sole reason for suppressing the book. In an interview with a reporter for the Associated Press, Willits claimed, "If they had published that book without that one picture, that one page, we'd have the book."

The *Biloxi Sun Herald* reported on January 10, 2005, that library patron Tara Skelton had tried to borrow a copy of the book from the library system in October 2004, but she was told it was not in circulation. A library worker explained that the book contained a photograph that "showed private parts." Other local residents also criticized the board's decision.

The story of the ban was circulated by the Associated Press and published in national newspapers, including the *New York Times*, the *Washington Post*, and the *Los Angeles Times*, and the story also appeared on CNN. The library system received over 400 e-mail messages, most of them from out of state and negative in tone. In response to the negative publicity, the Jackson-George Regional Library System board held a special meeting in Pascagoula on January 10, 2005. In a vote of 5-2, the library trustees decided to lift the ban and put the seven copies of *America (The Book)* into circulation. In a report published in the *Newsletter on Intellectual Freedom* in March 2005, library board chairman David Abies explained the reversal: "We don't decide for the community whether to read this book or not, but whether to make it available." One of the board members, David Ogborn, who opposed lifting the ban, disagreed: "Our libraries are not a trash bin for pornographic materials."

Although his suppression of the book had initiated the outcry, Willits praised the board members for acting promptly and fittingly and stated to reporters, "There were twelve to fifteen people in the audience and most spoke up in defense of the book. . . . The board responds to the community input and they made that decision." He also told a reporter for the *South Mississippi Sun-Herald*, "We got some absolutely nasty e-mails and telephone calls that you would not believe. . . . We were communists and fascists at the same time."

Despite such outcries—or because of them—*America (The Book)* enjoyed 15 weeks as the number-one nonfiction hardcover book on the *New York Times* best-seller list in late 2004, sold 1.9 million copies from September through December 2004, and became "the gift book of the year," according to Barnes & Noble vice president Daniel Blackman. In December 2004, *Publishers Weekly* named *America (The Book)* book of the year. Social studies and history teachers in various parts of the United States have credited the book with igniting their students' interest in historical events and figures, prompting students to ask if some of Stewart's quotations and interpretations of actions are true and even to research certain facts on their own.

FURTHER READING

"America Defeats Mississippi Ban." *American Libraries* 36 (February 2005): 13.

"*America* (The Winner)." *Publishers Weekly*, December 13, 2004, p. 5.

Bass, Warren. "Whether You're a Hawk or a Dove." *Washington Post*, October 10, 2004, p. T13.

Levinson, Martin H. *"America (The Book): A Citizen's Guide to Democracy Inaction."* Book review. *et Cetera* 62 (April 2005): 216–17.

"Librarian Bans Jon Stewart." *Los Angeles Times*, January 11, 2005, p. E3.

"Library Board Puts Jon Stewart's Book Back on Shelves." CNN broadcast, January 11, 2005.

"Library Board Reverses Ban on Stewart Book." *New York Times*, January 12, 2005, p. E2.

Maslin, Janet. "Politics 101, With All Its Mischief and Mirth." *New York Times*, September 16, 2004, p. E1.

Minzesheimer, Bob. "*America* Goes over the Top in Holiday Sales." *USA Today*, January 6, 2005, p. D1.

———. "Behind the Robes, Stewart Finds Controversy." *USA Today*, October 20, 2004, p. D1.

———. "Stewart's 'America' Offers Textbook Laughs." *USA Today*, September 17, 2004, p. E1.

Porter, Greg. "*America* Pulled from Shelves." *Daily Cardinal*, October 11, 2004.

"Success Stories: Libraries." *Newsletter on Intellectual Freedom* 54 (January 2005): 31–32.

"Success Stories: Libraries." *Newsletter on Intellectual Freedom* 54 (March 2005): 73.

Toppo, Greg. "Oh, Say Can You Snicker: Kids Take to *America (The Book)*, But Schools See a Mixed Blessing." *USA Today*, November 2, 2004, p. D6.

Wyatt, Edward. "Banned in Wal-Mart." *New York Times*, October 22, 2004, p. E1.

———. "Jon Stewart Book Is Banned." *New York Times*, January 11, 2005, p. E2.

AN AMERICAN TRAGEDY

Author: Theodore Dreiser
Original date and place of publication: 1925, United States
Original publisher: Boni & Liveright
Literary form: Novel

SUMMARY

An American Tragedy is a fictionalized version of the Chester Gillette murder case, which was tried in 1906. The story examines the manner in which one man's fate is determined by his background and personality and by the environmental conditions that lead him to desire luxuries and perquisites beyond his reach. The novel was originally published in two volumes: The first recounts events that lead to a death, and the second relates the story of the murder trial.

Clyde Griffiths is the son of street evangelists whose skid-row mission income cannot provide him with the fine clothes, high social status, and sophisticated friends that he craves. As a bellhop in an expensive Kansas City hotel, he comes into contact with wealthy people who have everything that he wishes to possess. He also explores his sexual needs in his infatuation with Hortense Briggs, on whom he spends his salary. After he accidentally kills a pedestrian in an automobile accident, Clyde leaves Kansas City and travels to Lycurgus, New York, where his uncle gives him a job as a supervisor in the family collar factory. Clyde also makes his first visit to a brothel in a scene that describes both the interior of the brothel and the variety of girls available to him. His chosen partner leads him upstairs to a room and "calmly, and before a tall mirror which revealed her fully to herself and him, began to disrobe."

Wishing for a "free pagan girl of his own," Clyde becomes sexually involved with Roberta Alden, a factory worker who believes that he loves her. Although their sexual activity is not graphically described, the reader is clearly aware that their relationship is not platonic as they struggle "in vain against the greater intimacy which each knew that the other was desirous of yielding to, and eventually so yielding, looked forward to the approaching night with an eagerness which was a fever embodying a fear." The affair proceeds, but Clyde becomes infatuated with and hopes to marry the daughter of a wealthy factory owner. When he tries to break off his relationship with Roberta, he learns that she is pregnant. Despite his efforts to arrange an abortion through visits to pharmacists and a doctor, Roberta remains pregnant and insists that Clyde honor his promise to marry her. They take a day trip into the Adirondack mountains, and Roberta drowns in an isolated lake when their boat tips and she tumbles overboard. Clyde fails to save her, and the author leaves unclear whether he even tries. Although Clyde runs away, he is caught and placed on trial. Eventually convicted, he is sentenced to die in the electric chair, but until his death he remains unsure whether he committed a murder.

CENSORSHIP HISTORY

In 1929, *An American Tragedy* was suppressed in Boston after a jury declared New York publisher Donald Friede guilty of violating the Massachusetts antiobscenity statute by selling the novel. In the case of *Commonwealth v. Friede*, Mass. 318, 171 N.E. 472 (1930), the attorney for the Watch and Ward Society read various passages in the courtroom, and neither the judge nor the members of the jury read the entire novel. After reading the passage regarding the scene in the brothel when the girl begins to undress, the prosecuting attorney stated to the all-male jury: "*Well*, perhaps where the gentleman who published this book comes from it is not considered obscene, indecent, and impure for a woman to start disrobing before a man, but it happens to be out in Roxbury where *I* come from."

When Friede's attorney Arthur Garfield Hays and Dreiser asked the court to consider the entire book rather than merely specific passages, the judge refused. The defense also brought in noted trial attorney Clarence Darrow, whose main role consisted of reading passages from the book aloud. Hays had intended to question Dreiser in a way that would allow the author to show that he had never intended to write an indecent or obscene book, but Dreiser was denied that opportunity as the judge excluded all of the defense attorney's questions. Friede was convicted of selling an "impure and obscene" book, although he received no sentence. In May 1930, the publisher appealed the case, but the Massachusetts Supreme Court upheld the conviction in *Commonwealth v. Friede*, 271 Mass. 318, 171 N.E. 472, 69 A.L.R. 640 (Sup. Jud. Ct. 1930) and forced Friede to pay a fine of $300. The trial judge refused to allow the entire book to be read in court, ruling that it would have been impractical to read the whole book to the jury and observing that omission of the allegedly obscene passages would have eliminated nothing essential from the novel. The court also overruled the appeal of the bookseller, who had been entrapped into selling the book. The irony is that, while the trial was in progress, the novel was required reading across the Charles River in a Harvard University English course.

The public outcry over *An American Tragedy* motivated the Massachusetts legislature to reform the laws regarding censorship. Of several bills that were proposed, a law that would have required the whole book rather than excerpts to be considered in court was defeated on April 1, 1929, in the Massachusetts Senate in a vote of 15 to 13. The bill was submitted a second time and again defeated, this time with a vote of 20 to 17.

FURTHER READING

Boyer, Paul S. "Boston Book Censorship in the Twenties." *American Quarterly* 15 (Spring 1930): 3–24.

Bullard, F. Lauriston. "Boston's Ban Likely to Live Long." *New York Times*, April 28, 1929, Sec. 3, pp. 1, 7.

Gilloti, Chris F. "Book Censorship in Massachusetts: The Search for a Test of Obscenity." *Boston University Law Review* 42 (Fall 1962): 476–91.

Grant, Sidney S., and S. E. Angoff. "Recent Developments in Censorship." *Boston University Law Review* 10 (November 1930): 488–509.

Markmann, Charles L. *The Noblest Cry: A History of the American Civil Liberties Union.* New York: St. Martin's, 1965.

"More of the Same: Massachusetts Supreme Court and Dreiser's *American Tragedy.*" *Outlook*, June 11, 1930, p. 214.

Schriftgiesser, Karl. "Boston Stays Pure." *New Republic*, May 8, 1929, pp. 327–29.

THE ARABIAN NIGHTS, OR THE THOUSAND AND ONE NIGHTS

Translator: Sir Richard Burton
Original dates and places of publication: 1881, England; 1885–88, Switzerland
Original publishers: Worthington Book Company; The Kama Shastra Society
Literary form: Collected folktales

SUMMARY

Long considered merely children's entertainment, the tales of *The Arabian Nights* were familiar to English readers through such stories as "Sinbad the Sailor," "Aladdin and His Lamp," and "Ali Baba and the Forty Thieves."

Of Persian, Indian, and Arabic folk origin, the tales were first collected in Cairo around 1450 and known as *The Book of a Thousand and One Nights.* The French translation by Antoine Galland, published privately from 1707 to 1717, brought the tales to the attention of Europeans, and countless adaptations were published in England and the United States in the 18th and 19th centuries.

All editions have followed the same story framework. The storyteller is Shahrazad (Scheherazade in other translations), who begins the tales as a means of staying alive. After ordering beheadings of his queen and 10 favorite concubines who had cuckolded him, the Sultan Shahryar (Schahriah in other translations) marries each night for three years a new wife who is strangled at daybreak. When his country protests the depletion of available young women, he marries Shahrazad, who asks that her sister Dinarzade remain with her. Shahrazad begins a story for her sister one hour before daybreak on her wedding night. Shahryar also listens and becomes intrigued, but Shahrazad stops mid-story at daybreak. Because Shahryar wants to know how the story ends, he spares her life and asks her to continue the story that evening. Cunning Shahrazad continues her story but ends mid-story each daybreak for 1,001 nights, by the end of which she has borne three children, told 270 tales, and earned her husband's trust and love.

Edward William Lane published privately the first English translation in 1840 and John Payne's *The Arabian Nights* appeared in 1881, but Sir Richard Burton's translation remains the most complete and alone captures the tone of the original, although it has generally remained unavailable. Lane translated fewer than half of the tales and omitted sexual references. Payne translated substantially more tales and many of the tales lack sexual incidents while other tales contain metaphoric sexual references: "She did off her clothes and I had a lover's privacy of her and found her an unpierced pearl and a filly no man had ridden." Animal-human intercourse is reported and thighs, breasts, and buttocks are frequently mentioned.

Burton, whose translation includes even more explicit sexual detail, wrote in his foreword that he translated the tales into language "as the Arab would have written in English." Thus, they are exuberant, earthy, and unembarrassed tales of lust, lesbianism, sodomy, bestiality, male transvestism, pederasty, incest, and sexual mutilation. His sexually willing slave girls, nubile virgins, omnipresent eunuchs, lecherous old women, and wine-induced lust entice the reader. Although most of the descriptions of sexual behavior are tastefully presented with euphemisms, the sexual nature of the actions is clear. One story details a porter's carousing with three ladies who admire and toy with his "prickle" while he teases about "thy slit, thy womb, thy coynte, thy clitoris." Several seductions began as a man and a woman "warm with wine" embrace with "kisses and murmurs of pleasure and amorous toyings," after which they indulge in "hot lust" before having "abated her maidenhead."

Included in Burton's translation is the lengthy "Terminal Essay," which devotes one-quarter of its 166 pages to analyzing, describing, and evaluating on a country-by-country basis the variations of pederasty and sodomy with which he had become familiar in his years of travel. Written in the language of the social anthropologist and quoting the writings of travelers, historians, and medical experts, he identifies known homosexual liaisons from history and describes the practices as well as the social roles of pederasts and homosexuals in history and in the 19th century.

CENSORSHIP HISTORY

The Obscene Publications Act was passed in 1857 with the express purpose of suppressing sexually explicit material, and fear of prosecution made Burton cautious. Although he did not expurgate his work, he did modify greatly the manner in which it was published. He had 1,000 copies of the work printed in Benares, India, at his own expense and named the Kama Shastra Society, of which he and fellow author Foster Fitzgerald Arbuthnot were founders and sole members, as the publisher. The first printing was sold to subscribers for the equivalent of $200 in today's currency. The books were financially successful, and Burton made a profit of 10,000 guineas ($25,000 in 1890s currency).

Burton claimed that *The Arabian Nights* was meant only for men and particularly for male scholars who wished to increase their understanding of other cultures. As Rice reports, Burton was denounced in the *Edinburgh Review* as "a man who knows thirty-five languages and dialects, especially that of pornography" and an authority on "all that relates to the bestial element in man." His lengthy work was called by another reviewer "an extraordinary agglomeration of filth."

After Burton's death, abridged forms of his work were published, but the full unexpurgated version remained unavailable to the public—and was banned by U.S. Customs—until after 1931. When Burton died, his wife, Lady Isobel, destroyed all of his private papers, as well as the original notes and manuscript for *The Arabian Nights*. She also entrusted William Coote, secretary of the National Vigilance Association, to burn books and papers after her death to remove all remaining "indecencies."

Payne's translation was one of a number of expensive editions of literary classics, including Boccaccio's THE DECAMERON, Queen Margaret of Navarre's THE HEPTAMERON, Rabelais's *GARGANTUA AND PANTAGRUEL*, Fielding's THE HISTORY OF TOM JONES, Rousseau's CONFESSIONS, and Ovid's THE ART OF LOVE, involved in the civil case *In re Worthington Company*, 30 N.Y.S. 361 (1894). In 1894, the New York Society for the Suppression of Vice, under the zealous leadership of Anthony Comstock, brought civil proceedings against the bankrupt Worthington Book Publishing Company, which was seeking the right to sell off assets. The receiver for the company asked the court to allow sale of the books, expensive volumes of world-renowned literary classics. Comstock appeared in the court record as opposing the sale.

In stating the decision of the court, Judge Morgan J. O'Brien wrote that "a seeker after the sensual and degrading parts of a narrative may find in all these works, as in those of other great authors, something to satisfy his pruriency," but he added that to simply condemn an entire literary work because of a few episodes "would compel the exclusion from circulation of a very large proportion of the works of fiction of the most famous writers of the English language." The court decision characterized the specific editions as being "choice editions, both as to the letter-press and the bindings . . . as to prevent their being generally sold or purchased, except by those who would desire them for their literary merit, or for their worth as specimens of fine book-making." In short, even though the text remained the same as that in cheaper editions, Judge O'Brien determined that the "very artistic character, the high qualities of style, the absence of those glaring and crude pictures [set these books] entirely apart from such gross and obscene writings as it is the duty of the public authorities to suppress."

The U.S. Customs Office continued to ban the import of Burton's unexpurgated translation until 1930, when the Tariff Act removed the ban on acknowledged literary classics.

FURTHER READING

"Anthony Comstock Overruled." *Publishers Weekly*, June 30, 1894, pp. 942–943.
Bercovici, Alfred. *That Blackguard Burton!* Indianapolis, Ind.: Bobbs-Merrill, 1962.
Brodie, Fawn M. *The Devil Drives: A Life of Sir Richard Burton.* New York: Norton, 1967.
Rice, Edward. *Captain Sir Richard Francis Burton.* New York: Scribner, 1990.
Thomas, Donald. *A Long Time Burning: The History of Literary Censorship in England.* New York: Praeger, 1969.

THE ART OF LOVE (ARS AMATORIA)

Author: Ovid (Publius Ovidius Naso)
Original dates and places of publication: CA. A.D. 1, Rome; 1926, England
Publisher: John Lane (England)
Literary form: Poetry collection

SUMMARY

The Art of Love is a guide to attracting and holding the attention of a member of the opposite sex, and it is composed in three parts. The first part gives wise advice to men concerning how to win a mistress, the second part advises men how to retain the interest of the mistress, and the third part tells women how they can satisfy the sensual desires of men. Ovid provides suggestions regarding the care of the body and the face, the ways of flattery, and the advantages of selecting a mature mistress. Critics have noted parallels between advice given by Benjamin Franklin in "Advice on Choosing a Mistress" and passages from *Ars Amatoria*, such as

> Let me see my girl with eyes that confess her excitement;
> Let her, after she comes, want no more for a while.
> What does youth know of delight? Some things ought not to be hurried.
> After some thirty-odd years, lovers begin to learn how.

Ovid also gives women advice regarding how to make the most of their good points, including the ways in which to pose themselves in various situations.

> Lie on your back, if your face and all of your features are pretty.
> If your posterior's cute, better be seen from behind . . . .
>
> If the breasts and thighs are lovely to look at,
> Let the man stand and the girl lie on a slant on the bed.

The advice to men is geared toward grooming them to be effective predators, and his advice for women prepares them to be desirable prey.

CENSORSHIP HISTORY

The Art of Love appears to have created difficulties for Ovid in A.D. 8, when Augustus banished Ovid from Rome for political reasons; historians note that the erotic content of the poems provided a contributing factor to Ovid's banishment. In 1497, in Florence, Italy, *The Art of Love* was burned with the works of Dante for their "immoral" content in Fra. Girolamo Savonarola's Bonfire of the Vanities. In 1564, the work was added to the list of books banned by the Tridentine Index in Rome, for "treating of lascivious or obscene subjects."

In 1892, *The Art of Love* was involved in the litigation of the Worthington Book Publishing Company, which was in financial difficulty. The receiver wanted to sell some of the company stock, including Burton's translation of THE ARABIAN NIGHTS, Fielding's THE HISTORY OF TOM JONES, Boccaccio's THE DECAMERON, Queen Margaret of Navarre's THE HEPTAMERON, Rabelais's GARGANTUA AND PANTAGRUEL, and Rousseau's CONFESSIONS to pay off creditors, but Anthony Comstock, leader of the New York Society for the Suppression of Vice, stepped in to oppose the sales. He demanded of the court that the books be officially burned. (See entry for *The Arabian Nights*.)

In 1926, United States Customs officers in San Francisco held up a new English edition of the *Love Books of Ovid*, illustrated by Jean de Bosschere, published by John Lane Company. The edition had been limited to only

300 copies and was already sold out. The work was banned from importation until the passage of the 1930 amendment to the Tariff Act eased restrictions on foreign classics.

FURTHER READING

Craig, Alec. *Suppressed Books: A History of the Conception of Literary Obscenity.* New York: World Publishing, 1963.
Hurewitz, Leon. *Historical Dictionary of Censorship in the United States.* Westport, Conn.: Greenwood, 1985.
Loth, David. *The Erotic in Literature.* New York: Dorset, 1961.

THE AWAKENING

Author: Kate Chopin
Original date and place of publication: 1899, United States
Original publisher: Henry S. Stone & Company
Literary form: Novel

SUMMARY

The Awakening, subtitled "A Solitary Soul" when it was first published in 1899, ignited strong feelings among reviewers, most of whom condemned author Kate Chopin for her portrayal of Edna Pontellier, a married woman and mother who dared to strive for personal and sexual freedom.

The novel opens on Grand Isle, where Edna, her husband, Leonce, and their children are on vacation from their home in New Orleans, staying at the pensione owned by Madam Lebrun. Edna, who "comes of sound old Presbyterian Kentucky stock," marvels at the lack of prudery among the other guests, who are all Creoles, unlike "Mrs. Pontellier, though she had married a Creole, was not thoroughly at home in the society of Creoles; never before had she been thrown so intimately among them." Although she finds the easy exchange of intimate details among both men and women shocking, "she had no difficulty in reconciling it with a lofty chastity which in the Creole woman seems to be inborn and unmistakable."

Edna enjoys a light flirtation with Madame Lebrun's son Robert, a self-professed romantic three years her junior who, each summer since the age of 15, "had constituted himself the devoted attendant of some fair dame or damsel. Sometimes it was a young girl, again a widow; but as often as not it was some interesting married woman." His most recent targets of adoration were Mademoiselle Duvigne, who died between summers, and Madame Ratignolle, the mother of three small children, whom Edna's husband views as the most perfect example of a mother-woman. "It was easy to know them, fluttering about with extended, protecting wings when any harm, real or imaginary, threatened their precious brood. They were women who idolized their children, worshipped their husbands, and esteemed it a holy privilege to efface themselves as individuals and grow wings as ministering angels." Edna Pontellier is not one of them. She "dabbles" in painting, chooses to live in "her own small life all within herself" as she has since childhood, and leaves her children to pick themselves up and brush themselves off when they fall.

Edna thinks of her marriage to Leonce Pontellier as "purely an accident," which occurred while she was secretly and hopelessly in love with a famous tragedian. Leonce expressed deep love and devotion to her, although she felt indifference, but the strenuous objections of her father and sister Margaret to Leonce's Roman Catholic faith provided the final motive to marry him. After a time, "she grew fond of her husband, realizing with some unaccountable satisfaction that no trace of passion or excessive and fictitious warmth coloured her affection, thereby threatening its dissolution." She feels a similar fondness for her children, but she does not miss them when they spend the summer with their grandmother; rather, she feels a relief at their absence and a freedom "of a responsibility which she had blindly assumed and for which Fate had not fitted her."

While on Grand Isle, Edna begins "to loosen a little the mantle of reserve that had always enveloped her," chiefly due to the influence of "mother-woman" Adele Ratignolle. Although their relationship remains within the boundaries of social propriety, Chopin describes their interactions in homoerotic terms: "The excessive physical charm of the Creole had first attracted her, for Edna had a sensuous susceptibility to beauty. Then the candor of the woman's whole existence, which every one might read, and which formed so striking a contrast to her own habitual reserve—this might have furnished a link. Who can tell what metals the gods use in forging the subtle bond which we call sympathy, which we might as well call love." The two escape one morning from their children and from the adoring Robert Lebrun to wander to the beach, where they share intimate memories. At one point, Adele places her hand on Edna's and, when "the hand was not withdrawn, she clasped it firmly and warmly. She even stroked it a little, fondly, with the other hand, murmuring in an undertone, "'Pauvre cherie.'" Edna is momentarily disconcerted by the action, "but she soon lent herself to the Creole's gentle caress." Despite the description, Adele takes on the role of mother surrogate to Edna and later warns Lebrun to refrain from his usual banter and flirting with Edna because "She's not one of us; she is not like us. She might make the unfortunate blunder of taking you seriously." Lebrun defends himself and points out that his flirtations are only in fun and not meant to compromise the reputations of anyone, unlike the effect that the behavior of Alcee Arobin had on the reputation of a consul's wife in Biloxi. The reference is imbued with irony because, although Edna's reputation remains safe with Lebrun, she later compromises her marriage and herself by engaging in an affair with Arobin.

The summer on Grand Isle serves as a catalyst to reveal that Edna has long felt trapped by her surroundings and in her life. Each time she hears Adele play a specific piano piece, she imagines "the figure of a man standing beside a desolate rock on the seashore. He was naked. His attitude was one of hopeless resignation as he looked toward a distant bird winging its flight away from him." When she takes a nighttime swim, after a summer of seeming failure in swimming lessons, she first exults in "her newly conquered power" to swim alone some distance from shore, but once she loses sight of the shore, a "quick vision of death smote her soul." She abandons the short feeling of freedom to hurry to shore after "her encounter with death and her flash of terror." When she tells her husband that she could have died out there alone, he dismisses her concern. The same night, she stubbornly remains in a hammock outside the pensione and refuses to return to their room both when he asks "fondly, with a note of entreaty" and later, when he commands her, "'I can't permit you to stay out there all night. You must come in the house instantly.'" The sound of his command increases her resistance and leads her to wonder how she could ever have responded to such commands, and she perceives "that her will had blazed up, stubborn and resistant."

As the summer continues, Edna becomes enamored with Lebrun, and he finds excuses to spend as much time with her as possible, although the relationship does not become overtly romantic. He shocks her when he decides without warning to leave for Mexico, a journey he had planned to take several months later. Edna retreats to her room, unnerved by his impending hasty exit and becomes "overheated and irritable." She explains her reaction to Adele as a result of the noise and confusion at the table. "'I hate shocks and surprises. The idea of Robert starting off in such a ridiculously sudden and dramatic way! As if it were a matter of life and death! Never saying a word about it all morning when he was with me.'" He does see her before he leaves, and they promise to write to each other, but she is overcome with grief. And she also recognizes that she is infatuated with him, as she had been hopelessly infatuated with the tragedian. She also realizes that she had learned nothing from her past experience. "The present alone was significant, was hers, to torture her as it was doing then with the biting which her impassioned, newly awakened being demanded."

When the Pontelliers return to their home in New Orleans, Edna's dissatisfaction with her conventional, orderly life increases. Her beautiful home begins to feel suffocating, her children become "part and parcel of an alien world which had suddenly become antagonistic." She begins to brood over the reason for her discontent. Overtly rejecting her former existence, Edna "began to do as she liked and to feel as she liked." Instead of directing the routine of her household, she begins to come and go "as it suited her fancy, and, so far as she was able, lending herself to any passing caprice." In a frenzy of activity, Edna begins to paint, ordering first her sons then various servants to pose for her. Her moods vary violently from great unhappiness one day to days when she is simply happy to be alive and breathing and "she found it good to dream and to be alone and unmolested."

Leonce Pontellier consults with Dr. Mandelet, an old friend and the family physician, in an attempt to learn what might be troubling Edna and seems to be genuinely surprised when the physician expresses no great concern for the situation. He advises: "'Don't contradict her. The mood will pass, I assure you. It may take a month, two, three months—possibly longer, but it will pass; have patience.'" In contrast, Edna's father, the Colonel, reproaches his daughter for her behavior and tells Leonce that he is "too lenient by far" and advises "'Authority, coercion are what is needed. Put your foot down good and hard; the only way to manage a wife. Take my word for it'" When Leonce leaves for an extended business trip to New York, Edna attends a dinner party where she meets Alcee Arobin and accepts a ride home from him. Days later, he visits the Pontellier home and tells her how different life might have been had he known her years earlier. Although she tells him that she is sorry if she misled him, she is excited by Arobin's attention and easily accepts his daily visits, notes, and professions of adoration. "They became intimate and friendly by imperceptible degrees, and then by leaps. He sometimes talked in a way that astonished her at first and brought the crimson into her face; in a way that pleased her at last, appealing to the animalism that stirred impatiently within her." She learns that Lebrun will return to New Orleans soon and becomes thrilled with the prospect, yet continues her relationship with Arobin. "When he leaned forward and kissed her, she clasped his head, holding his lips to hers. It was the first kiss of her life to which her nature had really responded. It was a flaming torch that kindled desire." After Arobin spends the night with Edna, she experiences "an overwhelming feeling of irresponsibility. There was the shock of the unexpected and the unaccustomed." She reproaches herself for having betrayed her husband, who has "provided for her external existence," and Lebrun, for whom she claims to feel "a quicker, fiercer, more overpowering love, which had awakened within her toward him." Most of all, however, she feels regret because "it was not the kiss of love which had inflamed her, because it was not love which had held this cup of life to her lips."

Edna decides to leave her large, well-furnished house and her husband to live in a small house of her own, paid for with her own small income. She grows despondent when she learns that Lebrun returned to New Orleans weeks before but had not contacted her. They meet by chance at an outdoor café, and he returns to her home, but his sense of honor leads him to refuse to listen to her professions of love. He knows about her affair with Arobin and reminds her that she is still married. In her despondence, she tells herself, "'Today it is Arobin; tomorrow it will be someone else.'" She leaves the city and goes to the beach, where she will take a final swim. Before jumping into the sea, "she cast the unpleasant, pricking garments from her, and for the first time in her life she stood naked in the open air, at the mercy of the sun." Memories of her father, her sister, and her old life run through her mind as she swims far out into the Gulf of Mexico, leaving the reader to believe that she is committing suicide.

CENSORSHIP HISTORY

The Awakening excited controversy when it was first published in 1899, and it was not until 1969 that the novel received acclaim. In an article that appeared in the May 4, 1899, edition of *The Mirror,* Francis Porcher condemned Chopin's novel and wrote that it is "a writer's responsibility to avoid 'morally diseased' characters and 'adult sin.'" In her 1990 biography *Kate Chopin,* Emily Toth relates that reviewers strongly condemned what they termed the "unwholesome attitude" of the novel. A review of the novel that appeared in the May 21, 1899, issue of the *St. Louis Post-Dispatch* called the work "too strong drink for moral babes" and suggested that it "should be labeled 'poison.'" Well-respected critic and editor for *Harper's Weekly* William Dean Howells criticized Chopin for writing about topics that are not acceptable in polite society and "certain facts of life which are not usually talked of before young people, and especially young ladies." The majority of reviewers were highly uncomfortable with the novel because, as Elaine Showalter observes in her introduction to the Everyman's Library edition, "Where previous works ignored sexuality or spiritualized it through maternity, *The Awakening* is insistently sexual, explicitly involved with the body and with self-awareness through physical awareness. Although Edna's actual seduction by Arobin takes place in the narrative neverland between chapters 31 and 32, Chopin brilliantly evokes sexuality through images and details." Per Seyersted, Chopin's biographer, writes that critics had expected the novel to be a regionalist work, to convey a sense of the Creole lifestyle as in her earlier works "Bayou Folk" and "A Night in Acadie." Instead, while reviewers praised her already established talent, they expressed regret that she applied her talent to "the overworked field of sex fiction."

In 1902, the Evanston, Illinois, Public Library removed *The Awakening,* JUDE THE OBSCURE by Thomas Hardy, THE DECAMERON by Giovanni Boccaccio, *A Lady of Quality* by Frances Hodgson Burnett, *McTeague* by Frank Norris, and *Oroloff and His Wife* by Maxim Gorky from the open shelves, along with other books that the library board believed were objectionable. The board moved the books to the attic, and patrons could not take then out unless they had permission from a member of the library board. Library board member William S. Lord told the *New York Times* that only new books were barred. "The fact that most people don't know the character of the offensive volumes is the primary cause of blacklisting them. . . . lately published books, which are indelicate or immoral, are dangerous because people do not know their character until after they have read them." Lord admitted that the Evanston Public Library contained books "now which are as bad or worse than those which have been withdrawn from general circulation but we do not disturb them because people know what they are. No parent would allow a son or daughter to read 'Venus and Adonis' or 'The Passionate Pilgrim.' The story of 'Jude the Obscure,' however well it may be told, is not the proper thing for a boy or girl to read, but if the boy or girl drew it from the library the parents would not interfere, not knowing its character. On this account we are compelled to protect the public." In support of the decision by the library board, Evanston mayor Patten stated, "They [the books] ought not to be allowed to circulate among all classes. They are harmful to many, but, on the other hand, they can be read freely by those of more mature mind."

In 2006, *The Awakening* was among nine books on the required reading list that were challenged in the second-largest high school district in Illinois, an act that "triggered debate over whether works praised in literary circles are high art or smut." The specific reason for banning the novel was what one board labeled its "unnecessary sexuality." The controversy began when Leslie Pinney, a Township High School district 214 board member, identified books on the reading list that she considered to "contain vulgar language, brutal imagery or depictions of sexual situations inappropriate for students." The novels Pinney identified as inappropriate reading material, in addition to *The Awakening*, were SLAUGHTERHOUSE-FIVE by Kurt Vonnegut, THE THINGS THEY CARRIED by Tim O'Brien, BELOVED by Toni Morrison, FREAKONOMICS by Stephen D. Levitt and Stephen J. Dubner, *The Botany of Desire: a Plant's-Eye View of the World* by Michael Pollan, THE PERKS OF BEING A WALLFLOWER by Stephen Chbosky, FALLEN ANGELS by Walter Dean Myers, and HOW THE GARCÍA GIRLS LOST THEIR ACCENTS by Julia Alvarez. The school board member admitted that she had not read most of the books she targeted and claimed that she did not want to ban the books from the district libraries but "to replace them with books that address the same themes without explicit material." The challenges were the first time in more than 20 years that someone had attempted to remove books from the reading lists in the Arlington Heights–based district, which employed an extensive review process based on established reading lists. In defense of the choices, English and fine arts department head Chuck Venegoni told a reporter for the *Chicago Tribune*, "This is not some serendipitous decision to allow someone to do what they felt like doing because they had something about talking about something kinky in front of kids. It's insulting to hardworking people who really do care about kids." He criticized Pinney's approach of taking a few passages out of context to condemn entire books and observed, "There is nothing in any of those books that even remotely approaches what an objective person would call pornography." Although the school district had an opt-out clause that allowed parents to request that their child read another book if they found the assigned material objectionable, Pinney found the current measures ineffectual "because unless you're digging around the student's backpack, looking at the books and reading them, how exactly will you know what your student is reading?"

Five hundred people attended the school board meeting on Thursday, May 25, 2006, to debate whether to keep *The Awakening* and the other novels on the school reading lists. Supporters of the ban asserted that their efforts were "to protect students from smut," and some people, such as Arlington Heights resident Bruce Ticknell, claimed that "teachers promoting the books were motivated by their own progressive social agendas." Students took the debate to the social networking site MySpace.com and sophomore Scott Leipprandt placed a petition against the ban on the Prospect High page, which nearly 500 students and alumni from the six high schools in the district signed. Leipprandt told a *Chicago Tribune* reporter that fighting the banning of books is important. "It's important because it shows us things. All these things happen in real life. By banning it, it doesn't give us the opportunity to talk about it before we encounter it in real life." After a long meeting during which hundreds of people spoke, the school board voted 6-1 in favor of approving the required reading list without change.

FURTHER READING

Doyle, Robert P. *2007 Banned Books Resource Guide*. Chicago: American Library Association, 2007.

Francisco, Jamie. "Book-Ban Debate Is Long, Impassioned: More Than 350 Sign Up to Speak to School Board." *Chicago Tribune*, May 26, 2006, p. 2NW.1.

_____. "Explicit Move Is Made to Ban Books from Reading List." *Chicago Tribune*, May 24, 2006, p. 2NS.8.

Keilman, John, and Jamie Francisco. "Book-Ban Fights Are Far from Over: Reading Lists Face Scrutiny Across the State." *Chicago Tribune*, May 28, 2006, p. 4C.1.

Seyersted, Per. *A Kate Chopin Miscellany*. Natchitoches, La.: Northwestern State University Press, 1979.

Showalter, Elaine. Introduction to *The Awakening: A Solitary Soul*. New York: Alfred A. Knopf, 1992.

Toth, Emily. *Kate Chopin*. New York: William Morrow and Sons, 1990.

"Western Town Has Literary Censors: The Evanston Public Library Makes Up a "Black List." *New York Times*, July 6, 1902, p. 9.

BESSIE COTTER

Author: Wallace Smith
Original date and place of publication: 1935, England
Original publisher: Heinemann
Literary form: Novel

SUMMARY

Bessie Cotter, praised highly as a literary work when it was first published in January 1935, depicts the life of a prostitute in realistic and unglamorized images. Set in Chicago in the early part of the 20th century, the novel relates the story of Bessie Cotter, who willingly enters the life of prostitution simply because it pays better than factory work. She is not a miserable victim of the streets, nor has she been drugged, tricked, or abused into selling her body. Neither is she consciously immoral or evil.

Instead, Bessie is a likable character, basically decent and caring toward others, whose simple philosophy of life is based on survival. She clearly does not like the "sporting life," but life in Miss Myrtle's "parlour house" is warm and secure. Bessie is content that she is fed well and earns $25 each night at Miss Myrtle's. She contrasts these earnings with the $10 per week that she would earn if she worked in a factory, the only other type of work that someone lacking in marketable skills might find. The other "ladies" working at Miss Myrtle's have chosen their line of work for similar reasons.

Although the main action of the book takes place in a house of prostitution, the sexual activity is only suggested and not overt. In a similar manner, the language of the women and their clients is inoffensive; "obscenities" are used at only one point in the novel, when two waiters are clearing away dishes from the previous night. The fault of the novel, according to its critics, lies in the failure of the author to condemn Bessie and the other ladies of Miss Myrtle's for their lifestyles, or to provide them with punishment for their actions.

CENSORSHIP HISTORY

Described by *New York Times* reviewers as simply a novel about "a fallen woman in Chicago" in the announcement of publication that appeared in the May 22, 1934, column "Books Published Today," *Bessie Cotter* was soon recognized by literary critics in the United States for its "realism, pathos, and humor" in its portrayal of a young woman's life in a house of prostitution.

The novel was published in England in January 1935 by Heinemann, one of England's leading publishers, and sold openly for four months until the bishop of London and chair of the Public Morality Council, A. F. Winnington-Ingram, issued a complaint to the authorities that the novel portrayed "an immoral life" without regrets or recriminations. The publisher was charged with selling an "obscene book" with "intent to corrupt" and was ordered to appear before the Bow Street magistrate.

During the hearing, Attorney General Sir Thomas Inskip declared in his opening statement for the crown that "The book deals with what everybody will recognize as an unsavory subject—gratification of sexual appetite." He rejected suggestions by the defense that publishers in doubt about a manuscript should be able to submit material before publication to the Attorney General or other official for review and stated: "Neither I nor any other public authority could undertake such a task. Publishers must shoulder their own responsibilities."

The court fined Heinemann £205 (about $1,000 at the time) "for publishing an allegedly indecent American book, Wallace Smith's *Bessie Cotter*," and ordered the book, which had sold 6,000 copies in four months, to be removed from distribution.

FURTHER READING

"Books Published Today." *New York Times*, March 22, 1934, p. 10.

"Britain Bans U.S. Book—Novel by Wallace Smith Is Called Indecent—Publisher Fined. *New York Times*, April 11, 1935, p. 19.

Craig, Alec. *The Banned Books of England and Other Countries*. London: Allen & Unwin, 1962.

Rolph, Cecil Hewitt. *Books in the Dock*. London: Deutsch, 1961.

BLESS ME, ULTIMA

Author: Rudolfo Anaya
Original Date and Place of Publication: 1994, United States
Original Publisher: Warner Books, Inc.
Literary Form: Young Adult Novel

SUMMARY

Bless Me, Ultima is the coming-of-age story of seven-year-old Antonio Marez, who struggles to make sense of the changes happening within his family and in life surrounding him in New Mexico in the years immediately following World War II. The novel resonates with sounds of the Spanish language, which Anaya uses in chapter titles and throughout the work, and with the cultural traditions and the beliefs that define Antonio's world.

In 22 chapters, titled from "Uno"(one) through "Veintidos" (22), Antonio observes the actions and reactions of his parents, his brothers, the people in his small town, and the healer, Ultima. Antonio's parents differ in their goals for his future, and both draw upon their own backgrounds to derive their dreams for the little boy. The daughter of farmers, Maria Marez is a devout Catholic who prays that Antonio will become a priest, while his father, Gabriel, once a vaquero who wandered the New Mexico llano, wants him to become a vaquero and to wander the great plains as he once did. Their argument over his future has already resulted in problems when Ultima reenters their lives. She is a well-respected healer with an extensive knowledge of plant lore and a reputation for using white magic to help the people of the small town of Guadalupe. As a midwife, she has been present at the births of many people in the town, and Antonio's parents believe that only Ultima truly knows their son's future because she helped him to enter the world and only she knows where she buried his afterbirth.

Ultima moves into the Marez home, and Antonio follows her around as she gathers herbs to make her healing concoctions. As they work together, he learns both about the plants and the nature surrounding him, as well as about the spiritual world, of which he has largely remained ignorant. Antonio is forced to begin thinking seriously about sin and death after seeing Lupito shot to death by a crowd in retaliation for Lupito's murder of the sheriff. Lupito suffers from post-traumatic shock disorder—a malady undiagnosed among soldiers of the time—which led to his momentary madness during which he shot and killed the sheriff. Ultima takes the troubled little boy to church with her the next morning and speaks with him about the moral choices all people must make in their effort to confront the world. Her words seem vague to him at the time, but he refers to that conversation later as his brothers return from the war and he senses in them the trauma that led Lupito to such a violent end.

When Antonio begins school, after helping his mother's brothers to harvest their crops, his parents become increasingly anxious about his future. Pressed by Maria to reveal Antonio's future, Ultima tells the family that he will "be a man of learning," a prediction that leaves Gabriel dissatisfied, and he turns his hopes for the success of the family to his older sons, who return from serving in World War II. Gabriel anticipates that their return will enable the entire family to leave New Mexico and move to California, where he feels the opportunities for success will be greater. Rather than fulfill his hopes, Antonio's older brothers are restless and angry and unable to achieve peace with their father and instead leave the small town to pursue independent lives without the family. Their exodus further confuses Antonio, who cannot understand why his father and his brothers were not able to be happy together. His mother is saddened when her older sons leave, and she is unable to explain their behavior to Antonio and can only tell him that he will understand many things when he has his First Holy Communion, an event to which he looks forward eagerly.

The world surrounding Antonio becomes increasingly complicated for him, as he hears stories and learns truths about Ultima that are difficult to reconcile with the Catholic faith his mother has worked hard to instill in him. His friend Samuel tells him about a river god in the form of a golden carp that protects mankind, and he feels guilty for believing the story because it conflicts with his religious upbringing. He learns that the satanic Trementina sisters have cursed his uncle Lucas and finds that the Catholic priest cannot rout the curse, but Ultima can with Antonio's help. He then worries how to reconcile his respect for Ultima's abilities with his Catholic faith.

Antonio faces a major crisis one afternoon in a blizzard when he sees a fight between Narciso, the town alcoholic, and Tenorio, whose daughters had cursed his uncle Lucas. One of the sisters has died, and Tenorio blames Ultima for her death and plans to kill Ultima. Narciso tries to prevent the murder, and Tenorio shoots and kills him while Antonio watches. Afterward, the young boy develops a life-threatening fever and experiences horrifying dreams.

Through all of the traumatic experiences, Antonio holds fast to the belief that he will understand everything that has occurred once he has experienced his First Holy Communion, and he struggles to balance the dissenting voices of his father, his mother, and his friend Florence, who points out to him the weaknesses in Catholic teachings. Antonio expects to experience an epiphany on Easter Sunday, when he takes his First Communion, and he feels seriously let down afterward because he feels no change. As Ultima helps Antonio to build moral independence and reinforces for him the very strong existence of good in the world, she also adds to his confusion. He helps her to exorcise ghosts from a house that Tenorio has put under a spell and learns that Tenorio's remaining daughter has become very ill after the incident. He also loses his friend Florence when she drowns in the river. Antonio is sent to stay on his uncles' farm to recover from losing his friend, but conflict follows him there as well. After a relaxing summer, he encounters Tenorio while walking from his uncles' farm to his grandfather's house, and the crazed man chases him and shoots at him. Antonio remains unharmed, but Tenorio shoots Ultima's owl, her spiritual familiar. When the owl dies, Ultima's death becomes inevitable. Antonio sits with the old woman as she dies, and he carries out her wish that he bury her owl after her death.

The novel does not sanitize Antonio's experiences. At school, he hears another classmate confess to spying through a hole in the wall into the girl's bathroom. "I made a hole in the wall . . . could see into the girls' bathroom. . . . could see everything . . . her ass, hear the pee." A friend brags, "I saw a boy and girl fucking in the grass," to which another classmate replies, "Aw, I see them every night under the railroad bridge . . . naked." Tenorio and other characters curse as they express their anger and intermittent sexual references appear in the text, if only briefly.

CENSORSHIP HISTORY

Bless Me, Ultima, which won the Premio Quinto Sol national literary award in 1972, has been praised by literary critics as "the masterwork" of Rudolfo Anaya, who is widely acclaimed as the founder of modern Chicano literature. President George W. Bush awarded the author a National Medal of the Arts "for exceptional contribution to contemporary American literature for bringing national recognition to the Chicano people," and First Lady Laura Bush placed the novel on her "must-read" list. The novel has also been chosen by the National Endowment for the Humanities for its "Big Read" program. In contrast, parents and administrators in several school districts have condemned the novel as "filthy" and asserted that it contains "excessive vulgarity" and removed it from classrooms.

Norwood superintendent of schools Bob Conder said in February 2005 that he removed two dozen copies of the novel from English classes at the high school after a parent complained that the book contained "filthy" language. He then turned the copies over to the complaining parents John and Rhonda Oliver, who "put them in a trash can and it goes to a landfill. . . . This is just our way of knowing it would be gone." When Luis Torres, a professor of Chicano studies at Metropolitan State College in Denver, offered to pay the school district $1,000 to rescue the books, Conder said that the school district "would not sponsor such garbage" and stated that he had given the books to the parents who complained, claiming he "wasn't certain if the books had been burned or otherwise destroyed." Torres told reporters that he and his colleagues were offering the school district far more than the original cost of $7 each because they were concerned about the misreading of the book. "We are offering such a deal to the Norwood School District because 'Bless Me, Ultima' is one of the most significant cultural treasures of the Chicano community in the United States, and we do not want the book destroyed. Its philosophical basis is the combining, or 'mestizage,' in Spanish, of the Spanish and European and Mexican indigenous cultural traditions, the cultural combination that resulted in today's Mexican and Chicano communities." Public outcry was strong. After 20 students staged an all day sit-in in the school gymnasium and took turns reading aloud from the book, Conder apologized to the students and promised that none of the students who demonstrated would be penalized for their action. He also wrote a letter of apology for removing the book "without enough information on the content of the book" and without reading either the book or the school board policy regarding such issues. He stated that he had formed a committee to review the book, as well as the existing curriculum, and to make recommendations about the book. A year later, an article appearing in the *Denver Post* on May 12, 2006, reported that two teachers who had been outspoken in defending the book during the controversy over *Bless Me, Ultima* were not recommended to be rehired in the Norwood School District. Interim superintendent Larry Raney asserted "The book issue never came up," and refused to comment on the teachers' fate, claiming that he could not talk about the situation because "they are personnel matters" and noting that the two teachers were at the end of their three-year probationary period.

On February 2, 2009, the Newman Crows Landing Unified School District school board voted 4–1 to ban *Bless Me, Ultima* from the sophomore reading list at Orestimba High School after a controversy of several months that began when a parent complained that the novel is "sexually explicit." Superintendent of Schools Rick Fauss concurred with the decision to remove the book and expressed his concern that "There was excessive vulgarity or profanity used throughout the book." The controversy began in the summer of 2008, after Nancy Corgiat, the mother of a sophomore student at the high school, contacted the school superintendent and "initially complained about the vulgar language, the sexually explicit scenes and an anti-Catholic bias." Fauss claimed he "followed district policy, had two committees review the book, and ultimately opted to remove it from the classroom. It went through all the procedures as outlined in the board policy and ended up with me." Teachers were told to find a replacement book for classes, despite the protests of parents who voiced concern about the ban and said the board was spending too much time counting "bad words." Fauss and members of the school board expressed concern about the language and noted, "The context didn't make it acceptable." When parents suggested that lawyers with the American Civil Liberties Union might launch a lawsuit to reinstate the book, the superintendent expressed confidence that his position and that of the board would prevail: "We're not afraid of that; we know what our rights are. We have insurance; we'll fight it." He denied that the school district had engaged in an act of censorship and asserted, "It's not censorship. It's simply a matter of determining our curriculum, which is left to the school district."

FURTHER READINGS

"Censorship Dateline: Schools." Newsletter on Intellectual Freedom 58, no. 2 (March 2009): 39–41.

Draper, Electa. "Norwood Book Ban Brings Offer: Metro Prof Will Pay $1,000 to Retrieve Copies of 'Bless Me, Ultima.'" Denver Post, February 4, 2005, p. B–05.

Florio, Gwen. "Award-Winning Book Headed for Landfill." Rocky Mountain News, February 4, 2005. Available online. URL: http://www.rockymountainnews.com/drmn/state/article/0,1299, DRMN_21_3522696,00.html. Accessed June 14, 2010.

Lofholm, Nancy. "Town Fights to Retain Teachers: 2 Vocal Advocates: Norwood School District Officials Deny That a Book-Banning Incident Last Year Imperiled the Educators' Jobs." Denver Post, May 12, 2006, p. B-05.

Mehta, Seema. "California District Bans Book Lauded by Laura Bush." Record, February 2009, p. A07.

THE BLUEST EYE

Author: Toni Morrison
Original date and place of publication: 1970, United States
Original publisher: Holt, Rinehart and Winston
Literary form: Novel

SUMMARY

The Bluest Eye is a sad and tragic novel that recounts the abuse and destruction of Pecola Breedlove, a young African-American girl whose mother knew that her very dark baby would grow into an unattractive young girl. The novel, which takes place in 1940, is narrated by Claudia MacTeer, two years younger than Pecola and her only friend. Black in a white-dominated world, Pecola begins to believe that life would be prettier and better if she were white, and she views blue eyes as symbolic of whiteness. She watches her father, Cholly Breedlove, become increasingly violent as his shattered dreams and constant humiliations as an African American heighten his frustrations, and her mother, Pauline, escapes into the clean and orderly life of working as a maid in a white family's home.

Pecola is raped by her father one spring afternoon when he returns home drunk and the two are alone. She becomes pregnant after he rapes her a second time. Traumatized by the attacks, she drifts further from reality and visits fraudulent minister Micah Elihue Whitcomb, known commonly as Soaphead Church, to ask him to give her blue eyes. For a fee, Soaphead claims that he can help her, but she must perform a task for him. He has wanted to rid himself of an old, sick dog, so he gives Pecola poisoned meat to feed the dog but tells her only that feeding the dog will result in a sign regarding her wish. Pecola is horrified as she watches the dog stagger around the yard and then die.

The combination of the rapes and this incident drives Pecola mad, leading to her complete loss of touch with reality. Pecola believes that she does have blue eyes and invents an imaginary friend who is always nearby for reassurance that her eyes are the bluest in the world.

CENSORSHIP HISTORY

Several incidents in the book have sparked controversy. The two rapes of Pecola have been criticized for being too graphic in description, and the novel describes the sounds that Pecola hears of her parents having sex in the room next to hers. Another incident that is specifically described is Cholly's first sexual encounter, during which he is surprised by three white hunters who focus a flashlight on the young people and force them to conclude their sexual act.

The Bluest Eye has been challenged in several school districts because of its "vulgar" and "obscene" language as well as for its "graphic sexual description." In 1994, the novel was removed from the 11th-grade curriculum at Lathrop High School in Fairbanks, Alaska, after parents complained that the language was "obscene" and that it contained explicit sexual episodes. School administrators ordered the book removed from the required reading list and stated as their reasons that "it was a very controversial book; it contains lots of very graphic descriptions and lots of disturbing language."

That same year, the novel was challenged in the West Chester, Pennsylvania, school district and at Morrisville (Pennsylvania) Borough High School. Parents in both districts complained to the school board of education about the "sexual content" of the novel and its "objectionable language." After reviewing the complaint and the book, the boards in both districts rejected the parents' request to remove the book from the school libraries and reading lists.

In November 2003, in Bakersfield, California, parents of a student attending East Bakersfield High School in the Kern High School district filed a complaint with the school superintendent requesting to have *The Bluest Eye* removed from the school district curriculum. Sue and Fred Porter initiated the process after their 16-year-old daughter brought the novel home from school and told her mother that the book made her feel uncomfortable, especially the sexual descriptions. Sarah was not bothered by the rape of Pecola by her stepfather; rather, it was "the description of how his genitalia enlarged while he was raping her that I had a problem with." In the formal complaint, Sue Porter asserted that the book "is obscene, according to a dictionary definition. When you say that an illegal act such as pedophilia or incest is not repulsive or offensive to modesty, that's just not true." She acknowledged that the novel "may be great literature—and may not—but it's not appropriate for children. Teachers are not qualified to speak on incest and pedophilia. We're going to put this in our kids' laps and we're not giving them any counseling for it?" Kern High School district superintendent William Hatcher organized a committee of parents, teachers, counselors, ministers, and librarians to review the book. In their report, they determined that the book is not obscene and stated, "It is neither prurient nor titillating. More importantly, taken as a whole, it has serious literary value." The committee and Hatcher did agree, however, that parents would be notified by letter that their child is reading *The Bluest Eye* and, at the parents' request, students can ask for an alternative assignment. The superintendent approved the use of the novel in the junior and senior honors and advanced placement classes. At the January 12, 2004, meeting of the Kern High School district school board, several school board trustees raised the issue of removing the novel from the classroom. Trustee Sam Thomas expressed "grave reservations about the book's sexually explicit material" and said that he could not support the book with a clear conscience, but he would not pull the book from class reading lists because "What I support is not the book, but the process." Board member Larry Starrh stated that he had read the book and several articles and letters discussing it, and he had decided that it was not appropriate for the classroom. "I would like to recommend that we overrule the superintendent," he stated, and asked to have the item added to the next board meeting agenda, scheduled for February 2, 2004. State law prevented the trustees from voting at the January 12th meeting because the public had not been previously informed that a vote would take place. The controversy attracted the attention of faculty at California State University, Bakersfield, who defended *The Bluest Eye*. In a resolution, the Academic Senate voted to

support the decision made by Kern High School District Superintendent Hatcher and urge the members of the Kern High School District Board of Trustees to vote against banning of *The Bluest Eye* from honors and advanced placement high school reading lists. . . . as a university faculty, we have an obligation to protect freedom and to guard against undue censorship. The complaint in question is an effort to ban *The Bluest Eye* from all high school classrooms, resulting in the censorship of a world-renowned and critically acclaimed literary work by Nobel laureate Toni Morrison.

The district school board trustees voted on February 2, 2004, to support the decision of the superintendent to retain the book in the honors and advanced placement classrooms. The Porter family, who initiated the review, filed a lawsuit against their daughter's English teacher "on the grounds that assigning the novel constituted sexual harassment." The lawsuit was dismissed.

In August 2005, the Littleton (Colorado) Public Schools district school board removed *The Bluest Eye* from the media-center shelves of the Heritage and Arahapoe High Schools after one parent complained of the book's "explicit description of sex in telling the story of an 11-year-old girl who is raped by her father." The book had been approved for students in the 10th grade and up, but the complaint came from the parent of a Heritage High School ninth-grade student who chose the book from a list of optional reading. The district formed a study group made up of parents, teachers, and administrators to review the complaint. The group recommended that the board restrict the book to juniors and seniors, a recommendation the board rejected in a 3-2 vote at the August meeting and, instead, voted to remove the book entirely. District policy required that the book could not be reconsidered until the end of the school year, but students and teachers actively voiced their displeasure and worked for reinstatement of the book. On October 5, 2005, high school students conducted sit-ins in their respective school libraries and read aloud excerpts from the novel. That evening, English teachers and students appeared in front of the school board to defend the book. Amanda Hurley, an English teacher in Heritage High School, acknowledged that the novel is "painful, difficult to read," but she also stated, "We have to discuss it, we have to learn from it." Students spoke in favor of the book and expressed fear that banning it was a dangerous precedent. Camille Okoren, Heritage High School senior, stated, "Once you ban one book, parents and teachers think it's OK to ban another book. Everyone is offended by different things." The board refused to reconsider the August decision and suggested that any member of the community can initiate the process of adding a book to the list of approved volumes, which would bring the issue back to the board before the end of the school year. Judy Vlasin, a Littleton High School English teacher, filed an application for reinstatement of the novel and included materials to support the educational value of the book. The novel has since been returned to the classroom for use by ninth and 10th grade students.

In Howell, Michigan, in 2007, the revision of the high school English curriculum and reading lists to comply with new state graduation requirements led to protests and complaints at a Howell Board of Education meeting that attracted the attention of national groups, including the National Coalition Against Censorship (NCAC), the American Booksellers Foundation for Free Expression (ABFFE), and the Woodhull Freedom Foundation. Members of the Livingston Organization for Values in Education (LOVE) singled out *The Bluest Eye* and BLACK BOY by Richard Wright as "smut," although the books had been read for two years in American literature classes. Anne Blaine, resident and author of a Christian novel, read aloud to school board members several graphic paragraphs and stated, "I've never read such smut like that in my life." On February 6, 2007, Chris Finan, ABFFE president, and the executive directors of NCAC and the Woodhull Freedom Foundation, respectively, Joan Bertin and Ricci Joy Levy, wrote an open letter to the Howell Board of Education and President Susan L. Drazic. The letter defended study of the novels in the classroom and asserted that the insistence upon the sexual references in the novels were distortions.

> The sexual content and profanity in *The Bluest Eye* and in *Black Boy* represent small but essential parts of the novels, consistent with the kind of material that high school students frequently read. Indeed, if students were precluded from reading literature with sexual content, they would be deprived of exposure to vast amounts of important material, including Shakespeare, major religious texts such as the Bible, the works of Tolstoy, Flaubert, Joyce, Faulkner, D.H. Lawrence, and Nabokov, and contemporary books such as *I Know Why the Caged Bird Sings*, and many of the texts regularly assigned in high schools throughout the State of Michigan.
>
> The challengers' focus on the sexual content of *The Bluest Eye* and *Black Boy* is misleading. These books are primarily concerned not with sexuality but with the important issues created by differences in social class and race.

At a heavily attended meeting on February 12, 2007, the school board voted 5-2 to return the novels to the Howell High School curriculum. Prior to the meeting, LOVE president Vicki Fyke contacted the county prosecutor David Morse and asked him to investigate the assignment of the books as a criminal violation. Fyke asserted that the assignment of the novels in a classroom was equivalent to the "distribution of sexually explicit materials to minors." Morse complied with the request and decided that no laws were being violated. In a letter to Fyke, Morse wrote that teachers assigning books that have been approved by the school board are exempt from prosecution: "Since the school board has approved use of these books, the teachers and administrators have complied with the school code and are excepted from criminal prosecution under the statute." Morse also asserted that the novels did not meet the criminal standard of being harmful to minors "because the sexually explicit scenes that Fyke and others objected to did not only appeal to readers' prurient interest in sex, and the books as a whole have substantial literary value." After the Howell School Board approved reinstatement of the novels, Fyke contacted the U.S. attorney for the Eastern District of Michigan, who forwarded her case to the Federal Bureau of Investigation (FBI) to investigate her claim that the school district teachers were distributing pornographic material to minors. In an interview on March 1, 2007, with reporter Tony Tagliavia of station WLIX, Fyke stated, "If anybody else gave them this material, it's against the law." On March 10, 2007, ABFFE released the following statement regarding Fyke's efforts: "Late yesterday, U.S. Attorney Stephen J. Murphy III and the Michigan attorney general's office announced that the complaints of obscenity by LOVE are without merit, and there has been no violation of federal law by placing the above-mentioned books on the Howell school approved reading list." Although represented as a local group, LOVE was assisted by the American Family Association, a larger organization that has initiated restrictions and banning in other states. The Michigan chapter assisted in filing the complaint with the state attorney general and the U.S. Department of Justice, claiming that the books violate laws against child pornography and child sexual abuse.

FURTHER READING

"Award Winning Books Challenged in Michigan School." Letter to the Howell School District Board of Education, February 6, 2007. Available online. URL: http://www. ncac.org/literature/20070206~MI-Howell~Award_Winning_Books_Challenged_ in_Michigan_School.cfm.

Butler-Evans, Elliott. *Race, Gender, and Desire: Narrative Strategies in the Fiction of Toni Cade Bambara and Toni Morrison.* Philadelphia, Pa.: Temple University Press, 1989.

"FBI Investigates Charge That Howell Books Are Porn." WLIX Broadcast Reported by Tony Tagliavia, March 1, 2007. Available online. URL: http://www.wilx.com/ news/headlines/6240036.htm. Accessed January 31, 2011.

Kuenz, Jane. "*The Bluest Eye:* Notes on History, Community, and Black Female Subjectivity." *African American Review* 27 (Fall 1993): 421–431.

National Coalition Against Censorship. "Michigan Board Retains Challenged Books." (Press Release, February 13, 2007). Available online. URL: http://www.ncac.org/ literature/related/howellpr.cfm. Accessed January 31, 2011.

Newsletter on Intellectual Freedom (May 1994): 86; (January 1995): 25; (March 1995): 44–45; (March 2004): 50–51; (May 2004): 118–119; (November 2005): 29; (January 2006): 13–15; (March 2007): 50–54; (May 2007): 117–118.

Staht, Jayne Lyn. "Howell: A Postscript—Atlantic Free Press—Hard Truths for Hard Times." Atlantic Free Press (March 10, 2007). Available online. URL: http://www. atlanticfreepress.com/news/1/1148-howell-a-postscript.html. Accessed January 31, 2011.

Tirrell, Lynne. "Storytelling and Moral Agency." *Journal of Aesthetics & Art Criticism* 48 (Spring 1990): 115–26.

Weinstein, Philip M. *What Else but Love? The Ordeal of Race in Faulkner and Morrison.* New York: Columbia University Press, 1996.

BOY

Author: James Hanley
Original date and place of publication: 1931, England
Original publisher: Boriswood Ltd.
Literary form: Novel

SUMMARY

Boy is a bleak novel of an impoverished young boy who runs away to sea, hoping for a better life than the ugliness and cruelty of the slums in which he is growing up. James Fearon is an undersized 13-year-old boy whose sensitive and inquisitive mind and feelings clash harshly with his surroundings. He has dreams of becoming a chemist and wants to remain in school, but his father is a heavy drinker who rarely works and his mother displays a hopelessness that leaves the family barely able to survive financially. The only solution is for James to leave school and to find a job to keep the family together financially. One of his teachers recognizes the boy's intellect and learns of his ambitions; she tries to find a way to keep him in school but is unsuccessful.

Disheartened by knowing that he will have to leave school and give up his dreams of an education, James spends time at the docks, watching the ships arrive and depart. He realizes that Liverpool will offer him nothing more than a continuation of the life his parents lead, and he determines to run away to sea. Impetuously, James stows away aboard a steamship bound for Egypt. After a few days he is discovered hiding in the bunkers and told that he will have to work to stay aboard. He also begins to experience the hardship and the abuses that the hardened seamen are ready to mete out. At first, James's future on the ship appears reasonably comfortable. When the lookout man on the ship dies suddenly, the captain assigns James to the position, thus starting what could be his career as an apprentice seaman. The outlook for the boy at this point in the novel is good, because historically apprentice seamen have become master mariners and even owners of ships and shipping companies. The respite from brutality does not last for long. Through subtle language and references, readers learn that the boy is subjected to sexual abuse by several members of the crew, brutal actions that the rest of the crew simply ignore.

When the ship docks in Alexandria, one of James's onboard shipmates insists on taking him to several brothels to introduce him to heterosexual intercourse. James contracts syphilis as a result of these interactions, and the disease is discovered after the ship leaves port. The captain considers the boy's syphilis a threat to the other sailors, and he murders James. Regarding this action, *New York Times* book reviewer Percy Hutchinson stated, "Nothing more brutal, nothing more grotesque in its brutality, is to be found in any literature."

Hanley's aim is not to titillate readers. Instead, his book contains a strongly moral tone that offers more of a warning than an invitation to those who might fantasize about a life on the open seas. The sailors are made to speak in the coarse and crude manner that dockers and sailors speak, and the brothel scenes are graphically recounted, without romanticizing the sexual encounters. As evidence of its serious intentions to produce a quality work, the publisher first issued the novel in an expensive limited edition.

CENSORSHIP HISTORY

Soon after it first appeared, *Boy* was expurgated by the publisher and reissued in a less expensive edition than the first. The second edition contained asterisks in the place of certain words spoken by the sailors and in descriptions of sexual activity. In a cheaply printed third edition published in 1934, the publisher replaced the asterisks with euphemisms and omitted certain passages entirely. Police seized copies of this edition in November 1934 from a lending library in Manchester and charged the librarian with distributing an "obscene publication." The directors of Boriswood Ltd. were prosecuted for aiding and abetting in the distribution, and the company was later arraigned as the principal perpetrator. On the advice of attorneys, the publisher pleaded guilty to the charges and paid fines totaling £400.

The action panicked other reputable publishers who became more conservative in signing works to publish. Author E. M. Forster publicly deplored the use of the law to punish the publication of what he called "a novel of much literary merit." His remarks were made in a paper entitled "Liberty in England," presented at the International Congress of Authors in Paris in June 1935. Forster wrote, in his foreword to Alec Craig's *The Banned Books of England*, that the novel had been out nearly four years and was "generally accepted as a serious and painful piece of work" but "it attracted the wrath of the authorities."

FURTHER READING

Craig, Alec. *The Banned Books of England and Other Countries*. London: Allen & Unwin, 1962.
Dangerfield, George. "Invisible Censorship." *North American Review* 244 (Winter 1937–38): 334–48.
Forster, E. M. *Abinger Harvest*. New York: Harcourt Brace, 1936.
Hutchinson, Percy. "Mr. Hanley Plumbs the Lowest Circle of Inferno." *New York Times Book Review*, April 10, 1932, p. 6.
"Miscellaneous Brief Reviews." *New York Times*, August 1, 1937, pp. 92–93.

THE BUFFALO TREE

Author: Adam Rapp
Original date and place of publication: 1997, Emeryville, Calif.
Original publisher: Front Street Inc.
Literary form: Young adult novel

SUMMARY

The Buffalo Tree relates six months in the life of a 13-year-old boy serving time in a juvenile detention center after being arrested for stealing hood ornaments from cars and selling them. Sura enters Hamstock six weeks before the book opens, and his early apprehensions quickly turn to fright as he experiences violence, abuse, bullying, and terror that are far worse than in his home and neighborhood environment. The administrators at Hamstock offer little protection to their charges and often bully them as well, leaving only the hope of escape or of completing their sentence as comfort.

Sura's bunk mate Coly Jo enters Hamstock at the same time as Sura and becomes a constant target of bullies Boo and Hodge, older adolescents who are serving longer terms. Sura and Coly Jo have had most of their personal belongings stolen by Boo, but Coly Jo proudly tells Sura that even though Boo has taken his beloved squirrel skin hat, he has managed to keep the squirrel tail hidden and he will eventually fight Boo to regain the hat. Early in the book, Sura learns that the large dead tree outside his window, the "buffalo tree," helps some of the boys deal with the constant challenges to fight. In Hamstock, a boy who is being taunted to fight ("buffaloed") has two options—he can either "chuck" (fight) or show his courage by climbing out of a window and up through the branches of the "buffalo tree," after which the boy taunting him will carve his initials on the lower trunk of the tree, similar to an old-time gunfighter putting a notch on his gun handle. Sura sees Coly Jo burying something at the base of the tree but does not ask him about it.

The boys can barely deal with the violence that occurs during the day, and the night is filled with terrors for Sura and Coly Jo, who fear that the only way they will survive is if they look out for each other. They agree to sleep in shifts, Coly Jo first and then Sura, each listening and watching for the danger that the other inmates pose. Even the small light that Coly Jo keeps on because he is afraid of the dark is no protection. One night, Sura is exhausted and falls asleep during his shift. When he awakens abruptly, the light is off and the air reeks with human waste and urine. While Sura dozed, another inmate had entered and defecated and urinated on Coly Jo, his bunk, and the surrounding area. As Coly Jo lies whimpering softly, Sura cleans everything up and tries to console the other boy. He gives him a clean sheet from his own bed and lends him a jacket to sleep in. A short time later, Coly Jo commits suicide by climbing the buffalo tree in the bitter cold, hanging his jeans and t-shirt and Sura's jacket on the highest branches, and then throwing his naked body onto the snow-covered ground below. Mister Roberts, their "cottage pop," finds the body lying in a frozen lump on the ground and tries unsuccessfully to revive Coly Jo while the other boys watch.

Sura's second bunkmate, Long Neck, begins as a bully, taking Sura's shirt and bunk, sitting at Sura's writing desk, and bragging about having committed a federal offense by blowing up a mailbox. He claims that the police surrounded him before taking him in and asks if Sura has ever been surrounded. Rather than assert himself, Sura simply bides his time, knowing that the six months must eventually end. After two weeks, Long Neck becomes the target of bullies and then loses a fight. Afterward, he changes his behavior toward Sura, returning both the shirt and the bunk and agreeing that they should probably should set up a watch arrangement at night for mutual protection.

Sura completes his six months of detention without serious physical injury, and he gladly returns to his mother, who is now living with a good, kind man named Flintlock. Before leaving Hamstock, Sura digs around the huge base of the "buffalo tree" to locate what Coly Jo buried and finds that it was the squirrel tail wrapped carefully in a handkerchief. He takes the tail with him. After the Hamstock van leaves him in front of his mother's house, Sura does not enter immediately. He first has to locate his "hoody" bag that he hid in a coffee can and placed under an old drain pipe. In a symbolic act of restitution, he uses electrical tape to attach each hood ornament to the car in the neighborhood from which he originally stole it. Some of the owners have had the ornament replaced, and others have not. Sura thinks briefly about the few boys he became friends with at Hamstock but finds that he feels no connection to that life and is comfortable in returning home. "It's like someone took an eraser and cleaned the image of myself out of my mind. . . . Something in those Sura bones feels like home."

The novel provides a gritty look at the juvenile detention system, and sexuality plays a minor role in contrast with the cruelty, abuse, and violence that rule the boys' lives. Early in the book, readers learn that the boys frequently sneak out of their room to stand outside the door of Mister Roberts's apartment, where they look through the window of the door at the pornographic movies he watches. During these escapades, some of the boys masturbate. In another scene in the book, one that caused controversy in a school system, Sura relates,

> Demetrius Gord always comes into the shower room sporting a sex pole. He can't even wear his towel cause that sex pole sticks straight out into the air like a treehand.
>
> If you wake up with a sex pole it usually goes away after you bust that morning piss. But Demetrius Gord's always got one. And he'll stand there and show it to you, too, like it's something he won at the carnival. It's probably the biggest sex pole you'll ever see.
>
> As long as he stays under his shower head and keeps it to himself I could care less if he put hotsauce on it.

Sura also talks about the differences in the appearance of the "sex poles" of boys who have been circumcised and those who have not. He relates that the soap flakes that the institution makes the boys use in the shower sometimes burn the eyes and other parts of the body. "One time I used so much soap that I got some all up in my dick hole and that made it burn when I pissed. So I went right over to Nurse Rushing's office and had her take a look at it and just about busted a sex pole when she started touching me with those smooth hands." The burning does stop, but he is tempted to visit her office again and claim that he is still in pain.

CENSORSHIP HISTORY

The Buffalo Tree provides readers with an unflattering view of one juvenile detention center, which, the narrator says, does not contain the most dangerous or most hardened juvenile detainees in the system. The brutal attacks and humiliation dealt by the boys to each other and the seeming lack of compassion of the administration make the setting of the novel bleak and the lives of the boys hopeless. Yet the language, the portrayal of violence and brutality, and the abuse were not the issues that led to the banning of this book at Muhlenberg High School in Pennsylvania; rather, the reason for the ban was the scene quoted above, in which the narrator describes another character's genitals.

In April 2005, Brittany Hunsicker, a 16-year-old student at Muhlenberg High School, attended a scheduled meeting of the board of education and asked to speak. When acknowledged, she addressed the board members, asking first, "How would you like if your son and daughter had to read this?" Hunsicker then proceeded to read the communal-shower scene in which Sura describes Demetrius Gord's sexual arousal. She concluded by telling the board, "I am in the 11th grade. I had to read this junk." The board members expressed shock at hearing that a book that had been a part of the 11th-grade reading list since 2000 contained such a "sexually explicit" passage but none of them could explain who had placed it on the list. The student claimed that she had not wanted to read the book but that her teacher insisted that all juniors were required to read it. District school superintendent Dr. Joseph S. Yarworth said that such a requirement was "a violation of school policy" and that "alternative reading material must be provided if parents object to what is on the list." Before the school board meeting ended, the board voted unanimously to ban the book from the Muhlenberg High School curriculum.

The *New York Times* reported that by 8:30 A.M. the next day, all copies of the book had been collected and stored in a vault in the high school principal's office, a move that had not been ordered by the school superintendent: "As soon as Dr. Yarworth discovered that an overzealous underling had had copies of the novel stored in the school vault, he ordered them returned to storage in the classrooms so it could still be read by students who sought it out." The superintendent told the *New York Times*, "I wanted us to comply with the narrowest possible interpretation of the board's decision."

In the weeks that followed, students circulated petitions to have the book reinstated in the curriculum. Teachers voiced their support of the book, as well. Conversely, editorials in the *Reading Eagle* praised Hunsicker for her "courage in challenging a book that never should have been part of the school's curriculum."

The school board met on May 4, 2005, the first meeting since the ban of *The Buffalo Tree*, and reconsidered the issue in front of 200 citizens. Mark Nelson, school board president, apologized for having voted to ban the book during the April meeting. He asserted that because he had not read the book he could not approve or disapprove of it, but he felt that "the decision had been hasty and in violation of the board's policy for book challenges." The policy required that all challenges to books must first be reviewed by a committee of teachers and administrators before the issue appeared before the board. Otto Voit, a board member who had read the book and voted to ban it, stated that the decision to remove a book from the curriculum was completely within the rights of the board.

Parents and students spoke before the board. One senior at the high school told the board, "Do not insult our intelligence by keeping this book from us." Tammy Hahn, mother of Brittany Hunsicker, who had initiated the complaint, told the board that she is a mother of four and responded that "the students' view is irrelevant. I am not about to let my daughter take part in a classroom discussion about erections." She added that such discussion amounted to "harassment to subject a girl to the smirks and innuendoes of male classmates who would have no sympathy for her discomfort." Other parents defended the book as presenting a look at "real life."

The board postponed a vote on the book for a week. On May 11, 2005, the school board met, and the well-attended session lasted until midnight. School board members spoke about the district policy of allowing alternative reading assignments when a student or a parent objects to a book on religious or moral grounds, and they stated that neither Brittany Hunsicker nor her mother Tammy Hahn objected. Hunsicker simply told her teacher that she "didn't like" the book and asked to read another, a request that her teacher refused. Hahn told the board that she would have made those specific objections based on moral grounds, had she known a formal objection was required rather than her daughter's singular expression of not liking the book.

The board voted to reconsider the ban and in 5-3 vote reversed its earlier decision, thus reinstating *The Buffalo Tree* in the Muhlenberg High School curriculum.

FURTHER READING

"Courage of Student Shown in Challenge." *Reading Eagle*, April 23, 2005.
"District Doesn't Need New Policy on Novels." *Reading Eagle*, June 10, 2005.
Weber, Bruce. "A Town's Struggle in the Culture War." *New York Times*, June 2, 2005, p. E1.

CANDIDE

Author: Voltaire (François-Marie Arouet)
Original date and place of publication: 1759, Switzerland
Publishers: Gabriel and Philibert Cramer
Literary form: Satire

SUMMARY

Candide, originally *Candide, ou l'optimisme*, is a satire of optimism and of the belief that "the world is the best of all possible worlds and everything in it is a necessary evil," a theory attributed to the philosopher Gottfried Leibniz. Voltaire refused to accept the philosopher's assertion that evil and death are part of a universal harmony, and he structured *Candide* to show the ridiculous nature of such thought. Voltaire hid his identity when publishing the book, noting that it was "translated from the German of Doctor Ralph with the additions which were found in the Doctor's pocket when he died at Minden in the Year of Our Lord 1759."

The work recounts the adventures of Candide, a young man educated by the optimist philosopher Pangloss to believe that the world in which he lives is "the best of all possible worlds." He lives at the castle of Baron Thunderten-tronckh and falls in love with the baron's beautiful daughter, Cunegonde. Caught kissing the young woman, Candide is ejected from the castle and begins to roam the world, penniless and hungry. He is witness to natural and social catastrophes, including the great earthquake of Lisbon and the terror of the Inquisition, in which numerous people suffer. On his journey, Candide becomes reacquainted with Cunegonde, who has her own adventures as the favorite of a series of men. Candide becomes, in turn, a captain in the army, a Jesuit priest, a sheepherder in South America, and a philosopher in Paris, where he also enjoys a love affair. When he finally finds Cunegonde once again, she has suffered several instances of rape and abuse, and she is now a servant. They settle on a farm with the string of characters who have joined Candide on his journey, but they soon become bored. To their good fortune, the group meets an old man who advises them to find contentment in cultivating their own garden.

CENSORSHIP HISTORY

In 1821, *Candide* was among the works to which Etienne Antoine, bishop of Troyne, referred when he wrote a pastoral letter to all clergy in France in which he reaffirmed all censorship orders previously issued by the clergy of France and the individual orders issued by the archbishops of Paris,

> in which these works were condemned as godless and sacrilegious, and as tending to undermine morals and the States. We prohibit, under canonical

law, the printing or sale of these books within the territory of this diocese, and we charge the vicar-generals to enforce this regulation and to see to the carrying out of the necessary penances for all who make confession of disobedience to these regulations.

The authority of the Catholic Church in France appears to have been considered sufficient for control of the matter, and no application was made to have the work placed on the Roman Index. Nonetheless, as a means of establishing authority, Pope Pius VII had placed *Candide* on the list of prohibited books of the Roman Index of 1806 and later renewed the prohibition.

In 1893, the American Library Association for the first time offered a 5,000-title book guide for small popular libraries and branches, calling it a collection that "one could recommend to any trustee." Geller observes that no works by Voltaire were included on the list because several of his works might prove to be "offensive" to some readers. Unlike Rousseau, whose biography, but not his works, the ALA at least included in the guide, no mention was made of Voltaire.

Candide was being studied in universities worldwide, was available in libraries, and appeared on college reading lists when United States Customs seized a shipment of the imported edition of the novel in 1928 and declared it obscene. The shipment was ordered by a professor of French at Harvard as assigned reading for his students. Relying on a previous ruling, a Customs official in Boston seized the shipment because the edition was unexpurgated. The professor and his Harvard colleagues contacted officials in Washington, demanding an explanation, and were told that Voltaire was on the list of banned works and that the Customs officer had acted correctly in confiscating the shipment. After the intercession of several influential politicians, the shipment was later released for use in the classroom. After a major setback in the 1933 litigation of ULYSSES, U.S. Customs recognized that a more discriminating appraisal of books was needed. The appointment of Baltimore attorney Huntington Cairns to assess the problems of Customs censorship resulted in new procedures that, by 1937, deprived Customs collectors and their deputies of their decision-making power. This ended the confiscation of accepted literature, such as *Candide*, in most cases, unless the editions contained illustrations that were "too vulgar or erotic," according to Customs bureau standards.

FURTHER READING

Ayer, Alfred Jules. *Voltaire*. New York: Random House, 1986.

Besterman, Theodore. *Voltaire*. New York: Harcourt Brace & World, 1969.

Geller, Evelyn. *Forbidden Books in American Public Libraries, 1876–1939*. Westport, Conn.: Greenwood, 1984.

Paul, James C. N. *Federal Censorship: Obscenity in the Mail.* New York: Free Press, 1961.

Putnam, George Haven. *The Censorship of the Church of Rome and Its Influence upon the Production and Distribution of Literature.* Vol. 2. New York: Putnam, 1906.

CANDY

Author: Maxwell Kenton (pseudonym for Terry Southern and Mason Hoffenberg)

Original dates and places of publication: 1958, France; 1964, United States

Original publishers: Olympia Press (France); G. P. Putnam's Sons (United States)

Literary form: Satire

SUMMARY

Candy is a satire that places its nubile and sexually acquiescent heroine, Candy Christian, from Racine, Wisconsin, in a series of adventures that culminate in a case of outrageous incest in a Tibetan temple. A clear spiritual descendant of Voltaire's *Candide*, Candy makes her way through numerous bizarre incidents that allow the authors to satirize social reformers, college professors, the American adoption of Zen mysticism, and the medical profession.

Candy is all body and no brains, a witless innocent who professes her virginity even as she is willing to yield to the advances first of her college ethics teacher, Professor Mephisto, who "needs" her, and then to those of a Mexican gardener to show him that she considers him her equal. She leaves home and travels to Greenwich Village, where she encounters an inarticulate man with a large hump on his back. Eager to show him that she does like him, and eager for him to like her, Candy invites the man to have dinner with her. His first words to her at her apartment are " 'I want' " as he unbuttons her jeans, "then he swiftly forced his hand across the panty sheen of her rounded tummy and down into the sweet damp . . . his stubby fingers rolling the little clitoris like a marble in oil. Candy leaned back in resignation, her heart too big to deprive him of this if it meant so much." He removes her jeans and panties, then adjusts her legs around his neck, "his mouth very deep inside her honey pot" as Candy continues to think, "It means so much to him." After being told by the hunchback, "I need fuck you!" Candy becomes the aggressor and shrieks, "Give me your hump!" He manipulates his body, "burying his hump between Candy's legs as she hunched wildly."

Candy then finds a gynecologist named Johns and a lecherous mystic named Grindle. She yields her body to both because "it means so much" to them. When he believes that Candy might be pregnant, Grindle, who has been her guru, gives her a one-way ticket to Tibet and tells her that she can achieve her spiritual acme there. Intellectually attracted to a mud- and dung-covered holy man, Candy is surprised to find him following her to a temple that contains a huge statue of Buddha. An earthquake occurs, causing the statue to topple. The holy man is thrown against Candy, the head of the Buddha statue rolls close behind her and its nose "moved slowly into Candy's coyly arched tooky. . . . *the Buddha, too, needed her!*" As she moves rhythmically in "esoteric Exercise Number Four," the movement has "definite effect on the situation in her honey-cloister as well, forcing the holy man's member deeply in and out." The rain washes away the mud and dung from the holy man's face as "the hopeless ecstasy of his huge pent-up spasm began," and Candy realizes: "Good grief—it's Daddy!"

CENSORSHIP HISTORY

Olympia Press publisher Maurice Girodias described his view of *Candy* as "a parody of pornography, rather than the real thing . . . done convincingly enough to satisfy the sex-obsessed whose sense of humor is notoriously blunted." One year after publication in Paris, *Candy* was banned by the Paris police while the publisher still had 2,000 of the original 5,000 printed copies unbound and at the printer. Because Girodias liked the book, he ordered the reprinting of the cover and the first few pages, giving the book the new name *Lollipop* to conceal the identity of the book from the French police. The publisher knew that this simple action would fool the inspectors because the police listed banned titles in alphabetical order and "a policeman's imagination seldom goes beyond the first letter of a word when it is not under orders to go any further."

The book continued to sell steadily and escaped further action until its publication in the United States by Putnam. Girodias recognized in the introduction to *The Olympia Reader* that *Candy* was not defensible on artistic grounds because it "dealt with the offensive subject of sex in such an open and unabashed manner that one would have expected a brutal reaction from the censors. In fact, very little happened, and this in itself is quite remarkable."

In 1964, members of the Illinois chapter of the National Organization for Decent Literature (NODL) issued a formal complaint against sale of the novel in Chicago bookstores. City officials warned booksellers not to sell or advertise *Candy* and told them that police would be watching to make certain that they complied. In light of court victories in recent years that had freed sales of Lolita, Tropic of Cancer, and Lady Chatterley's Lover, the booksellers organized to protest strict police censorship and threatened court action, charging that "the harassing of reputable book dealers is worse in Chicago than in any other city in the country" and that it had become the "Boston" of America. The NODL complaint was withdrawn and sales of *Candy* were permitted.

In 1966, law enforcement officials in Massachusetts responded to complaints of parents and educators who objected to sales of the novel to individuals under the age of 18. The case went to trial in *Commonwealth v. Corey*, 351 Mass. 331, 221 N.E.2d 222 (1966), and the prosecuting attorneys made clear that they did not seek to totally ban the book from sale. Rather, the question before the court was whether booksellers would be required to restrict sales of the book to people age 18 and over. After only brief testimony, during which booksellers did not offer resistance, the court ruled in favor of the prosecution.

FURTHER READING

Campbell, James. "Dirty Young Men." *New York Times Book Review*, June 6, 2004, p. 20.
Cook, Bruce. "Candy Comes to Chicago." *Nation*, September 14, 1964, pp. 125–126.
Girodias, Maurice. Introduction, in *The Olympia Reader*. New York: Grove, 1965.
Murray, D. M. "Candy Christian as a Pop-Art Daisy Miller." *Journal of Popular Culture* 5 (1971): 340–348.
Newman, M. W. *The Smut Hunters*. Los Angeles: All American Distributors, 1964.
Podhoretz, Norman, and Brian O'Doherty. "The Present and Future of Pornography." *Show* 4 (June 1964): 54–55+.
Sachs, Ed. "I Want *Candy*." *Focus/Midwest* 3 (February 1964): 11–13, 23–24.
Silva, Edward T. "From *Candide* to *Candy*: Love's Labor Lost." *Journal of Popular Culture* 8 (1974): 783–791.

THE CARPETBAGGERS

Author: Harold Robbins
Original date and place of publication: 1961, United States
Original publisher: Simon & Schuster
Literary form: Novel

SUMMARY

The Carpetbaggers, a novel containing numerous scenes of sex and of violence, is based loosely on the life of Howard Hughes. One reviewer, who estimated that "there is sex and/or sadism every 17 pages" of the novel, observed that the novel also "inaugurated a new mode of hard-boiled best-sellers." In many sections the novel combines both sex and violence.

Robbins takes his title from the name given to those Northern opportunists who overran the South after the end of the American Civil War, people who carried all of their worldly possessions in faded, multicolored bags made of remnants of carpet—carpetbags. In the same manner that the original carpetbaggers came to plunder the South, so do the characters in this novel exploit each other and Hollywood in its infancy. The story covers the years 1925 to 1945 in the lives of two men, Jonas Cord Jr. and Nevada Smith. The scion to the Cord Explosives empire, Jonas is used to having anything and anyone that he wants. Born Max Sand, Nevada Smith is the son of a white man and a Kiowa woman, and he has spent time in prison for murder and robbery. He is hired by old Jonas Cord Sr. as general companion, as well as to teach Jonas Jr. to ride. After the old man's death, young Jonas inherits his father's fortune and pays off his young stepmother, Rina, who tries in vain to convince Nevada to take her with him as he leaves the ranch.

As years pass, the paths of Jonas and Rina cross again in Hollywood, where Jonas becomes even wealthier by investing in movies, Nevada starts as a stuntman and becomes famous as a cowboy movie star, and Rina becomes an actress. Despite Rina's ongoing lesbian relationship, she marries Nevada in a media extravaganza and then divorces him soon after and marries again. The three thrive professionally in the growing film industry of the 1930s, but their personal lives are fraught with unhappiness as they drift from one sexual relationship to another. Eventually, Rina dies of encephalitis contracted while filming in Africa, but Jonas and Nevada survive. As the novel ends, Jonas has made the decision to reunite with his wife and daughter and Nevada has found a peaceful home life after the turbulence of his acting career.

Objections to the novel have centered on the explicit sexual descriptions, the frequent instances of adultery that pepper the novel, and the several instances of lesbian lovemaking that occur. Such lines as "her breasts rose like twin white moons against my dark, clenched fists" are common in the novel, as are such flowery euphemisms as "the foliage of her pubis" and terms such as "cunt," "fuck" and "bitch." The novel also contains a detailed rape sequence between Rina and her adoptive brother, in which Robbins places heavy emphasis on the specter of incest.

CENSORSHIP HISTORY

The Carpetbaggers was one of the most sensational paperback books of the early 1960s. In 1961, motivated by complaints filed by members of the National Organization for Decent Literature, police in Waterbury and Bridgeport, Connecticut, used informal censorship in asking that local wholesalers and retailers withdraw the book from sale because it was "obscene." Although booksellers and newsstand dealers in both cities complied with the ban on sales of the paperback edition of *The Carpetbaggers*, the Fairfield County chapter of the American Civil Liberties Union issued a formal protest to both Bridgeport Police Superintendent Joseph A. Walsh and Mayor Samuel J. Tedesco. In their letter to the mayor, the ACLU wrote that "no public official has the right to act as a censor." Mayor Tedesco sidestepped the issue and asserted, "This matter is entirely up to Superintendent Walsh." The police superintendent refused to reconsider the order to ban the book, pointing to the public support that the ban had received from parents "commending him for a campaign against obscene literature" and to the praise he had received from the Roman Catholic Bishop of Bridgeport, the Most Reverend Walter W. Curtis.

The paperback reprinter of the novel, Pocket Books, sued for damages and asked that a permanent injunction be granted, but the local court denied its request. In 1962, similar methods to ban the book were taken in Warwick, Rhode Island; Rochester, New York; and Mesquite, Texas, despite sales in the first two years that topped 2 million copies nationwide.

In 1965, booksellers in New Zealand experienced threats from local law enforcement officials, based on scattered complaints by individuals, that sales of *The Carpetbaggers* would be either banned or severely restricted. The firm of E. J. Hyams and Son Limited, acting on behalf of the publisher, New English Library Limited of London, submitted an application to the Indecent Publications Tribunal for review of the unexpurgated paperback edition of the novel to determine whether it was indecent. Although the counsel for the applicant offered brief submissions in support of the application, the counsel for the Department of the Secretary of Justice made no submissions. In its March 4, 1965, determination that the book "is not indecent within the meaning of the statute," the tribunal stated:

> It is a long story, prolix to the point of tediousness. There are accounts of sexual behaviour but we do not consider the narrative is such as to deprave a reader or to be injurious to the public good. We do not think there is any warrant for holding it to be indecent.

The novel was also banned in South Africa in 1965, and that government's Directorate of Publications later added two other novels by Robbins to the banned list: *The Betsy* and *Dreams Die First*.

FURTHER READING

"Bridgeport Police Scored on Book Ban." *New York Times*, March 15, 1962, p. 40.

Lewis, Felice Flanery. *Literature, Obscenity, & Law*. Carbondale: Southern Illinois University Press, 1976.

Perry, Stuart. *The Indecent Publications Tribunal: A Social Experiment*. London: Whitcombe and Tombs, 1965.

Robbins, Harold. "Master Harold." *Advocate: The National Gay and Lesbian Newsmagazine*, August 22, 1995, pp. 38–43.
"South Africa Bans a U.S. Novel." *New York Times*, August 4, 1978, p. B18.

CASANOVA'S HOMECOMING (CASANOVA'S HEIMFAHRT)

Author: Arthur Schnitzler
Original dates and places of publication: 1918, Germany; 1921, United States
Original publishers: S. Fischer (Germany); Thomas Seltzer (United States)
Literary form: Novel

SUMMARY

Casanova's Homecoming imaginatively re-creates the final conquest of the aged Casanova, who has become disgusting and contemptible to himself and to others. The novel begins with the 53-year-old impoverished Casanova waiting in Mantua to learn if he will be allowed to return to Venice, which he had left many years earlier after escaping from prison. He agrees to visit an old friend named Olivo, who has an attractive young niece as a guest. Remembering his past sexual conquests, among them Olivo's wife and her mother, Casanova becomes sexually aroused by Marcolina, Olivo's niece, whose unresponsiveness and seemingly incorruptible nature only arouse him further. He desires her more than he has desired any previous woman and observes that "Beneath the shimmering folds of her dress he seemed to see her naked body; her firm young breasts allured him."

Casanova deceives both the women with whom he has sex and his male friends, showing no regret for any of his actions. He is also highly disrespectful of the church and its representatives, and he refers to having been involved in an orgy with two nuns. When he learns that the seemingly pure Marcolina is sexually involved with Lieutenant Lorenzi, her young suitor, Casanova first thinks of denouncing her as "a lustful little whore" and then decides to take advantage of the situation. He plans to disguise himself one night and take Lorenzi's place in her bed. While he waits for the right moment to approach her, he seduces Olivo's daughter, gloating all the while that he had already seduced the girl's mother and grandmother. When night comes, Casanova enters Marcolina's window at midnight, wearing only the lieutenant's cloak over his nude body. He has sex with Marcolina and compliments himself on his performance: "From Marcolina's sigh of surrender, from the tears of happiness which he kissed from her cheeks, from the ever-renewed warmth with which she received his caresses, he felt sure that she shared his rapture."

When she awakens the next morning, Casanova must face reality when Marcolina reacts with horror, showing in her face her disgust for the "old man."

CENSORSHIP HISTORY

Casanova's Homecoming, translated from German by Eden and Cedar Paul, was one of three books published in 1922 by Thomas Seltzer and seized by the New York Society for the Suppression of Vice. Armed with a warrant issued by Magistrate Edward Weil, John Sumner led other society members on a raid of the publisher's offices on July 11, 1922, and seized more than 800 copies of *Casanova's Homecoming*, D. H. Lawrence's WOMEN IN LOVE, and the anonymously published A YOUNG GIRL'S DIARY. The publisher was forced to use his own trucks to transport the books to police headquarters. Stock was also taken from the shelves at Brentano's and Womrath's bookstores, resulting in what *Publishers Weekly* labeled "one of the most widely discussed cases in book censorship before the courts." The summons charged the publisher Thomas Seltzer with violations of Section 1141 of the Penal Code, which dealt with the publication and sale of obscene literature. Sumner claimed that he had received complaints from several sources, whom he refused to divulge, and refused to provide the publisher with any information until the trial. In signing for the books, Sumner indicated that they were receipted for by the Office of the District Attorney. Seltzer hired attorney Jonah J. Goldstein, and the two organized a comprehensive defense campaign, including newspaper publicity and letters of praise for the three books from literary figures and psychologists.

When the case went to trial on July 31, 1922, the magistrates' court contained highly respected witnesses for the defense, including Columbia University professor and literary critic Carl Van Doren, psychiatrist Adolph Stern, and magazine editors Gilbert Seldes and Dorothea Brand. The defense also argued against using isolated passages as the basis for deeming a book "obscene." Magistrate George W. Simms dismissed all charges against Seltzer on September 12, 1922, after praising the three novels as "a distinct contribution to the literature of the present day." Simms also cautioned the society:

> It has been said, with some justice, that the policy of pouncing upon books too frank for contemporary taste, without regard to the motive or purpose for which they were written, or the use to which they are to be put, is objectionable and should be curbed.

In 1923, Sumner succeeded in securing a grand jury indictment against *Casanova's Homecoming* and *A Young Girl's Diary*. The case never went to trial, and the society dropped the case two years after filing it when Seltzer withdrew the two books from distribution and agreed to destroy the plates. German-speaking Americans in the United States were free to enjoy the novel in its original language while litigation continued over the English-language version.

Simon & Schuster published the novel in 1930, and Sumner once again moved to block sales of the book. Armed with a search warrant and accompanied by a special agent and two police officers, Sumner seized an initial 477 copies of the novel from the publisher's office and served summonses on the firm and its sales staff. The society led by Sumner later seized more than 1,000 additional copies. The financially secure publisher, determined to fight the seizure and the tactics of the society, took the case to court and won a dismissal of charges. To avoid further unsavory maneuvers by Sumner and possibly expensive legal action, publisher Max Schuster traveled with a truck to the society headquarters and retrieved 1,500 confiscated copies of *Casanova's Homecoming.*

FURTHER READING

Boyer, Paul S. *Purity in Print: The Vice-Society Movement and Book Censorship in America.* New York: Scribner, 1968.
"Censorship Beaten in New York Court." *Publishers Weekly,* September 16, 1922, p. 801–804.
"The Law and the Censor." *New York Times,* September 14, 1922, p. 21.
"Seize 772 Books in Vice Crusade Raid." *New York Times,* July 12, 1922, p. 32.
Tanselle, G. Thomas. "The Thomas Seltzer Imprint." *Papers of the Bibliographical Society of America* 58 (Fourth Quarter 1964): 380–416.

THE CHINESE ROOM

Author: Vivian Connell
Original date and place of publication: 1942, United States
Original publisher: Dial Press
Literary form: Novel

SUMMARY

The Chinese Room is a psychological thriller that also attempts an indictment of upper-class English life, an approach that one reviewer called in "large part sheer nonsense." The plot focuses on London banker Nicholas Bude, who decides to experiment on his mind by writing anonymous letters to himself. Before he can begin, however, he receives several anonymous letters from someone else. While he attempts to sort out the puzzle, he isolates himself further from his already-estranged wife, Muriel. Long dissatisfied with her marriage, she takes the first of a series of lovers and discovers happiness through her reawakened sexuality. The psychological implications of this discovery are lost in the combined mystery story and attempts at psychological exploration. As a reviewer in the *Nation* observed, "If only because of the prurience of its sexual detail, a novel that might have been in the line of, say, D. H. Lawrence's LADY CHATTERLEY'S LOVER turns out to be in the line of adolescent reverie."

The novel presents a hard-hearted mistress in her slinky oriental silk pajamas, an elderly bank employee who goes home each night to become his version of a Chinese mandarin, and a man whose hands have personalities he cannot control, as well as opium smoking and hints of the supernatural. As Bude discovers his true self, he realizes that everyone carries inside a "Chinese room."

The sexual descriptions are suggestive. The village doctor propositions Muriel and twists "his kiss on her mouth as if he were twisting a cork into a bottle." She later begs him to kiss her again, crying out, "I want love so badly!" In their later lovemaking, Muriel discovers "the animal hunger of the woman," and readers learn that "his tongue never got tired." She also enjoys his "sadistic handling" and "felt that love-making, to be healthy, must be something nearer to a fight than a five-finger exercise on the body."

Bude has an affair with his secretary, Sidonie Coleman, a woman who "had as much humanity as a statue." In one scene, Bude "pressed his face into her breasts. . . . [H]e had seized her and taken her into the bedroom." Only then does she exhibit feeling: "[T]hen during the fierce, inarticulate conflict of their passion she would grip his shoulder with her teeth and never let go until the end." He later learns that she uses opium and also has a deformed foot, "the hoof of Pan" where her small toe should be.

As Muriel begins to exude sexuality, Bude finds himself attracted, once again, to her. Despite a near-fatal shooting, and after the discovery of the individual who is sending the letters, the Budes reunite and create a truly passionate marriage.

CENSORSHIP HISTORY

The Chinese Room was reprinted by Bantam Books in 1948 as a paperback and sold 2.5 million copies by 1951. In 1950, Middlesex County, New Jersey, prosecutor Matthew Melko collaborated with the local Committee on Objectionable Literature to produce a list of objectionable publications, which included *The Chinese Room*. He wrote to a major book distributor in the area, informing the New Brunswick News Dealers Supply Company in Elizabeth, New Jersey, of the list that contained books "of such a nature that they should be withdrawn from circulation."

Viewing the letter as a mandate to remove the books, the company manager, Ben Gelfand, did so immediately. Just as quickly, Bantam asked that the prosecutor review the books listed, which he did, clearing all but *The Chinese Room*. Bantam Books then sued Melko in *Bantam Books v. Melko, Prosecutor of Middlesex County*, 25 N.J. Super. 292, 96 A.2d 47 (1953). The complaint stated that a citizens' committee of self-appointed literary censors had been set up in Middlesex County and the prosecutor had acted on their advice in banning the book. By the time the case came to trial, Matthew Melko was no longer in office, so the action was directed against his successor, Alex Eber. In a complaint requesting that the court grant a restraining injunction, the publisher plaintiff charged that the prosecutor's action was illegal and beyond the scope of his office. Attorneys for the plaintiff wrote, "There is no legislative authority or any statute of the State of New Jersey under which the defendant could have acted where no crime has been committed or charged." Judge Sidney Goldman stated that he had read the novel and agreed with Bantam Books, writing in the decree, "Here we have a clear case of previous censorship in the area of literary obscenity. The way of the censor has been tortuous and tortured from earliest times. His story is one of arbitrary judgment and the suppression of much that we consider good, true and beautiful."

In rendering his decision, Judge Goldman questioned if the prosecutor had the authority to ban the sale of books, if he had issued an order to ban *The Chinese Room*, if the prosecutor should be restrained from further notifying distributors of the novel that it should not be sold in Middlesex County, and if Melko had acted illegally and beyond the scope of his authority. Judge Goldman ruled that *The Chinese Room* was not obscene and authorized an injunction against the prosecutor's interference with the sale of the book. He also stated, "I hold that neither the prosecutor nor the committee constituted by him had the authority to proscribe the distribution or sale in Middlesex County of books deemed by them, or by either of them, to be objectionable." In assessing the novel, Goldman stated, "It cuts a rather poor and pale figure in the colorful company of recent 'historical' novels of the *Forever Amber* [q.v.] type, which may be found in almost any public or circulating library, fresh from the best-seller lists." The prosecutor appealed the decision in *Bantam Books v. Melko, Prosecutor of Middlesex County*, 14. N.J. 524, 103 A.2d 256 (1954).

The New Jersey Supreme Court reversed the earlier decision and granted county prosecutors the right to ban the distribution and sale of publications they found objectionable or obscene, and the court further condoned the creation of censorship committees to aid prosecutors in such actions. After the decision, Middlesex County Prosecutor Eber stated that he viewed the decision as a blanket endorsement of his efforts at censorship and vowed to renew his efforts to block permanently the distribution and sale of materials he considered "objectionable." The decision of the high court agreed that *The Chinese Room* is not obscene and deleted from the initial judgment everything except the ban on the interference with the sale of the novel.

In July 1950, in Fall River, Massachusetts, authorities charged two local dealers and two store managers with intent to sell to persons under 18 years of age books that were "indecent, obscene or impure, or manifestly tend to corrupt the morals of youth." The resulting order to refrain from further distribution involved 14 books from six publishers, including *The Chinese Room* and Charles O. Gorham's THE GILDED HEARSE. The books were withdrawn from sale and the charges were rescinded.

FURTHER READING

Davis, Kenneth C. *Two-Bit Culture: The Paperbacking of America.* Boston: Houghton Mifflin, 1984.

De Grazia, Edward. *Censorship Landmarks.* New York: Bowker, 1969.

"In Brief: *The Chinese Room.*" *Nation*, January 9, 1943, p. 67

"Jersey Writ Bars Book Ban Attempt." *New York Times*, April 7, 1953, p. 27.

"Obscene-Book Ban Upheld in Jersey." *New York Times*, March 9, 1954, p. 34.

"A Reader's List: *The Chinese Room.*" *New Republic*, November 9, 1942, p. 618.

CHRISTINE

Author: Stephen King
Original date and place of publication: 1983, United States
Original publisher: The Viking Press
Literary form: Novel

SUMMARY

Christine is a macabre story of teenage love and tragedy, motivated by an automobile named Christine that has diabolical powers. Scrawny, pimple-faced Arnie Cunningham and his friend Dennis Guilder are two high school students driving home after work one summer afternoon when Arnie abruptly calls for Dennis to stop the car and back up. He has seen what he wants, a wreck of a 1958 Plymouth Fury with a For Sale sign on it. Arnie vehemently refuses to listen to Dennis when told that the car, with its cracked windshield, rusted and dented body, loose parts, and puddle of oil beneath, will be expensive to restore. He buys the car from its hate-filled, vulgar owner Rollins LeBay for $250 and then finds a lot in which to park and restore the car.

Dennis senses something sinister about the car. That fear is confirmed soon after when LeBay dies "suddenly" and Dennis speaks with LeBay's brother. He learns that LeBay's daughter had choked while riding in the car and then died by the side of the road, and LeBay's wife had committed suicide six months afterward, while seated in the car. Nothing dissuades Arnie from his new obsession, and Christine goes on homicidal rampages and kills anyone who hurts Arnie. Dennis realizes that LeBay's spirit has taken control of Arnie, the son of two college professors, and Arnie has rejected college plans in favor of his present work of smuggling liquor and cigarettes across state lines.

In the early stages of owning Christine, Arnie's life seems to become better as he gains new courage and strength to fight tormentors. His complexion clears and he acquires a girlfriend, Leigh, who also interests Dennis. This leads to several passages that describe her erect nipples or the sexual delirium that Arnie feels, as well as the boys' thoughts of having sex with Leigh. The love triangle soon evolves into Christine, Arnie, and Leigh, but Arnie is possessed by the spirit of the vengeful LeBay. Dennis battles furiously to save his friend, but the novel ends tragically with the deaths of not only Arnie's enemies but his parents and himself.

CENSORSHIP HISTORY

The novel has been censored and banned in many schools and libraries because it depicts the explicit sexual thoughts of teenage boys and contains sexual references. While numerous books by King have been banned or censored because of "vulgar language," "filthy" language, or other charges of being "obscene," *Christine* joins only a few King books, including *Carrie, Firestarter, The Shining*, and *The Stand*, that have been attacked for containing "explicit sex" and "sexual descriptions." Of these books, *Christine* has been most frequently attacked.

In 1985, parents of students in the Washington County, Alabama, school district complained to their school board that the novel contained "unacceptable language" and that it was "pornographic." After reviewing the novel, the county board of education banned the novel from all county school libraries. In 1987, the West Lyon Community School in Larchwood, Iowa, removed the book from its library, charging that "it does not meet the standards of the community." The book was removed from the Washington Middle School library in Meriden, Connecticut, in 1989, after parents complained that it contained "offensive" passages.

In 1990, parents of students attending the Livingston (Montana) Middle School complained that *Christine* and *The Shining* should be removed from the library because they contained "violence," "explicit sex," and "inappropriate language." The librarian agreed that the books were not "suitable for the intended audience," and the school principal commended the librarian for using "good judgment." In 1991, a school official in Hazel Park, Michigan, removed the novel from the curriculum after receiving verbal complaints from parents of high school students who objected to its use in an American novel class.

In 1992, parents in Peru, Indiana, petitioned the school board to remove from the high school library 12 novels written by Stephen King, claiming that they contained violence and obscenity. The board reviewed the novels and voted 5 to 1 to ban *Christine*, *CUJO*, and *The Dead Zone*. *Christine* was also challenged on the basis of "age appropriateness" in 1993 with all King novels contained in the Webber Township High School library and in 1994 in Bismarck, North Dakota, with eight other Stephen King novels. Neither challenge was successful.

FURTHER READING

Hohne, Karen A. "The Power of the Spoken Word in the Works of Stephen King." *Journal of Popular Culture* 28 (Fall 1994): 93–103.

King, Stephen. "Banned Books and Other Concerns: The Virginia Beach Lecture." In *The Stephen King Companion*, edited by George Beahm, 51–61. Kansas City, Mo.: Andrews & McMeel, 1989.

Newsletter on Intellectual Freedom (January 1986): 7; (May 1987): 86; (July 1987): 125; (May 1989): 75; (January 1991): 12; (July 1992): 106; (July 1993): 124; (May 1994): 84–85.

THE CLAN OF THE CAVE BEAR

Author: Jean Auel
Original date and place of publication: 1980, United States
Original publisher: Crown Publishing
Literary form: Novel

SUMMARY

The Clan of the Cave Bear is the story of Ayla, a prehistoric girl orphaned by an earthquake and forced to live for a time by herself in the forest. When a human tribe, the Clan of the Cave Bear, finds her and takes her in, Ayla tries hard to conform to their code despite her obvious differences from them. She is one of the "Others"—taller, blond, and blue eyed—and she also has more developed powers of speech than the members of the Clan, who still communicate largely by gesture. Cared for by the Clan medicine woman, Iza, and her brother, Creb, Ayla learns the customs and the language of the Clan, but she frequently violates their expectations because she does not share their racial memories. Ayla becomes adept at the skill of hunting, forbidden to women of the Clan, and her prowess makes an enemy of Broud, the son of the Clan leader. He torments her continuously as they grow up, and then rapes her when they are older. His actions are acceptable according to tradition, because any female must submit to a male at his will. The members of the Clan have not yet made the connection between sexual intercourse and reproduction, so they are amazed when Ayla becomes pregnant, more so because they had assumed that her differences would make her incapable of bearing children. She gives birth to a son, but when an earthquake destroys the Clan's cave, Broud, now the leader, blames Ayla. He curses her and expels her from the Clan, but she must leave her son behind.

CENSORSHIP HISTORY

In 1988, parents of students attending Berrien Springs High School in Michigan challenged the use of the novel in the classroom and asked that it also be removed from the high school library. Their complaints cited the passages of brutish behavior of the male clan members and the physical abuse and rape of Ayla as "vulgar, profane, and sexually explicit."

In 1992, one parent of a student attending Cascade Middle School in Eugene, Oregon, complained that the rape scene in the novel was offensive. The board of education considered the complaint and ordered the book removed from the middle school library and banned from future use.

The novel was challenged in 1993 at Moorpark High School in Sunneyville, California, after parents objected that the novel contained "hard-core graphic sexual content." It was kept on the recommended reading list.

FURTHER READING

Newsletter on Intellectual Freedom (January 1989): 28; (July 1992): 107; (January 1994): 14; (March 1994): 70; (May 1994): 99.

Wilcox, Clyde. "The Not-So-Failed Feminism of Jean Auel." *Journal of Popular Culture* 28 (Winter 1994): 63–70.

CONFESSIONS

Author: Jean-Jacques Rousseau
Original dates and places of publication: 1884, Switzerland; 1891, England
Original publishers: Waltham (Switzerland); Worthington (England)
Literary form: Memoir

SUMMARY

Jean-Jacques Rousseau's *Confessions* was published posthumously, but he had completed the work just before his death in 1778. In this extensive journal of his life, Rousseau re-creates the age in which he lived and brings to life the politics and society of 18th-century France. He also suffers from what one biographer refers to as "moral exhibitionism" and appears obsessed with revealing "the indecent and puerile details of his sex life." The work deals openly with his relationship with Therese Levasseur, his mistress for 16 years, whom he "always treated like a wife." The two had five children, all sent to the foundling hospital. Rousseau admits that he was so uninterested in the children that he did not even keep records of their identities or dates of birth.

Several specific passages in *Confessions* have motivated attempts at censorship. Rousseau traces his sexual development to when he was aged eight and the 30-year-old baby-sitter, the sister of a parson, spanked his bare bottom. He says that this act had the effect to "determine my tastes, my desires, my passions, my very self, for the rest of my existence . . . these strange tastes which persisted with a depraved and insane intensity." Several passages speak openly of Rousseau's addiction to masturbation, to the point that he risked his health and believed himself to be epileptic: "[S]educed by the vice which shame and timidity find so convenient . . . I set about destroying my sturdy constitution."

When he resides at a Roman Catholic hospice in Turin, after fleeing Protestant Geneva, the 16-year-old Rousseau condemns the sister converts at the hospice as being "the greatest set of sluttish, abandoned whores that had ever contaminated the Lord's sheepfold." The brother converts are no less lustful, particularly one who "frequently kissed me with an ardour which I found most displeasing. . . . He wanted to come into my bed . . . and finally took the most revolting liberties and, by guiding my hand, tried to make me take the same liberties with him." Rousseau claims to have been ignorant of the other young man's true intent.

Not only is the reader treated to a thorough discussion of Rousseau's sex life, but his prostate problems in later life are also detailed in *Confessions*. As Rousseau advanced in age, he found the need to urinate frequently, but the respected writer and philosopher usually found himself cornered at social events and unable to reach even a convenient corner of a courtyard in which to relieve himself. He relates, "In short, I can usually urinate only in full view of everybody and on some white-stockinged leg."

CENSORSHIP HISTORY

Rousseau's lengthy *Confessions* has been banned mainly for its sexual content and for his open discussion of life with his mistress of 16 years. In 1821, *Confessions* was among the works to which Etienne Antoine, bishop of Troyne, referred when he wrote a pastoral letter to all clergy in France in which he reaffirmed all censorship orders previously issued by the clergy of France and the individual orders issued by the archbishops of Paris:

> in which these works were condemned as godless and sacrilegious, and as tending to undermine morals and the States. We prohibit, under canonical law, the printing or sale of these books within the territory of this diocese, and we charge the vicar-generals to enforce this regulation and to see to the carrying out of the necessary penances for all who make confession of disobedience to these regulations.

The authority of the Catholic Church in France appears to have been considered sufficient for control of the matter, and no application was made to have the work placed on the Roman Index. Nonetheless, as a means of establishing authority, Pope Pius VII had placed *Confessions* on the list of prohibited books of the Roman Index of 1806 and later renewed the prohibition because of the sexual adventures that Rousseau recounted.

In 1892, Rousseau's *Confessions* was involved in the litigation of the Worthington Book Publishing Company, which was in financial difficulty. The receiver wanted to sell some of the company stock, including THE ARABIAN NIGHTS, THE HISTORY OF TOM JONES, THE ART OF LOVE, THE HEPTAMERON, *GARGANTUA AND PANTAGRUEL*, THE DECAMERON, and *Confessions* to pay off creditors, but Anthony Comstock, secretary of the New York Society for Suppression of Vice, stepped in to oppose the sales. He demanded of the court that the books be officially burned. The court disagreed.

A year later in 1893, the American Library Association for the first time offered a 5,000-title book guide for small popular libraries and branches, calling it a collection that "one could recommend to any trustee." No works by Rousseau were included on the list, yet a biography of the author was included. Based upon this observation, Geller notes, "This discrepancy between a writer's reputation and the acceptance of his work is a good indicator of censorship: exclusion on grounds other than significance."

U.S. Customs banned the book from entry in 1929, claiming that it was "injurious to public morals," but reversed the ban the following year.

FURTHER READING

Cranston, Maurice. *The Noble Savage: Jean-Jacques Rousseau.* Chicago: University of Chicago Press, 1991.

Geller, Evelyn. *Forbidden Books in American Public Libraries, 1876–1939.* Westport, Conn.: Greenwood, 1984.

Huizinga, J. H. *Rousseau: The Self-Made Saint.* New York: Grossman, 1976.

Putnam, George Haven. *The Censorship of the Church of Rome and Its Influence upon the Production and Distribution of Literature.* Vol. 2. New York: Putnam, 1906.

THE DECAMERON

Author: Giovanni Boccaccio
Original dates and places of publication: 14th century, Italy; 1921, England
Original publishers: Privately printed; The Navarre Society
Literary form: Collection of tales

SUMMARY

The Decameron is one of the oldest fictional works to have been charged as "obscene" in the United States. The premise of the collection of tales is that 10 young men and women, secluded for a time to escape the plague, divert themselves by telling stories on a variety of topics. Each must tell one story per day on a specific theme, for a total of 100 tales. Of the total, only eight tales are purely erotic; the remainder deal with social criticism, the outwitting of one person by another, and the criticism of nuns and priests.

In some of the tales, references to adultery or fornication are brief or oblique. In others, references are suggestive but not explicit. The stories contain figures of speech that replace explicit sexual description. Breasts and genitalia are spoken of metaphorically, and numerous metaphors are drawn from sowing, plowing, and reaping. Thus, a wife complains that her husband has neglected "tilling of my poor field." A lover boards his mate in the way that "the unbridled stallions . . . assail the mares of Parthia." Even common implements such as the mortar and pestle become metaphors for sexual activity, as in the story in which a man complains that "if she will not lend me her mortar, I will not lend my pestle."

Of the eight largely erotic tales, four are based upon a trick or joke. In one, the 10th story told on the ninth day, a priest persuades a man that changing his wife into a mare will help the man in his peddling business. Thus, the wife dutifully strips and stands on all fours, as the priest carefully explains to the husband that putting on the mare's tail is the most difficult part of the process. The wife waits patiently as the priest pretends to turn her various body parts into the body of a mare. He then engages in the sexual act that will make the mare's tail, but it is described through the use of metaphor:

> Ultimately, nothing remaining to do but the tail, he pulled up his shirt and taking the dibble with which he planted men, he thrust it hastily into the furrow made therfor and said, "And be this a fine mare's tail."

The 10th story of the third day contains the lengthiest description of an act of sexual intercourse, and it was rarely translated until recent years. In this story, a friar persuades a naive young girl that she is serving God by submitting to him, because he has a "devil" in him that can only be subdued if he places it into her "hell." Even this story is humorous, for the girl outpaces the friar in showing her enthusiasm in serving God, as she tires the friar with her ardor.

CENSORSHIP HISTORY

The Decameron was first placed on the Roman Index of Forbidden Books in 1559, by the order of Pope Paul IV, and the prohibition was confirmed in 1564. The objections centered on the "offensive sexual acts" in which clerics, monks, nuns, and abbesses in the work engaged. However, due to popular demand, in the form of an "urgent requirement" from the public, the Giunti of Florence, Italy, printed an expurgated edition in 1573, which contained a special authorization from Manrique, grand inquisitor, as well as one from de Pise, inquisitor-general of Florence. Revised under the authority of Pope Gregory VIII, the sexual activity and innuendo remained, but the religious characters were replaced by citizens, nobles, and bourgeoisie. Pope Sixtus V did not find the expurgation satisfactory, and the book was again placed on the Index, but the demand for copies by readers, ecclesiastics, and others was so great that Sixtus authorized another expurgated edition, with orders to remove more of the sexual activity and crude innuendo. This version was printed in 1588, but the new edition did not satisfy Pope Sixtus V, and the book remained on the Index. Yet it continued to be available in general reading and the authorities closed their eyes to this particular instance of disobedience, mainly because popular demand was so strong.

In a report entitled "How to Make a Town Library Successful," published in 1876, Frederick Beecher Perkins, assistant librarian of the Boston Public Library, recommended censorship of the collection:

> It should exclude such books as Rabelais, *The Decameron*, *The Heptameron*, the *Contes drolatiques* (*Droll Stories*) of Balzac, . . . all of which are sold in English translations for money by otherwise respectable American publishers. Few, indeed, are those who will object to this exclusion of ribald and immoral books from public circulating libraries.

In 1892, *The Decameron* was involved in the litigation of the Worthington Book Publishing Company, which was in financial difficulty. The receiver wanted to sell some of the company stock, including THE ARABIAN NIGHTS, THE HISTORY OF TOM JONES, THE ART OF LOVE, THE HEPTAMERON, *GARGANTUA AND PANTAGRUEL*, Rousseau's CONFESSIONS, and *The Decameron* to pay off creditors, but Anthony Comstock, secretary of the New York Society for the Suppression of Vice, stepped in to oppose the sales. He demanded of the court that the books be officially burned.

One year later, the American Library Association offered for the first time a 5,000-title book guide for small popular libraries and branches, calling it a collection that "one could recommend to any trustee." No works by Boccaccio were included on the list. When the American Library Association released its *Catalog* in 1904, works by Boccaccio were still excluded; Geller characterizes this situation as censorship by omission. In 1894, the U.S. Supreme Court applied the Hicklin rule, imported from England, that standard works of high literary quality were not obscene. The first case involved editions of *The Arabian Nights*, *The History of Tom Jones*, *The Decameron*, *The Heptameron*, and *The Art of Love*.

In 1903, the Boston Watch and Ward Society began a campaign of harassment against four area booksellers who were openly advertising and selling *The Decameron* and *Gargantua and Pantagruel* despite the request from the society that they refrain from doing so. Rather than acquiesce as in the past, the four met with other Boston booksellers and with publisher Little, Brown and Company to organize a resistance to this attempt at censorship. Booksellers, including the Old Corner, N. J. Bartlett, George E. Littlefield, Charles E. Goodspeed, and six others, joined Little, Brown to raise money for a legal defense fund. The case went to Boston municipal court, and the booksellers won judgment against the society.

The Decameron was declared to be an "obscene, lewd and lascivious book of indecent character" by a jury in Cincinnati, Ohio, in 1906. Edward Stiefel, president and general manager of the Queen City Book Company, was indicted by a grand jury for sending a copy of the book through the mail to Crawfordsville, Indiana. Stiefel gathered a strong defense, calling as witnesses a well-known judge, a member of the Cincinnati Board of Education, and a well-respected newspaper editor to testify to the status of the work as a classic. In addition, Stiefel offered into evidence library catalogs, catalogs from booksellers all over the world, and catalogs from public auctions of books in New York and Boston, all listing *The Decameron*. Despite the evidence, the jury deliberated only an hour and 15 minutes before finding Stiefel guilty of sending "obscene" materials through the mail. The judge, who appeared less punitive, only fined the defendant $5 and court costs.

In 1927, U.S. Treasury Department officials in Washington, D.C., rendered an opinion that reversed a ruling by New York Customs inspectors and admitted 250 copies of the work, imported by A. & C. Boni, thus ending forever the banning of this classic in the United States.

FURTHER READING

Boyer, Paul S. *Purity in Print: The Vice-Society Movement and Book Censorship in America.* New York: Scribner, 1968.
Geller, Evelyn. *Forbidden Books in American Public Libraries, 1876–1939.* Westport, Conn.: Greenwood, 1984.
Putnam, George Haven. *The Censorship of the Church of Rome and Its Influence upon the Production and Distribution of Literature.* Vol. 2. New York: Putnam, 1906.
Tebbel, John. *A History of Book Publishing in the United States.* Vol. 2. New York: Bowker, 1975.

THE DEER PARK

Author: Norman Mailer
Original date and place of publication: 1955, United States
Original publisher: G. P. Putnam's Sons
Literary form: Novel

SUMMARY

The Deer Park was originally subtitled "A Search for the Obscene," and Mailer crossed out but did not remove the subtitle when he first submitted the work. The main title is taken from the Deer Park of Louis XV, where the most beautiful maidens of France were brought as "ladies of pleasure awaiting the pleasure of the king." The title was appropriate for a novel about the fictional Hollywood resort Desert D'Or, "middle aged desperados of corporation land and the suburb" and the venal people in it. It is a setting of decadence, and of "drinking in that atmosphere, I never knew whether it was night or day. . . . afternoon was always passing into night, and drunken nights into the dawn of a desert morning."

The novel relates the story of a liberal movie director, Charles Francis Eitel, who is blacklisted by the studios for refusing to name his Communist friends at a congressional hearing, but who later relents because he needs to work again. Narrated by Sergius O'Shaugnessy, six feet tall, blond haired and blue eyed, movie-star handsome, and a fake Irishman who decided in the orphanage to assume that name and ethnic identity, the work concentrates on the mores of stars, starlets, producers, sensualists, and panderers. O'Shaugnessy had been a decorated first lieutenant in the United States Army Air Force in World War II, but he had a nervous breakdown when he realized how many thousands of faceless people he had killed. Remembering his victims has left him sexually impotent at the beginning of the novel, but blond and sensuous sex star Lulu, once married to Eitel, restores his prowess. After regaining his potency, O'Shaugnessy becomes a hard-drinking "stud."

The drama shifts from O'Shaugnessy to Eitel, whose depression over his lack of work leads him into an affair with Elena Esposito, an uneducated, sensuous woman and sometime actress who has been humiliated by many men. Their relationship is the main focus of the novel. Eitel considers Elena to be his intellectual and social inferior, but she does anything that Eitel wants, including experimenting sexually with other couples. Sex is a vital presence throughout the novel, and it was the reason that the novel was repeatedly rejected by publishers. One scene that described fellatio between Hollywood power broker Herman Teppis and a call girl named Bobby caused a furor:

> Tentatively, she reached out a hand to caress his hair, and at that moment Herman Teppis opened his legs and let Bobby slip to the floor. At the expression of surprise on her face, he began to laugh. "Just like this, sweetie," he said, and down he looked at that frightened female mouth, facsimile of all those smiling lips he had seen so ready to be nourished at the fount of power and with a shudder he started to talk. "That's a good girlie, that's a good girlie, that's a good girlie," he said in a mild lost little voice, "you're just an angel darling, and I like you, and you understand, you're my darling darling, oh that's the ticket," said Teppis.

The numerous couplings throughout the novel, although less detailed than the specified scene, aroused the "disgust" of potential publishers and later reviewers alike.

CENSORSHIP HISTORY

Mailer had a contract with Rinehart and Company for *The Deer Park*, but publisher Stanley Rinehart was uncomfortable with the book and asked critic John Aldridge to provide an outside opinion. In a careful analysis of the work, Aldridge said that the novel had "no morality," but he said that it was not pornographic. Mailer had avoided explicit language because he recognized the problems that his frank sexuality alone would create. Rinehart remained uncomfortable with the work, and Mailer agreed to rewrite it. When he showed it to Rinehart in May 1954, the publisher stated that he was still unhappy with the work's "sexual frankness[,] . . . extremely radical for 1954." In November 1954, three months before publication, Rinehart told Mailer that he would have to delete six lines of the fellatio scene. Rinehart claimed that he was "concerned about what his mother [mystery author Mary Roberts Rinehart] would think, since she was on the board of directors."

Once again, Mailer agreed to change words and to rewrite several lines, but then he changed his mind. One day after Mailer called with his refusal, Stanley Rinehart stopped publication of the book, which was already in galley form, and broke Mailer's contract. Charles "Cy" Rembar, an attorney and Mailer's cousin, challenged Rinehart's assertion that the novel was "obscene" and, as a result, "unpublishable." He offered to "test the issue in a suit for the advance of royalties." Threatened with a lawsuit, Rinehart maintained that the book was "obscene," but he paid the $10,000 advance to Mailer "for the privilege of not publishing his book."

Mailer then took the novel to seven other publishers, all of whom turned it down: Random House, Alfred A. Knopf, Farrar & Giroux, Charles Scribner's Sons, Harper and Row, Simon and Schuster and Harcourt Brace. Lawyers for several of the houses provided lists totaling 100 excerpts that "must be deleted," "must be changed," and "should be changed," but the passage protested by Rinehart did not appear in those lists.

Walter Minton, son of the president of G. P. Putnam's Sons, committed to buy the book sight unseen, convinced that a book turned down by so many other publishers "would sell because of the controversy. . . . It never occurred to me for an instant that there would be any censorship activity." Putnam capitalized on the notoriety with an advertisement that listed all of the negative comments made by reviewers: "Unfair," "Undiscriminating," "Embarrassing," "Unsavory," "Junk," "Moronic Mindlessness," "Nasty," "Disgusting." The book sold 50,000 copies and rose to number six on the best-seller list.

FURTHER READING

Balbert, Peter. "From *Lady Chatterley's Lover* to *The Deer Park:* Lawrence, Mailer, and the Dialectic of Erotic Risk." *Studies in the Novel* 22 (Spring 1990): 67–81.

Manso, Peter. *Mailer: His Life and Times.* New York: Simon & Schuster, 1985.

Mills, Hillary. *Mailer: A Biography.* New York: Empire Books, 1982.

Rembar, Charles. *The End of Obscenity.* New York: Random House, 1968.

Rollyson, Carl. *The Lives of Norman Mailer.* New York: Paragon House, 1991.

THE DEVIL RIDES OUTSIDE

Author: John Howard Griffin
Original date and place of publication: 1952, United States
Original publisher: Smith's Inc.
Literary form: Novel

SUMMARY

The Devil Rides Outside is an autobiographical novel about a young man, an unnamed war veteran interested in music, who goes to a French monastery to study manuscripts of Gregorian chants. While there, he decides to abandon his sensual life and embark on an ascetic course. The desire is newly born, because he has just left Paris and a mistress before coming to the monastery. The narrator resents the harsh life of the monks at first, until he realizes that those who immerse themselves in the effort to resist worldly pleasures achieve a deep peace and serenity. He becomes a close companion to Father Clement, in whom he confides and who voices the narrator's central problem when he asks: "If only you could say no just once, is that it?"

Throughout the first part of the novel, the narrator desires to return to his mistress in Paris, but he lacks the money to do so. When he suffers a severe attack of malaria during which the monks nurse him back to health, he begins to understand their strength of character, but his sexual desires remain, and he decides to go to the village of satisfy those desires. He encounters Madame Vincent, an attractive, middle-aged visitor, with whom he has a passionate encounter that Griffin describes in sensuous detail. Madame Vincent refuses to meet with him again, but the village women learn of her indiscretion, and she is forced to leave the town. When she returns some time later, she reveals that she is dying of cancer and wants only to spend her final days near the monastery in spiritual contemplation.

The second part of the novel begins as the narrator moves out of the unheated monastery and into a villa in the town nearby in order to avoid further illness. He continues his efforts to resist his sexual desires, and he deliberately chooses to take his meals with Madame Renee, who holds no attraction for him. An overbearing, middle-aged widow, she is nasty and cunning and soon tries to dominate him and to force him into intimacy with her, despite his feelings of repulsion. He eventually submits to her, but Griffin makes clear to the reader that his narrator is having sex with Madame Renee out of pity rather than desire.

After acquiescing to her, his descriptions of their encounters are grotesque, including visions of her "swollen into a gigantic serpentine voluptuousness . . . grasping, choking . . . suffocating me." When he finds himself actually sexually aroused by her, the possibility disgusts him and he calls upon the Virgin Mary for assistance, even as he struggles physically with Madame Renee. He pulls himself free and slaps the woman, pleased that he has finally become capable of saying no. In essence, even though he has rejected a woman whom he has grown to hate and who repulses him, he feels that he has achieved mastery over his sensual nature.

CENSORSHIP HISTORY

The Devil Rides Outside was the novel involved in the unanimous Supreme Court decision in *Butler v. Michigan*, 352 U.S. 380 (1957) that declared as unconstitutional the standards for defining obscenity that had been used for more than 70 years by federal and state censors. Before that final case, however, the novel attracted criticism from its first publication for the frank sexuality it portrayed. Reviewing the work in *Saturday Review*, B. R. Redman noted that "Mr. Griffin spares his hero and his readers nothing. He stops at no frontier of good taste—and, indeed, some saints have not—in his fusion of the sacred and the profane." The same reviewer questioned whether Griffin had exaggerated the sexual prowess of his hero and noted that "he errs in another way, and more importantly, when he asks us to believe in the absurd, unendurable, daily relationships, of the hero and Madame Renee." Another reviewer stated that Griffin out did Henry Miller in his frank treatment of sex and that interest in the work was "limited to specialists in psychopathia sexualis or mysticism."

The frankness of the sexual imagery resulted in charges that the novel contained "obscene, immoral, lewd, lascivious language." Censors objected to Griffin's lengthy descriptions of sexual activity, such as that between the narrator and Madame Vincent, of which Griffin provided a lengthy description:

> No longer do we kiss with our mouths drinking each other—our arms, our legs, our stomachs join in the kiss. . . . Hands descend the length of warm flesh, till they come to rest in the fleshiness of buttocks, the very feel of which fills us with profound drunkenness. Hands search further into our innermost selves . . . we become slowly united. . . . And the long sigh, unheard, pouring forth from the edges of consummation.

Even in the unwanted couplings with Madame Renee, the narrator exudes a wealth of sensuous detail as he relates "a vision of strong legs, deep navels, bursting milk-white breasts—insatiable, grasping, choking triangles of pubic greyness before my eyes," among other similarly graphic descriptions.

The novel was subject to suppression in Boston from its publication in 1952, but an important legal challenge to its sale occurred in Detroit, Michigan, in 1954, when a bookseller named Alfred E. Butler was found guilty and fined for selling the work to an undercover police officer. The judge in the Detroit trial determined that the sale was in violation of Michigan Penal Code, Section 343, that barred sales of books "containing obscene, immoral, lewd or lascivious language, or . . . descriptions tending to incite minors to violent or depraved or immoral acts, manifestly tending to the corruption of the morals of youth." Butler appealed to the United States Supreme Court, which reversed the decision. Writing the resulting opinion of the unanimous decision, Judge Felix Frankfurter called the statute "unreasonable" and determined that no bookseller should be sent to jail by the enforcement of such an unreasonable statute. He conceded that juveniles must be protected but viewed this antiobscenity law as excessive. He wrote the following:

> The State insists that, by thus quarantining the general reading public against books not too rugged for grown men and women in order to shield juvenile innocence, it is exercising its power to promote the general welfare. Surely,

this is to burn the barn to roast the pig. . . . We have before us legislation not reasonably restricted to the evil with which it is said to deal. The incidence of this enactment is to reduce the adult population of Michigan to reading only what is fit for children.

The decision in *Butler v. Michigan* was significant because it declared the view that whatever corrupted the morals of youth was obscene—a position that had been applied by American judges since the 1868 *Hicklin* ruling in England—to be an undue restriction on the freedom of speech.

FURTHER READING

Campbell, Jeff H. *John Howard Griffin.* Austin, Tex.: Steck-Vaughn, 1970.
"Court to Review Book Ban." *New York Times,* February 28, 1956, p. 11.
Egerton, John. *A Mind to Stay Here: Profiles from the South.* New York: Macmillan, 1970.
Henderson, R. W. "*The Devil Rides Outside.*" *Library Journal,* November 1, 1952, p. 77.
Kuh, Richard H. *Foolish Figleaves? Pornography In and Out of Court.* New York: Macmillan, 1967.
Paul, James C. N., and Murray Schwartz. *Federal Censorship: Obscenity in the Mail.* Glencoe, N.Y.: Free Press, 1961.
Redman, B. R. "*The Devil Rides Outside.*" *Saturday Review,* November 1, 1952, p. 16.

THE DIARY OF SAMUEL PEPYS

Author: Samuel Pepys
Original date and place of publication: 1970, United States
Original publisher: University of California Press
Literary form: Diary

SUMMARY

The Diary of Samuel Pepys is an intimate record of daily life in 17th-century London told with frankness by Pepys, who wrote in shorthand code and included his honest observations and feelings. Although originally written over the years 1660 to 1668, the volumes were willed to Magdalene College, Cambridge, where they remained untouched until 1818. The diaries were deciphered three years later and published in expurgated form at various times until the first fully unexpurgated edition appeared in 1970.

Eberhard Kronhausen and Phyllis Kronhausen view the book as a masterpiece of erotic realism, and they assert that "Samuel Pepys was a realist in politics and finance, as well as in whoring." The work employs down-to-earth language, "which did not leave out the erotic or excrementitious," and it contains numerous mentions of Pepys's extramarital sexual experiences, his observations of the sexual and hygiene habits of his contemporaries, and his often-sexual fantasies. In one usually expurgated passage, Pepys relates that "the Duke of York hath got my Lord Chancellor's daughter with child" but refuses to marry the girl despite promising to do so. The lord chancellor "do make light of it" and tells Pepys one of his father's old sayings: "that he that do get a wench with child and marry her afterwards is as if a man should shit in his hat and then clap it on his head." In another instance, Pepys is sorry to hear that a friend's maid had left service, "for I was in hopes to have had a bout with her before she had gone, she being very pretty."

Pepys speaks of strolling through the streets and trying hard to resist the "pretty strumpets . . . so apt is my nature to evil." He sometimes writes in polyglot, as when he fears that a woman of his acquaintance is pregnant by him. He visits her and is "met with the good news que elle ne est con child [that she is not with child] the fear of which she did give me the other day, had troubled me much." Pepys also has the uncomfortable experience of being caught by his wife while hugging and kissing their maid Deb, a revelation that costs him several nights of sleep and requires of him strong protestations of love for his wife. Soon after, when Deb is dismissed by Mrs. Pepys, he meets the girl in a coach, kisses her and gives her money with directions for future assignations.

CENSORSHIP HISTORY

The Diary of Samuel Pepys was heavily expurgated from its first publication, and the first complete edition did not appear until 1970, when the University of California Press created a new and complete transcription of the 2,500 pages. In 1825, Lord Braybrooke, a college trustee, edited the manuscript and, according to Perrin, omitted "a couple of thousand passages which he regarded as trivial as well as indecent." His first edition contained about half of the original work. When Sir Walter Scott wrote a review of the version, he stated, "something has been kept back, which would have rendered the whole more piquant, though perhaps less instructive." In 1848, Braybrooke admitted the expurgation and promised to produce another edition that would

> insert in its proper place every passage that had been omitted, with the exception of only those entries as were devoid of the slightest interest, and many others of so indelicate a character, that no one with a well-regulated mind will regret their loss; nor could they have been tolerated even in the licentious days to which they relate.

In 1875, Mynors Bright, the new president of Magdalene, published what he said was a more complete version of the diary. While he did add to the text and state that the reader now had the whole work "with the omission of but a few passages," he still left out more than 20 percent of the original. In 1893, Henry Wheatley claimed to have printed the whole diary "with the exception of a few passages which cannot possibly be printed." His omissions amounted to 30 pages, but that percentage was small compared to the original, and his edition contained 99 percent of the original. Until 1970, further editions of the diary based their text on Wheatley, thus continuing the publication of an expurgated edition. Nearly 150 years passed from the time the diaries were first deciphered until they were printed in their complete, original form.

FURTHER READING

Bryant, Arthur. *Samuel Pepys: The Man in the Making.* London: Cambridge University Press, 1943.
Craig, Alec. *Suppressed Books: A History of the Conception of Literary Obscenity.* New York: World Publishing, 1963.
Loth, David. *The Erotic in Literature.* New York: Dorset, 1961.
Perrin, Noel. *Dr. Bowdler's Legacy.* Boston: Godine, 1961.

DROLL STORIES

Author: Honoré de Balzac
Original dates and places of publication: 1832, France; 1884, England
Original publishers: Madame Louise de Bechet (France); Henry Vizitelly (England)
Literary form: Short story collection

SUMMARY

Published in France as *Contes drolatiques*, the work is a collection of stories that are written in the bawdy style of Rabelais in which the author gives free rein to his imagination. Balzac wrote the 30 tales in the style of his own interpretation of medieval French, including numerous archaic spellings to reinforce his efforts. He uses the ploy that he collected the tales in the monasteries of Touraine, but most are of his own creation whereas others are based only lightly on rumored misbehaviors among priests, nuns, and peasants. He also claims that he edited the tales considerably to avoid offending his readers. In the prologue to the tales, Balzac writes that he had omitted "such old words as, being yet a whit too fresh, might hurt the ear, shock the eye, bring a blush to the cheek and set on edge the teeth of betrousered virgins and of ladies who cultivate true virtue and three lovers."

Viewed as pornographic by his contemporaries, as well as by later critics, the stories were created as entertainment rather than as a means of plumbing the depths of human nature, as Balzac does in the numerous volumes of *La comedie humaine* (*The Human Comedy*). Graham Robb, a recent biographer of Balzac, observes that "to English readers, they are known as the *Droll Stories*, sometimes found lurking on the shelves of second-hand bookshops, with large-breasted women on their cover."

The topics of the stories range from necrophilia, nymphomania, and adultery to the bodily functions. In one story, a character is obsessed with "bowel evacuation" as a means of maintaining his health, while several other stories contain characters who urinate, defecate, and flatulate. Adultery is commonplace, and entertainment lies in watching the clever means by which the characters escape punishment for their behavior. The opening story, "The Beautiful Imperial," the story of a mistress, was first published in *Revue de Paris* in 1831. After its publication, Louis Veron, the editor, wrote to Balzac, "our subscribers are as prudish as ever, and to be perfectly honest, your writing is giving them erections. . . . Try to do something chaste if you can, if only to show them how versatile you are." In a later story, "The Wife's Appeal," an adulterous wife whose two children were fathered by a young priest is finally caught by her husband while in bed with the priest. As the husband advances with sword drawn, ready to kill both,

> she sprang at her husband with outstretched arms, half-naked, her hair dishev-elled, beautiful in shame, but more beautiful still in her love.
>
> "Stay, unhappy man!" she cried. "You are about to kill the father of your children!"

CENSORSHIP HISTORY

In a report entitled "How to Make a Town Library Successful," published in 1876, Frederick Beecher Perkins, assistant librarian of the Boston Public Library, recommended censorship of the collection:

> It should exclude such books as Rabelais, *The Decameron*, *The Heptameron* [qq.v.], the *Contes drolatiques* (*Droll Stories*) of Balzac, . . . all of which are sold in English translations for money by otherwise respectable American publishers. Few, indeed, are those who will object to their exclusion of ribald and immoral books from public circulating libraries.

In 1885, Anthony Comstock, secretary of the New York Society for the Suppression of Vice, saw an advertisement placed by the Globe Publishing Company of Paulsborough, New Jersey, for two books that suggested sexuality to him. Using a fictitious name, Comstock sent $2 for a copy of *Droll Stories* to John A. Wilson, who signed the advertisement. After he received the book, he then sent another $2 to purchase *The Heptameron* by Queen Margaret of Navarre. Comstock swore out a complaint and, in a case heard before a federal grand jury, obtained two indictments against Wilson for sending obscene literature through the mails. In dealing with the indictment against *Droll Stories*, the defense attorney argued that Balzac was accepted as a classic writer, and well-educated individuals had read and approved of his work, despite the existence of some "objectionable" passages that might also be found in the works of Shakespeare, Fielding, and Sterne. The jury refused to listen to this reasoning and delivered a verdict of guilty, leaving Wilson with no grounds to argue the second indictment, to which he pleaded no contest. Wilson was sentenced to two years in the state prison and fined $500 and court costs. The verdict had serious repercussions for publishing and bookselling, leading *Publishers Weekly* to write in the March 12, 1887, issue, "It is, to say the least, preposterous to class these books with the kind of literature intended to be prohibited by law, and if they are to be shut out from the mails on the score of decency it will be hard to say where dictation and persecution in this direction will stop."

In 1944, in New York City, Concord Books issued a sale catalog of 100 books, including *Droll Stories* and Voltaire's CANDIDE. The New York branch of the United States Department of the Post Office informed the publisher that mailing the catalog would violate the statute that banned the mailing of obscene literature, unless the offending titles were blackened out. The publisher complied with the demand.

Droll Stories was banned in Ireland on February 13, 1953. A prohibition order was published in the *Iris Oifigiuil*, "the only official source from which booksellers [and readers] might learn of a new prohibition order," in which all articles blacklisted by the Irish Board of Censors were listed. According to the Censorship of Publications Bill of 1928, "the notice in *Iris Oifigiuil* should be sufficient evidence in the courts of summary jurisdiction as to the character of the publication," despite the acknowledgment by justices quoted in Adams's thorough study of Irish censorship laws that "this gazette is not a publication which booksellers are addicted to reading." The Irish Board of Censors found the collection of stories "obscene" and filled with "indecent passages." The work was officially banned from sale in Ireland until the introduction of the Censorship Publications Bill in 1967 reduced to 12 years the duration of a prohibition order, and the work was among 5,000 titles released from the list of banned books.

FURTHER READING

Adams, Michael. *Censorship: The Irish Experience.* Tuscaloosa: University of Alabama Press, 1968.

Balzac, Honoré de. *Correspondence.* Edited by Roger Pierrot. Paris: Barnier, 1969.

Geller, Evelyn. *Forbidden Books in American Public Libraries, 1876–1939.* Westport, Conn.: Greenwood, 1984.

Gerson, Noel B. *The Prodigal Genius.* Garden City, N.Y.: Doubleday, 1972.

Loth, David. *The Erotic in Literature.* New York: Dorset, 1961.

Robb, Graham. *Balzac: A Biography.* New York: Norton, 1994.

Tebbel, John. *A History of Book Publishing in the United States.* Vol. 2. New York: Bowker, 1975.

Zweig, Stefan. *Balzac.* London: Cassell, 1970.

DUBLINERS

Author: James Joyce
Original date and place of publication: 1914, England
Original publisher: Grant Richards
Literary form: Short story collection

SUMMARY

Dubliners is a short story collection containing 15 stories that deal with incidents in childhood, adolescence, maturity, and married life. The characters and scenes are drawn from ordinary Catholic middle-class life, and many of the stories are tragic. Joyce not only created characters but also used the names of actual people and places in the stories.

The stories are realistic in setting and character. In "Two Gallants," a young man believes that he could settle down "if he could only come across some good simple minded girl with a little of the ready," while his friend Corley fears that a girl he meets periodically will "get in the family way." In "The Boarding House," a rather disreputable mother manipulates the situation so that her daughter will trap an older but naive man into marriage. In "The Dead," a husband learns that his wife once loved a young man now dead and realizes that he has never really known her. "Clay" relates the story of aging unmarried Maria, who recognizes the emptiness of her life. The same realism pervades the remaining stories.

CENSORSHIP HISTORY

Dubliners was printed in Dublin, Ireland, in 1912 after years of delay and wrangling. Twenty-two publishers and printers had already read the manuscript and refused to publish it. The edition of 1,000 copies was printed and then destroyed by the printer John Falconer, who decided that the stories contained objectionable passages. He was dismayed by reading about suggested infidelities in the stories as well as the suggestive nature of spinster Maria's self-assessment in a mirror in "Clay." Falconer kept only one copy from the print run. The work was finally published in 1914 by Grant Richards, who used the manuscript from the 1912 printing that was destroyed.

FURTHER READING

Johnson, B. S. "Pi Printers." *Censorship* 3 (Summer 1965): 43–45.

Joyce, James. "A Curious History." *Egoist*, January 5, 1914, pp. 26–27.

THE EARTH

See *LA TERRE*

EAT ME

Author: Linda Jaivin
Original dates and places of publication: 1995, Melbourne, Australia; 1997, New York
Original publishers: Melbourne Text Publishing (Australia); Broadway Books (United States)
Literary form: Novel

SUMMARY

Eat Me is a sexually explicit novel that relates the escapades of four Australian women: Julia, Chantal, Helen, and Philippa. The first chapter is presented as being the first chapter of the novel that Philippa is writing, called *Eat Me.* The setting is the produce section of a supermarket, and Philippa's character Ava very actively uses all manner of fruits and vegetables to stimulate her genitals. She slyly teases the store guard, who watches in amazement from behind shelves of food until he finally joins her in her play with figs, kiwis, bananas, and cucumbers, among many other items.

After the first chapter, the novel abruptly switches to the actual story and introduces the four bright, successful friends who meet in the designer cafes of Sydney, have dinner in the finest restaurants, and share the secrets of their sexual conquests. Their professions are varied. Julia is a photographer whose passions are Peking duck and younger men. Chantal is the editor of a fashion magazine, and her bisexuality gives her an active social life. Helen is a feminist scholar who proves that appearances are deceiving because her academic exterior belies the passionate woman beneath. Philippa is a writer who has been in a long-term lesbian relationship but enjoys an occasional "man on the side." Her novel *Eat Me* is a food- and sex-filled, thinly veiled account of the experiences that her friends share with her.

Food and sex are two great pleasures that the four women enjoy, and the imagery in this novel often blends both. Food and body parts are often compared. The fruits they eat are luscious, the men they devour are "succulent," and their sexual activities are presented as a buffet. "Eat me" takes on a multitude of meanings, both culinary and sexual. Philippa's novel develops throughout the larger novel, as each of her friends' and her own experiences is translated into the framework of her novel. In the final chapters of Jaivin's book, other friends Ellen, Jody, and Camilla see the publication of a book titled *Eat Me* and begin to celebrate that Philippa's book has finally come out. They then see that the name of the author is "Dick Pulse," and they suspect that something is wrong. As they flip through the novel, they see characters that remind them of themselves. They then become irate and upset for "poor Philippa," whom they believe has been cheated of the material by her writing teacher Richard, whom they believe to be "Dick Pulse." They promise each other not to say a word about the book to Philippa, in order to avoid hurting her. In the final chapter, Philippa lounges with her companion Cara and wonders if her friends are aware that the novel has been published and, if so, why they have not called.

CENSORSHIP HISTORY

Eat Me became the target of censors in Marion County, Florida, when in July 2003 an 83-year-old grandmother named Loretta Harrison took out the brightly colored book with the funny title believing it to be a comic novel. After reading only a few pages, Harrison filed an objection with the Marion County Free Library, charging that the novel was too obscene for general reading. She said that she had challenged the novel as "obscene" because she did not want any of her grandchildren to read it. The library advisory board reviewed the book and voted 2-1 to keep the book in the library, but library director Julie Sieg, who read the book, pulled the book from library shelves in August 2003. On August 26, 2003, she reported to the library board of trustees that she had overruled the recommendation of the three-person advisory board and had pulled the book from the circulation, because "we aren't in the habit of providing erotica or pornography." Marion Library policy allowed any patron to challenge a decision by the director, and former board chair Mary Lutes decided to do so. She wrote a letter to the editor of the local newspaper stating, "I'm confident that our library system is strong enough for the appeal process and can actually benefit from it."

The library board debated over the next few months who should have the final say as to whether a book stays or goes. The existing library policy determines that the library board "will review an appeal and subsequent ruling and at the end of the process take a roll call vote that amounts to a written recommendation to be submitted to the library director, the county administrator, and the complaining patron." Because the policy does not specify what follows, Sieg asserted that she had made the final decision to determine the fate of the book. She expressed her loathing for *Eat Me* and announced that it would remain off library shelves. In December 2003, the library board of trustees voted 7-3 to recommend that the book be placed in the library, but Sieg did not follow the recommendation. In February 2004, Sieg reversed her decision and stated, "I allowed my personal dislike for 'Eat Me' to overshadow my objectivity and adherence to policy."

FURTHER READING

American Library Association. "Florida Patrons Debate Whether Trustees Should Set Library Policy." *American Libraries* (February 27, 2004). Available online. URL: http://ala.org/ala/alonline/currentnews/newsarchive/alnews2004/may2004ab/ocala.cfm. Accessed February 1, 2011.

"Censorship Dateline: Libraries: Ocala, Florida." *Newsletter on Intellectual Freedom* 53 (January 2004): 7.

"Florida Director Swallows Her Ban of *Eat Me*." *American Libraries* (February 2004). Available online. URL: http://www.ala.org/ala/alonline/currentnews/newsarchive/alnews2004/february2004/marioneatme.cfm. Accessed December 10, 2009.

"Ocala, Florida." *Newsletter on Intellectual Freedom* 53 (January 2004). Formerly available online. URL: htpps://members.ala.org/nif/v53n1/dateline.html. Accessed December 10, 2009.

THE EPIC OF GILGAMESH

Author: Unknown
Original date and place of publication: 1928, London
Original publisher: Luzac & Company
Literary type: Epic poetry

SUMMARY

The Epic of Gilgamesh is the world's first epic poem, and versions of it have for decades appeared in world literature anthologies read by high school students throughout the United States. Until Stephen Mitchell published *Gilgamesh: A New English Version* (Free Press, 2004), most readers found the work dense and inaccessible although much of the same content was at their disposal, albeit in different form. Earlier translations of the poem were intended for scholars and students, but Mitchell created a new translation of the poem that was intended for the general reader, and it is accessible and understandable and in a easily read form.

The epic poem is older than the *Iliad*, and it remains only a fragment of a much longer work, although the fragments that have been found and translated create a relatively complete, if episodic, account of the journey of Gilgamesh, the young king of Uruk (now Iraq). Originally inscribed in the Akkadian language on stone tablets, the poem was buried during the fall of Nineveh and was not recovered and deciphered until the late 19th century. The existing fragments appear on 11 tablets, and scholars suggest that many more than that number of tablets have been lost.

The Epic of Gilgamesh opens with an arrogant Gilgamesh, possessed of great wealth, power, and physical attractiveness, who oppresses his people as he satisfies his own selfish needs. The gods hear the pleas of his subjects to free them from their oppression and create Enkidu, a ferocious wild man who is said to be the companion of animals, and they offer him as a double or second self for Gilgamesh. Upon first learning of Enkidu, the young king seeks to conquer him, and he sends Shambat, a temple priestess (sometimes translated as "harlot"), to find the wild man and to defuse his power by seducing him. The plan has the expected result, because coupling with Shambat for six days and seven nights awakens the humanity in Enkidu, pushing his animal identity into the background and strengthening his human characteristics. The wild animals no longer consider him one of their own, and they leave him.

Enkidu, seemingly tamed by his sexual experiences, is taken to the city of Uruk, where he meets Gilgamesh and defies the young king by blocking his attempt to enter a bridal chamber and assert his claim of first night with the bride. The two wrestle fiercely and are nearly equal in strength, but Gilgamesh is lauded as the nominal winner. After the fight, the men bond instantly, becoming soul mates, and they are represented in various translations as engaging in what in modern terminology might be labeled a man crush. Without preamble, Gilgamesh asks Enkidu to accompany him in an act of defiance of the gods as he enters the Cedar Forest with the goal of killing the monster Humbaba, who guards the forest. The sun god Shamash sends violent winds to attack Humbaba and to aid Gilgamesh in the fight. Gilgamesh and Enkidu cut off the monster's head and return triumphantly to Uruk.

Gilgamesh returns as a hero and attracts the attention of Ishtar, the goddess of sexual love, who wants him to be her lover. When the young king rejects her with insults and reminders of the many mortal men she has destroyed or turned into animals after tiring of them, she vows revenge. In a rage, she asks her father, the sky god Anu, to give her the Bull of Heaven to destroy Gilgamesh and his kingdom, which he does. Although the bull rampages and kills hundreds of people, Gilgamesh and Enkidu capture and kill it. Enkidu dreams that a council of gods has convened and determined that one of the two men must die as punishment for killing the bull, and that he is the chosen one. Shortly after having the dream, Enkidu becomes ill and dies after suffering for 12 days.

Gilgamesh grieves deeply after his friend's death, ripping off his clothes and tearing out his hair as he laments loudly. He makes elaborate plans to honor his dead friend and orders artisans to create an opulent statue of Enkidu. He offers jewels, gold, ivory, weapons, and other treasures to the gods and considers damming the Euphrates River to place Enkidu's tomb in the riverbed.

Both grief-stricken and now fearful of death, Gilgamesh goes on a quest for immortality. He begins to live as a wild man, killing lions, eating them, and wearing their skins as he searches for Uta-napishti, who found eternal life and whose secret Gilgamesh wants to learn. To find Uta-napisthi, Gilgamesh must travel to the edge of the world. Before reaching his destination, he must cross an ocean, which he does with the assistance of the ferryman Ur-shanabi, who helps him to avoid the Waters of Death. Uta-napishti does not relate the secret of eternal life to Gilgamesh, but he does give him a plant that is supposed to restore youth. On the journey home, however, Gilgamesh carelessly leaves the plant unguarded as he bathes in a pool and a snake steals it. After his many efforts, Gilgamesh returns to Uruk, not immortal in a traditional sense but able to continue his life and to serve as a much wiser and more compassionate ruler.

CENSORSHIP HISTORY

For decades, the standard text of *The Epic of Gilgamesh* used in schools was the Penguin Classics edition of the poem, translated by N. K. Sanders, which clearly conveys the lustful, sensual nature of the hero, beginning with the first tablet that contains the lament of the people: "Gilgamesh sounds the tocsin for his amusement, his arrogance has no bounds by day or night. No son is left with his father, for Gilgamesh takes them all, even the children; yet the king should be a shepherd to his people. His lust leaves no virgin to her lover, neither the warrior's daughter nor the wife of the noble." Shambat, the temple priestess or harlot, depending upon the translation, is instructed before her seduction of Enkidu: "Now, woman, make your breasts bare, have no shame, do not delay but welcome his love. Let him see you naked, let him possess your body. When he comes near uncover yourself and lie with him; teach him, the savage man, your woman's art." No challenges to these earlier versions have been reported.

In 2006, parents of students attending Clearview Regional High School in Harrison Township, New Jersey, challenged the use of the trade paperback *Gilgamesh: A New English Version* and demanded that the school remove the work from the 10th grade classrooms, where it had been an approved text for two years. In a statement to a reporter for the *Gloucester County Times*, Jennifer Low, the mother of a 10th grade student, said that she did not think the book should be in school. "I don't understand how the school can not allow girls to wear spaghetti straps but can allow them to read something so graphic." A new resident in the district who moved to New Jersey from Texas, the month before the article came out, Low claimed that she did not oppose the entire book, only a specific section that she described as "sexually descriptive and unnecessarily explicit." She said that other parents should be made aware of the offensive sections in the book and asserted that she would not have known about the content if her daughter had not told her that reading the passages "made her feel uncomfortable." Jeff Gellenthin, also a parent of a 10th grade student, told the reporter "Bottom line, that material is bizarre." He complained "in a fiery e-mail" to school officials that the translation is "pornography" and "sheer smut." School officials responded to the parent complaints by allowing students whose parents opposed the approved translation to read a different translation of the work.

FURTHER READNG

Ackerman, Susan. *When Heroes Love: The Ambiguity of Eros in the Stories of Gilgamesh and David.* New York: Columbia University Press, 2005.
"Censorship Dateline: Libraries." *Newsletter on Intellectual Freedom* 56, no.1. (January 2007). Accessed April 4, 2010.
Mitchell, Stephen, trans. *Gilgamesh: A New English Version.* New York: Free Press, 2004.

FANNY HILL, OR MEMOIRS OF A WOMAN OF PLEASURE

Author: John Cleland
Original dates and places of publication: 1748, England; 1821, United States
Original publishers: G. Fenton (England); Peter Holmes (United States)
Literary form: Novel

SUMMARY

Fanny Hill, or Memoirs of a Woman of Pleasure was written while John Cleland was incarcerated in a London debtor's prison. The story of an orphaned 15-year-old country girl who moves to London to find employment as a household worker but who instead enters a brothel is primarily composed of descriptions of her sexual experiences and those that she observes. Her first job is with a brothel keeper who trains Fanny for her future profession as a woman of pleasure. Those who have sought to ban the novel over the course of more than two centuries have complained that it contains numerous incidents of heterosexual and lesbian sexual activity, female masturbation, flagellation, and voyeurism. Typical of the criticism leveled at the novel is that of U.S. Supreme Court Justice Thomas C. Clark, who observed in a dissenting opinion in 1966:

> In each of the sexual scenes the exposed bodies of the participants are described in minute and individual detail. The pubic hair is often used for a background to the most vivid and precise descriptions of the response, condition, size, shape, and color of the sexual organs before, during and after orgasms.

Such criticism ignores the many instances in which the language is ornate and metaphorical as Cleland refers to genitalia through such euphemisms as "engine," "champion," and the "machine," as well as "the tender small part framed to receive it," the "pit," and the "wound." Although the novel may be "essentially a guidebook to erotic variations," the author presents them with humor. The author uses none of the "four-letter" words that are usually labeled "obscene," although he does use such candid terms as "maidenhead" and "defloration." The frequent labeling of the novel as priapic is also due to the fascination that Fanny shows with the male anatomy, as in the scene in which she and her first lover, Charles, have sex:

> a column of the whitest ivory, beautifully streak'd with blue veins, and carry-ing, fully uncapt, a head of the liveliest vermilion: no horn could be harder or stiffer; yet no velvet more smooth or delicious to the touch. . . . a pair of round-ish balls, that seem'd to pay within, and elude all pressure but the tenderest, from without.

At the end of the novel, after having experienced every variation of sexual intimacy, Fanny leaves her life of sin and marries Charles, providing the reader with her observation that "looking back on the course of vice I had run, and comparing its infamous blandishments with the infinitely superior joys of innocence, I could not help pitying even in point of taste, those who, immers'd in gross sensuality, are insensible to the so delicate charms of VIRTUE."

CENSORSHIP HISTORY

In 1749, less than one year after publication of *Fanny Hill, or Memoirs of a Woman of Pleasure,* John Cleland was imprisoned on the orders of Lord New-castle, the British secretary of state, on a charge of "corrupting the King's subjects." The action was taken after high-ranking officials of the Church of England had protested the nature of the book and demanded the arrest of Cleland, his publisher, and his printer. The bishop of London had person-ally contacted Newcastle, asking him to "give proper orders, to stop the progress of this vile Book, which is an open insult upon Religion and good manners, and a reproach to the Honour of the Government, and the Law of the Country."

The trial of *Fanny Hill* in 1821 in Massachusetts was the first obscenity case involving a book to be heard in the United States. The novel had been surreptitiously published in the United States for many years, beginning with several expurgated editions of the novel published by Isaiah Thomas between 1786 and 1814, but not until Peter Holmes published the first edition of the novel in its original form in 1821 did censors take notice. The publisher was convicted for publishing and printing a "lewd and obscene" novel. Hol-mes appealed to the Massachusetts Supreme Court, claiming that the court had not seen the book and that the jury had only heard the prosecution's description. In delivering a decision on the appeal, Chief Justice Isaac Parker observed that the publisher was "a scandalous and evil disposed person" who had contrived to "debauch and corrupt" the citizens of the commonwealth and "to raise and create in their minds inordinate and lustful desires." Of the novel, he stated that "said printed book is so lewd, wicked and obscene, that the same would be offensive to the court here, and improper to be placed upon the records thereof." In short, Holmes lost his appeal because the judge refused to review the book, to have the jury read the book, and to enter passages from the book into the court record, for to do so "would be to require that the public itself should give permanency and notoriety to indecency, in order to punish it."

In 1930, while the Massachusetts legislature debated a revision of censorship laws, *Fanny Hill* was among 300 books seized in a raid on a Philadelphia bookshop. The city district attorney led the raid and announced at the same time that Philadelphia officials would undertake an extensive campaign to curb sales of "obscene" literature.

In 1963, G. P. Putnam's Sons announced that it would issue an unexpurgated edition of *Fanny Hill.* New York City prosecutors with city attorney Leo A. Larkin decided to take legal action against the publisher. Because Putnam had a reputation as a responsible firm with book sales in many of New York City's largest bookstores, the city decided against arrests and criminal charges. Instead, city officials utilized the state injunctive procedure that allowed them to order the listing of inventories and to freeze stocks to prevent further sales until *Larkin v. G. P. Putnam's Sons,* 40 Misc. 2d 25, 243 N.Y.S2d 145 (Sup. Ct. N.Y. Co. 1963) was decided. A further advantage to the prosecution in proving the book was pornographic was that the injunctive procedure required the lesser proof of a civil case rather than the proof beyond a reasonable doubt of a criminal case. Judge Charles Marks issued an order to restrain sales of the novel. The case then went before the state supreme court and was tried without a jury before Justice Arthur G. Klein in *Larkin v. G. P. Putnam's Sons,* 14 N.Y.2d 399, 200 N.E.2d 760 (1964). Expert witnesses argued that the novel portrayed the economic realities of the times and emphasized its literary merit. The reporting of the British Profumo scandal, a sex-and-spy scandal that threatened to topple the British government, occurred while Justice Klein was deliberating. He dissolved the restraining order and dismissed the city's action, asserting that

> if the standards of the community are to be gauged by what it is permitted to read in its daily newspapers, then Fanny Hill's experiences contain little more than the community has already encountered on the front pages of many of its newspapers in the reporting of the recent "Profumo" and other sensational cases involving sex.

The prosecution appealed the decision in 1964, and in a 3 to 2 split decision in *Larkin v. G. P. Putnam's Sons,* 20 A.D.2d 702, case no. 2, 247 N.Y.S.2d 275 (1st Dep't 1964), the New York State intermediate appeals court reversed Justice Klein's action and ordered Putnam to refrain from selling the novel in the state of New York. Putnam then took the case to the New York Court of Appeals, which in a 4-3 decision reversed the decision of the lower court and granted final judicial amnesty to *Fanny Hill* in New York.

In 1963 the United States Supreme Court considered the validity of a Massachusetts Supreme Judicial Court decision that the novel was "pornographic" in *A Book Named "John Cleland's Memoirs of a Woman of Pleasure" v. Massachusetts*, 383 U.S. 413 (1966). The court cleared *Fanny Hill* of obscenity charges in a conditional decision. Justice William J. Brennan stated in the majority decision that historical importance is a factor, and "the circumstances of production, sale and publicity are relevant in determining whether or not the publication and distribution of the book is constitutionally protected."

In London in 1963, the publication of unexpurgated paperback versions of the novel motivated the director of public prosecutions to secure a seizure order for all copies of the novel that were currently displayed in the window of a small Soho bookstore. The store proudly proclaimed on a sign in the window that the novel was "Banned in America." The trial was held early in 1964; after four days of testimony, the novel was determined to be obscene and the seized copies were ordered to be destroyed.

In 1965, Paul's Book Arcade of Auckland, New Zealand, sought to avoid censorship and applied to the Indecent Publications Tribunal for a determination regarding the expurgated paperback edition of the novel, published by Mayflower Books Limited of London in 1964. In a decision rendered on May 20, 1965, the tribunal ruled:

> The book has no substance other than to relate the experiences of a prostitute and we think that it might arouse interest in the one form of perversion it describes . . . . We accordingly make a ruling which the statute permits classifying it as indecent in the hands of persons under eighteen years of age, though we feel considerable doubt as to how far, if at all, such a classification will have the effect sought.

FURTHER READING

Cooper, Morton. "Fanny Hill vs. the Constitution." *Pageant* 14 (June 1964): 14–20.

Foxon, David F. "John Cleland and the Publication of *Memoirs of a Woman of Pleasure.*" *Book Collector* 12 (Winter 1963): 476–487.

Kuh, Richard H. *Foolish Figleaves? Pornography In and Out of Court.* New York: Macmillan, 1967.

Rembar, Charles. *The End of Obscenity: The Trials of "Lady Chatterley's Lover," "Tropic of Cancer" & "Fanny Hill" by the Lawyer Who Defended Them.* New York: Random House, 1968.

Rolph, Cecil Hewitt. *Book in the Dock.* London: Deutsch, 1961.

Sebastian, Raymond F. "Obscenity and the Supreme Court: Nine Years of Confusion." *Stanford Law Review* 19 (November 1966): 167–189.

Stuart, Perry. *The Indecent Publications Tribunal: A Social Experiment*. Christchurch, New Zealand: Whitcombe and Tombs, 1965.

Wald, Emil W. "Obscene Literature Standards Re-examined." *South Carolina Law Review* 18 (Spring 1966): 497–503.

THE FIFTEEN PLAGUES OF A MAIDENHEAD

Author: Anonymous
Original date and place of publication: 1707, England
Original publishers: James Reade and Angell Carter
Literary form: Poetical bagatelles

SUMMARY

The Fifteen Plagues of a Maidenhood catalogs the troubles or "plagues" faced by young women still in possession of their maidenheads, making them burdens whose loss is to be desired. Each bagatelle offers encouragement to the virgin and often repetitive instructions by which she might accomplish this loss. The book represents what Loth has characterized as "a typical example of the new commercial smut." An excellent example of the character of the book lies in the middle bagatelle, the "Eighth Plague":

> Now I am young; blind Cupid me bewitches.
> I scratch my belly for it always itches,
> And what it itches for I've told before:
> Tis either to be wife or be a whore.
> Nay, any thing indeed, would poor I
> E'er maidenhead upon my hands should lie
> Which till I lose, I'm sure my wat'ry eye
> Will pay to love so great a sacrifice
> That my carcass soon will weep out all its juice
> Till grown so dry as fit for no man's use.

CENSORSHIP HISTORY

The Fifteen Plagues of a Maidenhead, John Garfield's *The Wandering Whore* (1660), and Edmund Curll's *Venus in the Cloyster* (1728) were involved in cases that helped to develop the legal concept of "obscene libel" in the 18th century. The move meant a change in the direction of censorship from a major emphasis upon controlling sedition, blasphemy, and heresy—issues with which the censorship courts were more familiar—to the effort to control published "obscenity." The responsibility for controlling obscenity also moved from the ecclesiastical to the secular courts, although creating the actual laws for these courts to enforce lagged behind the movement of jurisdiction.

In 1707, James Reade and Angell Carter were prosecuted for publishing *The Fifteen Plagues of a Maidenhead*. The defendants were brought before the king's bench and charged with "obscene libel," but they were acquitted after the defense counsel asserted that the court had no right to try the case because the defendants were not guilty of breaking any existing law. Lord Chief Justice Sir John Holt, one of the masters of English common law, admitted that he disliked the tone and the content of the book, calling it "bawdy." He also acknowledged in his ruling in *Rex v. Reade* that no common law or statute existed that "could warrant an indictment against even the filthiest book."

FURTHER READING

Foxon, David. *Libertine Literature in England, 1600–1745*. New Hyde Park, N.Y.: University Books, 1965.

Gerber, Albert B. *Sex, Pornography and Justice*. Secaucus, N.J.: Lyle Stuart, 1965.

Kearney, Patrick J. *A History of Erotic Literature*. Hong Kong: Parragon, 1982.

Loth, David. *The Erotic in Literature*. New York: Dorset, 1961.

FLOWERS FOR ALGERNON

Author: Daniel Keyes
Original date and place of publication: 1966, United States
Original publisher: Harcourt Brace Jovanovich
Literary form: Novel

SUMMARY

Flowers for Algernon is a novel about a daring human experiment that transforms a mentally retarded man with an IQ of 68 into a genius with an IQ of 185, thus forcing him to cope with the adult world. The experimental surgery that makes Charlie Gordon "normal" is only temporary, and he must suffer the growing realization that he will lose all that he has achieved and, once again, lapse into mental retardation.

Related as a series of progress reports written by Charlie, the novel shows his early inadequacies through the writing in the halting manner of expression, the considerable misspellings, and the lack of grammar skills, in the reports. As his abilities increase, so does the quality of the reports. Thirty-two-year-old Charlie has worked at a bakery for 17 years, after being "rescued" by his boss, Mr. Donner, from the Warren State Home, where his mother had committed him. Charlie attends classes three nights a week at the Beekman College Center for Retarded Adults, where he joins others in practicing speaking and writing skills. He has no memory of his family or other details from his past, only nightmarish flashes of his mother yelling at him and slapping him, and his father saying, "He can't help it if he gets an erection. It's normal."

After the surgery, which had also been performed on a mouse named Algernon who remains under study in the laboratory, Charlie works hard to obtain the needed skills to utilize his new intelligence, and his former teacher, Alice Kinnian, works with him. His rapidly developing mind can process great amounts of information, and he soon begins to trade ideas with experts in various fields, as he also enjoys artistic experiences. Newspaper accounts refer to him as the "moron-genius."

As he develops mentally, Charlie also develops emotionally and falls in love with Alice, who is attracted to him but urges him to become acquainted with other women. Charlie finds that he is haunted by the specter of the younger, retarded boy that he once was. He finally overcomes his fear by drinking a little too much and having sex with his neighbor, the bohemian painter Fay.

Through his scientific studies, Charlie learns that his improvement is only temporary and the deterioration will begin quickly. This fear is confirmed by abrupt changes in Algernon's behavior and the death of the mouse. Before the end, Charlie and Alice spend a long night making love and holding each other, fearing the inevitable. At the end of the novel, Charlie is living in the Warren State Home, his deterioration nearly complete.

CENSORSHIP HISTORY

The novel was banned from the public schools in Plant City, Florida, in 1976 because of its "references to sex" as well as for the sexual encounter between Charlie and his teacher. In 1977, the novel was removed from use in the 11th-grade classrooms in the Cameron County School District after parents protested to the district board of education. They complained that the book was "sexually oriented trash" and that it had no place in a high school classroom. The board agreed and ordered that all copies of the book be removed from the classrooms and that teachers no longer include references to the work in the curriculum.

In 1981, the novel was banned from the Glen Rose (Arkansas) High School library because parents complained about Charlie's first sexual encounter, claiming that it was too detailed and "explicit." In 1983, the novel was challenged, for the same reason, as a suggested reading at the Oberlin (Ohio) High School.

In 1984, parents of students at the Glenrock (Wyoming) High School challenged use of the novel as a required reading, claiming that several "explicit love scenes were distasteful." In 1986, the novel was removed from a 10th-grade supplemental reading list in the Charlotte-Mecklenburg (North Carolina) school district after parents protested its use and charged that the book was "pornographic."

FURTHER READING

Lambert, Robert. "Charley: Metamorphosis by Media." *Media and Methods* 5 (February 1969): 29–31.

Newsletter on Intellectual Freedom (July 1976): 85; (May 1977): 73; (July 1981): 91; (January 1984): 26; (July 1984): 122; (January 1987): 12; (March 1987): 54; (May 1987): 103; (July 1987): 150.

Shugert, Diane P. "Rationales for Commonly 'Challenged' Taught Books." *Connecticut English Journal* 15 (Fall 1983): 145–146.

THE FLOWERS OF EVIL (LES FLEURS DU MAL)

Author: Charles Baudelaire
Original dates and places of publication: 1857, France; 1909, England
Original publishers: August Poulet-Malassis (France); Constable and Company (England)
Literary form: Poetry collection

SUMMARY

First published as *Les Fleurs du Mal*, the collection contained 100 poems grouped under the following headings: Spleen and Ideal, Parisian Scenes, Wine, Flowers of Evil, Rebellion and Death. The sole collection of Baudelaire's poems to be published in his lifetime, the volume became notorious for its themes of eroticism, lesbianism, morbidity, perversity, and rebellion. His observations of and emphasis upon subjective experiences among prostitutes, drug users, the poor, and other images of Parisian ruin vie with images of unexpected beauty that he discerned beneath the perversity and corruption of modern civilization. To Baudelaire's contemporaries, the modernity of his rendering of the antithesis of good and evil was too great a deviation from contemporary work.

Although critics halfheartedly protested Baudelaire's "religious immorality" in such poems as "Saint Peter's Denial," "Abel and Cain," and "Satan's Litanies," the greater criticism was launched at his glorification of physical pleasures. Particular objections were raised against such lines as "Like a poor profligate who sucks and bites the withered breast of some well-seasoned trull" ("To the Reader") and the adoration of a lover's body in "Jewels," in which the poet glories in "the sleek thighs shifting, shiny as oil, the belly, the breasts—the fruit on my vine." When the book, author, and publisher were placed on trial in 1857 for "immorality," the prosecuting attorney made a point of quoting lines from "Jewels" and "Lethe" ("the reek of you that permeates your skirts . . . those entrancing pointed breasts"). He also declared that "the most intimate habits of lesbian woman" were depicted in "Lesbos," "Damned Women," and "Metamorphoses of the Vampire."

CENSORSHIP HISTORY

The Flowers of Evil was published in an edition of 1,100 copies in 1857 and immediately motivated an uproar among critics for the startling imagery and daring metaphors of the poems. Baudelaire had expected that his poems would offend readers, but he counted on the recent acquittal in the trial of MADAME BOVARY and the preoccupation of the government with elections to protect his work from prosecution. In a letter to his mother dated July 9, 1857, the poet stated, "People have been spreading the rumour that I am going to be prosecuted, but it won't happen. A government with the terrible Paris elections on its hands won't have time to prosecute a lunatic." He was wrong, for attacks on several poems had already begun in the form of articles in the satiric publication *Figaro*, which drew the attention of the courts to Baudelaire's work. On July 5, 1857, his publisher, Poulet-Malassis, received a letter from the Paris distributor stating that the rumor abroad, "especially in high society," was that *Les Fleurs du Mal* was going to be seized.

The minister of the interior declared *Les Fleurs du Mal* to be "one of those unhealthy and profoundly immoral works destined to have a *succes de scandale*, and he apprised the office of the public prosecutor of his opinion that the book was "an outrage of public morality." Police were sent to seize all copies of the work from the offices of the publisher and the printer. On August 20, 1857, Baudelaire appeared before the Sixth Criminal Court, faced by Deputy Imperial Prosecutor Ernest Pinard, a future minister of the interior. Pinard identified "Saint Peter's Denial," "Abel and Cain," "Litanies of Satan," and "The Murderer's Wine" as breaches of religious morality but did not press the point, so the court dropped the charge of blasphemy. Instead, the emphasis was placed upon the "immoral passages" of other poems, lines from which Pinard eagerly read, including "Jewels," "Lesbos," "Lethe," "Against Her Levity," "Metamorphoses of the Vampire," and two poems entitled "Damned Women." Baudelaire's defense attorney, Chaix d'Est-Ange, pleaded that the poet's work depicted vice in a way that made it odious to the reader, but the court was not convinced and ruled that the book contained "obscene and immoral passages or expressions." The poet was fined 300 francs, and the publisher and printer, were each fined 100 francs. All three were also deprived of their right to vote. Further, the court ordered the first five "immoral" poems named above and the version of "Damned Women" subtitled "Delphine and Hippolyta" to be deleted from future editions of *Les Fleurs du Mal*. The ban on the poems in France remained until May 31, 1949, when the French Appeals Court declared that the poems contained no words either obscene or vulgar, "though certain descriptions may, by their originality, have alarmed certain minds at the time."

FURTHER READING

Bergeron, Katherine. "The Echo, the Cry, the Death of Lovers." *Nineteenth Century Music* 18 (Fall 1994): 136–151.

Cohen, Emily Jane. "Mud into Gold: Baudelaire and the Alchemy of Public Hygiene." *Romanic Review* 87 (March 1996): 239–255.

Morgan, Edwin. *Flowers of Evil: A Life of Charles Baudelaire*. Freeport, N.Y.: Books for Libraries Press, 1943.

Pichois, Claude. *Baudelaire*. London: Hamish Hamilton, 1989.

Ramazani, Vaheed K. "Writing in Pain: Baudelaire, Benjamin, Haussmann." *Boundary* 223 (Summer 1996): 199–224.

FOREVER

Author: Judy Blume
Original date and place of publication: 1975, United States
Publisher: Bradbury Press
Literary form: Young adult novel

SUMMARY

Forever is a novel about first love and the chaotic feelings that accompany the romance and the sexual desire of teenagers Katherine and Michael. After meeting at a New Year's Eve party, the two date for several weeks, becoming closer and more sexually aroused each time that they meet. Katherine is a virgin and hesitant to "lose control," but Michael's passionate overtures eventually overcome her doubts. Their first few times having sex are unremarkable for Katherine because Michael reaches orgasm before she is completely aroused. After they finally synchronize their desire, Katherine becomes an enthusiastic aggressor, enjoying their lovemaking and seeking times to be alone with Michael. They pledge to love each other "forever," and for her 18th birthday, Michael gives Katherine a silver necklace on which her name is inscribed on one side of a disk with the words "forever, Michael" inscribed on the other.

Both partners act in a responsible manner, discussing their concerns regarding birth control and the prevention of sexually transmitted diseases and substituting mutual masturbation for sexual intercourse until birth control is available. Their encounters are detailed for the reader, who can trace the growing intensity of their desire from Michael's sensitive exploration of Katherine's breasts to their later frequent and varied lovemaking. Sexual activity is also integral to the subplots involving several friends. Sibyl, who "has a genius I.Q. and has been laid by at least six different guys," has a baby whose father she cannot identify. Erica seeks to help talented high school actor Artie determine if he is gay by having sex with him, but her efforts push him to attempt suicide.

Concerned that Katherine is too young to make a lifetime commitment to Michael, her parents urge her to date others and eventually demand that she work at a summer camp several hundred miles away to test the relationship. When her grandfather dies, Katherine rushes into the arms of fellow counselor Theo, who wisely tells her he wants her but "not with death for an excuse." This makes Katherine realize that she really will not love Michael "forever." When they next meet, she breaks off the relationship, leaving Michael angry and embittered.

CENSORSHIP HISTORY

Forever has been repeatedly challenged and banned in schools and libraries because of the detailed sexual descriptions and the perceived frequency of the sexual activity in the novel. In 1982, the parents of students attending Mid-valley Junior-Senior High School in Scranton, Pennsylvania, challenged the book, charging that it contained "four-letter words and talked about masturbation, birth control, and disobedience to parents." The book was also challenged that year in the Orlando, Florida, schools and at the Park Hill (Missouri) South Junior High School library, where librarians were required by the school board to place the book on the "restricted" shelves. In 1983, parents called for the removal of the book from the Akron, Ohio, school district libraries and from the Howard-Suamico (Wisconsin) High School library because "it demoralizes marital sex." In 1984, challenges to the book by parents resulted in its removal from the Holdredge (Nebraska) Public Library young adult section to the adult section because of claims that the "book is pornographic and does not promote the sanctity of family life." That same year, parents challenged inclusion of the book in the Cedar Rapids (Iowa) Public Library because it was "pornography and explores areas God didn't intend to explore outside of marriage."

The Patrick County, Virginia, school board, responding to parent complaints in 1986, ordered the novel placed on a "restricted" shelf in the high school library, and challenges were raised against its inclusion in the Campbell County (Wyoming) school libraries because it was "pornographic" and would encourage young readers "to experiment with sexual encounters." Parents of students in the Moreno Valley (California) Unified School District sought to remove the novel from the school libraries in 1987 and claimed that it "contains profanity, sexual situations, and themes that allegedly encourage disrespectful behavior." In 1987, charging that the "book does not paint a responsible role of parents," that its "cast of sex-minded teenagers is not typical of high schoolers today," and that the "pornographic sexual exploits are unsuitable for junior high school role models," parents of students attending Marshwood Junior High School in Eliot, Maine, demanded its removal from the classroom library. In 1988, the principal of West Hernando (Florida) Middle School yielded to parents' complaints that the novel was "inappropriate" and asked that it be removed from the school library shelves.

The challenges to *Forever* continued in the 1990s. In 1992, the novel was placed on the "reserve" shelf at the Herrin (Illinois) Junior High School library because it was "sexually provocative reading," and students could only check out the book if they had written permission from their parents. In 1993, the novel was removed from the Frost Junior High School library in Schaumberg, Illinois, after parents charged that "it's basically a sexual 'how-to-do' book for junior high students. It glamorizes sex and puts ideas into their heads." Also in 1993, the superintendent of schools in Rib Lake, Wisconsin, filed a "request for reconsideration" of the book after determining that it was "sexually explicit." The novel was placed on the "parental permission shelf," then later confiscated by the high school principal. High school guidance counselor Mike Dishnow, who spoke out against the district book policy and criticized the actions of the principal in restricting student access to the novel, was not rehired for the following academic year. He sued the school district, and a federal jury in Madison, Wisconsin, awarded him $394,560 in damages and lost wages. In summer 1996, the courts reversed their decision and, in agreement with the insurance company of the school district, determined that the board was responsible only for paying the legal fees and not lost wages to Dishnow. The school district took out a nine-year loan to pay off the settlement with interest, an amount of $232,000. In addition, teaching and administrative positions were cut and a bus route dropped to cover costs.

In 1994, school officials in Mediapolis, Iowa, responded to parent complaints about the novel and removed it from the school libraries because it "does not promote abstinence and monogamous relationships and lacks any aesthetic, literary, or social value." The book was returned a month later, but only to the high school library.

In 1995, parents in the Elgin Area School District U-46 in Elgin, Illinois, pressured the school board to remove *Forever* from the middle school library. The parents who lodged the complaint expressed concern about the sexuality in the book. Attempts to reinstate the book failed repeatedly for four years until school librarians in the district were able to convince a special faculty and parent committee to vote unanimously to lift the ban. The committee vote was presented to the Elgin Area School District U-46 Board, which voted 5-2 on January 22, 2002, to lift the ban and return *Forever* to the middle school library's bookshelves.

In 2003, *Forever* was challenged by a parent of a student attending the Spring Hill Elementary School in Hernando County, Florida. In the complaint, the parent charged that the novel is inappropriate for students at the elementary school level because it contains passages that speak openly about masturbation. After reviewing the complaint, the school board decided to retain the title but to make it available only to students who had written parental permission to read the novel.

In 2005, the *Pasadena Citizen* reported that Dr. Rick Schneider, Pasadena Independent School District superintendent, had banned the novel from all of the libraries in the school district after the parent of a student attending the Thompson Intermediate School submitted a formal complaint to the district. Before the district made the decision to remove the book, the district followed a formal policy that included the formation of a campus review committee composed of administrators, instructors, and parents who studied the book and presented their findings to the superintendent. The initial recommendation of the committee was that the district should remove the novel from only the intermediate school libraries and retain the novel in the high school libraries, but school superintendent Schneider made the decision to remove *Forever* from all of the libraries in the school system because he determined that the novel contains "sexually explicit content." A district spokesperson defended the decision. "The superintendent has the responsibility to put materials in the system that are educationally suitable and appropriate. In this particular case, after reading the book, he felt that, though the theme is not unsuitable, certain passages are and decided to remove the book. . . . Certain passages were not appropriate for any students of the school district." The same year, *Forever* was on a list of 50 books challenged by parents of students attending the Fayetteville middle and junior high school who charged that the books are too sexually explicit and promoted homosexuality.

The novel was not the object of any major challenges for several years until late 2009, when parents of students attending the Sugarloaf School in Summerland Key, Monroe County, Florida, became upset over the description of preteen sex in the book and asked school officials to remove the book from the shelves of the school district libraries. The challenge asserted that the novel contains "a distorted view of sex, promiscuity, [and is] usurping parental control." The school district refused the request until a committee could review the book and decide whether to remove access to the book for all levels of students or to make it accessible only to high school students. Sugarloaf school principal Theresa Axford reassured parents that the committee, which consisted of the principal, the school librarian, a district administrator, a teacher, and a member of community, would read the book and evaluate its literary merit. Tami Fletcher and Heather Fowler, two of the parents who initiated the request for removal of the book, asserted that their 13-year-old children had been subjected to listening to parts of the book being read aloud on the school bus. "This book was discussed with other children who had no choice but to hear it." The National Coalition Against Censorship (NCAC) urged its members to write letters to the school district to urge officials to retain the novel in the school libraries. In the letter, executive director of NCAC Joan Bertin reminded officials that "No book is right for everyone, and the role of the library is to allow students to make choices according to their own interest, experiences and family values. No one has to read something just because it's on the library shelf." NCAC reported in a posting on the organization's Web site dated February 18, 2010, that the school district review committee recommended keeping *Forever* in the school district libraries.

FURTHER READING

Doyle, Robert P. *Books Challenged or Banned in 2005–2006*. Chicago: American Library Association, 2006

"'Forever'—Banned." *Pasadena Citizen*. Available online. URL: http//www.freerepublic. com/focus/f-news/1381149/posts. Accessed September 20, 2010.

Forman, Jack. "Young Adult Books: 'Watch Out for #1.'" *Horn Book* 61 (January/February 1985): 85.

Guerra, John L. "Parents: Books too Racy for Youngsters." Available online. URL: http://ww.keysnews .com/node/20059. Accessed September 20, 2010.

"The Long and the Short of It." *Censorship News* 74 (Summer 1999).

Maynard, Joyce. "Coming of Age with Judy Blume." *New York Times Magazine*, December 3, 1978, pp. 80+.

Newsletter on Intellectual Freedom (July 1982): 124, 142; (May 1982): 84; (May 1983): 85–86; (March 1984): 39; (May 1984): 69; (March 1985): 59; (September 1985): 167; (March 1986): 39; (March 1987): 66–67; (July 1987): 125; (November 1987): 239; (March 1988): 45; (May 1992): 80; (May 1993): 70; (July 1993): 98, 104–05; (September 1993): 146–147; (May 1994): 83, 86; (July 1994): 109; (March 1995): 56; (January 2003): 8–9; (March 2004): 48–49; (May 2004): 95–96; (May 2005): 108; (July 2005):185–186.

"Parents in Florida Object to Judy Blume's 'Forever.'" Blog of the National Coalition Against Censorship. Available online. URL: http://ncacblog.wordpress. com/2010/02/18/parents-in-florida-object-to-judy-blumes-forever. Accessed September 21, 2010.

"Schools Liable for Censorship Damages." *Censorship News*, Iss. 62 (summer 1996). Available online. URL: http://www.ncac.org/projects/bit2.html. Accessed December 22, 2005.

Slivinski, Krystyna. "Schools Can Reinstate Banned Book: District 46 Board Will Let Libraries Stock Racy Novel." *Chicago Tribune*, January 24, 2002, p. 5.

Thompson, Susan. "Images of Adolescence: Part I." *Signal* 34 (1981): 57–59.

FOREVER AMBER

Author: Kathleen Winsor
Original date and place of publication: 1944, United States
Original publisher: Macmillan
Literary form: Novel

SUMMARY

Forever Amber relates the career of Amber, an illegitimate child born of noble lineage in 1644, from her rustic upbringing through her adventures in

London when she becomes a duchess and the mistress of Charles II. She has numerous lovers and gives birth to children by three different lovers. She does marry four times, but only her first marriage is legal, and she fails to marry the one man whom she truly loves.

The novel contains historically accurate detailed descriptions of the Restoration period, including Newgate Prison, the Great Plague, and the Great Fire in London, as well as numerous notable Restoration figures. The author achieves accuracy in re-creating the court of Charles II, as well as the costumes and the stage of the period. Amber forever loves Bruce, the first man who seduces her, but she is proud to become the mistress of King Charles II, assuring herself after their first encounter, "I'm somebody now! I've lain with the King!" After being moved into the palace, where she bears the king several children, she also makes several advantageous marriages, one to the older Lord Radclyffe, whose grown son she also seduces. Throughout the novel, Amber uses her sexuality to achieve her aims, actions befitting the times as portrayed in a novel in which most of the characters ignore traditional morality and use any means to achieve their ambitions.

Anatomical references are limited to descriptions of Amber's breasts, as "full and pointed, and upward tilting," and the sexual scenes are presented in general terms. Typical of such vague description is Amber's first seduction:

> At last his arm reached out, went around her waist, and drew her slowly toward him; Amber, tipping her head to meet his mouth, slid both her arms about him.
> The restraint he had shown thus far now vanished swiftly, giving way to a passion that was savage, violent, ruthlessly selfish. Amber, inexperienced but not innocent, returned his kisses eagerly. Spurred by the caressing of his mouth and hands, her desire mounted apace with his. . . .
> Amber, crying, half-mad with passion and terror, suddenly let herself relax.

CENSORSHIP HISTORY

Literary critics generally condemned the value of the novel, and the condemnation by *Atlantic* reviewer Frances Woodward that *Forever Amber* was "without any literary distinction" was typical. In 1946, the U.S. Department of the Post Office declared *Forever Amber* "obscene" and banned it from the mails, in theory until 1957, when the ban was officially lifted. The ruling had no significant effect upon sales of the book because mail distribution did not represent an important means of sales, although suggestive advertising materials sent through the mail had motivated the banning.

Forever Amber had been in print for four years, having sold 1.3 million copies in the United States and more than 100,000 copies in England, when it became the target of censors in the Commonwealth of Massachusetts in 1948. The case went to the highest court in the state as a civil rather than a criminal action under a new law that provided that whenever there was reasonable cause to believe that a book was "obscene, indecent or impure" the attorney general or any district attorney could ask a justice of the Superior Court to rule on the book. State Attorney General George Rowell charged that the book contained "70 references to sexual intercourse; 39 to illegitimate pregnancies; 7 to abortions; 10 descriptions of women undressing, dressing or bathing in the presence of men; 5 references to incest; 13 references ridiculing marriage; and 49 miscellaneous objectionable passages." The decision in *Attorney General v. Book Named "Forever Amber"*, 323 Mass. 302, 81 N.E.2d 663 (Sup. Jud. Ct. 1948) went against Rowell. Judge Donahue of the Massachusetts Supreme Court acknowledged the historical accuracy of the novel and stated that "these matters indicate a certain amount of study and research . . . that *Forever Amber* is sufficiently accurate for the purpose of representing a portrait of the period and its customs and morals; that it does not exaggerate or falsify any traits of the Restoration." The judge also noted that "sexual episodes abound to the point of tedium" and observed that they "are lacking in realistic detail, although some are coarse." Judge Donahue noted in closing statements that the book was "a soporific rather than an aphrodisiac" and noted that "while the novel was conducive to sleep, it was not conducive to a desire to sleep with a member of the opposite sex."

In 1952, the novel was banned in New Zealand after the Honourable Walter Nash, Minister of Customs, reviewed a copy seized by customs officers. Applying powers granted him by the Customs Act of 1913, Nash acted as censor and made the final decision to ban further importation of the novel. Perry notes that the law also allowed for the importer to "dispute the forfeiture, for the Attorney-General to lay an information against the importer for the condemnation of the book, to which the importer would file a defence. . . . I can, however, find no record in the *New Zealand Law Reports* of a case relating to books prohibited on grounds of indecency having been dealt with in this way." Only the Dunedin members of the New Zealand Library Association Fiction Committee raised a protest against the censoring of *Forever Amber*. Although they criticized the novel as "trivial and naive," they found the way in which the Minister of Customs had dealt with the work to be objectionable and they made the public statement that "the operation of censorship in New Zealand was 'casual, arbitrary and ill informed.'" Their views had no effect on the ban.

FURTHER READING

Ernst, Morris L., and Alan U. Schwartz. *Censorship: The Search for the Obscene.* New York: Macmillan, 1964.

Gilloti, Chris F. "Book Censorship in Massachusetts: The Search for a Test of Obscenity." *Boston University Law Review* 42 (Fall 1962): 476–491.

Morse, J. M. "*Forever Amber:* Defendant at Trial in Suffolk County Superior Court, Boston." *New Republic,* January 6, 1947, pp. 39–40.

Paul, James C. N., and Murray L. Schwartz. *Federal Censorship: Obscenity in the Mail.* New York: Free Press, 1961.

Perry, Stuart. *The Indecent Publications Tribunal: A Social Experiment.* London: Whitcombe and Tombs, 1965.

Woodward, Frances. "*Forever Amber.*" *Atlantic,* December 1944, p. 137.

FROM HERE TO ETERNITY

Author: James Jones
Original date and place of publication: 1951, United States
Original publisher: Charles Scribner's Sons
Literary form: Novel

SUMMARY

From Here to Eternity is a lengthy novel that chronicles the experiences of American soldiers stationed in Hawaii in the months preceding the Japanese attack on Pearl Harbor on December 7, 1941. Jones relates the daily lives of the men and the women whom they meet and love on the tropical beaches, in the cities, and in the numerous bars where soldiers yearning for girls back home meet women to quell their loneliness temporarily.

The soldiers speak in a realistic manner, and the descriptions of the bar girls and prostitutes they meet are described bluntly. At the New Congress Hotel and the Black Cat, the men hope to spend their money on

> the Chinese girls with their thin breastless side view and the startlingly curved front view, the Japanese girls with their stockiness of heavier breasts, shorter legs, and more voluptuous hips, but best of all the hapa-Portagee girls with their hot smoking, cat clawing sexiness, everywhere women, women, women, and them cockily feeling their load.

The novel focuses on several characters. The principal character is Robert E. Lee Prewitt, said to be the great-grandson of Confederate Robert E. Lee. Always on the side of the underdog, he rescues a "meek, frightened-faced little bundle of nerves" of a dog who is being held by two soldiers while they encourage a German Shepherd to mount her, and then gets into a fight that lands him in the stockade. While there, he murders a man; then he deserts. Prewitt is killed when he runs away from two military policemen after returning to camp.

The novel also focuses on the love affair between Sergeant Milton Warden and Karen Holmes, wife of Captain Dana Holmes. Karen has trouble dealing with the hysterectomy that she had to undergo several years earlier, after being infected with gonorrhea by her husband. She is bitter about the betrayal and bitter that she can no longer have children. As their love affair continues, Warden breaks through her defenses, and their love scenes are tenderly portrayed. The sergeant is also inspired to become a commissioned officer and does so near the end of the novel. The affair motivates several scenes of adultery, more suggested than explicit, and detailed discussions of Captain Holmes's infidelity and the result of the gonorrhea. As the novel ends, the war with Japan has begun, and Karen Holmes is on a ship with her son, going home and leaving Warden behind.

CENSORSHIP HISTORY

From Here to Eternity was the object of several attempts to censor it. In 1953, two years after the novel won the National Book Award, the police chief of Jersey City, New Jersey, "suggested" to booksellers and newsstand dealers that they remove the paperback edition of the book from their racks. The majority of book dealers complied with the "suggestion." The book was released for sale after a representative of the American Book Publishers Council informed the Jersey City legal authorities that this action violated earlier court decisions in the state.

The novel was banned from the mails in 1955 by the New York City post office four years after it had become a best seller. A carton of paperback copies broke open in a large mailing station, and one of the clerks happened to observe some "dirty words" on several pages. After the publisher entered a protest, the ban was reversed.

In 1956, the prosecuting attorney in Port Huron, St. Clair County, Michigan, ordered booksellers and distributors to cease displaying and selling all books that appeared on the disapproved list of the National Organization for Decent Literature, a Catholic censorship group founded in 1938. The books were identified as "objectionable," and the complaining organization cited the few erotic passages in each novel as the basis for identifying as objectionable *From Here to Eternity* and other novels such as John O'Hara's TEN NORTH FREDERICK, Bud Schulberg's *On the Waterfront,* Ernest Hemingway's *TO HAVE AND HAVE NOT,* and John Steinbeck's *The Wayward Bus.* The ban on all of the books was lifted after New American Library, paperback publisher of *From Here to Eternity,* joined with other publishers and obtained a federal district court injunction against the prosecution for "going beyond legal authority."

FURTHER READING

Champion, Laurie. "Jones's *From Here to Eternity,*" *Explicator* 54 (Summer 1996): 242–244.

Davis, Kenneth C. *Two-Bit Culture: The Paperbacking of America.* Boston: Houghton Mifflin, 1984.

Hempl, William J., and Patrick M. Wall. "Extralegal Censorship of Literature." In *Issues of Our Time*. Ed. by Herbert W. Hildebrandt. New York: Macmillan, 1963.

Oboler, Eli M. *The Fear of the Word: Censorship and Sex*. Metuchen, N.J.: Scarecrow, 1974.

Paul, James C. N., and Murray L. Schwartz. *Federal Censorship: Obscenity in the Mail*. New York: Free Press, 1961.

Tuttleton, James. *The Novel of Manners in America*. New York: Norton, 1972.

THE GENIUS

Author: Theodore Dreiser
Original date and place of publication: 1915, United States
Original publisher: John Lane Company
Literary form: Novel

SUMMARY

The Genius, the most thoroughly autobiographical of Dreiser's novels, relates the stormy history of artist Eugene Witla as he attempts to reconcile the twin drives of his life, a career in art and his powerful sexuality. Growing up in the last years of the 19th century in the United States, Witla faces a society in transition, in which the outward morality of a seemingly Victorian society clashes with new freedoms and increasingly flexible social and moral standards. These differing standards are emphasized by Witla's move from a small Illinois town to Chicago and, eventually, to New York City, as well as in his erratic love affairs in each setting.

Witla yearns for bohemian freedom and appears to have met a woman who allows him freedom while fulfilling his sexual desires when he becomes the lover of artists' model Ruby Kenny. Emotionally unsatisfied by their liaison, he becomes seriously involved with Angela Blue, a physically beautiful but emotionally distant school teacher. While courting Angela, Witla conducts brief sexual affairs with other women, who tempt him with their beauty or intellect, as he tries to penetrate Angela's sexual reserve. One evening, after another unsuccessful attempt at seduction, Witla asks Angela to marry him, but she puts him off. He leaves to make his mark as an artist in New York City, where "he must enter and do battle," but continues to think of Angela. When the incompatible young people eventually do marry, Witla's tribulations increase, as do his infidelities. Even when he tries to create a more stable life as the art editor for a huge publishing conglomerate, Witla becomes infatuated with and seduces Suzanne Dale, the daughter of a close friend of his employer. The seduction is revealed, and Witla is dismissed from his job right after learning that Angela is pregnant. Her pregnancy is difficult and she dies in childbirth, leaving Witla with a daughter, "Angela junior," to raise. As he determines to rebuild his life and to provide his daughter with a good future, Witla feverishly begins to paint and dreams of the lost Suzanne, not of his dead wife.

CENSORSHIP HISTORY

In 1916, eight months after publication of *The Genius* and after sales of about 8,000 copies, the novel caught the attention of John Sumner, the secretary of the New York Society for the Suppression of Vice. Sumner had received an unmarked envelope containing pages torn from a copy of the novel, as well as word from the Western Society for the Suppression of Vice in Cincinnati that a local clergyman had seen a young girl borrowing the novel from the local circulating library. Sumner warned the John Lane Company to withdraw the novel from circulation or face charges of distributing a lewd and profane novel, and he demanded that the publisher destroy the book's plates as well. He complained that the novel contained "seventeen profane and seventy-five lewd passages," and he expressed the view that it was "wholly conceivable that the reading of the book by a young woman could be very harmful." Many of the scenes to which he alluded depicted Witla as feeling passion, but there is little explicit sexual material in the novel. Alerted by Sumner to the moral danger posed by the novel, two postal inspectors also visited the publisher and expressed doubts about the novel.

In the initial contract with Lane, Dreiser had guaranteed the publisher that the novel contained "nothing of a scandalous, immoral, or libelous nature." After the New York Society for the Suppression of Vice threatened to prosecute Lane for violating the laws of the state against obscene literature, Lane withdrew the book from sale and discontinued its publication. Dreiser then bought the plates from Lane before suing the company, claiming that the publisher's refusal to continue sales of *The Genius* constituted a breach of the contract to which Lane had agreed if the sale, advertisement, or publication of the book did not constitute a violation of the law. Dreiser and the publisher took the matter to the Appellate Division of the New York State Supreme Court as a submitted controversy, a move that took the case directly to the body without previous adjudication. The publisher included in the brief the text of the threat of prosecution made by the society and asserted that he had withdrawn the novel from sale because of the threat. Dreiser declared his book to be fit and proper for general sale, and backing him were such prominent writers as H. L. Mencken, Robert Frost, Sinclair Lewis, Amy Lowell, Willa Cather, and Edwin Arlington Robinson. The Appellate Division ruled that determining if a publication was "objectionable" was a question of fact "to be decided as such in the proper manner," that is, in a criminal proceeding and not by the court as a matter of law, and it dismissed the case. No further litigation occurred because no charge of obscenity had been lodged formally, but the novel remained unpublished.

In 1923, Boni & Liveright reissued the novel. The power of the censors had lessened considerably by this time, and distribution of the novel was not again challenged. Although Dreiser appeared to have lost in the dismissal, his effort to fight the censors served to ease the way for a new generation of writers, including Sherwood Anderson, William Faulkner, and Ernest Hemingway.

FURTHER READING

Auerbach, Joseph S. "Authorship and Liberty." *North American Review* 207 (July 1918): 902–917.

Boyer, Paul S. *Purity in Print: The Vice-Society Movement and Book Censorship in America.* New York: Scribner, 1968.

Brooks, Van Wyck. *The Confident Years: 1885–1915.* New York: Dutton, 1952.

De Grazia, Edward. *Girls Lean Back Everywhere: The Law of Obscenity and the Assault on Genius.* New York: Random House, 1992.

Dudley, Dorothy. *Forgotten Frontiers: Dreiser and the Land of the Free.* New York: Smith & Haas, 1932.

Durham, Frank M. "Mencken as Missionary." *American Literature* 29 (January 1958): 478–483.

Gilmer, Walker. *Horace Liveright: Publisher of the Twenties.* New York: Lewis Publishing, 1970.

Tjader, Marguerite. *Theodore Dreiser: A New Dimension.* Norwalk, Conn.: Silvermine Publishers, 1965.

THE GILDED HEARSE

Author: Charles O. Gorham
Original date and place of publication: 1948, United States
Original publisher: Creative Age Press
Literary form: Novel

SUMMARY

The Gilded Hearse takes place on a single day in September 1938 in the lives of Richard Stiles Eliot and his wife Mary, who have reached a crisis in their marriage. Richard, the publicity director of a large New York publishing firm, is insecure in both his professional and his personal life, partly because Mary, a fabric designer for the firm of Golding and Jack, makes more money than he does. During the course of the day, they quarrel, review the sexual affairs that both have had, attempt to advance themselves economically and socially, and decide to reconcile. As they consider newspaper accounts of the Munich Conference and of Mr. Chamberlain's promise of peace with honor, they recognize the truth of Mary's statement, "most of us gave up our honor a long time ago. We'd settle for the peace without the honor."

Early in the novel, as Richard and Mary quarrel, the frustrated husband lashes out, "You dirty pig-Irish bitch. I suppose you're not screwing that Jew bastard, Golding, huh? I suppose you're not getting your nuccy from him?" In another part of the novel, a neurotic young society widow in whom Richard is romantically interested tells her roommate, "If I decide to copulate, I'll copulate."

In the incident that aroused the censors to action, Mary recalls accidentally meeting Monroe Golding on a train. The two retire to his train compartment and

> she pulled her dress up over her head. . . . [T]here were Monroe's hands at her underclothes, helping her to undress, and then they stood together in the dark, without any clothes. . . . She felt panic and moaned and tried to turn away, but then there was the fruity, sweet taste of the brandy mixed with the taste of his kiss as he bent her backward across the berth, and a lifeless giving-in at first as he took her. . . . [S]he lost her grip on time and place and let herself go coursing through to the end, through the waves and the breakers and the blinding lights.

Worried because she has a physical response to a man to whom she has no emotional attachment, Mary consults a doctor who reassures her with the following observations:

> An orgasm . . . is produced by suitable irritation of the clitoris, the walls of the vagina, and other parts of the body. I guess love helps, but it ain't necessary. Even women who have been mass raped have experienced automatic orgasm.

CENSORSHIP HISTORY

The Gilded Hearse was one of several novels published after World War II, including MEMOIRS OF HECATE COUNTY and END AS A MAN, that contained language that would have gotten a book banned in the years preceding the war. The language of the main couple's quarrels and the description of Mary's intimacy with her employer's son, Monroe Golding, provided the basis for complaints and resulted in legal difficulties for the publisher. The incident in which the doctor explains in clearly clinical terms how an orgasm occurs drew criticism, but the unemotional presentation and the absence of anatomical detail deprived it of erotic content.

In 1948, Harry Kahan, a special agent for the Society to maintain Public Decency, complained to the New York Society for the Suppression of Vice that the novel was "obscene." Acting in Kahan's interests, John Sumner, secretary of the society, brought an action against Creative Age Press, the publisher of the novel. The complaint charged that the work was in violation of Section 1141 of the Penal Code, which provides for banning books that are "obscene, lewd, lascivious, filthy, indecent and disgusting." Creative Age Press was represented in court by Harriet F. Pilpel, a member of the law firm of Greenbaum, Wolff & Ernst. Kahan attempted to provide Magistrate Frederick L. Strong with a copy of the book in which the passages that he considered objectionable were bracketed and underscored. The attorney for the publisher insisted that the book should be read as a whole, "not by selection of paragraphs alone," and offered Strong an unmarked copy of the book, which he accepted.

When the case went to court in *People v. Creative Age Press, Inc.*, 192 Misc. 188, 79 N.Y.S.2d 198 (1948), the magistrate in the case agreed to read favorable reviews of the book but not letters from "prominent members of the community" to attest to the author's character and intent in writing the book. Magistrate Strong stated the following regarding Gorham's purpose:

> The author testified that his primary purpose in writing the book was to express his conception that, at any given time, the condition of national morality is reflected by the then current condition of individual morality and that national policies of compromise at the expense of principle occur when it has become common practice for individual moral standards to be disregarded for the sake of material advantage.

Strong dismissed the action against Creative Age Press, stating that the two passages dealing with sexual relations "contain little anatomical detail" and that "neither husband nor wife derives any satisfaction from their infidelity." The magistrate asserted that "The characters are coarse and vulgar. The sex conversations are vulgar and nasty but they are aids to characterization. The sex passages are incidental, minor phrases and sentences." He ruled that more space was devoted to the lack of other moral qualities than to sex.

FURTHER READING

"Court Clears Novel of Obscenity Charge." *New York Times*, May 20, 1948, p. 27.
Dale, Virginia. "Literary Heel: *The Gilded Hearse*." *New York Times Book Review*, February 1, 1948, p. 26.
De Grazia, Edward. *Censorship Landmarks*. New York: Bowker, 1969.
"Hearing on Book Delayed." *New York Times*, March 30, 1948, p. 25.
Lewis, Felice Flanery. *Literature, Obscenity & Law*. Carbondale: Southern Illinois University Press, 1976.
"Publisher to Defend Seized Book in Court." *New York Times*, March 17, 1948, p. 27.
Smith, Harrison. "Practitioners of Culture." *Saturday Review of Literature*, February 28, 1948, p. 13.

THE GINGER MAN

Author: J. P. Donleavy
Original dates and places of publication: 1955, France; 1956, England; 1965, United States
Original publishers: Olympia Press (France); Neville Spearman (England); Seymour Lawrence (United States)
Literary form: Novel

SUMMARY

The Ginger Man is a comic study of life in Dublin as seen through the eyes of Sebastian Dangerfield, an American. Married and with a child, Dangerfield goes to Dublin to read law at Trinity College and to live out his particular philosophy of life that is far different from his former expectations of bourgeois respectability. Often broke and on the brink of starvation, Dangerfield drinks heavily, becomes involved in brawls, and generally sabotages his dreams of becoming a lawyer, although he professes to hope for success in that field.

Moody and difficult with those around him, Dangerfield lives a lunatic existence, as he moves from one pub to another and comes to know the alleyways of Dublin better than the legal reading rooms. He also has several affairs, one with a nurse named Chris in a prolonged scene that describes her act of undressing in minute detail until "she pressed her breasts together . . . swung her chest and flesh . . . and said she was ready." In another sequence, his friend Kenneth O'Keefe writes that he has "abandoned homosexuality for it has only succeeded in complicating my life further. I have been satisfying myself by hand as usual but find it very boring."

When Dangerfield's wife finally has enough of his behavior and leaves him, he decides to go to England but must first dodge his landlord Egbert Skully, to whom he owes months of back rent. In a funny scene, Dangerfield seduces the prim and straitlaced, aptly named Miss Frost, who complacently allows him to sleep on the floor of her room and charitably allows him into her bed, and then wails, "It's a mortal sin which I have to confess to the priest and it's adultery as well." Once in England, Dangerfield finds Mary, a seemingly dewy-eyed innocent whose sexually insatiable nature matches his own and who, as the novel ends, seems to promise him happiness at last.

CENSORSHIP HISTORY

The Ginger Man was published in unexpurgated form by Olympia Press in 1955, but the novel was not publishable in England, Ireland, or the United States. Donleavy submitted the manuscript for consideration to Charles Scribner's Sons in New York in 1954 but, as he states in a letter to Maurice Girodias of Olympia Press dated September 7, 1954, "Although impressed by it they felt they could not publish it because of obscenity. The obscenity is very much a part of this novel and its removal would detract from it." After deciding to publish the novel, Girodias stated in a letter dated January 7, 1955, that he believed the novel more than likely would be "banned in the U.K. and U.S." and noted that "the publicity created by banning often favours sales." The novel was published as part of "The Traveller's Companion Series" with the words "special volume" following the title listing. To Donleavy, this designation, meant by the publisher to set it apart from other titles, "could also be interpreted to mean in such context that *The Ginger Man* was a particularly raunchy variety of dirty book."

Publisher Neville Armstrong of Neville Spearman Ltd. required that Donleavy heavily censor the novel before publishing it in hardcover in England in 1956. In their initial meeting, Armstrong warned Donleavy,

> I think one must warn that as the book stands, it could also land the author and publisher in legal difficulties if not prison and involve the printer in the same plight. It's [*sic*] being an offense, as I am sure you know, to publish indecent books and to deprave and corrupt those into whose hands such publications may fall. If I am allowed to make some judicious cuts in the Paris edition and perhaps have an introduction written drawing attention to the work's literary merit, this will help allay a printer's misgivings and avoid the book's being prosecuted as an obscene publication.

In 1965, Seymour Lawrence launched his imprint with Houghton Mifflin of Boston by publishing the complete and unexpurgated edition of *The Ginger Man*.

FURTHER READING

Clancy, Ambrose. "Wild Irish Rogue." *Gentleman's Quarterly*, June 1991, pp. 60–68.
Donleavy, J. P. *The History of the Ginger Man*. Boston: Houghton Mifflin, 1994.

THE GOATS

Author: Brock Cole
Original date and place of publication: 1987, New York
Original publisher: Farrar, Straus & Giroux
Literary form: Young adult novel

SUMMARY

The Goats is the story of Laura Golden and Howie Mitchell, two 13-year-old campers designated the "goats" by their fellow campers, who strip them, take their clothes, and leave them in separate areas on "Goat Island" overnight.

The two meet; Laura finds a blanket to cover her body and Howie tries to preserve modesty by clutching a pillow to the front of his body. They become frightened when they think that several campers have returned late that night, fearing that even greater abuse will be dealt out, so they try to swim and float across the water from the island to the opposite shore. The two do not learn until nearly the end of the novel that the party that came to the island late at night contained camp counselors looking for them.

After swimming and floating on a log, the children are exhausted when they reach shore, and Laura collapses. Howie looks at her naked body, which Cole describes as follows: "It was long and white. She had no breasts, just two shriveled nipples. At the bottom of her belly was a small patch of hair, like a Hitler mustache. That meant she was more mature than he was. He didn't have any hair yet. The other boys called him Baldy." The two break into a vacant cottage and look for blankets and clothes. They lie down together in one bed, burrowing against each other for warmth, and Howie looks at the ceiling where he finds that someone has pinned a centerfold directly over the bed: "It was of a lady with her legs spread. She looked as if she were falling on him from an enormous distance." The joke lightens his fearful mood and the two sleep. After they awaken, Laura and Howie put on whatever clothes they can find, and they heat up some soup while they plan what to do next. Laura decides to call her mother, but Howie's parents are on an archaeological expedition in Turkey and he has left all contact information at camp. They agree that they will not return to camp.

Laura and Howie walk to a nearby municipal beach, where they take more suitable clothes from baskets in the bathhouse and search unlocked cars for spare change. Among the clothes that Laura takes are a pair of pink lace bikini panties, which she mischievously shows Howie as they walk away from the boat launch: "She unfastened her jeans and pushed them down a little. She was wearing tiny bikini panties. They were pink and mostly lace." A horrified Howie tells her, "Hey, you dope! Pull your pants up!" Laura calls her mother and begs to be taken home but does not tell her what has occurred, so Maddy Golden asks Laura to wait two more days until parents' weekend and advises her to try to enjoy the camp experience. After a frustrated Laura hangs up the telephone, the camp director, Mr. Wells, calls Maddy with the news that Laura is missing.

As Maddy Golden arrives at the camp and begins to search for her daughter, Laura and Howie try to find a way to survive until parents' weekend. They slip onto the bus of another camp, which appears to contain mainly older African-American campers who feed and shelter them for the night and keep the camp director in ignorance. When they leave the following day, Laura tries again to call her mother, but Maddy's secretary refuses the collect call, so she calls her mother's apartment and leaves a message on the answering machine in which she explains the entire ordeal until the money for the pay phone runs out. Laura begs her mother to also consider taking Howie when they leave the camp and promises to meet her in the camp parking lot on Saturday.

The two plot to obtain one more day of shelter at the Starlight Motel. Laura poses as a motel maid to obtain the key of a registered guest family that has just completed packing up their car. Laura then poses as Mrs. Hendricks and tells the clerk at the main desk that the family has had car trouble and would like to extend their stay another day. After, Laura and Howie leave the room to allow time for the maid to change the sheets and towels and to straighten up the room. When they return, they fall asleep in the same bed, after talking about their parents and revealing that both feel they have been burdens rather than sources of joy in their families. In bed, they cuddle, and Laura "touched the palm of his hand with the tip of her tongue experimentally," after which she learns Howie's name, and he learns that her true name is Shadow, not Laura. They fall asleep and then they awaken and go to dinner, planning to charge the meal to their room, but Laura is accosted by the motel manager when Howie goes to the bathroom. Mrs. Purse, the old, pink-haired maid, had watched as they left the room and reported to the manager that she had not seen any luggage when she cleaned the room. " 'They spent the afternoon in the same bed. At her age. . . . I don't know what this world's coming to.' " Howie creates a diversion by setting off car alarms and the fire alarm, which allows Laura the opportunity to run out to meet him.

They walk on the highway, and the next morning they are stopped by a man in a Jeep bearing the name "Hofstadter's Goat Farm" on the door. Flashing a badge, he tells them his name is Pearly Hofstadter. He assures them that he is a sheriff's deputy and will give them a ride. Once they are in the Jeep, they notice it smells like goats, a fact explained by the driver, who says that he had to carry one of his goats in the back seat a few weeks earlier. They notice that the door handles from inside the car have been removed, and they panic. Pearly tells Laura and Howie that he knows they are the kids who have run away from camp and set off the fire alarm the night before. He also leers and makes suggestive comments to them: " 'Getting a little nudgy, uh? . . . You know what I mean, Howie. Hell, I don't mind. I'm a liberal. It's okay by me if you kids have a little fun. I bet you and your girl have had a high old time. Ain't that right, Howie?' " Hofstadter pulls the truck onto a deserted road and steps out to make a call but makes the mistake of leaving the keys in the ignition. The children drive away, accidentally knocking him down, then crash the vehicle a short distance away and take off on foot. Laura finally manages to find her mother and speak with her, and she is surprised to hear Maddy cry with concern rather than express the anger she had expected. The novel ends with Howie and Laura hoping to continue the relationship they have forged, as they walk to Laura's waiting mother.

CENSORSHIP HISTORY

The Goats has provoked controversy for its perceived sexuality rather than for depictions or graphic description. In 1992, parents of students attending the Housel Middle School in Prosser, Washington, demanded that school librarian remove the book because "it contains a passage describing the rescue of a naked girl." Although that overly simplistic description is inaccurate, the *Newsletter on Intellectual Freedom* reported in March 1993 that parents expressed concern that middle school children should not be subjected to reading graphic descriptions as those of the girl's "two shriveled nipples" and the references to her pubic hair. The parents submitted a formal complaint to the Prosser School District board of education, which, in turn, directed the school library to remove the book from shelves and to make it unavailable to students.

In 1994, parents of students attending Timberland Regional Middle School in Plaistow, New Hampshire, challenged the inclusion of *The Goats* on the seventh-grade reading list. The January 1995 issue of the *Newsletter on Intellectual Freedom* reports that parents expressed concern about the language in the book, which they felt was "offensive and inappropriate" language for seventh-grade readers. Their objections included the use of the words *damn* and *bastard*, as well as references to nipples and the pink lace bikini panties that Laura steals from the municipal beach bathhouse.

In 2000, despite the absence of any sexual activity or sexual contact between the two main characters—or between any other characters in the book—two parents in Londonderry, New Hampshire, filed a formal complaint with the school board asking for a ban of the book, a required reading, which they believed was "not appropriate for 12- and 13-year-old students." As the September 6, 2000, issue of the (North Andover, Massachusetts) *Eagle-Tribune* reported, Malinda Scannell, one of the parents, claimed in her complaint that "it's sexuality that drives the book." Another parent, Rose Marie Haddad, had submitted a formal complaint against use of the book in the classroom in January 2000. In her complaint, Haddad objected to the descriptions of Laura's naked body and the centerfold on the cottage ceiling, and she also questioned the cruelty that the campers showed to Laura and Howie, saying that she "hoped children wouldn't put others in a similar situation." While waiting to consider the complaint, the school board did remove the book from the curriculum, although it remained in the school library. The school district then created a committee of parents, teachers and School Board Chairman Daniel J. Bever to review the book. After a month of deliberation, the committee rejected Haddad's challenge and the school board planned to return the book to the curriculum. In August 2000, Scannell appealed the decision, and the school board ordered *The Goats* removed from the library after receiving the formal complaint. On September 26, 2000, the Londonderry School

Board voted 4 to 1 to return *The Goats* to the curriculum, but the board also determined that, at the beginning of the academic year, middle school parents would receive a list of the books in the curriculum with a brief synopsis of each, so they could let teachers know if they did not want their children reading certain books. School board member Robert J. White stated in an *Eagle-Tribune* article, "It still gives parents the option to opt out."

FURTHER READING

Date, Terry. "Schools: Parental Objections to Reading Lists Are Rare." *Eagle-Tribune*, July 17, 2009. Available online. URL: http:/www.eagletribune.com/archivesearch/local_story_ 198003441.html. Accessed December 11, 2009.

Glenn, Wendy J. "Brock Cole: The Good, The Bad, and the Humorously Ironic." *The ALAN Review* 26, no. 2 (Winter 1999). Available oline. URL: http://scholar.lib.vt.edu/ejournals/ALAN/winter99/glenn.html. Accessed December 11, 2009.

Newsletter on Intellectual Freedom. (March 1993): 43; (January 1995): 25.

Rogers, David. "Author: Controversial Book Misunderstood." *Eagle-Tribune*, September 24, 2000.

———. " 'Explicit' Book Back in Class." *Eagle-Tribune*, September 27, 2000.

———. "Mom Wants Book Banned." *Eagle-Tribune*, September 6, 2000.

"These Kids Can Handle the Truth." *Eagle-Tribune*, September 22, 2000.

GOD'S LITTLE ACRE

Author: Erskine Caldwell
Original date and place of publication: 1933, United States
Original publisher: Grosset & Dunlop
Literary form: Novel

SUMMARY

God's Little Acre relates the story of a poor, illiterate Georgia farmer, Ty Ty Walden and his family. They struggle to survive on a rundown farm that barely provides a living while Ty Ty and his two sons, Buck and Shaw, dig holes all over the farm in search of gold, after hearing that nearly 15 years earlier gold nuggets had been found in the area. A pious man, Ty Ty once dedicated one acre of the farm to God, promising that all proceeds from that acre would go to the church, but he changes the site of the dedicated acre as he searches for gold to avoid discovering gold on God's acre. Because he never works the promised acre, whatever its location, the church receives nothing. In their search for gold, Ty Ty and his sons neglect farming, leaving the raising of cotton to two sharecroppers.

The sexual activities of his daughters Rosamund and Darling Jill, his sons, his son-in-law Will, and his daughter-in-law Griselda exist as a matter of course in the novel, as they become involved in numerous sexual relationships that lead to quarrels and violence. Even Ty Ty, who declares himself too old to be sexually active, is aroused by his son Buck's wife, Griselda, who has "the finest pair of rising beauties a man can ever hope to see." At one point, he tells her, "The first time I saw you, . . . I felt like getting right down there and then licking something." References to cunnilingus are made at other points in the novel. When Rosamund's husband, Will, decides that he will "take" Griselda, he tears off her clothes and refers to Ty Ty's earlier statement:

> He said you were so God damn pretty, a man would have to get down on his hands and knees and lick something when he saw you like you are now. Didn't he? Yes, so help me God, he did! And after all this time I've got you at last, too. And I'm going to do what I've been wanting to do ever since the first time I saw you. You know what it is, don't you, Griselda? You know what I want. And you're going to give it to me. . . . And I'm going to lick you, Griselda.

After the episode, Griselda tells Ty Ty that "after a woman has that done to her once, Pa, she's never the same again."

The family members generally have a casual attitude toward sex. Pluto, a millworker who is dating Darling Jill, complains to her father that she has been "fooling around with a lot of men," and Ty Ty expresses approval of her behavior and tells Pluto that "It's up to you to satisfy her." Darling Jill is caught in bed with Will, after enthusiastically having sex with him and screaming out her approval, but Rosamund only strikes Will and spanks Darling Jill with no further repercussions in the family. Ty Ty chances upon Darling Jill and the albino Dave Dawson having sex in the dark outside the Walden home, and he secretly watches them.

Near the end of the novel, Buck kills his brother, whom he believes tried to take Griselda from him. He then leaves the farm with a shotgun, leading the reader to assume that he will commit suicide. The novel ends as the father sees the dissension in his family and realizes that his attempts to keep peace among family members have failed. He despairs over the "blood on his land" and resumes digging for gold.

CENSORSHIP HISTORY

In 1933, John Sumner, secretary of the New York Society for the Suppression of Vice, brought a complaint of "obscenity" against Viking Press, publisher of *God's Little Acre*, and against Helen Schiller, a clerk employed by the publishers who sold the book to an agent of the society. The complaint cited specific passages from the book and maintained that they violated section 1141 of the Penal Law, placing the book within the meaning of that statute, "obscene, lewd, lascivious, filthy, indecent or disgusting." In hearing *People v. Viking Press*, 147 Misc. 813, 264 N.Y.S. 534 (1933), City Magistrate Benjamin

Greenspan observed that, to sustain the prosecution, "the court must find that the tendency of the book as a whole, and indeed its main purpose, is to excite lustful desire and what has been rather fancifully called 'impure imaginations.'" In defense, the publisher collected testimonials from literary critics, social workers, and educators, as well as literary reviews that supported the claim of high literary merit. After a careful reading, Judge Greenspan concluded that the book did not treat vice and lewdness as virtues, nor would it "incite lustful desires in normal minds." The court ruled against Sumner, stating:

> The court declines to believe that so large and representative a group of people would rally to the support of a book which they did not genuinely believe to be of importance and literary merit. The court is of the opinion, moreover, that this group of people, collectively, has a better capacity to judge of the value of a literary production than one who is more apt to search for obscene passages in a book than to regard the book as a whole.

Although the complaint against the publisher was dismissed, *God's Little Acre* suffered repeated prosecution for the next two decades. In 1934, faculty members at Columbia University complained that the novel was "indecent and tending to corrupt" and compelled its removal from the Teachers College library, even though the book was a required reading in several university English courses. In 1946, officials in St. Paul, Minnesota, banned sales of the book after a citizens group signed a complaint stating that the novel was "obscene" and "lewd." In 1947, officials in Denver, Colorado, banned the novel for similar reasons.

In 1948, *God's Little Acre* was among 25 books condemned as obscene by a fundamentalist minister in Philadelphia who complained to the police that obscene books were being sold in the city. A police officer purchased the identified books, and nine were determined to be obscene. Criminal proceedings were brought against five booksellers who were charged with possessing and intending to sell the following allegedly obscene novels: James Farrell's STUDS LONIGAN, Farrell's *A WORLD I NEVER MADE*, William Faulkner's SANCTUARY and THE WILD PALMS, Calder Willingham's *END AS A MAN*, Harold Robbins's *NEVER LOVE A STRANGER*, and *God's Little Acre*.

The case, *Commonwealth v. Gordon et al.*, 66 Pa. Dist. & Co. R. 101 (1949), went to trial without a jury in the Court of Quarter Sessions in Philadelphia County, Pennsylvania, presided over by Judge Curtis Bok, who read the books "with thoughtful care." He wrote the first carefully reasoned judicial opinion to interpret the limitations that First Amendment guarantees should exert upon obscenity proceedings. He determined that obscenity is an indeterminate term, "that it is not constitutionally indictable unless it takes the form of sexual impurity, i.e., 'dirt for dirt's sake' and can be traced to actual criminal behavior, either actual or demonstrably imminent." Judge Bok based his judgment on the books as a whole and upon their place in the arts. He discussed at length the concern whether in censoring obscenity the courts were contravening the principles of freedom of speech and of the press. Of *God's Little Acre*, Judge Bok observed, "It is a frank and turbulent story, but it is an obvious effort to be faithful to the locality and its people." He concluded, "I hold that the books before me are not sexually impure and pornographic, and are therefore not obscene, lewd, lascivious, filthy, indecent, or disgusting." This judgment was later sustained in the Superior and Supreme Courts of Pennsylvania.

The decision had important implications in later obscenity trials, and Judge Bok's exoneration of *God's Little Acre* and the other books in the case because they did not contain "dirt for dirt's sake" was used in the defense of other works. The questions raised in the *Commonwealth v. Gordon* case regarding the constitutionality of the statutes censoring obscenity were raised again in *United States v. Roth* (1957), and defendants cited the case in subsequent trials of LADY CHATTERLEY'S LOVER, TROPIC OF CANCER, and FANNY HILL.

In 1950, despite earlier exoneration in two major court cases, the book was banned from the state of Massachusetts in the case of *Attorney General v. Book Named "God's Little Acre,"* 93 N.E. 2d 819 (1950). The Watch and Ward Society of Boston initially brought a complaint against the book, calling it "obscene and pornographic," in the city of Boston, but the case was dismissed. The lower court judge conceded that the novel contained "racy, off-color or suggestive paragraphs," but stated the opinion that it did not have "a substantial tendency to deprave or corrupt its readers by inciting lascivious thoughts or arousing lustful desires." The society then took its case to the Supreme Judicial Court of Massachusetts, where the state attorney general argued that "the book abounds in sexual episodes and some are portrayed with an abundance of realistic detail. In some instances the author's treatment of sexual relations descends to outright pornography."

Despite evidence as to the literary merit of the book, Justice Spalding determined that evidence of the literary, cultural, and educational character of the work "does not change the substantive law as to what is obscene, indecent, or impure." Moreover, the judge stated that a discussion of the decisions in *People v. Viking Press, Inc.* (1933) and *Commonwealth v. Gordon* (1949) "would not be profitable" because "the interpretations placed on the statutes there involved differ materially from that which this court has placed on our statute." Justice Spalding also dismissed the contention that the rights of freedom of the press were at stake, claiming that such a concern "requires no discussion." The court reversed the lower court ruling and entered a new decree "adjudicating that the book in question is obscene, indecent, and impure."

FURTHER READING

Caldwell, Erskine. "My Twenty-five Years of Censorship." *Esquire*, October 1958, pp. 176–178.

———. "Protest against Columbia University's Ban on *Tobacco Road* and *God's Little Acre*." *New Republic*, June 27, 1934, pp. 184–185.

DeVoto, Bernard. "The Easy Chair: Liberal Decisions in Massachusetts." *Harper's Magazine*, July 1949, pp. 62–65.

Kauffman, Stanley. "God's Belittled Acre." *New Republic*, June 30, 1958, p. 21.

Klevar, Harvey L. *Erskine Caldwell: A Biography*. Knoxville: University of Tennessee Press, 1993.

St. John-Stevas, Norman. "Art, Morality and Censorship." *Ramparts* 2 (May 1963): 40–48.

Watson, Jay. "The Rhetoric of Exhaustion and the Exhaustion of Rhetoric: Erskine Caldwell in the Thirties." *Mississippi Quarterly* 46 (Spring 1993): 215–229.

"Worcester Library Directors Support Their Librarian." *Library Journal*, April 15, 1949, p. 649.

GOSSIP GIRL SERIES

Author: Cecily von Ziegesar
Original date and place of publication: 2002–Present, United States
Original publisher: Little, Brown and Company
Literary form: Young adult novel series

SUMMARY

The Gossip Girl series, written by Cecily von Ziegesar, is sophisticated, witty, edgy, and irreverent. It chronicles the alcohol- and sex-filled lives of the privileged children of wealthy parents in contemporary Manhattan. The novels are written from the perspective of an anonymous blogger who posts observations and interacts with e-mail correspondents on the Web site www.gossipgirl.net. She is mean and nasty and reveals awful details about everyone, all the while remaining anonymous. In a disclaimer that appears at the top of the gossipgirl.net Web page, the narrator states "All the names of places, people, and events have been altered or abbreviated to protect the innocent. Namely me."

Gossip Girl, the first book in the series, introduces readers to the world of "the people who are *born to it*—those of us who have everything anyone could possibly wish for and who take it all completely for granted." Manhattan is their playground and attending single-sex private schools is merely a diversion.

> Welcome to New York City's Upper East Side, where my friends and I live and go to school and play and sleep—sometimes with each other. We all live in huge

apartments with our own bedrooms and bathrooms and phone lines. We have unlimited access to money and booze and whatever else we want, and our parents are rarely home, so we have tons of privacy. We're smart, we've inherited classic good looks, we wear fantastic clothes, and we know how to party. Our shit still stinks, but you can't smell it because the bathroom is sprayed hourly by the maid with a refreshing scent made exclusively for us by French perfumers.

It's a luxe life, but someone's got to live it.

Although Gossip Girl is a member of the crowd she (or he) observes, the narrator freely shares their secrets and reports their adventures to anyone who ventures onto the Web site. "I'll be watching closely. I'll be watching all of us. It's going to be a wild and wicked year. I can smell it." In an interesting bow to the popularity of the Internet, the format of the novel alternates between presenting the Gossip Girl blog page and chapters of text that provide the back story for what the Web site only hints at.

The characters in the novels spend most of their time going to clubs, smoking marijuana, drinking Cosmopolitans in trendy bars, consuming scotch or whatever high-priced liquor is in their parents' liquor cabinets, agonizing over their social lives, and having sex. The continuity of characters in the novels has created a large following among adolescent girls. To many teenage girls, the novels represent "a stirring fantasy of freedom and an equally stirring fantasy of conspicuous consumption." Cindy Egan, an editor at Little, Brown and Company, which publishes the series, credits the popularity of the series to the way in which it speaks to young girls. "In 'Gossip Girl' you've got sophisticated subject matter with the girls having anxiety about dating and getting into college. But they're all doing the same things that high schoolers are doing, partying behind their parents' backs." The novels do not pretend to represent rites of passage or to provide a moral blueprint for readers. "In any event there is no discontent that can't be soothed through a tumble in the luxury marketplace." The novels are also not concerned about dealing with the emotional and psychological problems of their characters. In *All I Want Is Everything*, "As they kissed she couldn't help but think that sex with Dan would be a whole lot more meaningful than sex with Clark." "If sex is presented without much association to psychological tailspins, bulimia is depicted as a habit attached to even less. Bingeing and purging are shown more or less as another lifestyle choice available at relatively unburdensome cost."

One of the objections to the Gossip Girls novels is that the author has no moral tale to tell, and opponents have noted their "alarming lack of moralism about teen sex and drugs." "In von Ziegesar's universe, kids have sex without pregnancy scares; they get high in the Sheep Meadow and still make decent grades. Antiheroine Blair's bulimia is more of an icky weakness than a full-fledged pathology. At worst, von Ziegesar's characters end up embarrassed on the Internet or during an Ivy League interview" (Nussbaum 40).

CENSORSHIP HISTORY

Books in the Gossip Girls series have appeared on the American Library Association's list of the most frequently challenged books since 2006. The complaints have cited homosexuality, sexual content, drugs, material unsuited to its age group, and offensive language as the reasons for the challenges. According to the ALA record of challenges, the series has been challenged 13 times since 2004, in several states, including Florida, Texas, Arizona, and Indiana. The ALA also reports "It is unclear how many times libraries have banned the books."

The language in the novels is admittedly "steamy," and bookstore managers have made attempts to keep the novels out of the children's and junior sections. In Darien, Connecticut, Diane's Books and Barrett's Bookstore moved the novels out of the children's sections and into especially created teenage areas within the adult sections. Dottie Bush, the manager of the Barrett's Bookstore children's section, told a *New York Times* reporter, "We try to keep them separate. The language is bad and there's no value to them."

In August 2008, two mothers of students living in Leesburg, Florida, asked the Leesburg Public Library Advisory Board to remove two books from the Leesburg Public Library: *The Bermudez Triangle* by Maureen Johnson and *Only in Your Dreams: A Gossip Girl Novel* by Cecily von Ziegesar. Dixie Fechtel, who said she "was shocked" when she read parts of the two novels that her 13-year-old daughter brought home after checking them out from the Leesburg Public Library, told a reporter that "a parent or student walking into the youth section should not have to get something off the shelf as shocking as this." Fechtel was joined by another parent, Diane Venetta, in submitting the complaint. The two mothers expressed their outrage through letters to library officials accompanied by a signed petition containing 120 names of "friends and like-minded community members" that asked for the removal of both books and others, a request that Leesburg Public Library Director Barbara Morse denied. Dixie Fechtel claimed that she was horrified by what she read: "sexual innuendo, drug references, and other adult topics." After Morse denied her request, Fechtel engaged the formal book-challenge process of the public library in January 2009, which was designed to formally contest the book and to bring the decision to the five-member library board. Fechtel asserted that she welcomed the opportunity to speak with the board because "It's distasteful for youths. It's so farfetched that we would allow this to happen in the first place." In September 2009, the library board decided that the library should create a special shelf for high school reading and place the novels in the Gossip Girl series and similar teen-oriented books in that area. Librarians were told to place the label "High School" on the books and to place them on a special shelf in the young adult section. After achieving that goal, Fechtel told a reporter for the *Orlando Sentinel* that she would pursue the same goal in the nine municipal and six branch libraries of the Lake County system. She hopes to have all books that contain references to sex or illegal activities provided with a label stating: "Warning: Mature Content."

In 2007, a teen drama series *Gossip Girl* (based on the book's) was created and debated on the CW network. As of 2010, the show is in its fourth season and remains very popular.

FURTHER READINGS

Bellafante, Ginia. "'Gossip Girls' Series Aims Low, Sells High." *Chicago Tribune*, August 30, 2003, p. 7.

Burton, Connie O. "The Most Frequently Challenged Books of 2006." *Teacher Librarian* 35 (December 2007): 67.

Donald, David. "Gossip Girl Book at Center of Library Debate." Available online. URL: Daily Commercial.com/060909book. Accessed July 20, 2010.

Gay, Jason. "Dirty Pretty Things." *Rolling Stone* (April 2, 2009): 40–47.

Nussbaum, Evelyn. "Psst! Serena Is a Slut. Pass It On." *New York* 38 (May 30, 2004): 40–43.

O'Briant, Don. "Books with an Edge Lure Younger Set." *Atlanta Journal-Constitution*, July 6, 2005, p. E1.

Rippel, Amy C. "Leesburg Mom Not Giving Up on Library Book Warning-Label Campaign." *Orlando-Sentinal*. Available online. URL: http://articles.orlandosentinel.com/2010-04-16/news/os-lk-book-policy-leesburg-20100413_1_leesburg-library-six-branch-libraries-bermudez-triangle. Accessed July 18, 2010.

Steele, Margaret Farley. "Books for Teenage Girls Are a Little Too Popular." *New York Times*, August 20, 2006, p. 14NJ6.

THE GROUP

Author: Mary McCarthy
Original date and place of publication: 1963, United States
Original publisher: Harcourt Brace & World
Literary form: Novel

SUMMARY

The Group relates the story of eight women, members of the Vassar College class of 1933, who formed a clique while undergraduates. Six of the group are from wealthy Eastern families, one of the remaining two is the daughter of a wealthy self-made man, and the other is of middle-class background and raised in the West. All members of the group are determined to make their mark in the world and to have careers that will give them lives far different from those of their mothers. Inspired by the progressive thinking that they enjoyed at Vassar, the young women approach life with enthusiasm and with the expectations of those who have experienced privileged educations.

Comic and ironic at turns, the novel begins a week after commencement, as the group gathers to celebrate the first wedding of one of their numbers, Kay Strong, who had daringly lived with her finace Harald beforehand. As the other members of the group, whose nicknames include "Pokey," "Lakey," and "Priss" as well as Dottie, Libby, Polly, and Helena, assess the possible success of the marriage, they reveal their shallow personalities and equally shallow values. In the 10 years that follow, the group members dabble in "Trotskyite" politics, join the bohemian theater world, engage in numerous love affairs, and deal with abusive boyfriends and husbands. Lakey spends years in Europe, later bringing home her lesbian lover, the baroness, whose demeanor leaves the others insecure that "Lakey would now look down on them for not being Lesbians."

The novel ends with the funeral of Kay, said to have lost her balance and fallen from a window on the 20th floor of the Vassar Club in New York City while airplane-spotting only a few weeks before the United States enters World War II. Mrs. Davison, an older Vassar graduate present in the lounge when the incident occurs, refutes suggestions of suicide. She claims that Kay appeared to be in good spirits and "had left a cigarette burning in the ashtray by her bedside." She states that "'no young woman who was going to kill herself would do it in the middle of a cigarette.'"

References to sexual situations and graphic descriptions of the group's affairs aroused criticism when the novel was published. Later, the following passage was labeled "disgusting" in the 1970 President's Committee Report on Obscenity and Pornography:

Down there, she felt a quick new tremor. Her lips parted. Dick smiled. "You feel something?" he said. Dottie nodded. "You'd like it again?" he said, assaying her with his hand. Dottie stiffened; she pressed her thighs together. She was ashamed of the violent sensation his exploring fingers had discovered. But he held his hand there, between her clasped thighs, and grasped her right hand in his other, guiding it . . . over that part of himself, which was soft and limp, rather sweet, really, all curled up on itself like a fat worm. Sitting beside her, he looked into her face as he stroked her down there and tightened her hand on him. "There's a little ridge there," he whispered. "Run your fingers up and down it." Dottie obeyed, wonderingly. She felt his organ stiffen a little, which gave her a strange sense of power.

CENSORSHIP HISTORY

The Group was banned in Ireland on January 21, 1964. A prohibition order was published in the *Iris Oifigiuil,* "the only official source from which booksellers [and readers] might learn of a new prohibition order," in which all articles blacklisted by the Irish Board of Censors were listed. According to the Censorship of Publications Bill of 1928, "the notice in *Iris Oifigiuil* should be sufficient evidence in the courts of summary jurisdiction as to the character of the publication," despite the acknowledgment by justices quoted in Adams's thorough study of Irish censorship laws that "this gazette is not a publication which booksellers are addicted to reading." The Irish Board of Censors found the work "obscene" and "indecent," objecting particularly to the author's handling of the characters' sexuality, suggestions of homosexuality, and "promiscuity." The work was officially banned from sale in Ireland until the introduction of the Censorship Publications Bill in 1967 reduced to 12 years the duration of a prohibition order, and the work was among 5,000 titles released from the list of banned books.

In March 1964, New Zealand Customs placed the novel on its "Publications Restricted or Prohibited" list, classifying it under Category VI, reserved for "publications which, if imported, should be detained and copies referred for decision." The principal distributors' associations in New Zealand as well as the New Zealand Library Association quickly expressed their disapproval of the censorship. On May 20, 1964, the New Zealand Library Association wrote to the Ministry of Justice, reminding officials that the novel had been freely circulating for months and asking the Justice Department to refer the work to the Indecent Publications Tribunal for a decision rather than to allow the Customs department to have the final word. Newspaper reports ridiculed the Wellington Customs department's claim that it had delayed referring the work to the tribunal until they could obtain copies of the book, because libraries had received copies the previous year and the books were still being sold in bookstores. Faced with public disapproval, the comptroller of Customs announced on June 24, 1964, that the book would not be referred to the tribunal, nor would future imports of the book be detained.

FURTHER READING

Adams, Michael. *Censorship: The Irish Experience.* Tuscaloosa: University of Alabama Press, 1968.

Brightman, Carol. *Writing Dangerously: Mary McCarthy and Her World.* New York: Clarkson Potter, 1992.

Gelderman, Carol. *Mary McCarthy: A Life.* New York: St. Martin's, 1988.

Perry, Stuart. *The Indecent Publications Tribunal: A Social Experiment.* London: Whitcombe and Tombs, 1965.

United States President's Commission on Obscenity and Pornography. *The Report of the Commission on Obscenity and Pornography.* New York: Random House, 1970.

HAGAR REVELLY

Author: Daniel Carson Goodman
Original date and place of publication: 1913, United States
Original publisher: Mitchell Kennerley
Literary form: Novel

SUMMARY

Hagar Revelly is a naturalistic novel that deals with the problems that two poverty-stricken sisters, Thatah and Hagar Revelly, face in New York City.

Thatah appears to voice the author's views about sex in her statements that "virtue is not an affair of the body, it's an affair of the mind. . . . Nowadays it is only hypocrisy that the world calls virtue." In contrast, the naive Hagar is led astray, seduced by her employer, a department store manager. Unwilling to become the manager's mistress, she turns for comfort to a seemingly honest laborer, a man who later leaves her pregnant. The desperate young woman is tempted to become a prostitute to support herself but rejects that life. She decides, instead, to accept her former employer's long-standing offer to become his mistress, viewing this choice as morally superior to prostitution.

The daring subject matter of the novel is subtly presented, and the sexuality is only suggestive throughout. One of the most criticized passages of the novel describes Hagar's first drink of liquor and her ruin:

> For only a moment did Greenfield watch the drooping lashes, the quivering lips, the tremulous pulsation of her bosom. Then he lifted her into his arms, and despite a moment of slight resistance—carried her into the next room.

CENSORSHIP HISTORY

Hagar Revelly presented a significant challenge to the 1868 Hicklin test, which permitted juries to convict if even a single passage in an otherwise clean publication was judged obscene, when it was placed on trial for being "obscene." In 1913, Anthony Comstock, secretary of the New York Society for the Suppression of Vice, made an unannounced raid on the offices of publisher Mitchell Kennerley and arrested the publisher and his clerk on a federal writ. Boyer reports that reviews of the book had been generally favorable, and publications such as the *Review of Reviews* praised the "high plane" of Goodman's prose. The society seized the plates and all copies of *Hagar Revelly*, including the 2,000 being processed at the bindery. Comstock provided Judge Learned Hand with a copy of the novel, with specific passages underlined, but the judge reminded him that the book could only be assessed if the passages were read within the context of the entire book.

Judge Hand dismissed a demurrer filed by the publisher and expressed the opinion that popular ideas regarding the discussion of matters related to sex must be modified in order that the problems they involved might be seriously analyzed. He also stated that only a jury could determine whether the content of a book was obscene and refused to make a determination from the bench. Hand condemned those individuals who professed that they were shocked by passages that were "honestly relevant to the adequate expression of innocent ideas" and stated that legal obscenity must be defined simply as "the present critical point in the compromise between candor and shame at which the community may have arrived here and now" rather than as moral corruption.

When the case went to trial in the Criminal Branch of the United States District Court in *United States v. Kennerley*, 209 F. 119 (S.D.N.Y. 1913), the presiding judge ordered that all members of the jury be given copies of the novel, and they were told to read it in its entirety. In giving the jury its instructions, the judge cautioned jury members that finding Kennerley not guilty would set a dangerous precedent, and he directed them that their task was to determine if the book "might be injurious to the morals of any person." If it would, then it would be obscene under the statute. The defense attorney stressed the reformist intent of the author, a 30-year-old St. Louis physician and social hygienist who had written the book with the desire to teach "the innocent youth of the land . . . the wiles of vice. After five-and-a-half hours of deliberation, and a first ballot in which they had stood 6 to 6 for conviction, the jury announced a not guilty verdict." This loss was the last major case initiated by Anthony Comstock, who died a year later.

FURTHER READING

Boyer, Paul S. *Purity in Print: The Vice-Society Movement and Book Censorship in America.* New York: Scribner, 1968.
De Grazia, Edward. *Censorship Landmarks.* New York: Bowker, 1969.
Ernest, Morris L., and Alan U. Schwartz. *Censorship: The Search for the Obscene.* New York: Macmillan, 1964.
Lockhart, William B., and Robert C. McClure. "Literature, the Law of Obscenity, and the Constitution." *Minnesota Law Review* 38 (March 1934): 320–334.

THE HANDMAID'S TALE

Author: Margaret Atwood
Original date and place of publication: 1986, United States
Original publisher: Fawcett
Literary form: Novel

SUMMARY

The Handmaid's Tale provides a view of a frightening future in which racism and homophobia run rampant, personal freedom is lost, sexual practices are ritualized, and the earth has become polluted beyond reclamation. The satire depicts a postrevolutionary world run by religious and political conservatives who deport Jews to Israel, execute homosexuals, and resettle African Americans in North Dakota. Critics reviewing the novel have noted that these characteristics reflect real-world abuses, such as Romania's anti-birth-control edicts, the religious fanaticism of Iran's government, and the stringent rules of Puritan society in colonial New England.

Set in a thinly disguised Cambridge, Massachusetts, the novel is framed as a taped interview with narrator Offred, who is a Handmaid and one of the few remaining women who have not been made sterile by nuclear disasters and toxic waste. Her narrative poignantly alternates between her present mechanized life and a past when she was a young working woman with a loving husband and a child. All women have become enslaved, but the fertile Handmaids exist solely to be made pregnant by the Commanders (referred to throughout with the capital c), and their babies will be raised by the Commanders' Wives (referred to throughout with a capital w).

The novel contains numerous sexual scenes describing the fertilizations, encounters in brothels patronized by the high-ranking Commanders, and the secret sexual liaisons that spring up in this totalitarian state, yet their effect is more apocalyptic than erotic. The brothels are staffed by women who wear such prerevolutionary costumes as Playboy Bunny outfits and other fetish-related items. Working in one such brothel is Moira, a prerevolutionary lesbian friend of Offred's and a strong and rebellious character. Atwood not only depicts the excesses of conservatism but also presents the results of militant feminism gone awry. Pornography of all sorts has been outlawed, women shun all makeup and clothing that hints of sex appeal, and the Handmaids kill any man accused of rape. No one can be trusted, and even after Offred falls in love with Nick, the chauffeur of a Commander, she is uncertain if he will keep his promise to spirit her out of the United States into Canada or England.

CENSORSHIP HISTORY

In 1990, the novel was challenged as a reading assignment in a 12th-grade English class at Rancho Cotati High School in Rohnert Park, California, for being "sexually explicit" and "profane." A local minister asked that the book be withdrawn from the curriculum because the main character of the novel was a woman and young men were unable to relate to her. In a campaign to have the book removed from the schools, one parent circulated a letter to local residents stating, "If you as parents do not rise up and go to your schools over issues such as these, we will continue to educate our kids for the gutter." The school board formed a committee to review the novel, and the work was subsequently retained.

In 1992, parents in Waterloo, Iowa, challenged the use of the book as an optional reading in 12th-grade English classes because of "profanity," "lurid passages about sex," "themes of despair," and statements that they claimed were defamatory to minorities, women, God, and the disabled. The school board rejected the protestors' complaints by a vote of 6 to 1, and one member stated, "The objectors are trying to take away the rights of others to read the books." The protestors appealed to the Iowa Department of Education, which informed them that school districts determined the content of the reading lists.

The novel was removed from the Chicopee (Massachusetts) High School reading list in 1993 because parents complained that it contained "profanity" and "sex."

In 2001, the parents of several students enrolled in an Advanced Placement English class for seniors in Dripping Springs, Texas, challenged the use of the novel as part of the course curriculum, claiming they were offended by the sexual encounters described in the book. The school district board of education considered the parents' request for removal of the book, but the board decided to move the book from the curriculum to an optional reading assignment list.

In March 2006, one parent who felt it was her "duty to ensure no student be able to read *The Handmaid's Tale* in class" succeeded in having the book removed from the Judson Independent School District in San Antonio, Texas. Parent Cindy Pyo complained to Judson school superintendent that the book is "sexually explicit and offensive to Christians" after her son was assigned to read the book as part of the advanced placement English curriculum. Pyo requested an alternative assignment for her son, which the school honored, assigning him Aldous Huxley's BRAVE NEW WORLD with a few other students. Dissatisfied that other students in the school district were still reading the novel, Pyo submitted a complaint to Judson superintendent Ed Lyman, in the belief that she has "a responsibility to the country and our community to speak up for the values that will strengthen our society." *The Handmaid's Tale* had been in the school district's curriculum for advanced placement English for nearly 10 years, time during which some parents had requested an alternative reading assignment, but no one previously had formally challenged the book. Lyman made the unilateral decision to pull the novel from the AP curriculum despite the recommendations of a committee of teachers, students, and a parent who had approved its use. In an interview reported in the *Houston Chronicle*, the superintendent stated that he believed the book "does not meet community standards" and claimed that some of the descriptions in the book are too sexually explicit for high school students. "The tone of the book does not support, in my opinion, the effort by our state legislature to encourage abstinence outside the bonds of marriage." The recommendation committee appealed the decision to the Judson School District board of trustees, who met on March 23, 2006, to determine whether to uphold the superintendent's ban of the novel or to overrule his decision, which they did in a 5-2 vote. The well-attended meeting contained three hours of public comment and debate before the vote. Near the end of the meeting, board vice president Richard Lafoille stated that he did not see how the trustees could uphold the ban and told the audience of more than 200, "You kids want this book, I'm going to give it to you."

FURTHER READING

Benhuniak-Long, Susan. "Feminism and Reproductive Technology." *Choice* 29 (October 1991): 243.

Cooper, Pamela. "Sexual Surveillance and Medical Authority in Two Versions of *The Handmaid's Tale*." *Journal of Popular Culture* 28 (Spring 1995): 49–66.

Ferns, Chris. "The Values of Dystopia: *The Handmaid's Tale* and the Anti-Utopian Tradition." *Dalhousie Review* 69 (Fall 1989): 373–382.

"Judson Board Set to Write Final Chapter on Sci-Fi Book." *My San Antonio*, March 22, 2006. Available online. URL: http://www.mysanantonio.com/news/MYSA032206_01A_book_ban_86b7db6_html23805.html. Accessed December 12, 2009.

"Judson Makes Right Call, Restoring Book to Class." *My San Antonio*, March 27, 2006. Available online. URL: http://www.mysanantonio.com/opinion/MYSA032706_01O_judson2ed_56c2de7_html.html. Accessed December 12, 2009.

Newsletter on Intellectual Freedom (January 1991): 15; (July 1992): 126; (May 1993): 73; (July 2001): 174; (May 2006): 153–155.

"School's Purchase of Four Books Ignites a Furor in Waterloo." *Des Moines Register*, April 15, 1992, p. M2.

Stein, Karen. "Margaret Atwood's Modest Proposal: *The Handmaid's Tale*." *Canadian Literature* 23 (Spring 1996): 57–73.

Tait, Sue, and Christy Tyson. "Paperbacks for Young Adults." *Emergency Librarian* 16 (October 1988): 53–54.

Wilson, Sharon Rose. *Margaret Atwood's Fairy-Tale Sexual Politics*. Jackson: University of Mississippi, 1993.

THE HEPTAMERON (L'HEPTAMERON OU HISTOIRES DES AMANS FORTUNEZ)

Author: Marguerite d'Angoulême, Queen (Margaret) of Navarre
Original dates and places of publication: 1558, France; 1884, England
Original publishers: Privately published (France); Worthington (England)
Literary form: Collection of tales

SUMMARY

The Heptameron is a French classic of pornography and one of the few famous erotic works written by a woman, in this case a woman who was also a queen. The work is a frank imitation of Giovanni Boccaccio's THE DECAMERON, but the device used is that the 10 storytellers are trapped by a flood and must each day create stories that illustrate a subject that is newly assigned daily. Unlike *The Decameron*, the majority of the assigned subjects relate to sexual topics and the percentage of illicit affairs and fornicating clergy is higher in *The Heptameron*. The subject assigned on the first day is "the bad turns done by women to men and by men to women," while the eighth day requires that stories deal with "the most lecherous cases that can be conceived."

The work contains only 72 stories because Queen Marguerite died before reaching her goal. As in *The Decameron*, the stories contain many uncomplimentary portrayals of members of religious orders and sexual indiscretions of husbands and wives. Two major differences, however, are that *The Heptameron* contains stories of incest, not found in the earlier work, and a greater extent of emetic material. Overall, the stories also contain a greater amount of cruelty and manipulation of the opposite sex than appear in Boccaccio's work. The first story relates the adventures of a wife who takes a bishop for her lover because he pays her, and a young military officer for her lover because he gives her pleasure. When the officer protests and jilts her, she tells her husband, who kills the officer. Later, she learns that her husband is plotting to kill her, so she turns him in to the authorities. Afterward, "the wife, when her husband was removed, sinned more wickedly than before, and so died miserably."

Bizarre occurrences appear in other stories: One monk commits several murders in pursuit of a woman, another monk rapes a young girl as a form of chastisement, a husband kills his unfaithful wife, and a woman is soiled by feces in a monastery privy. In general, the stories in *The Heptameron* are not as playful and mischievous as those of Boccaccio, and the reason may lie in Queen Marguerite's stated intention to restrict her stories to true incidents.

CENSORSHIP HISTORY

The Heptameron was published posthumously in 1558 in a highly expurgated version. The complete version, clandestinely printed by private individuals, remained an underground work until late in the 19th century.

In a report entitled "How to Make a Town Library Successful," published in 1876, Frederick Beecher Perkins, assistant librarian of the Boston Public Library, recommended the following approach to censorship of the collection:

> It should exclude such books as Rabelais, *The Decameron*, the *Heptameron*, *The Contes Drolatiques* (Droll Stories) of Balzac, . . . all of which are sold in English translations for money by otherwise respectable American publishers. Few, indeed, are those who will object to this exclusion of ribald and immoral books from public circulating libraries.

In 1885, Anthony Comstock, secretary of the New York Society for the Suppression of Vice, saw an advertisement for the Globe Publishing Company of Paulsborough, New Jersey, which contained two books that would become his targets. Using a fictitious name, Comstock sent $2 for a copy of DROLL STORIES by Honoré de Balzac to John A. Wilson, who signed the advertisement. After he received the book, he then sent another $2 to purchase *The Heptameron*. Comstock then took his evidence to court and attained two federal grand jury indictments against Wilson for sending obscene literature through the mail. (See *Droll Stories*.)

The Heptameron was involved in the 1892 litigation of the Worthington Book Publishing Co., which was in financial difficulty. The receiver wanted to sell some of the company stock, including THE ARABIAN NIGHTS, THE HISTORY OF TOM JONES, THE ART OF LOVE, *The Decameron*, GARGANTUA AND PANTAGRUEL, Rousseau's CONFESSIONS, and *The Heptameron*, to pay off creditors, but Anthony Comstock stepped in to oppose the sales. He demanded of the court that the books be officially burned. The court disagreed. (See *Arabian Nights*.)

In 1900, a bookseller who had sold copies of the work was tried for obscene libel at the central criminal court in London in *Reg. v. Thomson*, 64 U.P. 456. The court record stated that Isabel Florence Thomson,

> then being a person of wicked and depraved disposition, and unlawfully and wickedly devising, contriving, and intending as much as in her lay to vitiate and corrupt the morals of the people of this kingdom unlawfully, wickedly, and wilfully did publish, sell, and utter a certain lewd, wicked, bawdy, and obscene libel in the form of a book entitled *The Heptameron of Margaret Queen of Navarre*.

The defense read extracts about the book from the *Encyclopedia Britannica* and the *Edinburgh Review* and stated that proceedings should never have been brought against the classic. The defense in this case also observed that

> in the Middle Ages things were discussed which if put forward now for the reading of the general public would never be tolerated. In towns buried from the corrupt times of the Roman Empire, now disinterred or in the course of being disinterred, there are discovered pictures of the most lewd and filthy character. Nobody would think of destroying those pictures, but to sell photographs in the streets of London would be an indictable offense.

The jury returned a not guilty verdict.

FURTHER READING

Geller, Evelyn. *Forbidden Books in American Public Libraries, 1876–1939.* Westport, Conn.: Greenwood, 1984.

Green, Virginia M. *Heroic Virtue, Comic Infidelity: Reassessing Marguerite de Navarre's Heptameron.* Amherst, Mass.: Hestia Press, 1993.

Rigolet, François. "Magdalen's Skull: Allegory and Iconography in *The Heptameron*." *Renaissance Quarterly* 47 (Spring 1994): 57–73.

Tebbel, John. *A History of Book Publishing in the United States.* Vol. 2. New York: Bowker, 1975.

Thomas, Donald. *A Long Time Burning: The History of Literary Censorship in England.* New York: Praeger, 1969.

THE HISTORY OF TOM JONES, A FOUNDLING

Author: Henry Fielding
Original dates and places of publication: 1749, England; 1931, United
  States
Original publishers: Andrew Millar (England); Brown House (United
  States)
Literary form: Novel

SUMMARY

The History of Tom Jones, A Foundling is a road novel that relates the adventures of the sexually impulsive young protagonist, from his illegitimate birth
through his marriage to the beautiful and virtuous Sophia Western. Found
as a baby in Squire Allworthy's bed, Tom is raised in the household and
treated like a family member. Although he falls in love with Sophia, he cannot resist the sexual charms of the gamekeeper's daughter, Molly Seagrim,
who becomes pregnant with what he thinks is his child. He confesses his
indiscretion to Allworthy and then goes to Molly to give her money, but he
finds her in bed with another man. Chastened, Tom decides to concentrate
on winning Sophia's love, but her father, Squire Western, refuses to let her
marry a foundling and tries to arrange a marriage to Allworthy's nephew
Blifil. Squire Allworthy becomes very ill, then recovers, and Tom becomes
drunk celebrating the recovery, but conspirators in the household claim that
he was celebrating the squire's impending death and his supposed inheritance, so the squire banishes Tom.

   While on the road, Tom has an affair with Mrs. Waters, whom he rescued from attack by a surly soldier named Northerton. He later meets Lady
Bellaston who, having heard of his attractiveness, seeks him out and seduces
him. This affair gave the most offense when the novel first appeared, because
he not only has the affair but also becomes her short-term gigolo. After Tom
ends the affair, he receives a letter from Sophia, telling him that she knows
about the two women and never wants to see him again. Further adventures
occur, and a series of coincidences reveal that Tom is the illegitimate child
of Squire Allworthy's late sister Bridget. Now that he is an Allworthy heir,
Squire Western welcomes Tom as his son-in-law, although Sophia pretends
reluctance. The two finally marry, and the novel ends happily as Squire
Western gives them his estate.

   Despite the lack of actual sexual material in the book, the numerous references to illegitimacy, references to Tom's numerous sexual liaisons, and
explicit anatomical references made the book a target of censors. In several
scenes, female characters suffer having their upper clothing torn from their
bodies as they fight to preserve their virtue. In the incident in which Tom
rescues Mrs. Waters,

> he had not entered far into the wood before he beheld a most shocking sight indeed, a woman stripped half naked, under the hands of a ruffian. . . . her clothes being torn from all the upper part of her body, her breasts, which were well formed and extremely white, attracted the eyes of her deliverer.

Although he loves Sophia, Tom continues to satisfy his desire for other women, more in the manner of boyish high spirits than in immorality. He views sex much as he views any challenge and "held it as much incumbent on him to accept a challenge to love as if it had been a challenge to fight." In addition to sexual references, Fielding's use of such taboo terms as *bitch, slut, hussy, harlot*, and *arse* also incited complaints.

CENSORSHIP HISTORY

The History of Tom Jones was attacked as "vulgar," "low," "indecent," and "devoid of moral sense" from its first publication. Critics claimed that Fielding had written "an enticement to moral corruption." Soon after the novel was published, *Gentleman's Magazine* observed that the "loose images" of the novel "perhaps invite to vice more than the contrast figures alarm us into virtue." In 1750, Bishop of London Thomas Sherlock warned that the novel had been written merely as an excuse to include "the most inexecrable Scenes of Lewdness." In 1772, Reverend Jonathan Edwards denounced *The History of Tom Jones* and warned the young against reading it.

Writing in 1879 regarding those works that should be contained in the well-stocked library, Samuel Green, a librarian in Worcester, Massachusetts, pointed out that he

> would place certain restrictions on the use of the novels of Smollett and Fielding, because while in many respects works of the first order, it is best that the young should read only such books as preserve a certain reticence in regard to subjects freely talked and written about in the last century.

In 1892, *The History of Tom Jones* was involved in the litigation of the Worthington Book Publishing Co., which was in financial difficulty. The receiver wanted to sell some of the company stock, including THE ARABIAN NIGHTS, THE DECAMERON, THE ART OF LOVE, THE HEPTAMERON, *GARGANTUA AND PANTAGRUEL*, Rousseau's CONFESSIONS, and *The History of Tom Jones* to pay off creditors, but Anthony Comstock, secretary of the New York Society for the Suppression of Vice, stepped in to oppose the sales. He demanded of the court that the books be officially burned. The court disagreed. (See *Arabian Nights*.)

In New York City in 1894, the Astor library removed all works by Fielding from its regular collection and placed them in the reference collection, after several patrons noted the "vulgar activities" depicted in the novel.

City and county officials in Dubuque, Iowa, staged a sudden raid on the public library in 1951. Under the authority of a warrant, they seized numerous books that were judged to be "obscene," including works of Rabelais, Boccaccio's *Decameron*, and *The History of Tom Jones*.

FURTHER READING

Geller, Evelyn. *Forbidden Books in American Public Libraries, 1876–1939*. Westport, Conn.: Greenwood, 1984.
Green, Samuel S. "Sensational Fiction in Public Libraries." *Library Journal* 4 (September–October 1879): 349–352.
Rolph, Cecil Hewitt. *Books in the Dock*. London: Deutsch, 1961.
Thomas, Donald. *Henry Fielding: A Life*. New York: St. Martin's, 1990.

HOMO SAPIENS

Author: Stanley Przybyszewski
Original dates and places of publication: 1898, Germany; 1915, United States
Original publishers: Hansson (Germany); Alfred A. Knopf (United States)
Literary form: Novel

SUMMARY

Homo Sapiens is an intense and introspective work written and first published in Germany by the Polish-born writer Stanley Przybyszewski and then translated and published in the United States. The author's best-known novel, *Homo Sapiens* uses ornate language to trace the dissolution of the hedonistic artist Erik Falk through alcohol and destructive eroticism, as he searches for something that will fill the emptiness he feels.

Falk embodies Przybyszewski's theories of a "libidinal unconscious" that drives him to engage in numerous affairs even as he protests that he loves his wife: "But at the same time, he loves his wife unqualifiedly. And he loves her so much that there can be no doubt of the reality of his love. In a word he loves both the one and the other." The protagonist, possessed of "an exceptional personality," is a close relative to Nietzsche's superman, aloof from the common herd yet conscious of the restraints of his existence.

Censors in the United States objected to the manner in which Falk expressed his uniqueness in relation to ordinary individuals in sexual terms:

"I have never suffered on account of a woman," boasts an old rake, Iltis.

"Because your organism is very tough, a peasant's organism, my dear Iltis. Your sensibilities have not yet reached the stage of dependence upon the brain. You are like a hydromedusa which suddenly parts with its feelers stocked with sexual organs and sends them off to seek the female, and then does not bother about them any more."

For Falk, the sexual instinct functions as the primary force in life, but his search for sexual union is part of the greater goal to find in woman the miraculous expression of his most intimate, "most precious I." Thus, even his dreams are imbued with sexuality. In one, Falk dreams of two elks fighting violently, one driving "his horns into the other's breast. He drove them in deeper and deeper, tore ferociously at his flesh and entrails. The blood spurted." As the two fight, near them "a female elk was pasturing unmindful of the savage struggle of the passion-mad males."

CENSORSHIP HISTORY

Homo Sapiens was praised when it was first published in Germany in 1898, and advance copies of the American publication of the book received praise in 1915. Writing in *The Little Review*, Alexander S. Kaun called the novel "the book of the age." Other reviewers agreed with the assessment, one stating that "Przybyszewski compels you to co-operate with him in analysing psychological phenomena." Praise did not save the novel from being banned, for preoccupation with "the sex-problem" was unsettling to American censors in 1915.

On December 23, 1915, 23-year-old Alfred A. Knopf, publisher of *Homo Sapiens* and only one year out of Columbia University, appeared before Magistrate Simms in Jefferson Market Court on charges brought by John Sumner and the New York Society for the Suppression of Vice. The society charged that the novel was obscene and should be removed from distribution. In the brief hearing, Knopf provided evidence that the book had received favorable reviews and was sold openly as a work of art. Knopf's attorney requested an adjournment to allow the presiding magistrate to read the book, but Assistant District Attorney Van Castile protested, "His Honor should not be subjected to such cruel punishment. The book is utterly stupid as well as indecent."

Despite the protest, an adjournment was granted and Knopf's wealthy father called in Wilson E. Tipple, his lawyer and a director of the vice society, to speak with young Knopf and convince him to change his mind. At a later meeting between young Knopf and Sumner, the publisher completely reversed his position, promising to withdraw the novel from sale and to melt down the plates. In return, Sumner withdrew the complaint. As Boyer relates, Knopf explained his actions in a letter to *Publishers Weekly*, dated January 22, 1916, in which he stated that the book had been "smirched" and that he did not "deign to satisfy the prurient demand which had been created."

FURTHER READING

Boyer, Paul S. *Purity in Print: The Vice-Society Movement and Book Censorship in America.* New York: Scribner, 1968.

"*Home Sapiens:* A Review." *The Little Review* 2 (December 1915): 25–27.

Kaun, Alexander S. "The Ecstasy of Pain." *Little Review* 2 (December 1915): 16–23.

"Publishing's Past Fifty Years, A Balance Sheet—II." *Saturday Review,* November 28, 1964, pp. 17–19, 69.

HOW THE GARCÍA GIRLS LOST THEIR ACCENTS

Author: Julia Alvarez
Original date and place of publication: 1991, United States
Original publisher: Algonquin Books
Literary type: Novel

SUMMARY

How the García Girls Lost Their Accents offers a realistic view of the experiences of young women whose previously secure and protected live have been disrupted. Carla, Sandra, Yolanda, and Sofia have enjoyed lives of privilege in the Dominican Republic, but their lives are reduced when they immigrate to the United States. The immigration is a hurried affair, enabled by the American Central Intelligence Agency to move the family to safety after their father, Carlos García, becomes the target of the Dominican secret police for working underground against the military dictatorship.

As the daughters of wealthy parents, the girls grew up being careless with their possessions and in their treatment of others who did not enjoy the same wealth and luxurious circumstances. While living in the Dominican Republic, they received expensive gifts from FAO Schwarz, which they viewed as located in what appeared at that time in their lives to be an almost mythical United States. Their perceptions change radically after they flee to New York City and confront their new material and cultural realities that do not include chauffeured cars, maids to pick up after them, and cooks to cater to their finicky eating habits. Their mother, Laura, also has a difficult adjustment to make, because she had always lived a life of privilege in the Dominican Republic. She was raised in a wealthy family and her drop in social and financial status are harsh realities.

The novel opens 29 years after the Garcías moved to the United States, and it is not until the 14th chapter, "The Blood of the Conquistadors," that the novel addresses the political situation in the Dominican Republic and identifies the reasons and the circumstances that made necessary the family's sudden move. The Dominican dictator Trujillo has been overthrown long before, the elder Garcías now have a house on Long Island, and the daughters have been in and out of marriages, relationships, professions, and mental institutions. Yolanda has returned to her homeland and finds that she is a stranger to both the culture and to the language that were once second nature to her. She mistakes farmworkers with machetes for criminals, travels unaccompanied unlike Dominican women who travel in pairs, and falters when speaking in Spanish. She has felt uncomfortable and foreign in the United States, but she is no more comfortable in her homeland and feels that she has no home.

Throughout the chapters that follow, moving between years in the girls' lives in the United States, the reader learns that Laura García sought to distinguish among her daughters when they were young by dressing them in specific colors and repeating symbolic stories for each. She dresses Carla in yellow and relates how she wanted red sneakers badly but the family finances only allowed for common white sneakers, so the young girl used her mother's red nail polish to paint her white sneakers red. Laura dresses Yolanda in pink and speaks of her daughter's abilities as a poet, while ignoring the truth that Yolanda makes her living as a teacher and has a mental breakdown because of the stress of living in two worlds but fitting into neither. Sofia is dressed in white, and Laura proudly supports her defiance of her father's overprotectiveness. Sandra, dressed in blue, is used by a sculptor in forming the face of the Virgin Mary, but her battle with anorexia and mental breakdown leave Laura without a story to tell because she feels that she is a failure as both a Dominican and an American mother.

The novel relates vignettes, some of them containing sexual references, that are integral to the growth and development of the four girls. Sofia has "nonstop boyfriends," and when she is sent as a punishment to the Dominican Republic for a year with her grandmother, she experiences a sexual relationship with her uncle's illegitimate son Manuel. As a young adult she has to go on vacation to Colombia in order to escape her father's prying nature and to evade his condemnation, as well as to have an opportunity to share an intimate relationship with another boyfriend. After having sex with her boyfriend while in Colombia, she leaves him, takes up with a German tourist named Otto, has sex with him four days after they meet, then returns to Germany with him. They later marry and present Carlos with a namesake grandson.

Yolanda was very close to her cousin Mundin, with whom she often played. He has a doll and modeling clay, which their grandmother bought at FAO Schwarz, and which Yolanda wants. When they are alone, he asks her to show him that she "is a girl." She complies and takes off her panties to show him her genitals in exchange for the doll and the clay. Yolanda experiences college life in the late 1960s and despite writing "pornographic poems" with classmate Rudy Elmenhurst, in a chapter titled with his name, she remains a virgin as an undergraduate. She is attracted to Rudy, but the language he uses to describe sexual acts—"balled," "laid," "fucked"—leaves her cold and detached. He accuses her of being "frigid" because she will not sleep with him. When she is in graduate school, the two meet again and he asks her "want to fuck?" She refuses him, then, drinks wine straight out of the bottle "like some decadent wild woman who had just dismissed her unsatisfactory lover."

Carla is at fault for a maid being fired from the family home when they were still living in the Dominican Republic and makes no effort to correct the error that leads to the firing. The girls were given iron banks bought at FAO Schwarz, and Carla's bank was in the form of the Virgin Mary. When Carla placed a coin in the slot, the figure's arms stretched outward, and the figure appeared to ascend to heaven. She left the bank on a shelf in her room and ignored it until one of the family maids asked if she could buy it from Carla with Christmas gift money. Carla simply gave the bank to the maid but did not tell her parents because she did not want to admit that she had not liked the gift and out of fear that they might deny her future gifts. When Laura discovers the bank missing from the shelf in Carla's room, then finds it in the maid's room, she accuses the girl of stealing the bank and dismisses her. Carla does not speak out. When the Garcías have been in the United States for a year, Carla is accosted by a sexual predator who lures her to his car and startles her when she sees he is naked from the waist down. After she runs home and her mother calls the police, both she and Laura feel humiliated because they do not have sufficient command of English to explain the incident completely to the police officers who arrive to take their statements, and no complaint is filed.

Sandra seems to have the most difficult time of the four girls growing up. She wants to be an artist, but she is asked to leave her art class because she wants to sketch and paint kittens and not follow the lessons provided by the teacher. She later encounters an apparently insane sculptor in his studio, where she finds him naked and chained and slashing violently at the face of the sculpture he is creating. He lunges for her, and she falls and breaks her arm, which takes months to heal correctly. In a gallery some time later, she and Laura see a sculpture with a face that is Sandra's. Her encounter with the sculptor had provided him with model for his vision of the Virgin Mary. She has the misfortune of witnessing her father being kissed on the lips by Mrs. Fanning, whose husband, a doctor, worked to help Carlos obtain a medical license in the United States. Rather than tell, Sandra insists that the couple buy her a flamenco doll despite her mother's protests that the girls should not receive any special gifts.

The novel ends with a story that takes place right before the Garcías leave the island. Yolanda has taken a very young kitten from its mother and named it Schwarz. When the mother cat appears, she hides the kitten in her drum that was bought at FAO Schwarz, then beats on the drum with spoons, sticks, and drumsticks in an effort to obscure the plaintive cries of the kitten trapped in the drum. She later pulls the kitten out of the drum and throws it to the ground, injuring its leg, then watches it limp away. That night and for many nights after, Yolanda dreams of the mother cat appearing and feels both fear and sadness for what she did to the kitten.

CENSORSHIP HISTORY

In 2006, *How the García Girls Lost Their Accents* was among nine books on the required reading list that were challenged in the second-largest high school district in Illinois, an act that "triggered debate over whether works praised in literary circles are high art or smut." The controversy began when Leslie Pinney, a Township High School district 214 board member, identified books on the reading list that she considered to "contain vulgar language, brutal imagery or depictions of sexual situations inappropriate for students." The novels Pinney identified as inappropriate reading material, in addition to *How the García Girls Lost Their Accents*, are *SLAUGHTERHOUSE-FIVE* by Kurt Vonnegut, *THE THINGS THEY CARRIED* by Tim O'Brien, THE AWAKENING by Kate Chopin, *FREAKONOMICS* by Steven D. Levitt and Stephen J. Dubner, *The Botany of Desire: A Plant's-Eye View of the World* by Michael Pollan, THE PERKS OF BEING A WALLFLOWER by Stephen Chbosky, *FALLEN ANGELS* by Walter Dean Myers, and *BELOVED* by Toni Morrison. The school board member admitted that she had not read most of the books she targeted and claimed that she did not want to ban the books from the district libraries, but in class she wanted "to replace them with books that address the same themes without explicit material." Her objection to *How the García Girls Lost Their Accents* identified the descriptions of sexual behavior in the novel, which she contended are entirely gratuitous. The challenges were the first in more than 20 years that someone had attempted to remove books from the reading lists in the Arlington Heights–based district, which employed an extensive review process based on established reading lists. In defense of the choices, English and fine arts department head Chuck Venegoni told a reporter for the *Chicago Tribune*, "This is not some serendipitous decision to allow someone to do what they felt like doing because they had something about talking about something kinky in front of kids. It's insulting to hardworking people who really do care about kids." He criticized Pinney's approach of taking a few passages out of context to condemn entire books and observed, "there is nothing in any of those books that even remotely approaches what an objective person would call pornography." Although the school district had an opt-out clause that allowed parents to request that their child read another book if they find the assigned material objectionable, Pinney found the current measures ineffectual "because unless you're digging around the student's backpack, looking at the books and reading them, how exactly will you know what your student is reading?"

Five hundred people attended the school board meeting on Thursday, May 25, 2006, to debate whether to keep *How the García Girls Lost Their Accents* and the other novels on the school reading lists. Supporters of the ban asserted that their efforts were "to protect students from smut" and some people, such as Arlington Heights resident Brude Ticknell, claimed that "teachers promoting the books were motivated by their own progressive social agendas." Students took the debate to the social networking site

MySpace.com, and sophomore Scott Leipprandt placed a petition against the ban on the Prospect High page which nearly 500 students and alumni from the six high schools in the district signed. Leipprandt told a *Chicago Tribune* reporter that fighting the banning of books is important. "It's important because it shows us things. All these things happen in real life. By banning it, it doesn't give us the opportunity to talk about it before we encounter it in real life." After a long meeting during which hundreds of people spoke, the school board voted 6-1 in favor of approving the required reading list without change. The following year, the school board voted to provide parents with the reading lists for courses before voting on materials.

In 2007, *How the García Girls Lost Their Accents* was removed from the school libraries in the Johnston County, North Carolina, school district after parents of students attending the West Johnston High School "challenged its sexual content and profane language to the school board." The removal of the novel led to the creation of a districtwide committee that was given the responsibility of reviewing titles in the schools and in the school libraries that might contain material similarly offensive to parents. The associate superintendent for curriculum and instructional services Keith Beamon asserted, "We are simply looking back through the titles to see if there are any red flags out there. It's not that we are looking for any particular title; it's a broad review to see if there is anything out there that jumps out at us. . . . If you've got a leak in one place in your house . . . we're just kind of checking everywhere else to make sure there are no other leaks."

The controversy in Johnston County began when the 15-year-old daughter of Georgia Roberts brought the novel home to read for her English class. Roberts said that her daughter told her multiple times that the book was very hard to read and that the deeper she got into the novel, the more upset she became. "She came to me and she was very upset and crying because the more you got into the book, the worse it got." The school assigned Roberts's daughter *All Quiet on the Western Front* as an alternative reading assignment and scheduled a parent-teacher conference. Roberts said that the teacher, school principal, and adviser defended use of the book by telling her that each of the scenes is a lesson in language barriers. That response angered Roberts, who told reporters, "I said to the teacher, 'Well, Ma'am, you can learn about language barriers at the DMV . . . you can go anywhere in Johnston County and come up with a language barrier situation. . . . It doesn't have to be done with a man's private parts rising and him taking care of himself." Roberts agreed that learning about diversity and different cultures is important, and said that she was willing to learn about the Latin culture "but not with the foul language and sexually explicit situations in the book." The West Johnston Media and Technology Advisory Committee reviewed the novel and suggested the book should stay on the library shelves and in the classroom curriculum. Ms. Roberts appealed the decision, and the matter was taken up by the district media and technology committee, who reviewed the work and recommended its removal from all county schools.

FURTHER READING

"Censorship Dateline: Libraries." *Newsletter on Intellectual Freedom* 57, no. 2 (March 2008): 59–61.
Francisco, Jamie. "Book-Ban Debate Is Long, Impassioned: More Than 350 Sign Up to Speak to School Board." *Chicago Tribune*, May 26, 2006, p. 2NW.1.
_____. "Explicit Move Is Made to Ban Books from Reading List." *Chicago Tribune*, May 24, 2006, p. 2NS.8.
Megan, Graydon. "Parents to Get Look at School Reading Lists: Controversy Led to Move by District in Arlington Heights." *Chicago Tribune*, May 12, 2007, p. 13.

HOW TO MAKE LOVE LIKE A PORN STAR: A CAUTIONARY TALE

Author: Jenna Jameson
Original date and place of publication: 2004, New York
Original publishers: Regan Books / HarperCollins
Literary form: Autobiography

SUMMARY

How to Make Love Like a Porn Star is a misleading title for this autobiography of Jenna Jameson, coauthored with former *New York Times* reporter Neil Straus, which is not the "how-to" manual that the title suggests. Instead, the book is a mixture of diary, interview, and narration, profusely illustrated, that tells of her transformation from Jenna Massoli, schoolgirl and cheerleader with braces, into Jenna Jameson, adult film star and current porn industry mogul. Pages purported to be from a diary she kept as an adolescent appear throughout the book, as do photographs of her as a child with her brother and stills from her movies and promotional material. The photographs of Jameson as a child with her brother and her father are poignant, and the stills from her movies are sexually explicit and contain portrayals of her nude and barely clothed in embraces and poses with other similarly clad women and men.

Jameson's mother, Judy, was a Las Vegas showgirl, and her father Larry, who served in Vietnam and at one point in the book claims to have shot 61 people dead in one afternoon, was first a television executive for Channel 13 in Las Vegas and then, after Judy's death, a police officer. Jameson's mother died of cancer when Jameson was two years old, and her father struggled to raise the children and pay off the medical bills. Larry Massoli also claims to have been a good friend to Frank Sinatra Jr.

and Bill Harrah (of Harrah's Casino), as well as a tough cop who had mobsters threatening him and his children. In several chapters, Jameson, her brother Tony, and her father alternate in telling stories about her early life and about their own problems. Tony had an extremely serious drug habit for years. Her father lived with a series of women who made his life miserable.

Jameson relates that she began to run wild when she was 15; met Jack, a tattoo artist who was part of a crowd of bikers; and eventually became involved with a group of bikers and partied with them at the beach and at bars. At the age of 16, she fell in love with Jack, whose neo-Nazi uncle, Preacher, raped her. That night she remained out all night, and when she returned home the next morning, she was confronted by her angry father who demanded to know where she had been. She returned his anger, immediately packed her belongings, and left home to move in with Jack, the tattoo artist who created what would later become one of her trademarks, the "Heart Breaker" tattoo on her backside.

Living with Jack, she had to find a job, so she tried out at several Las Vegas nightclubs, but she was not successful. Jack encouraged her to try stripping, which she did. She found work at the Crazy Horse Too, but only after she removed the braces from her teeth. But Jack also knew a way she could make even more money, and he helped her to do so. Within a few years, she went from high school cheerleader to stripper to nude model to porn actress. She also began to use drugs and became a crack addict. She quickly became a top nude model and porn star and the country's highest-paid feature dancer.

By day Jameson posed for magazine covers for what are euphemistically called "men's magazines," and at 19 she left stripping to act in adult films—mainly to retaliate against her boyfriend, who had been cheating on her. She shot her first scene in 1993 and a year later landed a contract with Wicked Pictures, which paid her $6,000 a month to perform in eight to ten feature films a year, doing three or four scenes in each. She found that her appearances in adult films made her more desirable as a stripper: "After I became famous, I made sick money stripping." At her peak she received $5,000 a show and typically did four shows a night. She also made extra money by posing for Polaroid photographs with patrons for $40 each and selling copies of her latest movie for $50. Jameson claims in the book that she often made $50,000 a week.

By 1998 Jameson had made approximately 40 films for Wicked, including hits like *Lip Service* and *Hard Evidence*. That year, at an awards ceremony in Las Vegas, she met Jay Grdina, who she says came from a wealthy cattle-ranching family and who had gotten into the adult film business after college. The two fell in love and moved to Scottsdale, Arizona, and Jameson decided to take a break from making movies. "Wicked launched me into superstardom," she says, "but I was determined to become my own boss."

The two formed ClubJenna as an Internet pornography company in 2000; ClubJenna.com was one of the first adult sites to feature fare beyond explicit picture and video content. Jameson provided diaries, advice on relationships and plastic surgery, even stock tips. They were profitable in their third week, but "dot-com became dot-bomb pretty quickly," so the couple decided to diversify. Web-site management and membership fees make up $12 million, or 40%, of ClubJenna's annual revenue. They also set up a movie production company. Jameson planned to do scenes only with women but decided she needed a man onscreen and persuaded Grdina to step in front of the camera. "If I were working with someone else, the audience could tell I wasn't into it—and stop buying movies," she writes. The two married in June 2003. Jameson writes at the end of her book that she hopes to continue to grow her business, but she wants to have a child.

CENSORSHIP HISTORY

How to Make Love like a Porn Star spent six weeks on the *New York Times* best-seller list. Many libraries did not order the book, and those that did place orders soon found themselves on lengthy waiting lists.

In January 2005, the Houston Public Library was ordered to move their 12 copies of *How to Make Love like a Porn Star* into closed stacks at the central library, from which the book could be obtained only by special request. The move was initiated when Councilwoman Pam Holm spoke out at a city council meeting and demanded that the Robinson-Westchase Library branch in her district remove the book from the best-sellers display at the front of the library. She claimed that an angry constituent had contacted her about the book and, although she admitted that she had not read the book or even looked through it, "It's a fine line with a best seller and what is considered pornography. I'm not a supporter of pornography, nor do I want it accessible to children." The complaint cited the "sexually explicit nature of the material" and the "vulgar language." The council contacted the library branch, and Sandra Fernandez, spokesperson for the Houston Library System, told them that Robinson-Westchase had no current plans to remove the book from the display, but promised that a review committee would study the issue. She also told the council that the display is really not an issue, because the book is constantly checked out and "the 12 books the library bought in October have all been almost continuously checked out at various locations." Houston Mayor Bill White contacted the library's interim director and told her to use "common sense" about the book. He claims that he did not order her to move the book and was "under the impression that she ordered the books to the private stacks." Despite White's efforts to downplay his role, Toni Lambert, the interim director, sent out a news release that stated: "I have reviewed the book and agree with Mayor White's recommendation on its placement. It was a reasonable solution to providing the book to customers while addressing the concerns raised. The mayor's intervention allowed us to provide a timely resolution to this issue. We are grateful for the mayor's support and assistance."

The local chapter of the American Civil Liberties Union threatened to sue the city for sequestering the book, and numerous Houston citizens complained that their First Amendment rights were being violated. The library review committee recommended on February 1 that the book should be shelved in the fine arts and recreation section along with other celebrity biographies. As the *Houston Chronicle* reported, the staff did not have to physically move any books, because all copies of the book had been in constant circulation for months. In mid-February, it had a waiting list of 41 patrons. Through a spokesperson, Mayor White claimed that the decision to move the book into closed stacks had been only a temporary measure and that the final decision was that of the review committee.

In a press release, Jenna Jameson chided the mayor and council, writing, "I think it is ridiculous and dangerous for a politician to dictate what kinds of books a public library should or should not have on its shelves. The selection of books should be solely up to the library director, not the mayor who is acting with political motivation. What's even more weird is that the original complaint came from a councilwoman named Pam Horn [*sic*], who admits she never even read the book."

FURTHER READING

Blumenstein, Lynn. "Porn Star Back on Houston Shelves." *Library Journal*, March 15, 2005, p. 2.

"Jenna Chides Library over Book Ban." Press release. Available online. URL: www.ainews.com/Archives/Story8430.phtml. Posted February 9, 2005. Accessed December 11, 2009.

Nissimov, Ron. "Mayor Wrote a New Page in Library History." *Houston Chronicle*, February 15, 2005.

"Porn Star Tell-All Slips Back on Shelves." *American Libraries* 36 (April 2005): 15.

"Success Stories: Libraries." *Newsletter on Intellectual Freedom* 54 (May 2005): 135.

IF IT DIE (SI LE GRAIN NE MEURT)

Author: André Gide
Original dates and places of publication: 1920, France; 1935, United States
Original publishers: Privately published (France); Modern Library (United States)
Literary form: Autobiography

SUMMARY

If It Die, titled *Si le grain ne meurt* when originally published, is André Gide's attempt to "give form to a confused inner agitation." Recounting his childhood through young manhood, the work contains his early revelation of a homosexual orientation, shown in one episode where the child Gide cries in his mother's arms and declares that he "is unlike the other schoolboys." The work is divided into two parts: Part one describes Gide's childhood and growth to young manhood, and a shorter part two describes his awareness of homosexual feelings and his adventures in acting on those feelings.

Gide relates adolescent incidents of masturbation and homoerotic desire in part one. He describes taking toys under the dining room table on the pretext of playing with a friend, but "we amused ourselves otherwise, beside each other but not with each other: we had what I afterwards learnt are called 'bad habits.' " As an adolescent at the École Alsacienne, he meets another boy for whom he "conceived an absolute passion," and later he meets another young man named Abel who makes Gide an "offer of his heart." With Lionel, he "made regular lovers' trysts, to which we hastened with beating hearts and agitated thoughts," and with Louis he feels "a kind of lover-like bashfulness . . . a sort of boiling agitation . . . a kind of passionate stammer."

In part two, which begins when Gide turns 20, the stirrings of sexual desire become reality. He and a friend travel to Tunisia and Algiers, where Gide has his first sexual experience with Ali, their young Tunisian guide. Ali undresses for their encounter and "he emerged naked as a god. . . . Though his body was perhaps burning, it felt as cool and refreshing to my hands as shade."

In Algiers, he meets Mohammed, who also thrills him and dominates his mind even though the two do not become intimate until later. Still, when Gide has sex with a native girl, he can only bear doing so "because I shut my eyes and imagined I was holding Mohammed in my arms." A short time later, when Oscar Wilde visits and arranges a sexual liaison for Gide with Mohammed, Gide is enthralled by his experience with "the perfect little body, so wild, so ardent, so lascivious" and brags that he "achieved pleasure five times with him" that one night.

Throughout, even as he relates his sexual adventures, Gide expresses feeling of guilt. The autobiography ends with Gide speaking of betrothal to his cousin Emmeline as a cure for his homosexual desires.

CENSORSHIP HISTORY

In 1935, a New York City policeman acting as an agent of the New York Society for the Suppression of Vice purchased a copy of *If It Die* from the Gotham Book Mart. Acting under orders from society secretary John Sumner, who considered passages in the book obscene, the officer then arrested the book mart owner for allegedly violating the New York Obscenity Statute. When the owner was placed on trial in *People on Com-*

plaint of Savery v. Gotham Book Mart Inc., in the City Magistrate's Court of New York City, Seventh District, Borough of Manhattan, on January 24, 1936, Sumner served as the prosecutor for the people. He directed his attack at 76 pages (20 percent) of the book, and only specific paragraphs contained in 22 of those pages, in the attempt to apply the Hicklin rule, which determined that paragraphs could be taken out of context and the test of obscenity of the entire work would be judged by assessing if the offending paragraphs had the tendency "to deprave the minds of those open to such influences and into whose hands a publication of this character might come."

Judge Nathan D. Perlman presided over the case and refused to grant Sumner the right to apply the Hicklin rule. Instead, in making a determination the judge cited the Woolsey decision in *United States v. One Book Entitled "Ulysses,"* in which the presiding judge emphasized consideration of the entire book and pondered the question: "Is the book dirt for dirt's sake?" Acknowledging that the book "contains a few paragraphs dealing with isolated instances of inversion, which, taken by themselves, are undoubtedly vulgar and indecent," Judge Perlman stated that they were, nonetheless, vital in "forming an essential part of the main theme." He asserted that these scenes were necessary for the author to present a truthful and accurate picture of his life: "It is as an entire creature we must study him, omitting nothing." Based on this assessment, the court ruled that *If It Die* "is not obscene, lewd, lascivious, or indecent within the meaning of the statute." He dismissed the complaint and discharged the owner of the Gotham Book Mart.

In 1938, after Gide publicly announced his disillusionment with communism, the Soviet Union banned all of his works, including *If It Die.* Soviet authorities in the occupation of East Berlin in 1954 banned all of Gide's works from East Germany.

In 1952, the work was placed on the Index librorum prohibitorum in Rome, on which it remained until the late 1960s. The Irish Board of Censors banned the work in 1953 for its blatant descriptions of Gide's homosexual relations, and the ban was not lifted until the relaxing of restraints in the 1970s.

FURTHER READING

Katz, Jonathan. *Gay/Lesbian Almanac.* New York: Carroll & Graf, 1994.

Kilpatrick, James J. *The Smut Peddlers.* New York: Doubleday, 1960.

Lucey, Michael. "The Consequences of Being Explicit: Watching Sex in Gide's *Si le grain ne meurt.*" *Yale Journal of Criticism* 4 (1990): 174–92.

Weightman, John. "Andre Gide and the Homosexual Debate." *American Scholar* 59 (Autumn 1990): 591–601.

ISLE OF PINES

Author: Henry Neville
Original date and place of publication: 1668, England
Original publisher: Allen Banks and Charles Harper at the Flower-
Deluice near Cripplegate Church
Literary form: Fictional journal

SUMMARY

Isle of Pines is a brief work that holds importance because it was the object
of the sole censorship action of the colonial period involving erotica in a
time when charges of blasphemy were common. The first part of the work
is purported to be the account of a man named George Pine, who writes of
his journey from England to being shipwrecked on an island in uncharted
waters near the coast of Madagascar. With him are three free women and
a female African slave, all of whom become his sexual partners after a few
months as "idleness and fulness of every thing begot in me a desire of enjoying the Women."

Between descriptions of the topography and vegetation of the island, Pine
recounts the gradual development of sexual intimacy on the island as he and
his companions begin "to grow more familiar" and he persuades two of the
women to let him "lie with them." Pine at first enjoys sexual intimacies in
private, with each woman individually. After a time, "custom taking away
the flame (there being none but us) we did it more openly, as our Lust gave
us liberty; afterwards my Masters [sic] Daughter was content also to do as
we did." He observes that the thought that they might never return home
lessened their inhibitions and "made us thus bold."

Pine only hesitates regarding the slave, "none remaining but my *Negro*,
who seeing what we did, longed also for her share." He waits until she makes
the move one night when he is asleep, crawling onto his grass mat close to
him, "to beguile me." Pine awakes and "feeling her, and perceiving who it
was, yet willing to try the difference, satisfied myself with her."

Although no indication is given of Pine's age at the beginning of the
account, he provides an accounting when he turns 60. Over the years, the
women had reproduced repeatedly and their children had similarly reproduced, to the point that Pine counted that he had 565 children, grandchildren and great-grandchildren.

The second, briefer part of the work is purported to be the work of a
Dutch sea captain who supposedly lands on the island 98 years after Pine's
first appearance. While there, he obtains the manuscript from one of
Pine's descendants, and it later reaches the hands of Henry Neville. The
story was translated into several European languages and viewed as a true
account.

146

CENSORSHIP HISTORY

The Isle of Pines was banned the year of its publication after authorities in the Massachusetts colony discovered it while searching for unlicensed material on the premises of the only two printers in the colony. Printer Marmaduke Johnson received a fine of £5 for possession of the pamphlet, but the fine was rescinded after he expressed penitence for possessing the suggestive material.

In 1711, Massachusetts passed a statute entitled "An Act against Intemperance, Immorality, and Profaneness, and for Reformation of Manners" that specifically decreed that no material considered obscene would be tolerated. The comprehensive act was directed toward anyone guilty of "composing, writing, printing or publishing of any filthy, obscene, or profane song, pamphlet, libel or mock sermon, in imitation or in mimicking of preaching, or any other preaching, or any other part of divine worship." Under this statute, suggestive literature like *The Isle of Pines* was banned.

FURTHER READING

Acts and Laws, Passed by the Great and General Court or Assembly of the Province of the Massachusetts-Bay in New-England, from 1692 to 1719. London: John Baskett, 1724.
Ford, Worthington Chauncey. *The Isle of Pines 1668: An Essay in Bibliography*. Boston: The Club of Odd Volumes, 1920.

IT'S PERFECTLY NORMAL

Author: Robie H. Harris
Original date and place of publication: 1994, Cambridge, Massachusetts
Original publisher: Candlewick Press
Literary form: Nonfiction

SUMMARY

It's Perfectly Normal, subtitled "A Book about Changing Bodies, Growing Up, Sex, and Sexual Health," combines text with illustrations by Michael Emberley to explain sexuality to preadolescent children. The author seeks to answer every possible question that children might have about sex through a pattern of presenting questions posed by two cartoon characters, a curious, adventurous bird and a squeamish, seemingly shy bee, and the answers they discuss and discover. The straightforward text and explicit illustrations provide clear explanations of the facts of life, without resorting to the use of euphemisms and without avoiding any topics. In the introduction, the author writes clearly that the book is created for preadolescent children, whose bodies will soon begin to undergo enormous, and sometimes frightening, changes. Through the persona of the curious bird, she reassures children that "It's perfectly normal for kids to be curious about and want to know about their changing bodies," while she uses the more reticent bee to represent children who might be unwilling to verbalize their curiosity about their changing bodies. The introduction also acknowledges to children that sex is an important aspect of life because it "is about a lot of things—bodies, growing up, families, babies, love, caring, curiosity, feelings, respect, responsibility, biology, and health," and reassures them that "it's also perfectly normal to want to know about sex."

The book is constructed in six parts, each profusely illustrated with anatomically correct sketches of boys and girls, as well as adult men and women of different races, ethnicities, and body types. Each of the six parts contains several chapters, each devoted to a specific question or concern of adolescents: Part 1—What is Sex? (Girl or Boy, Female or Male; Making Babies; Strong Feelings; Making Love; Straight and Gay), Part 2—Our Bodies (The Human Body; Outside and Inside—The Female Sex Organs; Outside and Inside—The Male Sex Organs; Words), Part 3—Puberty (Changes and Messages; The Travels of the Egg; The Travels of the Sperm; Not All at Once!; More Changes!; Back and Forth/Up and Down; Perfectly Normal), Part 4—Families and Babies (All Sorts of Families; Instructions from Mom and Dad; A Kind of Sharing; Before Birth; What a Trip!; Other Arrivals), Part 5—Decisions (Planning Ahead; Laws and Rulings), Part 6—Staying Healthy (Talk About It—Sexual Abuse; Checkup—Sexually Transmitted Diseases; Scientists Working Day and Night; Staying Healthy).

The book does not take a moral stance on the issue of sex, nor does it seek to frighten children through exaggeration. Instead, by using the dictionary definitions of the word *sex*, the author conveys the multiple meanings of the term as they relate to sexual desire, sexual reproduction, sexual intercourse, and gender. The text acquaints children with the scientific terms for the sexual organs and for sexual activity, but it also identifies the slang terms or common, everyday language that might be used to refer to the body and sex, such as referring to the breasts as "boobs" and the testicles as "balls." Sketches portray a heterosexual couple naked in bed in the act of sexual intercourse, same-sex and heterosexual couples embracing, naked girls and boys examining their genitals in mirrors, a baby in the uterus, and in a series of frames, the widening vagina in the act of giving birth. Each of these illustrations is accompanied by detailed text that explains the functioning of the male and female reproductive organs and the changes that the male and female bodies undergo during puberty, including such sometimes frightening phenomena as "wet dreams," menstruation, involuntary erections, and the processes of conception, gestation, and birth. In a separate chapter entitled "Planning Ahead: Postponement, Abstinence, and Birth Control," the author discusses these three options and provides detailed illustrations and explanations of available means of birth control and includes text and an illustration captioned "putting on a condom."

In addition to providing information about sexuality, the author deals with the highly sensitive topic of sexual abuse. The reticent bee remarks, "It's scary and creepy to hear about sexual abuse," to which the bird responds, "Yes, it is. But I do feel better just talking about it." Children are instructed as to what constitutes sexual abuse, and they are reassured that whatever happens is not their fault. They are told to reveal any abuse to a trusted adult. The final chapters of *It's Perfectly Normal* examine the causes and prevention of sexually transmitted diseases and remind children that they must make responsible choices.

CENSORSHIP HISTORY

It's Perfectly Normal has aroused controversy in California, Texas, Alaska, and Massachusetts, where challenges have been raised with varying success. In June 1999, parents in Auburn, California, demanded the removal of the book from the Placer County Library and charged that it posed a threat to children. Parent Carrie Gibson brought the issue of access to the book before the Placer County Library Board in May 1999, after her son brought the book home and she found that it contained "pornographic illustrations." In her complaint, Gibson stated, "The books that are sexually explicit or contain sexual education content should be placed behind the counter with only full, unrestricted access to adults. We must uphold community standards, and make the libraries safe once again for children." The director of library services, Elaine Reed, responded that "the overwhelming majority of the community wants to maintain our library policies of open access" and cautioned that limiting access to one book would encourage other restrictions, including the need to monitor newspapers and magazines. After the library board voted on June 29, 1999, not to restrict access to materials that certain members of the community viewed as sexually explicit or profane, the *Auburn Journal* reported that more than 50 people representing a newly formed group called Citizens for Safe Libraries assembled to protest on the library lawn. They demanded that the Placer County Library Board rescind the decision and threatened to call upon the Placer County Board of Supervisors to reverse the ruling of the library board. Their attempts were unsuccessful.

In May 2000, at the annual Holland, Massachusetts, town meeting, the Reverend Tom Crouse of the Holland Congregational Church announced that the library contained a book entitled *It's Perfectly Normal* and stated it was a threat to the moral well-being of children as it contained "pictures that are clearly pornographic." He called for its removal from the library. He was joined by other residents when he spoke at the library board meeting on June 3, 2000; library trustees promised a decision on the issue within three weeks. The *Southbridge Evening News* reported on June 26, 2000, that at the June 24, 2000, board meeting, library trustee Mary Fife stated, "All of the trustees felt that the book should remain in the juvenile section, but were willing to move it to the adult section." Crouse and his followers were not happy with the decision and promised to pursue the matter further. Crouse stated, "I wish it were out of the library. I'm definitely not pleased with the town's acceptance of the book. I'm not going to go away on this."

In 2001, two families whose children attended Oceanview Elementary School in Anchorage, Alaska, filed separate complaints in which they objected to the presence of *It's Perfectly Normal* in the school libraries of 16 Anchorage elementary and middle schools. They charged that the book is overly frank in dealing with such topics as masturbation, birth control, giving birth, and homosexuality and called upon Anchorage School District officials to limit library borrowing privileges of the book to students who had parental permission. Complainants Rick and Andrea Steele contended that the information contained in the book "should come from parents," while complainants Eric and Joan Egeland wrote in their petition that elementary school students "need basic information about sex. They don't need pictures of different positions, and marriage is mentioned once in the whole book, while homosexual relationships are allocated an entire section." On September 18, 2001, the Anchorage School District's Controversial Issues Review Committee voted 10-3 to keep the book on school library shelves. However, district school superintendent Carol Comeau recommended restricted access on October 3, 2001, days before the school was to vote on the issue. On October 8, 2001, the night of the school board vote on the issue, more than 100 people attended the meeting, including parents, teachers, and librarians. The *Anchorage Daily News* reported that when one of the parents, Susan Ratliffe, a mother of three, asked those who favored restriction of the book to stand, a majority did. Julie Cheverton, a mother of six, stated, "I think we need to focus on whether or not little Johnny can read, not whether or not he can masturbate." One middle school teacher gave the opinion that the book should be restricted because "most young people would go home themselves and try it out to see what they have been missing." After hours of debate, the board voted 6-1 to restrict *It's Perfectly Normal* at the elementary school level.

In 2002, in Montgomery County, Texas, after 12 area residents appeared at an August 26 commission meeting to call for the removal of *It's Perfectly Normal*, charging that the book "promotes homosexuality and abortion," county commissioners ordered the removal of the book from all libraries in the county. Library director Jerilynn Williams, attending the meeting to discuss a proposed capital bond issue, spoke up in favor of the book and asked that the complainants and the commission postpone action and allow the book to remain in the young adult nonfiction section of the library until someone filed a formal complaint to initiate reconsideration-committee review. Commission member Alan Sadler stated in an article that appeared in the August 27, 2002, issue of the *Conroe Courier* that the book "clearly tries to steer the child toward being pro-homosexual or at least neutral." Ten days after the initial meeting, a formal complaint was filed and a materials review committee was formed. On September 10, the *Conroe Courier* reported that more than 200 people appeared at the county commission meeting, where commissioner Alan Sadler told the crowd that the commission intended to "look up the methodology at how children's books get on the shelves and probably amend the process to include citizens."

The emotional outcry over books on sex education in the Montgomery County library expanded from *It's Perfectly Normal* to include another book entitled *It's So Amazing*. Because of the increased concern, the county commissioners doubled the size of the original five-member reconsideration committee and appointed five additional citizens. The controversy drew the attention of the area Republican Leadership Council (RLC), which supported removal of the books and widened the focus by campaigning for the removal of replicas of art containing nudes from a "Roman-themed" mall in Shenandoah, Texas. The *Conroe Courier* also reported that RLC party leader Jim German condemned defenders of the book and stated that they "are same people who spat on us when we came home from Vietnam [and] who will cry over their dead son's or daughter's casket because some child molester thought it was perfectly normal to molest their child." Throughout the ongoing controversy, library director Jerilynn Williams worked with her staff to provide information on the book to citizens of the county, despite personal threats and the continued call for her termination by outraged residents of the county, many of whom also demanded that the Montgomery County Library withdraw from membership in the American Library Association. After several months, the review committee determined that the book should remain on the library shelves, a decision the county commissioners accepted.

In 2005, Fayetteville, Arkansas, parent Laurie Taylor filed a complaint with the Fayetteville public school district school board and demanded the removal of *It's Perfectly Normal* from their library system. At a school board meeting on February 24, 2005, Taylor, the mother of two daughters ages 12 and 13, argued that the book contained sexually explicit material and should not be available for students in a school library. She also urged the removal of two other books, *It's So Amazing*, also by Robie Harris, and *The Teenage Guy's Survival Guide* by Jeremy Daldry. The school board president Steve Percival acknowledged Taylor's comments and reminded the board members and citizens that the school district had a process in place to handle library book complaints, which included the formation of a "materials evaluation committee" to review the book and to make a recommendation. The committee members disagreed whether the book should be only available in the parent libraries of the middle schools and elementary schools or housed in the general circulation in the junior high libraries. In its report, the committee wrote, "The materials selection committee represents the right of the parent to guide, direct and/or restrict their student's reading choices; however, it is not a right that translates to making a choice for the students of other parents. Therefore, the book should not be withdrawn from access for all students." Nonetheless, the final decision prevented students from obtaining the books, because the committee and the district decided to place the three books in parent libraries, which restricted student access. During a special meeting on September 15, 2005, the Fayetteville school board voted 4-3 to rescind its earlier action to restrict the books and authorized the creation of a committee to review and to recommend an overhaul of the district book selection policy. The board took action after the attorney for the school district Rudy Moore, Jr., advised the members that, after reviewing case law, he believed that restricting student access to the books was indefensible. He cited a Cedarville case decided in 2003 by U.S. District Judge Hendren of Fayetteville in which Hendren ruled that "even a minimal loss of First Amendment rights is injurious to students" and declared that such restrictions have a "stigmatizing effect" on students. Moore warned the school board, "It will be difficult to defend the restrictions placed on the books in May." Although some board members wanted to take more time to consider the situation, one member made the motion to rescind the earlier vote and to follow the review committee's recommendations for all three books. The board also authorized school superintendent Bobby New to organize a small working committee consisting of four librarians, one principal, one central office administrator, one high school student, and one parent to review the district book selection policy, much of which had not been changed for more than 30 years. Further, the committee was empowered to develop a procedure by which parents could review new books before they were placed on the library shelves and to develop a mechanism to review a group of books rather than only a single title, as was currently the case.

FURTHER READING

American Library Association. "Jerilynn Adams Williams Receives 2003 PEN/ Newman's First Amendment Award." Available online. URL: http://www.ala.org/ Template.cfm?Section=archive&template=/contentmanagement/contentdisplay. cfm&ContentID=27921. Accessed December 11, 2009.

"Anchorage Committee Retains *It's Perfectly Normal." American Libraries Online*. Available online. URL: http://www.ala.org/ala/alonline/currentnews/newsarchive/2001/ september2001/anchoragecommittee.htm. Accessed December 11, 2009.

"Anchorage Parents Object to *Perfectly Normal* Book." *American Libraries Online*. Available online. URL: http://www.ala.org/ala/alonline/currentnews/newsarchive/2001/ september2001/ALA_print_layout_1_22150_22150.cfm. Accessed December 12, 2009.

"Anchorage Schools Restrict *It's Perfectly Normal* After All." *American Libraries Online*. Available online. URL: http://www.lita.org/ala/alonline/currentnews/ newsarchive/2001/october2001/ALA_print_layout_1_22104_22104.cfm. Accessed December 11, 2009.

Newsletter on Intellectual Freedom (November 1999): 171; (September 2000): 143; (January 2002): 13; (May 2005): 135–136; (November 2005): 295–296; (March 2008): 77–80; (November 2008): 253–256.

Sherlin, Kit. "It's Only Normal to Question." *High Plains Reader*, October 11, 1997, pp. 6–7.

Sokolove, Michael. "Sex and the Censors." *Inquirer Magazine* (Philadelphia), March 9, 1997, 18+.

"Texans Further Stirred by Sex-Education Books." *American Libraries Online.* Available online. URL: http://www.ala.org/ala/alonline/currentnews/newsarchive/2002/september 2002/texansfurther.htm. Accessed December 11, 2009.

"Texas Commission Tries to Ban *It's Perfectly Normal.*" *American Libraries Online.* Available online. URL: http://www.ala.org/ala/alonline/currentnews/newsarchive/2002/september 2002/texascommission.htm. Accessed December 11, 2009.

"Texas Officials to Add Citizens to Materials-Review Committee." *American Libraries Online.* Available online. URL: http://www.ala.org/ala/alonline/currentnews/newsarchive/2002/september 2002/texasofficials.htm. Accessed December 11, 2009.

JANET MARCH

Author: Floyd Dell
Original date and place of publication: 1923, United States
Original publisher: Alfred A. Knopf
Literary form: Novel

SUMMARY

Janet March represented, in the words of author Floyd Dell, "an attempt to present a characteristic modern girl truly against her social-historical background." The novel stirred controversy throughout the United States for its frank account of the sexual coming of age of the female protagonist, a smart but vaguely discontented child of a successful Midwestern family. Dell hoped to make Janet his representative of the generation of young American adults, young people who had grown up in an America that had lost its earlier patriarchal framework but which had failed to create a new social order.

The novel is divided into four parts: Book One—"Once Upon a Time," Book Two—"Janet Herself," Book Three—"Roger," and Book Four—"Janet and Roger." The novel is a psychological study of a young girl's growing awareness of the world, and sex is at the heart of Janet's struggle for maturity. Her adventures include numerous impersonal sexual encounters with "respectable" boys as well as illicit love affairs, one of which leads to pregnancy and an abortion. Although unsettled by the experience, Janet refuses to feel guilty and, instead, she replays happily in her mind the afternoon of lovemaking that led to her pregnancy. In that passage, Janet recalls their sex as

> a rite that took one back out of civilization into some earlier world, it was a solemn and sacred ceremonial worship of nature. And it was the satisfying of some deep impersonal need, like hunger, like thirst, like the wish for sleep; it was rest, healing, quietness after tumult. . . . soaring into perilous heights of ecstasy, alone.

153

She continues to have affairs, engaging in relationships that reveal the confused mix of loneliness, adventurousness, innocence, and curiosity that characterize her discovery of life. When she becomes pregnant a second time, the father of her baby is Roger Leland, a man nearly twice her age whom she wants to marry.

CENSORSHIP HISTORY

Janet March shocked readers and reviewers in 1923 with its open depiction of abortion, free love, and sexual searching. In an incident that upset Dell, his literary hero and friend Upton Sinclair reviled the book in an article that appeared nationwide in Hearst newspapers. Calling the book "scandalous," Sinclair charged Dell with being too sympathetic in his portrayal of Janet's sexual curiosity and with failing to mention the possibility of disease in her sexual adventuring. Such criticism drove sales of the book up to 15,000 copies in only two months.

Soon after its publication in October 1923, the novel was banned in Boston under the "gentleman's agreement" that existed between the Watch and Ward Society and the Board of Trade of Boston Book Merchants. The two groups formed a joint committee to review works that had raised objections. When the representatives of both groups on the committee agreed that a particular book was in violation of the obscenity statutes, the board of trade warned its members. Anxious to avoid negative publicity, many dealers simply withdrew the book from sale, and newspapers in Boston also cooperated by refusing to advertise or to review such books.

In December 1923, John Sumner and the New York Society for the Suppression of Vice lodged a formal complaint with the New York City district attorney, charging that the book was "obscene." The office of the district attorney then informed publisher Alfred A. Knopf that steps might soon be taken to ban the book and to prosecute Knopf for publishing *Janet March*. Instead of fighting the threat, Knopf promised to cease printing further copies of the book and withdrew the book. The publisher also issued a statement that the action had been taken "rather than have it attain a large sale through a possible censorship court action." The author initially accepted the seemingly high-minded action, but he stated in his 1933 autobiography, *Homecoming*, that the publisher had let him down badly. Knopf claimed that this was its only recourse because Sumner's seeming omnipotence in the 1920s "made surrender the only feasible course," but the low number of convictions in cases brought by the vice society and the strong defeat of the "Clean Books" campaign of 1923–25 contradicted that fear. Advised by lawyers that various items in the original novel might be grounds for a jail sentence, Dell reluctantly acquiesced and later revised the novel, which was reissued by George Doran in its expurgated version.

FURTHER READING

Boyer, Paul S. *Purity in Print: The Vice-Society Movement and Book Censorship in America.* New York: Scribner, 1968.

Clayton, Douglas. *Floyd Dell: The Life and Times of an American Rebel.* Chicago: Ivan R. Dee, 1994.

"The Editor Recommends—." *The Bookman* 57 (February 1924): 459.

Hart, John E. *Floyd Dell.* New York: Twayne, 1971.

JUDE THE OBSCURE

Author: Thomas Hardy
Original dates and places of publication: 1895, England; 1895, United States
Original publishers: Osgood, McIlvaine (England); Harper (United States)
Literary form: Novel

SUMMARY

Jude the Obscure is the story of a man whose ambition and desire for knowledge are at war with his personal desires. Jude Fawley, a restless young man whose wanderings reflect his unsatisfied longings, works painfully to educate himself and to learn the classics and theology after his schoolmaster, Richard Phillotson, leaves for the great university town of Christminster. To earn his living, Jude becomes a stonemason and leaves Wessex for Christminster, where he hopes to advance his education as he works. His relationships with two significantly different women impede his progress.

Jude meets Arabella Donn, the daughter of a pig farmer, before he reaches Christminster. She and other young women are washing pig parts after slaughtering, and she captures Jude's attention by throwing a pig's "pizzle" (penis) at his head. Attracted by her appearance, Jude returns the missile of cold flesh to her and the two engage in a romantic dalliance while the "pizzle" lies draped over the nearby bridge railing. A short while later, Arabella seduces Jude and they marry. Unsuited for each other beyond their initial physical passion, the two eventually separate, though not before having a child.

Free again to pursue his goal of education, Jude goes to Christminster and meets his cousin, Sue Bridehead, an androgynous woman whose intellect and efforts for women's rights and the equality of the sexes make her a "new woman." Although the two are in love, Sue chooses to marry Jude's old schoolmaster, Phillotson. The marriage is not happy and, after Sue leaves Phillotson, she and Jude live together. They have two children who are murdered by Father Time, Jude's child with Arabella, and Father Time then commits suicide. When Sue leaves Jude, he returns to Arabella but does not live for long. Jude dies at the age of 30, wasting away within sight of the college that he had so desperately wanted to attend but which had rejected him. After discovering his dead body, Arabella decides to wait until the next morning to tell anyone, in order to enjoy a night at the festival with Jude's friends.

CENSORSHIP HISTORY

Hardy consented to the bowdlerization of several of his works before they reached the public, thus removing much of the potential controversy. Malcolm Cowley writes that because Hardy "adapted himself to the public" he became "a scandal even in academic circles." *Jude the Obscure* was serialized by *Harper's New Monthly* magazine in the United States but only after the author was willing to make changes in the novel. Pinion records that editor H. M. Alden reminded Hardy that "the Magazine must contain nothing which could not be read aloud in any family circle." Before the monthly installments were published, Hardy had to change the title to *Hearts Insurgent* and present as adopted orphans the two children who are born outside of marriage to Jude and Sue.

The excised material was restored when the novel was published in 1895, and *Jude the Obscure* was more savagely attacked by reviewers than any of Hardy's other works. Martin Seymour-Smith noted that reviewers called it a "grimy story" that was "steeped in sex" and accused Hardy of "wallowing in the mire." The London *World* labeled him "Hardy the Degenerate," and the *Guardian* condemned the novel as "a shameful nightmare to be forgotten as soon as possible." Novelist Mrs. Oliphant wrote in *Blackwood* that *Jude the Obscure* was "foul in detail" and claimed never to "have read a more disgusting book." Bishop How of Wakefield professed that he burned his copy of the novel and urged others throughout England to do the same. The bishop objected to the "crude image" of Arabella's means of introducing herself to Jude, as well as the hanging suicide of little Father Time. How was also successful in having the novel withdrawn from W. H. Smith's circulating library. The popular circulating libraries had significant influence on book sales during the second half of the 19th century. Novels were expensive and authors made little money in sales unless the circulating libraries accepted their books.

In 1903, Hardy revised the novel before it was published by his new English publishers, Macmillan and Company. The scene of the thrown pig pizzle was greatly modified out of concern for future sales. The references to the "clammy flesh" of the pizzle were deleted, as were references to it as the "indecent thing," "the lump of offal," "the fragment of pig," and "the limp object." He also toned down Arabella's seductive behavior and sensual nature.

Although Hardy lived for 33 years after *Jude the Obscure* was first published, it was his final novel. He lost heart when Bishop How burned the book, "the experience completely curing me of further interest in novel-writing." He acknowledges in the 1890 essay "Candour in English Fiction" that presenting morally imperfect characters who work out their destinies in a natural manner might result in a novel that contains cruelty, envy, or other evils, but that is merely reality. That such writing might have a negative influence on the weak-minded is also reality. As Hardy wrote in "Candour in English Fiction":

> Of the effects of such sincere presentation on weak minds, when the courses of the characters are not exemplary, and the rewards and punishments ill adjusted to deserts, it is not our duty to consider too closely. A novel which does moral injury to a dozen imbeciles, and has bracing results upon a thousand intellects of normal vigor, can justify its existence; and probably a novel was never written by the purest-minded author for which there could not be found some moral invalid or other whom it was capable of harming.

He also blames the libraries and the magazines for censorship, because they claimed that their readers were younger members of the family and felt it necessary to take precautions that would not be needed for adults. Inevitably, he concedes that satisfying "the prudery of censorship" is "the fearful price" that he has to pay "for the privilege of writing in the English language—no less a price than the complete extinction, in the mind of every mature and penetrating reader, of sympathetic belief in his personages."

FURTHER READING

Cowley, Malcolm. *After the Genteel Tradition.* Rev. ed. Carbondale: Southern Illinois University, 1964.

Hardy, Thomas. "Candour in Fiction." In *Thomas Hardy's Personal Writings: Prefaces, Literary Opinions, Reminiscences,* edited by Harold Orel, 125–133. Lawrence: University of Kansas Press, 1966.

Pinion, F. B. *Thomas Hardy: His Life and Friends.* New York: St. Martin's, 1992.

Seymour-Smith, Martin. *Hardy: A Biography.* New York: St. Martin's, 1994.

JURGEN: A COMEDY OF JUSTICE

Author: James Branch Cabell
Original date and place of publication: 1919, United States
Original publisher: Robert M. McBride & Co.
Literary form: Novel

SUMMARY

Jurgen is an exercise in double entendre that resembles THE DECAMERON in its view of the human preoccupation with sex, as well as in its subtle humor and reliance on fantasy and suggestion to ridicule human pretensions. The novel portrays the gods as vain, dense, and inept, while it depicts the concept of the ideal woman as merely a fantasy of man's imagination.

The title character is a poetry-writing pawnbroker who is given the opportunity to journey through dream kingdoms in the body of a young man while his mind remains mature. He is on a Faustian quest to satisfy his yearning for perfect love, beauty, and holiness, as well as to locate his aging wife, Lisa, whom he had wished would go to the devil and who was spirited away by the god-devil Koshchei. During his quest, Jurgen experiences numerous romantic adventures, both with women whom he once loved and with mythical women, such as Guenevere, Arthur's queen. His sexual encounters are often described, as in his experience with Guenevere: "He remembered always the feel of that warm and slender and yielding body, naked under the thin shift, as his arms first went about her."

The suggestive technique of the language is best illustrated in the episode with Guenevere during which Jurgen captures the magic sword Caliburn, used by the author as a phallic symbol throughout the novel. When Jurgen later meets Queen Sylvia Fereu, he offers her protection and praises its merits.

> "It is undoubtedly a very large sword," said Queen Sylvia. "There is something in what you advance."
>
> "There is a great deal in what I advance, I can assure you. It is the most natural and most penetrating kind of logic; and I wish merely to discharge a duty."

He is involved in a more erotic mythical encounter on the isle of Cocaigne with Anaitis, the daughter of the Sun. Before his marriage to her, Jurgen is given a ceremonial bath by four girls, who caress him throughout "with the tongue, the hair, the fingernails, and the tips of the breasts." For the marriage ceremony, Anaitis wears a tunic that "had twenty-two openings, so as to admit all imaginable caresses."

The novel uses symbolism, wit, and humor to provide discussions of philosophy. Jurgen visits Hell but leaves because it is too democratic. He finds Heaven too autocratic and concludes that there is no justice in Heaven because all is love. After his numerous sexually stimulating experiences, he happily welcomes back his wife, Lisa.

CENSORSHIP HISTORY

Jurgen was the subject of the first celebrated censorship case of the 1920s, and its author was the first prominent American author to have his works tested in court on charges of obscenity. The novel was highly praised by the literary community when it first appeared on September 17, 1919, and it was in its third edition after selling 4,000 copies when a letter to the editor published in the New York *Tribune* on January 3, 1920, drew attention to the sensual possibilities of the novel. The writer, Walter J. Kinsley, observed that Cabell "has said everything about the mechanics of passion and said it prettily" and cautioned that "once the trick of transposing the key is mastered—i.e., substituting sex words for poetic words—you can see the extreme sensuality that runs through the book."

Cabell had scattered double entendres throughout the novel in an attempt to get the work by the censors, and he even agreed to censor *Jurgen* before its first publication after his publisher warned him that many sexual references were still too easily perceived. Thus, in a prepublication letter to Burton Rascoe, Cabell noted that he had made 30 additional changes that resulted in "no real loss to literature."

John Sumner, secretary of the New York Society for the Suppression of Vice, saw a clipping of the letter and on January 14, 1920, sent society representatives with a warrant to the publisher's office, where they seized all plates and copies of the book. At a formal hearing held on January 23, 1920, Cabell's editor at McBride, Guy Holt, was charged with violating the antiobscenity provisions of the New York State Penal Code, and the court listened to a formal charge containing a long list of page numbers but heard no lines quoted from the novel for to have done so would have been "offensive to the court" and "improper to be placed in the court records." Authors and publishers then signed and circulated a letter of protest to exhibit their approval and support of the novel. *Jurgen* remained officially out of circulation for two years while the publisher waited for the case to go to trial. When the case went to court on October 16, 1922, Judge Charles C. Nott directed the jury to return a verdict of acquittal. In the decision, Judge Nott indicated that the nonrealistic character of the novel supported the argument against the obscenity charge:

> The most that can be said against the book is that certain passages therein may be considered in a veiled and subtle way of immorality, but such sugges-
> tions are delicately conveyed and the whole atmosphere of the story is of such an unreal and supernatural nature that even these suggestions are free from the evils accompanying suggestiveness in more realistic works.

The judge also referred in his ruling to medieval legends discussed in Cabell's preface as proof of the serious and artistic nature of the work. The irony is that the preface was facetious, and the author had only pretended to trace the "Jurgen legends" that he had made up to lend an aura of respectability to the book. Sumner eventually had the dismissal reversed, but Cabell's literary reputation became widespread, and the notoriety made his novel a best seller.

FURTHER READING

"Again the Literary Censor." *Nation*, September 25, 1920, p. 343.

Barlow, Samuel L. M. "The Censor of Art." *North American Review* 213 (March 1921): 346–350.

Boyer, Paul S. *Purity in Print: The Vice-Society Movement and Book Censorship in America.* New York: Scribner, 1968.

Colum, Padraic, and Margaret Freeman Cabell, eds. *Between Friends: Letters of James Branch Cabell and Others.* New York: Harcourt Brace & World, 1962.

Holt, Guy, ed. *Jurgen and the Law: A Statement with Exhibits, Including the Court's Opinion and the Brief of the Defendants on Motion to Direct an Acquittal.* New York: McBride, 1923.

Kallen, Horace M. "Protean Censorship." *Freeman,* June 29, 1921, pp. 370–372.

JUSTINE, OR THE MISFORTUNES OF VIRTUE

Author: Marquis de Sade
Original dates and places of publication: 1797, France; 1965, United States
Original publishers: En Hollande (France); Grove Press (United States)
Literary form: Novel

JULIETTE, HER SISTER, OR THE PROSPERITIES OF VICE

Author: Marquis de Sade
Original dates and places of publication: 1930, France; 1965, United States
Original publishers: Maurice Heine (France); Grove Press (United States)
Literary form: Novel

SUMMARY

The two interrelated works, created as opposites, form one of the most ambitious and outrageous works of literature ever written. *Justine,* written in 1787, while de Sade was imprisoned in the Bastille, first appeared in print in 1791, published privately in Paris. In 1797, the two works were published as a 10-volume set, four volumes of *Justine* and six volumes of *Juliette.* While Justine is virtue personified, Juliette is the embodiment of evil. The greater the crime, the more depraved the debauchery, the greater Juliette's pleasure. Her crimes include rape, incest, murder and even the defilement of Pope Pius VI, who is not permitted to enjoy her sexual favors until he has performed a black mass in St. Peter's Basilica. De Sade also pairs her with numerous major and minor personages of his time, including the French politician Saint Fond, Queen Caroline of England, and King Ferdinand of Naples.

The basic story of the combined works is that sisters Justine and Juliette are brought up at the Panthemont, where "for many a long year the prettiest and most libertine women gracing Paris have regularly emerged from that convent." The nuns in that convent regularly speak of "frigging" and utter such interjections as "O fuck!" The 13-year-old Juliette and her slightly younger sister soon learn about dildoes, sexual excesses, and strange rituals involving defecation and urination. Priests and bishops break their vows of celibacy with great frequency, and the nuns procure the most attractive of the young novices to please these men.

The sisters are forced to leave the convent when their parents die, and they make their way in an evil and corrupt world peopled by cross-dressing aristocrats, lords who sexually abuse their valets, and men who seek to prey upon the young women. In this world where murder is an aphrodisiac, every possible debauchery occurs, even bestiality with pecking geese, but de Sade punctuates the long passages of sexual activity with equally long digressions on the existence of God and the nature of man. Juliette thrives on evil and prospers, but Justine becomes the victim of everyone with whom she has contact. Despite increased violence against her, she remains unwilling to conform to the vice-ridden world, which makes her appear incorrigible. At the end, Justine dies when she is struck by a bolt of lightning that enters her mouth and exits through her vagina. Four libertines sexually desecrate the corpse while her sister Juliette watches and masturbates.

CENSORSHIP HISTORY

The 10 volumes telling the combined stories of Justine and Juliette were available freely in major bookstores in Paris for about a year after their publication in 1797. Then orders were issued by the French government to seize all copies and to prosecute any bookseller found dealing with the work. For nearly a century and a half afterward, the work was banned in France, although it circulated clandestinely in private editions.

In 1930, Maurice Heine in Paris issued a new edition of the combined novels, limited to 475 copies that were sold with discretion. Authorities under the Fourth Republic in France prosecuted the publisher and convicted him of committing an "outrage to public morals." In an essay that was included in this edition, Guillaume Apollinaire wrote that de Sade was "the freest spirit that ever lived," and he asserted that de Sade chose women as the protagonists of his novels as a means of professing his views that women should be as free as men. He wrote,

> Justine is woman as she has formerly been, enslaved, miserable, and less than human; her opposite, Juliette, represents the woman whose advent he anticipated, as a being of whom minds have yet no conception, who is arising out of humanity, who shall have wings and who shall renew the world.

Justine alone has also been subject to several instances of censorship. In Ireland, on January 21, 1936, a prohibition order was published in the

Iris Oifigiuil, "the only official source from which booksellers [and readers] might learn of a new prohibition order," in which all articles blacklisted by the Irish Board of Censors were listed. According to the Censorship of Publications Bill of 1928, "the notice in *Iris Oifigiuil* should be sufficient evidence in the courts of summary jurisdiction as to the character of the publication," despite the acknowledgment by justices quoted in Adams's thorough study of Irish censorship laws that "this gazette is not a publication which booksellers are addicted to reading." The Irish Board of Censors found de Sade's novel "obscene" and filled with "illicit sex behavior." The work was officially banned from sale in Ireland until the introduction of the Censorship Publications Bill in 1967 reduced to 12 years the duration of a prohibition order, and the work was among 5,000 titles released from the list of banned books.

In 1964, New Zealand Customs officers seized *Justine* and two works by Guillaume Apollinaire, MEMOIRS OF A YOUNG RAKEHELL and *The Debauched Hospodar,* originally published in one volume by Olympia Press in 1962. The importer, a Mr. D. W. Cheer of Christchurch, disputed the seizure, and the matter went before a magistrate, who issued an order prohibiting the publication of the titles of the books. The Indecent Publications Tribunal did not continue this order but did refuse to allow citations in the court records of passages that the defense counsel read in court. In testimony, the comptroller of Customs claimed that the books had been detained under the provisions of the Customs Act of 1913 as "Prohibited Imports," because they were indecent. As required by Section 12 of the Indecent Publications Act of 1963, proceedings for the condemnation were instituted by the comptroller before a magistrate who, in turn, was required to turn the matter over to the Indecent Publications Tribunal to determine the manner in which the books might be viewed as "indecent":

> whether the books were indecent within the meaning of the Act, or indecent in the hands of persons under a specified age, or indecent unless circulation was restricted to specified persons or classes of persons.

The counsel for the defense argued that even if a general ban were to be levied on the books, the importer should be free of restriction because he was a "serious collector of all sorts of books," with a library of from 5,000 to 6,000 volumes. Called to testify, the importer expressed his view "of the value of the books to a student of literature."

The tribunal placed *Justine* into an entirely different category than Apollinaire's novels, noting that it was "a well-known work written about 1787 whilst the author was in the Bastille." Acknowledging that the novel related "many sexual excesses and cruelties," they justified the work as being "a representation of de Sade's own character as depicting his disgust at conditions prevailing." Thus, on March 4, 1965, the tribunal concluded that the novel was "a seriously written work, somewhat philosophic in nature" and asserted that "though the episodes related are revolting the language used to describe them is not foul or offensive." Although the work was declared "indecent" as a narrative, "its circulation is restricted to psychologists or psychiatrists or any adult bona fide student of literature or philosophy."

FURTHER READING

Adams, Michael. *Censorship: The Irish Experience*. Tuscaloosa: University of Alabama Press, 1968.

Ciardi, John. "The Marquis de Sade II." *Saturday Review*, October 2, 1965, p. 36.

Lever, Maurice. *Marquis de Sade: A Biography*. New York: HarperCollins, 1993.

Perry, Stuart. *The Indecent Publications Tribunal: A Social Experiment*. London: Whitcombe and Tombs, 1965.

Thomas, Donald Serrell. *The Marquis de Sade*. Boston: New York Graphic Society, 1976.

Wainhouse, Austryn. "Foreword." *The Marquis de Sade: Juliette*. New York: Grove, 1968.

THE *KAMA SUTRA* OF VATSYAYANA

Author: Vatsyayana (translated by Sir Richard F. Burton and F. F. Arbuthnot)

Original dates and places of publication: 1883, Switzerland; 1962, United States

Publishers: Kama Shastra Society; E. P. Dutton

Literary form: Marriage manual

SUMMARY

The *Kama Sutra* of Vatsyayana is a Sanskrit classic written in India, circa 300 B.C., and it was well known among the educated classes. The English traveler and adventurer Sir Richard Burton translated the work into English in 1883, but the nature of the work limited publication to private editions.

The origin of the work is complicated. Also known as the *Kama Shastra* and the *Ananga Ranga*, the work is an Indian marriage manual. The manuscript used by Burton for translation was actually written by a 16th-century poet named Kalyana Malla, who drew much of his material on erotic subjects from earlier writers, particularly the sage Vatsyayana, who was largely credited as being the ancient author of the *Kama Sutra*. In the Indian vernacular, Kama was the love god, and Vatsyayana's writings were contained in a text known as the *Kama Sutra*, or "Love Verses," a manual of erotic instruction.

Burton had corresponded with Foster Fitzgerald Arbuthnot, who had possession of a copy of the work and had decided to have the erotic classic translated into English. They hired an Indian scholar named Bhagvanlal Indraji to create a rough draft in English, and then Burton polished the text and imposed his own view of how a man must treat a woman. As Rice observes, "Thus, many sections of the English version of the *Kama Shastra*

163

come not from Kalyana Malla's Sanskrit but from Burton's fertile brain, developing and improving upon a text that some Western scholars believe is poorer and more pedantic than its translation."

The work contains charts of how and where the man is to touch the woman, from forehead to big toe (the latter assuming the symbolic role of the clitoris) to provide "the touches by which passion is satisfied." The manual also contains significant use of scratching, biting, kissing, and chewing, actions that Burton justified by pointing out that the marriages in India often took place between children, so such "play" occurred in the process of becoming familiar with each other.

The following passage from the *Kama Sutra* has been cited by critics as being "a startlingly apparent" example of material that results in psychological disintegration:

> On the occasion of a "high congress" the Mrigi (Deer) woman should lie down in such a way as to widen her yoni, while in a "low congress" the Hastini (Elephant) woman should lie down so as to contract hers. But in an "equal congress" they should lie down in the natural position. What is said above concerning the Mrigi and the Hastini applies also to the Vadawa (Mare) woman. In a "low congress" the woman should particularly make use of medicine, to cause her desire to be satisfied quickly.
> The Deer-woman has the following three ways of lying down:
> The widely opened position.
> The yawning position.
> The position of the wife of Indra.
> When she lowers her head and raises her middle parts, it is called the "widely opened position." At such a time, the man should apply some unguent, so as to make the entrance easy.

In addition to providing instructions for various sexual positions, of which Burton commented that "one has to be an athlete to engage in," the work also provides women with instructions in how they may use men. The final sections relate "On the Means of Getting Money" and "Subjugating the Hearts of Others."

CENSORSHIP HISTORY

Burton and his collaborators in the Kama Shastra Society anticipated attempts of censorship as they approached the publication of the *Kama Sutra*. Their pretense was that the book was printed outside of England and that it was intended for scholars who wished to study "the great unknown literature of the East." Furthermore, by pricing the books at the equivalent in today's money of $200 each, the publishers also guaranteed that their readers had to be wealthy. The cover contained the words "For Private Circulation Only," and the place of publication was listed as Benares. After their problems in 1875, when the English printers refused to complete production of the book, Burton and his partners used two different printers to prevent confiscation of all copies should the authorities stage a raid. Soon after the first copies appeared in 1883, pirated copies appeared in Paris, Brussels, and the English Midlands.

The *Kama Sutra* was not sold openly in England, but pirated copies did appear in the United States. After spending 60 days in jail in 1930 for distributing unexpurgated copies of ULYSSES, Samuel Roth turned to more profitable publications and produced editions of the *Kama Sutra* and THE PERFUMED GARDEN. Agents of the New York Society for the Suppression of Vice brought complaint against Roth, who was prosecuted and sentenced to 90 days in jail for selling those books.

In hearings before the Subcommittee on Postal Operations of the Committee on Post Office and Civil Service in 1962, Robert W. Edwards, Deputy Collector of Customs, United States Customs Mail Division in Boston, testified that the *Kama Sutra* "bears the dubious distinction of being the filthiest book published today. . . . In my opinion, the human mind is scarcely able to withstand the impact of the overwhelming obscenity and sexually based desire for torture in the *Kama Sutra*." The President's Commission on Obscenity and Pornography recommended that books of its sort be "banned from the mails."

FURTHER READING

Lockhart, William B., and Robert C. McClure. "Censorship of Obscenity: The Developing Constitutional Standards." *Minnesota Law Review* 45 (November 1960): 19.
Rice, Edward. *Captain Sir Richard Francis Burton*. New York: Scribner, 1990.
Thomas, Donald. *A Long Time Burning: The History of Literary Censorship in England*. New York: Praeger, 1969.
United States President's Commission on Obscenity and Pornography. *The Report of the Commission on Obscenity and Pornography*. New York: Random House, 1970.

THE KREUTZER SONATA

Author: Leo Tolstoy
Original dates and places of publication: 1889, Russia; 1890, United States (translation)
Original publishers: Private (Russia); Pollard Publishing Co. (United States)
Literary form: Novel

SUMMARY

The Kreutzer Sonata is a novella that begins on a train on which the protagonist Posdnicheff tells his fellow travelers that he has killed his wife, whom he suspected of adultery. He slowly builds his case by blaming social conventions that he views as false and disastrous, beginning with an attack on romantic love. On the one hand, Posdnicheff claims that men feel lust, not love, and that, for them, a lifetime of love is impossible: "Every man feels what you call love, whenever he meets a pretty girl." As he rants, he blames doctors and others who encourage unmarried men to seek out prostitutes "for health's sake" and asserts that the lack of emotional involvement with and responsibility for one's partner in "voluptuousness without love" is immoral. The narrator has not always existed on so high a moral plain and admits having earlier been a "drunkard and a libertine."

> I did not consider, then, that debauchery did not consist in physical acts alone, but that the real wrong was in the relaxing of laws of morality with the woman with whom one has carnal relations. I even looked upon this loosening of moral ties as a thing to be proud of.

He claims that "woman has forged for herself, out of her charms, a weapon so powerful that no man, whether young or old, can resist her." He criticizes women for using sex as a weapon and contends that they deliberately appeal to man's sensual nature and regard men as mere sex objects; he includes in his criticism mothers who raise their daughters to marry rich men at any cost. Although Posdnicheff recognizes the efforts that society has made to liberate women, "they emancipate women in universities and in law courts, but continue to regard her as an object of enjoyment." He also observes that a woman, educated or otherwise, "is happy and attains all she can desire when she has bewitched man."

Marriage fails to produce moral behavior, and Posdnicheff claims that many "people marry regarding marriage as nothing but copulation. . . . [T]he husband and wife merely deceive people by pretending to be monogamists, while living polygamously." He claims that he and his wife had experienced "excessive sensuality" early in their marriage, leaving them "disenchanted, like two selfish beings." Therefore, he was moved to physically kill his wife as he had killed her spiritually long before.

CENSORSHIP HISTORY

The Kreutzer Sonata was among the first contemporary works by foreign writers to be involved in litigation in the United States. The novel had been banned from sale soon after publication in Russia by Czar Nicholas II for "immoral content." Tolstoy's wife appealed personally to the czar, and he relented in 1891 to allow the novel to appear in an expensive-to-produce compendium of the author's works.

In 1890, the postmaster general banned the work from general distribution and mailing through second- and third-class mail in the United States after an assistant attorney general declared it to be "of an obscene character." The impetus for the banning was a complaint initiated by Anthony Comstock, secretary of the New York Society for the Suppression of Vice, which charged Tolstoy's diatribe against promiscuity as being "pornographic" and "obscene," because it spoke of prostitution, sensuality, adultery, and lust. Yet the work contains no erotic scenes and speaks in condemnatory tones of lust and debauchery. The post office department in New York would permit the work to be sent only if it was placed in a sealed package and stamped with first-class postage. An editorial in the *American Law Review* observed that publicity generated by Civil Service commissioner Theodore Roosevelt calling Tolstoy a "sexual and moral pervert" and others who spoke out loudly against the book "resulted in the very object which it was intended to prevent, in giving enormous circulation to the book." The work received support from critics, who defended the book as one of literary importance. The question posed by Horace Traubel was echoed by many: "With Tolstoy in danger, who is exempt?"

As soon as the ban was enacted, street vendors in New York loaded pushcarts with copies and large signs stating "Suppressed." When they were arrested by police and their total stock of 240 books was confiscated, the vendors revealed that the Pollard Publishing Company had provided expurgated copies that contained none of the original offensive material. Publisher Walter Pollard confirmed their story and proved to the court that the books were bowdlerized copies. The judge dropped charges but insisted that the vendors remove the signs.

Later that year, a Philadelphia vendor was indicted for selling a translation of the novel and taken to court. When the case went to trial in *In re Arentsen*, 26 W.N.C. 359 (Q.S. Ct. Phil., 1890), the prosecutor pointed out that both the U.S. Post Office and the Russian government had censored the book. Despite the earlier judgments, Judge M. Russell Thayer, president judge of Common Pleas Court No. 4, declared the book "not obscene," and he wrote in the court decision that neither the post office officials nor the Russian czar had "ever been recognized in this country as a binding authority in questions of either law or literature." Instead, the judge pointed to both the content of the work and Tolstoy's preface, noting that the author's purpose appeared to encourage chastity:

> There is nothing in this book which can by any possibility be said to commend licentiousness or to make it in any respect attractive, or to tempt any one to its commission. On the contrary, all his teachings paint lewdness and immorality in the most revolting colors.

In his decision, Thayer declared the novel to possess "very little dramatic interest or literary merit" and acknowledged as bizarre Tolstoy's recommendation of complete celibacy for all people, married or otherwise, but he also stated that "it cannot, on that account, be called an obscene libel."

FURTHER READING

Flower, Benjamin O. "Conservatism and Sensualism: An Unhallowed Alliance." *Arena* 3 (December 1890): 126–128.

———. "The Postmaster-General and the Censorship of Morals." *Arena* 2 (October 1890): 540–552.

Gustafson, Richard F. *Leo Tolstoy, Resident and Stranger: A Study in Fiction and Theology.* Princeton, N.J.: Princeton University Press, 1986.

"*Kreutzer Sonata.*" *American Law Review* 25 (January–February 1891): 102–104.

Traubel, Horace L. "Freedom to Write and to Print." *Poet-Lore* 2 (October 1890): 529–531.

LADIES IN THE PARLOR

Author: Jim Tully
Original date and place of publication: 1935, United States
Original publisher: Greenberg
Literary form: Novel

SUMMARY

Ladies in the Parlor recounts the story of Leora Blair, a poverty-stricken young girl from the American Midwest, who enters a life of prostitution to escape her bleak early existence. The novel presents affecting details of her life in the small railroad town on the Ohio River, where she does everything possible to help her overburdened mother and suffering brothers and sisters, as well as to escape her brutal father. Tully also paints a sympathetic portrait of the prostitutes in the Chicago brothel where Leora eventually works, showing the women to be human beings who, although mercenary, are often the victims of their clients.

Leora has her first sexual experience at the age of 15 with Dr. Jonas Farway, whose seduction she encourages. Although she desires his affection and feels sexually attracted to him, she is also conscious that he has the means to help her family and to lessen their dire economic circumstances. After they are alone and he holds her close, "Her curiosity was stronger than his desire. An hour later they rose. Her body glowed. She forgot the slightest hurt he had caused." When they have sex a second time, "he was more patient. She responded slowly with the rhythm of her body. He crushed her to him, exclaiming, 'My God, my God.' "

Despite Farway's desire for her, Leora leaves for Chicago, where she enters a brothel owned by Mother Rosenbloom, a woman of many eccentricities. The prostitutes are friendly to Leora, and their language in describing customers and their past experiences is suggestive, containing anatomical references and the frequent use of "whore." Leora falls in love with powerful political boss Judge Slattery, an old friend of Mother Rosenbloom, and they enjoy one night together.

> She then removed her clothes and lay quiet, expectant, beside him.
> His touch burned her body.
> She half swooned under his embrace.
> Moments of wild delirium followed. Every particle of her body responded in ecstatic rhythm.
> When it was over, she held him close for a long time.

But her happiness is brief. By morning, the judge is dead and Leora is, once again, left to make her way in the world alone.

CENSORSHIP HISTORY

Ladies in the Parlor was one of eight American-authored works that became the subject of obscenity cases between 1934 and 1944, after the ban against importation of erotic classics was eased by the 1930 amendment of the Tariff Act and censors turned their attention to American works.

Other works that suffered in this period were Lillian Hellman's *The Children's Hour*, Erskine Caldwell's TRAGIC GROUND, James T. Farrell's *A WORLD I NEVER MADE*, William Faulkner's THE WILD PALMS, James M. Cain's SERENADE, Lillian Smith's *STRANGE FRUIT* and Kathleen Winsor's FOREVER AMBER. Three of these novels—*Tragic Ground, Strange Fruit,* and *Forever Amber*—became best sellers after their challenges in court.

The sexual encounter between the 15-year-old Leora and the middle-aged Dr. Jonas Farway was one of two incidents in the book that led to its condemnation, even though it is more suggestive than explicit. The subdued description of the sexual encounter between the prostitute Leora and Judge Slattery was the second incident identified in complaints.

Defenders of the book suggested that, because the material in *Ladies in the Parlor* was far less explicit than many books that the New York courts had previously cleared, the real reason for its ban may have been its nonliterary style, the concern with the characters and events in a house of prostitution, or its failure to make a moral judgment against prostitutes.

In a hearing on August 16, 1935, held in Yorkville Court, Magistrate Jonah Goldstein declared that *Ladies in the Parlor* was indecent and scheduled a trial for the defending corporation Greenberg Publishers Inc. in Special Sessions. Charles J. Bamberger, an agent of the New York Society for the Suppression of Vice, had obtained a copy of the book at Macy's department store for use in lodging the complaint. Magistrate Goldstein made the following statement in sending the case to trial:

> The manner in which the subject is treated, in my opinion, constitutes a violation of the law. You can call a spade a spade, but you don't have to give it a name that savors of the sewer. Throughout the book there are many evidences

of emphasizing dirt in the raw, and the book is barren of any effort to treat the subject in a literary way.

When the case appeared before the Special Sessions court, Bamberger insisted that more than thirty passages in the book were obscene. Although the court declared the novel obscene in a 2 to 1 decision and the publisher was fined $50, Judge Frederick L. Hackenberg warned against such censorship. In his dissenting opinion, published in the *New York Times,* he wrote,

> The daring attitude of yesterday may be considered quite reactionary tomorrow. The function of literary effort reaches beyond a bedtime story with an obligatory happy ending. Enforced silence about disturbing facts does not clear the air. Even vulgar language is one of the acknowledged mediums of literary effort.

FURTHER READING

"Court Bans Tully Book." *New York Times,* November 1, 1935, p. 19.
"Tully Book 'Indecent'." *New York Times,* August 17, 1935, p. 17.

LADY CHATTERLEY'S LOVER

Author: D. H. Lawrence
Original dates and places of publication: 1928, Italy; 1959, United States
Original publishers: Orioli; Grove Press
Literary form: Novel

SUMMARY

Lady Chatterley's Lover conveys Lawrence's bitter and deep dissatisfaction with the stultifying effects of industrialization and modern sterile society upon the natural life of all English classes. In general, he portrays the manner in which the upper classes have become devitalized and the lower classes debased by the increasing artificiality of their emotional and physical relationships. The novel relates the experiences of a young woman named Connie Chatterley, married to a baronet who is paralyzed from the waist down after severe injuries incurred fighting in World War I. She is sexually frustrated and becomes increasingly dissatisfied with the artificial and sterile nature of the society in which she lives. A brief affair with a man within her husband Clifford's social circle proves to be unsatisfying and leaves her even more restless and unhappy.

Repelled by her husband's suggestion that she become pregnant by another man and produce a child whom he might make his heir, Connie turns further away from him. Instead, she feels attracted to their game-keeper, Mellors, Lawrence's example of the "natural man," whom society has neither devitalized nor debased. His coarse exterior and verbal expression mask a highly developed spiritual and intellectual independence, and the two become lovers. Their affair is deeply passionate and their lovemaking extremely tender, as Mellors gradually leads Connie to abandon her preconceived views of propriety and her inhibitions. A number of passages contain detailed and candid descriptions of their sexual pleasures and their uncensored utterances and descriptions of both genitals and body functions.

> "Th'art good cunt, though, aren't ter? Best bit o'cunt left on earth. When ter likes! When tha'rt willin'!"
> "What is cunt?" she asked.
> "An' doesn't ter know? Cunt! It's thee down theer; an' what I get when I'm i'side thee; it's a' as it is, all on't."
> "All on't," she teased. "Cunt! It's like fuck then."
> "Nay, nay! Fuck's only what you do. Animals fuck. But, cunt's a lot more than that. It's thee, dost see: an' tha'rt a lot besides an animal, aren't ter? even ter fuck! Cunt! Eh, that's the beauty o' thee, lass."

Such passages, although relevant to the plot and to the development of the characters, became the basis for numerous attempts to ban the novel.

At the end of the novel, Connie is pregnant with Mellors's child and plans to marry him after obtaining a divorce from Clifford.

CENSORSHIP HISTORY

Lady Chatterley's Lover was suppressed long before the case of *Grove Press v. Christenberry* went to trial in 1959. The decision was made to publish the novel in Italy in 1928 and then to send copies to subscribers in England to avoid censors. Publishing in this way made it impossible for Lawrence to obtain an international copyright, so the author lost substantial money through the appearance of numerous pirated editions. The United States government had declared the novel obscene in 1929, and the post office ruled the novel barred from the mails. Travelers returning from Europe with copies of the novel faced having the book confiscated by United States Customs. Objections to the novel arose over both the explicit sexual description in the novel and the language used by the characters. As Charles Rembar, the lawyer who defended the novel in the 1959 trial, observed in his account of the case,

> not only did the Lawrence novel devote more of its pages to the act of sex and deal with it in greater detail than anything ever before sold over the counter; it had language that had never been seen in a book openly circulated, except when used for tangential and occasional purposes, and not often then. . . .

Lady Chatterley's Lover presented the forbidden acts in forbidden detail, and described them in forbidden language.

In 1929, John Sumner, secretary of the New York Society for the Suppression of Vice, alerted officials at the Boston Watch and Ward Society that bibliophile and former Yale librarian James A. DeLacey, now proprietor of Dunster House Bookshop, had ordered five copies of the novel. An agent went to the bookstore to purchase the book and, after repeated refusals, finally obtained a copy. The society then instituted legal proceedings against DeLacey and his clerk, Joseph Sullivan, who were found guilty on November 25, 1929, by Judge Arthur P. Stone in Cambridge district court. DeLacey was fined $800 and sentenced to four months in jail, and Sullivan was fined $200 and sentenced to two weeks in jail. The convictions were appealed, but despite strong community support for the two men and attestations to their character, on December 20, 1929, Judge Frederick W. Fosdick upheld the lower court conviction. The case was then taken to the state supreme court.

A year later, the novel was the key element of the "Decency Debates" that raged in the U.S. Senate between Senator Bronson Cutting of New Mexico and Senator Reed Smoot of Utah. Cutting worked to modify the censorship laws while Smoot opposed reform ("Senator Smoot Smites Smut," read one newspaper headline). That same year, a Philadelphia prosecutor authorized a raid on a bookshop and the seizure of 300 books, among them *Lady Chatterley's Lover*, Fanny Hill, and The Perfumed Garden, marking the beginning of an extensive campaign to eliminate the sale of "obscene literature" in that city. Also in 1930, the Massachusetts Supreme Court affirmed DeLacey's conviction, and he was sentenced to four months in jail.

In 1944, John Sumner, acting in the name of the New York Society for the Suppression of Vice, seized copies of *The First Lady Chatterley* (Dial Press, 1944), and the book remained on the blacklist of the National Organization of Decent Literature until 1953.

The novel had appeared in expurgated form over the 30 years since it had first appeared, but the Grove Press edition was the full edition with all of the "four-letter words" and sex scenes created by Lawrence. As soon as the novel was published by Grove, Postmaster General Christenberry issued an order to ban the novel from the mails. The publisher went to court and *Grove Press Inc. v. Christenberry*, 175 F. Supp. 488 (S.D.N.Y. 1959) was heard in federal district court by Judge Frederick van Pelt Bryan, who agreed with the publisher and lifted the ban. He stated in his opinion that the application of a rule of contemporary community standards to the case signals acceptance of the book throughout the country:

> the broadening of freedom of expression and of the frankness with which sex and sex relations are dealt with at the present time require no discussion. In one best selling novel after another frank descriptions of the sex act and "four-letter" words appear with frequency. These trends appear in all media of public expression, in the kind of language used and the subjects discussed in

polite society, in pictures, advertisements and dress, and in other ways familiar to all. Much of what is now accepted would have shocked the community to the core a generation ago. Today such things are generally tolerated whether we approve or not.

I hold that at this stage in the development of our society, this major English novel does not exceed the outer limits of tolerance which the community as a whole gives to writing about sex and sex relations.

In *Grove Press Inc. v. Christenberry*, 276 F.2d 433 (2d Cir. 1960), the circuit court of appeals agreed with Judge Bryan's decision.

In 1959, Postmaster General Summerfield made the decision to continue to suppress copies of *Lady Chatterley's Lover* from the mail, declaring that the book was filled with "filthy," "smutty," "degrading," "offensive," and "disgusting" words, as well as with descriptions of sexual acts. He claimed that such "filthy words and passages" outweighed any literary merit that the book might have.

In England in 1960, the director of public prosecutions brought a criminal action against Penguin Books, Ltd., when the publisher announced its intention to openly publish the first unexpurgated British edition of *Lady Chatterley's Lover*. The prosecutor, Senior Treasury Counsel Mervyn Griffith-Jones, asked jurors to test the obscenity of the book themselves by answering these two questions: "Is it a book that you would have lying around your house? Is it a book that you would even wish your wife *or your servants* to read?" The defense attorneys argued that the novel as a whole was not obscene, despite language and sexual content in various passages. Thirty-five defense experts stressed the literary merit of the work, and the jury deliberated for three days before acquitting Penguin Books of all charges. Kuh relates that when the House of Lords debated the trial that cleared the novel, with its sexual episodes between a lady and her gamekeeper, a peer who agreed with the decision was asked, "Would you want your wife to read it?" He replied, "I would not object to my wife reading it, but I don't know about my gamekeeper."

In 1965, the Indecent Publications Tribunal of New Zealand reviewed the paperback edition of *Lady Chatterley's Lover* to determine if it was indecent, despite an earlier decision that no action would be taken regarding the import or sale of the cloth-bound edition of the novel. At the time, the cloth-bound edition sold in New Zealand for 16 shillings and the paperback edition for 5 shillings. The tribunal acknowledged that the novel "is a seriously written work by an author who has an established place in the field of English literature" and that "the text of the story is in the case of each identical; there is no difference between the two editions save in regard to the preface of the one and the introduction of the other and the form of each respectively."

Nonetheless, tribunal members considered if the novel should be kept out of the hands of persons under 18 years of age, and the issue became the difference in cost between the cloth-bound and the paperback editions, the low price of the paperback making it easily available to minors. This consideration motivated dissent among the members of the tribunal, two of whom asserted that "the sale of the Penguin [paperback] edition should be restricted to persons of seventeen years or over. . . . They think it is a matter for regret that the free circulation of the hardcover edition should have prejudiced the issue, embarrassed the Tribunal and made it virtually impossible in a particularly clear instance to invoke the provisions of the statute." The other three tribunal members felt that, given the unrestricted circulation of the hardcover edition, "it would be futile to classify the paperback edition as indecent in the hands of juveniles." Viewing any restrictive action against the paperback edition as futile, the majority view of the tribunal determined on April 7, 1965, that "the paperback edition of *Lady Chatterley's Lover* published by Penguin Books is not indecent within the meaning of the Indecent Publications Act of 1963."

FURTHER READING

Boyer, Paul S. *Purity in Print: The Vice-Society Movement and Book Censorship in America.* New York: Scribner, 1968.

Grant, Sidney S., and S. E. Angoff. "Censorship in Boston." *Boston University Law Review* 10 (January 1930): 36–60.

———. "Recent Developments in Censorship." *Boston University Law Review* 10 (November 1930): 488–509.

Maddox, Brenda. *D. H. Lawrence: The Story of a Marriage.* New York: Simon & Schuster, 1993.

Paul, James C. N., and Murray L. Schwartz. *Federal Censorship: Obscenity in the Mail.* New York: Free Press, 1961.

Perry, Stuart. *The Indecent Publications Tribunal: A Social Experiment.* London: Whitcombe and Tombs, 1965.

Rembar, Charles. *The End of Obscenity: The Trials of Lady Chatterley's Lover, Tropic of Cancer & Fanny Hill by the Lawyer Who Defended Them.* New York: Random House, 1968.

Roeburt, John. *The Wicked and the Banned.* New York: Macfadden Books, 1963.

U.S. President's Commission on Obscenity and Pornography. *The Report of the Commission on Obscenity and Pornography.* New York: Random House, 1970.

LA TERRE (THE EARTH)

Author: Émile Zola
Original dates and places of publication: 1887, France; 1889, England; 1955, United States
Original publishers: Charpentier (France); Henry Vizitelly & Co., (England); Grove Press (United States)
Literary form: Novel

SUMMARY

La Terre (in English, *The Earth*) is the 15th in a 20-novel series entitled *Les Rougon-Macquart*, which traces the fortunes of two families, the Rougons and the Macquarts, as well as their expansion into the modern world and into all classes. Not merely the work of imagination, the novels were based on documented evidence obtained through books, newspaper clippings, and first-person investigations to ensure historical, social, and political accuracy. As for each volume in the series, Zola had a specific stated objective for this novel: "I want to write the living poem of the earth, but in its human rather than symbolic aspect." *La Terre* presents a horrifying view of French peasantry before the Franco-Prussian War and is characterized by a lack of idealism, for which Zola was widely criticized.

The setting of the novel is La Beauce, a rich agricultural area of France just before the 1870 Franco-Prussian War. The land breeds passion and obsession in the peasants, and their greed for land destroys their feelings of humanity. When old Fouan grows too old to farm, he divides his land among his daughter, Fanny; his younger son, Buteau; and his older son, Hyacinthe, also called "Jesus-Christ." In return for their shares of the land, Fougan expects that they will take care of him and his wife, Rose, and feed them until their death. He lives with each of his children in turn, but they victimize him and feel that he asks too much of them in return for his land.

Many incidents in the novel angered critics. The first pages of the novel describe a bull inseminating a cow as a boy and girl who are tending the animals look on with indifference. The character nicknamed "Jesus-Christ" pride himself on his flatulence, and his skill is that he "bombarded his enemies, bombarded the marshall who came to impound his possessions. . . . [H]e could in turn fire at will." Old Fouan's niece Lise is pregnant by Buteau, who lives with her but refuses to marry her and, instead, pursues her younger sister, Françoise, who marries and becomes pregnant by Jean Macquart. Lise and Françoise each have their own land, willed to them at the death of their father, Old Mouche. Buteau is greedy and wants not only his land and the land inherited by Lise, but Françoise's parcel as well, and he tries to drive Jean Macquart away. Fearful that Françoise's land will revert to Jean, Buteau rapes Françoise with Lise's assistance, hoping to produce a child to bind them. The jealous Lise later pushes Françoise against a scythe in the field, piercing her abdomen with the blade. Even as she is dying, Françoise refuses to will her land to Jean, viewing him as an outsider, and Jean is evicted.

Greedy to have all the land and fearful that Fouan might have seen the murder, Lise and Buteau smother the old man with a pillow and then set fire to his bed. Jean Macquart leaves to become a soldier, to defend the earth of France even if he cannot cultivate it.

CENSORSHIP HISTORY

The novel was first published as installments in the newspaper *Le Gil Blas*. Matthew Josephson relates that when the first installment appeared, writer Anatole France was outraged and accused Zola of having created "a heap of filth" and making "an effort to vilify humanity, to insult every aspect of beauty and love, to deny all that is good and decent." He further condemned Zola for portraying the peasants as "rolling about the fields, fornicating."

On the same day that Zola completed the final chapter, a lengthy denunciation of the book appeared in *Le Figaro*, a manifesto signed by five young novelists: Paul Bonnetain, Lucien Descaves, Gustave Guiches, Paul Margueritte, and J. H. Rosny aîné. The novelists accused Zola of having deserted the cause of truth and of showing less of a desire to present reality and more of "a violent bias towards obscenity." They speculated that this tendency may have been due to a discovery by Zola that "the profits of pornography were greater than those earned by serious literature" or possibly to some "affection [*sic*] of the writer's lower organs, the nasty habits of a solitary monk, which inclined him to dwell on filth and lechery in his fictional writing." Calling for Zola to withdraw the novel, the writers of the manifesto asserted that *La Terre* contained characters who "are in general simply human animals in rut." They accused him of sinking to a new low with his novel, stating that "in no other of his books does Zola accumulate so many scenes of goatish copulation, frustrated rape, actual rape, incest and sadistic murder."

In 1888, Zola's English publisher, Henry Vizitelly, came under attack by the National Vigilance Association (NVA), a group composed mainly of clergymen who founded it in 1886 to continue the work of the Society for the Suppression of Vice, which had ceased operations a few years before. All of Zola's works, translated from French into English by the publisher's son, were specifically cited, as were works by Flaubert, Goncourt, Maupassant, Daudet, and Bourget. The NVA gained the attention of Samuel Smith, M.P., who spoke in the House of Commons in May 1888 against Vizitelly, "the chief culprit in the spread of pernicious literature." Citing Zola's works as an example of "obscene publications," Smith asserted that "nothing more diabolical had ever been written by the pen of man; they are only fit for swine, and those who read them must turn their minds into cesspools." The House passed a motion that "the law against obscene publications and indecent pictures and prints should be vigorously enforced and, if necessary, strengthened." The government would leave the initiation of proceedings to private individuals.

Other politicians and the newspapers joined the campaign against pornography, widening the scope of the battle to include other works, but Zola remained the focus. In his account of his father's ordeal as the English publisher of Zola's works, Ernest Vizitelly reported that the Roman Catholic newspaper, the *Tablet*, attacked the author as "a pornographer." The *Globe* charged that Zola "sapped the foundations of manhood and womanhood," and the *Whitehall Review* demanded immediate action against his books.

The law firm of Collette & Collette, retained by the NVA, obtained a summons on August 10, 1888, against Henry Vizitelly for publishing three "obscene" novels by Zola: *The Earth* (*La Terre*), *Piping Hot* (*Pot-bouille*), and *NANA*. Henry Asquith, prosecutor for the Crown, referred to these novels as "the three most immoral books ever published." The defense argued that Vizitelly had carefully expurgated the books while translating them into English and pointed out that the unexpurgated French versions were being freely circulated and sold in England at the same time. The prosecution declared the fact irrelevant, and the publisher went to trial at the Old Baily in October 1888. Vizitelly was sentenced to four months in Holloway Prison and ordered not to publish any more of Zola's works. The court further agreed that all of Zola's works must be withdrawn from circulation in England, making Zola the only writer to have his works outlawed in England in the 19th century.

All of Zola's novels were banned at once in 1894 when they were placed on the Index librorum prohibitorum in Rome, in 1929 when Yugoslavia banned all of his works, and in 1953 when Ireland did the same. The major complaints centered on Zola's open portrayal of his characters' sexuality and their reflection of the often sordid sexuality of his society.

FURTHER READING

Hemmings, F. W. J. *The Life and Times of Emile Zola.* New York: Scribner, 1977.

Josephson, Matthew. *Zola and His Time.* Garden City, N.Y: Garden City Publishers, 1928.

Schom, Alan. *Emile Zola: A Biography.* New York: Holt, 1987.

Vizitelly, Ernest A. *Emile Zola, Novelist and Reformer: An Account of His Life and Work.* London: Lane, 1904.

LOLITA

Author: Vladimir Nabokov

Original dates and places of publication: 1955, France; 1958, United States; 1959, England

Original publishers: Olympia Press; Weidenfeld and Nicholson; G. P. Putnam's Sons

Literary form: Novel

SUMMARY

Lolita is structured as a psychiatric case study of the pedophiliac protagonist, Humbert Humbert, the middle-aged lover of 12-year-old Lolita. The book traces Humbert's sexual obsession with young girls; his marriage to Lolita's mother, Charlotte; and the long cross-country trip that he takes with Lolita after her mother's death. Near the end of the novel, the nymphet (as Humbert dubs her), now 16, married, pregnant, and physically worn out, writes and asks for money. Still obsessed with the image of the young Lolita, Humbert hysterically begs her to leave with him but she refuses. In desperation, he offers her a check for $3,600 and $400 in cash if she will reveal the name of the man with whom she ran off. That man is Quilty, a friend of her late mother's and Lolita's old lover from the time when Humbert was still ogling and desiring the 12-year-old.

Humbert seeks revenge, and he is later incarcerated for shooting and killing Quilty.

Humbert's obsession dominates his adult life as he considers every attractive adolescent a seductress. As he intellectualizes his lust, Humbert places the blame for his obsession on the girls, whom he feels lead him on deliberately. Sitting in parks, he "throbs with excitement," "pulses with anticipation," struggles to control the feelings that make him "race with all speed toward [his] lone gratification." Before meeting 12-year-old Dolores ("Lolita") Haze and her mother, Humbert has had three breakdowns and confinements in sanatoriums. He refers to adventures with a succession of girl-like prostitutes and relates that he frequents brothels looking for young girls.

The initial meeting with Lolita is sexually charged, as Humbert notes each sensuous detail of her childlike body and then becomes obsessed with determining how to appease his sexual desire. In one early scene, he teases Lolita by taking her apple as she sits beside him on the couch. Humbert experiences "a glowing tingle" that develops into a "deep hot sweetness" that he can barely control. He feels that "the nerves of pleasure had been laid bare" and "the least pressure would suffice to set all paradise loose." As he sits "suspended on the brink of that voluptuous abyss," he moves his hand up Lolita's leg "as far as the shadow of decency would allow."

After Humbert marries Charlotte, with the aim of having freer access to Lolita, he daydreams of "administering a powerful sleeping potion to both mother and daughter so as to fondle the latter through the night with perfect impunity." Charlotte dies when she runs into traffic after reading Humbert's secret diary that details his fantasies, and Humbert tries out his sleeping pill scheme when he retrieves the orphaned Lolita from camp. The pills don't make her comatose as he had planned, but he seduces her anyway. That begins their two years of travel, posing as father and daughter as they go from motel to motel, encountering the seedy side of the American landscape. After Lolita runs away, Humbert once again has a breakdown and enters a sanatorium, which he later leaves with the intent of finding Lolita and avenging his loss.

CENSORSHIP HISTORY

Lolita was denounced as "filth" and "sheer unrestrained pornography" when it was first published. Author Nabokov claimed that *Lolita* was a comedy and disagreed with those who considered it erotic writing, yet he argued strenuously to have the novel published anonymously in order to protect his career as a professor at Cornell University. American publishers were similarly reticent about an association with the topic, and the novel was promptly refused by many when Nabokov's agent circulated it in 1954. Pascal Covici of Viking Press and Wallace Brockway of Simon & Schuster thought it would strike readers as "pornographic." James Laughlin of New Directions refused the book because "we are worried about possible repercussions both for the publisher and the author" and suggested publication in France. Before giving up, Nabokov sent the manuscript to Roger Straus of Farrar, Straus and Young and to Jason Epstein of Doubleday, who also rejected the manuscript. When the novel failed to find a publisher in the United States, Nabokov's agent took it to Olympia Press in Paris, which published it in two volumes.

After Olympia Press published *Lolita* in English in 1955, France banned the book in December 1956. The publisher, Maurice Girodias, asked Nabokov for help in fighting the ban, but the author replied, "My moral defense of the book is the book itself." He also wrote an essay entitled "On a Book Entitled Lolita" that was a lengthy justification, later attached to the American edition, in which he claimed that readers who thought the work erotic were misreading his intentions. Rather, Nabokov stated, "That my novel does contain various allusions to the physiological urges of a pervert is quite true. But after all we are not children, not illiterate juvenile delinquents, not English public school boys who after a night of homosexual romps have to endure the paradox of reading the Ancients in expurgated versions."

Olympia Press won its case in 1957 in the Administrative Tribunal of Paris, and the novel was back on sale in January 1958. When the Fourth Republic fell in May 1958 and General Charles de Gaulle assumed power, the French minister of the interior appealed to the Conseil d'Etat, the highest court in France. By December of that year, the book was again banned in France after the government successfully appealed the initial judgment. No appeal was possible, but the publication of the novel in French by the prestigious French publisher Gallimard in April 1959 gave Olympia Press foundation for a suit. The publisher sued the French government on the basis that the legal principle of equality among French citizens had been violated by the banning of the Olympia Press edition of *Lolita* and not the Gallimard edition. The English version was placed back on the market in France in September 1959.

British Customs banned the book in 1955, the same year that Graham Greene, in the *Sunday Times*, named *Lolita* one of his three favorite books of the year. Greene's article led John Gordon to remark in the *Sunday Express:* "Without doubt it is the filthiest book I have ever read. Sheer unrestrained pornography." Several British publishers were eager to bid for the rights to the novel, but they waited for the enactment of the Obscene Publications Bill in 1959, which would permit literary merit to be taken into account should the book be placed on trial. They expected prosecution because reviewers were already waging a war against the novel, several stating that the novel should be suppressed in England if it could be proven that "even a single little girl was likely to be seduced as a result of its publication." Conservatives in Parliament urged Nigel Nicholson, a member of Parliament as well as a publisher, not to publish the book, claiming that it would be detrimental to the party image. He lost his next bid for reelection, partly because of *Lolita*.

In contrast, United States Customs determined in February 1957 that the book was not objectionable and could be admitted into the country. Therefore, the book could not be legally exported from France, but people who smuggled the book out could import it legally into the United States. Despite its admissibility by Customs, U.S. publishers refused to publish *Lolita* until G. P. Putnam's Sons took the chance in 1958. A year later, the bans in England and France were lifted and the book was published openly in those countries. In the United States, however, the Cincinnati Public Library banned the book from its shelves after the director observed that "the theme of perversion seems to me obscene."

The novel was also banned in 1959 in Argentina, where government censors claimed that the book reflected moral disintegration. In 1960, the minister of commons in New Zealand banned import of the novel under the Customs Act of 1913 that prohibited importing books deemed "indecent" within the meaning of the Indecent Publications Act of 1910. To fight the ban, the New Zealand Council of Civil Liberties imported six copies of the book and successfully challenged the Supreme Court. Mr. Justice Hutchin delivered the judgment, noting that the book had been written with no pornographic intent and for the educated reader. Basing his decision on the recommendation of a ministry advisory committee that individual orders should be permitted, the justice observed that New Zealand Customs did admit certain books addressed to authorized individuals or intended to be sold to restricted classes. The ban on *Lolita* in South Africa, instituted in 1974 because of the "perversion theme" of the novel, was lifted in 1982, and the South African Directorate of Publications gave permission for its publication in paperback form.

FURTHER READING

Baker, George. "*Lolita:* Literature or Pornography." *Saturday Review*, June 22, 1957, p. 18.

Centerwall, Brandon S. "Hiding in Plain Sight: Nabokov and Pedophilia." *Texas Studies in Literature & Language* 32 (Fall 1990): 468–484.

Dupee, F. W. "*Lolita* in America." *Encounter* 12 (February 1959): 30–35.

Feeney, Ann. "*Lolita* and Censorship: A Case Study. *References Services Review* 21 (Winter 1993): 67–74, 90.

Hicks, Granville. "Lolita and Her Problems." *Saturday Review*, August 16, 1958, pp. 12, 38.

Levin, Bernard. "Why All the Fuss?" *Spectator*, January 9, 1959, pp. 32–33.

"Lolita in the Dock." *New Zealand Libraries* 23 (August 1960): 180–183.

Patnoe, Elizabeth. "Lolita Misrepresented, Lolita Reclaimed: Disclosing the Doubles." *College Literature* 22 (June 1995): 81–104.

Roeburt, John. *The Wicked and the Banned.* New York: Macfadden Books, 1963.

Scott, W. J. "The *Lolita* Case." *Landfall* 58 (June 1961): 134–138.

THE LUSTFUL TURK

Author: Anonymous
Original date and place of publication: 1828, England
Original publisher: J. B. Brookes
Literary form: Novel

SUMMARY

The Lustful Turk, viewed by Kronhausen and Kronhausen as "an instance of the juncture of literature and pornography," is an epistolary novel in which Emily Barlow uses letters to reveal her adventures to her friend, Silvia Carey. The long central letter details her capture by Moorish pirates whose "renegade English" captain presents Emily as a gift to the dey of Algiers. She relates graphically her defloration by the dey:

> I quickly felt his finger again introducing the head of that terrible engine I had before felt, and which now felt like a pillar of ivory to me. . . . [S]ucking my lips and breasts with fury, he unrelentingly rooted up all obstacles to my virginity.

She becomes a willing victim in ensuing sexual episodes, and the deflorations of other harem members follow the same description as Emily's.

Silvia derides her friend's apparent acceptance of the imprisonment and writes that she is disgusted by Emily's "account of the libidinous scenes acted between you and the beast whose infamous and lustful acts you so particularly describe." The dey reads the letter and orders his men to abduct Silvia.

The book contains the subplot of two dishonest clerics, Father Angelo and Pedro, the abbot of St. Francis, who run a white-slave trade between France and North Africa. The only connection to Emily is that they supply women to the dey.

As the end of the book nears, the now-pregnant Emily jealously attempts to learn the identity of the Englishwoman rumored to be the dey's new sexual interest. With the help of a friendly eunuch, she enters the dey's private apartments and catches him with the woman. "The first object that met my eyes was a naked female half reclining on a table, and the Dey with his noble shaft plunged up to the hilt in her."

Emily faints and then is revived, after which she learns that the new woman is her friend Silvia, captured by the dey's men and deflowered by him. The two women decide to share him, but his sexual obsessions lead to disaster. A Greek girl, newly recruited to the harem, refuses to engage in anal sex ("buggery") with the dey and partially cuts off his penis. The dey orders a doctor to finish the job. He then pickles the testicles in "spirits of wine in glass vases" and gives Emily and Silvia one each before releasing them to return to England.

CENSORSHIP HISTORY

Such furtively circulated erotica as *The Lustful Turk* was frequently the target of societies for the prevention of vice in both England and the United States in the 19th century. In most cases, shipments of the book were confiscated and destroyed without protest by the publishers or distributors, who simply churned out new and cheaply printed copies. The novel was advertised in catalogs with other such pornographic pulp as *The Battles of Venus; The Bed-Fellows, or The Young Misses Manual; The Confessions of a Young Lady; The Ups and Downs of Life;* and *The Victims of Lust*, in which catalog copy promised "every stretch of voluptuous imagination is here fully depicted, rogering, ramming, one unbounded scene of lust, lechery and licentiousness." The nature of the works meant that they were freely pirated, so numerous editions emerged containing embellishments that varied from one edition to another.

William Dugdale, dubbed by erotica collector Henry Ashbee as "one of the most prolific publishers of filthy books," included *The Lustful Turk* among his stock. By 1857, he had been prosecuted nine times for his publications and suffered the seizure and loss of large amounts of his stock. In 1857, in response to complaints lodged by the Society for the Suppression of Vice, Dugdale appeared in court before Lord Chief Justice Campbell. The justice declared obscene the books seized, including *The Lustful Turk*. After referring to Dugdale as "London's most notorious pornographer," the justice sentenced him to a year in jail. An incensed Dugdale threatened the justice with a penknife, but the sentence was carried out. That same year, Chief Justice Campbell proposed the creation of the Obscene Publications Act of 1857 and worked to make it law, citing *The Lustful Turk* as among the works that the act would outlaw.

In the United States, *The Lustful Turk* was deemed pornography, and the work was automatically confiscated and destroyed in numerous raids on booksellers by Anthony Comstock and the New York Society for the Suppression of Vice. The book never went to trial because, as in England, publishers and distributors simply printed new copies of the pirated book and sold them furtively.

FURTHER READING

Boyer, Paul S. *Purity in Print: The Vice-Society Movement and Book Censorship in America.* New York: Scribner, 1968.

Broun, Heywood, and Margaret Leech. *Anthony Comstock.* New York: Albert & Charles Boni, 1927.

Kearney, Patrick J. *A History of Erotic Literature.* Hong Kong: Parragon, 1982.

Kronhausen, Eberhard, and Phyllis Kronhausen. *Pornography and the Law: The Psychology of Erotic Realism.* New York: Ballantine, 1959.

Perkins, Michael. *The Secret Record: Modern Erotic Literature.* New York: William Morrow, 1976.

MADAME BOVARY

Author: Gustave Flaubert
Original dates and places of publication: 1857, France; 1888, England
Original publishers: Michel Levy (France); Henry Vizitelly (England)
Literary form: Novel

SUMMARY

Madame Bovary relates the story of Emma Roualt, a young Frenchwoman married to hardworking doctor Charles Bovary, and the manner in which she allows impossible romantic ideals to destroy her marriage and her life. Despite her husband's infatuation with her, Emma feels little for him and, instead, seeks the passionate love she has read about in romance novels. When the couple attends a fancy dress ball at the estate of a marquis, Emma dances with royalty and mingles with the rich; she leaves believing that this was the life she was born to lead.

She becomes extremely unhappy, and Charles decides that she needs a change of scenery. As they move from Tostes to Yonville, Emma learns that she is pregnant. This knowledge and the attentions of notary clerk Leon, who shares her interests in art and literature, distract her at least until the baby is born. Having hoped for a boy, Emma is disappointed when a daughter is born, and she begins to borrow money from dry goods merchant Lheureux to buy luxury items that she believes she deserves.

As Emma becomes increasingly unhappy, she gravitates toward Leon and the two profess their love but do not begin an affair. Instead, to avoid temptation, Leon moves to Paris. Emma, however, begins an affair with a patient of her husband's, the wealthy Rodolphe Boulanger, who wants only to add her to his list of conquests. Each morning Emma obsessively rushes to Boulanger's estate, where the two make passionate love, and she meets him some evenings after Charles is asleep.

After the novelty wears off and Boulanger ends the affair, Emma sinks into a deep depression, staying in bed for two months. When she recovers,

Charles takes her to Rouen to enjoy the opera, but she secretly meets Leon, and they begin an affair. She lies to Charles, telling him that she will take weekly piano lessons in Rouen, but she meets Leon in a hotel room each week to continue their affair.

At the same time, her debt to Lheureux increases, and she begins to borrow money elsewhere to pay him back. She becomes desperate when he confronts her and threatens to confiscate all of her property unless she immediately pays him 8,000 francs. Unable to raise the money, Emma commits suicide by ingesting arsenic after writing a letter of explanation to Charles. Her death weakens Charles, who dies soon after, leaving their daughter, Berthe, to work in a cotton mill to earn her living.

CENSORSHIP HISTORY

Madame Bovary was censored before publication as a novel, when it appeared in installments in *Revue de Paris*, a literary publication run by Flaubert's friend Maxime DuCamp. Before agreeing to publish the work, DuCamp asked to excise a single passage, about a page and a half in length, near the end of the novel. The passage relates Emma's extended tryst with Leon behind the closed curtains of a cab, and DuCamp felt that getting it past the censors would be "impossible." Flaubert agreed, but he was not prepared for the following editorial note inserted by the editors in place of the passage: "Here the editors found it necessary to suppress a passage unsuitable to the policies of the *Revue de Paris;* we hereby acknowledge this to the author." The editors later requested that cuts be made in the sixth and final installment of the novel—a move that Flaubert first fought and then reluctantly accepted, adding his own disclaimer regarding the quality of the now-fragmented work.

The omission of the offensive passages did not prevent government action being taken against *Madame Bovary*, though Flaubert felt the action was aimed more at the overly liberal *Revue* than at his novel. *Madame Bovary* went on trial on January 29, 1857, in highly formal court proceedings in which Imperial Advocate Ernest Pinard admitted that the language of the law of 1819 was "a little vague, a little elastic." He also asserted that the prosecution faced "peculiar difficulty" because reading the entire novel to the jury would be too time consuming, but reading only the "accused passages" would be too restrictive. To solve the problem, Pinard summarized the novel in detail and read verbatim the offending passages. When his version reached the appropriate point in the narrative, Pinard called upon the jury to apply "limits and standards" and noted, "Yes, Mr. Flaubert knows how to embellish his pictures with all the resources of art, but without art's restraints. No gauze for him, no veils—he gives us nature in all her nudity and crudity!"

In defense, Flaubert's lawyer portrayed the novel as a handbook of bourgeois respectability, noting that it taught the consequences of straying from moral behavior. The jury, which waited a week to deliver a verdict, acquitted the author, publisher, and printer without costs on the basis that their guilt had been "insufficiently established." In essence, the jury asserted that Flaubert "committed the wrong of occasionally neglecting the rules which no self-respecting writer should transgress, and of forgetting that literature, like art, must be chaste and pure not only in its form but also in its expression, in order to accomplish the good effects it is called upon to produce." A few months later, the novel was published in its entirety, all cuts restored, and sold 15,000 copies in two months.

In 1888, Flaubert's English publisher, Vizitelly, came under attack by the National Vigilance Association (NVA), a group composed mainly of clergymen who founded it in 1886 to continue the work of the Society for the Suppression of Vice, which had ceased operations a few years before. *Madame Bovary*, translated from French into English by the publisher's son, was specifically cited, as were works by Zola, Goncourt, Maupassant, Daudet, and Bourget. The NVA gained the attention of House of Commons member Samuel Smith, M.P., who spoke in May 1888 against Vizitelly, "the chief culprit in the spread of pernicious literature." The House passed a motion that "the law against obscene publications and indecent pictures and prints should be vigorously enforced and, if necessary, strengthened." The government would leave the initiation of proceedings to private individuals.

Other politicians and the newspapers joined the campaign against pornography, widening the scope of the battle. The Roman Catholic newspaper *Tablet* attacked Vizitelly as a "pornographer." The law firm Collette & Collette, retained by the NVA, obtained a summons on August 10, 1888, against Henry Vizitelly. The defense argued that Vizitelly had carefully expurgated the books while translating them into English, and it pointed out that the unexpurgated French versions were being freely circulated and sold in England at the same time. The prosecution declared the fact irrelevant, and the publisher went to trial at the Old Bailey in October 1888, where a jury charged him with "uttering and publishing certain obscene libels." Vizitelly was fined and ordered to desist publishing the offensive works. When he repeated the offense in 1889, the publisher received a four-month prison sentence, despite impaired health.

In 1893, the American Library Association for the first time offered a 5,000-title book guide for small popular libraries and branches, calling it a collection that "one could recommend to any trustee." No works by Flaubert were included in the list.

FURTHER READING

Elliott, Desmond. "The Book That Shocked Paris: The Strange Story of *Madame Bovary*." *Books and Bookmen* 5 (June 1960): 11, 46.

Geller, Evelyn. *Forbidden Books in American Public Libraries, 1876–1939*. Westport, Conn.: Greenwood, 1984.

Kendrick, Walter. *The Secret Museum*. New York: Viking, 1987.

Mancuso, Ludwig. *The Obscene: The History of an Indignation*. London: MacGibbon & Key, 1965.

Steegmuller, Francis. *Flaubert and Madame Bovary*. Boston: Houghton Mifflin, 1970.

MADELEINE

Author: Anonymous
Original date and place of publication: 1919, United States
Original publisher: Harper & Brothers
Literary form: Autobiographical novel

SUMMARY

Madeleine is the anonymous autobiographical novel written by a purportedly reformed prostitute and madam of a house of prostitution. The work provides painstakingly recounted domestic details of life within a bordello, but the references to sexual activity are subtle and infrequent. The reader learns the routine of the establishment, including areas of responsibility for upkeep and the details of running the business.

Despite its sometimes jaded cynicism, as in the author's comment that the only difference between wives and prostitutes is that prostitutes "do not cheat in the delivery of the merchandise for which they are paid," the book makes an effort to deliver a moral message. Although Madeleine does not encourage others to follow her path, she does distinguish between her own entry into "the life" and those of contemporary young girls, noting that prostitutes in her youth were relatively moral compared to their modern counterparts. At one point, the author observes that, in her day, "no 'decent' house . . . would have tolerated some of the styles . . . on the streets today." She also condemns the "present-day craze for rag-time."

CENSORSHIP HISTORY

Madeleine was one of the books that emerged from the antiprostitution movement of New York City in the 1890s, despite its publication in the postwar period. Reviewers who were fully familiar with the "white-slave" investigations were not scandalized and neither were readers who were familiar with the vice commission reports. Still, John Sumner and the New York Society for the Suppression of Vice filed charges against Harper & Brothers in January 1920. Clinton T. Brainard, the president of Harper & Brothers, was convicted in the court of special sessions and fined $1,000. Although the vice society claimed to find *Madeleine* offensive to public morals and Sumner labeled the book "one of the worst and most dangerous books that has come to our attention in a long time," other factors appear to have been behind the charges.

Brainard had been secretary of a grand jury charged with investigating municipal scandals in the administration of John Hylan, New York mayor and a protégé of William Randolph Hearst. The Hearst publication *New York American* launched a campaign against *Madeleine* as soon as it appeared, and the publication pointedly mentioned Brainard in each article. In reporting the conviction, Hearst publications emphasized that Brainard had been "finger-printed like any other common law-breaker." Brainard appealed, and lawyers for the publisher stressed the book's reformist intent. On July 9, 1920, the appellate court of New York reversed the lower-court conviction, and *Madeleine* was vindicated in *People v. Brainard*, 192 App. Div. 816, 183 N.Y.S. 452. In its ruling, the court stated that "no one can read this book and truthfully say it contains a single word or picture which tends to excite lustful or lecherous desire."

FURTHER READING

"Brainard Innocent, Upper Court Holds." *New York Times*, July 10, 1920, p. 17.

Broun, Heywood. "Heywood Broun Comes to the Rescue of Immoral Books." *Current Opinion* 67 (December 1919): 315–316.

Ernst, Morris L., and Alexander Lindey. "The Censor Marches On . . ." *Esquire*, June 1939, pp. 174–177.

Loth, David. *The Erotic in Literature*. New York: Dorset, 1961.

Pringle, Henry F. "Comstock the Less." *The American Mercury* 10 (January 1927): 56–63.

MADEMOISELLE DE MAUPIN

Author: Théophile Gautier

Original dates and places of publication: 1835, France; 1887, England; 1900, United States

Original publishers: Ariel (France); Henry Vizitelly (England); C. T. Brainard Publishing Co. (United States)

Literary form: Novel

SUMMARY

Gautier begins *Mademoiselle de Maupin* with a preface that expresses his view of censors. Written in the voice of his narrator, Chevalier D'Albert, it characterizes the "great affectation of morality" of his era as "one of the greatest burlesques of the glorious epoch at which we have the good fortune to live." He observes that many who seek to censor or to ban art and literature ignore the beauty and value of the whole work and, instead, "if there is any nakedness in a picture or book they go straight to it like swine to the mire."

Mademoiselle du Maupin consists of letters, written to a friend by the 22-year-old Chevalier D'Albert, that satirize virtue and praise sensuality, adultery, and fornication. Relating his desires for certain women, D'Albert describes their physical attributes and then provides details of the scenes that lead to their sexual intimacy. He believes that being a gentleman demands that he have a mistress, and he accepts adultery as a social reality.

The first part of the novel details the young man's experiences with his first mistress, Rosette, who yields to all of his desires. D'Albert states, "I caress her as much as I like; I have her nude or dressed, in town or in country." He also claims that she arouses "the brute" in him and "in her society, vulgar and ignoble thoughts alone occur in me."

The second part of the novel describes the adventures of Magdalene de Maupin, who often masquerades as a man. She is also interested in Rosette, and a number of their scenes in which Rosette believes Magdalene to be a man named Theodore include highly sensual and passionate embraces. Magdalene relates one incident:

> I felt her breasts, half bare and excited, heaving against my bosom, while her clasped fingers clutched my hair. A thrill went through me and my bosoms swelled. Rosette did not let go of my mouth. Her lips sucked in my lips, her teeth touched my teeth, our breaths mingled. I drew back for a moment, and two or three times turned my head to avoid her kisses, but an invincible attraction made me turn again, and I kissed her in return almost as ardently as she had kissed me.

At one point Magdalene states that their kisses "agitated me to the highest degree, although they were those of a woman . . . which made me forget that after all I was not a man."

Later in the novel, Magdalene, still disguised as Theodore, seeks to save her landlady's 15-year-old daughter, Ninon, from becoming the mistress of a predatory chevalier and charms Ninon into becoming her mistress. Professing only altruistic intentions, Magdalene writes that "her body was a little marvel of delicacy" and concludes that "only a woman could love her with sufficient delicacy and tenderness." Her growing passion for Ninon leads to Magdalene's realization that "I belong to a third, distinct sex, which as yet has not a name."

Magdalene locates Rosette, now the mistress of D'Albert, who perceives that Theodore is really a woman. Eager for sexual experience, Magdalene invites D'Albert into her bedroom where, after a detailed description of her undressing, the two make love. Late the next day, Magdalene leaves D'Albert for Rosette's bedroom, which she does not leave until noon of the following day. The reader does not learn what occurs between Rosette and Magdalene, only that the maid found the bed in disarray with the imprint of two bodies and two pearls from Magdalene's hair in the sheets. Magdalene departs and asks only that Rosette and D'Albert kiss each other occasionally with her in mind.

CENSORSHIP HISTORY

The novel was severely criticized for its explicitly erotic scenes when it was first published, but the outcry that it should be suppressed because of its "lewdness" and "indecency" strengthened sales, and Gautier reaped a handsome financial profit. At the same time, he experienced a critical backlash when the French Academy voted to bar him from membership.

In 1917, the prosecution of *Mademoiselle de Maupin* in the United States made legal history for the publishing world. John Sumner, the secretary of the New York Society for the Suppression of Vice, saw a copy of the English translation of *Mademoiselle de Maupin* displayed in the window of booksellers McDevitt-Wilson and opened to what he perceived to be a "corrupting" illustration. He purchased a copy of the book from store clerk Raymond Halsey and then brought a charge against Halsey for violating section 1141 of the New York Penal Code, the obscenity statute. Halsey was arrested and brought to trial and acquitted in the Court of Special Session. The clerk then sued the society for malicious prosecution and won in a trial by jury. The society appealed and the Appellate Division affirmed the original decision. The society then took the case to the Court of Appeals, where *Halsey v. New York Society for the Suppression of Vice*, 234 N.Y. 1, 136 N.E. 219 (1922) was decided in favor of Halsey in a 5-2 decision. Halsey was awarded $2,500 and accrued interest in damages from the society. The court took the following points into considering in reaching a decision: the reputation of the author; the regard in which the novel had been held by eminent critics since first publication; the whole work, not simply specific passages; the nature of the language, which was "not of the street"; and the effect that translation from the French might have.

The significance of the case went beyond the victory of one bookseller. Although the presiding Court of Appeals Judge William S. Andrews acknowledged that the novel "contains many paragraphs, however, which taken by themselves are undoubtedly vulgar and indecent," he based his decision on the "whole book" concept and provided more specific criteria to strengthen the defense:

> No work may be judged from a selection of paragraphs alone. Printed by themselves they might, as a matter of law, come within the prohibition of the statute. So might a similar selection from Aristophanes or Chaucer or Boccaccio or even from the Bible. The book, however, must be considered broadly as a whole.

Dissenting Judges J. Crane and J. Hogan wrote that the book "counsels vice" and attempts "to impress upon the readers that vice and voluptuousness are natural to society, are not wrongs but proper practices to be indulged in by the young." They noted that if the activities in the book were expressed in the "language of the street, there would be no doubt in the minds of anybody that the work would be lewd, vicious and indecent." Moreover, the "polished style with exquisite settings and perfumed words makes it all the more dangerous and insidious and none the less obscene and lascivious."

FURTHER READING

Cusseres, Benjamin de. "Case of Prudery against Literature: Attack on Gautier's Novel Brings to Mind Many Historical Examples of Law's Moral Censorship of Books." *New York Times*, May 23, 1920, p. 3.

Marchand, Henry. *The French Pornographers: Including a History of French Erotic Literature.* New York: Book Awards, 1965.

Nelson, Hilda. "Theophile Gautier: The Invisible and Impalpable World." *French Review* 45 (June 1972): 819–830.

THE MAID OF ORLEANS (LA PUCELLE)

Author: François-Marie Arouet (Voltaire)
Original dates and places of publication: 1759, France; 1901, United States
Original publishers: Privately printed (France); E. R. Du Mont (United States)
Literary form: Satire

SUMMARY

The Maid of Orleans, translated sometimes as *The Virgin of Orleans,* is a highly suggestive work that relates stories of King Charles VII of France dallying with his mistress Agnes Sorel while the threat of an English attack looms. The disgusted nobleman St. Denis vows that "every wrong is righted by its opposite," and he looks for a virgin who can lead France to victory, despite the skepticism of other nobles who doubt that any virgins remain in France. When he finds Joan of Arc, many comment that "the key to France's salvation lies under her skirt," and many attempt to violate her chastity. She does come close to surrendering to Dunois, but she stops their lovemaking just in time to prevent defloration:

> "Beloved bastard," she cried, "do stop. Now is not the right time. Heaven knows of our love, so let us not ruin our future. To you alone I pledge my troth. I swear that you shall have my flower. But let us wait until your avenging arm has conquered the Briton and driven out the usurper. Then we shall lie together under our laurels."

After victory on the battlefield, Joan keeps her promise to Dunois.

Voltaire allows Joan her chastity, but the other characters in the satire show distinctly immoral behavior. The king's mistress is licentious, and her charms are described in detail. Voltaire observes:

> Below a neck whiter than alabaster were two separate mounds, shapely, stirring and throbbing, rounded by Eros, and tipped with little buttons of rose. Oh, charming, palpitating breasts, you invited the hand to squeeze, the eye to marvel, and the mouth to kiss.

At one point, King Charles surprises Agnes with a naked young page, Monrose, who is described as having "displayed a rear like that which Caesar in his youth shamelessly proffered to Nicodemus, that portion of the anatomy for which valiant warriors, alas, have such a weakness."

The author makes other graphic observations. He states that Robert d'Abriselle liked to lie "between two big-bottomed nuns, to caress four chubby hemispheres and fondle an equal number of breasts, and all that without sinning." In other incidents, an English chaplain sexually assaults

Agnes Sorel, and the English king turns over a "mother and daughter to his soldiers."

CENSORSHIP HISTORY

The Maid of Orleans became the object of a legal action in 1909 when a man who had ordered the 42-volume set of Voltaire's works refused to honor the contract and pay $200 for the set. Peter J. Quinn's claim that *The Maid of Orleans* and the PHILOSOPHICAL DICTIONARY were immoral made this the first case in which a person buying the book for personal use became a litigant in a literary obscenity case. The case went before the New York Municipal Court, which ruled that the books were immoral and the contract was illegal.

In an appeal to the Supreme Court of New York, the decision was reversed in *St. Hubert Guild v. Quinn*, 64 Misc. 336, 118 N.Y.S. 582 (Sup. Ct. 1909). In his decision, Judge J. Seabury, with Judges Gildersleeve and Giegerich concurring, asserted, "The rule against the sale of immoral publications cannot be invoked against those works which have been generally recognized as literary classics." Seabury added that "the question in a given case is not simply whether the publication be immoral, but whether it is sufficiently so to enable the criminal law to punish it as such." In ruling on *The Maid of Orleans*, he decided that the book in question was not sufficiently immoral.

FURTHER READING

De Grazia, Edward. *Censorship Landmarks*. New York: Bowker, 1969.
Lewis, Felice Flanery. *Literature, Obscenity, and Law*. Carbondale: Southern Illinois University, 1976.
Wellek, Rene, and Austin Warren. *Theory of Literature*. 3d ed. New York: Harcourt Brace & World, 1956.

MEMOIRES

Author: Giovanni Casanova de Seingalt
Original dates and places of publication: 1826, Germany; 1922, England
Original publishers: Brockhaus (Germany); The Casanova Society (England)
Literary form: Autobiography

SUMMARY

Casanova's *Memoires*, originally titled *Memoires: Ecrites par lui-meme*, is the world's most famous erotic autobiography. As researchers of sexual behavior

Eberhard and Phyllis Kronhausen point out, the work also provides "one of the most important sources for the cultural historian, and especially for the student of sexual customs, the psychologist, and the sexologist."

Throughout the work, Casanova reports in detail a wide and varied range of sexual experiences, and he also reveals important social information regarding contraception and the sexual customs of different classes. In one incident, Casanova and an agent who has procured the sexual services of three beautiful young girls have dinner, drink champagne, and then settle down to an amorous evening. The agent takes from his pocket a condom, "this admirable preservative from an accident which might give rise to a terrible and fruitless repentance." The girls are familiar with the item, and "they laughed heartily to see the shape these articles took when they were blown out." In another incident, Casanova not only describes contraceptives but also provides a detailed description of an ejaculation and its "abundant flow of liquid." He relates experiences in which various girls undress completely, allowing him to rhapsodize in detail about their naked bodies, particularly their breasts and buttocks, and then make his "bliss complete by presenting me with their maidenheads."

In one instance, Casanova meets a nun who has recently given birth in secret and who joins him in "exhausting all imaginable kinds of pleasure, exciting each other's desires, and only wishing to prolong our enjoyment." Remembering her earlier pregnancy, the next time they engage in sexual intercourse Casanova uses "a little article of transparent skin, about eight inches long, with one opening, which was ornamented with a red rosette . . . this preventive sheath." In another instance, he reports unlacing the corset of a young novice, "and affixing my lips to one of the blossoms of her breasts I sucked it with a voluptuous pleasure which is beyond all description." Afterward, he expresses the great pleasure that he has enjoyed, and she responds that it is no sin for her because it "will easily be wiped out with a little holy water. At all events we can swear that there has been no kissing between us."

Defenders of the work point out that beyond documenting the sexual adventures of a libertine, *Memoires* relates his attraction to a highly pregnant woman and gives details regarding the delivery of a baby and other realistic, antierotic material "which any pornographer worthy of the name would never introduce into his story."

CENSORSHIP HISTORY

Casanova's *Memoires* were published in highly expurgated form in 1826, but the complete work did not appear until 1922. The manuscript remained in the safe of the publisher until the moral climate appeared to have changed sufficiently to allow publication of the entire work. Even in expurgated form, the work created controversy. In 1834, the entire 12-volume set of the expurgated *Memoires* was placed on the Index librorum prohibitorum in Rome, where it remained until the dissolution of the Index in the 1960s. In 1863, the French government banned sales of the work without protest from booksellers or distributors. In 1929, United States Customs confiscated a shipment of books containing *Memoires* and other erotic classics, but the court refused to hear the case, so the books were released.

On September 20, 1932, a prohibition order was published in the *Iris Oifigiuil*, "the only official source from which booksellers [and readers] might learn of a new prohibition order," in which all articles blacklisted by the Irish Board of Censors were listed. According to the Censorship of Publications Bill of 1928, "the notice in *Iris Oifigiuil* should be sufficient evidence in the courts of summary jurisdiction as to the character of the publication," despite the acknowledgment by justices quoted in Adams's thorough study of Irish censorship laws that "this gazette is not a publication which booksellers are addicted to reading." The Irish Board of Censors found Casanova's memoirs "obscene" and filled with "illicit sex behavior." The work was officially banned from sale in Ireland until the introduction of the Censorship Publications Bill in 1967 reduced to 12 years the duration of a prohibition order, and the work was among 5,000 titles released from the list of banned books.

FURTHER READING

Adams, Michael. *Censorship: The Irish Experience.* Tuscaloosa: University of Alabama Press, 1968.

Kronhausen, Eberhard, and Phyllis Kronhausen. *Pornography and the Law: The Psychology of Erotic Realism.* New York: Ballantine, 1959.

Marchand, Henry L. *The French Pornographers.* New York: Book Awards, 1965.

MEMOIRS OF A YOUNG RAKEHELL

Author: Guillaume Apollinaire
Original dates and places of publication: 1962, France; 1969, United States
Original publishers: Olympia Press (France); Grove Press (United States)
Literary form: Novel

SUMMARY

The Memoirs of a Young Rakehell provides a brief narrative of a young boy's sexual awakening. Master Roger spies on his sister and then attempts to seduce the family maid, before finally becoming sexually involved with the pregnant wife of the bailiff. The work is written from the perspective of the adolescent Roger and notes with details his preoccupation with the "swelling nipples" and his "burning desire to know just what it was that women carried beneath their skirts which was so precious that they were always frantic to hide it." As he observes the women around him more closely, he finds opportunities to see one "fleshly triangular mound" after another.

The author describes Roger's frequent masturbation and fascination with the length, circumference, and firmness of his penis. His thoughts focus on sex, and he takes every opportunity to observe the breasts, buttocks, or vaginal areas of women, to the point of humor as he hides in various locations to spy on women in their private moments. Eventually, Roger and his sister experiment with sexual intercourse; then he seduces several of the maids. Each incident is fully described, from his initial bumbling forays under their skirts—"slipping my hand beneath her skirts, I discovered a very hairy mound"—to the point where he has one after another "trembling beneath her flimsy clothing" as he fondles breasts, buttocks, and thighs. He repeatedly "stands erect" and reaches "voluptuous climax," providing explicit description of each thrust.

In addition to the graphic details, the book contains numerous uses of the terms *fuck* and *prick* and descriptions of breasts and buttocks of all types. For the most part, the brief work consists of a series of adolescent sexual adventures that end with the narrator impregnating his aunt and two maids and then serving as the godfather to all three children. This is all done as part of his fulfillment of "patriotic duty, that of increasing my country's population."

CENSORSHIP HISTORY

In 1964, New Zealand Customs officers seized *Memoirs of a Young Rakehell* and *The Debauched Hospodar*, works by Apollinaire originally published in one volume by Olympia Press in 1962, and the Marquis de Sade's JUSTINE. The importer, a Mr. D. W. Cheer of Christchurch, disputed the seizure, and the matter went before a magistrate, who issued an order prohibiting the publication of the titles of the books. The Indecent Publications Tribunal did not continue this order but did refuse to allow citations in the court records of passages that the defense counsel read in court. In testimony, the comptroller of Customs claimed that the books had been detained under the provisions of the Customs Act of 1913 as "Prohibited Imports," because they were indecent. As required by Section 12 of the Indecent Publications Act of 1963, proceedings for the condemnation were instituted by the comptroller before a magistrate who, in turn, was required to turn the matter over to the Indecent Publications Tribunal to determine the manner in which the books might be viewed as "indecent":

> whether the books were indecent within the meaning of the Act, or indecent in the hands of persons under a specified age, or indecent unless circulation was restricted to specified persons or classes of persons.

The counsel for the defense argued that even if a general ban were to be levied on the books, the importer should be free of restriction because he was a "serious collector of all sorts of books" with a library of from 5,000 to 6,000 volumes. Called to testify, the importer expressed his view "of the value of the books to a student of literature."

In its decision, rendered on March 4, 1965, the tribunal asserted that the content of the two novels was "vile and revolting both to the episodes related and the language used to describe them." Although they acknowledged that Apollinaire had been viewed as a literary "bright light," their judgment was that the books were obscene and should not be circulated generally. However, the tribunal did find the books to be useful in the study of abnormal psychology and concluded that "we classify the translation of the two novels written by Guillaume Apollinaire as indecent unless circulation is restricted to persons professionally engaged in the study of abnormal psychology, who desire to use them for that purpose."

FURTHER READING

Perkins, Michael. *The Secret Record: Modern Erotic Literature*. New York: Morrow, 1976.
Perry, Stuart. *The Indecent Publications Tribunal: A Social Experiment*. London: Whitcombe and Tombs, 1965.

MEMOIRS OF HECATE COUNTY

Author: Edmund Wilson
Original date and place of publication: 1946, United States
Original publisher: Doubleday
Literary form: Short story collection

SUMMARY

Memoirs of Hecate County consists of six interconnected stories that relate the lives of the well-to-do residents of a New York suburb. All of the short stories—"The Man Who Shot Snapping Turtles," "Ellen Terhune," "Glimpses of Wilbur Flick," "The Milhollands and Their Damned Soul," "Mr. and Mrs. Blackburn at Home"—and the novella entitled "The Princess with the Golden Hair" are related by an unnamed male narrator, but only the novella contains candid accounts of sexual relations.

"The Princess with the Golden Hair" relates the narrator's experiences with two women: the "princess" of the title, Imogen Loomis, the beautiful, sheltered wife of a wealthy advertising magnate, and Anna Lenihan, a young working-class woman of immigrant background who is separated from her emotionally unstable husband. He relates through diary entries his efforts to seduce Imogen while he conducts a satisfying sexual relationship with Anna.

Using frank language, the narrator describes how he "liberated one little breast" of Anna's and relates that she becomes "so responsive to my kissing her breasts that I can make her have a climax in that way." After he contracts gonorrhea from Anna, the narrator sees a doctor and renews his efforts to seduce Imogen.

When the narrator and Imogen finally have an assignation, he learns that she wears a brace on her back. She claims to have tuberculosis of the spine, but the narrator later learns that her ailment is only in her imagination. Nonetheless, their sexual encounter is described at length. In a prolonged passage, the narrator describes Imogen's thighs and genitals:

> all that lay between them was impressively beautiful, too, with an ideal aesthetic value that I had never found there before. The mount was of classical femininity: round and smooth and plump; the fleece, if not quite golden, was blond and curly and soft; and the portals were a deep tender rose.

She does "something special and gentle" to him and then has an orgasm, "a self-excited tremor . . . brimming of female fluid."

The narrator visits Anna, who is hospitalized to undergo surgery to correct the damage the gonorrhea has done to her reproductive system. While she is at home recuperating, he urges her to marry another man whom she does not love. The novella ends as the narrator receives a letter from Anna telling him that she has taken his advice, and he now realizes that he will "never make love again."

CENSORSHIP HISTORY

The literary merit of *Memoirs of Hecate County* was established before the work was taken to court and found "obscene" in both California and New York. The *New York Times Book Review* called it "a good, distinguished book," and *Time* magazine named it "the first event of the year which can be described as 'literary.'" A further unusual aspect of the litigation is that the book was ruled "obscene" based only on one of the six stories, despite the increasing agreement of legal authorities to judge a work in its entirety and not according to specific sections that have been determined to be obscene. Wilson's fellow writers asserted that the sexual descriptions were boring rather than arousing. Raymond Chandler observed that Wilson had "made fornication as dull as a railroad time table," while Malcolm Cowley described the sex scenes as "zoological."

In 1946, booksellers in San Francisco and New York City were arrested for selling the work and taken to trial. That same year, copies of the book were confiscated in Philadelphia, and the publishers ceased shipment to Massachusetts because of its censorship laws. In San Francisco, a bookseller was charged with selling an "obscene" book, but the first trial was dismissed because it resulted in a hung jury. In the second trial of *People v. Wepplo*, 78 Cal. App. 2d 959, 178 P.2d 853 (1947), the jury acquitted the bookseller.

In New York City, the New York Society for the Improvement of Morals, formerly the New York Society for the Suppression of Vice, brought suit against Doubleday & Co. for violating section 1141 of the New York State Obscenity Statute. Police confiscated 130 copies of the work from four Doubleday bookstores after society secretary John Sumner charged that the book was the "most salacious and lascivious work issued for indiscriminate circulation." The next day, major bookstores such as Brentano's, Scribner's, and Hearn's had removed all copies from their shelves. Since its publication a few months earlier, 50,000 copies of the book had been sold. The publisher went to court and was convicted of obscenity for publishing *Memoirs of Hecate County* in *People v. Doubleday & Co., Inc.*, 272 App. Div. 799, 71 N.Y.S.2d 736 (1st Dep't). Literature professor and critic Lionel Trilling testified at the New York trial at the Court of Special Sessions and emphasized that the stories are related and constitute a study of good and evil. He also observed that the sexually frank passages contribute heavily to the "very moral" theme of the book. The district attorney, Frank Hogan, countered with evidence that the book contained "the most intensive concentration of sex episodes, with nothing omitted in the way of bare-skinned description." He asserted in the brief that

> There are 20 separate acts of sexual intercourse. . . . These take place between the protagonist and four different women. Eighteen of the acts occur in the space of an hour or two with two different women. Three of the acts occur with two married women.

The brief cited specific pages on which these acts occur and detailed further attempts at sexual intercourse, nocturnal dreams of intercourse, daydreams of intercourse and "filthy conversations about sex" in the book. The decision was affirmed by the State Supreme Court Appellate Division in *People v. Doubleday & Co., Inc.*, 297 N.Y. 687, 77 N.E.2d 6 (1947) and the publisher was fined $1,000. The state district attorney also warned that booksellers who sold the book would be sentenced to a year in prison. Writing about the decision, *Time* magazine observed that "the decision made thousands of citizens more impatient than ever to get their morals ruined. It also proved again that finding a yardstick for proving a serious book indecent is as difficult as weighing a pound of waltzing mice."

In 1948, the case then went to the U.S. Supreme Court, which refused to overturn the decision of the lower court and, instead, rendered a 4-4 curiam decision that the book was obscene after Justice Felix Frankfurter chose to not participate. The conviction remained, but the 4-4 decision meant that no opinion was written in *Doubleday & Co. v. New York*, 335 U.S. 848 (1948).

The book was not published in England until 1951 because publisher Frederic Warburg knew of the case against Doubleday & Co. in the United States and wanted to avoid the same action. He tried to have the text set in England but could not find a willing printer; he begged Wilson to edit the text, but Wilson refused. The work was published in 1951 by W. H. Allen.

In 1961, New American Library published the paperback edition of the work with the following legend on its cover: "Not for Sale in New York State." When Ballantine Books issued a paperback edition in 1966, the book was described on the cover as "authentic and unexpurgated" as well as "still banned in the State of New York."

FURTHER READING

Bates, Ralph. "Mr. Wilson's Visit to Suburbia." *New York Times Book Review*, March 31, 1946, pp. 7, 16.
"Evil in Our Time." *Time* 48, March 25, 1946, p. 102.
Lockhart, William B., and Robert C. McClure. "Literature, the Law of Obscenity, and the Constitution." *Minnesota Law Review* 38 (March 1954): 295–395.
Moskin, Morton. "Inadequacy of Present Tests as to What Constitutes Obscene Literature." *Cornell Law Quarterly* 34 (Spring 1949): 442–447.
"Pound of Waltzing Mice." *Time*, December 9, 1946, pp. 24–25.

THE MERRY MUSES OF CALEDONIA

Author: Robert Burns
Original dates and places of publication: 1800, Scotland; 1907, United States
Original publishers: Peter Hill (Scotland); Privately printed for members of the Caledonia Society (United States)
Literary form: Collection of bawdy poems and songs

SUMMARY

The Merry Muses of Caledonia is a collection compiled by Robert Burns of 85 poems and songs, many of which were selected for use as a private songbook by the drinking club to which Burns had belonged, the Crochallan Fencibles. The group gave the collection its name in 1800, four years after Burns's death, for he had left it untitled. The poet collected ancient and modern folk songs, leaving some as they were and adding his own bawdy endings to others, and he also wrote at least 20 new songs to complete the collection. Many of the songs first appeared in letters sent by the poet to his friends.

The complete collection that Burns commissioned to be printed disappeared after his death and did not resurface until 1815, when Allan Cunningham obtained Burns's own manuscript from a banker's son who claimed that the poet had presented the manuscript to the banker. Editions published before that contained 30 to 40 of the songs, as did many later editions, because the entire collection remained unavailable. Even Cunningham selected only 42 "suitable" items from the manuscript, bowdlerizing and eliminating as he chose. Included among song titles are "Nine Inch Will Please a Lady," "How Can I Keep My Maidenhead?" and "Nae Hair On't," as well as such lines as "Meg had a muff, and it was rough" and a plethora of such terms as "c---t," "f-----g," "f---s," and "a---e" presented with dashes, as well as euphemisms for sexual intercourse such as "mowing."

CENSORSHIP HISTORY

The Merry Muses of Caledonia collection was not published in an unexpurgated edition in Scotland until 1959, when the passage of the Obscene Publications Act liberated the material for publication, and distinguished scholarly editors James Barke and Sydney Goodsir issued privately a complete edition of the collection in Edinburgh. Twenty-nine earlier editions contained largely bowdlerized versions of the songs and poems. A 30th edition, in 1800, was not expurgated but was incomplete because the Crochallan Fencibles did not have Burns's complete manuscript, only selections that he had sent members individually. When Allan Cunningham obtained the complete collection in 1815, he took the liberty of selecting the least "offensive" songs and making changes in them, expurgating them to make them publishable. He noted the following in his preface:

> In several places small but necessary liberties have been taken with the language. It would have been unwise to omit verses so characteristic, and they would have offended many had they appeared as they stand in the original.

Until the complete text of the songs was published for public consumption in 1959, the only copy was kept in the Private Case of the British Museum Library with other risqué literature. Not only was the material expurgated but, as Perrin points out, Burns's biographers effectively expurgated his life by omitting mention of licentious songs to avoid tempting readers into seeking the material. Editors chose to ignore the existence of the songs in so-called standard, or complete, collections of the poet's works. As George Legman observes,

> Annandale of the Standard Edition pretended that there was no *Merry Muses*, as did President Eliot of Harvard (who gave Burns one of the fifty volumes of the Five-Foot Shelf [of the Harvard Classics] to himself). So did J. Logie Robertson, editing *The Poetical Works of Robert Burns* ("the text is presented entire") for Oxford University Press in 1910.

Other editors admitted to the existence of the *Merry Muses* and hinted at their contents but, like American editor James Hunter, who edited *The*

Complete Works of Robert Burns in 1886, believed, "To reproduce such pieces in a work dedicated to the genius of Scotland's bard would be sacrilege."

FURTHER READING

Craig, Alec. *Suppressed Books: A History of the Conception of Literary Obscenity.* New York: World Publishing, 1963.

Legman, George, ed. "Introduction." *The Merry Muses of Caledonia: Collected and Written in Part by Robert Burns.* New Hyde Park, N.Y.: University Books, 1965.

Perrin, Noel. *Dr. Bowdler's Legacy: A History of Expurgated Books in England and America.* Boston: Godine, 1992.

Thomas, Donald. *A Long Time Burning: The History of Literary Censorship in England.* New York: Praeger, 1969.

MOLL FLANDERS

Author: Daniel Defoe
Original date and place of publication: 1722, England
Original publisher: Privately printed
Literary form: Novel

SUMMARY

Moll Flanders is subtitled "The Fortunes and Misfortunes of the Famous Moll Flanders, who was born in Newgate, and during a Life of continu'd Variety, for Threescore Years, besides her Childhood, was Twelve Year a *Whore*, five times a *Wife* (whereof once to her own Brother), Twelve Year a *Thief,* Eight Year a Transported *Felon* in *Virginia*, at last grew *Rich*, liv'd *Honest*, and died a *Penitent.*" The author, thus, aptly summarizes his book and provides readers with advance warning about the heroine they will encounter.

The author relates in the preface that this is "a private history . . . where the names and other circumstances of the person are concealed." Taking the charade farther, Defoe seeks to appease potential critics by acknowledging that the story of a woman so "debauched" and "wicked" makes it difficult "to wrap it up so clean as not to give room, especially for vicious readers, to turn it to his disadvantage." Still, Defoe warns that, for the book to be a true lesson in morality, "the wicked part should be made as wicked as the real history of it will bear."

In this spirit, Moll's adventures and philosophy are presented. She "kept true to this notion, that a woman should never be kept for a mistress that had money to make herself a wife," a state that she enters repeatedly. Sexual relationships are Moll's means to marriage. She is widowed in several instances and marries her brother in one; thus, nothing is left for "a poor desolate girl without friends" but to try again. When the novel ends, Moll appears comfortable and ready to enjoy a secure old age.

CENSORSHIP HISTORY

Moll Flanders was popular when it first appeared, running to three editions in the first year and another edition annually for the next 60 years. The book then disappeared from publication as a single entity until 1896, when it resurfaced in an edition published in Holland. Perrin states, "It was not expurgated; it was also not reviewed." Until the publication of the Dutch edition, however, the highly popular novel was informally banned by acts of omission, but wealthy fans of the work were able to obtain copies if they were willing to buy expensive entire sets of Defoe's works. This strategy was used by the Victorians to allow "wealthy 'strong' readers" to read forbidden works. Thus, both *Moll Flanders* and the similarly racy *Roxana* (1724) were included unexpurgated in several sets of Defoe's works during the 19th century. Buyers of these volumes secondhand would find one or both novels missing for, as Desmond MacCarthy states in *Criticism*, "When I was a boy, it [*Moll Flanders*] was not an easy book to come by. . . . From second-hand sets of Defoe's works that volume was frequently missing."

In 1892, when Viking Portables decided to issue an anthology entitled *Selections from Defoe's Minor Novels*, meaning everything but *Robinson Crusoe*, editor George Saintsbury expurgated *Moll Flanders* freely. Perrin describes the expurgation:

> But first he got out his gelding knife. Having picked a group of the blander scenes, he lopped out all racy paragraphs. . . . Then he went through again, cutting out individual sentences. . . . Finally he poked through word by word—and fell abruptly to the ranks of the lower-grade bowdlerists.

Even Defoe's subtitle created consternation among Victorians. In his comprehensive 1878 *Dictionary of English Literature*, W. Davenport Adams summarizes the subtitle as follows: "The title of a novel written by Daniel Defoe; the heroine of which is a female of questionable reputation, who afterwards becomes religious." As Perrin observes, "The one thing Moll's reputation isn't, of course, is questionable."

Through the first three decades of the 20th century, *Roxana* and *Moll Flanders* were among books regularly seized by local U.S. Customs inspectors for being "obscene," the last time in 1929 in New York City. The ban was lifted when the passage of the 1930 amendment to the Tariff Act eased restrictions on the importation of classics.

FURTHER READING

Alkon, Paul. *Defoe and Fictional Time*. Athens: University of Georgia Press, 1979.
"Defoe's Works Banned." *Publishers Weekly* (October 19, 1929): 1,938.
MacCarthy, Desmond. *Criticism*. London: J. Dent, 1932.

Moore, John R. *Daniel Defoe: Citizen of the Modern World.* Chicago: University of Chicago Press, 1958.

Perrin, Noel. *Dr. Bowdler's Legacy.* New York: Atheneum, 1969.

Sutherland, James. *Defoe.* Philadelphia, Pa.: J. B. Lippincott, 1938.

MY LIFE AND LOVES

Author: Frank Harris

Original dates and places of publication: 1925, France; 1926, United States

Original publishers: Privately printed (France); Up-to-Date Printing Co. (United States)

Literary form: Autobiography

SUMMARY

In the foreword to *My Life and Loves,* Harris claims that he intends to reveal all that life has taught him, and to especially "begin at the A.B.C. of love." He also aims "to warn the young and impressionable against the shoals and hidden reefs of life's ocean . . . [as well as] to teach youths how to use their magazine gun of sex so that it may last for years." Harris observes in the foreword that an additional goal is to encourage other writers to develop characters evenly by including "the sex side of characters" and thus bring them fully to life. In short, he claims that "it is the first book ever written to glorify the body and its passionate desires and the soul as well and its sacred, climbing sympathies."

The four volumes of Harris's autobiography present his extraordinary observations of public figures and public and literary events across decades and continents. The work also relates in detail his even more extraordinary sex life, from young childhood through old age, during a life that afforded him the opportunity and the drive for variegated experience. These frankly presented descriptions of his sexual experiences evoked criticism of the book from its first publication.

Harris gives little attention to his first four years of life, during which his mother died, but moves quickly to relate that he caught the nursery maid in bed with a man and soon learned that he could use this knowledge to blackmail her to give him more sugar on his bread. Sent to a girls' boarding school after his mother's death, he repeatedly drops his pencils to the ground, then crawls under tables, ostensibly to retrieve his pencil. He actually moves closer to the girls' legs, once even touching a calf and experiencing "my first taste of Paradise and the forbidden fruit—authentic heaven!" He claims that he records this incident "because it proves that sex-feeling may show itself in early childhood." From these early experiences, Harris progresses to adulthood and numerous adult sexual experiences, including his initiation by an experienced Greek woman into the ways of cunnilingus, which he dubbed "mouth-worship."

Blended with Harris's accounts of events and figures of his day are other stories of his successes and failures with women, ranging across continents, nationalities, and races. He trades stories of sexual prowess with French writer Guy de Maupassant, chronicles meetings with philosophers such as Maeterlinck, comments on Asian culture while describing the passion and sexual skills of his Japanese mistress, and criticizes the United States government for its handling of conscientious objectors during World War I. The work is a valuable social and historical document, despite its notoriety and the candid descriptions of Harris's sexual exploits.

CENSORSHIP HISTORY

My Life and Loves appeared in Paris in 1925 in plain brown wrappers that were also used when the book was shipped into England. Some copies were seized by British Customs officials, but many copies of the book made it to Soho bookshops. After police received complaints from private English citizens, they confiscated and destroyed copies of the work by magisterial order or by virtue of "disclaimers" signed by prudent booksellers. In essence, the police "disclaimer" form was a system developed by the London Metropolitan Police that enabled them to destroy books that no one would care to defend in court. The disclaimer said, in essence, that the bookshop owner disclaimed ownership to specific items seized from the bookstore on a given day, thus indicating that he or she would not dispute the seizures and giving the police freedom to destroy the items. The practice saved time because no summons was issued or served and no hearing before or examination of documents by a magistrate occurred. The police simply obtained a signed disclaimer and destroyed the books that they had judged to be indecent, thus making the police the determiners of public morality. Should a bookseller dispute the proceeding, a lengthy and expensive legal battle was certain to ensue.

In 1926 at the urging of the New York Society for the Suppression of Vice, the New York City police raided the Up-to-Date Printing Company, which was printing the American edition of the book, and seized about 300 copies of Volume 2. They also arrested the president of Up-to-Date, Norman Pomerantz, and two employees, as well as Esar Levine, Harris's United States agent. In leading the campaign, John Sumner proclaimed the work to be "the most obscene book published in the present century." He led a raid on the bindery, confiscated an additional 680 copies of the book, and arrested bindery employees Jacob Sidowsky and Harry J. Lebovit.

When the case went to trial, Lebovit and Pomerantz received fines totaling $750, and Levine received a workhouse sentence of 90 days. In its report of the case, *Publishers Weekly* supported the censors and declared *My Life and*

Loves to be "unfit for publication under the standards of any country." At the same time, the book received the lead review in the February 14, 1926, issue of the *Saturday Review of Literature*. In an attempt to circumvent the censors, Harris and his supporters quickly organized the Frank Harris Publishing Co. and published a bowdlerized version of the book, which was also challenged but survived.

FURTHER READING

Harris, Frank. Foreword to *My Life and Loves*. New York: Grove, 1963.

Kronhausen, Eberhard, and Phyllis Kronhausen. *Pornography and the Law: The Psychology of Erotic Realism*. New York: Ballantine, 1959.

"*My Life and Loves* Unfit." *Publishers Weekly*, March 27, 1926, p. 1,136.

Rolph, Cecil Hewitt. *Books in the Dock*. London: Deutsch, 1961.

Tobin, A. I., and Elmer Gertz. *Frank Harris: A Study in Black and White*. Chicago: Mendelsohn, 1931.

NATIVE SON

Author: Richard Wright
Original date and place of publication: 1940, New York
Original publisher: Harper and Sons
Literary type: Novel

SUMMARY

Native Son is the story of Bigger Thomas, a character whom Richard Wright revealed was a composite of the many angry oppressed black men he knew growing up, those who "consistently violated the Jim Crow laws of the South and got away with it, at least for a sweet brief spell. Eventually, the whites who restricted their lives made them pay a terrible price. They were shot, hanged, maimed, lynched, and generally hounded until they were either dead or their spirits broken." As Arnold Rampersad writes in his introduction to the HarperPerennial edition of *Native Son*, the novel "is a story that is at one level a seedy melodrama from the police blotter and, at the same time, an illuminating drama of an individual consciousness that challenges traditional definitions of character."

The novel is divided into three parts, rather than chapters, each division named for the experiences and emotions that envelop Bigger Thomas, the eldest of three children living with the impoverished Mrs. Thomas in a seedy, rat-infested apartment on Chicago's South Side. The first third of the story is entitled "Fear," and it opens with a view of the grim little apartment in which four people share one bedroom and struggle to maintain their dignity and modesty while sleeping, dressing, and undressing in the same small cramped room. Of the three children, Bigger is the most rebellious and most aware of the many opportunities that have been denied him, and he is also the least likely to acquiesce to the demands of the white world. As the novel begins, Bigger and his brother, Buddy, attempt to kill a rat that has terrorized their sister, Vera, and their mother. As the women scream in fright, Bigger and Buddy corner the rat behind a trunk and, although the creature defiantly slashes Bigger's trousers with its sharp teeth, kill it by slamming it with a skillet, after which Bigger crushes the rat's skull by pounding it with his shoe. After the excitement subsides, Mrs. Thomas and Vera repeat their earlier reminders that Bigger has a job interview that day. Mrs. Thomas taunts him with the charge that they could afford to live in better and safer housing if he did have a job and warns him that the way he now lives, hanging out with friends at the pool hall and remaining unemployed, will land him in jail. Vera exhibits her conscientious nature and worries that she will be late for her sewing classes at the YWCA, and Buddy appears to share the same concerns for making a go of life, but Bigger expresses disdain for their concerns.

As the day passes and Bigger waits until his 5:30 P.M. appointment with Mr. Dalton, a very rich white man whose daughter is involved with a communist and whose picture often appears in the society news columns, Bigger considers robbing Blum's Delicatessen with his friends Gus, Jack, and G. H. They have robbed businesses owned by African Americans, but this would be their first robbery of a white-owned business. Gus expresses doubts about the robbery, and Bigger taunts him for being a coward, but Gus responds that Bigger is afraid, afraid that Gus will say "yes." Jack steps between the two when Bigger attempts to attack Gus and distracts Bigger by going with him to the movies. Earlier, Bigger and Gus had played a game they called "white," in which they spoke and acted as they perceived wealthy and snobbish white people did. When a skywriting plane passes overhead, Bigger states that he could fly a plane if he were given the chance, a remark that makes both young men laugh bitterly and conclude that no white people would ever give Bigger or any other Negro the chance.

The films Jack and Bigger see provide a startling dichotomy of the way in which the white and black races are represented. The first movie shows a married rich white woman, who takes a lover, and who is seen golfing, swimming, and going to cocktail parties and to exclusive nightclubs. She returns to her husband after communists try to kill him, which leads Bigger and Jack to try to ascertain what a "Red" is, and they conclude that they must be violent people who live in Russia. The second movie stereotypically depicts naked African tribal women and men dancing wildly to the sound of beating drums. Bored by the second film, Bigger thinks about how he will soon be "getting hold of money" if Dalton hires him as a chauffeur. He begins to express hopefulness about his life and rejects the idea of robbing Blum's because he sees a possibility of having a job that will lead to money and success. Once he arrives at the Dalton residence in the all-white neighborhood, his confidence falters as he agonizes over which door to knock on, the front or the back. When the white housekeeper admits him to the house, he feels uncomfortable in the elegant surroundings, with its fine artwork, smooth white walls, and lovely furniture. Mr. Dalton welcomes him and asks about Bigger's family and past, and the reader learns that the old man's company owns the slum in which Bigger and his family live. As Dalton explains the duties of a chauffeur, his daughter Mary appears and begins a brief inquisition, talking about capitalists and trade unions with a familiarity that aggravates Bigger, although Dalton seems indifferent to what she says. Dalton bluntly reveals that he knows Bigger's reputation as a troublemaker, but as a supporter of the National Association for the Advancement of Colored People, he will give him the job. After the interview, the housekeeper Peggy provides Bigger's supper and explains that he will also be expected to tend to the furnace. In the kitchen, he also meets Mrs. Dalton who, although blind, startles Bigger by her keen perception of where he is and what he is doing.

In his first act of employment, Bigger is expected to drive Mary to the university, but the spoiled young white woman has other plans. She tells him that they will pick up her friend Jan Erlone, and the two make a big show of interacting with Bigger as equals and asking him to use their first names, actions that embarrass Bigger and cause him to feel a "dumb, cold, inarticulate hate" toward them. Mary and Erlone sit in the front seat, and Mary presses against Bigger as he drives. When the two ask him to join them in eating at Ernie's Kitchen Shack, "a place where colored people eat," Bigger is seen by his friend Jack and his sometime girlfriend Bessie, which displeases him.

Mary and Jan direct Bigger to drive them around the park while they drink beer and then rum and talk idealistically about communism, before a very drunk Erlone is taken to the train. Bigger drives a similarly drunk Mary home, where she stumbles noisily, leading him to carry her upstairs and to place the unconscious and suppliant young woman into bed, where he kisses her and begins to go further. "He lifted her and laid her on the bed. Something urged him to leave at once, but he leaned over her, excited, looking at her face in the dim light, not wanting to take his hands from her breasts. She tossed and mumbled sleepily. He tightened his fingers on her breasts, kissing her again, feeling her move toward him. He was aware only of her body now; his lips trembled."

As her body begins to respond to him, the door opens and Mrs. Dalton enters the room and calls out Mary's name. Bigger panics when Mary mumbles a response and, afraid that his presence will be revealed, he briefly presses a pillow against her face to keep her quiet. Mrs. Dalton leaves after accusing Mary of being "dead drunk," and Bigger realizes that he may have escaped discovery but has accidentally suffocated the young woman. Faced with the problem of saving his own life, Bigger thinks of a way to cast suspicion on Erlone and devises a plan for getting rid of Mary's body by placing it in her trunk, which he was supposed to take to the train the next day, then attempts to burn it in the furnace in the basement. The plan is temporarily blocked when he cannot fit the body entirely in the furnace, and he is forced to cut off her head with a hatchet and put both her head and body into the furnace then place a fresh load of coal into the fire. After removing the large amount of cash from Mary's purse, he returns to his home and sleeps.

Book Two, "Flight," opens the next morning, a bright and sunny Sunday. He hides the evidence he has accidentally taken home with him and runs out of the house, feeling that he has created a new life for himself. Convinced that he has murdered and gotten away with the act, he feels invincible. He knows that white people might accuse him of robbing, getting drunk, or raping, but he feels that they would never believe a black man would have the audacity to kill a white woman. The thought makes him brazen, and he spends some of the money he took from Mary's purse buying cigarettes for Gus, Jack, and G. H., then takes a streetcar to the Dalton home. While on the way, Bigger thinks of the murder and begins to feel pride in what he did, considering her murder a justification for the fear that white people have caused him over the years. "Now that the ice was broken, could he not do other things? What was there to stop him?" The action takes on a greater importance in his mind, and he thinks of the relationship between the races, characterizing white people as a "great natural force" against which blacks should join in a group and fight back to "end fear and shame."

Once at the Dalton home, Bigger is momentarily shaken from his newfound confidence when he finds Peggy looking into the furnace, but she expresses no suspicions, so he merely adds more coal and pretends to wait for Mary to come downstairs. After Peggy chastises him for leaving the car out all night, he responds that Mary had told him to do so and mentions that a man had visited her that night. While the family speculates where Mary has gone, Bigger delivers her empty trunk to the train station, then returns to hear Peggy tell Mrs. Dalton that Mary had not packed any clothes. When questioned, Bigger repeats his story about the night before and says Erlone had gone up to Mary's room, in an attempt to shift the guilt onto the young communist. After leaving, he visits Bessie and shows her the roll of money, after which she responds to his kisses and "she drew him to her bed." Afterward, "his body felt free and easy now that he had lain with Bessie." She tells him about a kidnapping case that occurred in the neighborhood where she worked, the real life case of Leopold and Loeb, who sent ransom notes to the family of a young boy they kidnapped and killed. The case gives Bigger a further idea to cover his crime, and he enlists Bessie's help in creating a ransom note to extort $10,000 from the Dalton family.

Britten, a private investigator hired by Dalton, confronts Bigger when he returns to the Dalton home and asks rapid-fire questions intended to trap him into admitting involvement with the Communist Party. In a clever move, Bigger, although frightened by Britten's approach and suspicions, manages to turn suspicion more fully in Erlone's direction and make himself a potential witness against the other man.

After coercing Bessie into helping him write the ransom note, Bigger returns to the Dalton home to surreptitiously deliver it. He is confronted again by Britten and several policemen who question him, asking insistently about Jan's activities with Mary the night before in the car, "Did Jan lay the girl?" "Did he lay her?"

Bigger runs away from the Dalton house after Mary's bones are found in the furnace, and he runs to Bessie and confesses what he did. She cries and tells him that no one will believe the death was accidental and, instead, "They'll say you raped her."

> They would say he raped her and there would be no way to prove he had not. That fact had not assumed importance in his eyes until now. He stood up, his jaw hardening. Had he raped her? Yes he had raped her. Every time he felt as he had felt that night, he raped. But rape was not what one did to women. Rape was what one felt when one's back was against the wall and one had to strike out, whether one wanted to or not, to keep the pack from killing one. He committed rape every time he looked into a white face. He was a long, taut piece of rubber which a thousand white hands had stretched to the snapping point, and when he snapped it was rape. But it was rape when he cried out in hate deep in his heart as he felt the strain of living day by day. That, too, was rape.

He and Bessie bundle up some bedding and leave her apartment to hide in an abandoned house, where Bigger plans to kill her. First, however, he wants to have sex. "He kept kissing her until her lips grew warm and soft. A huge warm pole of desire rose in him, insistent and demanding; he let his hand slide from her shoulder to her breasts, feeling one, then the other; he slipped his other arm beneath her head, kissing her again, hard and long." Despite her pleading to stop, and her attempts to push him away, Bigger rapes her. Hours later, because she could identify him and "It was his life against hers," he smashes her head with a brick, killing her. After he throws her body and the bloody bedclothes down an air shaft, he realizes that the money he had stolen from Mary's purse was in her dress pocket, but he decides not to retrieve it.

The police identify Bigger as Mary's killer and a manhunt throughout the city results in thousands of young black men being detained and questioned, while Bigger moves from one hiding place to another. He is finally captured when the police direct the fire department to turn the powerful hose on him in the freezing night, in an attempt to avoid his shooting anyone. As he is dragged away, he hears the shout of the crowd, "Kill that black ape!"

In the final book, Bigger faces trial for killing Mary. Despite Bigger's attempts to frame him, Jan tries to help him and obtains the services of a communist lawyer named Max. As Max would later acknowledge, Jan tells Bigger that knowing him has taught him a lot about the suffering of black people and revealed a plethora of details about the relationship between the races. Bigger also uses the time in jail to analyze his familial relationships and his attitude toward the world. He recognizes that his anger has driven him to commit heinous acts that have destroyed his chance for a future and removed all possibility of a meaningful life. At the end, despite all efforts by Max to defend him, Bigger is found guilty and sentenced to die.

CENSORSHIP HISTORY

Native Son was the object of censorship while still in manuscript form. In the Introduction to *New Essays on Native Son*, Kenneth Kinnamon quotes from letters between Wright and his editor, Edward Aswell. The original manuscript contained a masturbation episode in the scene where Bigger and Jack view several movies on the day that Bigger has his job interview with Mr. Dalton. Kinnamon relates that the episode appeared in several drafts until it was removed from the galley proof.

> Bigger and Jack are hardly seated when the graphic description begins: 'I'm polishing my nightstick,' Bigger said. Seen by a passing woman, Bigger and Jack are reported to the manager. The masturbation scene continues for a full page, ending when the two change seats because of the mess they have made.
>
> As the original episode in the Regal Theatre continues, the movie begins with a newsreel showing wealthy young white women on a Florida beach. One of these is Mary Dalton, who is shown in a close-up embracing Jan Erlone as the narrator comments: *"Mary Dalton, daughter of Chicago's Henry Dalton, 4605 Drexel Boulevard, shocks society by spurning the boys of La Salle Street and the Gold Coast and accepting the attentions of a well-known radical while on her recent winter vacation in Florida."* Other sexy scenes with mildly lewd comments by the narrator follow. Recognizing the address as the one at which he will make application for employment that very afternoon, Bigger and Jack discuss the sexual possibilities with Mary.

Referring to the censored galley proof, Kinnamon identifies other passages that Wright removed after reading marginal notes written by Aswell. The scene in which Bigger drives Mary and Erlone around the park was initially more sexually explicit and included a reference to Bigger's response that included "fighting off the stiffening feeling in his loins." A similar excision occurred in the scene in which Bigger carries the drunk Mary up to her room. In the galley passage, "He tightened his arms as his lips pressed tightly against hers and he felt her body moving strongly. The thought and conviction that Jan had had her a lot flashed through his mind. He kissed her again and felt the sharp bones of her hips move in a hard and veritable grind. Her mouth was open and her breath came slow and deep." The daring nature of the instances of interracial sexuality were not only shocking, but they might have prevented the book from being distributed. Kinnamon writes, "As Aswell knew, and as he must have argued to Wright, to retain such highly charged sexual scenes would risk censorship and thus prevent the larger political message from being conveyed, or at best undercut that message by diverting the salacious reader's attention."

Native Son has been challenged many times since its publication. In 1978, parents in Goffstown, New Hampshire, and in Elmwood Park, New Jersey, challenged use of the book in high school classrooms due to "objectionable language." In 1981, parents of Drury High School in North Adams, Massachusetts, petitioned the school to keep the novel out of the classroom. A member of the parental rights committee, Gerald Delisle, told a reporter, "There's enough pornography in movies and television. Why teach the kids something like that?" In response, the principal Roger F. Cirone defended the decision, based on the report compiled by a committee of parents, teachers, and students who "indicated it was proper to use the book, which had been in the school system at least 10 years." The parents took their complaint to school superintendent Robert Maroni, calling it a "garbage book filled with sex and violence." The superintendent turned down the parents' request to ban the book, saying, "I firmly believe that no parent or group of parents has a right to determine what students other than their own children may or may not read." The group then launched an appeal to the school committee, which heard their arguments in September 1981, and denied their request.

In 1988, the novel was challenged for use in both the classrooms and in the library of Berrien Springs, Michigan, high school because parents asserted that the novel is "vulgar, profane, and sexually explicit." The novel was retained for use in the Yakima, Washington, schools in 1994 after a five-month dispute over what advanced high school students should study in class. Two parents complained to school officials about the profanity and "images of violence and sexuality" in the book and asked for it to be removed from the reading list. In 1996, parents of students enrolled in advanced placement English classes at Northwest High School in High Point, North Carolina, asked the school board to remove the novel because it is "sexually graphic and violent." In 1998, the novel was removed from the high school curriculum in Fort Wayne, Indiana, because of the "graphic language" and "sexual content."

FURTHER READING

Blades, John. "The Uncut Version of Richard Wright's Original 'Native Son,' 'Black Boy' Restores Power of His Themes." *Chicago Tribune*, October 7, 1991, p. 1.

Doyle, Robert. *2007 Banned Books Resource Guide*. Chicago, Ill.: American Library Association, 2007.

Kinnamon, Kenneth, ed. *New Essays on Native Son*. New York: Cambridge University Press, 1990.

"New England News Brief: 'Native Son' Ban Sought." *Boston Globe*, July 15, 1981, p. 1.

"New England News Briefs: School Book Ban Still Sought." *Boston Globe*, July 14, 1981, p. 1.

"New Try in N. Adams Tonight to Ban 'Native Son' at School." *Boston Globe*, September 1, 1981, p. 1.

Rampersad, Arnold. Introduction. *Native Son*. New York: HarperCollins, 1993.
Tolbert, Kathy. "Parents' Bid to Cut Book from Reading List Rejected." *Boston Globe*, July 24, 1981, p. 1.

A NIGHT IN A MOORISH HAREM

Author: Anonymous
Original date and place of publication: 1854, England
Original publisher: Privately published
Literary form: Novel

SUMMARY

A Night in a Moorish Harem is one of the most famous of the underground pornographic classics that circulated freely in Victorian England. Purported to be the account of "Lord George Herbert," who is described in the preface as "the handsomest man in the English nobility," the first-person narrative relates one night in a Moroccan harem containing nine women, each representing a different Mediterranean nationality. Herbert had anchored his ship, the *Antler*, off the coast of Morocco and gone for a swim to cool his sexual frustrations that had built up after months without one of "the beautiful women of London and the favours which some of them had granted me." After the swim, he fell asleep in a small boat that was initially attached to the ship but slipped free and floated away from the ship. When he awakened, he was near shore and under the wall of a large building from which nine women of the pasha's harem were watching him. They tied their shawls together and Herbert pulled himself up to their rooms using the shawl rope.

Once Herbert is inside, the women strip him of his wet clothes and then begin to strip themselves. Their pasha is away for the night, and they all are endlessly ardent and eager to gratify Herbert's desires. In between his sexual performances, with each woman in turn, Herbert listens to the stories of their sex lives, including various sexual adventures such as lesbian interludes and mating with a stallion.

The requisite responses are assigned to each girl, as they "swoon," "groan with pleasure," "undulate," or move "sinuously." For his part, Herbert exhibits great prowess, and his often "rigid shaft" or "swollen shaft" is said to "gush" great quantities of semen. The women, in turn, are all "tight and elastic and hot and juicy." At one point, the women all decide to measure Herbert and, one at a time, each takes her bracelet and "clasped it around my shaft. But the clasp would not fasten. The bracelet was not large enough." He turns the tables on the women and measures their thighs, breasts, and "the length of their slits."

The story ends as the dawn approaches, and Herbert weakly tells the women that he must return to his ship. They help him to dress and lower

211

him safely to his waiting boat below their window; he returns to his ship while they await the return of the pasha.

CENSORSHIP HISTORY

A Night in a Moorish Harem was a popular underground pornographic classic in Victorian England long before it crossed the Atlantic Ocean and appeared in the United States. The book was published privately, or by overnight presses, and no established publishing house made it part of the backlist. In December 1923, Maurice Inman and Max Gottschalk, two New York booksellers, were arrested for selling three underground literary classics: *A Night in a Moorish Harem*, *Only a Boy*, and FANNY HILL. The purchaser was Charles J. Bamberger, a longtime agent of the New York Society for the Suppression of Vice whose specialty in erotica made him a valuable aid to society secretaries Anthony Comstock and John Sumner for more than 40 years. The booksellers appeared in special sessions court in New York City in March 1924, were convicted for selling "obscene" material, and were fined $25 each. *Publishers Weekly* applauded the convictions and observed that the suppression of "such admittedly obscene books" was "a salutary measure of which the book trade may well approve."

In 1931, the vice society brought charges against bookseller Frances Stel-off for selling *Hsi Men Ching* and *A Night in a Moorish Harem*, but the court dismissed the charges.

Two years earlier, Reverend Philip Yarrow, leader of the Illinois Vigilance Association, launched a campaign against Chicago booksellers and used entrapment to obtain his evidence. Walter Shaver, owner of a chain of Chicago bookstores, was charged with selling Yarrow a copy of *A Night in a Moorish Harem*. Tried in municipal court in January 1930, Shaver testified that an agent of Yarrow's had badgered him into ordering a copy of the book and argued that his was a case of entrapment. The jury agreed and returned a verdict of not guilty. In retaliation, Shaver instructed his lawyer to file a damage suit against Yarrow, and the vice crusader fought back through his newspaper, *Vigilance*, claiming that "classical smut has no more standing under the law than low-down smut." He was supported by the *Christian Century*, which praised Yarrow for his "moral policing of the beasts who specialized in distributing moral sewage." The *Chicago Evening Post* exposed Yarrow's entrapment methods and published photographs of checks that Yarrow had received as informant fees in obscenity convictions. While the trial progressed, Shaver's business sank into bankruptcy, thus inflaming public opinion further against Yarrow. In April 1931, a Chicago superior court jury awarded Shaver $5,000 in damages, a judgment that was reversed on appeal a year later.

FURTHER READING

"Battling the Wolves." *Christian Century* 48 (April 8, 1931): 470–471.

Boyer, Paul S. *Purity in Print: The Vice Society Movement and Book Censorship in America.* New York: Scribner's, 1968.

"Chicago Bookseller Wins Case." *Publishers Weekly*, April 4, 1931, p. 1,790.

Farriman, Milton. "Bookseller Victorious in Chicago Reformer's Campaign." *Publishers Weekly*, February 1, 1930, pp. 566–568.

"Gottschalk Fined for Obscene Book Sale." *Publishers Weekly*, March 8, 1924, p. 834.

Marcus, Stephen. *The Other Victorians*. New York: Basic Books, 1966.

"Neither Censorship nor Puritanism Involved." *Christian Century*, March 19, 1930, pp. 357–358.

"Two Booksellers Arrested on Sumner Complaint." *Publishers Weekly*, December 23, 1923, p. 1,974.

NOVEMBER (NOVEMBRE)

Author: Gustave Flaubert

Original dates and places of publication: 1914, France; 1921, United States

Original publishers: Editions du Seuil (France); Roman Press (United States)

Literary form: Novel

SUMMARY

The sexual encounters in *November* were based on an actual relationship that the 18-year-old Flaubert had experienced with a 35-year-old woman named Eulalie Foucaud, the daughter of a hotel keeper named Delanglade, in Marseilles. Never certain if she was widowed or still married, the young author spent four passionate days with her and then left, fearful that she would encroach on his private life. They wrote for eight months but never met again.

The novel is divided into three sections. The first two sections present a young man at age 15 and then at age 18. In the first section, the young protagonist first becomes sexually aware. He expresses feelings about women in the abstract, relating how he watches the prostitutes and mingles with them on the streets. He also watches the women who entertain at the fairgrounds and becomes "tormented" as he dreams of "those strangely formed thighs so firmly encased in pink tights, those supple arms wreathed in bangles." At 15, he exhibits an inexperienced sensuality and yearns for the women, asserting that "there is no age at which we do not dream of women: as children we squeeze the breasts of the big girls who kiss us and hold us in their arms."

In the second section, the now-18-year-old protagonist desires a mistress. He decides suddenly to visit a prostitute and states, "I felt dimly the oncoming of my season of heat. . . . I felt a need for sensual pleasure. . . . [M]y passion overflowed." In his assignation with Marie, the young man provides the reader with his impressions before intercourse, as he watches "the shape of her breasts come and go in the motion of her breathing," and he marvels that "she had one of those splendid bosoms on which one would wish to die." The actual sexual experience is described in generalities:

> Her warm, tremulous flesh stretched beneath me, quivering. From head to foot I was all sensuality; my mouth pressed to hers, our fingers intertwined, shaken by one spasm, interlaced in one embrace.

Afterward, Marie tells the young man her story, and she begs him to love her. For some unexplained reason, however, he delays returning to her, by which time she has disappeared. He spends the rest of his life thinking of her and observes, "It was she that I pursued everywhere; in the beds of others I dreamed of her caresses."

CENSORSHIP HISTORY

November was completed in 1840, before Flaubert was 21 years old, but he refused to have it published during his lifetime. Although he avoided any explanation of his reticence, aside from references to the sexual content and the focus on the prostitute Marie, biographers have suggested that the intensely personal background of the narrative is a more likely reason. He claimed to have thought often of the model for Marie, Eulalie Foucaud, until the end of his life.

Therefore, the first French publication of the novel did not occur until 1914, and the first English translation emerged in 1921 when Ernest Reichl published *November* as part of the Individual Library series of books of his Roman Press imprint. Reichl made these books available in attractive leather bindings with specially designed title pages. The following year, the novel was seized by United States Customs as "obscene," but it was released after being reviewed by literature experts of the Customs bureau.

In 1935, a bookseller named Herbert Miller was charged by John Sumner, secretary of the New York Society for the Suppression of Vice, with selling an obscene book, the Roman Press edition of *November*. Miller was taken to City Magistrates Court of New York City, Fourth District, Borough of Manhattan. Sumner charged that the work lacked "decency" and that it violated "contemporary public morals." In reaching a determination in *People on Complaint of Sumner v. Miller,* 279 N.Y.S. 583 (1935), City Magistrate Goldstein observed that

> the criterion of decency is fixed by time, place, geography and all the elements that make for a constantly changing world. A practice regarded as decent in one period may be indecent in another. . . . To change standards of morals is the task of the school and church; the task of the judge is to record the tides of public opinion, not to emulate King Canute in an effort to turn back the tide.

Magistrate Goldstein dismissed the complaint and discharged the defendant, after noting that there was not sufficient cause to hold the defendant for trial.

FURTHER READING

Kilpatrick, James J. *The Smut Peddlers.* New York: Doubleday, 1960.
Lottman, Herbert. *Flaubert: A Biography.* Boston: Little, Brown, 1989.
Troyat, Henri. *Flaubert.* Paris: Librairie Ernest Flammarion, 1988.

THE 120 DAYS OF SODOM (LES 120 JOURNÉES DE SODOME)

Author: Marquis de Sade

Original dates and places of publication: 1904, Germany; 1962, France; 1966, United States

Original publishers: Fischer (Germany); Olympia Press (France); Grove Press (United States)

Literary form: Collection of tales

SUMMARY

The 120 Days of Sodom was a carefully planned work that de Sade completed while incarcerated, first in Vincennes and then in the Bastille. The work was written on both sides of numerous pieces of loose paper that the author then pasted end to end, rolled up, and hid in his cell for safekeeping. When de Sade left the Bastille in 1789, the work remained. The manuscript was found in the cell in 1832 by a man named Arnoux de Saint-Maxim, who passed it on to the Villeneuve-Trans family, but it remained unpublished until the 20th century.

The author originally planned to illustrate through 600 examples all possible perversions. The premise for the book is that four wealthy and jaded men join forces and send their agents throughout France to kidnap the handsomest boys and the prettiest girls from the country's richest and most distinguished families. The children then are taken to the mountaintop castle of one of the men, where they are locked in with the men and four of the most experienced brothel mistresses in Paris. The entrances are all walled up, and the sole bridge that connects the castle to the outside world is removed. The voluptuaries have provided themselves with every necessity and every possible luxury and, secure from the prying eyes of the outside world, they embark on a continuous orgy.

The brothel mistresses are assigned the task of relating the experiences of their lives, in an assigned order and in graphic detail. The plan is that each woman will tell five stories each day of the most interesting sexual perversions possible, beginning with the "simple passions" in November and ending with the "murderous passions" in February. As Marchand notes, "there were to be 600 different tales of sexual profligacy, systematically ordered, and proceeding in the direction of ever greater and rarer perversions." While the tales are told, the boys and girls are kept close at hand so that the men can immediately gratify any sexual arousal that may occur.

Only 150 of the stories, the "simple passions," are completed. The remaining stories exist in outline form. The stories tell of "buggering," "frigging," "fucking," and devouring of excrement, all in repeated and graphic detail. The tales tend more toward the grotesque than the erotic, with their "discharges of spittle," the burying of hatpins and other sharp objects in flesh, and the repeated episodes of pederasty.

CENSORSHIP HISTORY

The 120 Days of Sodom was banned from bookstores when it was first published in a limited edition in Germany, despite the learned notes to the text provided by psychiatrist Iwan Bloch, who had justified the publication by emphasizing its scientific importance. Authorities decried the pederasty and emphasis upon excrement throughout the work and the infliction of pain in the latter tales.

In 1966, Corgi Books in England planned to release the paperback edition of *The 120 Days of Sodom*, having already released the "complete and unexpurgated" edition of JUSTINE in 1965. Unfortunately for the publisher, the sensational Moors murder trial occurred in 1966 in England following the murders by Myra Hindley and Ian Brady of two children, aged 7 and 12, and one 17-year-old between December 1964 and October 1965. They photographed and tape-recorded their torture and mutilation of the victims. In court, Brady told the judge that he had studied carefully de Sade's instructions, "Is murder a crime in the eyes of Nature? . . . Destruction is Nature's method of progress. . . . Murder is often necessary, never criminal and essential to tolerate in a republic." The public outcry stifled plans to reprint additional books by de Sade. As reviewer Ludovic Kennedy stated in an April 29, 1966, article in *The Spectator* regarding the Moors trial and books, "No respectable publisher would print a novel containing what is alleged." Because de Sade's novels contained scenes similar to what occurred in the Moors murders, "no British publisher who valued his respectability should publish de Sade," as Sutherland states. The first English translation was published by Grove Press in 1966.

FURTHER READING

Hayman, Ronald. *De Sade: A Critical Biography*. New York: Crowell, 1978.

Kendrick, Walter. *The Secret Museum: Pornography in Modern Culture*. Baltimore: Penguin, 1988.

Kennedy, Ludovic. "The Moors Murders and de Sade." *Spectator*, April 29, 1966, pp. 23–25.

Lever, Maurice. *Sade: A Biography*. Translated by Arthur Goldhammer. New York: Farrar, Straus & Giroux, 1993.

Marchand, Henry L. *The French Pornographers: Including a History of French Erotic Literature.* New York: Book Awards, 1965.

Sutherland, John. *Offensive Literature: Decensorship in Britain, 1960–1982.* London: Junction Books, 1982.

OUR LADY OF THE FLOWERS (NOTRE-DAME-DES-FLEURS)

Author: Jean Genet
Original dates and places of publication: 1943, France; 1963, United States
Original publishers: L'Arbalete (France); Grove Press (United States)
Literary form: Novel

SUMMARY

Our Lady of the Flowers, written while Genet was serving a sentence in Fresnes prison in France, creates a world in which the author presents in a positive light every attribute despised by society and every crime. Sartre observed that the book is less an attempt at communication than it is "a willful perversion of the sexual act. . . . [I]t is the epic of masturbation."

Throughout, Genet fantasizes in this highly autobiographical novel about past lovers, giving them such names as Mimosa, Darling, First Communion, and Divine, and he imagines himself making love to them. The name Our Lady of the Flowers is given to the former butcher boy and brutal murderer, Adrien Baillon, who is on trial, while Darling is really a stereotypical muscleman, pimp, and shoplifter; Divine is a transvestite male streetwalker once named Louis Culafroy, whose companions and fellow transvestites are Mimosa, First Communion, and Lady Apple.

The novel does not contain a conventional plot. Rather, episodes are superimposed upon each other, moving from the beginning, which presents the funeral of Divine, to the end, which is "her" death. At the funeral gather "the girl-queens and boy-queens, the aunties, fags, and nellies" who are part of Divine's circle. From that point, the novel returns to the past to explain how Louis Culafroy became Divine and then recreates "her" life, affairs, and drug use. She becomes involved with Darling, who becomes her pimp, and the two live together and attend Mass regularly. The novel mixes graphic sexual imagery with religious symbolism, most pointedly mimicked in the name Our Lady of the Flowers. Repeated homosexual encounters are described, as if to prove the statement made by Darling that "a male that fucks another male is a double male." The novel ends with Darling in prison, sending a letter that contains a dotted line and the instruction "kiss it." Genet explains that "the dotted line that Darling refers to is the outline of his prick."

CENSORSHIP HISTORY

Our Lady of the Flowers contains images and references that for two decades were considered too "obscene" to encourage any publisher to put out an English edition of the book, and the French version met with opposition in England. In 1957, the reference department of Birmingham Public Library in England ordered the two-volume French-language version of the work, but it was seized by British Customs and refused entry into England. Craig states that

> if the books had reached their destination, they could have been understood only by advanced students of the French language, and the librarian would have been responsible that they were issued only to responsible readers.

Birmingham authorities failed to support sufficiently their ordering of the book, sending a representative ignorant of the French language to the Custom and Excise Office in London, where he was persuaded to avoid challenging the seizure in the courts. Further, the chair of the Public Libraries Committee, also ignorant of the French language, was present and "was dreadfully shocked at passages translated for their benefit which dealt with homosexual incidents."

The English version of *Our Lady of the Flowers*, published by Grove Press in 1963, was banned in Ireland on October 23, 1965. A prohibition order was published in the *Iris Oifigiuil*, "the only official source from which booksellers [and readers] might learn of a new prohibition order," in which all articles blacklisted by the Irish Board of Censors were listed. According to the Censorship of Publications Bill of 1928, "the notice in *Iris Oifigiuil* should be sufficient evidence in the courts of summary jurisdiction as to the character of the publication." The Irish Board of Censors found the novel "obscene" and "indecent," objecting particularly to the author's handling of the theme of homosexuality and brutal crime. The work was officially banned from sale in Ireland until the introduction of the Censorship Publications Bill in 1967 reduced to 12 years the duration of a prohibition order, and the work was among 5,000 titles released from the list of banned books.

FURTHER READING

Adams, Michael. *Censorship: The Irish Experience.* Tuscaloosa: University of Alabama Press, 1968.

Craig, Alec. *Suppressed Books: A History of the Conception of Literary Obscenity.* New York: World Publishing, 1963.

Molz, Kathleen. "The Public Custody of the High Pornography." *American Scholar* (Winter 1966–67): 93–103.

Perkins, Michael. *The Secret Record: Modern Erotic Literature.* New York: William Morrow and Company, 1976.

Sartre, Jean-Paul. *Saint Genet: Comedian and Martyr.* New York: Braziller, 1952.
White, Edmund. *Genet: A Biography.* New York: Knopf, 1994.

OUTLAW REPRESENTATION: CENSORSHIP AND HOMOSEXUALITY IN TWENTIETH-CENTURY AMERICAN ART

Author: Richard Meyer
Original date and place of publication: 2002, New York
Original publisher: Oxford University Press
Literary form: Nonfiction book

SUMMARY

Outlaw Representation is a profusely illustrated and heavily documented scholarly study of the censorship of works by gay artists from 1934 to 2000, with specific focus on the careers of Andy Warhol, Robert Mapplethorpe, David Wojnarowicz, Gran Fury, and Holly Hughes. In this work, Meyer analyzes the works of gay artists and the circumstances under which their works have been suppressed, attacked, and censored, as well as the manner in which these artists have responded to such threats. Meyer observes that, rather than give in to censors who have labeled their works indecent or obscene, most artists have produced their own "outlaw representations" of homosexuality and "used the outlaw status of homosexuality to propose new forms of social, sexual and creative life."

The study provides a detailed analysis of the confiscation from the Corcoran Gallery of Art in Washington, D.C., by the U.S. Navy in 1934 of the oil painting *The Fleet's In!* by Paul Cadmus. The painting portrays sailors on shore leave carousing with several highly made-up and sensuously dressed women and one effeminate-appearing rouged man with gay trademark red tie and seemingly bleached hair. Meyer's book includes more than 200 images, including photographs from physique magazines, illustrations from gay liberation posters, and paintings, to examine the conflicts surrounding homosexuality that have defined the direction of modern art in America. The author also examines the contemporary conflicts over federal funding for the arts and homoerotic art and, in particular, the insistence by the National Endowment for the Arts (NEA) on "general standards of decency," a vague statement that led the NEA to withdraw funding from four artists in 1990 and that resulted in a U.S. Supreme Court case, *Finley v. NEA*, 118 S.Ct. 2168 (1998). Overall, Meyer provides a carefully considered visual analysis of once-censored works and provides readers with a detailed historical context for each.

CENSORSHIP HISTORY

The censorship of *Outlaw Representation: Censorship and Homosexuality in Twentieth-Century American Art*, a scholarly book about censorship, offers an irony that must be examined. Meyer contracted with Oxford University Press in the United States in 1995 to write the book and gave the publisher worldwide rights as part of the agreement. After he had written the text and obtained signed permissions for the photographs that he planned to include in the book, editors at the Oxford University Press home office in England raised concerns about two of the photographs, which the company wanted Meyer to remove from the book. One photograph was a picture taken in 1979 by gay U.S. photographer Robert Mapplethorpe of two leather-clad homosexuals that the author planned to position in the book next to a 1953 coronation photograph of Queen Elizabeth and Prince Philip taken by gay British photographer Cecil Beaton. The second was a photograph of a naked five-year-old boy, Jessie McBride, photographed in 1976 by Mapplethorpe on a commission from Mrs. McBride, who was in the room when the photograph was taken. Oxford University Press officials asked Meyer to remove the photographs in the interest of good taste, but he refused to do so. The publisher was also concerned that the photograph of the naked young boy might result in criminal charges. As a result, Oxford University Press forbade the sale of *Outlaw Representation* in Great Britain and in Canada. Meyer stated in an interview with *The Advocate*, "I was informed that the London office of Oxford University Press would not distribute the book in England or anywhere in Europe. Attorneys representing the publisher said that publishing the picture of the child would violate two criminal statutes in England, the Protection of Children Act and the Criminal Justice Act, so the book was only made available in the United States." In an interview given to the *Washington Post*, Meyer stated, "Oxford has, in effect, censored a scholarly book on censorship."

In January 2002, Meyer was scheduled to speak at an event sponsored by Glad Day Bookshop, Canada's first and longest-existing lesbian and gay bookstore, and organizers planned to have copies of *Outlaw Representation* available for signing and sale. They discovered that Oxford University Press had not published the book in Canada nor was the press distributing it there. Glad Day considered canceling the event, but managed to obtain from an unidentified source 30 copies of the U.S. edition.

FURTHER READING

"Boys and the Banned: Michael Warner on *Outlaw Representation*." *Artforum International*, April 1, 2002, p. 35.
Bryan-Wilson, Julia. "Pictures at a Deposition." *Art Journal* 62, no. 2 (Summer 2003): 102.
D'Arcy, David. "Banned in Britain." *The Art Newspaper*. International edition. Formerly available online. URL: http://www.theartnewspaper.com/news/article. asp?idart+9612. Accessed November 30, 2005.

Houchin, Steve. "Professor of Art History Honored by Smithsonian for Book about Banned Homosexual Images." Available online. URL: http://www.hnn.us/articles/printfriendly/1722.html#book9-25-03. Posted September 25, 2003. Accessed January 3, 2006.

Kennicott, Philip. "'Gay' Art: Dolled Up and Still Dressed Down." *Washington Post*, November 30, 2003, p. N07.

Miller, Tim. "Taking on the Antigay Censors." *Advocate*. Available online. URL: http://www.advocate.com/html/stories/857/857_outlaw.asp. Accessed November 30, 2005.

PAMELA, OR VIRTUE REWARDED

Author: Samuel Richardson
Original date and place of publication: 1740, England
Original publisher: Privately printed
Literary form: Epistolary novel

SUMMARY

Pamela, or Virtue Rewarded is concerned with a domestic middle-class and predominantly feminine world of "domestic politeness." The novel grew out of a project that several booksellers commissioned of Richardson, a book of letters to be used as models by the less educated when they needed to write on special occasions. Among these models was a letter written by parents to their daughter, a servant whose master had tried to seduce her. Richardson's imagination was piqued by the idea, and he expanded it into the series of letters that became *Pamela*.

The letters from Pamela to her parents dramatize her sexual ordeal, as she describes the manner in which Mr. B attempts first to seduce and then to rape her. The story pits pure female innocence against ruthless and powerful male lust in letters that are frequently written by Pamela on the run, as she escapes one trap after another. Writing in her room, Pamela hears Mr. B at her door, so she hurriedly grabs her paper and pen and continues to scribble while slipping out through an open window. She runs from him, but not so quickly that he will not catch her.

Despite all protestations of innocence, Pamela provides her readers with detailed descriptions of her ravishment. Nearly swooning, she has the presence of mind to write, "he then put his hand in my bosom," before she "fainted away with terror." She repeatedly locks herself in a closet or her room but never takes any of the many opportunities to leave the estate. Mr. B finally marries Pamela.

CENSORSHIP HISTORY

Pamela's behavior motivated both praise and censure for the novel. Although Richardson's proclaimed intention was to show the reward (marriage) to be gained when a girl preserves her virtue, his contemporaries were skeptical. Author Henry Fielding attacked in a parody named *Shamela* (1741) what he viewed as Pamela's facile opportunism. His view was that, rather than an innocent victim, the servant girl was a coy temptress who, with bold calculation, constantly put herself in Mr. B's line of vision. Another contemporary, Charles Povey, blasted Richardson's "inflammatory novel" in his work *Virgin in Eden* (1741), stating, "What can youths and virgins learn from *Pamela*'s letters, more than lessons to tempt their chastity." The outraged moralist asserted that Pamela showed a lack of the very modesty for which Richardson had praised her when she exposed herself a second time to Mr. B's advances.

Pamela was condemned by the Roman Catholic Church in 1744 and was prohibited reading for Catholics. It appeared on the Index librorum prohibitorum mainly because it was a novel that related a suggestively romantic relationship, despite Richardson's pretense of presenting a moral. The work appears on the Index of Benedict XIV, issued in 1758, and the Indexes of Pope Leo XIII, issued in 1881 and 1900 and still in force in 1906. As Putnam observes, the selection of fiction that appears on various editions of the Index is "curiously disproportionate, and in fact almost haphazard in its character."

Both *Pamela* and Richardson's *Clarissa Harlowe* (1747) were published as long chapbooks in the United States in 1772, when Reverend Jonathan Edwards warned the young against reading both books more because they were fiction, "considered a sinful form of writing, than because of any intrinsic sin."

In 1893, the American Library Association created for the first time a 5,000-title book guide for small popular libraries and branches, claiming it to be a collection that "one could recommend to any trustee." *Pamela* and *Clarissa Harlowe* were omitted from the list, although works by Henry Fielding were included. When the ALA released its *Catalog* in 1904, the continued exclusion of *Pamela* and *Clarissa Harlowe* from the list implied censorship by omission. Many individuals agreed with Corinne Bacon, first a librarian at the Newark (New Jersey) Public Library and later the editor of the H. W. Wilson *Fiction Catalog*, in criticizing the heroine who "held out for a 'higher price' (marriage), as more immoral than Hester Prynne of *The Scarlet Letter.*"

FURTHER READING

Bacon, Corinne. "What Makes a Novel Immoral?" *Wisconsin Library Bulletin* 6 (August 1910): 83–95.

Geller, Evelyn. *Forbidden Books in American Public Libraries, 1876–1939.* Westport, Conn.: Greenwood, 1984.

Thomas, Donald. *A Long Time Burning: The History of Literary Censorship in England.* New York: Praeger, 1969.

PANSIES

Author: D. H. Lawrence
Original date and place of publication: 1929, England
Original publisher: Privately printed
Literary form: Poetry collection

SUMMARY

Pansies is a collection of poems, its title a play on the French term *pensees* (thoughts), that Lawrence first published privately in its entirety.

As Lawrence states in the introduction to *Pansies*, "I should wish these *Pansies* to be taken as thoughts rather than anything else; casual thoughts that are true while they are true and irrelevant when the mood and circumstance changes." In essence, the poems do not form a manifesto for Lawrence, nor did he consider that he was making any sort of statement in their publication. Rather, he expressed his personal philosophy on a range of issues, from censors to love, in poems entitled "All I Ask," "Let Us Talk, Let Us Laugh," and "Women Want Fighters for Their Lovers," as well as 225 others.

Censors were shocked by such verses as the following:

> The fighting cock, the fighting cock—
> have you got one, little blighters?
> Let it crow then, like one o'clock!
>   (from "Women Want Fighters for Their Lovers")

> They say I wrote a naughty book
> With perfectly awful things in it,
> putting in all the impossible words
> like b - - - - and f - - - - and sh - - .
>   (from "My Naughty Book")

CENSORSHIP HISTORY

Lawrence sent the manuscript of *Pansies* to agent Curtis Brown on January 7, 1929, and learned three weeks later that Brown had never received the package. Using powers granted by the Post Office Act of 1908, Home Secretary Sir William Joyson-Hicks ("Jix") had ordered the police to intercept and review all mail sent by Lawrence into England in the effort to locate copies of the Orioli edition of LADY CHATTERLEY'S LOVER. The postal inspector who intercepted the *Pansies* manuscript "was disturbed" by it and sent it to Joyson-Hicks, who agreed that the poems were "indecent" and sent the manuscript to the director of public prosecutions.

The fanfare surrounding the seizure led to a debate in Parliament, when the Labour Party representative of West Leicester, F. W. Pethick-Lawrence, asked Home Secretary Joyson-Hicks

> if he will give the names and official positions of the persons on whose advice he causes books and manuscripts to be seized and banned; what are the qualifications of such persons for literary censorship; and whether, to assist authors and publishers, he will state what are the rules and regulations, the contravention of which causes a book to be seized and banned by his Department?

Joyson-Hicks attempted to circumvent accountability for the seizure by pointing out that Lord Campbell's act gave a metropolitan police magistrate or any two justices of the peace powers that "on sworn information" they might issue a search warrant. But Pethick-Lawrence pressed the issue and asked Joyson-Hicks what that had to do with the government's confiscation of materials in the mails. The home secretary then stated that if a violation of rights had occurred, it was the responsibility of the police. However, he adamantly insisted that no violation had occurred because British postal laws decreed that the postmaster general should "refuse to take part in the conveyance of any indecent matter." In this case, Lawrence's manuscript was discovered "during a routine inspection of packages for concealed letters sent through the mails at lower than lawful postal rates." He added that the manuscript was then sent to his office and "by my directions forwarded to the Director of Public Prosecutions."

Pethick-Lawrence demanded to know who had determined the material to be "obscene." Joyson-Hicks responded that the postmaster general made the first determination and then sent it to him. He stated that in regard to the *Pansies* manuscript, "It is not a question of literary merit at all, and, if the honourable Member has any doubt, I will show him the book in question. It contains grossly indecent matter."

Publisher Martin Secker conceded that some of the poems "should be eliminated" and removed 14 poems—"The Noble Englishman," "Women Want Fighters for Their Lovers," "Ego-Bound Women," "There Is No Way Out," "My Naughty Book," "The Little Wowser," "The Young and Their Moral Guardians," "What Matters," "What Does She Want?," "Don't Look at Me!," "To Clarinda," "Demon Justice," "Be a Demon," and "The Jeune Fille"—before publishing the collection in 1931. Lawrence also authorized P. R. Stephenson to bring out an unexpurgated edition in collaboration with bookseller Charles Lahr. The government censorship made the poems more attractive to buyers, and the collection sold well.

FURTHER READING

DeGrazia, Edward. *Girls Lean Back Everywhere: The Law of Obscenity and the Assault on Genius.* New York: Random House, 1992.

Lawrence, D. H. *Literature and Censorship.* Ed. by Harry T. Moore. New York: Viking, 1959.

Nehls, Edward, ed. *D. H. Lawrence: A Composite Biography.* Madison: University of Wisconsin Press, 1959.

Pollnitz, Christopher. "The Censorship and Transmission of D. H. Lawrence's "Pansies": the Home Office and the "Foul-Mouthed Fellow." *Journal of Modern Literature* 28, no. 3 (Spring 2005): 44–71.

Rolph, Cecil Hewitt. *Books in the Dock.* London: Deutsch, 1961.

THE PERFUMED GARDEN

Translator: Sir Richard Burton
Original dates and places of publication: 1886, Switzerland; 1933, England
Original publishers: The Kama Shastra Society (Switzerland); Fortune Press (England)
Literary form: Sex manual

SUMMARY

The Perfumed Garden, attributed to the 15th-century Sheikh Nefzaoui, was first translated from Arabic into French by Isadore Liseux in 1885, and then from French into English by Burton, who called it "a manual of erotology." In his notes to the translation, Burton questions, "What can be more important, in fact, than the study of principles upon which rest the happiness of man and woman, by reason of their mutual relations?" The work functions as a book of sexual etiquette and does not simply describe sexual positions. Rather, chapters contain instructions and illustrative stories that suggest ways of improving coition, dealing with praiseworthy men and women, dealing with men and women who are worthy of contempt, improving the act of generation, curing impotence, eliminating body odor, determining the sex of a fetus, and dealing with deceitful spouses.

The work contains numerous Arabic words for male and female genitals, as well as definitions that are amusing and graphic but avoid the clinical aspect of 20th-century sex manuals. Included are recipes to cure impotence ("a glassful of very thick honey, twenty almonds, and one hundred grains of the pine tree") and to effect abortion, although Burton points out that many of the latter could prove to be dangerous. The work also contains prescriptions for "increasing the dimensions of small members and for making them splendid." One such remedy consists in washing the member first in warm water, then rubbing it vigorously with a mixture containing pepper, lavender, galanga, and musk combined with honey and preserved ginger. Following is another remedy:

wash the member in water until it becomes red, and enters into erection. Then take a piece of soft leather, upon which spread hot pitch, and envelop the member with it. It will not be long before the member raises its head, trembling with passion. The leather is to be left on until the pitch grows cold, and the member is again in a state of repose. This operation, several times repeated, will have the effect of making the member strong and thick.

CENSORSHIP HISTORY

Burton and his collaborators in the Kama Shastra Society anticipated attempts of censorship as they approached the publication of *The Perfumed Garden*. Their justification was that the book was printed outside of England and that it was intended for scholars who wished to study "the great unknown literature of the East." Furthermore, by pricing the books at the equivalent in today's money of $200 each, the publishers also guaranteed that their readers had to be wealthy. The cover contained the words "For Private Circulation Only," and the place of publication was listed as Benares. Soon after the first copies appeared in 1886, pirated copies appeared in Paris, Brussels, and the English Midlands.

The revised edition, which Burton called *The Scented Garden*, was nearly complete when he died, but his wife never approved of his preoccupation with erotic literature and had all of the notes to the revision destroyed within a fortnight of his death. Lady Isobel appointed William Coote, the secretary of the National Vigilance Association, as her husband's literary executor. Encouraged by the widow, Coote burned many of Burton's papers, including the complete translation of *The Perfumed Garden* from the original Arabic, with extensive notes and revisions, on which Burton had worked for 14 years.

The Perfumed Garden was not sold openly in England, but pirated copies did appear in the United States. After spending 60 days in jail in 1930 for distributing unexpurgated copies of Ulysses, Samuel Roth turned to more profitable publications and produced editions of *The Perfumed Garden* and the Kama Sutra. Agents of the New York Society for the Suppression of Vice brought a complaint against Roth, who was prosecuted and sentenced to 90 days in jail for selling those books.

In 1930, a district attorney in Philadelphia authorized the raid of a bookshop and seizure of 300 books, among them *The Perfumed Garden*, Fanny Hill, Lady Chatterley's Lover, and *Lysistrata*. He announced that the raid marked the beginning of an extensive campaign to eliminate the sale of "obscene literature" in Philadelphia.

In 1933, Fortune Press in London was raided by police using the authority of Lord Campbell's Act, and among the works confiscated was a bowdlerized version of *The Perfumed Garden*. The case was heard in Westminster police court, where Magistrate Mr. A. Ronald Powell stated that it was not his role to consider whether a work was of literary or other merit and asserted that even "a classical author might lapse into obscenity." Ruling out expert evidence that would show the authors to be people of importance or classical authors in their own countries, the magistrate and the court showed the contempt of the law for a range of books, including historical and religious works as well as novels. Of the books seized, only *The Perfumed Garden* was recognized as conventionally pornographic.

FURTHER READING

Burton, Sir Richard, trans. "Introduction." In *The Perfumed Garden of Sheikh Nefzaoui.* New York: Lancer, 1964.

Craig, Alec. *Suppressed Books: A History of the Conception of Literary Obscenity.* New York: World Publishing, 1963.

Kilpatrick, James J. *The Smut Peddlers.* New York: Doubleday, 1960.

Rice, Edward. *Captain Sir Richard Francis Burton.* New York: Scribner, 1990.

THE PERKS OF BEING A WALLFLOWER

Author: Stephen Chbosky
Original date and place of publication: 1999, United States
Original publisher: MTV Books
Literary type: Young adult novel

SUMMARY

The Perks of Being a Wallflower is an epistolary novel written by a 15-year-old high school student using the pseudonym "Charlie" to a friend whose name is never revealed. As Charlie tells the recipient of his letters, he is writing the letters because "I just need to know that someone out there listens and understands and doesn't try to sleep with people even if they could have." He does not want the reader to learn his identity and relates that he will call people by different names or by "generic names" because he does not want the reader to find him. For the same reason, he does not include a return address. Although this method of contact is secretive and might appear to be threatening, Charlie reassures the reader, "I mean nothing bad by this." Instead, he plans to relate the events and emotions he encounters as an adolescent making his way through an often confusing and sometimes painful life. "So, this is my life. And I want you to know that I am both happy and sad and I'm still trying to figure out how that could be." Each letter contains a specific date during the 1991–92 school year, and he greets the reader consistently as "Dear friend" and signs the letters, "Love always, Charlie."

The letters begin on August 25, 1991, a few months after his best friend, Michael, commits suicide, although the catalyst for the first letter appears to be his fear of high school. He ends the first letter by telling what he believes to be his reason for writing: "I don't know why I wrote a lot of this down for you to read. The reason I wrote this letter is because I start high school tomorrow and I am really afraid of going." Charlie writes about his reaction to the suicide and of his feelings that Michael could have talked to him if he were having problems. From that beginning, Charlie shares many experiences with the reader. He writes proudly of watching his brother on television playing football for Penn State. He talks about his family and home life, how his parents both cried after the final episode of *M*A*S*H*, and tells the reader about his beautiful mother and his hardworking father. At intervals, he inserts references to his Aunt Helen, and mentions his sister's love life, including an incident when he walked in while she is having sex with her boyfriend. "And I opened the door to the basement, and my sister and this boy were naked. He was on top of her, and her legs were draped over either side of the couch. And she screamed at me in a whisper. 'Get out. You pervert.'"

The novel does not shy away from dealing with controversial topics that are also a part of an adolescent's experience and growing awareness of the world. The letters explore Charlie's feelings and observations about drug use, homosexuality, oral sex, masturbation, teenage sexuality, and suicide. He asks if the reader knows what masturbation is, then answers his own question stating that the reader is older than he and must know, but he decides to tell anyway. "Masturbation is when you rub your genitals until you have an orgasm. Wow!" In the following letter, he informs the reader where he learned about it. "I guess I forgot to mention in my last letter that it was Patrick who told me about masturbation. I guess I forgot to tell you how often I do it now, which is a lot. I don't like to look at pictures. I just close my eyes and dream about a lady I do not know. And I try not to feel ashamed. . . . One night, I felt so guilty that I promised God that I would never do it again. So, I started using blankets, but then the blankets hurt, so I started using pillows, but then the pillows hurt, so I went back to normal."

Charlie also writes about a teenage couple and watching what amounts to an incident of date rape. He is ordered by his older brother and sister to stay in his room when they give a party while his parents are away, but couples repeatedly come into the room, trying to find a private place to make out. All of the couples except one leave when they see him, and he later learns that they are "very popular and in love." They ask if they can use the room even if he must remain present, and he agrees, then watches as they proceed to undress and as the girl protests.

> And the boy kept working up the girl's shirt, and as much as she said no, he kept working it. After a few minutes, she stopped protesting, and he pulled her shirt off, and she had a white bra on with lace. I honestly didn't know what to do by this point. Pretty soon, he took off her bra and started to kiss her breasts. And then he put his hand down her pants, and she started moaning. I think they were both very drunk. He reached to take off her pants, but she started crying really hard, so he reached for his own. He pulled his pants and underwear down to his knees.
>
> "Please. Dave. No."
>
> But the boy just talked soft to her about how good she looked and things like that, and she grabbed his penis with her hands and started moving it. I wish I could describe this a little more nicely without using words like penis, but that was the way it was.

After a few minutes, the boy pushed the girl's head down, and she started to kiss his penis. She was still crying. Finally, she stopped crying because he put his penis in her mouth, and I don't think you can cry in that position. I had to stop watching at that point because I started to feel sick, but it kept going on, and they kept doing other things, and she kept saying "no." Even when I covered my ears, I could still hear her say that.

Charlie also reveals a lot about his own life and his experiences navigating through the world of adolescence. He watches as two male friends of his kiss, then sees them having sex with each other in Patrick's room. Other than to tell the reader that "Brad assumed the role of the girl in terms of where you put things" and to reveal that Brad cried and would not allow Patrick to console him, Charlie refrains from providing graphic details. About two-thirds of the way through the novel, Charlie describes his own near-homosexual experience with Patrick which is limited, at first, to a long, slow kiss. "We didn't do anything other than kiss." Later, Charlie hopes that Patrick will want to spend more intimate time with him, as well.

For the most part, although he experiments with drugs and sex to a limited degree, Charlie is a "wallflower," an observer who stands on the sidelines, watching and reporting the activities surrounding him, but his observations about other people reveal much about his life and his fears. As he comments on the activities of his friends, Charlie also learns more about his feelings, and he becomes conscious of long-hidden memories that have had a negative influence in his life. In the final letter, Charlie writes that he has just returned home after spending two months in the hospital, where he was taken after his parents found him sitting in a catatonic state.

CENSORSHIP HISTORY

Stephen Chbosky has told interviewers that he was highly influenced by J. D. Salinger's THE CATCHER IN THE RYE, and that novel is one among many controversial novels that Charlie mentions reading. The protagonists of both novels experience the angst of adolescence and the feelings of being outsiders. Moreover, both novels portray the thoughts and feelings of teenage boys with realistic candor. As a result of this realism, *The Perks of Being a Wallflower* has shared a similarity with the earlier novel in having become a target of people who wish to ban the novel because of its honest discussion of suicide and references to sexuality.

In 2003, a group named Parents Against Bad Books in Schools challenged the retention of the novel in the Fairfax, Virginia, school libraries because of what the group claimed were "profanity and descriptions of drug abuse, sexually explicit conduct and torture." The following year, the novel was removed from the Massapequa (N.Y.) school district reading assignment list in an elective sociology course due to "offensive content." In 2005, the novel was challenged and retained as optional reading in the Arrowhead High School curriculum in Merton, Wisconsin.

In 2006, the grandmother of a sixth grade student in the Apache Junction, Arizona, school district sent a letter of complaint to the state school superintendent of public instruction Tom Horne, stating that her grandchild had brought home from school *The Perks of Being a Wallflower,* a book that contained numerous sexual references, including a scene where a girl is forced to have oral sex with a boy during a party. In an interview with the *Tucson Citizen,* Horne said that this was the only page of the book he read after receiving the complaint. "The page is not just oral sex. It's nonconsensual oral sex that's described in detail. There's nothing in *Catcher in the Rye* that's remotely comparable to this." He took action and sent a cautionary memorandum on November 22, 2005, to school districts statewide to look at their school policies regarding library books, which led many schools to remove the book from their libraries. He told a reporter, "I'm hoping that if they have this book on the shelves they make sure it is no longer available to minors or any other students for that matter and they will check to see if there are any other books like that on their shelves. I wouldn't dream of trying to stop adults from reading it, but schools should not make this book available to students in their charge." Although he did not ask that schools remove the book, he tells school principals and county superintendents that they should "reconsider keeping the book" since he believed that the accelerated reader had inappropriately labeled it as reading for fourth graders. Although he admitted to not have read the book in its entirety, he stated, "There's a page of description of forced oral sex. . . . That's a little much for a 12-year-old."

In February 2009, West Bend, Wisconsin, residents Ginny and Jim Maziarka sent a letter of concern to the West Bend Community Memorial Library asking for the removal and/or relocation of a long list of gay-positive titles and young adult books that contained sexual content. The following month, the Maziarkas sent the library a specific objection to *The Perks of Being a Wallflower* and asked the staff to relocate the novel and several other books to the adult book section. When the library trustees failed to comply, the town common council members asserted that the trustees were not serving the community interests. When trustee Reilly-Kliss approached Alderman Terry Vrana and tried to explain the library reconsideration policy, he told her, "I don't care about your policy. I want those books off the shelves." In April 2009, Reilly-Kliss and three other library trustees who were originally recommended for reappointment were removed from the board "for not satisfying the Maziarkas." After months of "nasty e-mails, phone calls and even accusatory comments at the grocery store," the library board voted on June 2, 2009, to maintain the collection exactly as it was— with young adult materials clearly marked as such and shelved geographically separated from both children's and adult titles. Additionally, the library agreed to add several reparative-therapy titles on becoming heterosexual that the couple had recommended.

Also in 2009, the novel was removed from the Portage High School classrooms in Indiana, after claims that it was inappropriate reading material because it contains such topics as homosexuality, drug use, and sexual behavior.

FURTHER READING

"Apache Junction, AZ." *School Library Journal* 52 (January 2006): 24.
Goldberg, Beverly. "Wisconsin Board, Staffers Cope with Would-Be Book Burners."
American Libraries 40 (August/September 2009): 23–24.
Newsletter on Intellectual Freedom 55 (January 55): 9–14.

PEYTON PLACE

Author: Grace Metalious
Original date and place of publication: 1956, United States
Original publisher: Julian Messner
Literary form: Novel

SUMMARY

Peyton Place opens with some of the most provocative lines in literature: "Indian summer is like a woman. Ripe, hotly passionate, but fickle, she comes and goes as she pleases so that one is never sure whether she will come at all, nor for how long she will stay." The novel is devoid of blatantly sexual passages, except in one instance near the end, but the aura of illicit sexuality remains, as does the reminder that it is the book that "lifted the lid off a small New England town." At its most basic, *Peyton Place* is the melodramatic story of the greed, revenge, destructive pettiness, and simmering sexuality that pervade many small towns. Neighbors spy on neighbors, people pry into each other's lives, and townspeople try strenuously to hide their own faults and desires.

The story revolves around Allison MacKenzie, whose mother, Constance Standish, had left the town years before to make a career in New York City. Constance had returned with her infant daughter, fathered by a married man, and told her neighbors she had been married and widowed. Unaware of the circumstances of her birth, Allison dreams of similarly escaping from Peyton Place and its pettiness after high school graduation and of becoming a writer in New York City. Selena Cross, the third main female character and a product of the poor neighborhood, is sexually victimized by her stepfather, but she becomes a strong and independent woman. The novel contains characters who engage in adultery and incest, and the women in the novel are among the first in popular fiction to seek sex rather than to act merely as pawns in sexual activity. Near the end of the novel, as Allison briefly becomes the lover of a married literary agent, she hesitates and says to him, "Then you think that sex between unmarried persons is excusable." Moments later, she is in his arms and "began to make moaning, animal sounds, and even then he continued his sensual touching and stroking and waited until she began the undulating movements of intercourse with her hips." She does not lose her virginity until 500 pages into the novel and seven pages before its end. Disappointed to learn that her lover is married, she returns to Peyton Place, no longer awed by its power over her.

CENSORSHIP HISTORY

Peyton Place created a sensation even before it was published; Allan Barnard, an editor at Dell Books, which bought the reprint rights in advance of publication, realized that company head Frank Taylor might refuse to take a chance on the book, so he told Taylor, "I have something I want to buy, but I don't want you to read it." Taylor agreed, but when he later asked about Barnard's earlier request, Barnard replied, "Because you wouldn't have let me buy it." The novel sold 3 million paperback copies in 1957 and more than 10 million paperback copies by 1967. Throughout years of enormous sales, the novel retained a notoriety that appeared to fuel sales.

In 1957, the city of Knoxville, Tennessee, activated a city ordinance that permitted the Knoxville City Board of Review to suppress any publication that it considered to be obscene. The target was *Peyton Place*; local dealers were forbidden to sell it. When one indignant newsstand owner tested the ordinance, it was ruled unconstitutional.

Peyton Place was banned in Ireland on May 6, 1958. A prohibition order was published in the *Iris Oifigiuil*, "the only official source from which booksellers [and readers] might learn of a new prohibition order," in which all articles blacklisted by the Irish Board of Censors were listed. According to the Censorship of Publications Bill of 1928, "the notice in *Iris Oifigiuil* should be sufficient evidence in the courts of summary jurisdiction as to the character of the publication," despite the acknowledgment by justices quoted in Adams's thorough study of Irish censorship laws that "this gazette is not a publication which booksellers are addicted to reading." The Irish Board of Censors found the work "obscene" and "indecent," objecting particularly to the author's handling of the characters' sexuality, acts of incest, and "promiscuity." The work was officially banned from sale in Ireland until the introduction of the Censorship of Publications Bill in 1967 reduced to 12 years the duration of a prohibition order, and the work was among 5,000 titles released from the list of banned books.

Also in 1958, a shipment containing copies of *Peyton Place* was confiscated by Canadian Customs officers and further copies of the book were refused entry. To determine if the novel was obscene, the Canadian Tariff Board held a hearing at which a professor of English and a former professor of history gave testimony on behalf of the book. Based on their testimony, the tariff board handed down a ruling that permitted the entry of *Peyton Place* into Canada. In its statement, the board observed that the witnesses' testimonies gave "a distinction between obscenity and realism in literature and an interpretation of modern fiction."

The novel was one of several paperback books considered objectionable for sale to youths under 18 in *State v. Settle*, 156 A.2d 921 (R.I. 1959). In 1959, the Rhode Island Commission to Encourage Morality in Youth brought action against Bantam and three other New York paperback publishers whose books were distributed throughout the state of Rhode Island by Max Silverstein & Sons. The commission notified Silverstein that the Bantam Books paperback editions of *Peyton Place* and *The Bramble Bush* were on their list of "objection-able" publications that they circulated to local police departments. Unwilling to risk court action, the distributor retrieved unsold copies of the books and returned them to the publishers, who appealed first to the Rhode Island Superior Court, which upheld the ban, and then to the United States Supreme Court, which reversed the decision. In rendering a decision, in *Bantam Books, Inc., et al., v. Joseph A. Sullivan et al.*, Supreme Court Justice William J. Brennan stated that "informal censorship may sufficiently inhibit the circulation of publications to warrant injunctive relief . . . [but] criminal sanctions may only be applied after a determination of obscenity has been made in a criminal trial." Although the commission had no legal means of extracting compliance from Silverstein, Justice Brennan noted, its means of intimidation and the threats to institute criminal proceedings followed by police visits "plainly serve as instruments of regulation independent of the laws against obscenity."

FURTHER READING

Adams, Michael. *Censorship: The Irish Experience*. Tuscaloosa: University of Alabama Press, 1968.

Beattie, A. M., and Frank A. Underhill. "Sense and Censorship: On Behalf of *Peyton Place*." *Canadian Library Association Bulletin* 15 (July 1958): 9–16.

Booth, Wayne C. "Censorship and the Values of Fiction." *English Journal* 53 (March 1964): 155–164.

Davis, Kenneth C. *Two-Bit Culture: The Paperbacking of America*. Boston: Houghton Mifflin, 1984.

Ernst, Morris L., and Alan U. Schwartz. *Censorship: The Search for the Obscene*. New York: Macmillan, 1964.

Loth, David. *The Erotic in Literature*. New York: Dorset, 1961.

Pearce, Lillian. "Book Selection and *Peyton Place*." *Library Journal* 83 (March 1958): 712–713.

THE PHILANDERER

Author: Stanley Kauffmann
Original dates and places of publication: 1952, United States; 1953, England
Original publisher: Simon & Schuster (United States); Secker & Warburg Ltd. (England)
Literary form: Novel

SUMMARY

The Philanderer was first published in the United States in 1952 under the title *The Tightrope*, and reviewers immediately compared it to James Joyce's *Portrait of the Artist as a Young Man* for its ability to excite the reader's feelings. In particular, although some critics lauded the author's ability to relate details that provided a realistic view of the protagonist, others observed that, as *New York Times* reviewer Richard Sullivan put it, "the effect of this kind of detail upon the reader gives rise to a pertinent question, that of simple propriety."

The novel provides a tawdry and maudlin view of life in which a 33-year-old man attempts to eliminate the desolation from his life by engaging in selfish and meaningless sexual affairs. The work provides an account of this man's extramarital affairs, as well as his thoughts regarding his wife and children and his unfathomable need to take revenge on the world. To avenge himself for wrongs that he never identifies, the main character decides to have an affair with every attractive woman he meets, viewing them as "the janes, the jazzy, jazzy janes" whose existence offers him a challenge. He is anxious, at first, in his mission of seduction, but he finds that the women whom he pursues offer little resistance. Seducing the wife of his boss almost costs the philanderer his job, but he manages to escape discovery and to continue his seductions until he finds that no amount of illicit sex can fill the emptiness that he feels.

CENSORSHIP HISTORY

The Philanderer received strong reviews by critics who approvingly noted that it condemned the behavior it portrayed. Walter Allen, writing in the April 25, 1953, issue of the *New Statesman*, observed that the novel provided "as devastating a criticism as any I've read of the consequences of the tradition of American adolescent competition in sexual experience that we have already had described for us by Dr. Margaret Mead and Mr. Gorer." Still, legal authorities on the Isle of Man had already condemned the novel after police received a complaint that a person could obtain the books at Boots' Library. The high bailiff had felt bound by existing law, however outmoded, to act in some manner, but he imposed only a one-pound fine on the work and created a criminal record for the novel.

The trial of *The Philanderer* in London in 1954 was influential in changing the obscenity law in England, a change motivated largely by the summation of Mr. Justice Stable, who presided over the trial in the Queen's Bench Division in the Old Bailey. Defendants in the case were Secker & Warburg Ltd., the publisher, and Frederic Warburg, a director of the firm. The author was not in court.

Justice Stable opened the trial by telling the jury to take the novel home and "Read it as a *book*. Don't pick out the highlights. Read it through as a whole. And then we'll all come back here on Friday and proceed with the case." Before the court adjourned, both counsels gave opening arguments. The prosecutor, Mervyn Griffith-Jones, told the jury he expected that after reading the book they would say it had the "tendency to deprave and to corrupt those whose minds were open to such immoral influences and into whose hands it might fall." Rodger Winn, defense counsel, stated that such thinking was 150 years old and that the problem was to determine "whether the impact of certain passages on a Victorian mind would be the same as on a modern mind." The judge added that in 1909, when he was 21 years old, his parents had discussed seriously whether or not his mother could attend a performance of George Bernard Shaw's play *Pygmalion:* "When the lady in the play said 'Not bloody likely' it was the biggest social shock I can remember. If I had used that word when I was twenty-one, I would have been ordered out of any respectable house in England." By 1954, he added, that taboo was gone.

When the jury returned and the case resumed, no expert witnesses were called by either side. The judge's summation to the jury, strongly sympathetic to the defendants, ended with the caution to the jury that if criminal law were to be driven too far in the desire to stamp out the "bawdy muck," there existed the risk of a revolt, "a demand for a change in the law, so that the pendulum may swing too far the other way and allow to creep in things that at the moment we can keep out." The jury delivered the expected verdict of not guilty, and the defendants were discharged without court costs. Justice Stable's decision was not binding on future cases because it was not a court of appeals judgment, and Customs and postal authorities continued to seize books in transit while other magistrates prosecuted other publishers, but this case set the stage for change in English obscenity laws.

FURTHER READING

Cummins, Anthony. "Why Stanley Kauffmann's Philanderer Still Rings a Bell." Available online. URL: http://www.guardian.co.uk/books/booksblog/2010/mar/11/ stanley-kauffmann-law-philanderer. Accessed August 17, 2010.

Mackay, R. S. "Hidden Rule and Judicial Censorship." *Canadian Bar Review* 361 (March 1958): 1–24.

Rolph, Cecil Hewitt. *Books in the Dock.* London: Deutsch, 1969.

"The Test of Obscenity." *Author* 65 (Autumn 1954): 1–5.

Warburg, Frederic. "A View of Obscenity." *New Yorker,* April 20, 1957, pp. 106–133.

POEMS AND BALLADS

Author: Algernon Charles Swinburne
Original date and place of publication: 1866, England
Original publisher: Moxon
Literary form: Poetry collection

SUMMARY

Poems and Ballads shocked Victorian sensibilities with its sadomasochistic eroticism that is repeated throughout such poems as "Anactoria," "Laus Veneria," "Dolores," "Faustine," and "Feline." The language does not evoke the pleasures of sexuality as much as it emphasizes the pains of sexual love with its "violent delights" that "have violent ends." Although Swinburne sought deliberately to shock Victorian readers, his equally important goal was to accomplish what he saw accomplished in THE FLOWERS OF EVIL by Charles Baudelaire, who portrayed normally ugly objects and images as sources of beauty and desire and who represented the immoral as moral.

Swinburne succeeded in creating images that had never before been heard in English poetry. The following lines appear in "Anactoria":

> My life is bitter with thy love; thine eyes
> Blind me, thy tresses burn me, thy sharp sighs
> Divide my flesh and spirit with soft sound,
> And my blood strengthens, and my veins abound.

Sexual passion is not portrayed in Swinburne's poems as sensuous and pleasurable; rather, bodies "crush" together and "bruise" each other:

> I feel my blood against my blood: my pain
> Pains thee, and lips bruise lips, and vein stings vein,
> Let fruit be crushed on fruit, let flower on flower,
> Breast kindle breast, and either burn one hour.

CENSORSHIP HISTORY

Soon after the publication of *Poems and Ballads*, in 1866, rumors arose that the *Times* was going to publish a review of the work by Eneas Sweetland Dallas and include a demand that the publisher be prosecuted. Moxon, the publisher, became frightened and withdrew the book from sale without consulting Swinburne. Copies that remained on the market commanded prices of more than five guineas (nearly $12 in current value). An unexpurgated version of the book was then published by John Camden Hotten, an English publisher of mainly flagellent pornography. Although reviewers and public opinion widely attacked the book, no legal action was brought. Public opinion did, however, influence Mudie's Library to withdraw the book from its shelves, thus removing a major source of sales for the publisher.

In August 1866, Swinburne wrote to Charles Augustus Howell, "I got an anonymous note today threatening to 'cut off my stones' within six weeks if my poems are not withdrawn."

FURTHER READING

Greenberg, Robert A. " 'Anactoria,' and the Sapphic Passion." *Victorian Poetry* 29 (Spring 1991): 79–87.
Mordell, Albert, ed. *Notorious Literary Attacks.* New York: Boni & Liveright, 1926.
Swinburne, Algernon Charles. *Letters of Algernon Charles Swinburne.* Vol. 1. Edited by C. Y. Lang. New Haven, Conn.: Yale University Press, 1959, 173–174.
Thomas, Donald. *A Long Time Burning: The History of Literary Censorship in England.* New York: Praeger, 1969.

Wagner-Lawlor, Jennifer. "Metaphorical 'Indiscretion' and Literary Survival in Swinburne's 'Anactoria.' " *Studies in English Literature, 1500–1900* 36 (Autumn 1996): 917–934.

POINT COUNTER POINT

Author: Aldous Huxley
Original date and place of publication: 1928, United States
Original publisher: Harper & Row
Literary form: Novel

SUMMARY

Point Counter Point presents a satiric portrayal of the members of English society and of the London intellectual set in the 1920s. The novel is dated by the frequent references to contemporary British politics, but numerous allusions are also made to literature, painting, music, and scientific information of the time. An elaborately constructed novel, the intricacy of its interrelationships is supposedly based on Bach's Suite no. 2 in B Minor. Philip Quarles, a major character in the novel, is writing a novel, thus creating a novel-within-the-novel structure that creates echoes or "counterpoints" between the two. Further complicating *Point Counter Point* is Huxley's admission that he patterned his characters after real literary figures. Thus, Mark and Mary Rampion are idealized portrayals of D. H. and Frieda Lawrence; the diabolical, sexually depraved Spandrell is based on Charles Baudelaire; and Everard Webley, assassinated by Spandrell, is based on Sir Oswald Mosley, leader of the British fascist movement. J. Middleton Murry and Katherine Mansfield are portrayed in the characters Denis Burlap and Beatrice Gilray. Quarles is Huxley.

For the most part, the long and complicated novel with its numerous characters concerns the broken marriages, adulterous affairs, and other interactions of this group. Their behavior is irreverent in regard to traditional social behavior, and their sexual proclivities are tolerated more within the group than they would be by the greater society.

CENSORSHIP HISTORY

Point Counter Point was one of numerous novels that were banned in Boston due to the efforts of the Watch and Ward Society. In 1928, the society placed the novel on its list of "unacceptable" books and then circulated the list to Boston booksellers, suggesting that it was in their best interests not to display advertising for the books or to sell the books that appeared on the list. Booksellers adhered to this "gentleman's agreement" and effectively, if unofficially, sales of the novel were banned in Boston.

In 1930, librarian Margery Quigley withdrew *Point Counter Point* from the Montclair (New Jersey) Public Library because she felt that, given its apparent approval of extramarital sex, "she had no moral right to distribute it from the library." She returned the novel to the shelves a few days later when a group of her most conservative clubwomen assigned it as a book for discussion.

Point Counter Point was banned in Ireland on May 13, 1930, for containing "immoral matter." A prohibition order was published in the *Iris Oifigiuil*, "the only official source from which booksellers [and readers] might learn of a new prohibition order," in which all articles blacklisted by the Irish Board of Censors were listed. According to the Censorship of Publications Bill of 1928, "the notice in *Iris Oifigiuil* should be sufficient evidence in the courts of summary jurisdiction as to the character of the publication," despite the acknowledgment by justices quoted in Adams's thorough study of Irish censorship laws that "this gazette is not a publication which booksellers are addicted to reading." The Irish Board of Censors found the novel to be "obscene" and "indecent." The ban against *Point Counter Point* was not revoked until 1970.

FURTHER READING

Adams, Michael. *Censorship: The Irish Experience.* Tuscaloosa: University of Alabama Press, 1968.

Lewis, Felice Flanery. *Literature, Obscenity, and the Law.* Carbondale: Southern Illinois University, 1976.

Quigley, Margery. "Books in Suburbia—The Suburban Library's Book-Buying Problems." *Library Journal,* April 1, 1930, p. 303.

RABBIT, RUN

Author: John Updike
Original date and place of publication: 1960, United States
Original publisher: Alfred A. Knopf
Literary form: Novel

SUMMARY

Rabbit, Run relates the story of onetime high school basketball star Harry "Rabbit" Angstrom, 26, who impulsively deserts his pregnant wife. The novel is set in the small town of Mt. Judge, a "suburb of the city of Brewer, fifth largest city in Pennsylvania," in the spring of 1959. Rabbit feels trapped in his life as a lower-middle-class family man who now demonstrates "a penny's worth of tin called a friggin' MagiPeeler in five-and-dime stores." His wife, Janice, pregnant with their second child, spends her days in an alcoholic stupor, watching television. Despite his contempt for her, Rabbit sometimes finds wisdom in *The Mickey Mouse Club*, especially in the daily advice offered by head Mouseketeer Jimmy.

Little in Rabbit's life is what it appears to be. The fame and success of his high school basketball career have left him with an idealized view of those years that extends to his old coach, Marty Tothero, now unemployed and living in a tenement. As Rabbit tries to recapture some of the order and certainty of his earlier life, he realizes that Tothero is only a broken old man with a penchant for being beaten by his stern lover, Margaret, who refers to him as "an old bloated bastard." The young minister, Jack Eccles, sent to find Rabbit and return with him to Janice and her family, is ineffective. Unable to make Rabbit return, Eccles suggests that they play golf sometime. Rabbit arrives at the Eccles house and finds the minister's young wife in tight orange shorts, and he cannot resist slapping "her sassy ass" and then ruminating on its firmness. When Rabbit eats in a Chinese restaurant, the waiters speak in heavily accented English as they take his order but speak in perfect English once he leaves.

Throughout the novel, Rabbit remains constantly aware of his sexuality. When he first runs off, he thinks of finding "hard-bodied laughers" in West Virginia and remembers the "young whores in Texas," whom he frequented when in the army. Through Tothero, Rabbit meets Ruth, a warmhearted, voluptuous prostitute into whose apartment he moves. He rhapsodizes about her body and their sexual relationship in specific detail at various points in the novel.

When Janice goes into labor, Rabbit returns home, but he moves out again when Janice rejects his sexual advances as signs of "his whore's filthiness." She accidentally drowns their baby while drunk. The day of his baby's funeral, Rabbit sees "two teenage girls in snug shorts" and is unable to resist ogling "their perky butts and expectant sex." After the funeral, Rabbit returns to Ruth, who is pregnant with his child, but she refuses to resume their relationship unless he chooses between his wife and her. The novel ends with the panicked Rabbit running blindly down the street.

CENSORSHIP HISTORY

Rabbit, Run was banned in Ireland on February 20, 1962. A prohibition order was published in the *Iris Oifigiuil*, "the only official source from which booksellers [and readers] might learn of a new prohibition order," in which all articles blacklisted by the Irish Board of Censors were listed. According to the Censorship of Publications Bill of 1928, "the notice in *Iris Oifigiuil* should be sufficient evidence in the courts of summary jurisdiction as to the character of the publication," despite the acknowledgment by justices quoted in Adams's thorough study of Irish censorship laws that "this gazette is not a publication which booksellers are addicted to reading." The Irish Board of Censors found the work "obscene" and "indecent," objecting particularly to the author's handling of the characters' sexuality, the "promiscuity," and the "explicit sex acts." The work was officially banned from sale in Ireland until the introduction of the revised Censorship Publications Bill in 1967.

In 1976, parents of students in six community high schools in Aroostook County, Maine, challenged the inclusion of *Rabbit, Run* in the high school libraries because of its references to sex and to an extramarital affair. Parents cited as one of several objectionable scenes Rabbit's first sexual encounter with Ruth, in which Updike first describes Rabbit caressing her breasts and then provides a detailed description of them having sex:

> He kneels in a kind of sickness between her spread legs. With her help their blind loins fit. . . . [S]he reaches her hand down and touches their mixed fur and her breathing snags on something sharp. Her thighs throw open wide and clamp his sides and throw open again so wide it frightens him. . . . His sea of seed buckles, and sobs into a still channel. At each shudder her mouth smiles in his and her legs, locked at his back, bear down.

They also raised objections to Rabbit's constant fantasizing about sexual experiences with most of the women he meets and the language in which he expresses such desires. His two-month affair with Ruth, after he leaves Janice for the first time, motivated further objections because the book "seems to make his wife at fault for the affair."

The county school board established a review committee to consider the complaints and recommended that the book be retained. In making the final decision on the book, the school board voted 8 to 6 against banning the book from the libraries but determined that some restriction was required. In a vote of 7 to 6, with one abstention, the board decided that the novel should be placed on the reserved shelf in each of the six county high school libraries and only charged out to students who brought signed permission slips from their parents.

In 1986, the novel was removed from the required reading list for the high school English classes in Medicine Bow, Wyoming, because of the sexual descriptions and profanity in the book. In their complaint to the school board, parents cited Rabbit's cursing, including "shit," "bastard," and "son of a bitch," and Tothero's use of the word "cunt." They also identified the sexually explicit passages between Ruth and Rabbit and his "sexually explicit fantasies."

FURTHER READING

Adams, Michael. *Censorship: The Irish Experience.* Tuscaloosa: University of Alabama Press, 1968.

Galloway, David D. *The Absurd Hero in American Fiction: Updike, Styron, Bellow.* Rev. ed. Austin: University of Texas Press, 1970.

Hunt, George W. *John Updike and the Three Great Secret Things: Sex, Religion, and Art.* Grand Rapids, Mich.: Wm. B. Eerdmans, 1980.

Markle, Joyce. *Fighters and Lovers: Theme in the Novels of John Updike.* New York: New York University Press, 1973.

Newsletter on Intellectual Freedom (March 1977): 36; (March 1987): 55.

Updike, John. "The Plight of the American Writer." *Change* 9 (April 1978): 36–41.

Wright, Derek. "Mapless Motion: Form and Space in Updike's *Rabbit, Run.*" *Modern Fiction Studies* 37 (Spring 1991): 35–44.

THE RAINBOW

Author: D. H. Lawrence

Original dates and places of publication: 1915, England; 1915, United States

Original publishers: Methuen and Company (England); B. W. Huebsch (United States)

Literary form: Novel

SUMMARY

The Rainbow spans three generations of the Brangwen family, moving from the beginning of the English industrial revolution in 1840 through the first decade of the 20th century. Lawrence shows the destruction of the traditional way of life and the ways in which the Brangwen family must accommodate themselves to their changing lives. The early Brangwens farm the land and live in harmony with their surroundings, but the second generation of Brangwens move into the industrial town of Beldover, where the seasonal cycle is replaced by a man-made calendar. Will and Anna no longer participate in the rhythms of nature, and their relationship suffers. They fall into a fixed domestic routine, and Anna begins to live through her children.

Ursula, daughter of Will and Anna, represents the modern woman, becoming the first Brangwen female to support herself and to enter a profession. She also rejects the traditional expectations of her family, such as religion, marriage, and love, becoming involved in unsatisfying relationships with fellow teacher Winifred Inger and shallow aristocrat Anton Skrebensky. She becomes pregnant by Skrebensky but takes ill with pneumonia and miscarries. The novel ends on a hopeful note as Ursula awakens one morning and sees a rainbow, "as if a new day had come on the earth."

CENSORSHIP HISTORY

The Rainbow contains several passages that have aroused challenges. Lawrence believed that the passage in the book that prosecutors found most offensive was likely the one in which the pregnant Anna dances naked in her bedroom:

> She would not have had any one know. She danced in secret, and her soul rose in bliss. She danced in secret before the Creator, she took off her clothes and danced in the pride of her bigness. . . . She stood with the firelight on her ankles and feet, naked in the shadowy, late afternoon, fastening up her hair.

Other passages that generated numerous complaints by editors at Methuen were scenes that were characterized in editorial notes as "lesbian" incidents. In one beach scene, Winifred suggests that she carry Ursula into the water, and in another the two are caught in the rain and "after a while the rain came down on their flushed, hot limbs, startling, delicious." B. W. Huebsch, the publisher of the first American edition of the *The Rainbow*, deleted these two passages and a third that had "generated the most complaints" from reviewers about the Methuen edition:

> Ursula lay still in her mistress's arms, her forehead against the beloved, maddening breast.
> "I shall put you in," said Winifred.
> —But Ursula twined her body about her mistress.

The Rainbow was censored by Lawrence before publication after editors at Methuen and Company sent the manuscript back to the author's agent, J. B. Pinker, "for alteration." Lawrence made cuts, but the altered manuscript was still unacceptable, and the editor again returned the work with portions marked for cutting. Lawrence refused to make further cuts, writing in a letter to Pinker, "I have cut out as I said I would, all the *phrases* objected to. The passages and paragraphs marked I cannot alter." The publisher recognized that the 13 passages the author refused to cut were likely to cause trouble. As soon as the novel was published, book reviewers alerted circulating libraries and legal authorities, calling it "an orgy of sexiness," "windy, tedious, boring and nauseating," and "a monstrous wilderness of phallicism."

The novel was condemned in 1915 after a private citizen complained to the London police. They, in turn, acquired a copy of the novel and took it to Sir John Dickinson, a Bow Street magistrate who issued a warrant under the Obscene Publications Act of 1857. The warrant called for the seizure of the 1,000 copies of the novel found on the publisher's premises. Dickinson also issued a summons that was served on Methuen, requiring that the publisher "show cause why the said books should not be destroyed." The police solicitor charged that the obscenity was so extensively distributed throughout the book that "I am at a loss, Sir, to understand how Messrs. Methuen came to lend their name to its publication."

Methuen claimed that Lawrence had been asked twice to modify the language of the manuscript but had refused, so they published as it stood. A destruction order was granted by the court under Lord Campbell's Act of 1857 to legal authorities without prosecution "or, therefore, any chance of its adequate defence." Thus, the police action against *The Rainbow* was not a criminal proceeding that would result in a jail term. The benefit to such a proceeding for the legitimate publisher was that it carried no risk of stigmatization by the government, nor did the publisher face fines or imprisonment.

The magistrate ordered all 1,000 copies to be destroyed and chided the publisher that he was sorry "that a firm of such high repute should have allowed their reputation to be soiled as it has been by the publication of this work." As publisher Algernon Methuen stated, "The [Scotland Yard] solicitors, in consideration of the reputation of our firm, kindly suggested that we might prefer to hand over the books rather than submit to actual search, and this we did." Aside from the loss of book stock, the publisher paid costs that amounted to 10 guineas, about $30 in contemporary currency. Methuen then requested that Lawrence return the advance it had paid him for the work, but he refused and the firm dropped the request. The novel was not available in an unexpurgated edition again until 1949, when Penguin Books published an edition.

In the United States, B. W. Huebsch published the novel in 1915, using the corrected proofs from Methuen and deleting the 13 "offensive" passages without obtaining permission from the author for the expurgations.

FURTHER READING

Ben-Ephraim, Gavriel. *The Moon's Dominion: Narrative Dichotomy and Female Dominance in Lawrence's Earlier Novels.* Rutherford, N.J.: Fairleigh Dickinson University Press, 1989.

DeGrazia, Edward. *Girls Lean Back Everywhere: The Law of Obscenity and the Assault on Genius.* New York: Random House, 1992.

Doherty, Gerald. "The Art of Appropriation: The Rhetoric of Sexuality in D. H. Lawrence." *Style* 30 (Summer 1996): 289–308.

Geller, Evelyn. *Forbidden Books in American Public Libraries, 1876–1939: A Study in Cultural Change.* Westport, Conn.: Greenwood, 1984.

Lawrence, D. H. *The Quest for Rananim: D. H. Lawrence's Letters to S. S. Koteliansky, 1914–1930.* Ed. and intro. by George J. Zytaruk. Montreal: McGill-Queen's University Press, 1970.

Rolph, Cecil Hewitt. *Books in the Dock.* London: Deutsch, 1961.

REPLENISHING JESSICA

Author: Max Bodenheim
Original date and place of publication: 1925, United States
Original publisher: Horace Liveright
Literary form: Novel

SUMMARY

Replenishing Jessica contributed to the reputation of its author as a libertine, yet the publisher and author both asserted that it was an essentially moral book. Although the main character uses erotic rebellion as her weapon against society, Bodenheim shows that she is essentially corrupted by her behavior and her life declines in a distasteful manner. Although she attempts to separate her sex life from the rest of her existence, Jessica's sexual adventures with more than a dozen men from all social levels, and on two continents, eventually harden and degrade her.

Although the very wealthy Jessica is worth $4 million, the novel does not make money the reason for her intense promiscuity. After a sexually adventurous existence, she marries Ted Purrel, an aggressive upstart who combines an acquisitive mentality with brutal sexuality. He earns a substantial salary, but he views Jessica as a property, an object whose acquisition will make him the envy of others. Although she is not in love with him, she "finally agreed to marry Purrel because he had become much less aggressive and blatant, and because she had determined to narrow most of her life to sexual pleasures."

Soon after, they both begin love affairs, but Purrel wants Jessica to remain faithful to him while he does as he pleases. One evening, returning after they have been separated for a while, Purrel beats Jessica so that her face becomes bruised and discolored. After the bruises heal, she sells her house, arranges a divorce, and then spends two years running around with a variety of men, one of whom introduces her to heroin use. When that lover dies of an overdose and another commits suicide, Jessica reevaluates her life and decides to become useful to society. She works with a children's group at a settlement house and, while on a trip to the art museum with them, meets a "tall, bony, crippled man" whose left side of the torso is paralyzed, left arm is doubled up, and left hand droops in a twisted fashion, "while his left leg was a little shorter than his right." She becomes close to him and eventually asks him to marry her, for he is the only man who can replenish her emotionally.

CENSORSHIP HISTORY

Early in the 1920s, publisher Horace Liveright paid the author $1,000 for a still-unwritten novel. When the novel was delivered, Liveright found it to be "filthy," despite his own permissive standards. After bitter discussions with Bodenheim, the publisher and author reached an agreement to rewrite portions of the book, a task that fell to editor T. R. Smith. After the most glaringly offensive passages were modified or removed, the book was published in 1925 as *Replenishing Jessica*. Liveright's expurgation did not go far enough, and the New York Society for the Suppression of Vice, led by John Sumner, obtained a grand jury obscenity indictment against Liveright for the book. The publisher retained as defense attorney Arthur Garfield Hays, who proclaimed the novel to be a "highly moral" work, written by "a great author and poet."

When the case was heard in general sessions court in March 1928, the judge ordered the entire 272 "smoldering pages" of the book read to the jury. Newspapers reported that jurors slept through the supposedly "juicy passages." Mayor Jimmy Walker commented. "No girl has ever been seduced by reading a book." Despite Sumner's presentation of damaging testimony regarding Liveright's earlier private opinion of the book, the jury took only 15 minutes to return a verdict of not guilty and to acquit Liveright. Despite the victory, Bodenheim was upset by the trial because he had wanted to testify. Instead, the defense thought it wiser that he leave town during the trial rather than risk his possibly disruptive testimony.

FURTHER READING

Boyer, Paul S. *Purity in Print: The Vice-Society Movement and Book Censorship in America.* New York: Scribner, 1968.

Gilmer, Frank Walker. *Horace Liveright: Publisher of the Twenties.* New York: Lewis, 1970.

Moore, Jack B. *Maxwell Bodenheim.* New York: Twayne, 1970.

SANCTUARY

Author: William Faulkner
Original date and place of publication: 1931, United States
Publisher: Cape & Smith
Literary form: Novel

SUMMARY

In brief, *Sanctuary* tells the story of sexually provocative 17-year-old Temple Drake, a socially prominent judge's daughter and college student, who accidentally witnesses a murder and then falls victim to a sadistic rape. Temple is taken to the isolated house of former convict Lee Goodwin and his common-law wife, Ruby, one evening by her date, Gowan Stevens, after the two have had too much to drink; Stevens wants to buy bootlegged liquor. While there, he remains drunk for three days. When he finally sobers up and realizes that he is outnumbered, he runs off and leaves Temple. Temple is sexually harassed and then raped with a corncob by an impotent bootlegger named Popeye, who also kills Tommy, a mentally retarded gang member who witnessed the act. Afterward, Popeye confines Temple in a Memphis brothel, where she is forced to engage in sexual acts with a stranger named Red while Popeye watches. When Temple begins to enjoy her involvement with Red, Popeye shoots him and then disappears.

Temple is located at the brothel by the lawyer assigned to defend Goodwin on the charge of murdering Tommy, but she falsely identifies him as the killer to protect her reputation. Both she and her prominent father want to hide her sexual involvement with Red and her experiences at the brothel, so they guarantee that her testimony and the trial will be over quickly by implicating Goodwin. Without remorse, Temple is escorted from the courtroom after testifying and leaves for vacation in Luxembourg. The innocent Goodwin is burned to death by a lynch mob.

Despite the persistent sexual undercurrent of much of the novel, none of the sexual acts is described in detail. Even the rape by corncob is referred to obliquely and only Temple's bleeding afterward is described. Throughout, anatomical references are limited to the thighs or the loins. The erotic passages emerge in images of Temple's appearance, with her short dress that permits "fleet revelations of flank and thigh," and the voyeurism in the brothel. Popeye's advances are detailed: "Then it touched me, that nasty little cold hand, fiddling around inside the coat where I was naked. . . . his hand was going inside the top of my knickers." Later in the novel, after becoming eroticized by Red, Temple sits "in a floating swoon of agonized sorrow and erotic longing, thinking of Red's body," and then begs him to have sex with her: "Please. Please. Please. Don't make me wait. I'm burning up." The novel was unusual for its time in its topics of rape and voyeurism as well as for the brothel setting, in which a major part of the action takes place.

CENSORSHIP HISTORY

William Faulkner's sixth novel, *Sanctuary* gained notoriety as much for its erotic passages and inclusion of rape, voyeurism, and prostitution as for the author's claim in his introduction to the 1932 Modern Library edition that he had written about these topics for financial rather than artistic reasons.

In 1948, *Sanctuary* was one of nine novels identified as obscene in criminal proceedings in the Court of Quarter sessions in Philadelphia County, Pennsylvania. Indictments were brought by the state district attorney, John H. Maurer, against five booksellers who were charged with possessing and intending to sell the books. The other allegedly obscene novels were Harold Robbins's NEVER LOVE A STRANGER, James Farrell's STUDS LONIGAN and A WORLD I NEVER MADE, Erskine Caldwell's GOD'S LITTLE ACRE, Calder Willingham's END AS A MAN, and Faulkner's THE WILD PALMS.

In his March 18, 1949, decision in *Commonwealth v. Gordon*, 66 D. & C. 101 (1949) that *Sanctuary* is not obscene, Judge Curtis Bok stated: "There are no vulgar Saxon words in the book, but the situations are stark and unrelieved. It makes one shudder to think of what can happen by misadventure." Bok refused to declare *Sanctuary* "obscene" because the definition in cases that he cited in his decision restricted the meaning of the term "to that of sexual impurity, and with those cases that have made erotic allurement the test of its effect." The work also failed to meet Bok's definition of sexual impurity in literature, which he defined "as any writing whose dominant purpose and effect is erotic allurement—that is to say, a calculated and effective incitement to sexual desire."

Faulkner was awarded the Nobel Prize in literature in 1950. Although *Sanctuary* did not go to court again, by 1954 it was again condemned as obscene by numerous local censorship groups throughout the United States, and the National Organization of Decent Literature placed it on the disapproved list. Also in 1954, Ireland banned *Sanctuary*, along with most of the author's other works, because of the language such as "son of a bitch," "whore," "slut," and "bastard" combined with the brutal violence of the story. Irish and U.S. censors also objected to the character Ruby, who prostitutes herself to obtain money to free her common-law husband from jail, to obtain legal fees, and to pay their expenses. Changes in society have removed most objections to the book, although scattered local censorship continues throughout the United States.

FURTHER READING

Gladstein, Mimi. *The Indestructible Woman in Faulkner, Hemingway, and Steinbeck.* Ann Arbor, Mich.: UMI Research Press, 1986.

Heller, Terry. "Mirrored Worlds and the Gothic in Faulkner's *Sanctuary.*" *Mississippi Quarterly* 42 (Summer 1989): 247–259.

Loe, Mary Hong. "Case Studies in Censorship: William Faulkner's *Sanctuary.*" *Reference Services Review* 23 (Spring 1995): 71–84.

Page, Sally R. *Faulkner's Women: Characterization and Meaning.* De Land, Fla.: Everett/Edwards, 1972.

Tanner, Laura E. "Reading Rape: *Sanctuary* and *The Women of Brewster Place.*" *American Literature* 62 (December 1990): 559–582.

Williams, David. "Faulkner's Women: The Myth and the Muse." Montreal: McGill–Queen's University Press, 1977.

Wilson, Andrew J. "The Corruption in Looking: William Faulkner's *Sanctuary* as a Detective Novel." *Mississippi Quarterly* 47 (Summer 1994): 441–460.

SARI SAYS: THE REAL DIRT ON EVERYTHING FROM SEX TO SCHOOL

Author: Sari Locker
Original date and place of publication: 2001, New York
Original publisher: HarperCollins
Literary form: Nonfiction

SUMMARY

Sari Says is a compendium of advice for teenagers who might be reluctant to ask their parents questions about fashion, life, sex, clothes, relationships, abortion, smoking, kissing—or even about talking to their parents. The author, an advice columnist for *Teen People* Online, purports to answer "real questions from real teens" and includes the following chapters: "There's No Place Like Home," "School Days," "Friends Forever," "You've Got Style," "You're No Body Till You Love Your Body," "Totally Crushing," "The Dating

Game," "Pucker Up," "Boyfriends and Girlfriends," "Breaking Up Is Hard to Do," and "Let's Talk about Sex."

The answers to teens' questions are carefully considered and advise young people to share their thoughts with their parents whenever they can. Many of the questions concern sex, a topic that young people are often reluctant to discuss with adults they know. In an interview quoted in the September 2002 issue of *American Libraries*, Locker states, "As a teen educator, I know that when a teen asks me a question about sex, they need an honest, accurate answer because otherwise they're going to be getting information from sources that are not positive value–based or encouraging sexual health." Girls write to ask whether their breasts are "normal." Questions regarding how to kiss, when to become sexually active, or how to protect oneself after becoming sexually active also appear frequently, as do questions about being gay or knowing someone who is gay.

The book covers the gamut of questions that concern young people.

CENSORSHIP HISTORY

In addition to providing advice to protect them emotionally and physically if they engage in sex, *Sari Says* recommends that teenagers work harder at getting along with their parents. Some parents, however, view Locker's advice as threatening to their own authority and have called for the book to be banned from their libraries.

On July 10, 2002, in Dyersville, Iowa, the board of trustees of the James Kennedy Public Library voted unanimously to forbid the recently purchased *Sari Says* from being added to the collection. After the decision, the library returned to the vendor several copies it had purchased. The issue was first brought to the library board in June by board trustee Betty Anne Scherrman, after she inspected a shipment of books that library director Shirley Vonderhaar was preparing for shelving. Scherrman looked through *Sari Says* and requested that Vonderhaar not place the book on the shelves because it was "inappropriate." Vonderhaar did not agree, so Scherrman took the matter before the library board. The chairman of the library board, Wayne Hermsen, told an Associated Press reporter that some of the contents of the book were "too sexually explicit" and that this was the first book banned by the library. In their unanimous vote on July 10, 2002, the library board did not vote to "remove" the book from the library, because as Scherrman stated, "We didn't buy the book—that's all!" Instead the vote was to "return" the book.

The ban on *Sari Says* attracted national attention, and the library board chairman received e-mail messages from throughout the country, as well as calls from library patrons. Some patrons called for the board to revisit its earlier decision, while others condemned the book as "disgusting" and "filthy." On August 12, 2002, the James Kennedy Public Library board met, and in a 6-3 vote defeated a motion by board member Kori Mahoney to rescind the ban. Chairman Hermsen said after the vote that the incident made the library evaluate its approval process and completely revamp its policies.

FURTHER READING

Associated Press. "Iowa Library Keeps Ban on Teen Advice Book." Posted on Freedom Forum. Available online. URL: www.freedomforum.org/templates/document. asp?documentID=16703. Accessed August 10, 2010.

Goldberg, Beverly. "Muzzling What Sari Says." *American Libraries* 33 (September 2002): 19.

Ishizuka, Kathy. "Iowa Library Reaffirms Ban on *Sari Says*." *School Library Journal*. 48 (September 2002): 21.

"Sari Says Nothing More in Dyersville, Iowa." *Newsletter on Intellectual Freedom* 51 (September 2002). Formerly available online. URL: www.ala.org/al_onlineTemplate.cfm? Section=july2002&Template=/ContentManagement/ContentDisplay.cfm& ContentID= 10168. Accessed January 3, 2006.

THE SATYRICON

Author: Gaius Petronius Arbiter
Original dates and places of publication: ca. A.D. 60, Rome; 1918, United States
Original publishers: Privately published (Rome); Boni & Liveright (United States)
Literary form: Satire

SUMMARY

The original version of *The Satyricon* consisted of prose interspersed with verse, but no complete text of the work remains, nor are historian certain by whom the work was actually written. Instead, because the text contains clues that it was written in the first century A.D., researchers have ascribed it to a member of the emperor Nero's court, Petronius, who lost favor with the emperor and was driven to suicide. Over centuries, anonymous forgers have pieced together the remaining fragments to present an irreverent and frequently racy account of the picaresque adventures of two witty and erudite rogues, Encolpius and Ascyltos, who wander with their young male companion, Giton, on the fringes of society and survive through petty thievery and trickery. The themes of the work champion the enjoyment of life at any cost and ridicule the fickleness of men and women and the absurdity of pretentiousness. Exaggerated, humorous, and ironic in their behavior, the characters avoid as far as possible contact with the usual social virtues of honesty, integrity, discretion, and dependability, preferring to indulge in a range of libidinal adventures, both heterosexual and homosexual.

The narrator, Encolpius, is sexually involved with the young boy Giton, and the two engage in numerous other sexual encounters with both men and women. Their relationship forms the chief motif of the work, as Ascyltos and others try to lure Giton away from Encolpius. The sex acts are briefly mentioned, more often suggestive rather than explicit, but licentiousness does punctuate the narrative. In the one extended sensual scene, the work depicts an orgy in the court of the priestess Quartilla, during which a catamite (a boy used in pederasty) is led in who, Encolpius says, "[o]ne minute . . . nearly gored us to death with his writhing, and the next, he befouled us . . . with his stinking kisses."

In another scene, Giton is placed in a room with a seven-year-old girl and the two are encouraged to engage in sexual exploration while Encolpius watches through a keyhole. In another extended scene, the trio are guests of the coarse and crude Trimalchio, modeled on Nero, who makes rude noises and speaks repeatedly of the "evacuation" of the body. The end of the work places Encolpius at home, criticized by servants and acquaintances for seeming to be sedentary and showing no sense of enterprise.

CENSORSHIP HISTORY

In 1921, John Sumner and the New York Society for the Suppression of Vice went to court against publishers Boni & Liveright for publishing *The Satyricon*. Their edition contained two volumes, sold for $20, and was limited to 1,200 sets. The case was dismissed by Magistrate Charles A. Oberwager in Magistrate's Court on September 27, 1922, in a decision that contained extensive quoting from the works of literary authorities, encyclopedias, and higher-court decisions. Oberwager established that, despite lewd passages, *The Satyricon* was a recognized classic and a significant historical document, and he pointed out that the obscenity statute was not meant "to anathematize all historical manners and morals different from our own, or to close the treasure house of the past." He also sharply reprimanded the society and warned that "no individual or private organization should be permitted to exercise general powers of censorship over literary works."

On October 1922, the New York district attorney reopened the case at the insistence of Sumner, who asserted in testimony that "the *Decameron* was a Sunday School book beside *Satyricon*. It is so bad that if it can be published, there is nothing which can be prevented." Chief City Magistrate William G. McAdoo, who was assigned the case, refused to take it. Instead, he warned Sumner that such attacks on "inert publications, which are . . . at once historic, classical, and erotogenic" were eroding the influence of both Sumner and the society. Unwilling to accept defeat, Sumner sought a grand jury indictment of the publisher with the help of District Attorney Joab A. Banton. The jurors, faced with having to read the entire two-volume *Satyricon*, quickly turned down the request for an indictment. As a result, *The Satyricon* was never banned, but printers remained cautious for many decades. To evade censors, those who reprinted the work usually set the potentially objectionable passages of the book in Latin. In 1927, Liveright published a one-volume, highly expurgated edition of the work that contained little to which even the vice society could object.

FURTHER READING

Boyer, Paul S. *Purity in Print: The Vice-Society Movement and Book Censorship in America.* New York: Scribner, 1968.
"Judge as Literary Critic." *Catholic World* 116 (December 1922): 392–399.
Schmeling, Gareth. "*The Satyricon:* Forms in Search of a Genre." *Classical Bulletin* 47 (1970): 49–53.

SEPTEMBER IN QUINZE

Author: Vivian Connell
Original dates and places of publication: 1952, United States; 1954, England
Original publishers: The Dial Press (United States); Hutchinson Publishing (England)
Literary form: Novel

SUMMARY

September in Quinze was written at the Gallia Palace Hotel at Cannes, and the author expresses his appreciation to the director and concierge in a note preceding the story. The title is a pun on the name Cannes (Quinze). The novel relates the love affairs and tragedies of a collection of disaffected individuals, including a Russian countess married to an opium addict and a Middle Eastern potentate who has settled in Quinze and dedicated himself to the pursuit of self-indulgence. Although aristocrats proliferate, the main focus is on Pietro Salvadori, a young Italian man who lost his family when Americans bombed his village during World War II. He serves as an insightful observer of the emptiness of others' lives.

Quinze is a city of lonely decadence, where "the whores [sit] at the bar" in the casino in which millions of francs are lost in single bets. King Sadook, ruler of an unnamed Middle Eastern nation, brags, "I've had a couple of hundred of women in bed," but feels "hungry in his loins" for "a woman with hair under her arms and sweat on her belly." Heloise, the cool and elegant Countess Saignor, attracts admiring glances, but she is dead inside and can feel no passion. Her opium-addicted husband Raymond, who has passed off the poetry of Baudelaire as his own, haunts her, and they both eventually commit suicide. Manuelo was born in Spain and educated at Harvard, but his passion is kindled by the young American Sara when he learns that her father is a wealthy businessman with European ties that can further his semilegal enterprises. The French Marcel is a pimp, and he bemoans

September in Quinze because business is slow. American Homer Barton seems to be the typical loud and obnoxious tourist until he receives word of his only son's death in the Korean War, which makes him evaluate his own wasted existence and seek love and happiness rather than material success.

Pietro also bears the scars of his family's deaths, and he appears to have no direction at the outset of the novel. To make food money, he walks poodles for the fashionable ladies, taking the dogs to the Poodle Club, where they are placed on cushions, given yellow tea, and pampered. He wins a million francs in one try at the roulette wheel with a coin acquired from a dead man, and then proceeds to sort out his life, eventually finding true love with a woman of similar background.

The novel contains several sexual scenes in which people "ached for love" "stripped" and the body of one or another "became an animal." Sadook disguises himself as a commoner and shares a night of lust with a woman who "wanted him because he savaged her with his manhood in the forest of hair and roared like a wild stallion." Pietro initiates a sexual experience as "he ripped off her skirt and imprisoned her with an angry hand and pulled the silk off her breasts. They glowed like gourds of love in the moonlight and Pietro stooped and smothered his face in her bosom." Other characters engage in sexual activity with varying degrees of explicitness in the novel.

CENSORSHIP HISTORY

September in Quinze was banned in Ireland on August 1, 1952, after the Irish Board of Censors found the novel "obscene" and "indecent." A prohibition order was published in the *Iris Oifigiuil*, "the only official source from which booksellers [and readers] might learn of a new prohibition order," in which all materials blacklisted by the Irish Board of Censors were listed. According to the Censorship of Publications Bill of 1928, "the notice in *Iris Oifigiuil* should be sufficient evidence in the courts of summary jurisdiction as to the character of the publication." The work was officially banned from sale in Ireland until the introduction of the Censorship Publications Bill in 1967 reduced to 12 years the duration of a prohibition order, and the work was among 5,000 titles released from the list of banned books.

In 1954, *September in Quinze* became the subject of litigation after the British Treasury Counsel examined the novel and determined it was "obscene." Both the government and Hutchinson Publishing wanted the case dealt with by the Marlborough Street magistrate, but Magistrate Frank Milton insisted on committing the case for trial at the Old Bailey. In preliminary hearings, Magistrate Milton allowed the defense to include supporting criticisms and reviews of the book, but these were later disallowed when the case was heard at the Old Bailey. Sir Gerald Dodson, the presiding judge in the case and also the recorder of London, determined that the novel did not meet his standard that all books must be suitable reading for "a callow youth, or a girl just budding into womanhood."

Hutchinson Publishing and its director, Katherine Webb, were each fined 500 pounds. In his summing up, Sir Dodson stated:

> I should have thought any reader, however inexperienced, would have been repelled by a book of this sort, which is repugnant to every decent emotion which ever concerned man or woman. It is a very comforting thought that juries from time to time take a very solid stand against this sort of thing, and realise how important it is for the youth of this country to be protected and that the fountain of our national blood should not be polluted at its source.

FURTHER READING

Adams, Michael. *Censorship: The Irish Experience.* Tuscaloosa: University of Alabama Press, 1968.

Craig, Alec. *Suppressed Books: A History of the Conception of Literary Obscenity.* New York: World Publishing, 1963.

Rolph, Cecil Hewitt. *Books in the Dock.* London: Deutsch, 1961.

SERENADE

Author: James M. Cain
Original date and place of publication: 1937, United States
Original publisher: Alfred A. Knopf
Literary form: Novel

SUMMARY

Serenade is the story of John Howard Sharp, a concert singer who has landed fundless in Mexico City because his voice has failed him. He meets Juana Montes, a "three-peso whore," who appears to be receptive to his advances until she hears him sing. She changes her mind because she hears a wooden quality in his voice that she associates with homosexuals. The two decide to join forces, nonetheless, and open a house of prostitution in Acapulco. On the way, they are caught in a rainstorm and take refuge in a church, where John rapes Juana. He justifies his action by saying, "Yes, it was rape, but only technically, brother, only technically. Above the waist, maybe she worried about the *sacrilegio,* but from the waist down she wanted me bad."

They live together, indulging frequently in such sex play as "smearing her nipples with soup." After a run-in with a Mexican official, the two move to California, where John regains his voice. When conductor Winston Hawes reenters John's life, their strong physical attraction to each other is evident. Desperate to "save" John from his homosexual feelings, Juana kills Winston and must escape from the United States into Mexico. John follows her, but Juana runs away only to be reunited with him as she is about to die at the hands of the official who originally forced them to flee Mexico.

CENSORSHIP HISTORY

Serenade was not the object of attempted censorship until a decade after publication. In 1949, after receiving complaints from patrons of the Free Public Library in Worcester, Massachusetts, the state attorney general ordered that copies of *Serenade* and GOD'S LITTLE ACRE be removed from the library shelves. The case appeared before the Superior Court of Suffolk County, Massachusetts, which judged the book "not obscene." The attorney general filed an appeal with the Supreme Judicial Court where, in September 1950, *Serenade* was again cleared in a 4-3 decision in *Attorney General v. Book Named "Serenade,"* 326 Mass. 324, 94 N.E. 2d 259 (1950). In presenting the majority decision, Judge Spalding wrote that the sexual episodes in *Serenade* were "not portrayed in a manner that would have a 'substantial tendency to deprave or corrupt readers by inciting lascivious thoughts or arousing lustful desires.' "

FURTHER READING

DeVoto, Bernard. "The Easy Chair: Liberal Decisions in Massachusetts." *Harper's Magazine*, July 1949, pp. 62–65.
Frohock, W. M. *The Novel of Violence in America.* Dallas, Tex.: Southern Methodist University, 1950.
"Worcester Library Directors Support Their Librarian." *Library Journal*, 1949, p. 649.

SEX

Author: Madonna
Original date and place of publication: 1992, New York
Original publisher: Warner Books
Literary form: Pictorial

SUMMARY

Sex is a 128-page book of erotica and sexual fantasies written by Madonna. It was produced in a spiral-bound format with sheets of aluminum as covers, wrapped in silver, and accompanied by a copy of "Erotica" on a single CD. As Madonna writes in the introduction, "This is about sex. Sex is not love. Love is not sex. But the best of both worlds is created when they come together." She defends the sexual activity portrayed in the book as not meant to encourage others to engage in unsafe sex and explains that all of the photographs are based on her fantasies. She explains, "when I let my mind wander, when I let myself go, I rarely think of condoms. My fantasies take place in a perfect world, a place without AIDS." She cautions readers that everything they see in the book is "a dream, pretend. But if I were to make my dreams real, I would certainly use condoms. Safe sex saves lives. Pass it on." The brief essays in the book that are interspersed with the pictures are all written by Dita Parlow, a persona created by Madonna. On her CD *Erotica*, Madonna also shares performance credits with this imagined self.

The photographs in the book explore diverse forms of sexual behavior, including homosexuality and fetishism. Madonna appears in photographs with various celebrities, including model Naomi Campbell, actress Isabella Rossellini, rappers Big Daddy Kane and Vanilla Ice, and gay porn star Joey Stefano. She is fully naked in some pictures and partially clothed in others; the photographs cover a range of locales.

CENSORSHIP HISTORY

Sex sold 1.5 million copies worldwide and appeared in the number-one position on both the *Washington Post* and the *New York Times* best-seller lists.

Japan banned the book because its controversial photographs violated the country's censorship law. In New Delhi, India, police announced they would confiscate copies of *Sex* that entered the country. On November 26, 1992, in Paris, the Catholic group The Future of Culture filed two lawsuits against Madonna and her publisher for corrupting French youths with pornography and petitioned the court to have all copies of the book in France destroyed. On December 7, 1992, the group lost its court battle to have the book destroyed.

In December 1992, Judith Sees, chairperson of the Monroe County Library System board of trustees in Michigan, was warned by 20 families that they would remove their children from the 4-H program run by Sees because she had supported the inclusion of Madonna's book in the library collection.

In 1992, the Mesa, Arizona, Public Library System cancelled its orders for copies of the book after local residents called and protested the proposed purchase.

In October 1993, *Library Journal* reported that Kay Clark, vice president of the library board of trustees in Beloit, Wisconsin, had sided with the librarians of the Beloit Public Library in their fight to keep the book as part of the library collection. She was not reappointed after she allowed the book to enter the public library collection with no attached age restriction.

In Austin, Texas, the library formed its first Reconsideration Committee, composed of staff librarians, in response to the numerous complaints the library received about the Austin Public Library's acquisition of *Sex*.

For the most part, as Will Manley wrote in his column in the October 1997 issue of *American Libraries*, librarians avoided the controversy:

> The number of libraries that own the book is minuscule. Clearly it was far too explicit. Very few librarians wanted to have to defend it in front of angry library

boards, city councils, county commissions, or parent groups. So they simply decided not to buy the book. But this was not an act of censorship, it was an act of selection. Every librarian I talked to said that he or she passed on the book not because of its X-rated content, but because it was published with a metal cover and spiral binding that were not conducive to practical library use.

The hypocrisy of this little white lie becomes obvious when we think about what would happen if Danielle Steele's next bestseller were to appear in a similar heavy-metal format. No doubt we would buy it in multiple copies and congratulate the publisher for putting Steele into steel, a material that can withstand the abuse of the hundreds of patrons eager to get their hands on the book.

FURTHER READING

"Board Member Axed over Access to *Sex*." *Library Journal* October 1, 1993, p. 16.

Flagg, Gordon. "After Four Months, Libraries Are Still in the Hot Seat over *Sex*." *American Libraries* 23 (April 1993): 290–291.

Flagg, Gordon. "For *Sex*, See Librarian . . . Maybe." *American Librarians* 23 (December 1992): 900.

Harris, Daniel. "*Sex*, Madonna, and Mia: Press Reflections." *The Antioch Review* 51 (4): 503–518.

Manley, Will. "Are We Free to Talk Honestly about Intellectual Freedom?" *American Libraries* (October 1997). Formerly available online. URL: http://lists.webjunction. org/wjlists/web4lib/1997-october/022143.html. Accessed January 3, 2006.

SEXUS

Author: Henry Miller
Original dates and places of publication: 1949, France; 1965, United States; 1969, England
Original publishers: Obelisk Press (France); Grove Press (United States); Calder & Boyars (England)
Literary form: Novel

SUMMARY

Sexus is the first of three volumes in a series that Miller called *The Rosy Crucifixion*. The second volume is *Plexus*, published in 1953 by Olympia Press in Paris, in 1963 by Weidenfeld & Nicolson in London, and in 1965 by Grove Press. *Nexus*, the third volume, was published in 1960 by Obelisk Press, in 1964 by Weidenfeld & Nicolson, and in 1965 by Grove Press. *Sexus* is largely autobiographical, and it provides graphic details of the promiscuous behavior of its principal characters.

The novel, which began as custom-written erotica for a wealthy individual collector, contains two plotlines that run simultaneously throughout it. The first plot is the narrator's affair with a woman for whom he has left his wife and child, and the second is his beginnings as a writer and the frustrations that he faces in his boring job that provides financial survival. The novel contains numerous unadorned sex scenes, many recounted in flashback, that are simple physical couplings in bushes or on bare and dirty slum floors. The novel also contains several homosexual episodes, one incident in which the narrator has consecutive sex with two female partners in one bed, and many instances of fellatio, cunnilingus, and mutual masturbation. Sex plays a major role in the book, and the author never raises any questions of morality, but he does discuss the ills of society as well as the cures for these ills.

CENSORSHIP HISTORY

Sexus became involved in an obscenity trial in Norway in 1959, the first in 70 years in that nation. The prosecutor in Oslo decided to test whether the national law against obscene literature still had meaning and brought charges against a Norwegian novel called *The Song of the Red Ruby*. The defense claimed that there were many other more pornographic books being sold undisturbed in Norway and named *Sexus* as the best example. The novel had been translated into Danish in 1957, and the similarity of the languages meant that the book was also sold in Norway.

The prosecutor ordered the several hundred copies in Danish and a few copies of the English version confiscated for being "obscene writing" and brought proceedings against two Oslo booksellers in the Oslo Town Court. They were found guilty the following year, but an appeal of the case to the Norwegian Supreme Court resulted in a reversal of the decision against the two booksellers. In a letter in defense of the novel, Miller stated,

> It is not something evil, not something poisonous, which this book Sexus offers the Norwegian reader. It is a dose of life which I administered to myself first, and which I not only survived but thrived on. Certainly, I would not offer it to infants, but then neither would I offer a child a bottle of *aqua vitae*. I can say one thing for it unblushingly—compared to the atom bomb it is full of lifegiving qualities.

Despite his efforts, the ban on *Sexus* remained.

FURTHER READING

Loth, David. *The Erotic in Literature*. New York: Dorset, 1961.
Miller, Henry. "Defense of the Freedom to Read—A Letter to the Supreme Court of Norway in Connection with the Ban on *Sexus* (*The Rosy Crucifixion*)." In *Versions of Censorship: Anthology,* edited by John McCormick and Mairi MacInnes, 223–230. Garden City, N.Y.: Doubleday, 1962.
Sutherland, John. *Offensive Literature: Decensorship in Britain, 1960–1982*. Totowa, N.J.: Barnes & Noble, 1982.

SHANGHAI BABY

Author: Wei Hui (Zhou Weihui)
Original dates and places of publication: 1999, Shanghai; 2001, United States
Original publishers: Chunfeng Literature and Art Publishing House (Shanghai); Simon & Schuster (New York)
Literary form: Novel

SUMMARY

Shanghai Baby is one of the first novels published in China that portrays the author's generation of women, born in the 1970s and seeking to manage the constant tensions between traditional values and more liberal Western influences. The book is filled with social issues that have long been taboo in China, including female masturbation and homosexuality.

The novel relates the sexual adventures of Coco, a 25-year-old waitress and sometime writer. Her real name is Nikki, but she prefers the name Coco, which she associates with the elegant couturier Coco Chanel. She lives in relative contentment with Tian Tian, whose wealthy mother sends him substantial money each month. Tian Tian continually urges her to leave her job as a waitress and to write, claiming that he has known from the first time he saw her that she is "cut out to be a writer," but she resists for a time. Once Coco acquiesces to write full time, Tian Tian becomes obsessed with pushing her "to write a genuine book of enchantment. This became the core of his life." Despite her new freedom to write and the gentle attentions of Tian Tian, Coco remains sexually frustrated because Tian Tian is sexually impotent. She has a series of erotically charged dreams from which she awakens with tears in her eyes and with Tian Tian lying helpless by her side.

The couple attend a party at the residence of Tian Tian's friend Madonna, where Coco meets a wild group of partygoers, including Flying Apple, a handsome bisexual who claims to be saving money for a sex-change operation, and Mark, an arrogant German investment consultant attached to a Shanghai firm. Coco and Mark dance and flirt while Tian Tian sits on a couch and smokes marijuana, becoming oblivious to his surroundings and eventually falling asleep next to a urinal in the bathroom. Mark helps Coco take Tian Tian home in a cab and put him to bed, after which she excitedly anticipates a few sensual moments with Mark. Instead, he kisses her on both cheeks and leaves, having first placed his business card in her hand.

As Coco contemplates the pleasures of an affair with Mark, "a tall Western man," she reveals that she admires tall men "because of my loathing for a pint-size ex-boyfriend" who "was also a sex maniac" and who used her body "to try out all sorts of positions from porn videos." He had fascinated her, at first, with his ability to recite famous works by Shakespeare "in Oxford English," but his penchant for sex in public places and voyeuristic fantasies soon saddened her and his later stalking terrorized her. Coco believes that a tall man will treat her differently, and she encourages a relationship with Mark. He sends two invitations for an art exhibition at the Liu Haisu Art Museum, which Tian Tian refuses to attend. Coco and Mark slip away from the exhibit to Mark's apartment where, after several drinks of rum, Mark performs cunnilingus on Coco and then startles her by entering her with "his huge organ." She returns to her apartment guiltily and recalls another of her past boyfriends, Ye Qian, who she says "restored my healthy attitude to sex. He patiently taught me how to distinguish between clitoral and vaginal orgasms, and often made me climax both ways at once." Her memories provide details of their many and varied sexual encounters, after which she reconsiders her relationship with Tian Tian and describes him as "a fetus soaking in formaldehyde."

Coco vows to avoid further sexual contact with Mark, but she succumbs to his seductive behavior toward her at another art exhibition, which they leave hurriedly. At the party afterward, Mark and Coco have sex in "a grubby women's restroom," in a graphically detailed scene that leaves her disgusted with herself and penitent. She berates herself for being "a bad girl" and thinks of the many times her parents have expressed disappointment about her and praised her cousin Zhu Sha, who has always acted ladylike and followed conventional morality. With shock, she learns that her seemingly perfect cousin has divorced her husband because he was sexually unable to fulfill her, and she is living for a time with Coco's parents. Coco is even more surprised to learn that Zhu Sha works at the same investment firm as Mark.

As the affair between Coco and Mark advances, Tian Tian decides to leave for a few months to travel but gives restlessness as his excuse instead of hinting at any knowledge of the affair. Lonely, Coco calls Mark at home and learns that he is married and his wife is visiting from Germany for a month. Despite misgivings, she continues to meet her German lover whenever possible for sexual encounters, including one that occurs while Tian Tian calls from Haikou, where he has decided to settle for a time.

In a rare visit to her parents' home, on the occasion of her father's 53rd birthday, Coco shares memories with Zhu Sha and they speak about Mark. Coco learns that Mark will represent his company team in a competitive football match and tells Zhu Sha that she wants to attend to meet Mark's wife, Eva, and their two children. Meeting Mark's family confuses Coco, because she genuinely likes Eva, and Mark admits to her that he loves his wife although he enjoys their affair. She calls Tian Tian and becomes alarmed when his speech sounds slurred; he calls her back and tells her to send money because he has depleted the large amount of money he took with him, using much of it to buy morphine. Despite her infidelity, Coco loves Tian Tian and tries to save his life by compelling him to enter a detoxification program in Haikou while she returns to Shanghai to continue writing her novel.

SHANGHAI BABY

With Tian Tian in a drug treatment facility and Mark in Mexico, Coco
fantasizes about a series of old boyfriends in graphically explicit sexual situations. As she becomes increasingly lonely, her agent Deng calls her with
the good news that her short story collection, *Shriek of the Butterfly*, is going
to be republished in an edition of 10,000 copies, and he invites her to lunch
with several influential people. During lunch, Coco considers an affair with
a man whom she has always called Godfather, who had been two years ahead
of her at Fudan University and who always dressed in black with dark glasses,
but she does not pursue the desire.

She works on her novel and receives a surprise visitor one day, Tian Tian's
mother Connie, who has returned to Shanghai from Spain despite her son's
refusal to see her. When Connie learns that Tian Tian is in a drug treatment
facility, she cries and berates herself for having neglected and alienated him,
but Coco calms her and the two become friends. Tian Tian returns to Coco
unannounced, cured of his addiction and capable and eager to be her sexual
partner. The two young people vow to stay with each other through whatever life brings, and Coco asks him to create healing in another area of his
life by having dinner with his mother Connie and her Spanish husband Juan.
Although reluctant, Tian Tian agrees, and the evening is uncomfortable.

In their apartment, Tian Tian and Coco feel secluded from the world and
both continue their creative works, but Coco does not refuse Mark when he
calls and asks her to meet him. After a movie premiere party, the two go to
Mark's apartment, and Coco find that she cannot resist his "pair of wicked
blue eyes, a cute butt, and that monstrous plaything." The author describes
their lovemaking in the shower and in bed in meticulous detail. Love and
sex fail to motivate Coco's creativity and the novel languishes, so she takes
Madonna's advice to throw a party in the hope of driving away her lifeless
mood. The suggestion works and, after cleaning up the empty pill contain-
ers, liquor bottles, cigar butts, and leftover food the following day, Coco
finds that she is able to write again.

Tian Tian agrees to create murals for his mother's new Spanish restaurant and spends long days away from the apartment. Alone in the apartment
when Mark calls her and tells her that his company is transferring him back
to Germany, Coco rushes to meet him and realizes that she has fallen deeply
in love with him. The two spend several days together, and Coco finds Tian
Tian missing when she returns to the apartment. She finds him in a drug-
induced stupor and learns that he has returned to using morphine. As his
habit worsens, Coco watches him being led away by police "again and again"
until he dies one morning, naked and next to her in bed.

CENSORSHIP HISTORY

Shanghai Baby was banned in China after 100,000 copies had already been
sold, and after the English translation was published in England in June
2001 and released in the United States in September 2001. Wei Hui, whose

full name is Zhou Wei Hui but who only uses one name, is the first author to be banned in China for pornography. The Chinese banned the book because it contains "too much decadence and too much sexual description" and officials believed that it would "give a bad influence to a new generation." Police publicly raided book fairs and confiscated copies of the novel. Forty thousand copies of a new printing of the book were burned, operations at the publishing house were suspended for three months, and the publisher was replaced. The publisher was required to destroy the page proofs, and tens of thousands of copies were confiscated and destroyed throughout the country. *The People's Daily*, the Communist Party's propaganda organ, harshly ridiculed and criticized the author, calling her "decadent, debauched, and a slave of foreign culture."

Wei Hui claimed that the sexual adventures alone of her character were not the only reason the book was banned in China. In an interview given to reporter Kerry O'Brien for the Australian Broadcasting Corporation, she stated, "I think the book irritated some Chinese men because a Chinese woman sleeps with a Western guy. In China, it's like a big deal. If you sleep with a Western man, you also sleep with the whole Western culture, you betray your country." She said that the older Chinese statesmen were probably upset by the freedom displayed by women in this book and in the books of other young Chinese women writers.

In an interview with a reporter for the *Washington Post*, Wei Hui discussed the relation between a book signing she did in Chengdu in March 2000 and the timing of the banning. Because the advance publicity had been heavy, she knew that numerous television and print reporters would be present at the signing, so she dressed for the event in a diaphanous, low-cut top. Photographs of her were on every area newspaper and television station. She learned later that several retired Communist Party leaders responded to the explosion of publicity by writing letters to the Chinese central authorities and demanding an investigation. An inquiry was led by Zeng Qinghong, one of China's top Communist Party officials. With weeks, the book was officially labeled "pornographic" and thousands of copies were destroyed. Her editor believed that the book was banned because Wei Hui exhibited too much of her body at the Chengdu publicity fete: "It was banned because Wei Hui was outrageous. It wasn't her book so much as her 'performance art' in Chengdu."

FURTHER READING

"China-Censorship: China Inadvertently Creates a Media Darling." *World News Digest*, Available online. URL: www.canoe.ca/jul00/world_digest_jul8.html. Accessed February 3, 2011.

"An Interview with Wei Hui." *Bibliofemme*. Available online. URL: www.bibliofemme. com/interviews/weihui.shtml. Accessed February 3, 2011.

Kunhikrishnan, K. "The New Face of China." *Hindu*. Available online. URL: www. hinduonnet.com/2001/11/04/stories/1304017r.htm. Accessed January 3, 2006.

O'Brien, Kerry. "Shanghai Writer Challenging Stereotypes." Television broadcast transcript. Australian Broadcasting System. Available online. URL: www.abc.net.au/7.30/content/2001/s337692.htm. Accessed August 23, 2010.

Pomfret, John. "Letter from China; The Coveted Stamp of Disapproval." *Washington Post*, June 27, 2000, p. C1.

Sheng, John. "Afterthoughts on the Banning of 'Shanghai Baby.' " *Perspectives* 2. Available online. URL: www.oycf.org/perspectives/8_103100/afterthoughts_on_the_banning_of.htm. Accessed August 12, 2010.

Smith, Craig S. "Sex, Lust, Drugs: Her Novel's Too Much for China." *New York Times*, May 11, 2000, p. A4.

SIMON CALLED PETER

Author: Robert Keable
Original date and place of publication: 1921, United States
Original publisher: E. P. Dutton and Company
Literary form: Novel

SUMMARY

Simon Called Peter is the story of Peter Graham, an Anglican chaplain serving in France during World War I, who struggles to deal with what he views as the lax standards of those around him. As the months of the war drag out, Graham becomes close to those whose behavior he disdained earlier and he struggles with the growing awareness that he is much less effectual than he has hoped to be. As his standards of personal behavior become increasingly lower, Graham learns to feel compassion for others around him and for prostitutes, one of whom, Louise, becomes his friend. As his self-image deteriorates and he becomes discouraged and angry with himself, Graham turns to Louise in a moment of temptation and begs her to have sex with him:

> "That's just it, Louise," he cried. "I am a wild beast tonight. I can't stand it any longer. Kiss me."
>
> He put his arms around her, and bent her head back, studying her French and rather inscrutable eyes, her dark lashes, her mobile mouth, her long white throat. He put his hand caressingly upon it, and slid his fingers beneath the loose lace that the open wrap exposed. "Dear," he said, "I want you tonight."
>
> "Tonight, cherie?" she questioned.
>
> "Yes, now," he said hotly. "And why not? You give to other men—why not to me, Louise? . . . I've a body, like other men."

Although Graham passionately demands that Louise have sex with him, she refuses, knowing that he would only regret the experience.

Continuing to struggle with his duties and with his growing desires, Graham later falls in love with Julie, an unconventional young woman he plans to marry. Toward the end of the novel, the two spend a few passionate days in a London hotel without any expression of hesitation or guilt regarding their behavior. Obsessed by Julie, Graham proclaims, "I believe I'd rather have you than—than God!" To Graham, "she was his bride, his wife, coming to him consecrate—not by any State convention, not by any ceremony of man-made religion, but by the pure passion of human love, virginal, clean."

In spite of their proclamations of love and desire, the two decide that they should not marry because Graham's allegiance is to his church. As the novel ends, he concludes that "the things of the spirit were, after all, so much greater than the things of the flesh."

CENSORSHIP HISTORY

Simon Called Peter aroused the ire of censors because it portrays a cleric who exhibits no guilt when he breaks the moral code by engaging in a premarital sexual relationship. Although the view of the main character is that sincere emotion is sufficient sanctification for his sexual relationship, it was not enough for those who wanted the novel banned.

In October 1922, *Simon Called Peter* became the center of attention of the Boston Watch and Ward Society. The public demand for the novel became "irresistible" after newspapers reported that the novel had been favorite reading of the victims in the sensational double murder of Mrs. James Mills and her minister-lover Reverend Edward Hall in September 1922 in New Jersey. The Boston Watch and Ward Society brought charges against Edith Law of Arlington, Massachusetts, the owner of a Boston rental library, who was convicted in the Cambridge District Court in October 1922 and fined $100 by Judge Arthur Stone for stocking *Simon Called Peter* in her rental library. In an appeal, Judge Stone suspended the fine but warned Law that she faced a jail sentence if she were ever again convicted in an obscenity case. The case drew particular attention because the novel had been a best seller for more than a year.

In New York City, John Sumner, secretary of the New York Society for the Suppression of Vice, tried without success to have the book banned, but the courts refused to hear the complaint. Nonetheless, a second conviction for the sale of *Simon Called Peter* occurred in 1923, brought by the Boston Watch and Ward Society against Morris Honigbaum of Boston's Modern Bookshop. Despite continuing strong sales of *Simon Called Peter* in other areas of the country, Honigbaum was fined $100 for selling the novel.

FURTHER READING

"Boston Clean Book Case." *Publishers Weekly*, January 26, 1924, p. 240.

Boyer, Paul S. *Purity in Print: The Vice-Society Movement and Book Censorship in America*. New York: Scribner, 1968.

"Finds Keable Book Obscene." *New York Times*, October 19, 1922, p. 2.

Fuller, Richard F. "How Boston Handles Problems." *Publishers Weekly*, May 26, 1923, pp. 1, 624–1,625.

"Sumner Denounces Book in Hall Case." *New York Times*, October 20, 1922, p. 3.

1601—A FIRESIDE CONVERSATION IN YE TIME OF QUEEN ELIZABETH

Author: Mark Twain (Samuel Langhorne Clemens)
Original date and place of publication: 1876, United States
Original publisher: Privately printed
Literary form: Satire

SUMMARY

1601—A Fireside Conversation in ye Time of Queen Elizabeth is Mark Twain's underground classic, and one of his few attempts at erotica. Regarding the work, he stated, "If there is a decent word in it, it is because I overlooked it." Written just after Twain completed *The Adventures of Tom Sawyer* and before he started *Adventures of Huckleberry Finn*, the work is as highly crafted as his most popular works. Despite its extensive use of language usually labelled "obscene," the author claimed to have put great care into the writing of *1601* and once stated, "I built a conversation which *could* have happened—I used words such as were used at that time—1601."

Twain set the work in the court of Queen Elizabeth I and gathers to her fireside such contemporary luminaries as William Shakespeare, Sir Walter Raleigh, Ben Johnson, and a number of imaginary women who are identified as ladies of the queen's household. The fictional conversation is recounted by the queen's cupbearer, who relates that the flatulence of one of those present motivates the queen to question all present about the identity of the culprit and then to state, "I have not heard the fellow [admit] to this fart."

In the conversation that follows, each individual present speaks in the style and manner expected—the learned and pompous Bacon, the poetic Shakespeare and Jonson, and the sharp and arrogant queen. The talk moves quickly to tales of sexual prowess and sexual misconduct. One participant tells the story of a king (unnamed) who could claim having deflowered 10 virgins in one night, while his wife "serviced" twice as many young men in the same period. References are made to the custom of a "far-off land" in which widows wear phallic symbols in their hair, prompting the queen to state tartly that English widows use them, too, but "prefer them between their thighs." When the ladies of the court appear to enjoy too heartily the accounts of others' adventures, they must bear a discussion of their own sexual adventures.

CENSORSHIP HISTORY

Twain wrote *1601* in 1876 for his friend, the Reverend Joseph Twitchell, with the proclaimed purpose of disclosing "the picturesqueness of par-lor conversation in Elizabeth's time." In 1880, Secretary of State John

Hay received a copy and then sent it to his friend, Alexander Gunn, in Cleveland. Gunn wrote Hay that he intended to print the book, to which Hay protested that he could not condone this. However, he added that if Gunn was willing to go ahead with the printing without his consent, he would like Gunn to save him a copy. C. E. S. Wood, a West Point lieutenant, is also said to have had a finely made edition printed on the West Point presses—one that was circulated among "popes and kings and such people," Twain wrote. Some of these copies were taken abroad and, as a result of Twain's large international reputation, many limited-run editions in English and in translation appeared in Europe, some with expensive illustrations. In 1900, higher-quality editions of the book were worth 20 guineas in England. Ernst and Schwartz have called the work "one of the outstanding American examples of high literary pornography," but the author's self-banning of the work and the surreptitious manner in which pirated copies were circulated kept the work out of the sight of official book banners.

In 1962, *1601* appeared in Volume 1, Number 4, of *Eros*, a deluxe hardbound quarterly magazine published by Ralph Ginzburg that became the subject of an obscenity trial in *Ginzburg v. United States*, 383 U.S. 463 (1966). Its existence went unmentioned in the company of a story entitled "Madame Tellier's Brothel," photographs of male prostitutes, French postcards with buxom women nude from the waist up, and a photographic essay of an African-American man having sex with a Caucasian woman. Edward De Grazia, an author and attorney who defended in many such trials, stated that the Department of the United States Post Office had received more than 35,000 complaints against Ginzburg's use of the mails "to peddle his 'sex and love' publications," but Attorney General Robert Kennedy remained reluctant to prosecute because he feared that people would "blame it on [his] Catholicism." He waited until prosecution was initiated by a U.S. attorney in Philadelphia. When the case appeared before the U.S. Supreme Court, Ginzburg was sentenced to serve five years in prison for "pandering," but the appeals filed by defense attorneys kept Ginzburg free on bail for eight years. When Ginzburg again faced the Supreme Court, his sentence was lowered to eight months, and the charges of "commercial exploitation," "pandering," and "titillation" remained.

FURTHER READING

Ernst, Morris L., and Alan U. Schwartz. *Censorship: The Search for the Obscene*. New York: Macmillan, 1964.

De Grazia, Edward. *Girls Lean Back Everywhere: The Law of Obscenity and the Assault on Genius*. New York: Random House, 1992.

Lewis, Felice Flanery. *Literature, Obscenity, & Law*. Carbondale: Southern Illinois University Press, 1976.

Loth, David. *The Erotic in Literature*. New York: Dorset, 1961.

SLEEVELESS ERRAND

Author: Norah C. James
Original date and place of publication: 1929, England
Original publisher: Scholartis Press
Literary form: Novel

SUMMARY

Sleeveless Errand is one of the many novels written after World War I that depict what Gertrude Stein labeled the Lost Generation, that rootless group of young people who found the destruction caused by the war so emotionally devastating that they could not bring themselves to trust in the future. Paula Cranford, the main character, is a neurotic who blames her behavior on complications resulting from the war. She has just broken off a relationship with a man she loved very much and finds herself at a loss about what to do with her life, which bores her. Eventually Paula becomes disgusted with the time she spends drinking and moving about without purpose, and she decides to commit suicide.

Soon after Paula decides to end her life, she meets Bill Cheland in a restaurant in Lyons. He has just learned that his wife Laura has recently had an affair and, filled with hopelessness that seems to have developed from his wartime experiences, he also thinks of suicide. The main portion of the novel is concerned with the 36 hours that Paula and Bill spend together after they meet. During that time, the two share stories of what has brought them to their present states of mind, and the author uses the stream-of-consciousness technique to allow readers to learn the characters' thoughts as they ruminate over what has happened in their separate lives. As Paula reveals her life and speaks of the many types of people that have been part of her circle, Bill begins to understand that Laura has not been lacking in virtue after all. In revealing their most intimate thoughts, desires, and fears, the characters use language that is natural to the segment of the population they represent but that censors found obscene. The sentences include such terms as "balls," "bloody," and "poor little bugger," and the characters offer no words of condemnation in discussing an adulterous friend. The terms "God" and "Christ" pepper their speech, and, in an instance to which the prosecution pointed as an example of the "shocking depravity" of the book, one character demands, "For Christ's sake give me a drink."

At the end of the novel, Bill has gained a new appreciation for his marriage and for his wife, but Paula has become entrenched in her despair and drives a car over a cliff to her death.

CENSORSHIP HISTORY

Sleeveless Errand was banned soon after publication, in proceedings that started when a reviewer sent his copy of the novel to British Home Secretary Sir William Joyson-Hicks. Known as "Jix," the home secretary was a staunch conservative who had made sex his target in the censorship of bookshops and the theater, and his policemen had been sent on repeated raids to confiscate "obscene" books and to close down "immoral" productions. He sent the case to Director of Public Prosecution Sir Archibald Bodkin, who ordered that police seize copies at the premises of Scholartis Press, the publishing house. Publisher Eric Partridge was summoned and was ordered to show cause that the book should not be destroyed. Bodkin also ordered that the case be heard in front of the Bow Street magistrate on March 3, 1929, and applied for a destruction order for the book, which he claimed "tolerated and even advocated adultery." The prosecution cited the "obscene" language used by the characters as evidence of its "shocking depravity."

The defense asserted that the intent of the author had been "to portray and condemn the mode of life and language of a certain section of the community" and that the book merely reflected life as it was in that community. The magistrate ruled in favor of the prosecution and granted the destruction order, stating that the novel suggested "thoughts of the most impure character" to readers of all ages. In a speech to the House of Commons, Joynson-Hicks attributed the seizure of the books to an "indirect form of censorship" but insisted that nothing that could properly be described as literary censorship had occurred. He reminded critics that "The law has decided that indecent publications are not to be permitted," and stated that he had only acted in accordance with the law: "In regard to *The Sleeveless Errand*, it is grossly obscene."

FURTHER READING

"Books and Authors—*Sleeveless Errand*. *New York Times Book Review*, March 19, 1929, p. 8.
"British Deny Censorship." *New York Times*, March 1, 1929, p. 3.
Elliott, Desmond. "Field Day for the Righteous." *Books and Bookmen* 5 (December 1959): 17.
MacCarthy, Desmond. "Literary Trends." *Life and Letters* 1 (October 1928): 329–341.
Partridge, Eric. *The First Three Years*. London: Scholartis, 1930.
"*Sleeveless Errand* and Other Works of Fiction." *New York Times Book Review*, June 9, 1929, pp. 5–8.

SNOW FALLING ON CEDARS

Author: David Guterson
Original date and place of publication: 1994, United States
Publisher: Harcourt Brace Jovanovich
Literary form: Novel

SUMMARY

Snow Falling on Cedars takes place in 1954 on San Piedro Island, off the coast of Washington in the Pacific Northwest. The story opens on December 6, one day before the 13th anniversary of the bombing of Pearl Harbor, and the tension between Japanese Americans and Anglo citizens in the town remains high. Kabuo Miyamoto, who fought on the American side in World War II, is on trial, charged with killing Carl Heine, also a veteran of World War II and the son of a man who once had an agreement to sell land to the Miyamoto family before they were sent to internment camps. Kabuo and Carl had been childhood friends, despite the simmering anti-Japanese tensions on the island. Watching the trial are Ishmael Chambers, another World War II veteran who has lost an arm in the war and who is now editor of the town newspaper, the *San Piedro Review*, and Hatsue, Kabuo's wife. Many years earlier, Ishmael and Hatsue had had a secret romantic relationship, which Hatsue ended without explanation. Ishmael has information that could clear Kabuo, but he hesitates to bring it up, hoping that he might be able to recapture Hatsue's love if Kabuo is convicted.

Sheriff Art Moran appears on the witness stand and describes pulling Carl Heine's body out of a net on Carl's boat. He explains that he arrested Kabuo after learning from the island's coroner, Horace Whaley, that the autopsy showed that Carl had head injuries consistent with injuries inflicted with gun butts by Japanese soldiers trained in stick fighting, or kendo. Kabuo is an expert in kendo. The sheriff also learns that 14 years earlier, Heine's father, Carl Sr., had made an arrangement to sell seven acres to Kabuo's family and had accepted installment payments. When the family had only two more payments left, the Miyamoto family and other Japanese-American families were moved to internment camps as the other citizens of San Piedro Island stood silent. Carl Sr., promised to hold the land and take the final two payments when the families return, but he died before the war ended, and his wife Etta, who holds a bitter hatred for the Japanese Americans, sold the land to Ole Jurgensen. When Kabuo returned from the war, he was upset by the betrayal but decided to remain patient and wait until Ole decided to sell. His chance came a few days before Carl's death; he learned that Ole decided to sell but found that Carl Heine already had made an offer. Based on the accumulated information, the sheriff decides that Kabuo had substantial reason to want Carl dead.

The novel takes place in a series of flashbacks interspersed with the events of the trial, and readers are made aware of the complicated relationships that exist among the major characters. Detailed descriptions of the heated love affair between Ishmael and Hatsue suggest that the two would have stayed together had prejudice not created obstacles to their love. The efforts of Zenhichi Miyamoto, Kabuo's father, to buy the land and the fair agreement of Carl Heine, Sr., provide a stark contrast to the hatred that Etta Heine holds for Japanese Americans and her disgust that anyone of Japanese background might own her family's land.

Kabuo testifies that he pleaded with Carl, his childhood friend, to sell him the parcel of land that Zenhichi had paid for years earlier and that he felt hopeful that Carl would sell it to him. He also tells the court that he saw Carl the night of the murder. Carl had taken his boat out on the foggy night of September 15, 1954, to think about Kabuo's request, but his boat ran out of power and stranded him in the dense fog in the middle of a shipping lane, leaving him in a dangerous position should a large freighter come through the channel. Kabuo found Carl and the disabled boat and helped him, a kindness that led Carl to decide to sell the land to Kabuo. Later that night, a large freighter passed through the shipping channel, and the force of its huge wake shook Carl's boat violently, knocking him from the mast he had climbed to untangle a lantern and throwing him to the deck. Unconscious, he fell into the water and drowned.

The only person who can save Kabuo's life is Ishmael, who on the evening of the second day of the trial acquires the logbook of a nearby lighthouse. The radioman's assistant is no longer stationed at the lighthouse, but he had recorded that on the night of the murder a large freighter lost its way and the radioman attempted to put it back on course by advising the crew to steer directly through the channel in which Carl was fishing. The logbook reports that the freighter passed through the channel just five minutes before the time on Carl's waterlogged watch. Ishmael struggles between his desire to turn over the logbook to clear an innocent man and his desire for Hatsue. The trial ends, and all but one of the jurors declare Kabuo guilty, leading the judge to adjourn for that day. In the evening, Ishmael reveals the contents of the logbook to Hatsue and then to the sheriff. After a reexamination of Carl's boat, the sheriff finds the rope on the mast where the lantern hung, as well as the blood and hair where Carl hit his head when he fell. The charges against Kabuo are dropped.

CENSORSHIP HISTORY

Snow Falling on Cedars was on the *New York Times* best-seller list for more than a year, and it was cited as best book of the year by the American Booksellers Association and awarded the PEN/Faulkner Award in 1995, but two school districts in Texas and another in the state of Washington found the book "obscene" and "vulgar." In Boerne, Texas, Lake Highlands High School principal Sam Champion officially reprimanded teacher Frances Riley for using "poor judgment" in teaching the book although she had obtained prior permission from the head of the English department to do so. Parents and students complained that the book was "offensive" because it contained racial epithets, and they objected to "sexually graphic passages." Labeling the book "highly offensive," school superintendent John Kelly ordered the book to be removed from the high school curriculum and the library shelves until a study could be made of the contents. The Texas office of the American Civil Liberties Union (ACLU) contacted the school, and the superintendent responded to the query that the book "contained elements that are deemed obscene and graphic and inappropriate by parents and others." In the official school board record of the incident, officials stated that the book was removed from the curriculum because of "obscenity, graphic depiction of sex, mutilation." The *Spokane Spokesman Review* reported on September 11, 1999, that 17-year-old student Jerald Meadows told a reporter that students were annoyed with the length of the book (460 pages) and "complained to their parents about it just to get out of reading it."

Also in 1999, parents of students attending Vidor (Texas) Junior High School in the Vidor Independent School District formally requested the removal of *Snow Falling on Cedars* from the school library. The complaint charged that the novel contains "profanity" and "inappropriate language" for readers in junior high school. According to the 1999–2000 report by the Texas ACLU, the book was banned from the library.

In May 2000, the South Kitsap school board in Port Orchard, Washington, voted 3 to 2 not to place the novel on the district-approved reading list, after critics complained about "sexual content" and "profanity" in the book. The *Newsletter on Intellectual Freedom* reported that a parent, Doug Bean, addressed the board and charged, "This book is extremely vulgar. This book doesn't teach respect; it teaches self-indulgence." The book was withheld until committees at the high school and district levels could review it. Both committees recommended inclusion of the novel in the approved reading list, but students were not required to read it if they or their parents disapproved of it.

In January 2007, school district officials in the Dufferin-Peel Catholic District in Ontario, Canada, removed *Snow Falling on Cedars* from the high school library after one parent complained that the novel contains "objectionable sexual content." The novel was on the reading list for the 11th grade English class at Father Michael Goetz Secondary School in Mississauga, before teachers and librarians were directed by district administrators to remove the book from circulation until a board-appointed committee could review the book. Although the school officials insisted that they were not banning the novel from the district, only making it inaccessible to students until the review committee completed its work, teachers in the district viewed the action differently. One teacher-librarian, who requested to remain anonymous, stated in a news article for the *Star* that "Pulling a book off the shelf and 'banning' it are pretty much the same thing, since they both mean nobody will be able to read the book in the school library." The district "challenged materials" policy required that a committee consisting of library services and religious education coordinators, two trustees, a parent, and the superintendent of schools review the novel and recommend whether to retain the novel in the curriculum or to support its removal. The parent who filed a formal complaint with the school district objected to the detailed description of the young married couple's first sexual encounter and to a description of a sexual relationship between two teenagers.

In January 2008, the school board in the Coeur d'Alene School District voted 3-2 to retain the novel as a reading choice for high school junior English classes after a lengthy review process that was initiated by parents who objected to the "adult material in the novel." Mary Jo Finney, one of several parents who filed a complaint to have the book removed from the curriculum, objected to "depictions of masturbation, genitalia and intercourse" and asserted that the book contains "vulgar language" and that "the 'F-word' appears nine times on one page." The parents told the school board that the book is "too explicit for high school readers, who don't have the life experience or sophistication to read controversial scenes in context." The school district created an 11-member committee that included Finney to review the book. Other members of the committee praised the manner in which the novel deals with racism and prejudice, and the majority agreed that the "adult content" was "tastefully written, not gratuitous, and important to the plot and character development." The majority report issued by the committee stated that mature students need challenging literature that "comes with the realities of life and [is] rich in human experience." The committee voted to reinstate the novel in the curriculum and to allow students who object to the content to request another novel.

FURTHER READING

American Civil Liberties Union. *Free Speech: Banned and Challenged Books in Texas Public Schools 1999–2000*. Austin: Texas ACLU, 2000.
Kalinowski, Tess. "Peel Board Pulls Novel After Parent Complains." Available online. URL: http: //www.thestar.com/News/article/ 17655. Accessed August 13, 2010.
Kramer, Beeky. "'Snow Falling' Survives School Curriculum Challenge." Available online. URL: http:// www.spokesmanreview.com/breaking story.asp?ID=13078. Accessed August 10, 2010.
Newsletter for Intellectual Freedom (November 1999): 163; (July 2000): 106.

SONG OF SOLOMON

Author: Toni Morrison
Original date and place of publication: 1977, United States
Original publisher: Alfred A. Knopf
Literary type: Novel

SUMMARY

Song of Solomon by Toni Morrison examines the ramifications that the actions of past generations have on their descendants and explores the topic largely through the experiences and emotional conflicts of the third Macon Dead.

The novel opens on February 18, 1931, on the sidewalk outside of Mercy Hospital, a charity hospital in Michigan given the name "No Mercy Hospital" by African-American residents of the area because only white patients are admitted for treatment. A crowd has gathered to watch as insurance agent Robert Smith, wearing blue silk wings and positioning himself on the hospital roof, prepares to leap into the air as the promised at three o'clock in the afternoon and to fly to the other side of Lake Superior. Among the onlookers is a very pregnant Ruth Foster Dead, the daughter of a deceased African-American doctor who had never been given hospital privileges by Mercy and whose patients, aside from two who were white, had never been granted admittance. As the crowd watches with excitement, the scene takes on a further surreal cast. Red velvet rose petals fall from the basket Ruth holds and swirl around in the air, and a woman sings loudly, "O Sugarman done fly away" while Smith prepares to soar. Ruth's labor pains begin when the insurance agent hits the ground. The shock of the man's leap appears to overcome the racial prejudices of the hospital attendants, who take Ruth into the hospital where, the next day, her son Macon becomes the first African-American child born in Mercy Hospital.

The third Macon Dead, whose grandfather received the name during the American Civil War from "a drunken Yankee in the Union Army" who completed his paperwork and ignored whatever the true name may have been, is pampered and babied by his mother, Ruth. Born 15 years after his two sisters First Corinthians and Magdalene, he acquires the nickname "Milkman" when a janitor named Freddy looks through a window of the Dead home and sees Ruth nursing the boy who is old enough that his feet nearly touch the floor. She knows that her husband would be horrified to see her sitting with her son at her breast. "She sat in this room holding her son on her lap, staring at his closed eyelids and listening to the sound of his sucking. Staring not so much from maternal joy as from a wish to avoid seeing his legs dangling almost to the floor." Ruth views the nursing as "a pleasure she hated to give up," but discovery by Freddy makes her panic. "Ruth jumped up as quickly as she could and covered her breast, dropping her son on the floor and confirming for him what he had begun to suspect—that these afternoons were strange and wrong." Freddy realizes that his discovery gives him a hold over Ruth. Macon Dead Jr. hears his son's nickname used repeatedly by people in the town, but no dares to reveal its origin because he is a difficult man to approach and most are afraid of him. Still, "he guessed the name was not clean. . . . He knew that wherever the name came from, it had something to do with his wife and was, like the emotion he always felt when thinking of her, coated with disgust." He is also estranged from his sister, Pilate, because he disapproves of the way in which she lives her life.

Milkman has an unhappy childhood in which he is hated at first by his father, who recognizes that his son has replaced him in Ruth's affections. Later, the young man distances himself from Ruth and works with his father, who has become a brutal landlord. He also becomes sexually involved with his cousin Hagar, who is unable to maintain a casual relationship and, instead, pursues him, to the amusement of the people in town. As Milkman grows older, his life appears to lack direction and he feels stifled working with his ruthless father, but he sees no way out. He is also disheartened to learn that his mother had tried repeatedly to abort him because his father had not wanted her to remain pregnant so many years after the birth of his two sisters. He feels as if "everybody was using him for something or as something. Working out some scheme of their own on him, making him the subject of their dreams of wealth, or love, or martyrdom. Everything they did seemed to be about him, yet nothing he wanted was part of it. Once before he had a confidential talk with his father, and it ended up with his being driven further from his mother. Now he had a confidential talk with his mother, only to discover that before he was born, before the first nerve end had formed in his mother's womb, he was the subject of great controversy and strife."

The chance to escape and to start a new life appears when his father tells him that a green tarpaulin suspended from the ceiling of Pilate's dilapidated house may contain millions of dollars in gold, a possibility that leads Milkman to plot a robbery with his friend Guitar Bains. While Milkman views the promised riches as a means of escaping his present life, Guitar seeks the money to fund his work with a secret society named the Seven Days, which murders randomly selected white people in retaliation for the centuries of injustices African Americans have experienced.

The expected bounty consists of only a few rocks and a human skeleton, which Milkman learns is that of his grandfather, the first Macon Dead. Unable to give up the possibility of finding gold to start a new life, he travels to the old farm in Pennsylvania his father owns and believes that he will find gold hidden in a cave on the farm, after promising Guitar half of any gold he finds. Rather than gold, he discovers his family's history when he meets Circe, the midwife who delivered his father and aunt, and he learns his grandparents' names, Jake and Sing, an Indian woman. The search for his family's history, and his own, intensifies as he travels to Shalimar in Virginia, where his grandfather once lived. Guitar follows Milkman secretly and plans to murder him and take the gold that he believes Milkman has found. The family history Milkman uncovers is tragic. He learns that his great-grandfather Solomon, known as the legendary flying African, escaped slavery by flying to Africa but abandoned his family to do so. He left behind a wife who went insane and 21 children who were scattered when they were taken in by different families. Milkman's grandfather Jake, the first Macon Dead, was raised by an Indian woman named Heddy, whose daughter Sing he married.

The discovery of his family's history and of information regarding his immediate ancestors transforms Milkman into a mature man. He survives Guitar's attempt to murder him and returns home to reveal his discovery to his father and his aunt. When he arrives, he learns that Hagar has died and that the family continues to deal with several tragic events. His aunt Pilate returns with him to Shalimar, where the two bury his grandfather's bones on the mountain that is known as Solomon's Leap because that is the promontory from which his great-grandfather jumped as he began his "flight" to Africa. After the burial, Milkman watches as Pilate is struck and killed by a bullet fired by Guitar. After she dies in Milkman's arms, he shouts to Guitar to take his life if he needs it, then "he leaped. . . . For he knew now what Shalimar knew: If you surrendered to the air, you could *ride* it."

CENSORSHIP HISTORY

The winner of both the National Book Critics Circle Award and the American Academy of Arts and Letters Award, *Song of Solomon* is also the first novel by an African-American woman to become a Book-of-the-Month Club selection. That pedigree did not prevent people from labeling it a "filthy and inappropriate piece of trash" in the 1990s, nor has it prevented efforts to remove it from schools as recently as 2009.

In 1993, parents in Columbus, Ohio, submitted a complaint to the school administration asserting that the novel "contains language degrading to African Americans" and charged that it is "sexually explicit." Their objections focused on the early scene that described Ruth Foster Dead breast-feeding Milkman and her admitted shame at being discovered in the act with a child who appears to be nearly the age of an adolescent. Parents in the Richmond City, Georgia, school district voiced a similar complaint in 1994 regarding that passage and others that they labeled "filthy and inappropriate." In this later challenge, those complaining specified additional scenes that they felt were "sexually graphic," including Milkman's sexual affair with his cousin Hagar and one particular scene that takes place after Hagar attempts to kill Milkman with a knife when he tries to end the affair, but he escapes taunts her: "If you keep your hands just that way and then bring them down straight, straight and fast, you can drive that knife right smack into your cunt."

In 1998, the superintendent of the St. Mary's County, Maryland, public schools removed *Song of Solomon* from the required reading list for the advanced placement English class, despite the recommendations of a faculty committee that advised the school administration to retain the book. Parents who filed the complaints told the superintendent that they were "troubled" by the "sexual matter" in the book and labeled the novel "repulsive filth," and "trash" and demanded its removal from the schools. African-American community leaders asserted that the removal of the book was racially motivated and threatened to file a lawsuit if the superintendent's decision was supported by the school board. In response to the threat, Barbara Thompson, president of the St. Mary's County Board of Commissioners, stated that the superintendent had the right to remove the novel from the required reading list, a decision that the board voted unanimously to support. In defense of her move, Thompson told reporters, "She did not ban the book from the school library. She just said it wasn't required reading. Unfortunately, people keep misinterpreting it and making a much bigger issue of it. If you read the book, you know that it has very sexually explicit things in it." The board president admitted that she did not read the entire book, only the two pages she presented to the board. She claimed that after she read the passage, she ripped up the book.

FURTHER READING

Doyle, Robert P. *2007 Banned Books Resource Guide*. Chicago: American Library Association, 2008.
Zeitchik, Steven M. "Md. Schools Veto Morrison, Angelou Titles." *Publishers Weekly*, January 19, 1998, 236.

SOPHIE'S CHOICE

Author: William Styron
Original date and place of publication: 1979, United States
Original publisher: Random House
Literary form: Novel

SUMMARY

Sophie's Choice is a novel set in 1947 in New York City that describes the intertwined lives of three people renting rooms in the same house: Stingo, a young aspiring writer from the South whose small legacy has allowed him to move north to Brooklyn and write; Sophie Zawistowska, a beautiful Polish emigrant who has survived the Nazi concentration camps at great personal cost; and Nathan Landau, a mentally unstable Jewish man who suffers from paranoid schizophrenia. The story is told by Stingo, who describes his interactions with Nathan and Sophie and who acts as an observer of their individual lives and of their relationship.

Through a series of monologues and flashbacks, Stingo slowly reveals the misery that preceded Sophie's arrival in the United States and her growing unhappiness in her relationship with Nathan. She arrived in America a broken woman, suffering both mentally and physically, after having been widowed twice and losing her two children in the concentration camps. When she meets Nathan in the library, she feels that she has found a man who will help her to forget her painful past and offer her true happiness. At the beginning of their relationship, Nathan, a financially successful biologist, is a commanding presence in Sophie's life. He nurses her back to health and shows her a tender love that makes her feel secure once again. The two become lovers, and Sophie learns that Nathan has a very dark side and is filled with hate. He is a paranoid schizophrenic who drinks excessively and suffers from an addiction to benzedrine sulfate. He frequently flies into rages during which his face becomes contorted and he screams and hits anyone near him, including Sophie. He taunts her: "You're a cheater. You're worse than any little yenta that ever came out of Brooklyn." Despite Sophie's loyalty and fidelity to him, he accuses her of having sex with other men. At one point, he threatens her and hits her, shouting, "Let me out of here before I murder you—you whore! You were born a whore and you'll die a whore!"

Nathan increases his drug use, and on one occasion, the depth of his psychological problems is shown when he takes six amphetamines and snorts two lines of cocaine. He pulls Sophie into a car with him and begins to drive recklessly at high speed, while Sophie screams for him to stop. Stresses continue to build and, after Stingo returns to his family farm in Virginia, Sophie travels there for a break and the two become lovers for a night. Sophie is torn between staying with Stingo, with whom she would be able to relax, and her concern for Nathan, despite his hate for life and his abuse of her. She also reveals the horrible choice that the Nazis had forced her to make: to select which of her two children she will keep and which will be taken by the Nazis. For the rest of her short life, she questions, "Suppose I had chosen Jan to go . . . to go to the left instead of Eva. Would that have changed anything?" Sophie returns to Brooklyn, followed by Stingo a few days later. He arrives at the rooming house to find police, an ambulance and a milling crowd, and he learns that Nathan and Sophie have committed suicide by ingesting sodium cyanide. Although the newspapers glamorize the suicides as the result of love and devotion, Stingo recognizes that the two chose suicide because they could no longer stand the pain they suffered.

CENSORSHIP HISTORY

Sophie's Choice, which won the National Book Award in 1980, was removed from the school library of La Mirada High School in La Mirada, California, on September 17, 2001, after a parent complained that the book contains "profanity" and "extreme sexual content." Students in the district who fought the ban were joined in their efforts by the American Civil Liberties Union (ACLU) of Southern California; the law firm of Greines, Martin, Stein, and Richland; and the American Library Association.

The problem began when Joseph Feres took his 17-year-old daughter to the local public library to obtain a copy of *Sophie's Choice*, which she had selected from the 12th-grade English literature supplemental reading list. As Feres looked through the book, he came across passages that contained sexual activity and found several instances of profanity. He then sent a large number of letters to school administrators, local church leaders, and school board members expressing his outrage. He also confronted principal Andrew Huynh and voiced concerns about the judgment of the teacher who provided the supplemental list. In an interview with the *Los Angeles Times*, Feres stated, "There are ways to teach the lessons without getting into the gutter to teach it. You don't have to use profanity and extreme sexual content." In the same interview, he claimed that he was "saying the book should be banned. . . . It's just not appropriate for high school kids."

Huynh wrote to Feres, saying that he had held a conference with the 12th-grade English teacher, and he had spoken with her about the book and directed her to remove *Sophie's Choice* from the supplemental reading list. Huynh also reassured Feres that the book had been removed from the school library. School board members defended the principal's action and told reporters that instructional materials should be reviewed to determine their appropriateness and that Huynh acted appropriately to review instructional material that a parent found to be objectionable.

Student Kat Kosmala and other students contacted the ACLU, charging that the school district had committed an act of censorship and calling for a return of the novel to the school library. In December 2001, the ACLU, in coordination with the private law firm of Greines, Martin, Stein, and Richland, began to prepare a case against the Norwalk–La Mirada Unified School District, threatening to sue the school district if the book was not restored. The ACLU expressed concern regarding the way the decision to ban the book was made. Attorneys pointed out that the school district had an established policy that allowed for a systematic review of materials that are challenged, but the school principal circumvented the policy and removed the book without review.

Reporters contacted author William Styron, telling him about the ban, and the author expressed outrage at the action. He told a reporter for the *Los Angeles Times* that he found the action "reprehensible" and "shocking," and stated, "It's improper to allow people to be browbeaten about books in this country." When told that the ban was based on charges that the book contained "profanity" and "extreme sexual content," Styron defended the use of language and the sexual activity as being very important in developing the nature of the characters and integral to the story.

On January 11, 2002, the ACLU of Southern California issued a press release stating that the novel had been returned to the La Mirada High School Library and that the school district had agreed to return the novel "after First Amendment issues were cited." The school district had also received letters and calls from a number of organizations dedicated to free expression, including the American Library Association and the National Coalition Against Censorship. The ACLU stated in the press release, "Once the district was informed of the possible First Amendment violations, it was swift in reviewing and remedying the situation and we appreciate the prompt action."

FURTHER READING

"ACLU Announces 'Sophie's Choice' Has Been Returned to La Mirada High School Library." ACLU Press Release. Formerly available online. URL: http://www. aclu-sc.org/print/NewsRelease/100039. Accessed November 30, 2005.

"ACLU Takes Action after Acclaimed Novel *Sophie's Choice* Is Removed from School Library." ACLU News and Publications. Formerly available online. URL: http://www.aclu-sc.org/News/Releases/100030. Accessed November 21, 2005.

"Censorship: Whose 'Standards' Are They?" *Los Angeles Times*, December 28, 2001, p. B16.

Goldberg, Beverly. "Second-Guessing Sophie's Choice." *American Libraries* 33 (March 2002): 25.

Helfand, Duke. "Students Fight for 'Sophie's Choice.'" *Los Angeles Times*, December 22, 2001, p. B1.

"Local High School Backs Off Censoring *Sophie's Choice*: Quick Action Brings Novel Back to School Library." *ACLU Open Forum* (Winter 2002). Formerly available online. URL: http://www.aclu-sc.org/News/OpenForum/1004/100441. Accessed October 10, 2004.

Perera, Andrea. "Controversial Novel Returns to Library." *Los Angeles Times*, January 12, 2002, p. B4.

Stillman, Peggy, and Andrea Kross. "Why Is Everyone Reading *Sophie's Choice*?" *Digital Library and Archives—Virginia Libraries* 46, no. 3 (July/August/September 2000).

A STORY TELLER'S HOLIDAY

Author: George Moore
Original date and place of publication: 1918, England
Original publisher: Henry Vizitelly
Literary form: Collection of tales

SUMMARY

A Story Teller's Holiday is a rambling 500-page work that contains dozens of Irish folk stories and legends, many relating amorous activities in convents and monasteries. Written in a carefree and flowing style, the work offers a lighthearted commentary on human behavior, although critics have complained that the dialogue in many of the tales is somewhat contrived. The stories are highly suggestive, but the language is delicate and restrained, allowing little explicit description of these sexual goings-on to emerge. The story of Adam and Eve is typical:

> In spite of her silence, perhaps because of it, he [Adam] began to speak once more of Iahveh's providence and his design, saying: "Eve, if it be within his design that we beget children the secret how we shall beget them will not be withheld from us." "Adam," she answered, "I cannot talk any more," and fell back amid the mosses, and his joy was so great that he could not get a word past his teeth, and when relief came they lay side by side, enchanted lovers, listening to the breeze that raised the leaves of the fig-tree, letting the moonlight through.

Overall, although the stories are drawn from folktales and legends, they present carefully detailed depictions of human behavior that revealed the vices and follies of society in Moore's time.

CENSORSHIP HISTORY

In 1929, the United States Customs seized an inscribed first edition copy of *A Story Teller's Holiday* when noted book collector Paul Hyde attempted to import a copy, because the book was on the Customs banned list. The ban was appealed to the United States Customs court, and prominent bookmen, including John Macrae Sr., Donald Friede, and Arthur Krock, appeared in the U.S. Customs court to testify on behalf of *A Story Teller's Holiday*. In May 1930, the court upheld the ban. The United States Customs court declared *A Story Teller's Holiday* to be "obscene within any fair meaning of the word." In rendering judgment, the court referred to the following formulation of the Hicklin rule: "What is [the] probable, reasonable effect [of this book] on the sense of decency, purity and chastity of society extending to the family made up of men and women, young boys and girls—the family, which is the common nursery of mankind?" The application of this standard established for the court that Moore's novel was unfit, and the novel was banned.

Three years later, the United States Department of the Treasury reversed the ban, using its so-called classics option that existed in the newly reconstructed Section 305 of the *Fordney-McCumber Tariff of 1922*, which governed seizures by Customs.

A Story Teller's Holiday was banned in Ireland on January 20, 1933. A prohibition order was published in the *Iris Oifigiuil*, "the only official source from which booksellers [and readers] might learn of a new prohibition order," in which all articles blacklisted by the Irish Board of Censors were listed. According to the Censorship of Publications Bill of 1928, "the notice in *Iris Oifigiuil* should be sufficient evidence in the courts of summary jurisdiction as to the character of the publication," despite the acknowledgment by justices quoted in Adams's thorough study of Irish censorship laws that "this gazette is not a publication which booksellers are addicted to reading." The Irish Board of Censors found the novel to be "obscene" and "indecent." In 1944, a Council of Action, composed of individuals representing literary and civil liberties groups, examined the incidence of censorship in Ireland in the years 1930 to 1943. The ban against the work remained in force until the 1970s, when it was among the many books removed from the banned list.

FURTHER READING

Adams, Michael. *Censorship: The Irish Experience*. Tuscaloosa: University of Alabama Press, 1968.
Boyer, Paul S. *Purity in Print: The Vice-Society Movement and Book Censorship in America*. New York: Scribner, 1968.
Paul, James C. N., and Murray L. Schwartz. *Federal Censorship: Obscenity in the Mail*. New York: Free Press, 1961.

STUDS LONIGAN

Author: James T. Farrell
Original date and place of publication: 1935, United States
Original publisher: Vanguard Press
Literary form: Novel

SUMMARY

Studs Lonigan consists of three independently titled volumes that trace the physical and moral disintegration of a young Chicago man of Irish descent in the period from 1916 to 1933. The story begins with Studs Lonigan's graduation from a parochial school and ends with his death. For most of the 1920s, Studs and his family enjoy financial prosperity, leading them to embrace wholeheartedly the myth that democratic capitalism guarantees success to anyone with sufficient ambition and ability. The economic devastation brought by the Great Depression reverses this optimism, destroying the economic and spiritual foundations of the Lonigan family. Studs dies at the end of *Judgment Day*, his ill health caused by excessive consumption of the cheap bootleg liquor that he uses as an escape from the bleakness of his life.

Young Lonigan takes place in 1916 and follows the 15-year-old Studs in the year after he graduates from parochial school. Studs spends most of his time on the streets with his friends, smoking, fighting, stealing small items, and bragging about sexual exploits. He believes that being a man means being tough, and his language is peppered with such terms as *goddam, son of a bitch,* and *whore,* as well as terms censored in the text by Farrell such as *s---t* and *kiss my ---.* Stud's sexual arousal by girls, even his 13-year-old sister, is described at many points in the novel. When his sister accidentally brushes her breast against him, "Dirty thoughts rushed to his head like hot blood. He told himself he was a bastard because—she was his sister." Farrell describes Studs's first sexual experience, his involvement in a "gang-shag" with a girl named Iris.

Characters mention "show parties," in which younger children disrobe and exhibit their genitals. When his friend Helen Shires tells him that Weary Reilley "tried to do that to me," Studs thinks about mothers and fathers "doing it." He also considers the appearances of girls in detail, determining that "if they had good legs they were supposed to be good for you-know, and if they didn't they weren't; [that he should] notice their boobs, if they were big enough to bounce."

The Young Manhood of Studs Lonigan takes place over 12 years, from 1917 through 1929. Studs cuts high school and drinks heavily and brawls in the streets, having detailed sexual fantasies and trading graphic stories of sexual conquests with his friends. Although he eventually takes a job and seems to begin planning for a future, his drinking blurs his judgment. On New Year's

Eve, 1929, Studs reaches his lowest point when he and his friends host a wild party that gets out of hand after several of the women they have invited refuse to have sex. Studs dances with one girl and vows that "he was going to give it to her like she'd never gotten it before." His friend Weary later knocks Studs out and then rapes the girl after beating her severely. The volume ends with the unconscious Studs lying drunk in his own vomit on a sidewalk, his clothes bloody and torn.

In *Judgment Day*, Studs and his remaining friends recall the many men of their group who have died after destroying their health by drinking. They look forward to changing their former ways of being "drunk and whoring all the time, with no ambition." Studs is aware that he has wasted numerous opportunities in life, and he regrets his choices. As he plans to marry Catherine, who is pregnant with his child, Studs learns that he has a serious heart condition. He develops pneumonia soon after and dies, leaving Catherine destitute.

CENSORSHIP HISTORY

Young Lonigan was published in 1932 with a note warning that its buyers were "limited to physicians, social workers, teachers, and other persons having a professional interest in the psychology of adolescence."

In 1942, the trilogy was dropped by the American Library Association, as it was among the books the ALA identified as immoral and damaging in their efforts to portray American lifestyles. As a result, British publishers Constable & Co. were refused a permit to import the American printings, which amounted to a ban in England because there was insufficient paper there to print the books. After two years, paper stock was made available, and 5,000 copies of the trilogy were printed. That same year, the trilogy was banned from entry into Canada when Canadian Customs officials labeled the book as being of "an indecent and immoral characters."

In 1948, the three novels were among nine novels identified as obscene in criminal proceedings in the Court of Quarter sessions in Philadelphia County, Pennsylvania. (See GOD'S LITTLE ACRE for a complete discussion of the case.) Indictments were brought by the state district attorney, John H. Maurer, against five booksellers who were charged with possessing and intending to sell the books. The other allegedly obscene novels were Harold Robbins's *NEVER LOVE A STRANGER*, Farrell's *A WORLD I NEVER MADE*, Erskine Caldwell's GOD'S LITTLE ACRE, Calder Willingham's *END AS A MAN*, and William Faulkner's SANCTUARY and THE WILD PALMS.

In his March 18, 1949, decision in *Commonwealth v. Gordon*, 66 D. & C. 101 (1949) that the trilogy was not obscene, Judge Curtis Bok stated:

> It is not a pleasant story, nor are the characters gentle and refined. There is rape and dissipation and lust in these books, expressed in matching language, but they do not strike me as out of proportion. The books as a whole create a

sustained arc of a man's life and era, and the obvious effort of the author is to be faithful to the scene he depicts.

No one would want to be Studs Lonigan.

Bok refused to declare the trilogy "obscene" because in cases cited in his decision the definition restricted the meaning of the term "to that of sexual impurity, and with those cases that have made erotic allurement the test of its effect." The work also failed to meet Bok's definition of sexual impurity in literature, which he defined "as any writing whose dominant purpose and effect is erotic allurement—that is to say, a calculated and effective incitement to sexual desire."

The Select Committee on Current Pornographic Materials, in hearings authorized by the United States House of Representatives in 1953, recommended that the trilogy be removed from sale because of its "indecent" content. The National Organization for Decent Literature (NODL) also placed the trilogy on its blacklist, and the work was banned from sale in St. Cloud, Minnesota, as the result of efforts by local NODL members. The novel was banned in Ireland that same year because of its "excessive sexuality" and discussion of abortion.

In 1957, the United States Information Agency banned the trilogy from its overseas libraries because it portrayed "brutality" and sexual content.

FURTHER READING

Elliott, Desmond. "Scandal over Studs (Trial over James Farrell's *Studs Lonigan*)." *Books and Bookmen* 5 (November 1959): 23–26.

Farrell, James T. "The Author as Plaintiff: Testimony in a Censorship Case." In Farrell's *Reflection at Fifty and Other Essays:* 188–223. New York: Vanguard, 1954.

———. "Lonigan, Lonergan, and New York's Finest." *Nation*, March 18, 1944, p. 338.

Huntington, Henry S. "The Philadelphia Book Seizures." *Elation*, August 21, 1948, pp. 205–207.

Smith, Gene. "The Lonigan Curse." *American Heritage* 46 (April 1995): 150–151.

SUSAN LENOX: HER FALL AND RISE

Author: David Graham Phillips
Original date and place of publication: 1917, United States
Original publisher: D. Appleton Company
Literary form: Novel

SUMMARY

Susan Lenox is the story of a small-town girl of illegitimate birth who lives with her uncle and aunt after her mother dies giving birth to her. Viewed by her family and townspeople as bound to "suffer for her mother's sins," she is blamed when her cousin's boyfriend falls in love with her. Branded a "loose" woman, she is quickly married off to a coarse local farmer who terrifies her on their wedding night: "He crushed her. He kissed her with great slobbering smacks and gnawed at the flesh of her neck with teeth that craved to bite."

With the help of journalist Rod Spenser, Susan runs away, assumes a new name, and begins a career as a singer on a riverboat. When the boat is wrecked and her manager-lover, Robert Burlingame, contracts typhoid fever, she becomes a prostitute to support them, but he dies. Susan then works in a sweatshop for a time, but she discovers that life as a streetwalker is more lucrative. Spenser reenters her life, reforms her, and takes her with him to New York City, where he hopes to have a career as a playwright, but Susan soon leaves him after his friends tell her that she is hampering Spenser's career. As a model in the garment district, Susan must often have sex with business owners to keep her job, so she returns to streetwalking. When she becomes addicted to opium and alcohol, she lands in a brothel for a time, but then escapes and ponders "abandoning her body to abominations beyond belief at the hands of degenerate oriental sailors." Spenser also sinks into drug addiction.

Susan meets Spenser again, and they become each other's salvation. She becomes a successful actress and inherits the estate of a bachelor director, thus achieving emancipation. As the novel closes, Susan, finally financially secure, realizes, "Yes, she has learned to live. But—she has paid the price." Spenser rebuilds his career as a journalist.

Both the main character's lifestyle and her philosophy of life were sources of criticism when the novel first appeared. At one point in the novel, a girl who works for the Salvation Army calls out, "The wages of sin is death." Susan responds, "The wages of weakness is death . . . but the wages of sin—well, it's sometimes a house on Fifth Avenue."

CENSORSHIP HISTORY

The novel, inspired by the "white slave" furor in New York City in the 1890s, was completed at the author's death in 1911 but did not appear in publication until 1917, when *Hearst's Magazine* took advantage of a renewed public interest in prostitution and published the novel in serialized form. When the book was first published, the *New York Times* branded the story "essentially false" and "profoundly immoral." The New York Society for the Suppression of Vice brought charges against the magazine for printing "obscene" material, but the case was promptly dismissed. When D. Appleton Company published the entire novel in 1917, John Sumner and the New York Society for the Suppression of Vice threatened the company with legal action.

Joseph H. Sears, president of Appleton, was not intimidated and responded to Sumner that the novel had been published "to awaken the American people to a high moral sense, in order that the terrible evils going on daily about them might be eliminated." Sears defiantly promoted the book, and the society initiated proceedings. The author's sister intervened and persuaded Sears to establish a compromise so that "this last product of her brother's genius [would] reach as wide an audience as possible." Appleton agreed to withdraw the first edition of *Susan Lenox* and to publish an expurgated version. Mollified, the society withdrew its complaint and scored a partial victory.

FURTHER READING

Filler, Louis. *Voice of Democracy: David Graham Phillips*. University Park: Pennsylvania State University, 1968.

Goldman, Eric F. "David Graham Phillips, Victorian Critic of Victorianism." In *The Lives of Eighteen from Princeton*, edited by Willard Thorp, 118–153. Princeton, N.J.: Princeton University Press, 1946.

Marcosson, Isaac F. *David Graham Phillips and His Times*. New York: Dodd, Mead, 1932.

Ravitz, Abe C. *David Graham Phillips*. New York: Twayne, 1966.

SWEETER THAN LIFE

Author: Mark Tryon (pseud.)[1]
Original date and place of publication: 1958, United States
Original publisher: Vixen Press
Literary form: Novel

SUMMARY

Sweeter Than Life, a forerunner of the sexually oriented pulp novels that were so numerous in the 1960s, contains a prominent lesbian theme. The novel relates the life and death of Nym Bardolph, a young woman who lives in Okeechee, Florida. After an unhappy marriage, her mother, Lucy, teaches Nym to hate all men and inadvertently introduces her daughter to lesbian lovemaking when Nym finds her mother and the red-haired schoolteacher on the couch. Both are completely naked, the teacher's face is "a mask of frantic ecstasy" and "deep-throated hoarse animal groans poured from the little redhead."

Nym is not so much traumatized by the incident as she is liberated to seduce both men and women. Nym's adventures with her future husband, Sean Bardolph, are described in highly suggestive but not explicit language. She manipulates his libido,

---

[1]The Library of Congress catalog indicates that this name is pseudonym and lists no other books by this author. An extensive search of diverse sources has not revealed the author's true indentity.

arousing him, helping him remove his clothes and then letting her educated fingers and hands roam over his trembling body, their search and skillful stimulation growing gradually in intimacy, only to stop her little game short when his face contorted with the painful ecstasy of the ultimate moment.

Determined to gain control over a valuable plot of land, she needs Bardolph to aid her, so she willingly fulfills "his wildest dreams of blissful satiety in her arms." The task is aided by "her breasts quivering with the most apparent physical desire, . . . her mouth a moist cavern of accomplishment." When Bardolph's ardor cools, Nym seduces Johnny Martel in scenes that contain similar long passages of undressing, nudity, and foreplay.

The change of pace in this novel occurs when Nym seduces Lynn, a young girl who works in Bardolph's real estate office. The action starts as a rape, with Lynn "straining to push Nym away" and Nym clinging tightly as "with one hand she held the girl down and . . . stripped the dress from Lynn." After giving readers a detailed description of Lynn's underwear, the author writes: "Nym's hand found the nubile breasts, molding and caressing until she felt the tips harden." Nym's breasts are also described, "so full that they seemed swollen, their great dark eyes gleaming dully against the white flesh"; then "there were no sounds in the office but the sounds of love."

CENSORSHIP HISTORY

Sweeter Than Life was a distinct departure from earlier works that had been condemned for erotic content. As Lewis observes, "that novel contains numerous long, sensual passages which, since they contribute little no plot or characterization, might be termed 'dirt for dirt's sake.'" Edward De Grazia, a prominent defense attorney in such high-profile censorship cases as those involving Aristophanes' *Lysistrata*, William Burroughs's NAKED LUNCH, Henry Miller's TROPIC OF CANCER, and the Swedish film *I Am Curious—Yellow*, states that *Sweeter Than Life* "seems to have had no appreciable literary value." Supreme Court Justice Felix Frankfurter told his law clerk, Paul Bender, that the book was "horrible filthy junk!" Yet all agreed that the defendant's constitutional right to due process of law had been violated in the lower court decisions involving the book.

In 1958, bookseller Eleazar Smith was charged with "disseminating obscene matter" and was ordered to appear in municipal court where Judge James H. Pope declared Smith guilty of the charge. The bookseller appealed the conviction of the appellate department of the Los Angeles Superior Court, which upheld the prior decision in *People v. Smith*, 161 Cal. App. 2d 860, 327 P.2d 636 (1958), but Judge David did not discuss the nature of the novel or the criteria that led to his decision. Under the California obscenity statute, knowledge of the obscene nature of the book was required before the court could establish guilt. Therefore, when the decision was appealed to the United States Supreme Court, in *Smith v. California*, 361 U.S. 147

(1959), the court reversed the decisions of the lower courts. Smith claimed that, even though the book might be "obscene," he never read the books in his stock and should be immune from prosecution. His attorney persuaded the Supreme Court that his client was innocent of "disseminating obscene matter," even though the book might be labeled "obscene" under prevailing standards.

Justice William J. Brennan delivered the court's opinion that it was unconstitutional for the California legislature to punish a bookseller for selling a book called *Sweeter Than Life*, found by a judge to be obscene, without proof that the bookseller knew of the sexually oriented content of the book. "Every bookseller would be placed under an obligation to make himself aware of the contents of every book in his shop. It would be altogether unreasonable to demand so near an approach to omniscience." Thus, the decision in the case was based on the legality of the municipal ordinance rather than on the content of the novel.

FURTHER READING

De Grazia, Edward. *Censorship Landmarks*. New York: Bowker, 1969.
———. *Girls Lean Back Everywhere: The Law of Obscenity and the Assault on Genius*. New York: Random House, 1992.
Lewis, Felice Flanery. *Literature, Obscenity, and the Law*. Carbondale: Southern Illinois University Press, 1976.
"Obscenity Appeal Set." *New York Times*, January 13, 1959, p. 19.

TEN NORTH FREDERICK

Author: John O'Hara
Original date and place of publication: 1955, United States
Original publisher: Random House
Literary form: Novel

SUMMARY

Ten North Frederick opens with the funeral of prominent Gibbsville resident Joseph B. Chapin and then examines the circumstances that shaped him and eventually led to his death. The novel offers an unadorned view of the "real" man hidden behind the apparently successful attorney, as it also uncovers the social structure, codes, and values of Gibbsville.

Yale graduate Chapin grows up with a domineering mother who smothers him and expresses ambitions that create in him an exaggerated sense of his own importance. Chapin's subservience to his mother influences his choice of wife, the ambitious, cold, shrewd, and tough Edith Stokes, who wants to own Joe. Mrs. Chapin thoroughly approves of Edith, for "no girl with a face as plain as Edith's could inspire a love or even a passion that would cause a son to reject his mother." The couple move in with Joe's parents, beginning their married life at 10 North Frederick Street. The scene depicting their wedding night reveals Edith's demanding nature, and it is also one of the passages cited in efforts to ban the novel:

> He put his knee between her legs and she made a sound like a moan. . . . He felt her breasts and she pulled up her nightgown.
> "Do it to me, do it to me," she said. "Hurry." She made it difficult for him to find her; she was already in the rhythm of the act and could not stop. "For God's sake," she said. "For God's sake."
> "I'm trying, dearest."
> "Do it then," she said angrily.
> The moment he entered her she had her climax, with a loud cry. His own climax followed and immediately she wanted him again.

Between the obsessions of his wife and his mother, Chapin becomes dispirited and allows himself to be manipulated by them and by others. Chapin lives in an emotional straitjacket and lacks vitality for much of the novel. Stagnated by the desire to maintain appearances as Gibbsville aristocracy, Chapin and his wife ruin their daughter's marriage to an amiable Italian musician, whom she truly loves, and force her to have an abortion. They also try to stop their son from dropping out of Yale and becoming a jazz pianist.

Edith and other characters in the novel are involved in extramarital relationships, but most of the sexual acts are implied rather than described explicitly. When Chapin falls deeply in love with his daughter's New York roommate, Kate, they spend one night together that is referred to but not described. Kate loves Chapin but refuses to talk of marriage and the future, knowing fully that the 50-year-old man would be miserable if he were to give up his friends, home, and family for her. She sends him away and he returns to 10 North Frederick Street, Gibbsville, Pennsylvania, where he begins to drink heavily and dies of cirrhosis of the liver.

CENSORSHIP HISTORY

Between 1956 and 1958, *Ten North Frederick* was the object of a series of local bans and seizures in Port Huron, Michigan; Detroit, Michigan; and Albany, New York, despite its continued steady sales in other parts of the nation. Law enforcement officials applied local obscenity standards, threatened prosecution, and then raided booksellers to remove the "obscene" novel.

In 1956, the prosecuting attorney in Port Huron, St. Clair County, Michigan, ordered booksellers and distributors to cease displaying and selling all books that appeared on the disapproved list of the National Organization for Decent Literature, a Catholic censorship group founded in 1938. The complaining organization cited the few erotic passages in the novel as the basis for identifying as "objectionable" *Ten North Frederick*, along with other novels such as James Jones's FROM HERE TO ETERNITY, Bud Schulberg's *On the Waterfront*, Ernest Hemingway's *TO HAVE AND HAVE NOT* and John Steinbeck's *Wayward Bus*. The ban was lifted after Bantam Books, paperback publisher of *Ten North Frederick*, joined with other publishers and obtained a federal district court injunction against the prosecution for "going beyond legal authority."

In 1957, a year after *Ten North Frederick* won the National Book Award for fiction, Detroit, Michigan, police commissioner Edward S. Piggins banned sales of the paperback version of the book. Acting on the strength of a 119-year-old Michigan statute against obscenity, he directed the head of the Detroit Police Censor Bureau Inspector Melville E. Bullac to notify bookstores and libraries that the book had been placed on the city's "objectionable list" and banned from sale, although the book could still be obtained at public libraries. As the *New York Times* reported on January 19, 1957, "Sale of the 50-cent paperback edition was banned last week by the Police Department's eleven-man Censor's Bureau, which held its price made it attractive to a minor's pocketbook." The president of the Detroit Library Commission, Thomas Long, challenged the police commissioner's ruling and the issue went to court. In a decision handed down on March 29, 1957, Circuit Judge Carl M. Weideman declared that the ban violated the United States Constitution and ordered Police Commissioner Piggins to lift the ban on sales of the book. Judge Weideman cautioned the police against "directly or indirectly" influencing a person to stop selling the book or threatening to arrest distributors. He also asserted that both the police commissioner and the police censor had "circumvented the judicial process" by ordering the book banned from sale by Detroit booksellers. The police commissioner complied with the decision to lift the ban on the sale of the book and, in a letter to Judge Weideman, wrote that the department would not "do anything that might be interpreted as a ban or a threat of a ban."

One year later, a local censorship group in Albany, New York, gained an indictment in the Albany County Supreme Court against Bantam Books, John O'Hara, and the distributors of the novel "for conspiring to publish and distribute an obscene book." Lawyers for the defendants reviewed the testimony and argued that only specific passages, rather than the entire work, had been read to the grand jury. This challenge represented the first time following the decision in *Roth v. United States*, 354 U.S. 476 (1957), that an indictment involving a charge of obscenity had been opposed on the basis that the entire work had not been read to or by the grand jury. The publishers successfully defended their position and the ban was lifted.

FURTHER READING

"Book Ban Opposed—Detroit Library Head to Keep O'Hara Novel Available." *New York Times*, January 19, 1957, p. 13.

"Detroit Book Ban Void—Court Enjoins the Police from Barring O'Hara Novel." *New York Times*, March 30, 1957, p. 17.

Hempl, William J., and Patrick M. Wall. "Extralegal Censorship of Literature." In *Issues of Our Time*, edited by Herbert W. Hildebrandt, 130–143. New York: Macmillan, 1963.

Oboler, Eli M. *The Fear of the Word: Censorship and Sex.* Metuchen, N.J.: Scarecrow, 1974.

"Police Aide Cleared in Book Ban Fight." *New York Times*, May 5, 1957, p. 60.

Tuttleton, James. *The Novel of Manners in America.* New York: Norton, 1972.

TESS OF THE D'URBERVILLES

Author: Thomas Hardy

Original dates and places of publication: 1891, England; 1892, United States

Original publishers: Osgood, McIlvaine (England); Harper (United States)

Literary form: Novel

SUMMARY

Tess of the D'Urbervilles was subtitled "A Pure Woman Faithfully Presented," and Hardy intended to portray a woman whose intentions had been good throughout despite eventually becoming a mistress and a murderess. The novel opens as John Durbeyfield learns that he is the last descendant of one of England's oldest and most powerful families. A poor and powerless working man and a heavy drinker, Durbeyfield sends his eldest daughter, Tess, to the still-wealthy branch of the D'Urbervilles at their estate at Trantridge to claim kinship.

The D'Urbervilles are actually wealthy people named Stokes who have taken the unused ancestral title as their own, and innocent Tess is unaware that Alec D'Urberville is not her cousin. He gives Tess a job caring for his mother's chickens to keep her nearby and rapes her one night in the woods. She stays with him for a few weeks and then returns home pregnant. Their child dies soon after birth.

Grieving for her child and disgraced, Tess takes a job on a distant farm, where she meets Angel Clare, who claims to follow the spirit but not the letter of the Bible. They fall in love, and, on their wedding night, Tess and Angel confess to each other. Angel tells of a brief affair, and Tess forgives him. She then tells him about Alec, and Angel rejects her.

Angel leaves for Brazil, and Tess returns briefly to her family before taking a job at another dairy at Flintcomb-Ash, where she again meets Alec, now a fire-and-brimstone preacher. He wants her back, but she is still married to Angel and does not love Alec. When Tess's father dies the family loses its home, and Alec steps in, promising to educate her brothers and sisters and to protect her mother if only Tess will live with him. She resists Alec and sets up camp with her family at the ancient D'Urberville burial vaults. Alec reappears, and a disheartened Tess relents, because her letters to Angel have gone unanswered.

Angel returns, ready to forgive Tess, and finds her at the luxurious sea resort of Sandbourne, where he begs her forgiveness. She tells him about Alec and orders him to leave. He refuses, and Tess loses control of her senses. She murders Alec, the source of her unhappiness, and then runs away with Angel, whom she believes will now truly forgive her because she has eliminated the root of their problems. They hide in a deserted mansion and then move on to Stonehenge, where Tess falls asleep on a sacrificial altar. The police arrive and arrest her, and Tess is tried for murder. Before she is hanged, Tess asks Angel to care for and to marry her innocent younger sister 'Liza-Lu. The novel ends as Angel and 'Liza-Lu watch the hanging, then walk off together, hand in hand.

CENSORSHIP HISTORY

Hardy consented to the bowdlerization of many of his works before they reached the public just to get them published, and his experience with *Tess of the D'Urbervilles* was no exception. Hardy had great difficulty finding a publisher for the novel, and magazines demanded radical revisions before serializing it. Tillotson and Son, a Lancashire newspaper syndicate, contracted with Hardy in 1889 to serialize the novel, but their suggestions that he make changes in the scene in which Tess is seduced and in the improvised baptism of her dying baby alienated the author. He refused to agree to their suggestions and, instead, asked the publishers to cancel the contract. Hardy then took the still incomplete work to *Murray's Magazine*, whose editor, Edward Arnold, rejected the piece because the magazine "preferred girls to grow up in ignorance of sexual hazards." Mowbray Morris, editor of *Macmillan's Magazine*, rejected the novel because he was "profoundly upset by the book's sexuality."

Before offering the novel to another magazine, Hardy revised the work to produce a version that would not cause offense. In November 1890, Hardy agreed to terms with *Graphic* to begin serialization in July 1891 and for serialization in *Harper's New Monthly* in the United States soon after. Several passages were excised from the novel. Hardy had to remove the seduction scene and the improvised baptism. He was also forced to include a mock marriage staged by Alec to make Tess believe that she was actually his legal wife. The illegitimate baby was also omitted.

In addition to objections to the illicit relationship between Tess and Alec, Hardy was accused of taking a "low" view of women. His sensuous descriptions of Tess were labeled "French" and critics said that it was "degrading" to see women portrayed as in the following example from the novel:

She had stretched one arm so high above her coiled-up cable of hair that he could see its delicacy above the sunburn; her face was flushed with sleep and her eyelids hung heavy over their pupils. The brimfulness of her nature breathed from her. It was a moment when a woman's soul is more incarnate than at any other time; when the most spiritual beauty inclines to the corporeal; and sex takes the outside place in her presence.

In 1891, the novel was banned by Mudie's and Smith's circulating libraries, leading to a virtual censorship over popular reading in England. The popular circulating libraries had significant influence on book sales during the second half of the 19th century. Novels were expensive and authors made little money in sales unless the circulating libraries accepted their books. The same year, the novel was also the object of banning by the Watch and Ward Society in Boston, which charged that the novel contained illicit sexuality and immorality. The society forced Boston booksellers to agree that they would not advertise or sell *Tess of the D'Urbervilles*, and most adhered to the request.

While attempting to find a publisher for *Tess*, Hardy published in 1890 in *New Review* an essay called "Candour in English Fiction," in which he noted that "the novels which most conduce to moral profit are likely to be among those written without a moral purpose." Hardy, far in advance of the court decisions in such novels as James Joyce's ULYSSES, D. H. Lawrence's LADY CHATTERLEY'S LOVER, Henry Miller's TROPIC OF CANCER, and others, recognized the need to portray life honestly: "the passions ought to be proportioned as in the world itself." Viewing life as a "physiological fact," he felt that life's "honest portrayal must be largely concerned with, for one thing, the relations of the sexes, and the substitution for catastrophes as favor the false coloring best expressed by the regulation finish that 'they married and were happy ever after,' of catastrophes based upon sexual relationship as it is. To this expansion English society opposes a well-nigh insuperable bar." He concedes that satisfying "the prudery of censorship" is "the fearful price that he has to pay for the privilege of writing in the English language—no less a price than the complete extinction, in the mind of every mature and penetrating reader, of sympathetic belief in his personages."

FURTHER READING

Cowley, Malcolm. *After the Genteel Tradition*. Rev. ed. Carbondale: Southern Illinois University, 1964.

Hardy, Thomas. "Candour in English Fiction." In *Thomas Hardy's Personal Writings: Prefaces, Literary Opinions, Reminiscences*, edited by Harold Orel, 125–133. Lawrence: University of Kansas Press, 1966.

Pinion, F. B. *Thomas Hardy: His Life nd Friends*. New York: St. Martin's, 1992.

Seymour-Smith, Martin. *Hardy: A Biography*. New York: St. Martin's, 1994.

THEIR EYES WERE WATCHING GOD

Author: Zora Neale Hurston
Original date and place of publication: 1937, United States
Original publisher: J. B. Lippincott and Company
Literary type: Novel

SUMMARY

Their Eyes Were Watching God is the story of the past 20 years of Janie Craw-
ford's life as it she perceives it to have happened and as she tells it to her
best friend Pheoby Watson. Janie returns to town looking younger than
her 40 years and dressed in a man's shirt and coveralls, giving the town
women enough to gossip about. Then she increases their resentment by not
acknowledging them but simply walking past them to her house. "Seeing the
woman as she was made them remember the envy they had stored up from
other times. So they chewed up the back parts of their minds and swallowed
with relish. They made burning statements with questions, and killing tools
out of laughs. It was mass cruelty." Fully aware of their gossip about her
and about the way she had left town some time before with a man 10 years
younger, Janie decides to tell her story to Pheoby and let her friend decide
how much to tell the rest. "You can tell 'em what Ah say if you wants to. Dat's
just de same as me 'cause mah tongue is in mah friend's mouf."

Janie recalls her early years being raised by her grandmother Nanny, who
grew up under slavery and whose daughter, Leafy, Janie's mother, was the
product of a rape by a white man. Leafy suffered a similar fate and gave birth
to Janie after being raped by a white schoolteacher. Soon after Janie's birth,
Leafy abandoned her daughter to the care of Nanny. Janie recalls growing
up and living in the backyard of a white family named the Washburns and
the close friendships she shared with their children. "Ah was wid dem white
chillum so much till Ah didn't know Ah wuzn't white till Ah was round six
years old." After a roving photographer takes photographs of the children
and Janie sees her image, she realizes, " 'Aw, aw! Ah'm colored!' "

Nanny has had a difficult life, always feeling repressed and never having enough money to buy what she wanted and only barely able to buy
what was needed. She wants more for her granddaughter and, when she
sees 16-year-old Janie let Johnny Taylor kiss her at the front gate, the old
woman decides that Janie should marry Brother Logan Killicks, an older
settled man who she believes will protect the girl. When Janie rejects the
idea, Nanny explains the great hopes that she has always held for her granddaughter, and she shares her sorry story with the girl. She recounts the abuse
she suffered at the hands of "Mistis," the wife of the plantation owner who
knew that her husband had been Nanny's lover and had fathered Leafy, a
baby "wid gray eyes and yaller hair." A week after the birth, Nanny had been
forced to flee the plantation with her infant, because Mistis planned to have

the overseer tie her to the whipping post and have her whipped until the skin peeled off her back. Although she is helped by a good white family in West Florida and raises her daughter with the hope of educating Leafy to become a teacher, she cannot protect her from rape by a white schoolteacher. Sadly, Nanny relates that soon after Janie's birth Leafy began to drink and run around with men, eventually leaving altogether.

Janie does marry Killicks, but she is not able to love him. Two months after the marriage, she tells her grandmother that despite his seeming adoration and the way he does everything for her, she hates the way his head looks, feels that his belly is too big, thinks that his toenails are like those of mules, and "He don't even never mention nothin' pretty." Instead of sympathizing with her, Nanny tells her to feel proud that people tip their hats to her and call her "Mis' Killicks," yet she is distressed by Janie's unhappiness and dies a month later.

After less than a year of marriage, Killicks stops treating her well and orders her to work hard on the farm. When he leaves one day to buy a mule in a nearby town, Joe Starks walks into her life, "a cityfied [sic], stylish dressed man with his hat set at an angle that didn't belong in these parts." He is well-dressed and a glib speaker "from Georgy" who dazzles the young woman with his plans to turn the $300 in his pocket into a fortune by exploiting the new opportunities "down heah in Floridy." They laugh and joke together and promise to meet each day in the scrub oaks across the road until he would move on. Starks tells Janie, "Ah wants to make a wife outa you" and promises to treat her like a lady, swearing that he is a man of principles. That night, she asks Killicks what he would think if she ran away from him, but he dismisses that suggestion and tells her that no other man would want her given her family history. The next morning, after Killicks insists that Janie help him move the manure pile, she makes up her mind to leave with Starks. The two drive off in a hired rig to Green Cove Springs, where they marry the same day and he buys her new clothes of wool and silk.

Starks and Janie move into a small town named Eatonville, where his money buys them land and a house and where he builds a general store and acquires a post office for the town. As a man of position, he becomes mayor, which forces Janie to play the role of hostess both in his store and for the functions that his new position requires. Rather than enjoy a happy and love-filled marriage as she had expected, Janie is confined to the store six days of the week, and her thoughts and opinions are ignored by Stark. He is jealous of her beautiful hair and forces her to wear a headrag so no other man can see its beauty. After her great hopes, the marriage is a disappointment to her. Seven years later, Starks becomes physically abusive, slapping Janie when dinner is spoiled or when she talks back to him. Soon, after a particularly violent argument in front of customers in the store, Starks begins to deteriorate physically, and suspicions around Eatonville are that Janie has been poisoning him, a rumor fed by a root-doctor who is profiting from the illness. When he is too sick to leave his bed, he refuses to see Janie and depends, instead, on a parade of people from the town to look after his needs. Janie learns from a physician that Starks is suffering from kidney failure and will die soon, and she enters his sickroom shortly before his death to let him know how disappointed she has been with their marriage. "All dis bowin' down, all dis obedience under yo' voice—dat ain't what Ah rushed off down de road tuh find out about you."

After Starks dies, Janie enjoys her freedom for the first time in her life. She refuses the offers of many men to help her with the business, and she rejects their claims that she needs someone to protect her. After six months, she changes from mourning black to her mourning white clothing and with the change appears a suitor more than 10 years younger than she, who was born Vergible Woods but who tells her "Dey calls me Tea Cake for short." Janie becomes enamored of his carefree attitude and with the way he listens to her and makes her laugh. She also enjoys his impetuous behavior. Her store clerk warns her about Tea Cake and tells her "Dat long-legged Tea Cake ain't got doodly squat. He ain't got no business makin' hisself familiar wid nobody lak you." Janie thanks him, but she already knows she is infatuated with Tea Cake. "He looked like the love thoughts of women. He could be a bee to a blossom—a pear tree blossom in the spring. He seemed to be crushing scent out of the world with his footsteps. Crushing aromatic herbs with every step he took. Spices hung about him. He was a glance from God." After they spend the first night together, she "awoke the next morning by feeling Tea Cake kissing her breath away. Holding her and caressing her as if he feared she might escape his grasp and fly away."

The town watches as Janie and Tea Cake become a couple and "got mad." Pheoby's husband tells his wife to warn Janie about the gossip that Tea Cake is after her money and that she is wearing colors too soon after her husband's death. Eager to shed her past, Janie looks forward to marriage with Tea Cake and proclaims "Dis ain't no business proposition, and no race after property and titles. Dis is uh love game." The two marry, and life with the unpredictable Tea Cake both frightens and fascinates Janie. He persuades her to go with him to the Everglades to go "on de muck" where the soil is rich and fertile. While they wait for the season to begin, Tea Cake teaches her to shoot with pistol, shotgun, and rifle. She is soon so good a shot that she could "shoot a hawk out of a pine tree and not tear him up." They work side by side picking beans from the rich soil, and their house becomes the center of social activity for the workers. Other women try to lure Tea Cake away from her, and, after finding him wrestling in the cane field with a woman named Nunkie, Janie strides angrily home and later physically attacks him when he comes in. They struggle from room to room. "They wrestled on until they were doped with their own fumes and emanations; till their clothes had been torn away; till he hurled her to the floor and held her there melting her resistance with the heat of his body, doing things with their bodies to express the inexpressible; kissed her until she arched her body to meet him and they fell asleep in sweet exhaustion."

Mrs. Turner, a light-skinned African American, creates trouble for Janie when she brings her brother to the house, hoping to make Janie like him enough to leave Tea Cake and to bring her inheritance from Starks with her.

That night, Tea Cake "whipped Janie. Not because her behavior justified his jealousy, but it relieved that awful fear inside him. Being able to whip her reassured him in possession." Aware as they are of Mrs. Turner's pretentiousness and her disdain for dark skin, the men join Tea Cake in concocting a plan to run her out of town, and they destroy her restaurant in the effort.

A violent hurricane drives the couple and the other muck workers out of the Everglades. As Tea Cake and Janie struggle to reach dry ground, he is bitten by a rabid dog while protecting Janie. Four weeks later, Tea Cake becomes sick with headaches and is unable to drink water without gagging. The doctor tells Janie that the dog bite has infected Tea Cake with rabies and that too much time has passed to cure him. The rabies soon makes him go mad, and he attempts to shoot her, but Janie grabs a rifle and shoots at nearly the same time, killing him but not moving quickly enough to avoid "his teeth in the flesh of her forearm." Janie is arrested but given a speedy trial and acquitted of murder. Afterward, as she tells Pheoby, she gave away everything she and Tea Cake owned and returned to Eatonville. As Janie ends her story, she tells Pheoby that she is home again and she is satisfied to be there because she has truly known love.

CENSORSHIP HISTORY

Their Eyes Were Watching God received a mixed reception when it was first published in 1937. Critics such as Lucille Tompkins, writing in the September 26, 1937, *New York Times Book Review*, praised the novel as being "a well nigh perfect story—a little sententious at the start, but the rest is simple and beautiful and shining with humor" and commended the author for "not being too much preoccupied with the current fetish of the primitive" (Sheila Hibben, *New York Herald Tribune Weekly Book Review*, September 26, 1937). In a review published in *New Republic* on October 13, 1937, Otis Ferguson opened his review with the statement, "It isn't that this novel is bad, but that it deserves to be better." He writes that the inclusion of dialect selectively throughout the novel "is to set up a mood of Eddie Cantor in blackface." Richard Wright is harsher in his criticism. In an article published in *New Masses* on October 5, 1937, he chastises Hurston for seeming "to have no desire whatever to move in the direction of serious fiction." With a dismissive tone, he contends that "Miss Hurston can write; but her prose is cloaked in that facile sensuality that has dogged Negro expression since the days of Phillis Wheatley. Her dialogue manages to catch the psychological movements of the Negro folk-mind in their pure simplicity, but that's as far as it goes." Instead of furthering the cause of literature, Wright asserts that Hurston "voluntarily continues in her novel the tradition which was forced upon the Negro in the theater, that is the minstrel technique that makes the 'white folks' laugh."

More recently, *Their Eyes Were Watching God* was challenged for being sexually explicit by parents of students attending Stonewall Jackson High School in Brentsville, Virginia. In 1997, the parents asked school officials to remove Hurston's novel as well as *The House of the Spirits* by Isabel Allende and *One Hundred*

Years of Solitude by Gabriel García Márquez from the international baccalaureate program, a standardized interdisciplinary program for advanced students. The parents contended that students should not have to read the novels, which contain "explicit sexual descriptions, including necrophilia and rape scenes." In a letter to the school board, parent Jeff Smelser described the offensive passages in the books as "graphic descriptions of sexual perversion" and "glorified fornication." A committee consisting of parents, teachers, and administrators approved retaining the work on the advanced reading list, but Smelser appealed the decision. In response, associate superintendent for instruction Pamela K. Gauch appointed a countywide committee consisting of teachers, parents, students, and a librarian to consider the appeal. The new committee did not contain members from Stonewall High School because the original decision to approve retaining the book was made by an all-Stonewall committee. For the appeal, the school officials chose to create a committee having geographic, gender, and ethnic diversity. The original challenge occurred when Amy Smelser selected to read *Their Eyes Were Watching God* for the summer reading program prior to her junior year in high school. The family was troubled by the book, but the two alternatives they selected were equally disturbing. After circulating flyers and "numerous meetings with Stonewall teachers and administrators," the Smelsers filed a formal complaint. When the appointed committee responded that the IB program is optional and that the books would remain in the curriculum, Jeff Smelser filed his appeal and the countywide committee was formed. The decision of the earlier committee was upheld by both the countywide committee and the elected school board, and the books have remained in the IB curriculum at Stonewall Jackson High School.

FURTHER READING

Gates, Henry Louis, Jr., and K. A. Appiah. *Zora Neale Hurston: Critical Perspectives Past and Present.* New York: Amistad, 1993.

Hurston, Zora Neale. *Their Eyes Were Watching God.* New York: J. B. Lippincott, 1965.

O'Hanlon, Ann. "Family Appeals Book Decision: County School System Asked to Reconsider Reading List." *Washington Post,* October 12, 1997, p. 1:4.

THEN AGAIN, MAYBE I WON'T

Author: Judy Blume
Original date and place of publication: 1971, United States
Original publisher: Bradbury Press
Literary form: Young adult novel

SUMMARY

Then Again, Maybe I Won't focuses on a few years in the life of Tony Miglione, beginning when he is 13 years old. The adolescent is growing up in Jersey

City, New Jersey, in a two-family home that also contains his parents, his grandmother, his older brother Ralph, and Ralph's wife. Tony's father is an electrician, his mother is a clerk in a department store, and his grandmother does the family housekeeping. Ralph is a teacher, a profession that his father hopes Tony will also enter. The novel examines the manner in which each generation deals with its specific needs and concerns as the family encounters increasing financial burdens.

The family's difficulties begin after Tony's father becomes the manager of an electronics plant in Queens and the family moves to an upper-middle-class suburb on Long Island. Once there, the Migliones are caught up in the competition of keeping up with the neighbors. Tony's father trades in his pickup truck for a fancy car, and his mother hires a live-in housekeeper, which leaves his grandmother with nothing to do except watch television alone. The changes place the family in financial jeopardy, and Tony experiences continuing and severe stomach pains.

In addition to all of this change, Tony awakens sexually and becomes strongly attracted to 16-year-old Lisa, the daughter of the snobbish family living next door. Each night, he watches from his bedroom window as she undresses, even though he feels guilt and shame as his sexual awareness grows. He becomes even more upset after he has several wet dreams, and he fears that his parents know when his father unexpectedly decides to have a "man-to-man" talk about sex. Given a pair of binoculars for Christmas, Tony uses them to take closer looks at Lisa, which makes his guilt feelings increase. Tony begins to suffer severe gastric attacks as the result of the combined anxieties of the family's financial problems, his sexual urges, and his fears that he will be implicated in his friend Joel's shoplifting. He is hospitalized for 10 days of tests and observation, after which the doctors conclude that his problems are psychological, and Tony begins treatment by a psychiatrist. By the end of the novel, he has learned to control his fears and resolves to act more responsibly. He surmises that he might even stop watching Lisa undress at night, but "then again, maybe I won't."

CENSORSHIP HISTORY

Then Again, Maybe I Won't has been challenged in many schools because of its references to masturbation, nocturnal emissions, erections, and "immorality and voyeurism." In 1980, the novel was removed from the Gilbert, Arizona, elementary school libraries and the school board ordered that students who wanted to check out the book from the junior high school library could only do so if they had written parental consent. In 1982, the book was challenged in the Tuscaloosa, Alabama; Orlando, Florida; and Harford County, Maryland, school systems for being "sexually offensive." In 1983, the Elk River, Minnesota, school board responded to parent complaints about the book and decided to restrict the title to students who had written parental permission.

Several parents who supported the book contacted the Minnesota Civil Liberties Union, which sued the school board, forcing it to reverse the decision later in the same year.

In 1984, the novel was removed from all of the school libraries in the St. Tammany Parish, Louisiana, school district, after parents complained that its "treatment of immorality and voyeurism does not provide for the growth of desirable attitudes." The book was later reinstated. In Peoria, Illinois, that same year, parents complained that the book contained "strong sexual content" and "vulgar" language and alleged that the book lacked social or literary value. The school board voted to remove the book from all libraries in the school district, but the decision was later changed to restrict the book to students who brought written parental permission.

A year later, the book was challenged as being "profane, immoral, and offensive," but after consideration the school board decided to retain the book in the school district libraries. In 1988, parents complained that "sexual content" made the book unsuitable to be included in the Des Moines, Iowa, elementary school libraries, but the district officials rejected the challenge. In 1989, a group of parents of students attending elementary and middle schools in the Salem-Keizer, Oregon, school district complained that the book is a "dismal tale of a young boy's inability to cope and his very inappropriate responses to the changes taking place in his life." They asked the school board to remove the book from the school district libraries, but the move was rejected.

In 1990, parents in Tyrone, Pennsylvania, challenged the inclusion of the novel in the elementary school libraries, claiming that the main character is a voyeur and that the book deals with masturbation and alcohol abuse. The school board considered their complaint and in a 6-2 vote retained the book. The same group of parents then objected to the appearance of the novel on the suggested reading list, and the school board agreed to form a committee to review the policy and guidelines for creating reading lists. The book was retained on the reading list. In 1991, a parent in Hartford, Wisconsin, asked that the school board remove the novel from the elementary school library, charging that it contained "profanity" and "promoted shoplifting and voyeurism." The board-appointed school review committee voted to retain the book.

FURTHER READING

Donelson, Kenneth L., and Alleen Pace Nilsen. *Literature for Today's Young Adults.* Glenview, Ill.: Scott Foresman, 1989.

Foerstel, Herbert N. *Banned in the U.S.A.: A Reference Guide to Book Censorship in Schools and Public Libraries.* Westport, Conn.: Greenwood, 1994.

Newsletter on Intellectual Freedom (July 1982): 124; (September 1982): 155–156; (May 1983): 71; (September 1983): 153; (May 1984): 69; (July 1984): 121; (January 1985): 8; (March 1985): 33, 42, 58; (July 1985): 112; (January 1990): 4–5; (July 1990): 127; (March 1991): 62.

THE THIEF'S JOURNAL

Author: Jean Genet
Original dates and places of publication: 1954, France; 1964, United States
Original publishers: Olympia Press (France); Grove Press (United States)
Literary form: Novel

SUMMARY

The Thief's Journal is a semiautobiographical novel in which the author relates his life from his birth as the illegitimate child of parents who abandon him through his years as a vagabond. Raised by foster parents whom he robbed, Genet was incarcerated in a juvenile facility and then spent years in a series of correctional institutions. He gives detailed accounts of his imprisonments for theft and dope smuggling or peddling, as well as of his homosexual relations with other prisoners and with a French police detective and British soldiers at Gibraltar. The work also details his wanderings as a beggar and tramp from one end of Europe to the other.

At times philosophical, Genet repudiates good throughout all of his accounts, often reversing accepted moral values and embracing the evil he encounters. He purports to find God in the places that traditional, middle-class society has abandoned—"the dark corners of crime, vice and shame." He unabashedly speaks openly of one of his lovers, Stilitano, a notorious criminal and pimp.

Throughout, Genet purports to function for the good of others. One example of such thinking is his sexual encounter with a "coast guard" stationed on the shores of Spain, which keeps the man occupied when he should be on duty. As Genet sleeps in a shack near the sea, the man stumbles in, looking for fishermen and sailors who are smuggling goods between Morocco and Spain. The thirtyish guard shares supper with Genet, who is several years younger; "then he began to caress me. . . . He knew he ought to leave, but my caresses grew more artful. He couldn't bear to tear himself away; the smugglers must have landed peacefully." He perceives himself as "the favorite mistress who, beneath a starry sky, soothes the conqueror" and grants the man "the loveliest of my nights" as the sounds of smugglers' boats landing can be heard through an open window.

CENSORSHIP HISTORY

The Thief's Journal was banned in Ireland on December 21, 1961. A prohibition order was published in the *Iris Oifigiuil*, "the only official source from which booksellers [and readers] might learn of a new prohibition order," in which all articles blacklisted by the Irish Board of Censors were listed. According to the Censorship of Publications Bill of 1928, "the notice in *Iris Oifigiuil* should be sufficient evidence in the courts of summary jurisdiction as to the character of the publication," despite the acknowledgment by justices quoted in Adams's thorough study of Irish censorship laws that "this gazette is not a publication which booksellers are addicted to reading." The Irish Board of Censors found the novel "obscene" and "indecent," objecting particularly to the author's handling of the theme of homosexuality and the poetic treatment of crime. The work was officially banned from sale in Ireland until the introduction of the Censorship Publications Bill in 1967 reduced to 12 years the duration of a prohibition order, and the work was among 5,000 titles released from the list of banned books.

FURTHER READING

Adams, Michael. *Censorship: The Irish Experience.* Tuscaloosa: University of Alabama Press, 1968.
Kronhausen, Eberhard, and Phyllis Kronhausen. *Pornography and the Law.* New York: Ballantine, 1959.
White, Edmund. *Genet: A Biography.* New York: Knopf, 1994.

THIS BOY'S LIFE

Author: Tobias Wolff
Original date and place of publication: 1989, United States
Original publisher: Grove Press
Literary form: Memoir

SUMMARY

This Boy's Life relates incidents of the author life that take place in the United States during the 1950s and the 1960s, in the post–World War II period that is often portrayed as a time of peace, prosperity, and strong family values. The memoir opens as the adolescent Toby Wolff joins his mother, Rosemary, on a journey to Utah, where she hopes to reverse their luck and to provide a financially secure future for herself and for her son by mining uranium. Rosemary has recently left Florida and her second husband, Roy, an abusive and volatile man who follows Toby and his mother as they travel to Utah. The pair feel constantly oppressed by their fugitive status and by their impoverished circumstances. In contrast, Toby's father, who abandoned his wife and youngest son shortly after Toby was born, is living a life of luxury in Connecticut after marrying a wealthy woman. Toby's brother, Geoffrey, attends Princeton University.

Toby romanticizes his nomadic existence and renames himself Jack both to honor his favorite author Jack London and to distance himself from his father and from the shabbiness of life with his mother. Their shared troubles make him emotionally close to his mother, who loves him very much, although she finds herself unable to overcome her abusive childhood and to function as the strong protective parent he needs. Rosemary's emotional scars run deep, and she continuously becomes involved in relationships with men who abuse her and Jack, both physically and emotionally. After Toby/Jack's father leaves her, she marries Roy, whose volatile nature provides a harrowing environment for Jack and his mother, and they attempt to escape their nightmare by leaving Florida and traveling to Utah. When Roy leaves Rosemary, she uproots Toby/Jack and moves to Seattle, where she meets Dwight, the man who will become a major force in her son's life and the source of his most intense discomfort. Dwight is a bully who constantly belittles and berates Jack, assigning him chores for no better reason than to exhibit the control that he exerts over Rosemary and her son. He taunts and criticizes Jack and claims that he wants to make a man out of the boy, but his behavior shows him to be petty and mean-spirited. To obtain spending money, Jack must deliver newspapers, but Dwight takes all of Jack's earnings and uses it for his own needs. Whatever Jack does is never quite good enough for Dwight, who expresses little genuine interest in him aside from making him an object of ridicule and bullying. Dwight tries to turn Jack into the aggressive individual he is and teaches the boy to fight, then expresses one of his few moments of approval when Jack appears ready to engage in a confrontation with Arthur Gayle, a "notorious sissy" with whom Jack had once been friends.

The attempts to cope with his miserable existence lead Jack to escape into his vivid imagination, and he fantasizes a life that is far from the reality of his life in Chinook. In the effort to escape Dwight and Chinook, Jack applies to private boarding schools and forges praise-filled letters of his accomplishments to accompany his applications. Although he is a member of a group of boys that are repeatedly in trouble with the authorities, Jack creates a perfect self for his applications, one in which he is a straight-A student, a star athlete, and a model student. He writes the lies so often that he soon becomes convinced that he is a gifted student and virtuous human being, despite the daily evidence to the contrary.

As Jack grows older, he makes several attempts to run away, but his plans always go awry. He plans to run away with Arthur to Alaska after a Boy Scout meeting, but he is sidetracked by another troop's request for help. In the process of offering help, Jack alienates Arthur and is defrauded of all of his money. He decides to run away to live with his brother, Geoffrey, at Princeton, but he sabotages his own plans when he is caught forging a bank check.

Despite all of his often self-imposed troubles, Jack receives the opportunity to escape Dwight and Chinook when he is accepted into the prestigious Hill School. An alumnus of the school, Mr. Howard, interviews Jack and attempts to serve as his mentor. The attention that both Mr. and Mrs. Howard give Jack in buying him a new wardrobe and preparing him to attend the school enhances Jack's self-esteem, and he thrives on their attention. Shortly before he is supposed to leave home to attend the school, he has an altercation with Dwight, who pushes Jack in front of Rosemary, an action that motivates her to leave Dwight and to take Jack with her. At Jack's request, Rosemary allows him to live with the family of his friend Chuck Bolger, and Jack promises that he will keep out of trouble while living with the Bolgers. He is unable to keep that promise and is caught stealing gasoline from the nearby farm owned by the Welch family. Despite his remorse for the action, Jack refuses to apologize for his action. At the same time, Jack watches as his friend Chuck Bolger faces arrest on a statutory rape charge. Tina Flood might be pregnant, but the sheriff lets Chuck know that he can avoid arrest if he agrees to marry her, a deal that Chuck refuses. Fortunately for Chuck, a third friend Huff agrees to marry Tina.

Jack's chaotic life continues when he chooses to visit his father and brother the summer before beginning the Hill School. When Jack arrives, his father leaves immediately for Las Vegas with his latest girlfriend. Jack feels alone and detached from his surroundings. Attending Hill does not improve his life because he has lied his way into the school and he cannot keep up with its academics. Midway through his senior year, Jack is expelled from the school. He feels that he has few options left, and the memoir ends as Jack enlists in the army and faces service in Vietnam.

CENSORSHIP HISTORY

This Boy's Life was nominated for the National Book Award in 1994 and praised extensively by critics, but such esteem has failed to insulate the work from challenges. In 2003, parents of high school students in the Blue Valley school district in Overland Park, Kansas, petitioned the school board to remove the memoir and Walter Dean Myers's *FALLEN ANGELS* from district classrooms "due to vulgar language, sexual explicitness, or violent imagery that is gratuitously employed." The school board reviewed *This Boy's Life* and decided in August 2005 to remove the work from the school curriculum but allowed it to remain in the school library. The decision was the result of a long debate. In 2003, Janet Harmon and her husband challenged the use of the memoir in the classroom "because of references to alcohol and sexual explicitness" and cited passages in which the adolescent Jack speaks of watching the Mickey Mouse Club and turns the wholesome activity "disgusting" by noting that "It was understood that we were all holding a giant bone for Annette." They also raised objections to the repeated uses of such "sexually graphic language" as "fuck you" and references to the homosexual kiss between Jack and his friend Arthur, as well as a range of sexual fantasies in which Jack engages. In one passage during which the adolescent boys trade fantastic stories, Jack relates that "they were good friends with a guy who lost his dick in an automobile accident. He crashed his convertible into a tree and his girlfriend was thrown high into the branches. When the police got her down, they found the guy's dong in her mouth." After receiving the initial challenge filed by the Harmons, school officials refused their request and retained the book in the curriculum but created a special review committee to assess the suitability of the work and other books and plays assigned in the Blue Valley communications arts classes. The review of all books being used in the district was conducted by 25 to 30 communication arts teachers who developed new rationales for use of the books and who provided information regarding content of the works and explanations of how each work fits into the school curriculum. After two years, the special review committee recommended removal of *This Boy's Life* because it was "no longer the best fit for the curriculum." On August 8, 2005, the school board voted to remove the work from use in the school district. Vermeda Edwards, director of curriculum and instruction in the school district, asserted that "No titles were removed because of violence, language, or sexual content." The parents who led the challenge to *This Boy's Life* and 13 other books viewed the move as verification of the initial challenge, and one told a reporter for the *Kansas City Star* that she and other "concerned parents" would remain vigilant and "see that the best and the highest quality books are taught and used."

FURTHER READINGS

Newsletter on Intellectual Freedom 54 (November 2005): 282–283.

THREE WEEKS

Author: Elinor Glyn
Original dates and places of publication: 1907, England; 1907, United States
Original publishers: Gerald Duckworth (England); Duffield & Co. (United States)
Literary form: Novel

SUMMARY

Three Weeks tells the simple and dramatic story of Paul Verdayne, a handsome and wealthy English nobleman in his early twenties, sent by his parents first to France and then to Switzerland after he is caught embracing the parson's daughter, Isabella Waring. Once in Switzerland, Verdayne pines for the earthy Isabella until he sees a beautiful older woman, in her 30s, who is dressed in black and has a face "like a magnolia bloom." After several days of smoldering glances, Paul and the Lady (as she is referred to throughout the novel) meet, and she boldly asks him to visit her in her suite. Rich in the exotic decor of sumptuous silks, satins, and brocades, the Lady's suite also contains a huge tiger skin draped over her couch, upon which she reclines provocatively, "while between her red lips was a rose not redder than they—an almost scarlet rose. . . . [T]he whole picture was barbaric."

The two begin a passionate sexual relationship that lasts only three weeks, during which the Lady is repeatedly described as "undulating" on the tiger skin and whispering such lines as "This is our souls' wedding." The Lady reads Apuleius in Latin to Paul and sings as she plucks the strings of a guitar, but reviewers did not criticize the novel for these incidents. Rather, criticism emerged because of the numerous times in which Paul and the Lady "melted into one another's arms" and "the spirit of their natures melted as One." The Lady is fierce in her passion and tireless in her lovemaking, and the physicality of the descriptions shocked many reviewers.

Paul learns that the Lady is really the queen of a small (unnamed) Balkan kingdom and that her husband is abusive. When she vanishes after three weeks have passed, Paul becomes physically ill, and his father takes him home to England. Nine months later, Paul receives a letter from the Lady informing him that she has given birth to their son. Through his father's efforts, Paul learns her identity, but she is murdered by her husband before they reunite. Overcome by grief, Paul roams the world for five years and then arranges to see his son.

CENSORSHIP HISTORY

Three Weeks was viewed by critics of the time as one of many novels written in England by women in 1907 that contained what *Publishers Weekly* viewed as "questionable morality" and "morbid or abnormal conditions." Many critics were unremittingly hostile to what amounted to an illicit love affair. Even Glyn's friends in society professed to be scandalized by the book; her grandson recounts in his biography of her that "among her friends in society she was abused and reviled, called an immoral woman and a glorifier of adultery." The novel was banned at Eton, and the headmaster. Dr. Edward Lyttleton, informed Glyn of the ban. The author assumed that he had not yet read the book, so she sent him a copy. After reading it, he wrote to her and stated that he had enjoyed the book and admitted to having been misled by its reputation. The ban, however, remained in place.

Although the book raised an uproar among reviewers in the United States, the lurid eroticism of the novel fascinated American readers, selling 50,000 copies in the first three weeks after publication in the United States, and then averaging 2,000 sales daily for the three months following. The novel also created a new standard for sexual content in novels.

In 1908, the Boston Watch and Ward Society placed pressure on booksellers to agree to withhold the novel from sale, thus effectively banning the work in Boston. Backed by the New York publisher of the novel, Duffield & Company, Joseph E. Buckley deliberately incited a confrontation with legal authorities by selling a copy of the novel to Inspector McCarr of the Boston police. Buckley was indicted and charged with "selling a certain printed book entitled *Three Weeks*, containing in and upon certain pages certain obscene, indecent and impure language, manifestly tending to corrupt the morals of youth."

In the case that followed, *Commonwealth v. Buckley*, 200 Mass. 346, 86 N.E. 910 (1909), the grand jury asserted that the language of the offending sections of the book could not be included in the transcript of the proceedings, because it was too "improper to be placed upon the court records and offensive to the court." The jury in the Superior Court of Suffolk County case declared the book "obscene" and the court fined Buckley $100. Duffield & Company appealed the decision, but the Supreme Judicial Court of Massachusetts upheld the Superior Court decision. The ruling became an important guide for judicial interpretation of the obscenity laws of Massachusetts for decades to come.

In the appeal, the publisher questioned whether the presiding Superior Court judge had properly instructed the jury in the term *obscene* and regarding the author's purpose. In writing the Supreme Judicial Court opinion, Judge Hammond asserted that terms such as *obscene* and *impure* were not technical terms and, therefore, need not be explained to a jury. The judge further asserted that the author's purpose need not be considered in judging the effect of a book. More specifically, Judge Hammond observed:

An author who has disclosed so much of the details of the way to the adulterous bed as the author of this book has and who has kept the curtains raised in the way that she has kept them, can find no fault if the jury says that not the spiritual but the animal, not the pure but the impure, is what the general reader will find as the most conspicuous thought suggested to him as he reads.

Writing about the case a few years later, conservative literary critic Brander Matthews, usually a strong supporter of the Watch and Ward Society, condemned the court action. He observed that *Three Weeks* was "a cheap tale of superficial cleverness" that would have sunk "swiftly beneath the waters of oblivion" without the publicity generated by the trials. Instead, sales of the novel became even stronger throughout the United States and stimulated sales in England as well.

The Watch and Ward Society savored its victory and achieved increased power as a result of the case. Sporadic bannings, similar to that imposed by the Society, occurred throughout the nation but without litigation. Massachusetts booksellers, unwilling to risk more arrests and losses in court, joined forces with the Watch and Ward Society in a "gentleman's agreement" to keep much of modern fiction out of Commonwealth bookstores for more than a decade, until H. L. Mencken challenged the Society's edict in 1926 by selling a copy of *American Mercury* on Boston Common and was cleared by a municipal judge.

Three Weeks remained scandalous for a long while. As late as 1932, a Mickey Mouse cartoon was banned from publication in Ohio newspapers because it depicted a cow reclining in a field, reading *Three Weeks.*

FURTHER READING

Etherington-Smith, Meredith, and Jeremy Pilcher. *The "It" Girls: Elinor Glyn, Novelist, and Her Sister Lucile, Couturiere.* New York: Harcourt Brace Jovanovich, 1986.

Glyn, Anthony. *Elinor Glyn.* Garden City, N.Y.: Doubleday, 1955.

Grant, Sidney S., and S. E. Angoff. "Censorship in Boston." *Boston University Law Review* 10 (January 1930): 36–60.

Matthews, Brander. "Books That Are Barred." *Munsey's Magazine*, December 1913, pp. 493–497.

McCoy, Ralph E. *Banned in Boston: The Development of Literary Censorship in Massachusetts.* Urbana: University of Illinois, 1956.

Rolph, Cecil Hewitt. *Books in the Dock.* London: Deutsch, 1961.

TOBACCO ROAD

Author: Erskine Caldwell
Original date and place of publication: 1932, United States
Original publisher: Charles Scribner's Sons
Literary form: Novel

SUMMARY

Tobacco Road presents an unflinching look at the Lester family, a rural family whose grim experiences living on the edge of starvation jolt readers into an awareness of the plight of the rural poor. The novel is filled with acts of brutality and the hopeless futility felt by the derelict family living on a barren and poverty-ridden Georgia tobacco farm.

Amoral rather than immoral in behavior, patriarch Jeeter Lester boasts of his potency, having fathered 17 children by his wife, Ada, and untold numbers of children with women living on area farms. He and Ada abuse Jeeter's elderly mother, denying her food, ignoring her, and, finally, refusing to go to her aid when Jeeter's son Dude backs over her with a car and leaves her lying facedown in the dust. Hours later, when Jeeter does turn his attention to his mother, she has stopped bleeding and makes no sound although "she ain't stiff yet, but I don't reckon she'll live." While neighbor Lov Bensey is around to help, Jeeter takes her out to the field, digs a ditch, and buries her without worrying whether she is dead yet.

Jeeter gives his 12-year-old daughter Pearl in marriage to Lov Bensey in trade for "some quilts, nearly a gallon of cylinder oil, besides giving him all of a week's pay, which was seven dollars." He attempts to marry off his hare-lipped daughter, Ellie May, but settles for sending her to comfort Lov after Pearl runs away, with the demand that Ellie May return the following morning with food and some of Lov's clothes. His son, Dude, marries Bessie, an older woman and self-styled preacher whom the women call a "hussy" because of her affinity for men. Jeeter tries to climb into bed with Dude and Bessie, "a right smart piece to live with," when the three stay at a hotel after a trip to Augusta to sell firewood. He is foiled in his attempt when the manager knocks at their door and tells them that he has another room available, but Bessie is the one who leaves. The next morning, she is sleepy and tired, reports that she had been asked to move from bed to bed, and concludes that "there sure is a lot of men staying there."

The final tragedy of the novel occurs because years of agricultural mismanagement have left the fields barren, and the Lesters are too poor to buy needed fertilizer to grow anything. In desperation, Jeeter follows an old tradition of burning the broom sedge off the fields, but he and Ada burn to death when their cabin catches fire. He could have left the farm and worked in the cotton mills, but he stubbornly clung to the land as his ancestors had.

CENSORSHIP HISTORY

The novel escaped extensive attempts at censorship in part because major efforts were directed at the stage version, closely adapted from the novel. In 1935, Chicago mayor Edward J. Kelly banned performances of the play, backed by expert witnesses including a former governor, a circuit judge, and members of the bar who claimed that the play "offered more obscenity than Chicagoans wished to tolerate." The ban was upheld by the Seventh Circuit Court of Appeals, which determined Kelly's assessment of community standards to be accurate justification. The stage version was also banned in Detroit, Michigan; St. Paul, Minnesota; Minneapolis, Minnesota; Utica, New York; and Tulsa, Oklahoma. Also in 1935, a member of the House of Representatives from Georgia appealed to Congress to forbid staging of the novel, because it presented an "infamous, wicked, and untrue portrait" of his district. Six assistant district attorneys viewed the play to address the charge, after which they refused the representative's request.

Attempts to ban the novel also occurred in several instances. In 1934, several faculty members at Columbia University condemned *Tobacco Road* and Caldwell's GOD'S LITTLE ACRE as "indecent and tending to corrupt" and demanded the withdrawal of both books from the Teachers College library. The action was taken even though both books were on required reading lists of several university English courses. In 1941, the novel was barred from the mails by the postmaster general, who claimed that the book was "indecent and immoral." At the same time, the novel continued to be sold in bookstores. In 1953, *Tobacco Road* was banned from import and sale by the Irish government, which claimed that the novel was "obscene."

FURTHER READING

Caldwell, Erskine. "My Twenty-five Years of Censorship." *Esquire*, October 1958, pp. 176–178.

Caldwell, Erskine. "Protest against Columbia University's Ban on *Tobacco Road* and *God's Little Acre*." *New Republic*, June 1934, pp. 184–185.

Haskins, Doug. "The Many Faces of Censorship." *Canadian Forum* 33 (June 1953): 57–58.

Klevar, Harvey L. *Erskine Caldwell: A Biography*. Knoxville: University of Tennessee Press, 1993.

Mikva, Abner J. "Chicago: Citadel of Censorship." *Focus/Midwest* 2 (March–April 1963): 16–17.

Miller, Dan B. *Erskine Caldwell: The Journey from Tobacco Road*. New York: Knopf, 1994.

TRAGIC GROUND

Author: Erskine Caldwell
Original date and place of publication: 1944, United States
Original publisher: Grosset & Dunlap
Literary form: Novel

SUMMARY

Tragic Ground relates the existence of the Douthits, a Georgia family who relocates from their rural surroundings to an urban industrialized area on the Gulf Coast to take advantage of the work opportunities in a munitions factory during World War II. The end of the war brings a closing of the factory, leaving the family destitute and unable to cope with their impoverished life in the city. The efforts of social workers to assist the family are ineffective, so patriarch Spence Douthit decides to solve their problems by finding a rich husband for his 13-year-old daughter, Mavis. Much of the comedy, and most of the erotic references, emerge from this quest and from the inability of the family to cope with precarious urban life. Nonetheless, Caldwell makes an important statement about the fate of the illiterate and transient workers who are unprepared to survive in what becomes an alien environment once their source of income—jobs at the munitions factory—ends.

As Spence pursues his mission, he speaks of young girls becoming prostitutes and refers freely to the genitals of both males and females. In one incident he is lured by a prostitute into a hotel room, where he is beaten and robbed of his money. Finding his older daughter, Libby, in bed with her boyfriend, who has just returned from the war, he expresses surprise rather than anger because of all the Douthits, Libby is the one who usually follows social rules.

In describing the manner in which recruiters for the munitions jobs persuade rural wives to withhold sex until their husbands agree to take the jobs, Spence says that he felt "like a rabbit with his balls caught in a sewing machine." He tells a sexily dressed prostitute in a nightclub, "Your tits are showing." In efforts to interest a man in marrying Mavis, he states, "She keeps me pricked up around the house." His wife is similarly blunt, pointing out when she feels threatened by the attractiveness of the social worker, "If I had my looks back . . . I could go out and get sported, too. . . . I'd hist [*sic*] my skirt and have the men poking hards at me all over this part of the world. . . . You've worked my region to a frazzle."

CENSORSHIP HISTORY

Tragic Ground was one of eight works by American authors that became the subject of obscenity cases between 1934 and 1944, after the ban against importation of erotic classics was eased by the 1930 amendment of the Tariff Act and censors turned their attention to American works. Other works that suffered in this period were Lillian Hellman's *The Children's Hour*, Jim Tully's LADIES IN THE PARLOR, James T. Farrell's WORLD I NEVER MADE, William Faulkner's THE WILD PALMS, James M. Cain's SERENADE, Lillian Smith's *STRANGE FRUIT*, and Kathleen Winsor's FOREVER AMBER. Three of these novels— *Tragic Ground, Strange Fruit*, and *Forever Amber*—became best sellers after their challenges in court.

The language of *Tragic Ground*, natural to the characters, raised objections among critics when the novel appeared. In the same year that the novel was published, members of the Boston Watch and Ward Society lodged a complaint with the police, claiming the novel was "obscene" and dealt with "low life matters." Acting on the complaint, a detective purchased a copy of the book from Miss E. Margaret Anderson of the Dartmouth Book Stall in Boston and then arrested her for "distributing obscene material." The case went to municipal court, in a hearing presided over by Municipal Judge Elijah Adlow, who ridiculed the obscenity charge and stated, "I'm not interested in these crusades against literature, and I'm getting tired of books being banned." When the arresting detective pointed out that one scene in the book depicted a woman and man together, the man naked to the waist, the judge asked, "Do you think anybody would be astounded to hear that?"

In delivering a ruling, Judge Adlow observed to the police, "It's not for me or for you to try to establish literary tastes of the community." He stated that he had found *Tragic Ground* to be "dull," but concluded that "the judges of the Municipal Court and the members of the Police Department were not qualified to pass on the literary value of books."

FURTHER READING

Burgum, Edwin Berry. "Erskine Caldwell and His Jeeters." *New York Times Book Review*, October 15, 1944, p. 46.

Caldwell, Erskine. "My Twenty-five Years of Censorship." *Esquire* 50, October 1958, pp. 176–178.

"Caldwell Novel Cleared as 'Dull.' " *New York Times*, December 29, 1944, p. 13.

Daniels, Jonathan. "American Lower Depths." *Saturday Review of Literature*, October 14, 1944, p. 6.

Miller, Dan B. *Erskine Caldwell: The Journey from Tobacco Road*. New York: Knopf, 1995.

TRILBY

Author: George du Maurier
Original date and place of publication: 1894, United States
Original publisher: Harper & Brothers
Literary form: Novel

SUMMARY

Trilby may now be a forgotten novel, rarely read, but it remains a part of the American idiom as manipulating managers and image makers continue to be dubbed "Svengali," a reference to the villainous character in this novel. The novel is also responsible for introducing Americans to the common romantic conception of the bohemian artistic life of Paris in the 19th century. Set in the Latin Quarter in Paris, the novel portrays a glamorous and free place where parties and activities are spontaneous and continuous, but Du Maurier also conveys a sense of the darkness that underlies some of this gaiety. To provide authenticity, the author uses concrete details and the names of real people and places.

Du Maurier wrote *Trilby* in French and then translated it into English for publication in America. Today, the novel reads like a classic melodrama, complete with a sinister villain who is both mysterious and extremely intelligent and talented, and who possesses hypnotic, diabolical powers. He is joined by a weak-willed young heroine, a mediocre singer who is completely mesmerized by the cadaverous and evil-appearing Svengali, who exerts his power and will to turn her into a singing star in Europe.

When Svengali and Trilby meet, the young woman is earning a living posing as an artist's model. She is lovely and sweet-tempered and is adored by the artist Gecko, for whom she has only sympathy. Trilby also sings in local cafes, but her mediocre singing voice evidences no especial talent, although it does bring her many male admirers, several of whom want to marry her. While she juggles admirers, Svengali attempts to lure her away with promises of an international career and great riches, but she experiences feelings of deep loathing for him and resists. Instead, she falls in love with Little Billee and the two hope to marry. Svengali intrudes upon Trilby's friendships with other entertainers Taffy and the Laird, and insinuates himself into her romance with Little Billee. He is present when Little Billee announces to his parents that he and Trilby want to marry. They are horrified at the idea of their son marrying a café singer and condemn the union. Their reaction disheartens Trilby and leaves her vulnerable to Svengali, who smiles fiendishly and lures her away to begin manipulating her life and creating her career.

Trilby is afraid of Svengali, but she is also unable to resist his powers. "He seemed to her a dread, powerful demon, who . . . oppressed and weighed on her like an incubus." For five years, they tour the world while Trilby sings under the stage name of La Svengali, pretending to be married although others suspect they are not. Trilby is a brilliant singer as long as Svengali wields the baton during her performances, but in the rare case when she chooses to sing without him present, her voice becomes flat and unappealing.

After Svengali dies in a fit of apoplexy during one of Trilby's performances, she seems to awaken from the trance in which she has lived for five years but cannot remember anything that has occurred, nor does she remember any of her performances. She becomes ill and Little Billee visits her, but she sends him away. After he leaves, a messenger delivers a package, which she unwraps to find a portrait of the evil and leering Svengali. The portrait briefly comes to life and then shrinks to a mere photograph, but it has the intended effect. Trilby has once again come under the spell of the evil Svengali; he calls her from the grave, and she dies.

CENSORSHIP HISTORY

In 1894, *Trilby*, one of the literary crazes of the 1890s and one of the most widely read books ever published in America to that date, became the target of censors in Philadelphia, who demanded that the board of education and the city council remove the novel from the public library in the 21st ward. The request was made by three district residents, two of them clergymen. The objections centered on the doubtful marriage between Trilby and Svengali, as well as Svengali's diabolical hold upon his protégée.

The board created a committee to consider the request, but they were unable to come to a decision. One committee member illogically suggested that the problem might be due to the translation, noting that "Many a book that may appear perfectly harmless in French becomes harmful when read here in a translation." This was unlikely because the author created his own translation for Harper & Brothers. The committee chairman disagreed and asserted that the book would probably have to be removed, because the board had already been forced to remove many books from the shelves. After the decision was moved to the library committee of the Philadelphia Board of Education, chose to retain the book, given that hundreds of thousands of Americans were already reading it.

FURTHER READING

Haney, Robert W. *Comstockery in America: Patterns of Censorship and Control.* Boston: Beacon, 1960.
Tebbel, John. *A History of Book Publishing in the United States.* New York: Bowker, 1975.

THE TRIUMPH OF DEATH

Author: Gabriele D'Annunzio
Original dates and places of publication: 1889, Italy; 1896, United
  States
Original publishers: Da Palmo (Italy); George H. Richmond & Co.
  (United States)
Literary form: Novel

SUMMARY

The Triumph of Death is an autobiographical novel that relates the fatal romantic infatuation of a young man that closely parallels D'Annunzio's love affair
with Elvira Leoni. Tindall characterizes the novel as "artificial, morbid, without simplicity or sanity," and the work does provide numerous scenes of
depression and long introspective passages that far outnumber the erotic
scenes. Although the novel details the orgiastic abandon of characters George
and Hippolyte, many nonerotic passages convey the feelings of George toward
his mother and father and toward the beloved uncle, Demetrius, who commits
suicide, as well as George's thoughts regarding music and religion.

George's intellect remains at war with his sensuality, and he comprehends
"that he would in no way succeed in realizing the type of exuberant life . . .
that his intellectual and moral faculties, too disproportioned, would never
succeed in finding their equilibrium and their model." He also experiences
the frustration of knowing that he can never fully possess his ideal woman
Hippolyte, who is married, and he can never be fully sure of her love nor can
he control his desire for her.

The sexual attraction between George and Hippolyte is evident in the
novel, but the descriptions are not explicit. Traveling by train together, "they
spoke in low tones, communicating the ardor of their blood, exchanging burning promises. . . . Their desire grew. . . . They united their lips." Although this
description is the reader's introduction to the coming stolen week of love, no
explicit erotic activity is presented. The most erotic scene in the novel occurs
when George thinks in detail about Hippolyte's physical beauty, belaboring
his description of her body. Beyond an adoring mention of her "serpentine ele-
gance" and "the narrowness of her thigh," George describes her "sterile abdomen" with its "virginal purity," her "alabaster" skin and the graceful curve of
her back. He turns his most specific attention to her breasts, "firm and small,
as if sculptured in very delicate alabaster, and the points of her extraordinarily
erect breasts [which] were of a rose-violet hue."

The lovers' downfall is George's fascination with death, which emerges
after they learn of a suicide that leads George to exclaim, "Happy are the
dead! They have no more doubts!" As George's feelings of insecurity in his
love for Hippolyte increase, he thinks of being released from his torment
through death—hers or his own. At the end of the novel, George causes the
death of both of them.

CENSORSHIP HISTORY

The Triumph of Death captured the attention of the New York Society for the Suppression of Vice and its secretary Anthony Comstock in 1897. Comstock purchased a copy of the book and then brought charges against the clerk who sold it to him, George H. Richmond Jr., and Richmond's father, who was both a reputable book dealer and the American publisher of the novel. The defendants appeared for arraignment before Magistrate Leroy B. Crane in a New York City court on March 4, 1897, before which the Richmonds were held on $500 bail.

When the case went to court on March 25, 1897, Judges Hinsdale, Jerome, and Jacob of the Court of Special Sessions presided. A number of literary critics and literature professors were present, ready to testify to the critical value of the book, but the court refused to permit expert testimony. The judges refused to assess the book simply based on passages pointed out by Comstock and, instead, admitted the whole book into evidence. On April 5, 1897, the judges acquitted the Richmonds of all charges. In response, George Richmond threatened to sue Magistrate Crane for saying at the end of the arraignment hearing, "If a man were to put that book into the hands of my daughter I should not wait for the law; I would shoot him."

The publicity surrounding the arraignment of the Richmonds increased sales of the novel, making it suddenly popular. When Comstock made efforts to ban the novel in Asbury Park, New Jersey, the *New York Times* published an article about the effort and ridiculed his activities, noting that

> until that illustrious maker of reputations took the matter in hand the Italian's books were a drug in the market. The make-believe decadents and the like who "wrote them up" in weekly journals of small circulation found them hopeless as a topic. Now Mr. COMSTOCK has taken one of them up and is pushing its circulation beyond that of a penny newspaper with plenty of crude pictures of ladies' footwear.

In 1898, the Boston Watch and Ward Society attempted to acquire the cooperation of city book dealers to repress sales and advertising of the novel. The society was unsuccessful because sales of the book had already been so numerous as to convince booksellers that the book should remain. The ensuing publicity further increased sales.

FURTHER READING

"D'Annunzio at Asbury Park." *New York Times*, July 24, 1897, p. 6.

De Grazia, Edward. *Girls Lean Back Everywhere: The Law of Obscenity and the Assault on Genius.* New York: Random House, 1992.

"Offended at the Magistrate." *New York Times*, April 16, 1897, p. 5.

Tindall, William York. *Forces in Modern British Literature, 1885–1956.* 2d ed. New York: Vintage, 1956.

"*Triumph of Death* Exonerated." *New York Times,* April 6, 1897, p. 5.

TROPIC OF CANCER

Author: Henry Miller
Original dates and places of publication: 1934, France; 1961, United States
Original publishers: Obelisk Press (France); Grove Press (United States)
Literary form: Novel

TROPIC OF CAPRICORN

Author: Henry Miller
Original dates and places of publication: 1939, France; 1962, United States
Original publishers: Obelisk Press; Grove Press
Literary form: Novel

SUMMARY

Tropic of Cancer relates the loneliness, futility, shallow pleasure-seeking, degradation, and squalor of one American's life in France in the early 1930s. Begun as Miller's autobiography and written in the form of a diary, with a main character named for the author, the novel relates Miller's life in Paris and includes portraits of his many friends and acquaintances there. Despite the link to his life, the novel is neither chronologically organized nor specific as to dates and places. Rather, Miller uses a technique of free association in recalling events and creates an impressionistic rather than reportorial interior monologue.

An American expatriate in Paris who depends upon his friends for meals and lodging, the main character enjoys sexual adventures with diverse women. His erotic life is graphically described, although the frequent exaggerations turns the seemingly erotic material into outlandish situations that point up the absurdity of human existence more than they arouse.

The sexual imagery and the language used to relate Miller's views are blunt throughout the novel, as the following passage that appears early in the novel illustrates:

O Tania, where now is that warm cunt of yours, those fat, heavy garters, those soft, bulging thighs? There is a bone in my prick six inches long. I will ream out every wrinkle in your cunt, Tania, big with seed. I will send you home to your Sylvester with an ache in your belly and your womb turned inside out. Your Sylvester! Yes, he knows how to build a fire, but I know how to inflame a cunt. . . . I am fucking you, Tania, so that you'll stay fucked. And if you are afraid of being fucked publicly I will fuck you privately. I will tear off a few hairs from your cunt. . . . I will bite into your clitoris and spit out two franc pieces.

Miller also includes numerous excretory references in the work. In one instance, he describes the continuous droning speech of a dinner companion as feeling "exactly as if he had taken out that circumcised dick of his and was peeing on us." In another instance, he offers social criticism and notes, "for a hundred years or more the world, *our* world has been dying. And not one man, in these last hundred years or so, has been crazy enough to put a bomb up the asshole of creation and set it off."

Tropic of Capricorn is also semiautobiographical. The novel covers the years from 1920 to 1924 in Miller's life, before he left America for Europe. During this period, he worked for Western Union, called the Cosmodemonic Telegraph Company of North America in the work. Once again, as in the earlier novel, Miller recounts his agony in trying to "find" himself and to be true to himself despite the pressures to conform brought on artists by an industrial society. Although he was married to his first wife during the years covered by *Tropic of Capricorn*, Miller relates a series of sexual adventures with prostitutes, the wives and sisters of friends, and casual acquaintances.

Strewn throughout the novel are numerous "four-letter" words, not only relating to sexual and excretory incidents but also infused in casually related incidents. At one point, he states, "I had a good time because, as I said before, I really didn't give a fuck about anything." In another section, he notes, "I wasn't a good ass licker." He criticizes America in equally blunt language: "I think of all the streets in America combined as forming a huge cesspool, a cesspool of the spirit in which everything is sucked down and drained away to everlasting shit. . . . In the belly of the trombone lies the American soul farting its contented heart out."

As in *Tropic of Cancer,* Miller uses exceedingly frank language in this novel in referring to bizarre sexual activity with "Mona," who represents his second wife. After spying on Mona, who is masturbating in the bathroom, Miller approaches her:

She just stood there quietly and as I slid my hand up her legs she moved one foot a little to open her crotch a bit more. I don't think I ever put my hand into such a juicy crotch in my life. . . . I had my whole four fingers inside her, whipping it up to a froth. Her mouth was stuffed full and the juice pouring down her legs. Not a word out of us, as I say. Just a couple of quiet maniacs working away in the dark like gravediggers. It was a fucking Paradise and I knew it, and I was ready and willing to fuck my brains away if necessary. She was probably the best fuck I ever had.

Despite the blunt language, sexual descriptions, and references to urine and feces, Miller manages to impart to readers the absurdity of the human condition.

CENSORSHIP HISTORY

Tropic of Cancer was first published in Paris in 1934 and remained officially banned from the United States for three decades, but college students smuggled thousands of copies into the United States in that time until Grove Press published the novel in the United States. Of nearly 2 million copies of the book distributed, nearly three-quarters of a million were returned to the publisher. The book was involved in at least 40 criminal cases against wholesalers and booksellers, even after the federal government refused to ban the book. An untold number of civil suits to suppress the book have also occurred, as have "voluntary" withdrawals from sale after local intimidation.

In 1950, Ernest Besig, the director of the American Civil Liberties Union in San Francisco, attempted to import both *Tropic of Cancer* and *Tropic of Capricorn* into the United States and initiated the first court case involving the novels. Citing Section 1305 of the U.S. Code, Customs department officials held the books, and Besig sued the government. Before the case went to trial, Besig requested a motion to admit 19 depositions from literary critics testifying to the literary value of the novels and to Miller's stature as a serious writer. The motion was denied by Judge Louis A. Goodman, who stated bluntly:

> In my opinion the dominant effect of the two respondent books is obscene. Both books are replete with long passages that are filthy and revolting and that tend to excite lustful thoughts and desires. While the books also have passages, and indeed chapters, that may be said to have literary merit, the obscene portions have no literary value; they are directly, completely and wholly filthy and obscene and have no reasonable relation to any literary concept inherent in the books' theme.

The case went to trial without a jury in 1951 with Judge Goodman presiding. Despite the presentation by Besig of literary reviews of Miller's work and the statements from critics describing the literary merits of the books, the judge condemned the books and declared them obscene. In closing statements, Judge Goodman wrote,

> The many long filthy descriptions of sexual experiences, practices and organs are of themselves admitted to be lewd. . . . It is sufficient to say that the many obscene passages in the books have such an evil stench that to include them here in footnotes would make this opinion pornographic. . . . There are several passages where the female sexual organ and its function are described and referred to in such detailed and vulgar language as to create nausea in the

reader. If this be importable literature, then the dignity of the human person and the stability of the family unit, which are the cornerstones of society, are lost to us.

Besig appealed the decision to the Ninth Circuit Court of Appeals, and on October 23, 1953, the novels were again declared "obscene" by a unanimous decision in *Besig v. United States*, 208 F. 2d 142 (9th Cir. 1953). In his written decision, Circuit Judge Albert Lee Stephens characterized the books as being the "unprintable word of the debased and morally bankrupt" and claimed that, even taken as a whole, they lacked literary merit. He stated:

Practically everything that the world loosely regards as sin is detailed in the vivid, lurid, salacious language of smut, prostitution, and dirt. And all of it is related without the slightest expressed idea of its abandon. Consistent with the general tenor of the books, even human excrement is dwelt upon in the dirtiest words possible.

The 1961 Grove Press edition of *Tropic of Cancer* attracted numerous later legal actions because no test case had been heard by the Supreme Court, as there had been in the case of LADY CHATTERLY's LOVER. Grove Press delayed appealing the earliest cases to the Supreme Court, and the delay in securing a definitive judgment proved costly because the publishing firm committed itself to assisting every bookseller prosecuted. Five state courts declared the novel "obscene" in *State v. Huntington*, no. 24657, Super. Ct., Hartford County, Conn. (1962) (Connecticut); *Grove Press, Inc., v. Florida*, 156 So. 2d 537 (Fla. Dist. Ct. App. 1963) (Florida); *Haiman v. Morris*, Ill. Sup. Ct., June 18, 1964 (opinion not printed; later withdrawn) (Illinois); *Commonwealth v. Robin*, no. 3177, C.P. Phila. Co. Penn. (1962) (Pennsylvania); and *People v. Fritch*, 13 N.Y.2d 119, 192 N.E.2d 713 (1963) (4-3 decision) (New York). Within the same period, California, Massachusetts, and Wisconsin declared the novel "not obscene" in *Zeitlin v. Arnebergh*, 31 Cal.800, 383 P.2d 152 (1963) (unanimous); *Attorney General v. Book Named "Tropic of Cancer,"* 345 Mass. 11, 184 N.E.2d 328 (1962) (4-3 decision); and *McCauley v. Tropic of Cancer*, 20 Wisc. 2d 134, 121 N.W.2d 545 (1963) (4-3 decision).

On June 22, 1964, in a 5-4 decision in *Grove Press, Inc., v. Gerstein*, 378 U.S. 577 (1964), the U.S. Supreme Court reversed the Florida decision of *Grove Press, Inc., v. Florida*, 156 So. 2d 537 (Fla. Dist. Ct. App. 1963). The judgment was reversed by a per curiam order in which Justice William J. Brennan Jr. declared that "material dealing with sex in a manner that advocates ideas, or that has literary or scientific or artistic value or any other form of social importance, may not be branded as obscenity and denied the constitutional protection."

Grove Press vigorously defended *Tropic of Cancer* in numerous jurisdictions, but the publisher was forced to issue a statement that it did not have the financial means to defend booksellers in cases regarding Miller's *Tropic of Capricorn*.

FURTHER READING

"Another Furor over Books." *Ohio State University Monthly* 55 (December 1963): 8–12.

Ciardi, John. *"Tropic of Cancer."* *Saturday Review*, June 1962, p. 13.

De Grazia, Edward. *Girls Lean Back Everywhere: The Law of Obscenity and the Assault on Genius.* New York: Random House, 1992.

Hutchison, E. R. *Tropic of Cancer on Trial.* New York: Grove, 1968.

Kilpatrick, James J. *The Smut Peddlers.* New York: Doubleday, 1960.

Kincaid, Larry, and Grove Koger. *"Tropic of Cancer* and the Censors: A Case Study and Bibliographic Guide to the Literature." *Reference Services Review* 25 (Spring 1997): 31–38, 46.

Kuh, Richard H. *Foolish Figleaves? Pornography In and Out of Court.* New York: Macmillan, 1967.

Moore, Everett T. *"Tropic of Cancer"* (Second Phase). *ALA Bulletin* 56 (February 1962): 81–84.

"Obscenity-Evidence Admission of Contemporary Critical Evaluation of Libeled Book." *Minnesota Law Review* 35 (February 1951): 326–330.

Roeburt, John. *The Wicked and the Banned.* New York: Macfadden, 1963.

Smith, Roger H. "Cops, Counselors, and *Tropic of Cancer."* *Publishers Weekly*, October 23, 1961, p. 35.

U.S. President's Commission on Obscenity and Pornography. *The Report of the Commission on Obscenity and Pornography.* New York: Random House, 1970.

TWILIGHT SERIES

Author: Stephenie Meyer
Original date and place of publication: United States, 2005–2008
Original publisher: Little, Brown and Company
Literary type: Novel

SUMMARY

The Twilight series, written by Stephenie Meyer, consists of four books: *Twilight, New Moon, Eclipse,* and *Breaking Dawn.* Like *Romeo and Juliet*, the series centers upon teen lovers from widely disparate worlds who must overcome forces and people that seek to separate them. The additions of the paranormal and the macabre suggest the stories of Edgar Allan Poe, whose works contain several instances of love between human beings and vampires. The four novels span several years and take the main character, a human teenager named Isabella (Bella) Swan, from first love in high school through marriage and early motherhood. Throughout the four novels, the forces of good and evil clash, and high levels of melodrama characterize the works.

In the first novel, Bella has moved from Phoenix, Arizona, to Forks, Washington, where she lives with her father because her mother has to travel extensively with her new husband, a minor league baseball player. Bella meets the 100-year-old, still-teen Edward Cullen, a darkly handsome, brooding member of a vampire family who drinks animal rather than human blood. The two fall in love, but she also attracts the attention of the sadistic James, a member of a rival vampire family. James pursues Bella, and the Cullen family tries to protect her, but she feels compelled to run away to Phoenix, where James follows her and attacks her. Edward's family retaliates and kills James, after which Bella feels she can return safely to Forks.

In the second novel, *New Moon*, Bella sinks into a deep depression after Edward and his vampire family leave Forks because they feel that their continued presence has endangered her life. After the Cullen family leaves, Bella becomes emotionally close to Jacob Black, a member of a werewolf tribe, whose family joins him in protecting Bella when James's mate Victoria tries to avenge his death by killing Bella. A misunderstanding ensues, and, like Romeo, Edward believes that his beloved is dead and travels to Italy, where he plans to commit suicide. Bella finds him and stops him, but they are detained by members of the powerful vampire coven the Volturi, who release them only after the couple promises that she will shortly become a vampire. Having found each other again, Bella and Edward return to Forks.

The conflict increases in *Eclipse*, the third novel, in which Victoria has gathered a large number of vampires in an attempt to destroy Edward's family and to kill Bella as vengeance for the murder of James. At the same time, Bella is forced to choose between Jacob and Edward. She chooses Edward, but Jacob's wolf family joins forces with the Cullen family to combat Victoria's vampire family, over which the vampire-wolf forces triumph. After the victory, Bella agrees to marry Edward.

In the final novel, *Breaking Dawn*, Edward and Bella shorten their honeymoon on an island off South America after they discover she is pregnant. The rapidly progressing pregnancy debilitates Bella, and she nearly dies giving birth. Edward saves her by injecting her with his venom. The member of a rival vampire coven mistakenly believes that Bella and Edward's half-vampire, half-human daughter, Renesmee, is an "immortal child," a being against vampire law. She reports the assumed violation to the Volturi, and the couple struggles to acquire evidence and testimony to prove that Renesmee is no danger to the vampires or to their secrets. The series ends happily, as Jacob makes peace with Bella's love for Edward and the Volturi leave the couple in peace.

The novels are written from the first-person point of view and relate events largely through Bella's perspective, although the epilogue of *Eclipse* and a segment in *Breaking Dawn* are related by Jacob Black. The vampires in the Twilight series differ in several ways from those that appear in other novels featuring vampires, a fact that Stephenie Meyer explains is the result of her not having been "informed about the canon vampires." "*Twilight* vampires have strong piercing teeth rather than fangs; they glitter in sunlight rather than burn; and they can drink both animal as well as human blood." Meyer claims that she was not concerned with creating stories about vampires and that her emphasis was upon creating relationships among her characters without regard to their status as human or vampire.

CENSORSHIP HISTORY

The novels in the Twilight series have been honored by critics. *Twilight* was named one of the Best Children's Books of 2005 by *School Library Journal* and identified as "Best Book of the Year" by *Publishers Weekly*, in addition to being named one of the "Top Books of 2008" by *USA Today*. In 2009, *New Moon* won the "Young Reader's Choice Award," and *Eclipse* and *Breaking Dawn* were both top-selling works. The reception by parents and educators has not always been as enthusiastic because of what reviewers have described as "adolescent erotic tension, but note that the sexual themes are tastefully presented and the star-crossed lovers remain chaste until married."

In October 2008, instructional materials specialist Linda Myers in the Capistrano unified school district ordered the library staff in the 12 middle schools of the district to remove the books in the Twilight series from their shelves and to send them to the school district office, which would place them in the high school libraries. She noted in her e-mail directive the school district coordinator of literacy programs had reviewed the books and "determined them to contain subject matter which is deemed too mature for our middle school–level students." Four days later, the school district reversed the decision and announced that the books would remain in the middle school libraries until a committee could undertake a more thorough review of the books and their content. Julia Hatchel, a spokesperson for the school district, assured a reporter for *School Library Journal* that "no one in the district is interested in banning the books." Instead, she noted, "We had some concern that we might be pushing this too quickly and held off on a decision until we have more to determine the proper placement. I think of it as a realignment." The district announced that they will follow an existing procedure to make the final decision: "There's a process that we go through to determine the appropriateness of placement of library books, and we will go through that process to determine the best placement for these books." The article notes that Hatchel had been a school principal when she participated in an earlier "realignment" in which she ordered an atlas containing images of ancient Greek and Roman statues removed from the district elementary schools because "It was inappropriate for kindergartners through fifth graders."

In April 2009, Deseret Books, a store owned by the Church of Jesus Christ of the Latter-day Saints, more commonly known as the Mormon Church, of which the author Stephenie Meyer is a member, announced that it had removed the Twilight series from sale in its 38 stores because the books "are met with mixed reviews." The chain did not so much ban the book as make it inconvenient to acquire, because would-be purchasers have to place a special order to buy it from Deseret Books.

Conservative Christian groups have been divided in their reactions to the series. The Christian Coalition of America gave serious thought in July 2009 to launching a campaign against both the books and the movies in the Twilight series after having attempted to ban the HARRY POTTER series several years earlier. In an interview with a reporter for *USA Today*, Roberta Combs, president of the Christian Coalition, claimed that despite the pro-abstinence stance of the books the presence of vampires as role models is troubling. "We can let our voices be heard, and anytime you do that you have an effect one way or another. These Twilight books are very disturbing books for family values. Teen marriage is not a standard, but the part that is more troubling is the vampire. It's just not normal for young people to idolize a vampire." In contrast, Gordon Robertson, chief executive officer of the Christian Broadcasting Network, which condemned the Harry Potter books "for fear that the books would inspire young people to try casting spells," has taken a more liberal view of the Twilight series and suggests using the books as a means of opening a dialogue with children. Kathryn Darden, a Christian freelance writer and frequent contributor to faith-based publications, observes that the distinction emerges because of references in the Bible: "One reason for the division is that witches are specifically condemned in the Bible, while vampires are not even mentioned."

In September 2009, school administrators and school librarians at Santa Sabina College in New South Wales determined that *Twilight* is "too racy for schoolchildren to read" and removed copies of the novel from the school library shelves. The school also cautioned parents that they should not allow their children to bring their private copies of the novel to school. The concern about the sexual and supernatural themes in the book motivated teachers in the school to run a seminar for Year 6 students during which they could discuss the themes and deal with what they considered to be issues of concern. Helen Schutz, the head librarian of the school, told a reporter for the *Daily Telegraph* that "We don't have a policy of censorship but the issues in the Twilight series are quite different from the Harry Potter classics. It is not available in our junior library for these reasons. . . . We wanted to make sure they realise [sic] it's fictitious and ensure they don't have a wrong grasp on reality." Not all Catholic schools in New South Wales agreed with the decision. Mark Rix, a spokesperson for the Catholic Education Office, stated that "Individual schools had to decide whether the books were suitable. It comes down to the discretion of the school to keep an eye on what the kids read. Some primary students are not ready to read *Twilight*. That said, some secondary students may not be either." At the Balmoral Queenwood School for Girls, only senior school students were allowed to borrow the novels from the school library, and school officials at St. Anthony's Catholic elementary school in Picton, New South Wales, refused students' requests to bring their copies of the books to school.

FURTHER READING

Barack, Lauren. "CA District Reinstates Twilight Books after Ban." *School Library Journal* (November 2009): 207–208.

Dickson, Lauren. "Schools Ban Racy Twilight Books by Stephenie Meyer." *Daily Telegraph*. Available online. URL: http://www.dailytelegraph.com.au/entertainment/schools-ban-racy-twilight-books-by-stephanie-meyer/story-e6frewyr-1225772090737. Accessed October 13, 2010.

Gaulin, Pam. "Banned Books Week: The Twilight Series." *Yahoo! News*. Available online. URL: http://news.yahoo.com/s/ac/20100924/en_ac/6833034_banned_books_week_the_twilight_series. Accessed September 26, 2010.

Martindale, Scott. "School District Briefly Bans Vampire Book from Middle Schools." *Orange County Register*. Available online. URL: http://www.ocregister.com/common/printer/view.php?db=ocregister&id=194237. Accessed September 27, 2010.

Puente, Maria. "Adults Fret That *Eclipse* Lacks Good Role Models for Teens." *USA Today*. Available online. URL: http://www.usatoday.com/life/movies/news/2010-07-07-eclipse07_CV_N.htm. Accessed September 27, 2010.

Thomas, Ethan. "Twilight Loses Luster with Deseret Books." *Deseret News*. Available online. URL: http: www.deseretnews.com/article/print/705299108/Twilight-loses-luster-with-Deseret -Book.html. Accessed September 26, 2010.

"Twilight Banned at Australian School—Deemed Too Racy." Available online. URL: http://www.lisnews.org/twilight_banned_australian_school_deemed_too_racy. Accessed September 26, 2010.

ULYSSES

Author: James Joyce
Original dates and places of publication: 1918, England; 1933, United States
Original publishers: Sylvia Beach's Shakespeare & Co. (England); Random House (United States)
Literary form: Novel

SUMMARY

Written in the stream-of-consciousness style, *Ulysses* takes places on one day, June 16, 1904, and relates the thoughts, feelings, words, and actions of Leopold Bloom, his wife Molly, and Stephen Dedalus. The novel was severely criticized because it explicitly describes physical and sensual pleasures, makes excretory references, and depicts sexual incidents in frank terms. In addition, complaints were made about the language, which contains numerous uses of "fuck," as well as frequent genital references such as "vagina," "scrotum," "penis," "hymen," and euphemisms for the genitals.

Most of the erotic references emerge through the characters of Bloom and Molly. Wandering through the city of Dublin and stopping at various bars throughout the day, Bloom reflects the journey of the epic hero Ulysses, who wandered 10 years before reaching his home and family. Bloom, who is obsessed with physical and sensual pleasures, recalls his sexual experiences while on his daylong journey, remembering one instance in which "Wildly I lay on her, kissed her; eyes, her lips, her stretch neck, beating, woman's breasts full . . . fat nipples upright." He is also explicit in excretory references, describing in detail a bowel movement in the outhouse and relating the physical sensations produced. He enjoys eating "grilled mutton kidneys which gave to his palate a fine tang of faintly scented urine."

Molly is equally concerned with excretory matter and sex. When she has run out of a skin cosmetic, she thinks, "I suppose Ill [sic] only have to wash in my piss." She thinks of sex with her lover, Blazes Boylan, noting, "I think he made them a bit firmer sucking them like that so long he made me thirsty titties he calls them I had to laugh yes this one anyhow stiff the nipple gets for the least thing Ill [sic] get him to keep that up." Molly describes the male sexual organ as a "tremendous big red brute of a thing" and "some kind of a thick crowbar" as she prepares to have sex near the end of the novel. In rhapsodizing about the encounter, she describes taking off her clothes and experiencing "one the size of that to make you feel full up . . . like a stallion driving it up into you. . . . I made him pull it out and do it on me considering how big it is so much the better in case any of it wasnt [sic] washed out properly the last time I let him finish it in me." The sexual references are numerous, but the descriptions emerge in a fragmentary manner, most appearing as interior monologues of the characters.

CENSORSHIP HISTORY

In 1922, the U.S. Department of the Post Office burned 500 copies of the novel when an attempt was made to import the book and court decisions ruled against the book. The first court trial of the book, however, actually occurred in 1921, when John Sumner, the secretary for the New York Society for the Suppression of Vice, and his followers seized an issue of the *Little Review*, which contained one chapter of the serialized version of the novel. The trial took place in the court of general sessions with magazine editors Margaret Head and Jane Heap as defendants. Author John Cowper Powys and playwright Philip Moeller, called as witnesses, testified that Joyce's style was too obscure to be understood by most people, but the court ruled against the *Little Review* and the novel.

Bowdlerized and bootlegged copies of the novel appeared, but no further action occurred until 1932, when the collector of Customs seized a copy of the book sent to Random House and declared it obscene under the Tariff Law of 1930. Random House intervened in the case because the publisher was, at that time, producing copies of the book with the intent to distribute it to the American reading public. The publisher demanded the court hearing required by the tariff law and asked for exculpation of the work. In pleas to the Federal Court of New York, Random House asked that the book be read in its entirety and that the passages declared to contain "the dirtiest language" be viewed in the context of the whole. In *United States v. One Book Entitled "Ulysses,"* 5 F. Supp. 182 (S.D.N.Y. 1933), later affirmed in *United States v. One Book Entitled "Ulysses,"* 72 F.2d 705 (2d Cir. 1934), Judge John M. Woolsey rejected the claims of obscenity, stating that despite the "unusual frankness" of the novel, "I do not anywhere detect the leer of the sensualist. I hold, therefore, that it is not pornographic." He further observed that he viewed the language and actions to be entirely consistent with the types of people whom Joyce describes. As to "the recurrent emergence of the theme of sex in the minds of his characters, it must always be remembered that his locale was Celtic and his season Spring." Judge Woolsey ruled that the book was not obscene when judged by its effect on the average man, *l'homme moyen sensuel*. He stated the following:

> In many places it seems to be disgusting, but although it contains, as I have mentioned above, many words usually considered dirty, I have not found anything that I consider to be dirt for dirt's sake. Each word of the book contributes like a bit of mosaic to the detail of the picture which Joyce is seeking to construct for his readers.

The government appealed the decision in the circuit court of appeals where, in *United States v. One Book Called "Ulysses,"* Judge Augustus Hand and Judge Learned Hand upheld the earlier decision. In the majority decision, they noted, "We think that *Ulysses* is a book of originality and sincerity of treatment, and that it has not the effect of promoting lust." The government chose not to appeal to the Supreme Court, and thus ended a decade-long struggle with the United States government and local censorship groups. It also provided a step toward freedom in the struggle between the moralists and publishers. In essence, the court ruled that the harm of an "obscene" book must be judged not from reading select passages but as a result of the whole book. Therefore, if the book as a whole had merit and the allegedly obscene parts were germane to the purpose of the book, then the book could not be viewed as obscene. In summing up the new interpretation of the law, Judge Augustus Hand stated:

> We believe that the proper test of whether a given book is obscene is its dominant effect. (I.e., is promotion of lust the dominant effect of reading the whole book?) In applying this test, relevancy of the objectionable parts to the theme, the established reputation of the work in the estimation of approved critics, if the book is modern, and the verdict of the past, if it is ancient, are persuasive pieces of evidence; for works of art are not likely to sustain a high position with no better warrant for their existence than their obscene content.

A significant result of the verdict was that it led judges and prosecutors to examine a book in its entirety rather than according to isolated passages. The decision also admitted *Ulysses* into the United States.

The controversy over *Ulysses* appeared to have been settled by the court in 1932, and the length of the novel and its difficult language have made it an unpopular choice for students when it has appeared on high school suggested reading lists. As a result, Apple's decision to demand cuts from *Ulysses Seen*, a graphic adaptation of the novel by Rob Berry and Joseph Levitas, before the company would approve the application for use on their iPhone and iPad surprised many people and resulted in such cyber headlines as "Joyce's *Ulysses* Banned Again—by Apple," "A Publishing Tradition: Apple Censors Joyce's *Ulysses*—a Century After the U.S. Did the Same," and "Tiny Cartoon Penis Disqualifies Ulysses Comic from iPad Store." The offending panel contains the sketch of a nude, physically out-of-shape Buck Mulligan diving into the sea. Although the application does not contain offensive language and the cartoon is an abstract rendering, which the authors thought they "might have to pixelate or cover with 'fig leaves,' " Apple's policy forced them "to either scrap the idea of moving the tablet with Apple or re-design our pages." Berry and Levitas chose to crop the images "to remove any offending genitalia." The outcry against Apple's act of censorship was quick and strong. By June 16, 2010, the day that Bloomsday is celebrated worldwide by readings from Joyce's tome, Apple reversed its decision. Berry told an interviewer, "They said they had decided to change their policy in our case and we should resubmit the original unedited versions of all the pages. They told us they'd push it through for Bloomsday." Eight hours after Berry and Levitas resubmitted *Ulysses Unseen*, the application was available from the iTunes Store "for free download but restricted to users aged 17 or older."

FURTHER READING

"Another Repeal: Joyce's *Ulysses* Is Legal at Last." *Nation*, December 20, 1933, p. 693.

Arnold, Bruce. *The Scandal of "Ulysses": The Sensational Life of a Twentieth-Century Masterpiece*. New York: St. Martin's, 1994.

Brown, Damon. "A Publishing Tradition: Apple Censors Joyce's Ulysses—a Century After the the U.S. Did the Same." Available online. URL: http://www.bnet.com/blogmedia/a-publishing-tradition-apple-censors-joyces-ulysses-a-century-after-the-us-did-the-same/8534. Accessed August 21, 2010.

Bryer, J. R. "Joyce, *Ulysses*, and the *Little Review*." *South Atlantic Quarterly* 66 (Spring 1967): 148–64.

Ernst, Morris L., and Alan U. Schwartz. *Censorship: The Search for the Obscene*. New York: Macmillan, 1964.

"In Reversal, Apple Approves 'Ulysses' Comic with Nudity." Available online. URL: http://www.google.com/hostednews/afp/article/ALeqM5i5NWT-KZ7ilmOyU47WzdRw28SmxA. Accessed August 23, 2010.

Kelleher, Kevin. "Joyce's *Ulysses* Banned Again—by Apple." Available online. URL: http://www.thebigmoney.com/blogs/app-economy/2010/06/09/joyce-s-ulysses-banned-again-apple-not-government?page=full. Accessed August 21, 2010.

Marcuse, Ludwig. *The History of an Indignation.* London: MacGibbon & Key, 1965.

Paul, James C. N., and Murray L. Schwartz. *Federal Censorship: Obscenity in the Mail.* New York: Free Press, 1961.

St. John-Stevas, Norman. *Obscenity and the Law.* London: Secker & Warburg, 1956.

Spence, Nick. "Ulysses Seen iPad Webcomic Gets Apple Approval After Cuts." Available online. URL: http://www.macworld.com/article/151821/2010/06/ulysses.webcomic.html. Accessed August 17, 2010.

United States President's Commission on Obscenity and Pornography. *The Report of the Commission on Obscenity and Pornography.* New York: Random House, 1970.

VENUS AND TANNHAUSER (UNDER THE HILL)

Author: Aubrey Beardsley

Original dates and places of publication: 1903, United States; 1904, England

Original publishers: Dodd, Mead and Company (United States); John Lane Company (England)

Literary form: Novel

SUMMARY

Venus and Tannhauser contains constant references to the sensuality of Venus and her court, including homosexual practices, orgies, and such perversions as bestiality. The tone of the work is fantasy, and the literary style and the minute descriptions of the characters, as well as what they wear and say, provide a mocking air that blunts the sexual tone of the work.

Beardsley appeared to have consciously sought to shock his readers, as he has Venus, the queen of his fantasy empire, engage in sexual play with her tame unicorn named Adolphe. In one incident, Venus tries mightily to please her pet:

> Poor Adolphe! How happy he was, touching the Queen's breasts with his quick tongue-tip. . . . After the first charming interchange of affectionate delicacies was over, the unicorn lay down upon his side and, closing his eyes, beat his stomach wildly with the mark of manhood.
>
> Venus caught that stunning member in her hands and laid her cheek along it; but few touches were wanted to consummate the creature's pleasure.

Other passages that have been identified as offensive contain excretory references:

Felix always attended Venus upon her little latrinal excursions, holding her, serving her, and making much of all she did. To undo her things, lift her skirts, to wait and watch the coming, to dip a lip or finger in the royal output, to stain himself deliciously with it, to lie beneath her as her favours fell, to carry off the crumpled, crotted paper—these were the pleasures of that young man's life.

Passages of both types were expurgated when the work first appeared.

CENSORSHIP HISTORY

Venus and Tannhauser was not published in unexpurgated form until 1959, when Grove Press published the novel under the title *Under the Hill.* The work first appeared in heavily expurgated form in the January 1897 and April 1898 issues of *The Savoy,* and publisher Arthur Symons hailed it as reflecting "undoubted, singular, literary ability." In 1903, Dodd, Mead and Company published an equally heavily expurgated version that was later "mutilated" further when John Lane published another version in 1904.

In 1954, Samuel Roth, denounced by the post office as the "leading smut king" in America, was charged with 26 indictments of obscenity. Among these counts was the charge that the fragment of *Venus and Tannhauser* included in volume three of Roth's quarterly magazine *American Aphrodite* was obscene. The government obtained the needed evidence when a post office inspector, using the pseudonym of Archie Lovejoy, ordered and received that issue of the magazine through the mails. Roth was convicted on 22 counts of distributing "obscene materials," sentenced to five years in jail, and fined $5,000. The conviction was upheld in *Roth v. United States,* 237 F.2d 796 (2d Cir. 1956) in the United States Court of Appeals, Second Circuit, on September 18, 1956. Roth then appealed the decision to the United States Supreme Court, which ruled on the constitutionality of the statute under which Roth was convicted. In a decision in *Roth v. United States,* 354 U.S. 476 (1957), the Supreme Court voted 6 to 3 to uphold Roth's sentence.

FURTHER READING

Ernst, Morris L., and Alan U. Schwartz. *Censorship: The Search for the Obscene.* New York: Macmillan, 1964.

De Grazia, Edward. *Girls Lean Back Everywhere: The Law of Obscenity and the Assault on Genius.* New York: Random House, 1992.

Lewis, Felice Flanery. *Literature, Obscenity, & Law.* Carbondale: Southern Illinois University Press, 1976.

Magrath, C. Peter. "The Obscenity Cases: Grapes of Roth." *Supreme Court Review* 139 (1966): 9–13.

THE WILD PALMS

Author: William Faulkner
Original date and place of publication: 1939, United States
Original publisher: Random House
Literary form: Novel

SUMMARY

The Wild Palms counterpoints two stories, each containing a male character who is forced into a relationship with a woman who eventually becomes his inadvertent destroyer. In "The Wild Palms," medical student Harry Wilbourne falls in love with Charlotte Rittenmeyer, married and the mother of two children. The two run away together to find the romantic love that Charlotte craves, but Wilbourne's inability to support them adequately places the couple in an increasingly perilous financial situation. When Charlotte becomes pregnant and demands that Wilbourne perform an abortion, he resists at first and then gives in to her demands.

Charlotte dies of the complications, feeling angered and betrayed. Yet, before dying, she makes her husband promise that he will not prosecute Wilbourne. Rittenmeyer, however, does prosecute but then offers Wilbourne cyanide as an alternative to life imprisonment. Recalling Charlotte's motto, "Between grief and nothing I will take grief," Wilbourne refuses and prepares to spend his life in prison.

"Old Man," the second story, parallels the first but reverses the situation. A convict, imprisoned after committing a robbery to obtain gifts for his girlfriend who soon marries another man, is on a work gang when a flood arises. He is sent to rescue a pregnant woman from a tree, which he does, but their boat rushes off course, stranding them for seven weeks on an island. In that time, the woman gives birth to a son with the help of the convict, who uses a tin-can lid to cut the umbilical cord.

He protects the woman and her child until they can return home, where he is promptly imprisoned and given 10 additional years in jail for attempting to escape. Rather than protest, he takes his punishment, viewing prison as a sanctuary. He lands in the same prison as Wilbourne. The irony of the two stories is that the apparently unheroic convict, a man who fears women, has acted heroically while the romantic Wilbourne has failed in his effort to play the role of hero.

The stories are relatively free of graphic sexuality, but censors objected to the discussion of abortion and the graphic description of Charlotte's pregnancy in "The Wild Palms." In one scene in that story, Charlotte and Wilbourne share a room with another couple and hear a "stallion-like surge from the other bed, the violent blanket-muffled motion ceasing into the woman's panting moans and at times a series of pure screams tumbling over one another." This is followed by "fierce breathing, the panting and shuddering woman moans." Also objectionable were the references to the birth of the baby in "Old Man" and the cutting of the cord.

CENSORSHIP HISTORY

The Wild Palms received complimentary reviews when it was first published, and no protests arose regarding its content until nearly a decade later. In 1948, *The Wild Palms* was one of nine works identified as obscene in criminal proceedings in the Court of Quarter Sessions in Philadelphia County, Pennsylvania. (See God's Little Acre for a complete discussion of the case.) Indictments were brought by State District Attorney John H. Maurer against five booksellers who were charged with possessing and intending to sell *The Wild Palms* and other allegedly obscene works, including Erskine Caldwell's God's Little Acre, Harold Robbins's *NEVER LOVE A STRANGER*, James Farrell's Studs Lonigan, and *A WORLD I NEVER MADE*, Calder Willingham's *END AS A MAN*, and Faulkner's Sanctuary.

Judge Curtis Bok, who presided in *Commonwealth v. Gordon et al.*, 66 D.&C. 101 (1949), stated in his decision that "the redeeming feature of this tale ['The Wild Palms'] is that an acid loneliness comes through, the awful loneliness that pervades lost people, even in company. No one could envy these two miserable creatures." He discussed at length the concern whether in censoring obscenity the court were contravening the principles of freedom of speech and of the press. Judge Bok concluded, "I hold that the books before me are not sexually impure and pornographic, and are therefore not obscene, lewd, lascivious, filthy, indecent, or disgusting."

The Wild Palms was banned in Ireland on April 16, 1954. A prohibition order was published in the *Iris Oifigiuil*, "the only official source from which booksellers [and readers] might learn of a new prohibition order," in which all articles blacklisted by the Irish Board of Censors were listed. Based on tenets established in the Censorship of Publications Bill of 1928, the Irish Board of Censors found the novel "obscene" and filled with "indecency." The work was officially banned from sale in Ireland until the introduction of the Censorship Publications Bill in 1967 reduced to 12 years the duration of a prohibition order, and the work was among 5,000 banned titles released.

FURTHER READING

Adams, Michael. *Censorship: The Irish Experience*. Tuscaloosa: University of Alabama Press, 1968.
McHaney, Thomas L. *William Faulkner's* The Wild Palms: *A Study*. Jackson: University of Mississippi, 1975.
Page, Sally R. *Faulkner's Women: Characterization and Meaning*. De Land, Fla.: Everett/Edwards, 1972.

WOMEN IN LOVE

Author: D. H. Lawrence
Original date and place of publication: 1920, United States
Original publisher: Thomas Seltzer
Literary form: Novel

SUMMARY

Women in Love deals with the psychological explorations and the interrelationships of sisters Ursula and Gudrun Brangwen as they deal with love and life in a small English mining town. Alike in many respects, the sisters mirror the goals and desires of other modern young women of the early 20th century in their reservations about getting married and having children, as well as in their hatred of their middle-class origins. Ursula, however, is different from Gudrun in her ability to respond both spiritually and physically to Rupert Birken, although the two struggle mightily before Ursula and Rupert reach an understanding in which "He wanted sex to revert to the level of the other appetites, to be regarded as a functional process, not as a fulfillment." When they do consummate their relationship, Lawrence blends the physical passion with a spiritual bonding.

> They threw off their clothes, and he gathered her to him, and found her, found the pure lambent reality of her forever invisible flesh. Quenched, inhuman, his fingers upon her unrevealed nudity were the fingers of silence upon silence. . . . She had her desire fulfilled. He had his desire fulfilled.

In another segment of the novel, their sexual interaction is more fully revealed: "Kneeling on the hearth-rug before him, she put her arms around his loins, and put her face against his thighs."

Gudrun, on the other hand, and her lover Gerald are too self-absorbed to establish any true communication, and references to their sexual relationship are brief.

Beyond the sensual passages between Ursula and Rupert, critics have objected to Rupert's desire for intimacy with Gerald Crich. Rupert believes that men are capable of establishing an intimate friendship that a man can never attain with a woman. At one point in the novel when the two men wrestle in the nude, Rupert believes that he and Gerald are about to reach a plateau of trust and understanding, but Gerald appears unable to surrender his feelings entirely to anyone.

CENSORSHIP HISTORY

Overall, although *Women in Love* does not contain language that is usually identified as "obscene," nor are passages graphically sexual, the sexual relationship between Ursula and Rupert and the homoerotic relationship of Rupert and Gerald evoked strong objections from critics. The novel first appeared in 1920 in a limited edition of 1,250, marked "for subscribers only." The title page omitted Seltzer's imprint and carried, instead, the phrase "Privately Printed" to protect the company from attacks by censors. That move alone might have signaled to would-be censors that even the publisher thought the book too erotic to be published as part of the company's usual list. Two years later, Seltzer published the novel in a regular trade edition with the company imprint. In 1922, the limited edition of *Women in Love* became one of three titles published by Thomas Seltzer that were involved in a well-publicized censorship case. The other two were Arthur Schnitzler's CASANOVA'S HOMECOMING and the anonymous A YOUNG GIRL'S DIARY. The magistrate's court ruled in favor of the publisher.

In 1923, Supreme Court Justice John Ford tried to suppress *Women in Love* after his daughter brought the book home from the circulating library that had recommended it to her. Ford founded the Clean Books League and worked with John Sumner, secretary of the New York Society for the Suppression of Vice, to achieve the passage of a "clean books" bill in the New York legislature. He also favored upholding and strengthening existing obscenity laws. Incensed by the action, Lawrence sent Ford a telegram from Taos, quoted on page 580 of the February 24, 1923, issue of *Publishers Weekly*:

> Let Judge John Ford confine his judgment to courts of law, and not try to perch in seats that are too high for him. Also let him take away the circulating library tickets from Miss Ford, lest worse befall her. She evidently needs an account at a candy shop, because, of course, 'Women in Love' wasn't written for the Ford family. . . . Father and mother and daughter should all leave the tree of knowledge alone. The Judge won't succeed in chopping it down, with his horrified hatchet. Many better men have tried and failed.

FURTHER READING

Boyer, Paul S. *Purity in Print: The Vice-Society Movement and Book Censorship in America.* New York: Scribner, 1968.
"Censorship Beaten in New York Case." *Publishers Weekly*, September 16, 1922, pp. 801–904.
De Grazia, Edward. *Girls Lean Back Everywhere: The Law of Obscenity and the Assault on Genius.* New York: Random House, 1992.
Ford, John. *Criminal Obscenity, a Plea for Its Suppression.* New York: Revell, 1926.
Lawrence, D. H. "On Obscenity." *Publishers Weekly*, February 23, 1923, p. 580.
Loth, David. *The Erotic in Literature.* New York: Dorset, 1961.

WOMEN ON TOP: HOW REAL LIFE HAS CHANGED WOMEN'S SEXUAL FANTASIES

Author: Nancy Friday
Original date and place of publication: 1991, New York
Original publisher: Simon & Schuster
Literary form: Nonfiction

SUMMARY

Women on Top contains an accumulation of sexual fantasies, compiled and documented by Nancy Friday as a followup to her earlier books about women's sexual fantasies, *My Secret Garden* (1973) and *Forbidden Flowers* (1975). Published in 1991, nearly twenty years after the first book, the entries are, as the introduction states, written by women "for the most part in their twenties, the generation that followed the sexual revolution and the momentum of the women's movement." The book is divided into three parts, "Report from the Erotic Interior," "Separating Sex and Love: In Praise of Masturbation," and "The Fantasies."

In Part I, "Report from the Erotic Interior," Friday offers a prelude to the explicit sexual fantasies that follow and observes that great differences exist between the sexual desires voiced by women in the present book in contrast with those voiced in 1973, the generation of their mothers.

> Here is a collective imagination that could not have existed twenty years ago, when women had no vocabulary, no permission, and no shared identity in which to describe their sexual feelings. Those first voices were tentative and filled with guilt, not for having done anything but simply for daring to admit the inadmissible: that they had erotic thoughts that sexually aroused them.

The sexual fantasies detailed in *Women on Top* are far from tentative. Friday compiled the material from 1980 through 1990, selecting from interviews and letters women wrote to her after she issued invitations at the end of her previous books to women who wished to contribute to a future book about women's sexual fantasies. In the request, promising anonymity, she provided a Post Office box number to which contributors could send their submissions. In the book, Friday categorizes the sexual fantasies into three chapters that reflect the most commonly expressed themes: women in control, women with women, and sexually insatiable women. The author represents this accumulation of detailed sexual fantasies as more of a political and social statement than as an effort to titillate, as accusers have charged. She observes that in the early 1970s the women's movement for economic and political equality and the sexual revolution appeared to be "one campaign," but that time has shown that to be untrue: "Society adapted more readily to women's entry into the workplace than to their growing into full sexuality. It is seldom discussed but nonetheless true that economic parity is less threatening to the system than sexual equality."

Friday contends that the social and legal climate has increasingly sought to deprive women of the right to control their own bodies and, even as women move closer to economic parity, they are being forced into "a form of sexual slavery" as society deprives them of the right to fully express their sexuality. In highly charged language in Part I, the author derides men for seeking to control women's sexuality and "the angry feminists, having little sympathy for men of the women who loved men, [who] turned up their noses at the sexual revolution." She offers the antidote to these ills in the form of the MTV generation, "whose fantasies fill this book," and especially such exhibitionistic singers and performers as Madonna.

> There stands Madonna, hand on crotch, preaching to her sisters: Masturbate. Madonna is no male masturbatory fantasy. She is a sex symbol/model for other women. Nor is she just a lesbian fantasy—though she is that, too—but rather she embodies sexual woman/working woman, and I think you could put mother in there too. I can see Madonna with a baby in her arms, and, yes, the hand still on her crotch.

The second part of the book, "Separating Sex and Love: In Praise of Masturbation," provides a historic view of society's condemnation of female masturbation and identifies many of the female disorders once attributed to the action by eminent physicians, as well as the cure that was once common: the clitoridectomy. "That was in your grandmother's or great-grandmother's time, when some of the most eminent, celebrated surgeons in the land routinely took knife in hand and skillfully removed various parts of a woman's genitalia for reasons of insanity, hysteria, and, oh yes, hygiene." In contrast, the author asserts that masturbation represents sexual freedom, and she lauds the role of sexual fantasy in providing that freedom. She explores the history of society's view of both male and female masturbation in sections titled "What We Win from Masturbation," "The Mother/Daughter Deal," "How Masturbation Helps Men Separate Love and Sex," "The Nice Girl Rules," and "The Swept Away Phenomenon."

Additional sections in Part II also question if social norms have really changed as much as those who lived through the sexual revolution of the 1960s profess they have. Friday discusses "The Cloaca Concept" [*cloaca* is Latin for "sewer"] and advises women that a large portion of their aversion to masturbation lies in "their repugnance to the clitoris, urethra, vagina, and anus [that] have come to thought of as one filthy, indistinguishable mass 'down there.'" Blaming mothers for imparting this viewpoint, Friday asks, "How can we think well of ourselves if we harbor a sewer?"

In the final section of Part II, "What Is a Real Woman?," the author suggests ways in which women can free their daughters from the negative feelings and sexual restrictions experienced by past generations of women. She reviews in brief the most popular sexual fantasies reported by women and urges mothers to encourage such fantasies, ending the section with "Mother, let your little girl masturbate."

The third and most lengthy section of *Women on Top* presents detailed sexual fantasies of women who range in age from 14 to 62, although the majority of the respondents are in their 20s. As a means of organization, Friday divides the fantasies into three categories and then subdivides the categories even further to create thematic unity. The first group of fantasies is entitled "Seductive, Sometimes Sadistic, Sexually Controlling Women" and contains the subcategories "The Great Seductress: The Power of the Pleasure Giver," "Good Mother/Good Orgasm," "All I Want Is to Control Everything," "Angry Women/Sadistic Fantasies," and "Look at Me! The Power of the Exhibitionist." The second group of fantasies, entitled "Women with Women" includes "Only Another Woman Knows," "Am I Gay?," and "The Other Woman as Mirror." In "Insatiable Women: The Cry for 'More!' " fantasies are categorized as "The Thrill of the Forbidden," "Women with Bigger Appetites Than Men," "One Woman, Many Fantasies," " More Oral, Please," "Taking It All In," "Groups," "Watching Two Men Having Sex," and "If I Had a Penis."

The carefully developed categories are clear indicators of the nature of the fantasies that appear in each. Although the content of the fantasies and the ages and state of life of each respondent vary—single, married, virgins, experienced, orgasmic, nonorgasmic, working class, professional, and so forth—all of the sexual fantasies appear to have been selected for their attention to detail and to the lack of reticence on the respondents' parts to express their desires in the clearest language possible. The female and male genitalia are spoken of in scientifically/anatomically correct language, as well as in slang, with as many references to "vagina" and "penis" as to "cunt" and "cock," and so forth.

Friday provides no final summation chapter to the book and allows the final story in the section "If I Had a Penis" to end the work.

CENSORSHIP HISTORY

Women on Top has experienced challenges and bans in several public library systems, for reasons that have included objections to the frank language used to concerns that the fantasies related by women were "over the top."

In Buford, Georgia, in 1997 Connie Cosby and Sheila Blahnik filled out complaint forms about the compilation of women's sexual fantasies and submitted them to the Gwinnett Public Library. Cosby told a reporter for the *Atlanta Journal-Constitution* that she did "not think the incestuous fantasies in Nancy Friday's book 'Women on Top' were suitable reading for children." The complaints prompted a staff review of the book and its removal from the library. Library director Jo Ann Pinder told reporters that the book was removed mainly because it had been purchased in 1991 when the book was a best seller and the author was on a national publicity tour. She said that it is no longer popular at the library: "Some books are right for the time and wrong at others." Library board chairwoman Dorothy Roberts observed, "We did change the material review process, and the book no longer fell under the guidelines for the nonfiction collection." After the decision was made to remove the book, complainant Cosby expressed shock that the book was removed altogether and said that she had just wanted the book removed from the general collection.

In Gainesville, Georgia, in December 1994, 150 Hall County residents appeared at a library board meeting and demanded that the Chestatee Regional Library System remove *Women on Top* from the library. The library turned the complaint over to the book review committee that handled book challenges. In late December 1994, the committee report was issued in which committee members labeled the book as "pornographic and obscene" and claimed that it lacks "literary merit" before the committee voted 4-2 to remove the book from the library. The library board waited until January 1995 to take final action on the book. When the library board met in late January 1995, the vote on whether to remove *Women on Top* from the library was split 5-5. In article that appeared in the *Atlanta Journal-Constitution*, board members said that the motion to remove the book died with the split vote. The 60 citizens who attended the meeting disagreed, but the library board cited library policy. Board members who had supported retention of the book told onlookers that only a court of law can decide whether a book "declared obscene and not subject to Constitutional protection should be removed." Board members expressed a reluctance to "open up endless sorts of ramifications." The chairman of the Coalition of Concerned Citizens, Don DeLozier, told a reporter, "This is a moral issue the community is upset about and it will not die."

Two weeks after the library board's 5-5 vote defeated the proposal to remove *Women on Top* from the library, the library board announced that they had called an emergency meeting for February 15, 1995, to take a second vote on the issue. One member had been absent, and the board chairwoman admitted that she had been mistaken when she cast her vote that produced a tie and allowed the book to stay on the shelves. As chairperson, she should cast a vote only to break a tie. When a new vote was taken, the board voted 5-4 to remove the book.

FURTHER READING

"Editorial: Ideas for Our Community: A Library for Everyone." *Atlanta Constitution*, July 21, 1997, p. A1.

"Library Restrictions vs. Parental Restrictions." *Atlanta Journal–Constitution*, March 30, 1997, p. J9.

McCafferty, Dennis. "Library Board Refuses to Ban Sex Fantasy Book." *Atlanta Constitution*, January 25, 1995, p. B2.

———. "*Women on Top* May Yet Be Pulled from Hall Library." *Atlanta Constitution*, February 8, 1995, p. C2.

Sibley, Celia, and Beth Burkstrand. "Banning of Book Surprises Petitioner." *Atlanta Journal-Constitution*, May 19, 1997, p. J1.

———. "Gwinnett Libraries Ban *Women on Top*." *Atlanta Constitution*. March 19, 1997, p. B2.

Skube, Michael. "The Search for Smut Ends in a Circular Rut." *Atlanta Journal–Constitution*, July 10, 1994, p. N10.

Torpy, Bill. "Library Committee Votes to Ban Book." *Atlanta Journal-Constitution*, December 30, 1994, p. D3.

A YOUNG GIRL'S DIARY

Author: Anonymous
Original dates and places of publication: 1919, Switzerland; 1921, England; 1921, United States
Original publishers: Internationaler Psychoanalytischer Verlag (Switzerland); George Allen & Unwin (England); Thomas Seltzer (United States)
Literary form: Journal

SUMMARY

The anonymously written *A Young Girl's Diary* contains a preface by Sigmund Freud, who proclaimed the diary to be a "gem" that was the first work "enabling us to see so clearly into the soul of a young girl, belonging to our social and cultural stratum, during the years of puberal development." The work is a diary written by the pseudonymous Grete Lanier, an adolescent Viennese girl of the upper class who writes without self-consciousness about her reflections on sex.

The work is divided into four parts, each covering a year in Grete's life from the ages of 11 through 14 ½, when her father dies of a stroke. Now orphaned, she and her sister are sent to live with relatives in a provincial city. In one passage, the writer observes that her friend told her that "when one is dark under the eyes one has *it* and that when one gets a baby then one doesn't have it any more until one gets another." She also reflects that her friend Bertha "told us how one gets it, but I didn't really believe what she said. . . . She said it must happen every night, for if not they don't have a baby. . . . That's why they have their beds so close together. People call them *marriage beds!!*" The final part of the journal contains the author's excited and hazy impression of what she observes while watching the young couple living next door to her engaged in sexual intercourse.

CENSORSHIP HISTORY

In 1921, Sir Archibald Bodkin, director of public prosecutions in England, summoned publisher Stanley Unwin to his office and shouted loudly that *A Young Girl's Diary*, published recently by Allen & Unwin, was "Filth, my dear Sir, filth." Ready to refute the charge, Unwin pointed out that each invoice for the book carried a label that stated, "This psychological study is intended for the use of members of the educational, medical and legal professions only." Bodkin retorted that one of his policemen had purchased a copy; he then warned Unwin that "in the future you must obtain the name, address and occupation of the bookseller's customer before supplying the book." Bodkin pressed Unwin "to eliminate the objectionable passages and then distribute it" but backed down when Unwin asked him to identify specifically the "objectionable" passages. In reply to Unwin's request for specificity, Bodkin wrote,

> I must make it quite clear to you that to adopt any such suggestion would place me in the position of acting as a censor, a position I entirely decline to fill and one which would be contrary to my duty to fill.

In 1922, the limited edition of *A Young Girl's Diary*, translated from German by Eden and Cedar Paul, became involved in a well-publicized censorship case with two other Seltzer titles: Arthur Schnitzler's CASANOVA'S HOMECOMING and D. H. Lawrence's WOMEN IN LOVE. John Sumner, secretary of the New York Society for the Suppression of Vice, led raids that seized copies of the books from the publisher's office and took stock of *A Young Girl's Diary* from shelves at Brentano's bookstore. The society also arrested Mary H. Marks, a clerk at Womrath's circulating library chain, for lending *A Young Girl's Diary* to a borrower, and they also removed stock of the three books from store shelves. The magistrate's court ruled in favor of the publisher, and Mary Marks, who had been made a codefendant in the trial, was also cleared. (See *Casanova's Homecoming*.) After Magistrate George W. Simpson in Municipal Term court rendered his decision, counsel for the defendants Jonah J. Goldstein announced plans to sue John Sumner and the New York Society for the Suppression of Vice for damages incurred during the six-year suit. In his decision, Magistrate Simpson cited *People v. Brainard & Harper & Bros.*, 192 App. Div. 816, and wrote, "Books will not be banned by law merely because they do not serve a useful purpose nor teach any moral lesson." He wrote further that he had read the book "with sedulous care" and determined:

> Following the tests laid down by the cases in this State, both as to the manner of judging publications and a to the meaning of the statutes, I do not find anything in these books which may be considered obscene. On the contrary, I find that each of them is a distinct contribution to the literature of the present day. Each of the books deals with one or another of the phases of present thought.

One year later, Sumner again secured a grand jury indictment against *A Young Girl's Diary* and *Casanova's Homecoming*. In this case, the presiding judge declared immaterial the fact that the judge in the previous case had allowed experts to testify regarding the merits of the books. Instead, without testimony from experts, the books were found to be obscene. Faced with financial difficulties that prevented the expense of further litigation, Seltzer withdrew the books from circulation and agreed to destroy the plates. The criminal case was withdrawn but Seltzer's firm never recovered.

FURTHER READING

"Book Censorship Beaten in Court." *New York Times*, September 13, 1922, p. 20.

Boyer, Paul S. *Purity in Print: The Vice-Society Movement and Book Censorship in America.* New York: Scribner, 1968.

"Censorship Beaten in New York Court." *Publishers Weekly*, September 16, 1922, pp. 801–804.

"Confer in Boston on Banned Books." *New York Times*, March 13, 1927, p. 2.

Gunn, Daniel, and Patrick Guyomard. Introduction to *A Young Girl's Diary*, edited by Daniel Gunn and Patrick Guyomard. New York: Doubleday, 1990.

"The Law and the Censor." *New York Times*, September 14, 1922, p. 21.

Tanselle, G. Thomas. "The Thomas Seltzer Imprint." *Papers of the Bibliographic Society of America* 58 (Fourth Quarter 1964): 380–416.

Unwin, Sir Stanley. *The Truth about Publishing*. London: Allen & Unwin, 1960.

BIOGRAPHICAL PROFILES

ALVAREZ, JULIA (1950–   )

Julia Alvarez was born in New York City of Dominican parents who returned, when she was three months old, to their native Dominican Republic, where she lived for the first 10 years of her life. Her father was involved in rebel political activities, and the family was forced to the United States when Alvarez was 10, providing a difficult assimilation experience that served as the inspiration for her widely acclaimed novel *How the García Girls Lost Their Accents*, the first novel by a Dominican-American woman to attract critical acclaim in the United States. Alvarez has depicted her life and the histories of other Dominican Americans in her novels and uses her ability to connect with a reading public to highlight the particular problems of women of Hispanic descent. She has been acclaimed by critics as being the most influential Latina writer of her generation.

ANAYA, RUDOLFO (1937–   )

Born in a small rural village in New Mexico, Rudolfo Anaya has an intimate knowledge of the legends and the superstitions, as well as the farming and ranching traditions, that he depicts in his novels. His insight-filled work depicting the lives and traditions of Mexican Americans has brought him literary acclaim as one of the founders of Chicano literature and earned him the praise of critics. Anaya's first novel, *Bless Me, Ultima*, (1972) won the Premio Quinto Sol award and has become a classic. It was included among works selected for the Big Read, a community arts program created by the National Endowment for the Humanities. In 2007, the novel was selected to be among works chosen for the United States Academic Decathlon. Anaya has also written novels for children and young adults and is the author of a mystery series starring detective Sonny Boca.

APOLLINAIRE, GUILLAUME (1880–1918)

Born Wilhelm Apollinaris de Kostrowitzki in Rome, Italy, the French poet, theorist, and art critic was a major force in the avant-garde movements of early 20th-century art. Among his noteworthy contributions were a famed analysis and defense of cubism and his creation of the term *surrealism*. He also wrote fiction, including the highly controversial *Memoirs of a Young Rakehell* and *The Debauched Hospadar*.

ARBITER, GAIUS PETRONIUS (PETRONIUS) (d. A.D. 66)

Born in Rome, Italy, at an undetermined date, the prose and verse author left no historical evidence of his life, aside from mentions of him in the 16th book of the *Annals* of Tacitus. *The Satyricon* (A.D. 60) was censored in 1921 for its openly sexual descriptions.

ATWOOD, MARGARET (1939–)

Born in Ottawa, Ontario, the Canadian poet and novelist is also a political activist. Recurrent themes in her work revolve around the interlocked issues of power and language and the struggle of individuals, particularly women, to persevere in an indifferent society. All these elements come together in *The Handmaid's Tale* (1986), a hotly debated novel about state control of reproduction in a totalitarian state.

AUEL, JEAN (1936–)

Born in Chicago, Illinois, the former technical writer, circuit board designer, and credit manager first conceived of *The Clan of the Cave Bear* (1980) as a short story. After developing the story into the controversial 450,000-word novel, she followed with two sequels, *The Valley of Horses* (1982) and *The Mammoth Hunters* (1985).

BALZAC, HONORÉ DE (1799–1850)

Born in Tours, France, the novelist and short story writer was a founder of the realistic school and faithfully depicted ordinary and undistinguished lives. *Droll Stories (Contes Drolatiques)* (1832), a departure from realism, attracted the attention of censors for its excretory references and graphic sexual descriptions.

BAUDELAIRE, CHARLES (1821–1867)

Born in Paris, France, the poet, critic, and translator was a key member of the French Symbolist movement. He introduced the works of Edgar Allan Poe to Europe through his translations, making them French classics. *The Flowers of Evil (Les Fleurs du Mal)* (1857), the only volume of poetry published in Baudelaire's lifetime, was the object of a highly publicized censorship trial and was later banned for its sexual and lesbian references.

BEARDSLEY, AUBREY (1872–1898)

Born in Brighton, England, the artist and illustrator was part of the English aesthetic movement of the 1890s. Known for his black-and-white drawings on erotic and fabled subjects, he was one of the most important illustrators of his day. His few efforts at fiction were collected as *Venus and Tannhauser (Under the Hill)* (1904), a work censored for its sexual and excretory imagery.

BLUME, JUDY (1938–   )

Born in Elizabeth, New Jersey, the author writes books for young people and has earned a reputation for dealing candidly with problems of early adolescence.Most of her more than a dozen books have ignited challenges as to their appropriateness for school libraries and classrooms due to their language, religious references, and sexual content, especially *Then Again, Maybe I Won't* (1971), *Blubber* (1974), and *Forever* (1975).

BOCCACCIO, GIOVANNI (1313–1375)

Born in Uffizi, Florence, and acknowledged as the father of Italian prose style, the pastoral allegorist, epic poet, and novella writer is also viewed by critics as one of the first Renaissance humanists. His work influenced the writings of Geoffrey Chaucer and William Shakespeare, despite the notoriety that the 100 tales of *The Decameron* have engendered over the centuries.

BODENHEIM, MAXWELL (1893–1954)

Born in Clinton, Mississippi, the poet, novelist, and playwright was influenced in his early work by the Romantic and Imagist movements. His notoriously bohemian life ended when he and his third wife were found murdered in a dingy, heatless room. *Replenishing Jessica* (1927) became the target of censors and the subject of a widely publicized trial because of its sexual content.

BURNS, ROBERT (1759–1796)

Born in Alloway, Ayrshire, Scotland, the poet is best known for his lyrical poems on the subjects of nature, love, patriotism, and peasant life. His fascination with old Scottish airs led to the compilation of the posthumously published *The Merry Muses of Caledonia* (1800), censored for its bawdy language and frank sexuality.

BURTON, SIR RICHARD FRANCIS (1821–1890)

Born in Torquay, Devonshire, England, the explorer, linguist, and translator became in 1858 the first white person in modern times to view Lake Tanganyika in Africa. In addition to his travels, he produced books on swordsmanship and falconry; he is widely remembered for his translation of *The Arabian Nights*, as well as a number of sexually frank Eastern erotic manuals, including *The Kama Sutra*, that aroused the interest of censors. His widow burned his papers and unpublished translations.

CABELL, JAMES BRANCH (1879–1958)

The American author wrote more than 50 works of fiction, essays, and reminiscences, using his novels to attack modern orthodoxies. His best-known work, *Jurgen* (1919), whose symbolism was persistently sexual, earned him a popularity that faded when the elegant, sophisticated style he used passed from fashion. Among the best of his allegorical and fantastical novels are *The Cream of the Jest* (1917), *Figures of the Earth* (1921), and *The High Place* (1923).

CAIN, JAMES M. (1892–1977)

Born in Annapolis, Maryland, the newspaperman, novelist, and playwright was a member of the hard-boiled school of writers, publishing such novels as *The Postman Always Rings Twice* (1934), *Serenade* (1937), and *Mildred Pierce* (1941). The candidly sexual *Serenade* was censored in 1949 in Massachusetts.

CALDWELL, ERSKINE (1903–1987)

Born in Moreland, Georgia, the American author chronicled rural southern life and values in his major works. Among his best-known novels are *Tobacco Road* (1932), *God's Little Acre* (1933), and *Tragic Ground* (1944), all of which drew the complaints of censors. The 1933 stage version of *Tobacco Road* excited controversy and set Broadway records with its run of seven years.

CASANOVA DE SEINGALT, GIOVANNI JACOPO (1725–1798)

Born in Venice, Italy, the gambler and adventurer made a name for himself as a prodigious lover throughout Europe. His sole literary contribution is the 12-volume compilation of his *Memoires* (1826), which was not completely translated into English until 1966. *Memoires* was banned because of the graphic descriptions of Casanova's sexual exploits.

CHBOSKY, STEPHEN (1972–   )

Stephen Chbosky is an author, editor, screenwriter, and film director who was born and raised in Pittsburgh, Pennsylvania. His early film *The Four Corners of Nowhere* premiered at the Sundance Film Festival in 1995 and won the Narrative Features award at the Chicago Underground Film Festival. Chbosky also wrote the screenplay for the film version of the Broadway play *Rent* and received the Abraham Polonsky Screen Writing Award for his screenplay *Everything Divided*. His novel *The Perks of Being a Wallflower* has attracted the most attention of his works, largely because of the protests that adults have voiced to their perceptions of teen drug use, sexuality, and homosexuality in the novel. Chbosky is an vocal gay rights activist who now lives in California.

CHOPIN, KATE (1850–1904)

The feminist themes of Kate Chopin's novels, particularly *The Awakening*, were ahead of their times, and she found little acceptance or acclaim during her lifetime. Her early short stories published in *Vogue*, *Atlantic Monthly*, and other periodicals reflected the Louisiana Creole society into which her marriage transplanted her, and her fiction provided women characters who were strong-willed and who espoused decidedly feminist principles, even though they were bound by the rules of society. Chopin identified strongly with French author Guy de Maupassant, whom she admired for having recorded life and real human emotions in his short stories, traits that she sought to emulate in her own writing. Critics assert that she wrote her own life into her stories and that her work represents a chronicle of both the historical times in which she lived and of the Louisiana bayou she inhabited.

CLELAND, JOHN (1710–1789)

Born in Kingston-upon-Thames, Surrey, England, the novelist, playwright and essayist is best known as the author of *Fanny Hill, or Memoirs of a Woman of Pleasure* (1748). The novel has been censored repeatedly for its multiple sexual pairings and graphic sexual description.

COLE, BROCK (1938–   )

Born in Pittsburgh, Pennsylvania, Cole is a philosophy professor turned painter, illustrator, and writer who has created critically acclaimed picture books and three young adult novels that have won numerous awards for their realistic portrayal of contemporary issues. His first picture book, *The King at the Door* (1979), is a moral fable that won the 1980 Juvenile Award from the Friends of American Writers. Several more picture books followed: *No More Baths* (1980), *Nothing but a Pig* (1981), *The Winter Wren* (1984), and *The Giant's Toe* (1986). *The Goats* (1987) was Cole's first young adult novel, and it won the 1988 Carl Sandburg Award from the Friends of Chicago Public Library; it was also named a *New York Times* notable book and the American Library Association best book for young adults in 1987. In 1989, he published *Celine*, which won the *Booklist* Editors' Choice citation and the Notable Children's Book of the Year citation from *Publishers Weekly. The Facts Speak for Themselves* (1997) was on the *School Library Journal*'s Best Books of 1997 list and was nominated for the 1997 National Book Award.

CONNELL, VIVIAN (1905–1981)

Born in Cork County, Ireland, the playwright and novelist lived most of his life in France. He published six novels and three plays; his most successful works, *The Chinese Room* (1942) and *September in Quinze* (1952), were both objects of censors for their celebration of sexual openness.

D'ANNUNZIO, GABRIELE (1836–1938)

Born in Abruzzi, Italy, the novelist, poet, dramatist, and soldier typified the fin de siècle decadence that defied bourgeois ethics. His works omit any concern for morality or conscience and profess, instead, that meaning in life comes from the pleasures of the senses. *The Triumph of Death* (1894) was attacked by American censors who were offended by the novel's decadence.

DEFOE, DANIEL (1660–1731)

Born Daniel Foe in London, England, the pamphleteer, journalist, political agent, and novelist wrote frank and dramatically realistic fiction. His novel *Moll Flanders* (1922) was heartily received upon publication, but late-19th-century censors found its frank portrayal of sexuality immoral.

DELL, FLOYD (1887–1969)

Born in Barry, Illinois, the celebrated novelist, playwright, critic, editor, and poet became one of the brightest lights in American avant-garde and Greenwich Village bohemianism in the early years of the 20th century. A major member of the Chicago Literary Renaissance of the early 1920s, Dell moved to New York City where, in the late 1920s and the 1930s, this proponent of free love and champion of feminism, socialism, and Freudianism flourished as a writer. His novel *Janet March* created a controversy in 1923 with its portrayal of a sexually active modern young woman.

DONLEAVY, JAMES PATRICK (1926–)

Born in Brooklyn, New York, the novelist and short story writer has lived mostly in Ireland, which figures prominently in his work. *The Ginger Man* (1955), an autobiographical novel, is his most celebrated and most censored book. An unexpurgated version did not appear in the United States until 1965.

DREISER, THEODORE (1871–1945)

Born in Terre Haute, Indiana, the American journalist, magazine editor, playwright, and prolific novelist pioneered the literary movement known as naturalism. Dreiser depicted the lives of common people in such novels as *Sister Carrie* (1900) and *An American Tragedy* (1925). *Sister Carrie* was attacked and heavily censored as an immoral treatment of a scandalous woman's rise to success. Dreiser also suffered failure due to censorship of *The Genius* (1915), an autobiographical novel about power and sex that was labeled "pornography" and attacked by moralists. In 1925, he published *An American Tragedy*, widely regarded as his finest achievement. Critics labeled it "immoral," and the novel became the subject of a notorious trial.

DU MAURIER, GEORGE (1834–1896)

Born in Paris, France, the novelist and illustrator was famous for his caricatures in *Punch* before achieving success through his novels. *Trilby* (1894), censored in Philadelphia, incorporates memories of his days as an art student in Paris.

FARRELL, JAMES THOMAS (1904–1979)

Born in Chicago, the poet, critic, journalist, and novelist often depicted in his fiction the lives of Irish-Americans in Chicago from 1900 through the Great Depression of the 1930s. His best-known novel is *Studs Lonigan*, which, with *A World I Never Made* (1936), were repeatedly subjected to banning attempts for their language and sexual situations. Farrell's fiction is a part of the tradition of naturalistic writing.

FAULKNER, WILLIAM (1897–1962)

Born in Oxford, Mississippi, this major figure of contemporary American literature and one of America's most innovative novelists depicted ordinary society in terms of ageless human dramas. In 1949, Faulkner won the Nobel Prize for literature. He repeatedly explored the question of human freedom and the obstacles to it—racism, regimentation, shame, fear, pride, and overly abstract principles—infusing his novels with this honesty. Such works as *As I Lay Dying* (1930), *Sanctuary* (1931), and *The Wild Palms* (1939) have been attacked as being "vulgar" and "immoral" precisely because they depict realistically how people think, speak, and feel.

FIELDING, HENRY (1707–1754)

Born in Sharpham Park, Glastonbury, Somerset, England, the lawyer, playwright, and novelist contributed significantly to the development of the English novel. He became London's first police magistrate and organized the "Bow Street runners," the first paid police force. Fielding's *The History of Tom Jones, A Foundling* (1749) stirred controversy upon publication and suffered censorship for nearly two centuries.

FLAUBERT, GUSTAVE (1821–1880)

Born at Rouen in Normandy, France, the novelist aimed to create reality through exactness, accuracy of detail, and careful portrayal of object and event. Typical of his realistic method is *Madame Bovary* (1856), censored because of its suggestions of sexual activity and its theme of adultery.

FRIDAY, NANCY (1933–   )

Born in Pittsburgh, Pennsylvania, Friday began her writing career as a journalist in San Juan, Puerto Rico, before writing books about women's sexuality in the early 1970s. Critics have labeled Friday's books unscientific because the author solicited responses by including a mailing address in her early books. *My Secret Garden: Women's Sexual Fantasies* (1973) and *Forbidden*

Flowers: More Women's Sexual Fantasies (1975) told women that their fantasies were not uncommon. In 1978, after interviewing 300 mothers and daughters nationwide, Friday published *My Mother/My Self: The Daughter's Search for Identity.* She next wrote about men in *Men in Love: Men's Sexual Fantasies; The Triumph of Love over Rage* (1980).

GAUTIER, THÉOPHILE (1811–1872)

Born in Tarbes, France, the poet, novelist, journalist, travel writer, and critic became the leader of France's "art for art's sake" movement. His first important novel, *Mademoiselle de Maupin* (1835), epitomized the movement and was banned after motivating controversy. Gautier's sensitivity to beauty and his insistence on formal perfection inspired Charles Baudelaire and the Parnassian movement.

GENET, JEAN (1910–1986)

Born in Paris, France, the dramatist and novelist was the son of a prostitute and spent many years after the age of 10 in jail. He was released from a life sentence in 1947 through the intervention of Jean-Paul Sartre, after writing *Our Lady of the Flowers (Notre-Dame-des-Fleurs)* (1943), an autobiographical account of life in the criminal underworld. The novel was censored because it contained graphic descriptions of heterosexual and homosexual acts.

GIDE, ANDRÉ (1869–1951)

Born in Paris, the novelist, critic, and dramatist addressed in his work the problems of personal freedom within the confines of conventional moral and ethical codes. Through such works as the controversial autobiography *If It Die* (1920), he defended the right of each person to choose and to change his or her mind. Gide won the Nobel Prize in literature in 1947.

GLYN, ELINOR (1864–1943)

Born in Ottawa, Canada, but raised in England, the writer of romantic novels enjoyed shocking the public with a lifestyle replete with tiger skin rugs and stories of her violent passions. She defined "it" for film audiences, when the movie based on her novel *It* (1927) became a box office hit starring Clara Bow. Considered scandalous, *Three Weeks* (1909) became a best seller because of efforts to ban it.

GOODMAN, DANIEL CARSON (1883–1957)

Born in Chicago, Illinois, the physician, film company executive, novelist, and playwright practiced medicine for only 12 years before turning to writing full time. He served as the executive officer of the International Films

Corporation from 1922 to 1924. *Hagar Revelly* (1913) created a controversy with its depiction of a young woman who resorts to prostitution to support herself and her baby.

GORHAM, CHARLES O. (1911–1975)

Born in Philadelphia, Pennsylvania, the novelist and nonfiction writer produced five novels and two biographical studies. *The Gilded Hearse* (1948), his first novel, is about the advertising industry and was written while the author was a publicity director for Doubleday Publishing Company. The ensuing uproar over its sexual content produced enormous sales.

GRIFFIN, JOHN HOWARD (1920–1980)

Born in Dallas, Texas, the author worked as a photographer, lecturer, and journalist before publishing nine books, including *The Devil Rides Outside* (1952), banned for its frank sexuality, and *Black Like Me* (1961), for which Griffin is best known. The Caucasian author used chemicals and ultraviolet light to darken his skin and then traveled throughout the South as a black man. The resulting realism was disturbing to society.

GUTERSON, DAVID (1956–   )

Born in Seattle, Washington, Guterson made his literary debut with the collection of short stories *The Country Ahead of Us, the Country Behind* (1989). Five years later his first novel, *Snow Falling on Cedars* (1994), became a phenomenal best seller and won the prestigious PEN/Faulkner Award. Guterson's more recent novels, *East of the Mountains* (1999) and *Our Lady of the Forest* (2003), have further demonstrated the depth of his talent.

HANLEY, JAMES (1901–1985)

Born in Dublin, Ireland, the novelist, short story writer, playwright, and biographer was prolific in his literary output and sometimes used the pseudonym Patric Shone in his writing. *Boy* (1931), his second and most acclaimed novel, was impounded under British obscenity laws for its graphic violence and brutal sexuality, becoming a cause célèbre and securing the author's literary reputation.

HARDY, THOMAS (1840–1928)

Born in Upper Bockhampton, Dorset, the novelist, short story writer, and poet introduced the concept of fatalism into Victorian literature. The final two of his 15 novels, *Tess of the d'Urbervilles* (1891) and *Jude the Obscure* (1895), explored the classic conflict between human passions and an indifferent universe, creating controversy and motivating efforts to ban them because of their treatment of sexuality and marriage. The outrage of the puritanical Victorian public over these books made Hardy stop writing fiction and return to his first artistic love, poetry, for the final 30 years of his life.

HARRIS, JAMES THOMAS "FRANK" (1856–1931)

Born in Galway, Ireland, the journalist, biographer, and playwright was one of the most controversial authors of the early 20th century. He won considerable acclaim through his fictionalized biographies of Oscar Wilde, William Shakespeare, and George Bernard Shaw, but he is best remembered for his frequently censored autobiography, *My Life and Loves* (1923–27), which describes his sexual adventures and his early life in America.

HARRIS, ROBIE (1940–)

Born in Buffalo, New York, Harris has written for children and young adults, dealing with the changes and challenges that concern young people. Her first published book, *Before You Were Three: How You Began to Walk, Talk, Explore, and Have Feelings* (1977), was intended to help middle-grade readers appreciate how much they had learned since birth. With *It's Perfectly Normal: Changing Bodies, Growing Up, Sex, and Sexual Health* (1994), she aroused outrage among parents throughout the United State, but it was also named the Notable Children's Book selection of the American Library Association, the Editor's Choice for *Booklist*, and a Blue Ribbon winner for the *Bulletin of the Center for Children's Books.*

HOFFENBERG, MASON (1922–1986)

The avant-garde poet was born in New York City but lived mainly in Paris after World War II. He wrote erotica for Olympia Press under such pseudonyms as Chamberlain Drake and Faustine Perez, as well as poetry under the pseudonym of Maxwell Kent. The author claimed in interviews given soon after the publication of *Candy* (1964) that coauthor Terry Southern had conceived of the book and began writing it alone. When Southern ran into difficulties in 1957, he called upon Hoffenberg to help complete it.

HURSTON, ZORA NEALE (1891–1960)

The daughter of a Baptist minister, Zora Neale Hurston was a member of the Harlem Renaissance of the 1920s, the movement of black artists who sought to create their own artistic dimension. Hurston received acclaim as a novelist, folklorist, and anthropologist, talents and interests that she combined to produce writing of stark clarity, which exposed black culture and inspired pride in her race. Critics have acclaimed *Their Eyes Were Watching God* as her greatest novel and assert that Hurston achieves in the novel a distinctly valuable blend of a well-told story that details African-American lives in the United States before the Civil Rights movement.

HUXLEY, ALDOUS LEONARD (1894–1963)

Born in Goldaming, Surrey, England, the novelist, essayist, and critic is best known for his witty and humorous satiric portraits of early-20th-century upper-class British society in *Antic Hay* (1923) and *Point Counter Point* (1928), as well as for his scathing indictment of oppressive government and the dangers of technology in *Brave New World* (1932). All three works have been subject to censorship attempts. His disillusionment led him toward mysticism and the use of hallucinatory drugs and to write such works as *Eyeless in Gaza* (1936), *The Doors of Perception* (1954), and *Heaven and Hell* (1956), in which he describes the use of mescaline to induce visionary states.

JAIVIN, LINDA (1955–   )

Born in Connecticut, Jaivin currently lives in Australia. Her first novel, *Eat Me* (1996), is sexually graphic and received mixed reviews from critics. Jaivin has also written books about China: *The Year the Dragon Came* (1996) and *The Monkey and the Dragon: A True Story about Friendship, Music, Politics, and Life on the Edge* (2001), a biography of pop star Hou Dejian, a singer-songwriter who grew up in Taiwan and later defected to China.

JAMES, NORAH C. (1902–1987)

Born Norah Cordher in London, England, the novelist and short story author was working as the advertising and publicity manager for publisher Jonathan Cape, Ltd., when her sensational best seller, *Sleeveless Errand*, appeared in 1929. It became the most famous of her more than 40 novels, most of them romances.

JAMESON, JENNA (1974–   )

After a decade of making adult films, she coauthored her autobiography, *How to Make Love Like a Porn Star* (2004) with Neil Straus, a former critic for *Rolling Stone* magazine.

JONES, JAMES (1921–1977)

Born in Robinson, Illinois, the novelist used his five-year army career as background for his writing. *From Here to Eternity* (1951), a brutal depiction of the army life, attracted attention from censors because of its graphic sexuality and theme of adultery.

JOYCE, JAMES (1882–1941)

Born in Dublin, the short story writer, novelist, and poet is known for his extensive use of interior monologue, as well as other technical innovations. Dublin is the setting for all his writing, including *Dubliners* (1914) and *Ulysses* (1922), which were pirated by publishers and banned by censors.

KAUFFMANN, STANLEY (1916–)

Born in New York City, the writer, editor, actor, and director is also a well-respected theater and film critic. *The Philanderer* (1952) became Kauffmann's best-known novel after attempts to censor it led to a well-publicized London trial.

KEABLE, ROBERT (1887–1927)

Born in Bedfordshire, England, the novelist used his experiences as an Anglican chaplain during World War I as the basis for the controversial *Simon Called Peter* (1921), the most successful of his 13 novels. His financial success allowed the author to move to Tahiti, where he continued to write and rebel against prudery and convention.

KENTON, MAXWELL

(*See* Hoffenberg, Mason, and Southern, Terry.)

KEYES, DANIEL (1927–)

Born in Brooklyn, New York, the novelist has written several works that focus on psychological themes. *Flowers for Algernon* (1966), the best-known of Keyes's works, has been banned because of the sexually related thoughts and actions of the developmentally slow main character. Keyes's other works include the novels *The Touch* (1968) and *The Fifth Sally* (1980), as well as the nonfiction works *The Minds of Billy Milligan* (1981), *The Milligan Wars* (1993), and *Algernon, Charlie, and I: A Writer's Journey* (2000).

KING, STEPHEN (1947–)

Born in Portland, Maine, the writer of suspense and horror novels and stories is one of America's best-selling authors, under both his own name and the pseudonym Richard Bachman, whose works have gained both critical acclaim and popular success. At the same time, many of his better-known works, among them *Carrie* (1974), *The Shining* (1977), *Cujo* (1981), *Christine* (1983), *Pet Sematary* (1983), and *The Stand* (1990), have been singled out by censors who have sought to remove these novels and, in some cases, all of King's works from school and public libraries.

LAWRENCE, DAVID HERBERT (1885–1930)

Born in Nottinghamshire, England, the novelist, poet, critic, travel writer, and social commentator is best remembered for such controversial novels as *The Rainbow* (1915), *Women in Love* (1920), and *Lady Chatterley's Lover* (1928), banned because of Lawrence's candid portrayal of sexuality. His regard of sexual relations as the decisive element in human behavior shocked readers and became an integral part of his crusade against the constrictive and sterile values of modern civilization.

LOCKER, SARI (1970–)

Locker provided sexual advice to listeners weekly on WBAI radio in New York City. She has discussed teen issues on daytime talk shows and serves as the advice columnist for *Teen People Online*. In 2001, Locker published *Sari Says: The Real Dirt from School to Sex*, which answered the many questions that adolescents and teenagers had asked her in letters and e-mails.

MADONNA (MADONNA LOUISE VERONICA CICCONE) (1958–)

Madonna, one of the best-selling recording artists of all time, has also been responsible for a number of books, including a series of children's picture books and several controversial illustrated books for adults, the first of which was *Sex* (1992).

MAILER, NORMAN (1923–2007)

Born in Long Branch, New Jersey, the novelist, journalist, essayist, and political candidate is known for his brash politics and controversial views. His first novel, *The Naked and the Dead* (1948), based on his World War II combat experience in the Pacific, is viewed by critics as the finest of the modern war novels. Ensuing works such as *The Deer Park* (1955) and *An American Dream* (1965) continued this vision. All three books have been the targets of censors because of the author's blunt language and sexual imagery. Mailer won the National Book Award for *The Armies of the Night* (1968), his personal account of the 1967 peace march on the Pentagon. Mailer has also ignited controversy for *Oswald's Tale* (1995), which reviews the life of Lee Harvey Oswald and ponders his involvement in the death of President Kennedy.

MARGUERITE D'ANGOULÊME DE NAVARRE (QUEEN MARGARET OF NAVARRE) (1492–1549)

Born in Angoulême, France, the author became queen when she married Henri d'Albret, king of Navarre. Although she was highly religious, her work *The Heptameron* (1558) was a bawdy collection of tales patterned after Boccaccio's *Decameron*. The work did not arouse the interest of censors until the end of the 19th century.

McCARTHY, MARY THERESA (1912–1989)

Born in Seattle, Washington, the novelist, critic, and short story writer scrutinized the fads that influenced women's lives in the 1930s and 1940s in her best-selling novel *The Group* (1963), which also drew the attention of censors for its sexual content. In other novels and nonfiction, McCarthy examined national politics, United States policy in Southeast Asia, the Nixon administration scandals, and terrorism. McCarthy was married for a time to novelist Edmund Wilson, with whom she worked on *The Partisan Review* and whose *Memoirs of Hecate County* was also banned.

METALIOUS, GRACE (1924–1964)

Born Grace de Repentigny in Manchester, New Hampshire, Metalious wrote only four novels, but *Peyton Place* (1956) made her a literary celebrity. Highly critical of the small town in which she and her educator husband lived, the book resulted in the author and her family being shunned by local residents, which in turn led to her self-isolation.

MEYER, RICHARD E. (1966–   )

A professor of art history at the University of Southern California, Meyer's only book to date is *Outlaw Representations: Censorship and Homosexuality in Twentieth-Century Art* (2002).

MEYER, STEPHENIE (1973–   )

The author is a member of the Church of Jesus Christ of Latter-day Saints and considers herself to be morally conservative, despite the claims by parents in many school districts that her books are sexually explicit. Meyer achieved instant success as a writer with the publication of the Twilight series, which sold 29 million copies in 2008 and an additional 26.9 million copies in 2009. To date, more than 100 million books in the series have been sold, and the novels have been translated into 37 languages. Before writing the series, the idea for which Meyer claims came to her in a dream, she had never written a short story or other novel, and her only job was as a receptionist in a property company. After the release in 2005 of *Twilight*, the first book in the series, it reached the top position on the *New York Times* Best Seller List for Children's Chapter Books. *Publishers Weekly* named the novel Best Book of the Year, and it was also a *New York Times* Editor's Choice book in 2005. In 2008 and 2009, the four novel in the series—*Twilight, New Moon, Eclipse,* and *Breaking Dawn*—occupied the top four places on the *USA Today* year end best-seller list, making Meyer the first author to achieve this feat. Meyer broke more records as the books remained on the *USA Today* list of top 10 books for 52 weeks straight in 2009 and spent 102 weeks on the *New York Times* Best Seller List. After completing the Twilight series, Meyer published a science fiction novel for adults entitled *The Host,* which has not attracted either the sales or the following of her series.

MILLER, HENRY (1891–1980)

Born in New York City, the novelist lived for nine years in France, where he produced several major novels. His writing was mainly autobiographical, detailing his sexual misadventures and his compulsion to acknowledge the body. *Tropic of Cancer* (1934), *Tropic of Capricorn* (1939), and *Sexus* (1949) were banned for many years because of their sexual content and language.

MOORE, GEORGE (1852–1933)

Born in County Mayo, Ireland, the novelist and playwright was active in the Irish Literary Renaissance of the early 1900s. His best-known novel, *Esther*

Waters (1894), relates the story of a religious young woman with an illegitimate son. The novel was attacked for sexual content and banned, as were *A Modern Lover* (1883) and *A Story Teller's Holiday* (1918), a collection of short stories.

MORRISON, TONI (1931–)

Born in Lorain, Ohio, the editor, novelist, educator, and playwright proudly embraces her designation as "a black woman writer." Her novels focus on the struggles of female characters faced with the difficulties of growing up in a predominantly white society. *The Bluest Eye* (1970) was the target of censors for its sexual violence and theme of incest.

NABOKOV, VLADIMIR (1899–1977)

Born in St. Petersburg, Russia, the novelist, poet, short story writer, and expert on butterflies first received international recognition with *Lolita* (1955), a highly successful as well as controversial novel. He was noted for his superb control of language and plot and for his satire of American mores in fiction and nonfiction.

NAYLOR, PHYLLIS REYNOLDS (1933–)

Born in Anderson, Indiana, Naylor has published more than 100 nonfiction and fiction books for children and young adults. Some of her works are humorous, while others deal with serious issues. The Alice series, which follows the development of an adolescent girl; and the Shiloh series, which relates the moral struggles of an adolescent boy, all have a large following of young readers. Naylor has also written five books for adults, including *Crazy Love: An Autobiographical Account of Marriage and Madness* (1977), a nonfictional account of a difficult marriage to a paranoid schizophrenic. Naylor has gained notoriety for the Alice series, which some parents have sought to restrict because of the discussions between adolescent girls about sex and other "inappropriate topics." The author has won numerous awards, including the 1978 Golden Kite Award for nonfiction from the Society of Children's Book Authors and the 1979 International Reading Association (IRA) Children's Choice citation for *How I Came to Be a Writer* (1978), the 1985 American Library Association Notable Book citation and the IRA 1986 Children's Choice Citation for *The Agony of Alice* (1985), and the 1992 John Newbery Medal from Association for Library Service to Children for *Shiloh* (1991), among many others.

NEVILLE, HENRY (ca. 17TH CENTURY)

That *Isle of Pines* was written by a British author about whom no information is available leads literary historians to believe that *Henry Neville* is a pseudonym. The work was the first to be censored in the United States for containing sexual content.

O'HARA, JOHN (1905–1970)

Born in Pottsville, Pennsylvania, the novelist and short story writer was one of the best-selling writers of the 20th century. His ear for irony and acute powers of observation made his first novel, *Appointment in Samarra* (1934), a great success, and many later novels, including *Butterfield 8* (1935), *A Rage to Live* (1955), *Ten North Frederick* (1955), and *From the Terrace* (1958) became popular films. He set most of his novels in the fictitious community of Gibbsville, Pennsylvania, and infused the works with realistic portrayals of the American upper-middle class, including its sex and drinking patterns. *Appointment in Samarra* and *Ten North Frederick* both shocked reviewers and motivated censors who complained of the "vulgarity" in the novels and the sexual suggestiveness.

OVID (PUBLIUS OVIDIUS NASO) (43 B.C.–A.D. 17)

Born in Rome, the poet, dramatic monologuist, and historian, hailed as the successor to Virgil, is considered the greatest poet of his age. His *The Art of Love* (*Ars Amatoria*) (ca. A.D. 1) was an instant success, establishing him as the leading interpreter of upper-class Roman society of his day. The suggestiveness and psychological content of the poems were enjoyed for many centuries, but the poems became the object of censors in the late 19th and early 20th centuries.

PEPYS, SAMUEL (1633–1703)

Born in London, the government employee and onetime secretary of the admiralty did not have literary ambitions. His *Diary* (1660–69) was written in shorthand that was not deciphered until 1824. In addition to providing an accurate view of the age, the diary also offers an uninhibited view of the author's personal life, which led to its suppression until the 19th century.

PHILLIPS, DAVID GRAHAM (1867–1911)

Born in Madison, Indiana, the journalist and novelist earned a reputation as a fierce crusader for the lower classes early in his career. He boldly attacked the United States Senate as being corrupt, earning from President Theodore Roosevelt the label of the "Man with the Muck Rake." The posthumously published *Susan Lenox: Her Fall and Rise* (1917) gained notoriety for its sexually liberal heroine.

PRZYBYSZEWSKI, STANISLAW ("STANLEY") (1868–1927)

Born in Kujawy, Poland, the dramatist, novelist, essayist, editor, and poet was one of the most influential writers in Polish literature. His work emphasized sexual instinct as the primary force in human life, an element that led to the banning of his novel *Homo Sapiens* (1898).

RAPP, ADAM (1968–)

Born in Chicago, Rapp is a playwright as well as a novelist. Rapp's novels for young adults address the difficult issues of peer abuse and dysfunctional families. *Missing the Piano* (1994), his first novel, won the 1995 American Library Association Best Books for Young Adults and Best Books for Reluctant Readers citations. His sixth book *Under the Dog* (2004) was nominated in 2004 for the *Los Angeles Times* Book Award. Challenges have been raised against his second novel, *The Buffalo Tree* (1997), based on Rapp's experiences in a reform school; it has been challenged by parents for being "sexually graphic." Other novels published by Rapp are *The Copper Elephant* (1999), *Little Chicago* (2002), and *Thirty-three Snowfish* (2003).

RICHARDSON, SAMUEL (1689–1761)

Born in Derbyshire, England, the printer and novelist expanded the novel form to include psychological aspects of character and a highly emotional tone. He began *Pamela, or Virtue Rewarded* (1740) as a manual on letter writing, but the provocative behavior of the main female character led to censorship in the 19th century.

ROBBINS, HAROLD (1916–1997)

Born in New York City, the novelist produced a large number of financially successful novels that have been derided by critics for being sensationalist and poorly constructed. His autobiographical first novel, *Never Love a Stranger* (1948), was the target of censors for its frank language and references to sexuality, and *The Carpetbaggers* (1961) suffered attempts at suppression for its blatant portrayal of sexual activity. Changing mores have prevented further censorship of Robbins's increasingly sexually explicit novels.

RODRIGUEZ, LUIS J. (1954–)

Born in El Paso, Texas, Rodriguez spent the first two years of his life in Mexico, before his parents moved to the United States. He worked as a school bus driver, lamp factory worker, truck driver, paper mill utility worker, millwright apprentice, steel mill worker, carpenter, chemical refinery worker, and computer typesetter before becoming a journalist and full-time writer in 1980. Despite parents' challenges to the use of the book in schools, *Always Running* won the 1993 Carl Sandburg Literary Award for nonfiction, was named the 1993 *New York Times Book Review* Notable Book, and won the 1994 *Chicago-Sun Times* Book Award for nonfiction. Rodriguez's collections of poetry have won numerous awards, and his books have been published in German, French, Arabic, and Spanish, as well as English.

ROUSSEAU, JEAN-JACQUES (1712–1778)

Born in Geneva, Switzerland, the French philosopher and essayist engendered controversy through his emphasis upon individual liberty in such writings as his major political treatise, *The Social Contract* (1762), and his work on education, *Emile* (1762). The graphic accounts of his sexual activities included in his posthumously published *Confessions* (1884) led to their frequent banning.

SADE, MARQUIS DE (1740–1814)

Born Donatien-Alphonse-François in Paris, France, the author and libertine spent nearly 27 years in prison, after his first imprisonment in 1768 for mistreating a prostitute. He died in the insane asylum of Charenton. *Justine, or the Misfortunes of Virtue* (1791), which chronicles the sexual maltreatment of a young girl, is the best-known novel by de Sade, from whose name the word for the psychopathic behavior *sadism* is derived. The posthumously published *The 120 Days of Sodom* (1904) became an underground pornographic classic in the early 20th century.

SCHNITZLER, ARTHUR (1862–1931)

Born in Vienna, Austria, the dramatist and novelist was a physician before turning to writing. His works often delved into psychological themes related to sexuality and marriage that are evident in both his drama and such novels as the controversial *Casanova's Homecoming* (1918).

SMITH, WALLACE (1888–1937)

Born in Chicago, Illinois, the novelist, short story writer, and newspaper reporter was a veteran of four Mexican military campaigns before writing screenplays for the early Hollywood "talkies." *Bessie Cotter* (1934) was his most serious novel, and in it he returned to his Chicago roots to explore his realistic theme.

SOUTHERN, TERRY (1924–1995)

Born in Alvarado, Texas, the novelist, humorist, and screenwriter blended black humor, parody, and satire in his fiction, which includes *The Magic Christian* (1960); *Candy* (1964), his parody of an erotic novel; and *Red-Dirt Marijuana and Other Tastes* (1967). The controversy over *Candy* arose because censors did not realize that Southern and coauthor Mason Hoffenberg were parodying pornographic novels in the work and meant the exaggerated graphic sexuality to be funny.

STEWART, JON (1962–)

Host of *The Daily Show* on Comedy Central from 1999 to the present, Stewart has also appeared in films. Stewart's books *Naked Pictures of Famous*

People (1998) and *America* (2004) contain the same irreverent humor as his television shows.

STYRON, WILLIAM (1925–2006)

Born in Newport News, Virginia, Styron was the author of novels, plays, short stories, and nonfiction works. His works reflect the sensibility of the South and the acknowledgment of the importance of the past. Styron's first novel, *Lie Down in Darkness* (1951), was critically acclaimed for depicting modern life in tragic rather than pathetic terms and for making use of an elevated form of language. Although his sprawling second novel, *Set This House on Fire* (1960), was unsuccessful, *The Confessions of Nat Turner* (1967) was both critically and financially successful. *Sophie's Choice* (1979) portrays the doomed relationship of a mentally unstable New York Jewish intellectual with a young Polish refugee who has experienced the horrors of the Nazi concentration camps. It also invited controversy and achieved great success.

SWINBURNE, ALGERNON CHARLES (1837–1909)

Born in London, England, the poet exhibited in his work rebellion against Victorian manners and morals and sympathies with the political movements of his time. *Poems and Ballads* (1866) contained lyrics that dealt mainly with sensual love, leading censors to call for suppression of the work.

TOLSTOY, COUNT LEO (1828–1910)

Born at the family estate, Yasnaya Polyana (Clear Glade), a few miles south of Moscow, the Russian novelist and philosopher displayed in his work a genius for description and psychological acuity. Best known for his novels *War and Peace* (1865–69) and *Anna Karenina* (1875–77), Tolstoy achieved notoriety when censors banned *The Kreutzer Sonata* (1890), in which he explored the conflict between sexual passion and morality.

TRYON, MARK (N.D.)

The Library of Congress catalog lists this name of the author of *Sweeter Than Life* (1958) as a pseudonym, with no further information.

TULLY, JIM (1891–1947)

Born in St. Mary's, Ohio, the prizefighter, publicity man, and writer spent several years as a publicist for film star Charlie Chaplin. *Ladies in the Parlor* (1935) was censored for its theme of prostitution and one sexually graphic scene.

TWAIN, MARK (1835–1910)

Born Samuel Langhorne Clemens, the humorist, novelist, journalist, lecturer, and travel writer took his pseudonym from a phrase meaning "two fathoms deep" used by Mississippi River boatmen. He is largely associated with life on the Mississippi River because of the literary successes of *The Adventures of Tom Sawyer* (1876), *Life on the Mississippi* (1883), and *Adventures of Huckleberry Finn* (1884–85). Two of Twain's most popular works are also among the most frequently banned or censored in the United States: *The Adventures of Tom Sawyer* and *Adventures of Huckleberry Finn.*

UPDIKE, JOHN (1932–2009)

Born in Shillington, Pennsylvania, the novelist, short story writer, and poet often explored the conflict between mundane existence and the possibility of higher purpose. His novels examine middle-class manners from every possible perspective, exhibiting the flaws behind the finely created facade. *Rabbit, Run* (1960), typical of Updike's novels, aroused the interest of censors because of the sexual relationships among the characters and the graphic descriptions of sexual activity.

VOLTAIRE (1694–1778)

Born François Marie Arouet in Paris, France, the novelist, dramatist, and philosopher also wrote histories, essays, reformist tracts, poetry, and satirical tales such as *Candide* (1759) and *The Maid of Orleans* (1762), both of which were banned for their sexual content. A fighter for reform, Voltaire violently denounced intolerance and injustice, often aiding victims. He mercilessly satirized the social, political, and religious figures and ideas of his time.

WEI HUI (1973–)

Born in Yu Yoa City, China, in 1973, Wei Hui was a reporter, an editor, a television host, and a coffee shop waitress before becoming a full-time writer. Using the name Wei Hui, she published four novellas—*The Shriek of the Butterfly, Virgin in the Water, Crazy like Weihui,* and *Desire Pistol*—before publishing her first full-length novel, *Shanghai Baby* (1999). Although popular in China, Wei Hui's work did not receive international attention until 2000, when the Chinese government banned the novel and ordered the publisher to destroy all remaining copies. The novel may have been banned both for its sexually graphic text and for the outspoken behavior of the author, who claims that she represents the younger generation of women in China who are testing sexual limits and breaking free of the old restrictions.

WILSON, EDMUND (1895–1972)

Born in Red Bank, New Jersey, the critic, novelist, short story writer, play-wright, and poet was a highly respected literary critic as well as a writer. *Memoirs of Hecate County* (1946) was banned after publication because of the candid sexuality of one of the stories. Wilson was married for a time to novelist Mary McCarthy, with whom he worked on *The Partisan Review* and whose novel *The Group* was also banned.

WINSOR, KATHLEEN (1919–2003)

Born in Olivia, Minnesota, the novelist and former newspaper reporter is best known for her Restoration romance, *Forever Amber* (1944). The novel created controversy when it first appeared, which led to its being banned in Boston and other cities.

WOLFF, TOBIAS (1945–)

Born in Birmingham, Alabama, Tobias Wolff won the Wallace Stegner fellowship in creative writing in 1975–76, the National Endowment for the Arts fellowship in 1978, the Mary Roberts Rinehart grant in 1979, as well as the PEN/Faulkner Award for fiction and the O. Henry award for his short stories. Although his work is labeled fiction, many of his published works are nonfiction accounts thinly disguised as fiction. As Wolff stated in his *Contemporary Authors* biography, "Sometimes they're autobiographical in the actual events they describe, sometimes more in their depiction of a particular character." Critics have described Wolff as a realist and a minimalist, because he does not force happy endings on his characters' lives. Instead, he focuses on creating realistic lives for his characters that reflect his own experiences in which neither great suffering nor joy have been present.

WRIGHT, RICHARD (1908–1960)

Richard Wright was born in Roxie, Mississippi, but his writing and natural curiosity to study and to record the African-American experience led him to Chicago in the 1920s and New York in the 1930s, and eventually to Paris, where he became a permanent expatriate in 1946. A longtime member of the Communist Party, Wright traveled extensively to disseminate information about communism and to make efforts to secure equality for all individuals, not only African Americans. Even the Party disappointed him, with racism among the leadership and his denial of housing because of his race. He won a Guggenheim Fellowship that gave him the resources to write *Native Son*, a novel that many critics view as being mediocre in literary style but which they praise for its influence in revealing the world of African Americans.

VON ZIEGESAR, CECILY (1970–)

Know primarily for her series Gossip Girl, Cecily von Ziegesar was raised in the rarefied atmosphere that she explores in the series. Von Ziegesar offers an insider's view into a high-end teen lifestyle. The book-series became a highly successful TV show, which started its fourth season in fall 2010.

359

ZOLA, ÉMILE (1840–1902)

Born in Aix-en-Provence, France, the journalist and novelist used his fiction to campaign for social reform and justice and became the major proponent of literary naturalism. Zola created a cycle of 20 novels collectively called *Les Rougon, Macquart*, which were criticized for their gratuitous brutality and obscenity. Today they are valued as fictionalized sociology. Of particular interest are *Nana* (1880) and *La Terre*, the latter translated variously as *The Earth* and *The Soil* (1887). In later years, Zola also became known for his defense of Captain Alfred Dreyfus—and in particular for writing his famous "J'accuse" letter.

BIBLIOGRAPHY

BOOKS

Ackerman, Susan. *When Heroes Love: The Ambiguity of Eros in the Stories of Gilgamesh and David*. New York: Columbia University Press, 2005.

Acts and Laws, Passed by the Great and General Court or Assembly of the Province of the Massachusetts-Bay in New-England, from 1692 to 1719. London: John Baskett, 1724.

Adams, Michael. *Censorship: The Irish Experience*. Tuscaloosa: University of Alabama Press, 1968.

Alkon, Paul. *Defoe and Fictional Time*. Athens: University of Georgia Press, 1979.

American Civil Liberties Union. *Banned and Challenged Books in Texas Public Schools 2002–2003*. Report of the American Civil Liberties Union of Texas. Austin, Tex.: ACLU, 2003.

Arnold, Bruce. *The Scandal of "Ulysses": The Sensational Life of a Twentieth-Century Masterpiece*. New York: St. Martin's, 1994.

Ayer, Alfred Jules. *Voltaire*. New York: Random House, 1986.

Balzac, Honoré de. *Correspondence*. Edited by Roger Pierrot. Paris: Barnier, 1969.

Ben-Ephraim, Gavriel. *The Moon's Dominion: Narrative Dichotomy and Female Dominance in Lawrence's Earlier Novels*. Rutherford, N.J.: Fairleigh Dickinson University Press, 1989.

Bercovici, Alfred. *That Blackguard Burton!* Indianapolis, Ind.: Bobb-Merrill Co., 1962.

Besterman, Theodore. *Voltaire*. New York: Harcourt Brace & World, 1969.

Boyer, Paul S. *Purity in Print: The Vice-Society Movement and Book Censorship in America*. New York: Scribner, 1968.

Brightman, Carol. *Writing Dangerously: Mary McCarthy and Her World*. New York: Clarkson Potter, 1992.

Brodie, Fawn M. *The Devil Drives: A Life of Sir Richard Burton*. New York: Norton, 1967.

Brooks, Van Wyck. *The Confident Years: 1885–1915*. New York: Dutton, 1952.

Broun, Heywood, and Margaret Leech. *Anthony Comstock*. New York: Albert and Charles Boni, 1927.

Bryant, Arthur. *Samuel Pepys: The Man in the Making*. London: Cambridge University Press, 1943.

Burton, Sir Richard. "Introduction." In *The Perfumed Garden of Sheikh Nefzaoui*. New York: Lancer, 1964.

Butler-Evans, Elliott. *Race, Gender, and Desire: Narrative Strategies in the Fiction of Toni Cade Bambara and Toni Morrison*. Philadelphia: Temple University Press, 1989.

Campbell, Jeff H. *John Howard Griffin*. Austin, Tex.: Steck-Vaughn, 1970.

Chbosky, Stephen. *The Perks of Being a Wallflower*. New York: MTV Books, 1999.

Clayton, Douglas. *Floyd Dell: The Life and Times of an American Rebel*. Chicago: Ivan R. Dee, 1994.

Colum, Padraic, and Margaret Freeman Cabell, eds. *Between Friends: Letters of James Branch Cabell and Others*. New York: Harcourt Brace & World, 1962.

Cowley, Malcolm. *After the Genteel Tradition*. Rev. ed. Carbondale: Southern Illinois University, 1964

Craig, Alec. *Suppressed Books: A History of the Conception of Literary Obscenity*. New York: World Publishing, 1963.

Cranston, Maurice. *The Noble Savage: Jean-Jacques Rousseau*. Chicago: University of Chicago Press, 1991.

Davis, Kenneth C. *Two-Bit Culture: The Paperbacking of America*. Boston: Houghton Mifflin, 1984.

De Grazia, Edward. *Censorship Landmarks*. New York: Bowker, 1969.

———. *Girls Lean Back Everywhere: The Laws of Obscenity and the Assault on Genius*. New York: Random House, 1992.

Donelson, Kenneth L., and Alleen Pace Nilsen. *Literature for Today's Young Adults*. Glenview, Ill.: Scott Foresman, 1989.

Donleavy, J. P. *The History of the Ginger Man*. Boston: Houghton Mifflin, 1994.

Doyle, Robert. *2007 Banned Books Resource Guide*. Chicago: American Library Association, 2007.

Dudley, Dorothy. *Forgotten Frontiers: Dreiser and the Land of the Free*. New York: Smith & Haas, 1932.

Egerton, John. *A Mind to Stay Here: Profiles from the South*. New York: Macmillan, 1970.

Ernst, Morris L., and Alan U. Schwartz. *Censorship: The Search for the Obscene*. New York: Macmillan, 1964.

Etherington-Smith, Meredith, and Jeremy Pilcher. *The "It" Girls: Elinor Glyn, Novelist, and Her Sister Lucile, Couturiere*. New York: Harcourt Brace Jovanovich, 1986.

Farrell, James T. "The Author as Plaintiff: Testimony in a Censorship Case." In Farrell's *Reflection at Fifty and Other Essays*. New York: Vanguard Press, 1954.

Filler, Louis. *Voice of Democracy: David Graham Phillips*. University Park: Pennsylvania State University, 1968.

Foerstel, Herbert N. *Banned in the U.S.A.: A Reference Guide to Book Censorship in Schools and Public Libraries*. Westport, Conn.: Greenwood, 1994.

Ford, John. *Criminal Obscenity: A Plea for Its Suppression*. New York: Revell, 1926.

Ford, Worthington Chauncey. *The Isle of Pines 1668: An Essay in Bibliography*. Boston: The Club of Odd Volumes, 1920.

Forster, E. M. *Abinger Harvest*. New York: Harcourt Brace, 1936.

Foxon, David. *Libertine Literature in England, 1600–1745*. New Hyde Park, N.Y.: University Books, 1965.

Frohock, W. M. *The Novel of Violence in America*. Dallas, Tex.: Southern Methodist University, 1950.

Galloway, David D. *The Absurd Hero in American Fiction*. Rev. ed. Austin, Tex.: University of Texas Press, 1970.

Gates, Henry Louis, Jr., and K. A. Appiah. *Zora Neale Hurston: Critical Perspectives Past and Present*. New York: Amistad, 1993.

Gelderman, Carol. *Mary McCarthy: A Life*. New York: St. Martin's, 1988.

Geller, Evelyn. *Forbidden Books in American Public Libraries, 1876–1939*. Westport, Conn.: Greenwood, 1984.

Gerber, Albert B. *Sex, Pornography, and Justice*. New York: Lyle Stuart, 1965.

Gerson, Noel B. *The Prodigal Genius*. Garden City, N.Y.: Doubleday, 1972.

Gilmer, Frank Walker. *Horace Liveright: Publisher of the Twenties*. New York: Lewis, 1970.

Girodias, Maurice. "Introduction." *The Olympia Reader*. New York: Grove, 1965.

Gladstein, Mimi. *The Indestructible Woman in Faulkner, Hemingway, and Steinbeck.* Ann Arbor, Mich.: UMI Research Press, 1986.

Glyn, Anthony. *Elinor Glyn.* Garden City, N.Y.: Doubleday, 1955.

Goldman, Eric F. "David Graham Phillips, Victorian Critic of Victorianism." In *The Lives of Eighteen from Princeton,* edited by Willard Thorp, 118–153. Princeton, N.J.: Princeton University Press, 1946.

Green, Virginia M. *Heroic Virtue, Comic Infidelity: Reassessing Marguerite de Navarre's Heptameron.* Amherst, Mass.: Hestia Press, 1993.

Gunn, Daniel, and Patrick Guyomard. Introduction to *A Young Girl's Diary,* edited by Daniel Gunn and Patrick Guyomard. New York: Doubleday, 1990.

Gustafson, Richard F. *Leo Tolstoy, Resident and Stranger: A Study in Fiction and Theology.* Princeton, N.J.: Princeton University Press, 1986.

Haney, Robert W. *Comstockery in America: Patterns of Censorship and Control.* Boston: Beacon, 1960.

Hardy, Thomas. "Candour in Fiction." In *Thomas Hardy's Personal Writings: Prefaces, Literary Opinions, Reminiscences,* edited by Harold Orel, 125–133. Lawrence: University of Kansas Press, 1966.

Harris, Frank. Foreword to *My Life and Loves.* New York: Grove, 1963.

Hart, John E. *Floyd Dell.* New York: Twayne, 1971.

Hayman, Ronald. *De Sade: A Critical Biography.* New York: Crowell, 1978.

Hemmings, F. W. J. *The Life and Times of Emile Zola.* New York: Scribner, 1977.

Hempl, William J., and Patrick M. Wall. "Extralegal Censorship of Literature." In *Issues of Our Time,* edited by Herbert W. Hildebrandt. New York: Macmillan, 1963.

Holt, Guy, ed. *Jurgen and the Law: A Statement with Exhibits, Including the Court's Opinion and the Brief of the Defendants on Motion to Direct an Acquittal.* New York: Robert M. McBride, 1923.

Huizinga, J. H. *Rousseau: The Self-Made Saint.* New York: Grossman, 1976.

Hunt, George W. *John Updike and the Three Great Secret Things: Sex, Religion, and Art.* Grand Rapids, Mich.: Eerdmans, 1980.

Hurston, Zora Neale. *Their Eyes Were Watching God.* New York: J. B. Lippincott, 1965.

Hurwitz, Leon. *Historical Dictionary of Censorship in the United States.* Westport, Conn.: Greenwood, 1985.

Hutchison, E. R. *Tropic of Cancer on Trial.* New York: Grove, 1968.

Josephson, Matthew. *Zola and His Time.* Garden City. N.Y.: Garden City Publishers, 1928.

Katz, Jonathan. *Gay/Lesbian Almanac.* New York: Carroll & Graf, 1994.

Kauffmann, Stanley. Introduction to *The Philanderer.* 2d ed. London: Secker & Warburg, 1954.

Kearney, Patrick J. *A History of Erotic Literature.* Hong Kong: Parragon, 1982.

Kendrick, Walter. *The Secret Museum: Pornography in Modern Culture.* Baltimore: Penguin, 1988.

Kilpatrick, James J. *The Smut Peddlers.* New York: Doubleday, 1960.

King, Stephen. "Banned Books and Other Concerns: The Virginia Beach Lecture." In *The Stephen King Companion,* edited by George Beahm. Kansas City, Mo.: Andrews & McMeel, 1989.

Kinnamon, Kenneth, ed. *New Essays on Native Son.* New York: Cambridge University Press, 1990.

Klevar, Harvey L. *Erskine Caldwell: A Biography.* Knoxville: University of Tennessee Press, 1993.

Kronhausen, Eberhard, and Phyllis Kronhausen. *Pornography and the Law: The Psychology of Erotic Realism.* New York: Ballantine, 1959.

Kuh, Richard H. *Foolish Figleaves? Pornography In and Out of Court.* New York: Macmillan, 1967.

Lawrence, D. H. *The Quest for Rananim: D. H. Lawrence's Letters to S. S. Koteliansky, 1914–1930.* Ed. and intro. by George J. Zytaruk. Montreal: McGill-Queen's University Press, 1970.

Legman, George, ed. Introduction to *The Merry Muses of Caledonia: Collected and Written in Part by Robert Burns.* New Hyde Park, N.Y.: University Books, 1965.

Lever, Maurice. *Sade: A Biography.* Trans. by Arthur Goldhammer. New York: Farrar, Straus & Giroux, 1993.

Lewis, Felice Flanery. *Literature, Obscenity, & Law.* Carbondale: Southern Illinois University Press, 1976.

Loth, David. *The Erotic in Literature.* New York: Dorset, 1961.

Lottman, Herbert. *Flaubert: A Biography.* Boston: Little, Brown, 1989.

MacCarthy, Desmond. *Criticism.* London: Dent, 1932.

Maddox, Brenda. *D. H. Lawrence: The Story of a Marriage.* New York: Simon & Schuster, 1993.

Mancuso, Ludwig. *The Obscene: The History of an Indignation.* London: MacGibbon & Key, 1965.

Manso, Peter. *Mailer: His Life and Times.* New York: Simon & Schuster, 1985.

Marchand, Henry. *The French Pornographers: Including a History of French Erotic Literature.* New York: Book Awards, 1965.

Marcosson, Isaac F. *David Graham Phillips and His Times.* New York: Dodd, Mead, 1932.

Marcus, Stephen. *The Other Victorians.* New York: Basic, 1966.

Marcuse, Ludwig. *The History of an Indignation.* London: MacGibbon & Key, 1965.

Markle, Joyce. *Fighters and Lovers: Theme in the Novels of John Updike.* New York: New York University Press, 1973.

Markmann, Charles L. *The Noblest Cry: A History of the American Civil Liberties Union.* New York: St. Martin's, 1965.

McCoy, Ralph E. *Banned in Boston: The Development of Literary Censorship in Massachusetts.* Urbana: University of Illinois, 1956.

McHaney, Thomas L. *William Faulkner's* The Wild Palms: *A Study.* Jackson: University of Mississippi, 1975.

Miller, Dan B. *Erskine Caldwell: The Journey from Tobacco Road.* New York: Knopf, 1995.

Miller, Henry. "Defense of the Freedom to Read—A Letter to the Supreme Court of Norway in Connection with the Ban on *Sexus (The Rosy Crucifixion)*." In *Versions of Censorship: An Anthology,* edited by John McCormick and Mairi MacInnes. Garden City, N.Y.: Doubleday, 1962.

Mills, Hillary. *Mailer: A Biography.* New York: Empire, 1982.

Mitchell, Stephen, trans. *Gilgamesh: A New English Version.* New York: Free Press, 2004.

Moore, Jack B. *Maxwell Bodenheim.* New York: Twayne, 1970.

Moore, John R. *Daniel Defoe: Citizen of the Modern World.* Chicago: University of Chicago Press, 1958.

Mordell, Albert, ed. *Notorious Literary Attacks.* New York: Boni & Liveright, 1926.

Morgan, Edwin. *Flowers of Evil: A Life of Charles Baudelaire.* Freeport, N.Y.: Books for Libraries Press, 1943.

Morrison, Toni. *Song of Solomon*. New York: Alfred A. Knopf, 1977.

Newman, M. W. *The Smut Hunters*. Los Angeles: All American Distributors, 1964.

Oboler, Eli M. *The Fear of the Word: Censorship and Sex*. Metuchen, N.J.: The Scarecrow Press, 1974.

Page, Sally R. *Faulkner's Women: Characterization and Meaning*. De Land, Fla.: Everett/Edwards, 1972.

Partridge, Eric. *The First Three Years*. London: Scholartis, 1930.

Paul, James C. N., and Murray L. Schwartz. *Federal Censorship: Obscenity in the Mail*. New York: Free Press, 1961.

Perkins, Michael. *The Secret Record: Modern Erotic Literature*. New York: Morrow, 1976.

Perrin, Noel. *Dr. Bowdler's Legacy: A History of Expurgated Books in England and America*. Boston: Godine, 1992.

Perry, Stuart. *The Indecent Publications Tribunal: A Social Experiment*. London: Whitcombe and Tombs, 1965.

Pichois, Claude. *Baudelaire*. London: Hamish Hamilton, 1989.

Pinion, F. B. *Thomas Hardy: His Life and Friends*. New York: St. Martin's, 1992.

Putnam, George Haven. *The Censorship of the Church of Rome and Its Influence upon the Production and Distribution of Literature*. Vol. II. New York: Putnam's, 1906.

Ravitz, Abe C. *David Graham Phillips*. New York: Twayne Publishing, 1966.

Rembar, Charles. *The End of Obscenity: The Trials of* Lady Chatterley's Lover, Tropic of Cancer, & Fanny Hill *by the Lawyer Who Defended Them*. New York: Random House, 1968.

Rice, Edward. *Captain Sir Richard Francis Burton*. New York: Scribner, 1990.

Robb, Graham. *Balzac: A Biography*. New York: Norton, 1994.

Roeburt, John. *The Wicked and the Banned*. New York: Macfadden, 1963.

Rollyson, Carl. *The Lives of Norman Mailer*. New York: Paragon House, 1991.

Rolph, Cecil Hewitt. *Books in the Dock*. London: Deutsch, 1961.

St. John-Stevas, Norman. *Obscenity and the Law*. London: Secker & Warburg, 1956.

Sartre, Jean-Paul. *Saint Genet: Comedian and Martyr*. New York: George Brazillier, 1952.

Schom, Alan. *Emile Zola: A Biography*. New York: Holt, 1987.

Seyersted, Per. *A Kate Chopin Miscellany*. Natchitoches, La.: Northwestern State University Press, 1979.

Seymour-Smith, Martin. *Hardy: A Biography*. New York: St. Martin's, 1994.

Showalter, Elaine. Introduction to *The Awakening*. New York: Alfred A. Knopf, 1992.

Steegmuller, Francis. *Flaubert and Madame Bovary*. Boston: Houghton Mifflin, 1970.

Stuart, Perry. *The Indecent Publications Tribunal: A Social Experiment*. Christchurch, New Zealand: Whitcombe and Tombs, 1965.

Sutherland, James. *Defoe*. Philadelphia: Lippincott, 1938.

Sutherland, John. *Offensive Literature: Decensorship in Britain, 1960–1982*. London: Junction, 1982.

Swinburne, Algernon Charles. *Letters of Algernon Charles Swinburne*. Vol. I. Edited by C. Y. Lang. New Haven, Conn.: Yale University Press, 1959.

Tebbel, John. *A History of Book Publishing in the United States*. Vol. II. New York: Bowker, 1975.

Thomas, Donald Serrell. *A Long Time Burning: The History of Literary Censorship in England*. New York: Praeger, 1969.

———. *The Marquis de Sade*. Boston: New York Graphic Society, 1976.

Tindall, William York. *Forces in Modern British Literature, 1885–1956.* 2d ed. New York: Vintage, 1956.

Tjader, Marguerite. *Theodore Dreiser: A New Dimension.* Norwalk, Conn.: Silvermine, 1965.

Tobin, A. I., and Elmer Gertz. *Frank Harris: A Study in Black and White.* Chicago: Madelaine Mendelsohn, 1931.

Toth, Emily. *Kate Chopin.* New York: William Morrow and Sons, 1990.

Troyat, Henri. *Flaubert.* Paris: Librairie Ernest Flammarion, 1988.

Tully, Jim. *A Dozen and One.* Hollywood: Murray & Gee, 1943.

Tuttleton, James. *The Novel of Manners in America.* New York: Norton, 1972.

United States President's Commission on Obscenity and Pornography. *The Report of the Commission on Obscenity and Pornography.* New York: Random House, 1970.

Unwin, Sir Stanley. *The Truth about Publishing.* London: Allen & Unwin, 1960.

Vizitelly, Ernest A. *Emile Zola, Novelist and Reformer: An Account of His Life and Work.* London: Lane, 1904.

Wainhouse, Austryn. "Foreword." *The Marquis de Sade: Juliette.* New York: Grove, 1968.

Weinstein, Philip M. *What Else but Love? The Ordeal of Race in Faulkner and Morrison.* New York: Columbia University Press, 1996.

Wellek, Rene and Austin Warren. *Theory of Literature.* 3d ed. New York: Harcourt Brace & World, 1956.

White, Edmund. *Genet: A Biography.* New York: Knopf, 1994.

Williams, David. *Faulkner's Women: The Myth and the Muse.* Montreal: McGill-Queen's University Press, 1977.

Wilson, Sharon Rose. *Margaret Atwood's Fairy-Tale Sexual Politics.* Jackson: University Of Mississippi, 1993.

Wright, Richard. *Native Son.* New York: Harper & Row, 1979.

Zweig, Stefan. *Balzac.* London: Cassell, 1970.

PERIODICALS

"Again the Literary Censor." *Nation,* September 25, 1920, p. 343.

"*America* Defeats Mississippi Ban." *American Libraries* 36 (February 2005): 13.

"*America* (The Winner)." *Publishers Weekly,* December 13, 2004, p. 5.

"Another Furor over Books." *Ohio State University Monthly* 55 (December 1963): 8–12.

"Another Repeal: Joyce's *Ulysses* Is Legal at Last." *Nation,* December 20, 1933, p. 693.

"Anthony Comstock Overruled." *Publishers Weekly,* June 30, 1894, pp. 942–43.

"Apache Junction, AZ." *School Library Journal* 52 (January 2006): 24.

Auerbach, Joseph S. "Authorship and Liberty." *North American Review* 207 (July 1918): 902–17.

Bacon, Corinne. "What Makes a Novel Immoral?" *Wisconsin Library Bulletin* 6 (August 1910): 83–95.

Baker, George. "*Lolita:* Literature or Pornography." *Saturday Review,* June 22, 1957, p. 18.

Balbert, Peter. "From *Lady Chatterley's Lover* to *The Deer Park:* Lawrence, Mailer, and the Dialectic of Erotic Risk." *Studies in the Novel* 22 (Spring 1990): 67–81.

Barlow, Samuel L. M. "The Censor of Art." *North American Review* 213 (March 1921): 346–50.

Bass, Warren. "Whether You're a Hawk or a Dove." *Washington Post,* October 10, 2004, p. T13.

Bates, Ralph. "Mr. Wilson's Visit to Suburbia." *New York Times Book Review*, March 31, 1946, pp. 7, 16.

"Battling the Wolves." *Christian Century*, April 8, 1931, pp. 470–71.

Beattie, A. M., and Frank A. Underhill. "Sense and Censorship: On Behalf of *Peyton Place*." *Canadian Library Association Bulletin* 15 (July 1958): 9–16.

"Behind the Robes, Stewart Finds Controversy." *USA Today*, October 20, 2004. p. D1.

Bellafante, Ginia. "'Gossip Girls' Series Aims Low, Sells High." *Chicago Tribune*, August 30, 2003, p. 7.

Benhuniak-Long, Susan. "Feminism and Reproductive Technology." *Choice* 29 (October 1991): 243.

Bergeron, Katherine. "The Echo, the Cry, the Death of Lovers." *Nineteenth Century Music* 18 (Fall 1994): 136–51.

Blades, John. "The Uncut Version of Richard Wright's Original 'Native Son,' 'Black Boy' Restore Power of His Themes." *Chicago Tribune*, October 7, 1991, p. 1.

Blumenstein, Lynn. "Porn Star Back on Houston Shelves." *Library Journal*, March 15, 2005, p. 2.

"Board Member Axed over Access to *Sex*." *Library Journal*, October 1, 1993, p. 16.

"Book Ban Opposed—Detroit Library Head to Keep O'Hara Novel Available." *New York Times*, January 19, 1957, p. 13.

"Book Censorship Beaten in Court." *New York Times*, September 13, 1922, p. 20.

"Books and Authors—*Sleeveless Errand*." *New York Times Book Review*, March 19, 1929, p. 8.

Booth, Wayne C. "Censorship and the Values of Fiction." *English Journal* 53 (March 1964): 155–64.

"Boston Clean Book Case." *Publishers Weekly*, January 26, 1924, p. 240.

Boyer, Paul S. "Boston Book Censorship in the Twenties." *American Quarterly* 15 (Spring 1930): 3–24.

"Boys and the Banned: Michael Warner on *Outlaw Representation*." *Artforum International* 4, no. 8 (April 1, 2002): 35.

"Bridgeport Police Scored on Book Ban." *New York Times*, March 15, 1962, p. 40.

"British Deny Censorship." *New York Times*, March 1, 1929, p. 3.

Broun, Heywood. "Heywood Broun Comes to the Rescue of Immoral Books." *Current Opinion* 67 (December 1919): 315–16.

Bryan-Wilson, Julia. "Pictures at a Deposition." *Art Journal* 62, no. 2 (Summer 2003): 102.

Bryer, J. R. "Joyce, *Ulysses*, and the *Little Review*." *South Atlantic Quarterly* 66 (Spring 1967): 148–64.

Bullard, F. Lauriston. "Boston's Ban Likely to Live Long." *New York Times*, April 28, 1929, Sec. 3, pp. 1, 7.

Burgum, Edwin Berry. "Erskine Caldwell and His Jeeters." *New York Times Book Review*, October 15, 1944, p. 46.

Burton, Connie O. "The Most Frequently Challenged Books of 2006. *Teacher Librarian* 35 (December 2007): 67.

Caldwell, Erskine. "My Twenty-five Years of Censorship." *Esquire*, October 1958, pp. 176–78.

"Caldwell Novel Cleared as 'Dull.' " *New York Times*, December 29, 1944, p. 13.

Campbell, James. "Dirty Young Men." *New York Times Book Review*, June 6, 2003, p. 20.

"Censorship Beaten in New York Court." *Publishers Weekly*, September 16, 1922, pp. 801–4.

"Censorship: Whose 'Standards' Are They?" *Los Angeles Times*, home edition, December 28, 2001, p. B16.

"Censorship Dateline: Libraries." *Newsletter on Intellectual Freedom* 56, no. 1 (January 2007): 54–58.

"Censorship Dateline: Libraries." *Newsletter on Intellectual Freedom* 57, no. 2 (March 2008): 59–61.

"Censorship Dateline: Schools." Newsletter on Intellectual Freedom 58, no. 2 (March 2009): 39–41.

Centerwall, Brandon S. "Hiding in Plain Sight: Nabokov and Pedophilia." *Texas Studies in Literature & Language* 32 (Fall 1990): 468–84.

Champion, Laurie. "Jones's *From Here to Eternity*." *Explicator* 54 (Summer 1996): 242–44.

"Chicago Bookseller Wins Case." *Publishers Weekly*, April 4, 1931, p. 1,790.

Ciardi, John. "The Marquis de Sade II." *Saturday Review*, October 2, 1965, p. 36.

———. "*Tropic of Cancer*." *Saturday Review*, June 1962, p. 13.

Clancy, Ambrose. "Wild Irish Rogue." *Gentleman's Quarterly*, June 1991, pp. 60–68.

Cohen, Emily Jane. "Mud into Gold: Baudelaire and the Alchemy of Public Hygiene." *Romanic Review* 87 (March 1996): 239–55.

"Confer in Boston on Banned Books." *New York Times*, March 13, 1927, p. 2.

Cook, Bruce. "Candy Comes to Chicago." *Nation*, September 14, 1964, pp. 125–26.

Cooper, Morton. "Fanny Hill vs. the Constitution." *Pageant* 14 (June 1964): 14–20.

Cooper, Pamela. "Sexual Surveillance and Medical Authority in Two Versions of *The Handmaid's Tale*." *Journal of Popular Culture* 28 (Spring 1995): 49–66.

"Court Bans Tully Book." *New York Times*, November 1, 1935, p. 19.

"Court Clears Novel of Obscenity Charge." *New York Times*, May 20, 1948, p. 27.

"Court to Review Book Ban." *New York Times*, February 28, 1956, p. 11.

Cusseres, Benjamin de. "Case of Prudery against Literature: Attack on Gautier's Novel Brings to Mind Many Historical Examples of Law's Moral Censorship on Books." *New York Times*, May 23, 1920, Sec. 7, p. 3.

Dale, Virginia. "Literary Heel: *The Gilded Hearse*." *New York Times Book Review*, February 1, 1948, p. 26.

Dangerfield, George. "Invisible Censorship." *North American Review* 244 (Winter 1937–38): 334–48.

Daniels, Jonathan. "American Lower Depths." *Saturday Review of Literature*, October 14, 1944, p. 6.

"D'Annunzio at Asbury Park." *New York Times*, July 24, 1897, p. 6.

"Defoe's Works Banned." *Publishers Weekly*, October 19, 1929, p. 1,938.

"Detroit Book Ban Void—Court Enjoins the Police from Barring O'Hara Novel. *New York Times*, March 30, 1957, p. 17.

De Voto, Bernard. "The Easy Chair: Liberal Decisions in Massachusetts." *Harper's Magazine*, July 1949, pp. 62–65.

"Director Gags over *Eat Me*." *American Libraries* 34 (December 2003): 19.

Doherty, Gerald. "The Art of Appropriation: The Rhetoric of Sexuality in D. H. Lawrence." *Style* 30 (Summer 1996): 289–308.

Draper, Electa. "Norwood Book Ban Brings Offer: Metro Prof Will Pay $1000 to Retrieve Copies of 'Bless Me, Ultima.'" *Denver Post*, February 4, 2005, p. B-05.

Dupee, F. W. "*Lolita* in America." *Encounter* 12 (February 1959): 30–35.

Durham, Frank M. "Mencken as Missionary." *American Literature* 29 (January 1958): 478–83.

"Editorial: Ideas for Our Community: A Library for Everyone." *The Atlanta Constitution*, July 21, 1997, p. A1.

"The Editor Recommends—." *The Bookman* 57 (February 1924): 459.

Elliott, Desmond. "The Book That Shocked Paris: The Strange Story of *Madame Bovary*." *Books and Bookmen* 5 (June 1960): 11, 46.

———. "Field Day for the Righteous." *Books and Bookmen* 5 (December 1959): 17.

———. "Scandal over Studs (Trial over James Farrell's *Studs Lonigan*). *Books and Bookmen* 5 (November 1959): 23–26.

Ernst, Morris L., and Alexander Lindey. "The Censor Marches On. . . ." *Esquire*, June 1939, pp. 174–77.

"Evil in Our Time." *Time*, March 25, 1946, p. 102.

Farrell, James T. "Lonigan, Lonergan, and New York's Finest." *Nation*, March 18, 1944, p. 338.

Farriman, Milton. "Bookseller Victorious in Chicago Reformer's Campaign." *Publishers Weekly*, February 1, 1930, pp. 566–68.

Feeney, Ann. "*Lolita* and Censorship: A Case Study." *References Services Review* 21 (Winter 1993): 67–74, 90.

Ferns, Chris. "The Values of Dystopia: *The Handmaid's Tale* and the Anti-Utopian Tradition." *Dalhousie Review* 69 (Fall 1989): 373–82.

"Finds Keable Book Obscene." *New York Times*, October 19, 1922, p. 2.

Flagg, Gordon. "After Four Months, Libraries Are Still in the Hot Seat over *Sex*." *American Libraries* 23 (April 1993): 290–91.

———. "For Sex, See Librarian . . . Maybe." *American Librarians* 23 (December 1992): 900.

Flower, Benjamin O. "Conservatism and Sensualism: An Unhallowed Alliance." *Arena* 3 (December 1890): 126–28.

———. "The Postmaster-General and the Censorship of Morals." *Arena* 2 (October 1890): 540–52.

Forman, Jack. "Young Adult Books: 'Watch Out for #1.' " *Horn Book* 61 (January–February 1985): 85.

Foxon, David F. "John Cleland and the Publication of *Memoirs of a Woman of Pleasure*." *Book Collector* 12 (Winter 1963): 476–87.

Francisco, Jamie. "Book-Ban Debate Is Long Impassioned: More Than 350 Sign Up to Speak to School Board." *Chicago Tribune*, May 26, 2006, p. 2NW.1.

———. "Explicit Move Is Made to Ban Books from Reading List." *Chicago Tribune*, May 24, 2006, p. 2NS.8.

Fuller, Richard F. "How Boston Handles Problems." *Publishers Weekly*, May 26, 1923, pp. 1,624–25.

Gay, Jason. "Dirty Pretty Things." *Rolling Stone* (April 2, 2009): 40–47.

Gilloti, Chris F. "Book Censorship in Massachusetts: The Search for a Test of Obscenity." *Boston University Law Review* 42 (Fall 1962): 476–91.

Goldberg, Beverly. "Muzzling What Sari Says." *American Libraries* 33 (September 2002): 19.

———. "Second-Guessing Sophie's Choice." *American Libraries* 33, no. 3 (March 2002): 25.

———. "Wisconsin Board, Staffers Cope with Would-Be Book Burners." *American Libraries* 40 (August/September 2009): 23–24.

"Gottschalk Fined for Obscene Book Sale." *Publishers Weekly*, March 8, 1924, p. 834.

Grant, Sidney S., and S. E. Angoff. "Censorship in Boston." *Boston University Law Review* 10 (January 1930): 36–60.

———. "Recent Developments in Censorship." *Boston University Law Review* 10 (November 1930): 488–509.

Green, Samuel S. "Sensational Fiction in Public Libraries." *Library Journal*, September–October 1897, pp. 349–52.

Greenberg, Robert A. " 'Anactoria,' and the Sapphic Passion." *Victorian Poetry* 29 (Spring 1991): 79–87.

Harris, Daniel. "*Sex*, Madonna, and Mia: Press Reflections." *Antioch Review* 51 (4): 503–18.

Haskins, Doug. "The Many Faces of Censorship." *Canadian Forum* 33 (June 1953): 57–58.

"Hearing on Book Delayed." *New York Times*, March 30, 1948, p. 25.

Helfand, Duke. "Students Fight for *Sophie's Choice*." *Los Angeles Times*, December 22, 2001, home edition, p. B1.

Heller, Terry. "Mirrored Worlds and the Gothic in Faulkner's *Sanctuary*." *Mississippi Quarterly* 42 (Summer 1989): 247–59.

Henderson, R. W. "The Devil Rides Outside." *Library Journal*, November 1, 1952, p. 77.

Hicks, Granville. "Lolita and Her Problems." *Saturday Review*, August 16, 1958, pp. 12, 38.

Hohne, Karen A. "The Power of the Spoken Word in the Works of Stephen King." *Journal of Popular Culture* 28 (Fall 1994): 93–103.

"*Homo Sapiens:* A Review." *The Little Review* 2 (December 1915): 25–27.

Huntington, Henry S. "The Philadelphia Book Seizures." *Elation*, August 21, 1948, pp. 205–7.

Hutchinson, Percy. "Mr. Hanley Plumbs the Lowest Circle of Inferno." *New York Times Book Review*, April 10, 1932, p. 6.

"In Brief: *The Chinese Room*." *The Nation*, January 9, 1943, p. 67.

Ishizuka, Kathy. "Iowa Library Reaffirms Ban on *Sari Says*." *School Library Journal* 48 (September 2002): 21.

"Jersey Writ Bars Book Ban Attempt." *New York Times*, April 7, 1953, p. 27.

Johnson, B. S. "Pi Printers." *Censorship* 3 (Summer 1965): 43–45.

Joyce, James. "A Curious History." *Egoist*, January 5, 1914, pp. 26–27.

"Judge as Literary Critic." *Catholic World* 116 (December 1922): 392–99.

Kallen, Horace M. "Protean Censorship." *Freeman*, June 29, 1921, pp. 370–72.

Kauffman, Stanley. "God's Belittled Acre." *New Republic*, June 30, 1958, p. 21.

Kaun, Alexander S. "The Ecstasy of Pain." *Little Review* 2 (December 1915): 16–23.

Keilman, John, and Jamie Franisco. "Book-Ban Fight Are Far from Over: Reading Lists Face Scrutiny Across the State." *Chicago Tribune*, May 28, 2006, p. 4 C.1.

Kennedy, Ludovic. "The Moors Murders and de Sade." *The Spectator*, April 29, 1966, pp. 23–25.

Kennicott, Philip. " 'Gay' Art: Dolled Up and Still Dressed Down." *Washington Post*, November 30, 2003, p. N07.

Kincaid, Larry, and Grove Koger. "*Tropic of Cancer* and the Censors: A Case Study and Bibliographic Guide to the Literature." *Reference Services Review* 25 (Spring 1997): 31–38, 46.

"*Kreutzer Sonata*." *American Law Review* 25 (January–February 1891): 102–4.

Kuenz, Jane. "*The Bluest Eye:* Notes on History, Community, and Black Female Subjectivity." *African American Review* 27 (Fall 1993): 421–31.

Lambert, Robert. "Charley: Metamorphosis by Media." *Media and Methods* 5 (February 1969): 29–31.

"The Law and the Censor." *New York Times*, September 14, 1922, p. 21.

Lawrence, D. H. "On Obscenity." *Publishers Weekly*, February 23, 1923, p. 580.

Levin, Bernard. "Why All the Fuss?" *Spectator*, January 9, 1959, pp. 32–33.

Levinson, Martin H. *"America (The Book): A Citizen's Guide to Democracy Inaction."* Book review. *et Cetera* 62 (April 2005): 216–17.

"Librarian Bans Jon Stewart." *Los Angeles Times*, January 11, 2005, p. E3.

"Library Board Puts Jon Stewart's Book Back on Shelves." CNN broadcast. January 11, 2005.

"Library Board Reverses Ban on Stewart Book." *New York Times*, January 12, 2005, p. E2.

"Library Restrictions vs. Parental Restrictions." *The Atlanta Journal–Constitution*, March 30, 1997, p. J09.

Lockhart, William B., and Robert C. McClure. "Censorship of Obscenity: The Developing Constitutional Standards." *Minnesota Law Review* 45 (November 1960): 19.

———. "Literature, the Law of Obscenity, and the Constitution." *Minnesota Law Review* 38 (March 1954): 295–395.

Loe, Mary Hong. "Case Studies in Censorship: William Faulkner's *Sanctuary.*" *Reference Services Review* 23 (Spring 1995): 71–84.

Lofholm, Nancy. "Town Fights to Retain Teachers: 2 Vocal Advocates: Norwood School District Officials Deny That a Book-Banning Incident Last Year Imperiled the Educators' Jobs." *Denver Post*, May 12, 2006, p. B-05.

"Lolita in the Dock." *New Zealand Libraries* 23 (August 1960): 180–83.

Lucey, Michael. "The Consequences of Being Explicit: Watching Sex in Gide's *Si le grain ne meurt.*" *Yale Journal of Criticism* 4 (1990): 174–92.

MacCarthy, Desmond. "Literary Trends." *Life and Letters* 1 (October 1928): 329–41.

Mackay, R. S. "Hidden Rule and Judicial Censorship." *Canadian Bar Review* 361 (March 1958): 1–24.

Magrath, C. Peter. "The Obscenity Cases: Grapes of Roth." *Supreme Court Review* 139 (1966): 9–13.

Maslin, Janet. "Politics 101, With All Its Mischief and Mirth." *New York Times*, September 16, 2004, p. E1.

Matthews, Brander. "Books That Are Barred." *Munsey's Magazine*, December 1913, pp. 493–97.

Maynard, Joyce. "Coming of Age with Judy Blume." *New York Times Magazine*, December 3, 1978, pp. 80+.

McCafferty, Dennis. "Library Board Refuses to Ban Sex Fantasy Book." *Atlanta Constitution*, January 25, 1995, p. B2.

———. *"Women on Top* May Yet Be Pulled from Hall Library." *Atlanta Constitution*, February 8, 1995, p. C2.

Megan, Graydon. "Parents to Get Look at School Reading Lists: Controversy Led to Move by District in Arlington Heights." *Chicago Tribune*, May 12, 2007, p. 13.

Mehta, Seema. "California District Bans Book Lauded by Laura Bush." *Record* (February 2009): A07.

"Mesquite, TX: School Officials at Pirrung Elementary School are Reviewing *Alice the Brave.*" *School Library Journal* 50 (November 2004): 23.

Mikva, Abner J. "Chicago: Citadel of Censorship." *Focus/Midwest* 2 (March–April 1963): 16–17.

Minzesheimer, Bob. "*America* Goes over the Top in Holiday Sales." *USA Today,* January 6, 2005, p. D1.

———. "Stewart's 'America' Offers Textbook Laughs." *USA Today,* September 17, 2004, p. E01.

"Miscellaneous Brief Reviews." *New York Times,* August 1, 1937, pp. 92–93.

Molz, Kathleen. "The Public Custody of the High Pornography." *American Scholar* (Winter 1966–67): 93–103.

Moore, Everett T. "*Tropic of Cancer* (Second Phase)." *ALA Bulletin* 56 (February 1962): 81–84.

"More of the Same: Massachusetts Supreme Court and Dreiser's *American Tragedy.*" *Outlook,* June 11, 1930, p. 214.

Morse, J. M. "*Forever Amber:* Defendant at Trial in Suffolk County Superior Court, Boston." *New Republic,* January 6, 1947, pp. 39–40.

Moskin, Morton. "Inadequacy of Present Tests as to What Constitutes Obscene Literature." *Cornell Law Quarterly* 34 (Spring 1949): 442–47.

"Murfreesboro, TN: A Book Review Committee is Considering Whether to Remove *Alice on the Outside.*" *School Library Journal* 49 (April 2003): 30.

Murray, D. M. "Candy Christian as a Pop-Art Daisy Miller." *Journal of Popular Culture* 5 (1971): 340–48.

"Neither Censorship nor Puritanism Involved." *Christian Century,* March 19, 1930, pp. 357–58.

Nelson, Hilda. "Theophile Gautier: The Invisible and Impalpable World." *French Review* 45 (June 1972): 819–30.

"New England News Brief: 'Native Son' Ban Sought." *Boston Globe,* July 15, 1981, p. 1.

"New England News Briefs: School Book Ban Still Sought." *Boston Globe,* July 14, 1981, p. 1.

Newsletter on Intellectual Freedom. Judith F. Krug, ed. Chicago, Ill.: American Library Association, Intellectual Freedom Committee. Numerous issues from July 1976 through May 2004.

"New Try in N. Adams Tonight to Ban 'Native Son' at School." *Boston Globe,* (September 1, 1981, p. 1.

Nussbaum, Evelyn. "Psst! Serena Is a Slut. Pass It On." *New York* 38 (May 30, 2004): 40–43.

O'Briant, Don. "Books with an Edge Lure Younger Set." *Atlanta Journal-Constitution,* July 6, 2005, p. E1.

"Obscene-Book Ban Upheld in Jersey." *New York Times,* March 9, 1954, p. 34.

"Obscenity-Evidence Admission of Contemporary Critical Evaluation of Libeled Book." *Minnesota Law Review* 35 (February 1951): 326–30.

"Offended at the Magistrate." *New York Times,* April 16, 1897, p. 5.

O'Hanlon, Ann. "Family Appeals Book Decision: County School System Asked to Reconsider Reading List." *Washington Post,* October 12, 1997, p. PWE, 1:4.

Patnoe, Elizabeth. "Lolita Misrepresented, Lolita Reclaimed: Disclosing the Doubles." *College Literature* 22 (June 1995): 81–104.

Pearce, Lillian. "Book Selection and Peyton Place." *Library Journal,* March 1958, pp. 712–13.

Perera, Andrea. "Controversial Novel Returns to Library." *Los Angeles Times*, January 12, 2002, home edition, p. B4.

Podhoretz, Norman, and Brian O'Doherty. "The Present and Future of Pornography." *Show* 4 (June 1964): 54–55+.

"Police Aide Cleared in Book Ban Fight." *New York Times*, May 5, 1957, p. 60.

Pomfret, John. "Letter from China; The Coveted Stamp of Disapproval." *Washington Post*, June 27, 2000, p. C01.

"Porn Star Tell-All Slips Back on Shelves." *American Libraries* 36 (April 2005): 15.

"Pound of Waltzing Mice." *Time*, December 9, 1946, pp. 24–25.

Pringle, Henry F. "Comstock the Less." *American Mercury* 10 (January 1927): 56–63.

"Protest against Columbia University's Ban on *Tobacco Road* and *God's Little Acre*." *New Republic*, June 27, 1934, pp. 184–85.

"Publisher to Defend Seized Book in Court." *New York Times*, March 17, 1948, p. 27.

"Publishing's Past Fifty Years, a Balance Sheet—II." *Saturday Review*, November 28, 1964, pp. 17–19, 69.

Quigley, Margery. "Books in Suburbia—The Suburban Library's Book-Buying Problems." *Library Journal*, April 1, 1930, p. 303.

Ramazani, Vaheed K. "Writing in Pain: Baudelaire, Benjamin, Haussmann." *Boundary 2* 23 (Summer 1996): 199–224.

Rampersad, Arnold. Introduction to *Native Son*. New York: HarperCollins, 1993.

"A Reader's List: *The Chinese Room*" *The New Republic*, November 9, 1942, p. 618.

Redman, B. R. "The Devil Rides Outside." *Saturday Review*, November 1, 1952, p. 16.

Rigolet, François. "Magdalen's Skull: Allegory and Iconography in *The Heptameron*." *Renaissance Quarterly* 47 (Spring 1994): 57–73.

Robbins, Harold. "Master Harold." *Advocate: The National Gay and Lesbian Newsmagazine*, August 22, 1995, pp. 38–43.

Sachs, Ed. "I Want *Candy*." *Focus/Midwest* 3 (February 1964): 11–13, 23–24.

St. John-Stevas, Norman. "Art, Morality, and Censorship." *Ramparts* 2 (May 1963): 40–48.

Schmeling, Gareth. "*The Satyricon*: Forms in Search of a Genre." *Classical Bulletin* 47 (1970): 49–53.

"School's Purchase of Four Books Ignites a Furor in Waterloo." *Des Moines Register*, April 15, 1992, p. M2.

Schriftgiesser, Karl. "Boston Stays Pure." *New Republic*, May 8, 1929, pp. 327–29.

Scott, W. J. "The *Lolita* Case." *Landfall* 58 (June 1961): 134–38.

Sebastian, Raymond F. "Obscenity and the Supreme Court: Nine Years of Confusion." *Stanford Law Review* (November 1966): 167–89.

"Seize 772 in Vice Crusade Raid." *New York Times*, July 12, 1922, p. 22.

Sherlin, Kit. "It's Only Normal to Question." *High Plains Reader*, October 11, 1997, pp. 6–7.

Shugert, Diane P. "Rationales for Commonly 'Challenged' Taught Books." *Connecticut English Journal* 15 (Fall 1983): 145–46.

Sibley, Celia, and Beth Burkstrand. "Banning of Book Surprises Petitioner." *The Atlanta Journal–Constitution*, May 19, 1997. p. J1.

———. "Gwinnett Libraries Ban *Women on Top*." *Atlanta Constitution*, March 19, 1997, p. B2.

Silva, Edward T. "From *Candide* to *Candy*: Love's Labor Lost." *Journal of Popular Culture* 8 (1974): 783–91.

Skube, Michael. "The Search for Smut Ends in a Circular Rut." *Atlanta Journal–Constitution*, July 10, 1994, p. N10.

"*Sleeveless Errand* and Other Works of Fiction." *New York Times Book Review*, June 9, 1929, pp. 5–8.

Smith, Craig S. "Sex, Lust, Drugs: Her Novel's Too Much for China." *New York Times*, May 11, 2000, p. A4.

Smith, Gene. "The Lonigan Curse." *American Heritage* 46 (April 1995): 150–51.

Smith, Harrison. "Practitioners of Culture." *Saturday Review of Literature*, February 28, 1948, p. 13.

Smith, Roger H. "Cops, Counselors and *Tropic of Cancer.*" *Publishers Weekly*, October 23, 1961, p. 35.

Sokolove, Michael. "Sex and the Censors." *Inquirer Magazine* [Philadelphia], March 9, 1997, pp. 18+.

"South Africa Bans a U.S. Novel." *New York Times*, August 4, 1978, p. B18.

Steele, Margaret Farley. "Books for Teenage Girls Are a Little Too Popular." *New York Times*, August 20, 2006, p. 14NJ6.

Stein, Karen. "Margaret Atwood's Modest Proposal: *The Handmaid's Tale.*" *Canadian Literature* 23 (Spring 1996): 57–73.

Stillman, Peggy, and Andrea Kross. "Why Is Everyone Reading *Sophie's Choice?*" *Digital Library and Archives–Virginia Libraries* 46, no. 3 (July/August/September 2000).

"Sumner Denounces Book in Hall Case." *New York Times*, October 20, 1992, p. 3.

Tait, Sue, and Christy Tyson. "Paperbacks for Young Adults." *Emergency Librarian* 16 (October 1988): 53–54.

Tanner, Laura E. "Reading Rape: *Sanctuary* and the Women of *Brewster Place.*" *American Literature* 62 (December 1990): 559–82.

Tanselle, G. Thomas. "The Thomas Seltzer Imprint." *Papers of the Bibliographic Society of America* 58 (Fourth Quarter 1964): 380–416.

"The Test of Obscenity." *Author* 65 (Autumn 1954): 1–5.

Thompson, Susan. "Images of Adolescence: Part I." *Signal* 34 (1981): 57–59.

Tirrell, Lynne. "Storytelling and Moral Agency." *Journal of Aesthetics & Art Criticism* 48 (Spring 1990): 115–26.

Tolbert, Kathy. "Parents' Bid to Cut Book from Reading List Rejected." *Boston Globe*, July 24, 1981, p. 1.

Toppo, Greg. "Oh, Say Can You Snicker: Kids Take to *America (The Book)*, but Schools See a Mixed Blessing." *USA Today*, November 2, 2004, p. D6.

Torpy, Bill. "Library Committee Votes to Ban Book." *The Atlanta Journal–Constitution*, December 30, 1994, p. D3.

Traubel, Horace L. "Freedom to Write and to Print." *Poet-Lore* 2 (October 1890): 529–31.

"*Triumph of Death* Exonerated." *New York Times*, April 6, 1897, p. 5.

"Tully Book 'Indecent.' " *New York Times*, August 17, 1935, p. 17.

"Two Booksellers Arrested on Sumner Complaint." *Publishers Weekly*, December 23, 1923, p. 1,974.

Updike, John. "The Plight of the American Writer." *Change* 9 (April 1978): 36–41.

Wagner-Lawlor, Jennifer. "Metaphorical 'Indiscretion' and Literary Survival in Swinburne's 'Anactoria.' " *Studies in English Literature, 1500–1900* 36 (Autumn 1996): 917–34.

Wald, Emil W. "Obscene Literature Standards Re-examined." *South Carolina Law Review* 18 (Spring 1966): 497–503.

Warburg, Frederic. "A View of Obscenity." *New Yorker*, April 20, 1957, pp. 106–33.

Watson, Jay. "The Rhetoric of Exhaustion and the Exhaustion of Rhetoric: Erskine Caldwell in the Thirties." *Mississippi Quarterly* 46 (Spring 1993): 215–29.

Weber, Bruce. "A Town's Struggle in the Culture War." *New York Times*, June 2, 2005, p. E1.

Weightman, John. "Andre Gide and the Homosexual Debate." *American Scholar* 59 (Autumn 1990): 591–601.

"Western Town Has Literary Censors: The Evanston Public Library Makes Up a 'Black List.'" *New York Times*, July 6, 1902, p. 9.

Wilcox, Clyde. "The Not-So-Failed Feminism of Jean Auel." *Journal of Popular Culture* 28 (Winter 1994): 63–70.

Wilson, Andrew J. "The Corruption in Looking: William Faulkner's *Sanctuary* as a Detective Novel." *Mississippi Quarterly* 47 (Summer 1994): 441–60.

Woodward, Frances. *"Forever Amber." Atlantic* (December 1944): 137.

"Worcester Library Directors Support Their Librarian." *Library Journal*, April 15, 1949, p. 649.

Wright, Derek. "Mapless Motion: Form and Space in Updike's *Rabbit, Run.*" *Modern Fiction Studies* 37 (Spring 1991): 35–44.

Wyatt, Edward. "Banned in Wal-Mart." *New York Times*, October 22, 2004, p. E1.

———. "Jon Stewart Book Is Banned." *New York Times*, January 11, 2005, p. E2.

Yevish, I. A. "Attack on *Jude the Obscure:* A Reappraisal Some Seventy Years After." *Journal of General Education* 18 (January 1967): 239–48.

Zeitchik, Steven M. "Md. Schools Veto Morrison, Angelou Titles." *Publishers Weekly*, January 19, 1998, 236.

ONLINE RESOURCES

"Anchorage Parents Object to *Perfectly Normal* Book." *American Libraries Online.* Available online. URL: www.ala.org/ala/alonline/currentnews/newsarchive/2001/september2001/anchorageparents.htm. Accessed August 10, 2010.

Associated Press. "Iowa Library Keeps Ban on Teen Advice Book." Posted on Freedom Forum. Available online. URL: www.freedomforum.org/templates/document.asp?documentID=16703. Accessed August 10, 2010.

Donald, David. "Gossip Girl Book at Center of Library Debate." Available online. URL: Daily Commercial.com/060909book. Accessed July 20, 2010.

"Florida Director Swallows Her Ban of *Eat Me.*" *American Association of School Librarians.* Available online. URL: www.ala.org./aaslTemplate.cfm?Section=informationpower_Books_and_Products&templ ate=/ContentManagement/ContentDisplay.cfm&ContentID=58408. Accessed August 12, 2010.

Florio, Gwen. "Award-Winning Book Headed for Landfill." *Rocky Mountain News*, February 4, 2005. Available online. URL: http://www.rockymountainnews.com/drmn/state/article/0,1299,DRMN_21_3522696,00.html. Accessed June 14, 2010.

Frey, Christine. "Parents Notify 3 SJUSD Trustees of Their Intention to Recall Them." *Willow Glen Resident.* Available online. URL: www.svcn.com/archives/wgresident/07.29.98/CoverStory.html. Accessed August 10, 2010.

Gaura, Maria Alicia. "Parents in San Jose Criticize School Book—District Reviewing Use of Explicit Novel." *San Francisco Chronicle.* Available online. URL: http://articles.sfgate.com/1998-05-16/news/17720887_1_shelves-book-reading. Accessed August 10, 2010.

Glenn, Wendy J. "Brock Cole: The Good, The Bad, and the Humorously Ironic." *The ALAN Review* 26, no. 2 (Winter 1999). Available online. URL: http://scholar.lib.vt.edu/ejournals/ALAN/winter99/glenn.html. Accessed August 19, 2010.

"An Interview with Weihui." *Bibliofemme.* Available online. URL: www.bibliofemme.com/interviews/weihui.shtml. Accessed August 13, 2010.

"Jenna Chides Library over Book Ban." Press release. Available online. URL: www.ainews.com/Archives/Story8430.phtml. Accessed August 16, 2010.

Kunhikrishnan, K. "The New Face of China." *Hindu.* Available online. URL: www.hinduonnet.com/2001/11/04/stories/1304017r.htm. Accessed February 3, 2011.

"Missouri Librarians Latest to Discover: Banning Makes Books Popular." Associated Press. Available online. URL: www.freedomforum.org/templates/document.asp?documentID=17008&printerfriend. Accessed August 18, 2010.

"Modesto School Board Votes to Allow Controversial Book to Stay on List." KXTV News 10 broadcast. Available online. URL: www.kxtv.com/storyfull.asp?id=5992. Accessed August 12, 2010.

Nissimov, Ron. "Mayor Wrote a New Page in Library History." *Houston Chronicle.* Available online. URL: www.chron.comdisp/story.mpl/metropolitan3040041. Accessed August 18, 2010.

O'Brien, Kerry. "Shanghai Writer Challenging Stereotypes." Television broadcast transcript. Australian Broadcasting System. Available online. URL: www.abc.net.au/7.30/content/2001/s337692.htm. Accessed August 23, 2010.

"Ocala, Florida." *Newsletter on Intellectual Freedom* 53 (January 2004). Available online. URL: htpps://members.ala.org/nif/v53n1/dateline.html. Accessed August 14, 2010.

Rippel, Amy C. "Leesburg Mom Not Giving Up on Library Book Warning-Label Campaign." *Orlando-Sentinel.* Available online. URL: http://articles.orlandosentinel.com/2010-04-16/news/os-lk-book-policy-leesburg-20100413_1_leesburg-library-six-branch-libraries-bermudez-triangle. Accessed July 18, 2010.

"Sari Says Nothing More in Dyersville, Iowa." *Newsletter on Intellectual Freedom* 51 (September 2002). Formerly available online. URL: www.ala.org/al_onlineTemplate.cfm?Section=july2002&Template=/ContentManagement/ContentDisplay.cfm&ContentID=10168. Accessed August 18, 2010.

Sheng, John. "Afterthoughts on the Banning of 'Shanghai Baby.' " *Perspectives.* 2. Available online. URL: www.oycf.org/Perspectives/8_103100/afterthoughts_on_the_banning_of.htm. Accessed August 12, 2010.

"Success Stories—Libraries: Modesto, California." *Newsletter on Intellectual Freedom* 53 (January 2004). Available online. URL: http://members.ala.org/nif/v53n1/success_stories. html. Accessed August 12, 2010.

"Success Stories: Ocala, Florida." *Newsletter on Intellectual Freedom* 53 (May 2004). Available online. URL: htpps://members.ala.org/nif/v53n3/success_stories.html. Accessed August 12, 2010.

"Texas Commission Tries to Ban *It's Perfectly Normal.*" American Libraries Online. Available online. URL: www.ala.org/ala/alonline/currentnews/newsarchive/2002/september2002/texascommission.htm. Accessed August 12, 2010.

"Texans Further Stirred by Sex-Education Books." American Libraries Online. Available online. URL: www.ala.org/ala/alonline/currentnews/newsarchive/2002/september2002/texansfurther.htm. Accessed August 12, 2010.

"Texas Officials to Add Citizens to Materials-Review Committee." American Libraries Online. Available online. URL: www.ala.org/ala/alonline/currentnews/newsarchive/2002/september2002/texasofficials.htm. Accessed August 12, 2010.

"These Kids Can Handle the Truth." *Eagle-Tribune,* Posted September 22, 2000.

"Webb City District Bans Trio of Books." *Columbia Daily Tribune,* Available online. URL: http://archive.showmenews.com/2002/Aug/20020815News017.asp. Accessed August 12, 2010.

Works Discussed in Other Volumes of This Series

THE BASTARD OF ISTANBUL
Elif Shafak

BLACK BOY
Richard Wright

*BLOODS: AN ORAL HISTORY OF THE VIETNAM WAR BY
   BLACK VETERANS*
Wallace Terry

BORN ON THE FOURTH OF JULY
Ron Kovic

BOSS: RICHARD J. DALEY OF CHICAGO
Mike Royko

BURGER'S DAUGHTER
Nadine Gordimer

BURY MY HEART AT WOUNDED KNEE
Dee Brown

BUS STOP (CHEZHAN)
Gao Xingjian

*BY WAY OF DECEPTION: THE MAKING AND UNMAKING
   OF A MOSSAD OFFICER*
Victor Ostrovsky and Claire Hoy

CANCER WARD
Aleksandr Solzhenitsyn

CAT'S CRADLE
Kurt Vonnegut, Jr.

THE CHINA LOBBY IN AMERICAN POLITICS
Ross Y. Koen

THE CIA AND THE CULT OF INTELLIGENCE
Victor Marchetti and John D. Marks

CITIES OF SALT
Abdul Rahman Munif

CITIZEN TOM PAINE
Howard Fast

THE COMMERCIAL RESTRAINTS OF IRELAND CONSIDERED
John Hely-Hutchinson

COMPARATIVE POLITICS TODAY: A WORLD VIEW
Gabriel A. Almond, general editor

THE CORPSE WALKER: REAL-LIFE STORIES, CHINA FROM THE BOTTOM UP
Liao Yiwu

CRY AMANDLA!
June Goodwin

DAS KAPITAL
Karl Marx

DAUGHTER OF EARTH
Agnes Smedley

THE DAY THEY CAME TO ARREST THE BOOK
Nat Hentoff

DECENT INTERVAL
Frank Snepp

DID SIX MILLION REALLY DIE? THE TRUTH AT LAST
Richard Harwood

DOCTOR ZHIVAGO
Boris Pasternak

THE DRAPIER'S LETTERS
Jonathan Swift

A DRY WHITE SEASON
André Brink

DU PONT: BEHIND THE NYLON CURTAIN
Gerard Colby Zilg

FAIL-SAFE
Eugene Burdick and Harvey Wheeler

FIELDS OF FIRE
James Webb

THE FRAGILE FLAG
Jane Langton

THE FUGITIVE (PERBURUAN)
Pramoedya Ananta Toer

FUGITIVES (TAOWANG)
Gao Xingjian

GIRLS OF RIYADH
Rajaa Alsanea

THE GRAPES OF WRATH
John Steinbeck

THE GULAG ARCHIPELAGO 1918–1956
Aleksandr Solzhenitsyn

GULLIVER'S TRAVELS
Jonathan Swift

HANDBOOK FOR CONSCIENTIOUS OBJECTORS
Robert A. Seeley, editor

THE HOAX OF THE TWENTIETH CENTURY
Arthur R. Butz

I AM THE CHEESE
Robert Cormier

INSIDE RUSSIA TODAY
John Gunther

INSIDE THE COMPANY: CIA DIARY
Philip Agee

IN THE SPIRIT OF CRAZY HORSE
Peter Matthiessen

AN INTRODUCTION TO PROBLEMS OF AMERICAN CULTURE
Harold O. Rugg

THE INVISIBLE GOVERNMENT
David Wise and Thomas B. Ross

IT CAN'T HAPPEN HERE
Sinclair Lewis

JOHNNY GOT HIS GUN
Dalton Trumbo

THE JOKE (ŽERT)
Milan Kundera

A JOURNEY FROM ST. PETERSBURG TO MOSCOW
Aleksandr Nikolaevich Radishchev

JULIE OF THE WOLVES
Jean Craighead George

THE JUNGLE
Upton Sinclair

KEEPING FAITH: MEMOIRS OF A PRESIDENT
Jimmy Carter

KISS OF THE SPIDER WOMAN
Manuel Puig

THE LAND AND PEOPLE OF CUBA
Victoria Ortiz

LAND OF THE FREE: A HISTORY OF THE UNITED STATES
John W. Caughey, John Hope Franklin, and Ernest R. May

LAUGHING BOY
Oliver La Farge

EL LIBRO NEGRO DE LA JUSTICIA CHILENA
   (THE BLACK BOOK OF CHILEAN JUSTICE)
Alejandra Matus

THE MAN DIED: PRISON NOTES OF WOLE SOYINKA
Wole Soyinka

THE MANIFESTO OF THE COMMUNIST PARTY
Karl Marx and Friedrich Engels

MARXISM VERSUS SOCIALISM
Vladimir G. Simkhovitch

MEIN KAMPF
Adolf Hitler

LES MISÉRABLES
Victor Hugo

A MONTH AND A DAY: A DETENTION DIARY
Ken Saro-Wiwa

MY BROTHER SAM IS DEAD
James Lincoln Collier and Christopher Collier

MY NAME IS ASHER LEV
Chaim Potok

MY PEOPLE: THE STORY OF THE JEWS
Abba Eban

NELSON AND WINNIE MANDELA
Dorothy Hoobler and Thomas Hoobler

1984
George Orwell

NOVEL WITHOUT A NAME
Duong Thu Huong

OIL!
Upton Sinclair

ONE DAY IN THE LIFE OF IVAN DENISOVICH
Aleksandr Solzhenitsyn

*ONE PEOPLE, ONE DESTINY: THE CARIBBEAN AND
    CENTRAL AMERICA TODAY*
Don Rojas

*THE OPEN SORE OF A CONTINENT: A PERSONAL NARRATIVE
    OF THE NIGERIAN CRISIS*
Wole Soyinka

OUR LAND, OUR TIME: A HISTORY OF THE UNITED STATES
Joseph Robert Conlin

PARADISE OF THE BLIND
Duong Thu Huong

THE PATRIOT (HA PATRIOT)
THE QUEEN OF THE BATHTUB (MALKAT AMBATYA)
Hanoch Levin

THE POLITICS OF DISPOSSESSION
Edward W. Said

THE PRINCE
Niccolò Machiavelli

PRINCIPLES OF NATURE
Elihu Palmer

PROMISE OF AMERICA
Larry Cuban and Philip Roden

REPORT OF THE SIBERIAN DELEGATION
Leon Trotsky

THE RIGHTS OF MAN
Thomas Paine

RUSSIA
Vernon Ives

SECRECY AND DEMOCRACY: THE CIA IN TRANSITION
Stansfield Turner

EL SEÑOR PRESIDENTE (THE PRESIDENT)
Miguel Angel Asturias

SLAUGHTERHOUSE-FIVE, OR THE CHILDREN'S CRUSADE
Kurt Vonnegut, Jr.

SNOW
Orhan Pamuk

SPYCATCHER
Peter Wright

THE STATE AND REVOLUTION
Vladimir I. Lenin

STRONG WIND (VIENTO FUERTE)
THE GREEN POPE (EL PAPA VERDE)
Miguel Angel Asturias

THE STRUGGLE IS MY LIFE
Nelson Mandela

A SUMMARY VIEW OF THE RIGHTS OF BRITISH AMERICA
Thomas Jefferson

SYLVESTER AND THE MAGIC PEBBLE
William Steig

TEN DAYS THAT SHOOK THE WORLD
John Reed

THE THINGS THEY CARRIED
Tim O'Brien

THIS EARTH OF MANKIND
CHILD OF ALL NATIONS
Pramoedya Ananta Toer

365 DAYS
Ronald J. Glasser

TODAY'S ISMS: COMMUNISM, FASCISM, CAPITALISM, SOCIALISM
William Ebenstein

THE UGLY AMERICAN
William J. Lederer and Eugene Burdick

UNCLE TOM'S CABIN
Harriet Beecher Stowe

UNITED STATES–VIETNAM RELATIONS, 1945–1967
(THE PENTAGON PAPERS)
U.S. Department of Defense

THE VANĚK PLAYS
Václav Havel

WAITING
Ha Jin

WHY ARE WE IN VIETNAM?
Norman Mailer

THE BOOK OF COMMON PRAYER
Thomas Cranmer and others

THE CARTOONS THAT SHOOK THE WORLD
Jytte Klausen

CHILDREN OF THE ALLEY
Naguib Mahfouz

THE CHRISTIAN COMMONWEALTH
John Eliot

CHRISTIANITY NOT MYSTERIOUS
John Toland

CHRISTIANITY RESTORED
Michael Servetus

*CHURCH: CHARISM AND POWER: LIBERATION THEOLOGY
AND THE INSTITUTIONAL CHURCH*
Leonardo Boff

COLLOQUIES
Desiderius Erasmus

COMMENTARIES
Averroës

COMPENDIUM REVELATIONUM
Girolamo Savonarola

CONCERNING HERETICS
Sebastian Castellio

THE COURSE OF POSITIVE PHILOSOPHY
Auguste Comte

CREATIVE EVOLUTION
Henri Bergson

THE CRITIQUE OF PURE REASON
Immanuel Kant

THE DA VINCI CODE
Dan Brown

DE ECCLESIA
Jan Hus

DE INVENTORIBUS RERUM
Polydore Vergil

DE L'ESPRIT
Claude-Adrien Helvétius

DIALOGUE CONCERNING THE TWO CHIEF WORLD SYSTEMS
Galileo Galilei

DIALOGUES CONCERNING NATURAL RELIGION
David Hume

DISCOURSE ON METHOD
René Descartes

DON QUIXOTE
Miguel de Cervantes Saavedra

DRAGONWINGS
Laurence Yep

ÉMILE
Jean-Jacques Rousseau

ENCYCLOPÉDIE
Denis Diderot and Jean Le Rond d'Alembert, eds.

AN ESSAY CONCERNING HUMAN UNDERSTANDING
John Locke

ESSAYS
Michel de Montaigne

ETHICS
Baruch Spinoza

THE FABLE OF THE BEES
Bernard Mandeville

THE GUIDE OF THE PERPLEXED
Maimonides

HARRY POTTER AND THE SORCERER'S STONE
J. K. Rowling

HARRY POTTER AND THE CHAMBER OF SECRETS
J. K. Rowling

HARRY POTTER AND THE PRISONER OF AZKABAN
J. K. Rowling

HARRY POTTER AND THE GOBLET OF FIRE
J. K. Rowling

HARRY POTTER AND THE ORDER OF THE PHOENIX
J. K. Rowling

HARRY POTTER AND THE HALF-BLOOD PRINCE
J. K. Rowling

HARRY POTTER AND THE DEATHLY HALLOWS
J. K. Rowling

THE HIDDEN FACE OF EVE: WOMEN IN THE ARAB WORLD
Nawal El Saadawi

HIS DARK MATERIALS TRILOGY, BOOK I: *THE GOLDEN COMPASS*
Philip Pullman

HIS DARK MATERIALS TRILOGY, BOOK II: *THE SUBTLE KNIFE*
Philip Pullman

HIS DARK MATERIALS TRILOGY, BOOK III: *THE AMBER SPYGLASS*
Philip Pullman

HISTORICAL AND CRITICAL DICTIONARY
Pierre Bayle

HISTORY OF THE CONFLICT BETWEEN RELIGION AND SCIENCE
John William Draper

THE HISTORY OF THE DECLINE AND FALL OF THE ROMAN EMPIRE
Edward Gibbon

HOLT BASIC READING SERIES
Bernard J. Weiss, sr. ed.

IMPRESSIONS READING SERIES
Jack Booth, gen. ed.

INFALLIBLE? AN INQUIRY
Hans Küng

AN INQUIRY CONCERNING HUMAN UNDERSTANDING
David Hume

INSTITUTES OF THE CHRISTIAN RELIGION
John Calvin

INTRODUCTION TO THEOLOGY
Peter Abelard

*AN INTRODUCTION TO THE PRINCIPLES OF MORALS AND
   LEGISLATION*
Jeremy Bentham

INTRODUCTORY LECTURES ON PSYCHOANALYSIS
Sigmund Freud

THE JEWEL OF MEDINA
Sherry Jones

THE KORAN (QUR'AN)

LAJJA (SHAME)
Taslima Nasrin

THE LAST TEMPTATION OF CHRIST
Nikos Kazantzakis

LETTER ON THE BLIND
Denis Diderot

LETTERS CONCERNING THE ENGLISH NATION
Voltaire

LEVIATHAN
Thomas Hobbes

THE LIFE OF JESUS
Ernest Renan

MARY AND HUMAN LIBERATION
Tissa Balasuriya

MEDITATIONS ON FIRST PHILOSOPHY
René Descartes

THE MERITORIOUS PRICE OF OUR REDEMPTION
William Pynchon

THE METAPHYSICS
Aristotle

MEYEBELA: MY BENGALI GIRLHOOD
Taslima Nasrin

THE NEW ASTRONOMY
Johannes Kepler

THE NEW TESTAMENT
William Tyndale, trans.

NINETY-FIVE THESES
Martin Luther

OF THE VANITIE AND UNCERTAINTIE OF ARTES AND SCIENCES
Henricus Cornelius Agrippa

OLIVER TWIST
Charles Dickens

ON CIVIL LORDSHIP
John Wycliffe

ON JUSTICE IN THE REVOLUTION AND IN THE CHURCH
Pierre-Joseph Proudhon

ON MONARCHY
Dante Alighieri

ON THE INFINITE UNIVERSE AND WORLDS
Giordano Bruno

ON THE LAW OF WAR AND PEACE
Hugo Grotius

ON THE ORIGIN OF SPECIES
Charles Darwin

ON THE REVOLUTION OF HEAVENLY SPHERES
Nicolaus Copernicus

OPUS MAJUS
Roger Bacon

PENGUIN ISLAND
Anatole France

THE PERSIAN LETTERS
Charles-Louis de Secondat, baron de La Brède et de Montesquieu

PHILOSOPHICAL DICTIONARY
Voltaire

THE POLITICAL HISTORY OF THE DEVIL
Daniel Defoe

POPOL VUH

THE POWER AND THE GLORY
Graham Greene

THE PRAISE OF FOLLY
Desiderius Erasmus

PRINCIPLES OF POLITICAL ECONOMY
John Stuart Mill

THE PROVINCIAL LETTERS
Blaise Pascal

THE RAPE OF SITA
Lindsey Collen

THE RED AND THE BLACK
Stendhal

RELIGIO MEDICI
Sir Thomas Browne

RELIGION WITHIN THE LIMITS OF REASON ALONE
Immanuel Kant

THE RIGHTS OF THE CHRISTIAN CHURCH ASSERTED
Matthew Tindal

THE SANDY FOUNDATION SHAKEN
William Penn

THE SATANIC VERSES
Salman Rushdie

SHIVAJI: HINDU KING IN ISLAMIC INDIA
James W. Laine

A SHORT DECLARATION OF THE MISTERY OF INIQUITY
Thomas Helwys

THE SHORTEST WAY WITH THE DISSENTERS
Daniel Defoe

THE SOCIAL CONTRACT
Jean-Jacques Rousseau

THE SORROWS OF YOUNG WERTHER
Johann Wolfgang von Goethe

THE SPIRIT OF LAWS
Charles-Louis de Secondat, baron de La Brède et de Montesquieu

SPIRITS REBELLIOUS
Kahlil Gibran

THE STORY OF ZAHRA
Hanan al-Shaykh

A TALE OF A TUB
Jonathan Swift

THE TALMUD

THEOLOGICAL-POLITICAL TREATISE
Baruch Spinoza

THREE-PART WORK
Meister Eckhart

TOUBA AND THE MEANING OF NIGHT
Shahrnush Parsipur

THE VEIL AND THE MALE ELITE: A FEMINIST INTERPRETATION OF WOMEN'S RIGHTS IN ISLAM
Fatima Mernissi

VOODOO & HOODOO: THEIR TRADITIONAL CRAFTS AS REVEALED BY ACTUAL PRACTITIONERS
Jim Haskins

VOYAGES TO THE MOON AND THE SUN
Savinien Cyrano de Bergerac

THE WITCHES
Roald Dahl

WOMEN WITHOUT MEN: A NOVEL OF MODERN IRAN
Shahrnush Parsipur

ZHUAN FALUN: THE COMPLETE TEACHINGS OF FALUN GONG
Li Hongzhi

ZOONOMIA
Erasmus Darwin

BANNED BOOKS ON SOCIAL GROUNDS

THE ABSOLUTELY TRUE DIARY OF A PART-TIME INDIAN
Sherman Alexie

ADVENTURES OF HUCKLEBERRY FINN
Mark Twain

THE ADVENTURES OF SHERLOCK HOLMES
Sir Arthur Conan Doyle

THE ADVENTURES OF TOM SAWYER
Mark Twain

ALICE'S ADVENTURES IN WONDERLAND
Lewis Carroll

THE AMBOY DUKES
Irving Shulman

*THE AMERICAN HERITAGE DICTIONARY OF THE
   ENGLISH LANGUAGE*

AM I BLUE?
Marion Dane Bauer

AND STILL I RISE
Maya Angelou

AND TANGO MAKES THREE
Justin Richardson and Peter Parnell

ANNE FRANK: THE DIARY OF A YOUNG GIRL
Anne Frank

ANNIE ON MY MIND
Nancy Garden

ANOTHER COUNTRY
James Baldwin

APHRODITE
Pierre Louÿs

APPOINTMENT IN SAMARRA
John O'Hara

AS I LAY DYING
William Faulkner

THE AUTOBIOGRAPHY OF BENJAMIN FRANKLIN
Benjamin Franklin

THE AUTOBIOGRAPHY OF MALCOLM X
Malcolm X, with Alex Haley

THE AUTOBIOGRAPHY OF MISS JANE PITTMAN
Ernest J. Gaines

BABY BE-BOP
Francesca Lia Block

THE BASKETBALL DIARIES
Jim Carroll

BEING THERE
Jerzy Kosinski

THE BELL JAR
Sylvia Plath

BELOVED
Toni Morrison

THE BEST SHORT STORIES BY NEGRO WRITERS
Langston Hughes, ed.

BLACK LIKE ME
John Howard Griffin

BLESS THE BEASTS AND CHILDREN
Glendon Swarthout

BLUBBER
Judy Blume

BRAVE NEW WORLD
Aldous Huxley

BRIDGE TO TERABITHIA
Katherine Paterson

CAIN'S BOOK
Alexander Trocchi

CAMILLE
Alexandre Dumas, Jr.

THE CANTERBURY TALES
Geoffrey Chaucer

CAPTAIN UNDERPANTS (SERIES)
Dav Pilkey

CATCH-22
Joseph Heller

THE CATCHER IN THE RYE
J. D. Salinger

THE CHOCOLATE WAR
Robert Cormier

A CLOCKWORK ORANGE
Anthony Burgess

THE COLOR PURPLE
Alice Walker

CUJO
Stephen King

DADDY'S ROOMMATE
Michael Willhoite

A DAY NO PIGS WOULD DIE
Robert Newton Peck

DELIVERANCE
James Dickey

A DICTIONARY OF AMERICAN SLANG
Harold Wentworth

DICTIONARY OF SLANG AND UNCONVENTIONAL ENGLISH
Eric Partridge

DOCTOR DOLITTLE (SERIES)
Hugh John Lofting

DOG DAY AFTERNOON
Patrick Mann

DOWN THESE MEAN STREETS
Piri Thomas

DRACULA
Bram Stoker

GO ASK ALICE
Anonymous

GONE WITH THE WIND
Margaret Mitchell

GORILLAS IN THE MIST
Dian Fossey

GO TELL IT ON THE MOUNTAIN
James Baldwin

THE GREAT GATSBY
F. Scott Fitzgerald

GRENDEL
John Gardner

HEATHER HAS TWO MOMMIES
Leslea Newman

A HERO AIN'T NOTHIN' BUT A SANDWICH
Alice Childress

HOWL AND OTHER POEMS
Allen Ginsberg

I KNOW WHY THE CAGED BIRD SINGS
Maya Angelou

IN THE NIGHT KITCHEN
Maurice Sendak

INVISIBLE MAN
Ralph Ellison

JAKE AND HONEYBUNCH GO TO HEAVEN
Margot Zemach

JAMES AND THE GIANT PEACH
Roald Dahl

JAWS
Peter Benchley

JUNKY
William S. Burroughs

KING & KING
Linda de Haan and Stern Nijland

KINGSBLOOD ROYAL
Sinclair Lewis

THE KITE RUNNER
Khaled Hosseini

LAST EXIT TO BROOKLYN
Hubert Selby, Jr.

LEAVES OF GRASS
Walt Whitman

A LIGHT IN THE ATTIC
Shel Silverstein

LITTLE BLACK SAMBO
Helen Bannerman

LITTLE HOUSE ON THE PRAIRIE
Laura Ingalls Wilder

LITTLE RED RIDING HOOD
Charles Perrault

LORD OF THE FLIES
William Golding

MANCHILD IN THE PROMISED LAND
Claude Brown

MARRIED LOVE
Marie Stopes

MOTHER GOOSE'S NURSERY RHYMES AND FAIRY TALES
Unknown

MY HOUSE
Nikki Giovanni

THE NAKED APE
Desmond Morris

NAKED LUNCH
William S. Burroughs

NANA
Émile Zola

NEVER LOVE A STRANGER
Harold Robbins

NEW DICTIONARY OF AMERICAN SLANG
Robert L. Chapman
(discussed with *A DICTIONARY OF AMERICAN SLANG*)

OF MICE AND MEN
John Steinbeck

OF TIME AND THE RIVER
Thomas Wolfe

THE OLD MAN AND THE SEA
Ernest Hemingway

ONE FLEW OVER THE CUCKOO'S NEST
Ken Kesey

ORDINARY PEOPLE
Judith Guest

THE OX-BOW INCIDENT
Walter Van Tilburg Clark

THE RED PONY
John Steinbeck

THE SCARLET LETTER
Nathaniel Hawthorne

A SEPARATE PEACE
John Knowles

SISTER CARRIE
Theodore Dreiser

SOUL ON ICE
Eldridge Cleaver

STEPPENWOLF
Hermann Hesse

STRANGE FRUIT
Lillian Smith

STRANGER IN A STRANGE LAND
Robert A. Heinlein

THE SUN ALSO RISES
Ernest Hemingway

TO HAVE AND HAVE NOT
Ernest Hemingway

TO KILL A MOCKINGBIRD
Harper Lee

UNCLE REMUS
Joel Chandler Harris

UNLIVED AFFECTIONS
George Shannon

WE ALL FALL DOWN
Robert Cormier

WELCOME TO THE MONKEY HOUSE
Kurt Vonnegut, Jr.

THE WELL OF LONELINESS
Radclyffe Hall

WHALE TALK
Chris Crutcher

WOMAN IN THE MISTS
Farley Mowat
(discussed with *GORILLAS IN THE MIST*)

*WORKING: PEOPLE TALK ABOUT WHAT THEY DO ALL DAY
  AND HOW THEY FEEL ABOUT WHAT THEY DO*
Studs Terkel

A WORLD I NEVER MADE
James T. Farrell

INDEX

DATE DUE